INSPIRE / PLAN / DISCOVER / EXPERIENCE

SPAIN

SPAIN

CONTENTS

La Muralla Roja in Calpe on the Costa Brava

DISCOVER 6

EXPERIENCE 68

NEED TO KNOW 580

DISCOVER

The Barcelona skyline seen from Park Güell

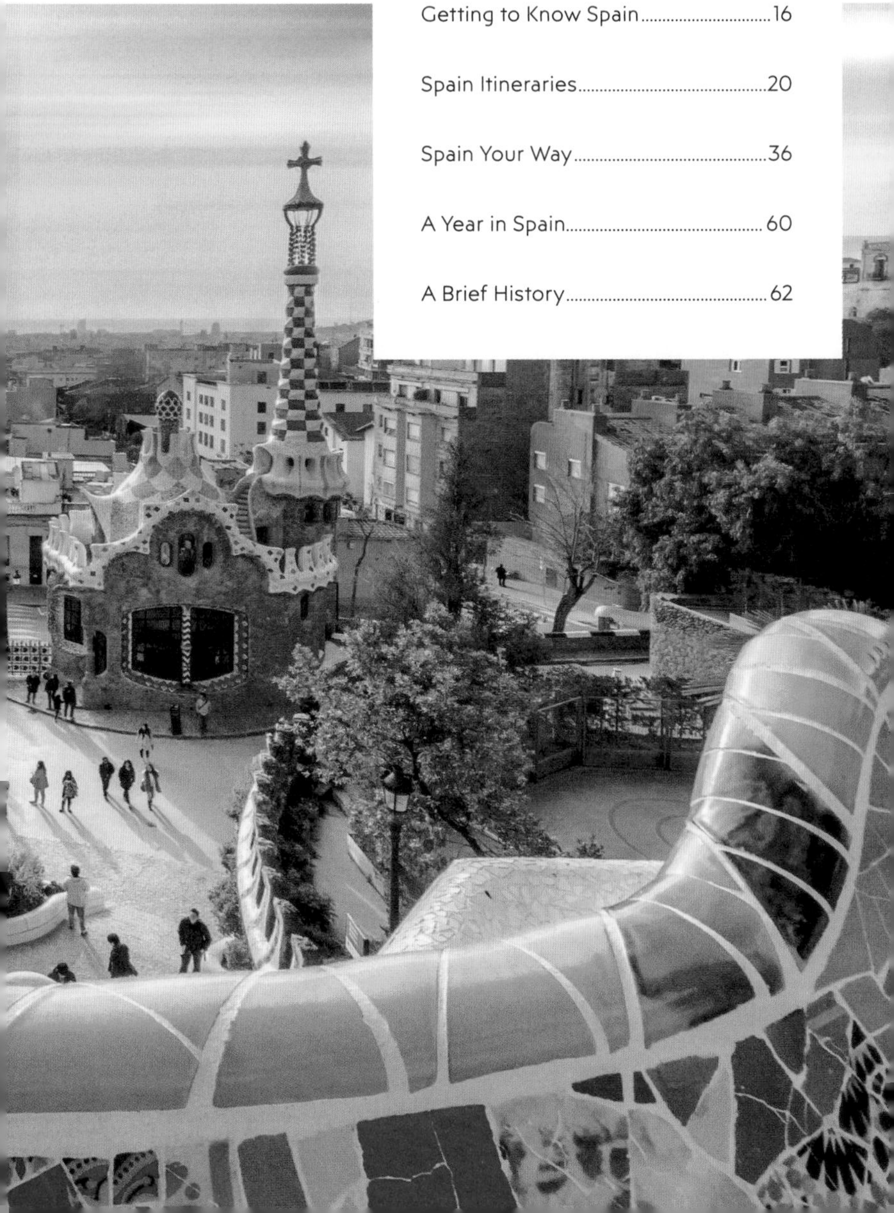

WELCOME TO
SPAIN

Fiery flamenco, tables covered with tasty tapas and the scent of jasmine – Spain is an intoxicating country. Infinitely varied, it's home to Roman ruins and Gaudí's fairy-tale creations, beautiful beaches and a sizzling foodie scene. Whatever your dream trip to Spain includes, this DK Eyewitness travel guide is the perfect companion.

1 A couple watching the sun set over Granada.

2 Corks for Rioja wine, made in Northern Spain.

3 The gleaming exterior of Gehry's Museo Guggenheim.

4 Overlooking the beach at Peñíscola, near Valencia.

The largest country in southern Europe, Spain is bounded to the east by the turquoise Mediterranean and to the west by the wild Atlantic. Consequently, it's framed by secret coves, long golden strands and wind-whipped cliffs. The towering peaks of the Pyrenees form the country's northern border, and, further south, badlands and vineyards give way to the high, sun-baked plains of Central Spain and the undulating olive groves of Andalucía.

The cities, too, are equally beguiling. In Madrid, Spain's fizzing capital, a trio of glittering galleries rub shoulders with jumbled flea markets. The spirit of Madrid's rival – sun-kissed Barcelona – is embodied in Picasso's paint, Gaudí's bricks and, now, on plates. The Catalan capital has a stellar foodie reputation, with experimental chefs reinventing classic cuisine. But San Sebastián is hot on its heels, serving up just-caught seafood and hearty *pintxos*. Bilbao – the other jewel in the Basque Country's crown – has transformed from an industrial has-been to an artistic trail-blazer thanks to the Museo Guggenheim. While this futuristic building crowns the north, in the south Andalucía's three seductive cities – Seville, Cordoba and Granada – are characterized by their Moorish structures, and shaded patios perfumed by orange blossom.

So, where to start? We've broken the country down into easily navigable chapters, with detailed itineraries, expert local knowledge and colourful comprehensive maps to help you plan the perfect visit. Whether you're staying for a weekend or longer, this DK Eyewitness travel guide will ensure that you see the very best that Spain has to offer. Enjoy the book, and enjoy Spain.

REASONS TO LOVE
SPAIN

The architecture is amazing; the natural landscape awe-inspiring. It has a packed calendar of curious festivals and comes alive after dark. Ask any Spaniard and you'll hear a different reason why they love their country.

1 THE ALHAMBRA

Nowhere encapsulates the spirit of al-Andalus quite like the Alhambra *(p494)*. Its salons are replete with icing-sugar ceilings of delicate stucco and its courtyards have impossibly still, reflective pools.

THE MEZQUITA 2

Casting shadows across the marble floor, 856 columns support the red-and-white horseshoe-shaped arches in the stunning hypostyle hall of Córdoba's Great Mosque *(p484)*.

3 BEAUTIFUL BEACHES

With more than 8,000 km (5,000 miles) of coastline, Spain has a stunning array of beaches *(p54)*. Take your pick from glorious sweeps of golden sand on the Costa Blanca, enchanting little coves on the Costa Brava or the Costa Verde's dramatic cliffs.

WALKING THE CAMINO DE SANTIAGO 4

You'll be presented with a coveted Compostela Certificate if you tackle the final 100 km (62 miles), or cycle the last 200 km (124 miles), of the celebrated pilgrim path *(p232)*.

TAKING A TAPEO 5

One of Spain's most delightful traditions is the *tapeo* – a stroll from tapas bar to tapas bar, sampling different dishes at each *(p41)*. Head to the charming historic centres of Madrid *(p288)* or Seville *(p448)* to join the locals on their hungry night-time hop.

LATE NIGHTS 6

Get into the Spanish rhythm by taking a siesta in the afternoon, when temperatures are highest, and waiting until the cover of darkness before joining the locals for dinner and drinks *(p56)*.

GAUDÍ'S BARCELONA 7

Spain's most famous architect has left his indelible mark on Catalonia's capital, with countless buildings bearing roofs modelled on scaly dragons and façades that look like whipped cream *(p98)*.

MADRID'S MUSEUMS 8

The capital packs a serious cultural punch with its superb trio of museums. The Prado *(p316)*, Thyssen-Bornemisza *(p320)* and Reina Sofía *(p322)* contain a millennia's worth of world-class art, and all within a stone's throw of each other.

9 DANCING THE FLAMENCO

There's nowhere more atmospheric to experience flamenco than Seville *(p461)*. Seek out an authentic *peña* to feel the *duende* – the "magic spirit" – as you watch the *bailaora* skirt swirl while the *tocadores* strum their guitars *(p56)*.

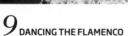

10 SEMANA SANTA

Hooded men and veiled women carrying flickering candles, crosses and decorated floats process through Spain's streets during Holy Week *(p61)*. Seville's festivities are the most elaborate *(p465)*.

SAVOURING SHERRY 11

Sip this fortified wine in the "Sherry Triangle" – the region around Jerez de la Frontera *(p503)*. Here, you can tour historic *bodegas* and enjoy a tipple in a typical *taberna (p48)*.

BASQUE CULTURE 12

The Basques have a unique language and traditions *(p277)*. Visit in August for the Semanas Grandes to see some *herri kirolak* (rural sports), such as stone-lifting, as well as dancing *(p61)*.

EXPLORE
SPAIN

This guide divides Spain into 17 colour-coded sightseeing areas, as shown
on this map. Find out more about each area on the following pages.

ASTURIAS AND CANTABRIA
p244

NORTHERN SPAIN

GALICIA
p222

CASTILLA Y LEÓN
p366

COMUNIDAD DE MADRID
p354

MADRID
p288

CENTRAL SPAIN

Atlantic Ocean

PORTUGAL

EXTREMADURA
p426

SEVILLE
p448

SOUTHERN

ANDALUCÍA
p472

Ortigueira
Ferrol
A Coruña
Avilés
Gijón
Santander
Santiago de Compostela
Lugo
León
Burgos
Pontevedra
Ponferrada
Ourense
Vigo
Braga
Benavente
Valladolid
Peñafiel
Vila Real
Porto
Salamanca
Aveiro
Ciudad Rodrigo
Ávila
Madrid
Coimbra
Plasencia
Aranjuez
Castelo Branco
Coria
Toledo
Leiria
Cáceres
Trujillo
Santarém
Badajoz
Mérida
Ciudad Real
Lisbon
Setúbal
Évora
Puertollano
Zafra
Linares
Beja
Córdoba
Jaén
Seville
Estepa
Lagos
Huelva
Granada
Faro
Jerez de la Frontera
Málaga
Motril
Cádiz
Marbella
Algeciras
Gibraltar (U.K.)
Tangier
MOROCCO

0 kilometres   100
0 miles   100

N

Canary Islands

WESTERN CANARY ISLANDS
p554

Santa Cruz
de la Palma
La Palma
La Gomera
San
Sebastián
Valverde
El Hierro

Santa Cruz
de Tenerife
Tenerife
Los
Cristianos

EASTERN CANARY ISLANDS
p564

Las Palmas de
Gran Canaria
*Gran
Canaria*

Lanzarote
Arrecife
Puerto del
Rosario
Fuerteventura

0 kilometres   100
0 miles   100

N

*Bay of
Biscay*

San
Sebastián
Biarritz
Bilbao

FRANCE

THE BASQUE COUNTRY, NAVARRA AND LA RIOJA
p260

Logroño
Tudela
Soria
Jaca
Huesca

ANDORRA
Andorra la Vella
La Seu
de Urgell

Perpignan
Figueres

CATALONIA
p150

Vic
Girona

ARAGÓN
p174

Zaragoza
Calatayud

Manresa
Lleida

EASTERN SPAIN

Alcañiz
Tortosa

Sitges
Barcelona
Tarragona

BARCELONA
p70

Guadalajara

Teruel
Benicarló

*Mediterranean
Sea*

Cuenca

Benicàssim
Castellón de la Plana

Menorca
Ciutadella

Sagunto
Requena
Valencia

Mallorca
Alcudia
Palma

THE BALEARIC ISLANDS
p532

CASTILLA-LA MANCHA
p402

Tormelloso
Albacete

Ibiza

Valdepeñas

Hellín

Gandia
Xábia

Ibiza

VALENCIA AND MURCIA
p192

Elda
Benidorm
Alicante

Úbeda
Huéscar

SPAIN

Lorca

Murcia
Cartagena

SOUTH WEST EUROPE

REP OF
IRELAND
UNITED
KINGDOM
GERMANY
BELGIUM
CZECH
REP.

*Atlantic
Ocean*

FRANCE
SWITZ.
AUSTRIA
ITALY

SPAIN
Barcelona
PORTUGAL
● Madrid
*Balearic
Islands*
● Seville

MOROCCO
TUNISIA

*Canary
Islands*
area of
Canary Islands
inset map

ALGERIA
LIBYA

Aguillas
Mojácar
Almería

GETTING TO KNOW
SPAIN

Stretching 1,085 km (674 miles) from east to west, and 950 km (590 miles) from north to south – without counting its islands – it's not surprising that Spain's 17 autonomous communities differ so greatly. We've split the country into seven regions, which each contain diverse areas.

BARCELONA

PAGE 70

The Catalan capital traces the history of architecture in its cityscape. As well as contemporary constructions, it features Europe's largest, and best preserved, medieval quarter and the greatest concentration of Modernista buildings found anywhere in the world. The most famous of these fantastical structures is the Sagrada Família, the still unfinished work of Antoni Gaudí i Cornet. Throw in almost 5 km (3 miles) of beaches, a superb dining scene and fabulous nightlife, and it's easy to see why this stylish, laid-back city on the Mediterranean coast draws so many visitors.

Best for
Amazing architecture

Home to
Old Town, Eixample, Montjuïc

Experience
Panoramic, city-wide views from the famous tiled bench in Gaudí's Park Güell

PAGE 144

EASTERN SPAIN

The rugged, craggy coves of the Costa Brava, the sun and sand of the Costa Blanca, and the mountains of the Pyrenees await in Eastern Spain. It's a fantastic destination for a huge range of outdoor sports and activities, including hiking, skiing, cycling and sailing. The region has a wealth of historical sights, too, including Catalonia's monasteries, Mudéjar towers in Aragón, and the great cathedrals of Valencia and Murcia. Foodies are also in for a treat – Valencia is the original home of paella and Catalan chefs are feted around the world for their dazzlingly imaginative creations.

Best for
Outdoor activities

Home to
Catalonia, Aragón, Valencia and Murcia

Experience
Tucking into a steaming bowl of paella at a seafront restaurant in Valencia

PAGE 216

NORTHERN SPAIN

This is the wild corner of Spain that few visitors discover. Seek out the mystical Celtic culture of Galicia, hike along the dramatic peaks of the Picos de Europa or walk the Camino de Santiago and explore the glorious coastline, with its wind-whipped cliffs and charming fishing towns. But this is also a sophisticated region, and the wealthiest in Spain, home to buzzing Bilbao and sleek San Sebastián. The Basque Country is world-renowned for its spectacular cuisine, while La Rioja is equally famous for its superb wines.

Best for
Dramatic scenery

Home to
Galicia, Asturias and Cantabria, the Basque Country, Navarra and La Rioja

Experience
Heading out on the pintxos trail in San Sebastián

$\rightarrow$

PAGE 288

MADRID

The enchanting Spanish capital has a host of glittering attractions – from the enormous Palacio Real, with its lavishly decorated chambers, to the massive Museo del Prado, whose collection comprises over 20,000 art works – but it somehow also feels surprisingly intimate. This is particularly true of the city's historic heart, where the cobbled streets and tiled taverns have barely changed in centuries. But the capital is far from staid and after dark Madrid really comes to life, with revellers spilling onto the streets from chic cocktail bars and tiny tapas bars.

Best for
Massive museums

Home to
West Madrid, East Madrid, sights just beyond the city

Experience
Browsing El Rastro flea market on a Sunday morning

PAGE 346

CENTRAL SPAIN

There's nowhere better to soak up the history of Spain than at its heart. Admire glorious Roman monuments in Segovia and Mérida, wander around Toledo's medieval core to discover its multicultural heritage in the form of churches, synagogues and Moorish fortresses, and gasp at the stunning Renaissance architecture of Salamanca. As you'd expect from their names, Castilla y León and Castilla-La Mancha teem with castles, but Central Spain is also home to some of the country's most beautiful and remote landscapes, particularly in Extremadura and the Sierra Centro de Guadarrama.

Best for
Historic towns and cities

Home to
Comunidad de Madrid, Castilla y León, Castilla-La Mancha, Extremadura

Experience
Strolling along the magnificent walls of Ávila, admiring the mountain views

SOUTHERN SPAIN

PAGE 442

When you think of Spain, you're probably thinking of the south: the strumming sound of flamenco, the heady scent of jasmine and orange blossom, and savouring a refreshing glass of ice-cold manzanilla sherry on a pretty square. Al-Andalus may have been vanquished centuries ago, but its spirit lives on in Seville's Alcázar, the Mezquita of Córdoba and Granada's Alhambra. Away from the cities, beautiful beaches and fishing villages stretch along the Mediterranean coast, perfect for escaping the summer heat.

Best for
Beaches and whitewashed villages

Home to
Seville, Andalucía

Experience
A flamenco show at one of Seville's peñas – flamenco clubs run by true aficionados of the art

SPAIN'S ISLANDS

PAGE 526

The sun-kissed Balearic Islands – Mallorca, Menorca, Ibiza, Cabrera and Formentera – provide the perfect Mediterranean escape. Despite their diminutive size, they offer a whole range of activities, whether you're looking for fun and glamour in one of Ibiza's raucous nightclubs, ancient history in the form of Menorca's Neolithic remains or a blissful rural retreat on unspoiled Formentera. Head for the subtropical Canary Islands to soak up stunning volcanic landscapes, breathtaking beaches and superb hiking routes all year round – it's the perfect winter-sun destination.

Best for
Nightlife and stunning scenery

Home to
The Balearic Islands, the Western and Eastern Canary Islands

Experience
The views from Spain's highest mountain, Mount Teide

←

1 An aerial view of Barceloneta's beach.

2 The Glory façade of the Sagrada Família.

3 A group eating dinner at La Dama, an airy restaurant.

4 A sculpture on display in the Museu Picasso.

Spain offers endless options for exploration, from weekends spent discovering the charming cities to longer tours through dramatic landscapes. Wherever you choose to go, our handpicked itineraries will help you plan the perfect trip.

3 DAYS
in Barcelona

Day 1

Morning Start your trip to Barcelona at its historic heart – the Barri Gòtic (p104) – stopping for a coffee at Els 4 Gats (p79). Next, visit Barcelona Cathedral, where the cloister is guarded by a gaggle of honking geese (p84). There are dozens of excellent places in the area for lunch, such as Bistrot Levante (www.bistrotlevante.com), which serves up creative vegetarian dishes.

Afternoon Stroll down La Rambla (p86), pausing to check out the market stalls on the way to Port Vell, which glistens with yachts (p102). Go from here to the traditional fishermen's neighbourhood of Barceloneta and spend the rest of the afternoon lounging on the beach (p102).

Evening Take a tapeo along the seafront, popping into tapas bars to nibble on their offerings. Once you've had your fill, head to 1881 on the roof of the Museu d'Història de Catalunya for cocktails with a view (www.sagardi.com).

Day 2

Morning Make a beeline for the spectacular Sagrada Família (p110). The length of the entrance queue can be almost as mind-boggling as the building itself, so book a tour to make the most of your visit (www.toursbylocals.com). After exploring the nave, take the lift up to the tower for panoramic city views, but bear in mind that the descent is by foot.

Afternoon After a lazy lunch at La Yaya Amelia (www.layayaamelia.com), it's a short stroll to the Sant Pau Recinte Modernista (p120), an enchanting complex of pavilions, set in peaceful gardens, that once functioned as a hospital.

Evening Staying with the architectural theme, take a taxi to La Dama, a stunning Modernista apartment that houses a restaurant and bar (www.la-dama.com).

Day 3

Morning Start on the pretty Passeig del Born, a former jousting ground now lined with cafés, such as the Bar el Born (www.barelborn.es). While away the rest of your morning at the Museu Picasso, tracing the evolution of the artist's style (p90). Almost as essential a stop is El Xampanyet (p101), the legendary cava and tapas bar opposite.

Afternoon Wander down the fashionable Passeig de Gràcia, which is as famous for its Modernista architecture as it is for its shopping. Don't miss the block known as the Ila de la Discòrdia (p121), where you'll see three delightfully clashing façades. Explore one of these architectural gems on a guided tour (book online in advance).

Evening As evening falls, you might want to experience the light show at La Pedrera, where the espanta-bruixes are illuminated in a riot of colour (p118). Later, head for dinner at El Nacional (p121), a stunning indoor food court.

7 DAYS
on the Mediterranean

Day 1

Board the train for Sitges (p169) from Barcelona's Passeig de Gràcia station. After speeding along the coast, you'll reach this enchanting town in time for a stroll and a steaming bowl of paella at seafront El Tambucho (Port Alegre 49; 938 94 79 12). After lunch, wander up to Sant Bartomeu i Santa Tecla, and then drop into the Museu Cau Ferrat, which has an extraordinary collection of Modernista art. Round off your day at Casablanca Cocktail Bar & Art Lounge with a fruity drink (p169).

Day 2

Board a mid-morning train bound for Tarragona (p171). Once the capital of an important Roman province, it's dotted with impressive remains. Buy a joint ticket and spend the day ticking off the sights, breaking for a hearty lunch at La Cuineta (Carrer Nou Patriarca 2; 977 22 61 01). Next, walk the Roman walls, before savouring a moment of reflection in the shaded cloisters of the cathedral. Feast on Catalonia's unique cuisine at soulful Les Coques (www.les-coques.com).

Day 3

In the morning, it's all aboard the train to Peníscola (p201). Take a taxi to the Old Town and spend some time browsing the streetside stalls for souvenirs before visiting the Castell del Papa Luna. Have a lazy lunch at Casa Jaime Peñiscola (www. casajaimepeñiscola.com), then ride the rails south to Valencia (p196). The walls of Spain's third-largest city are festooned with street art, so take a walking tour to learn more about the murals. Look out for any pieces that pertain to Valencia's status as the birthplace of paella, and sample this iconic dish for yourself at Restaurante Navarro (p198).

Day 4

Spend the day sightseeing in Valencia, beginning with a visit to the cathedral, where you can climb the bell tower for tremendous views. Then push on to El Mercado Central to check out its fresh produce and Modernist architecture. There are plenty of tapas bars in El Carmen so peruse a few before choosing one for lunch. In the afternoon, walk down the

1 Sitges bathed in golden light at sunset.

2 Façade of the 12th-century cathedral in Tarragona

3 The Roman theatre in Cartagena, lit up at night.

4 The futuristic exterior of the Ciutat de les Arts i de les Ciències in Valencia.

5 Peñíscola, crowded on a rocky promontory.

6 Walking down Murcia's lively Calle de la Trapería.

repurposed riverbed to the gleaming Ciutat de les Arts i de les Ciències to take in the interactive science museum. For dinner, decide whether the paella at legendary La Pepica beats the rest *(p198)*. Valencia is renowned for its nightlife so get ready to party with the city's movers-and-shakers at L'Umbracle in the Ciutat de les Arts i de les Ciències *(p199)*, where you can sip on cocktails under a canopy of palm trees.

Day 5

It's an easy and enjoyable train journey south through the hills to Alicante *(p208)*, a vibrant seaside city that offers great shopping and after-dark entertainment, as well as a lively cultural scene. Start with a Mediterranean lunch at Restaurante La Ereta *(www.laereta.com)*. Then, take in the fabulous views from the clifftop Castillo de Santa Bárbara and wander around the winding streets of the Old Town. In the evening, try gastro tapas bar La Taberna del Gourmet *(www.latabernadel gourmet.com)* and then see what the Costa Blanca has to offer once the sun goes down at the lively 26 Cafe Lounge Bar *(p209)*.

Day 6

Arrive in the port city of Cartagena *(p213)* in time for lunch at El Barrio de San Roque *(www.elbarriodesanroque.com)*. One of the oldest cities in Spain, Cartagena preserves a slew of Phoenician, Roman and Moorish monuments, including a spectacular Roman theatre and a lofty castle (now home to a history museum), from which there are fabulous panoramic views. Finish the day with dinner at much-loved Magoga, in the Old Town *(www.restaurantemagoga.com)*.

Day 7

Dominated by a vast Gothic cathedral, Murcia *(p210)* is an hour's train journey away. Start by sampling the Spanish version of pizza at Mano A Mano *(p211)*. Next, take a tour of the dazzling casino, a sort of Spanish social club. Then, check out the huge *pasos* at the Museo Salzillo. How does anyone carry these through the streets on Good Friday? End your week with an evening *tapeo* in one of Murcia's pretty squares, crammed with great tapas bars.

7 DAYS
in the Basque Country

Day 1

Start your trip in Bilbao, a vision from the future *(p264)*. The spectacular Museo Guggenheim deserves a day to itself *(p266)*. Admire the gleaming curves of Frank Gehry's magnificent building, and say hello to Jeff Koons' flower-covered *Puppy* at the entrance. After exploring the collection, spend the evening scouring the city for the best *pintxos* with Bilbao Food Tours *(www.mybilbaofoodtours.com)*.

Day 2

Spend the morning at Bilbao's other fantastic art museum, the Museo de Bellas Artes *(p264)*. Don't miss the pieces by big-names El Greco, Goya and Sorolla. From here, ride the steep tram to the Mercado de la Ribera for lunch at one of the brimming stalls *(p265)*. Come after-noon, drive the 40 minutes to Gernika-Lumo, which was bombed on the orders of General Franco in 1937 *(p272)*. After exploring the poignant peace museum, try the grilled meats at Restaurante Víctor Montes *(www.victormontes.com)*.

Day 3

Today, you'll explore the spectacular Costa Vasca, with its plunging cliffs and beautiful bays *(p273)*. Stop off at a string of enchanting towns, such as Lekeitio, Zumaia, Zarautz and pretty little Getaria. Any of them is ideal for a seafood lunch by the beach, but we love Bodega Katxiña in Orio *(www.bodegakatxina.com)*. If you're feeling energetic, spend your afternoon learning to surf at the North Shore Surf Camp in Zarautz *(www.northshorezarautz. com)*. When the sun goes down, head to San Sebastián *(p268)* for an evening of gourmet *pintxos* along the Calle 31 de Agosto. Don't miss out Gandarias *(p271)*.

Day 4

Ease yourself into the day with a stroll around the narrow streets surrounding the magnificent Basilica de Santa María *(p268)*, before a visit to the Museo de San Telmo *(p270)*. Set in a 16th-century monastery, its collection includes some of the Basque Country's most impressive masterpieces. After lunch at the Bodegón Alejandro *(www.bodegonalejandro.com)*,

1 Louise Bourgeois' towering *Maman* statue, outside the Museo Guggenheim in Bilbao.

2 Vines rolling down to the coast in the Rioja Alta wine region.

3 The beautiful Playa de la Concha in San Sebastián.

4 The Santuario de Arantzazu, high on a rocky mount.

5 Al fresco dining in Vitoria.

hike to the top of Monte Urgull (*p268*) to enjoy the panoramic views of the Playa de la Concha. Then, head down to this beach to relax on the sand. After watching the sun set over the bobbing boats on the horizon, it's time to seek out some dinner. If you're feeling flashy, why not splash out at one of this culinary city's many Michelin-starred restaurants – Arzak is our favourite (*p271*).

Day 5

From San Sebastián, drive inland through verdant countryside to the captivating Santuario de Loiola (*p274*). This lavish 18th-century complex was built on the site where the founder of the Jesuits Ignatius of Loyola was born in the 1490s. After admiring the paintings on the inside of the domed cupola here, continue to the elegant little university town of Oñati (*p275*) and enjoy a light lunch at Bizipoz (*Portu Kalea; 943 08 35 08*). In the afternoon, make a detour to take a look at the Franciscan Santuario de Arantzazu en route to the vibrant Basque capital of Vitoria, which is a 30-minute drive away (*p276*). There are plenty of spots for dinner here.

Day 6

Begin your exploration in the charming Plaza de la Virgen Blanca, where you can pick up breakfast. Then explore the older of Vitoria's two cathedrals, the Catedral de Santa María. After a late lunch at El Clarete (*www.elclareterestaurante.com*), visit the Museo de Arqueologia y Naipes (BIBAT), which has a curious collection of playing cards. Look out for the tarot cards designed by Salvador Dalí. In the evening take a *poteo* (*pintxos*-crawl) in the Old Town.

Day 7

Your last day will take you back to Bilbao but first stop off in Haro (*p275*). Browse the many wine shops in the capital of the Rioja Alta region, before gorging on the hearty *pintxos* and tapas served at Bar Benigno (*p275*). Even the designated driver will be rewarded by a detour to the Marqués de Riscal vineyard this afternoon (*p278*). They can indulge in a "barrel bath" or "Crush Cabernet Scrub" at the spa here instead of a wine tasting. Then, drive on to Bilbao and end your trip to the north with a traditional meal at Bikandi Etxea (*p265*).

→

① The lighthouse, perched on a cliff edge, in Castro Urdiales.

② The sweeping Playa del Sardinero, one of the beaches that frame Santander.

③ Exploring the haunting El Monte Castillo cave system.

④ A cable car climbing to the heights of the Parque Nacional de los Picos de Europa.

10 DAYS
in the North

Day 1

Kick off with two of Cantabria's prettiest and most popular beach resorts, Castro Urdiales *(p259)* and Laredo *(p259)*. Start with a stroll around Castro Urdiales' port, popping into its Gothic Iglesia de Santa María, which has a pinkish hue. Once you've worked up an appetite, order a seafood lunch at Arboleda *(Calle Ardigales 48; 942 87 19 93)* and then spend an afternoon on the sand in Laredo. Although the town's beaches get busy in summer, you'll find breathtaking, emptier stretches the further you walk from the centre. After basking in the sun, head for dinner at La Marina Company *(www.lamarinacompany.es)*.

Day 2

Next up is the Cantabrian capital Santander *(p258)*, which was completely rebuilt in the 1940s after a devastating fire destroyed its historic heart. Still an atmospheric port city, it has good seafood restaurants and some wonderful beaches. Try the lively Marucho *(www.maruchorestaurante.es)* for lunch. In the afternoon, take in some of the city's cultural highlights, such as one of the exhibitions at the Centro Botín or the fishy delights at the Museo Marítimo, including a skeleton of a gargantuan whale. In the evening, some of the best tapas in town are to be found at Cañadío *(www.restaurantecanadio.com)*.

Day 3

Drive southwest to Puente Viesgo for El Monte Castillo, a complex of caves *(p258)*. They are not as well known as the nearby Cuevas de Altamira *(p257)*, but they are just as impressive. From here, it's a 20-minute drive to Santillana del Mar *(p258)*, which, despite its name, is not quite located on the coast. It's an enchanting and beautifully preserved town, paved with cobblestones and dotted with churches, palaces and mansions. Don't miss La Colegiata, the Romanesque monastery at the heart of the town. Good places for lunch or dinner include Los Blasones *(www.restaurantelosblasones.es)* or Casa Uzquiza *(Calle Jesús Otero 5, 942 84 03 56)*.

Day 4

It's around an hour's drive to the extraordinary little town of Potes *(p254)*, which easily merits a couple of hours' strolling around, but also acts as a springboard for the stunning Parque Nacional de los Picos de Europa *(p248)*. You could spend weeks here, but in one day you can at least enjoy a fantastic hike (visit the tourist office for suggested routes), some rock climbing, or simply pick up some picnic provisions in Potes and enjoy lunch among some of the most spectacular mountain scenery that Spain has to offer. On your return to town have dinner in Casa Cayo *(www.casacayo.com)*.

→

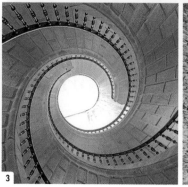

Day 5

Leave the Parque Nacional de los Picos de Europa via the Lagos de Covadonga, two picturesque lakes in the park's northwest corner, and continue to Covadonga itself, a charming mountain town that is worth a stroll. From here it's a ten-minute drive to the ancient Asturian capital of Cangas de Onís (*p255*), which enjoys a spectacular mountain backdrop. After a scrumptious tapas lunch at Restaurant El Molin de la Pedrera (*www.elmolin.com*), have a wander over the town's Romanesque bridge to the 8th-century chapel. Come evening, it's worth a detour from Cangas de Onís to the other side of Arriondas for the Michelin-starred Casa Marcial (*www.casamarcial.com*), which showcases the finest of the region's hearty cuisine.

Day 6

Continue west to Gijón (*p252*), a port city with a charming Old Town piled up on a narrow isthmus. While away the morning at the Palacio de Revillagigedo (Centro Cultural Cajastur), which hosts temporary exhibitions, and then wander along one of Gijón's long beaches, perhaps ending up at one or two of the tapas bars around Playa de San Lorenzo. Once you've soaked up the sun here, head back into town to walk the Roman walls and explore Gijón's museums. End up at Auga (*www.restaurante auga.com*), one of the finest restaurants in town, for a decadent dinner.

Day 7

Spend a day in handsome Oviedo (*p252*), a historic city gathered around a splendid Gothic cathedral. Check out the royal tombs and the 9th-century chapel, before lunch at Taberna Salcedo (*www.taberna salcedo.es*). Famous across Spain for its vibrant cultural gems, Oviedo has pre-Romanesque churches located on the hills overlooking the city. The best preserved is Santa María del Naranco, a couple of miles northwest of the centre. Next, have a look at the superb art, including paintings by El Greco, Goya and Dalí, in the Museo de Bellas Artes de Asturias. Afterwards, try the celebrated *fabada asturiana* (regional bean stew) at Casa Fermín (*www.casafermin.com*).

[1] The Basílica de Santa María la Real de Covadonga. ↑

[2] Surfers walking along Gijón's Playa de San Lorenzo.

[3] A spiral staircase in the Museo do Pobo Galego, Santiago de Compostela.

[4] The pretty seaside town of Cudillero, on the Costa Verde.

[5] Walking through the Puerta del Obispo Aguirre Izquierdo in Lugo.

[6] *La Regenta*, dedicated to Leopoldo Alas y Ureña's novel, Oviedo.

Day 8

Head west along the coastal road that skirts the glorious Costa Verde (p250). With its cliffs and coves, verdant hills and picturesque villages, this is easily one of Spain's loveliest and least spoiled stretches of coastline. Stop off and explore charming towns such as Cudillero, where you can dine on tapas at one of the outdoor cafés in the town's main square, Plaza Marina – try Bar Casa Julio at No 7 (617 43 82 54). Later head to Luarca, for a mooch around its pretty harbour, and perhaps end up in Castropol for a seafood dinner on the waterfront at El Risón (Paseo del Muelle s/n, 985 63 50 65).

Day 9

Cross the border into Galicia and aim for the ancient city of Lugo (p240). Once an important Roman settlement, Lugo is still ringed by spectacular and remarkably intact Roman walls, which you can climb to enjoy fabulous views. First, have a hearty Galician lunch outside the city at charming Taberna do Labrego (www. tabernadolabrego.com). Once you breach the walls, you'll find that the old city is a jumble of narrow streets and pretty squares – perfect for a wander before visiting Lugo's Romanesque cathedral. Round off your day with dinner at Terra Taberna do Miño (www.tabernaterra.com).

Day 10

End your journey in the magical city of Santiago de Compostela – the culmination of the famous pilgrimage and a fitting stop for your trip (p226). An enchanting city built of cool grey stone, it is dominated by a magnificent cathedral, said to contain the bones of St James (Santiago). Allow plenty of time to visit the cathedral, and then head to the Mercado de Abastos for a glass of wine and a plate of prawns at any of the bars in the area. In the late afternoon, visit the Museo do Pobo Galego for an interesting look into local life over the centuries. In the evening, head for Dezaseis and be sure to try the city's star dishes – scallops or octopus (www. dezaseis.com). What better way to end your trip to the north coast than with a delicious plate of seafood?

←

① The busy streets of the Plaza Mayor.

② Admiring Caravaggio's *St Catherine of Alexandria* in the Museo Thyssen-Bornemisza.

③ A flamenco show at Villa Rosa in Huertas.

④ Dipping a churro in sauce.

24 HOURS
in Madrid

▌ *Morning*

Nothing sets you up for a weekend in Madrid like a breakfast of fried churros dipped in hot chocolate, and nowhere has been serving them as long as the Chocolateria San Ginés (*www.chocolateria sangines.com*). Check out the photos of its famous patrons on the walls. From here, it's a short walk to the grand, arcaded Plaza Mayor (*p302*). Built by the Habsburgs in the 17th century, it's still the hub for many of the city's celebrations. Exit down the elegant flight of steps under the Arco de los Cuchilleros and turn immediately right for the Mercado de San Miguel (*p306*), a handsome century-old iron and steel market building, which has been converted into a gourmet food court. Admire the glistening vegetables and perfectly sliced fish, and try to resist your rumbling tummy. Exiting at the far end, you'll be close to the Plaza Conde Miranda, a graceful, quiet square where you can buy biscuits via a revolving panel in the wall of the Convento de las Carboneras – the perfect souvenir. Stroll back through the Plaza Conde Barajas to find the legendary El Sobrino de Botín, the world's oldest restaurant and a great spot to savour suckling pig, roasted in an oak-wood oven (*p306*).

▌ *Afternoon*

Choosing between the trio of museums in Madrid's Golden Triangle of Art is tough but, containing masterpieces from almost every movement from Flemish masters to Russian constructivism, the Museo Thyssen-Bornemisza is the ultimate all-rounder (*p320*). Here, you'll see works by El Greco and Edward Hopper, Salvador Dalí and Canaletto, Picasso and Gauguin. It's a vast collection, so leave some time to recuperate with an ice-cold *caña* (beer) in the nearby Plaza de Santa Ana. This square is at the heart of the Huertas neighbourhood, famous for its literary past but blessed with a present that moves to the soulful rhythm of flamenco. Take a tour of the shops and taverns connected with this most Spanish of arts, before taking in an authentic performance that will finish just in time for dinner (*www.theflamencoguide.com*).

▌ *Evening*

Huertas heaves with superb bistros these days, but one of the best is tiny and friendly TriCiclo (*p330*). Chow down on meaty prawns and delicate *amuse-bouches* before indulging in a nightcap in one of the nearby bars. For something a little out of the ordinary, head back past the Museo Thyssen-Bornemisza to the NH Suecia hotel, a side entrance of which will take you downstairs through some bathrooms to Hemingway – an Art Deco speakeasy open until the early hours (*Calle Marqués de Casa Riera 4; 91 051 35 92*).

←

1 The city's skyline at dusk, bathed in golden light.

2 Patio de las Doncellas in the Real Alcázar.

3 Young women dancing the flamenco on the Plaza de España.

4 Café culture on the Calle de las Sierpes.

2 DAYS
in Seville

Day 1

Morning Arrive early to beat the queue for one of Seville's most recognizable landmarks, La Giralda, the minaret-cum-bell tower next to the vast cathedral *(p452)*. The tomb of Christopher Columbus can be found inside the cathedral, along with a wealth of lavish artworks, but the highlight is the extraordinary view from the top of the tower. Nearby, the Bodega Santa Cruz makes an excellent tapas stop – try the spinach with chickpeas, a local speciality *(Calle Rodrigo Cano 1; 95 421 86 18)*.

Afternoon Walk off your lunch with a gentle stroll through the Jardines de Murillo and the charming Parque María Luisa *(p456)*, pausing on one of its colourful benches to listen to the tinkling fountains. Close by is the former Real Fábrica de Tabacos, the workplace of Carmen in the opera of the same name and now part of the Universidad *(p465)*. Seville features in many operas, and one way to learn more is to take a tour with a soprano, who – with musical accompaniment – will show you the sights that inspired composers *(www.sevillaofficial tours.com)*.

Evening Round off your journey through Seville's musical heritage at Tablao El Arenal *(p56)*. Sip on Rioja and savour the delicate dishes as you watch the swirling skirts, stamping feet and strumming fingers of the guitarists. Flamenco is the city's heart and soul.

Day 2

Morning Start your day admiring the superb art collection in the Museo de Bellas Artes *(p458)*. Seek out *La Servilleta*, an image of the Virgin and Child, which is said to have been painted on a napkin *(servilleta)*. Next, window-shop along Calle de las Sierpes, admiring the flamenco dresses and *mantilla* shawls *(p460)*. Cross over the river to soulful Triana – the city's working-class heart *(p466)*. Head straight for the neighbourhood's bustling market and discover its best-loved tapas bars on a culinary walking tour, starting at 12:30pm *(www.azahar-sevilla.com)*.

Afternoon While away the remainder of the afternoon in the Barrio Santa Cruz, an enchanting warren of narrow lanes lined with whitewashed houses sporting geranium-filled balconies. Wrought-iron gates give tempting glimpses of the leafy patios and gardens so typical of this neighbourhood, but don't miss out on visiting the grand courtyard and garden of the Casa de Pilatos *(p463)*, a breath-taking mansion that is still home to the Dukes of Medinaceli.

Evening For an unforgettable experience, book a night visit to the sumptuous Real Alcázar *(p454)*, where actors posing as Fernando III, Isabel la Católica or Lope de Vega will act as your guide. After exploring this must-see Mudéjar sight, join the locals for a late dinner at Bar Las Teresas, famous for its hulking hams *(www.lasteresas.es)*.

←

1 Cycling along the river, with Triana on the opposite bank.

2 The Puente Nuevo, linking the two sides of Ronda.

3 A decorated house in the Albaicín, Granada.

4 An art installation in Málaga's town centre.

5 DAYS
in Andalucía

Day 1

The spirit of old al-Andalus is strongest in Granada (*p492*). Start off your tour in the old Moorish neighbourhood of the Albaicín (*p498*), whose narrow lanes are lined with craft shops, bathhouses and cafés. Stop for lunch at Carmen Verde Luna (*www.carmenverdeluna.com*), then head up to explore the Alhambra's honeycomb-like rooms and arcaded patios (*p494*), as well as the Generalife gardens (*p496*). In the evening, take in a clandestine flamenco show in one of the caves in Sacromonte, where the art form originated. We love Zambra Maria la Canastera, where the eponymous dancer performed (*www.marialacanastera.com*).

Day 2

A two-hour drive west of Granada is Córdoba (*p482*). When you reach the city, head straight for the Mercado Victoria – a gourmet food hall (*p483*). At Córdoba's heart is the Mezquita (*p484*), where you can easily spend a couple of hours walking beneath the hallowed arches. Next, wander the narrow lanes of the former Jewish Quarter to the Sinagoga (*p482*). Take in the beautiful interior before seeking out the statue of Maimonides, the philosopher. Finish your day with supper at Bodegas Campos (*www.bodegascampos.com*), where you can dine in the library, office or the Sala los Célebres (Room of Celebrities).

Day 3

Wake up early to allow yourself plenty of time to explore the endlessly romantic city of Seville (*p449*). After the 90-minute drive there, potter around the evocative Barrio Santa Cruz (*p470*) and then climb La Giralda (*p452*). When you're peckish, nibble on tapas at time-warped Casa Plácido (*p459*). Allow a couple of hours to visit the Real Alcázar, one of Spain's most dazzling buildings (*p454*). In the evening, cross the river to Triana for some spontaneous flamenco (*p466*).

Day 4

It's best to arrive early in Ronda (*p480*), so that you beat the inevitable coach-trippers. It's a beautiful city in its own right, perched astride a deep gorge, but its bullring steals the show. Marvel at the colonnaded stands curving around the vast sandy stage. Then, stroll across the vertigo-inducing Puente Nuevo for lunch at Bardal (*www.restaurantebardal.com*) in the Old Town. It's a 90-minute drive from Ronda to Málaga. Start your trip to the city by visiting the Museo Picasso Málaga, before seeking out the old-school seafood bars (*p507*). Our favourite is El Tintero II, where the waiters carry around dishes for diners to peruse (*p507*).

Day 5

Begin your day with a visit to the imposing Alcazaba and perhaps a little window-shopping along the nearby Calle Marqués de Larios. Then, it's time to head for the beach at El Pedregalejo for a long lunch at one of the seafood restaurants, before you sleep it off in the shade. The Centre Pompidou Málaga is open until 8pm so explore this collection of contemporary art once the sun has gone down. Andalucía is Spain's most traditional region, so round off your tour with a typical Spanish meal of crispy-skinned lamb at Restaurante Miguel (*www.restaurantemiguel.es*).

Take a Tour

Tread in the footsteps of one of your favourite artists, or discover new galleries, on one of Spain's many art tours. In Barcelona, the official tourist board runs a Picasso walking route (bcnshop.barcelonaturisme.com) and Art Space Tours (artspacetours.com) offers guided gallery visits, art-themed dinners and photography tours. On the other side of the country, visitors can take in the capital's museums with an artist or art historian with Insider's Madrid (www.insiderstravel.io).

→

Taking a tour of Barcelona's street art with Art Space Tours

SPAIN FOR
ART LOVERS

As the home of Picasso, Velázquez and Miró, Spain has good reason to shout about its art. Big-name artists are showcased in spectacular museums across the country, but Spain's masterpieces aren't confined to the past – the country's contemporary art scene has never been more vibrant.

Gargantuan Galleries

Three of the world's finest museums form Madrid's glittering Golden Triangle of Art - the Prado (p316), Thyssen-Bornemisza (p320) and Reina Sofía (p322). Highlights at the Prado include works by Velázquez and Goya; Impressionist paintings stand out at the Thyssen-Bornemisza; and Picasso's Guernica takes centre stage at the Reina Sofía. Elsewhere, Barcelona is home to the MNAC (p133) and Bilbao has the glorious Guggenheim (p266).

↑ Richard Serra's *The Matter of Time* in the Museo Guggenheim Bilbao

Open-Air Galleries

From graffiti to outdoor sculptures, Spain is packed with some amazing public art. Check out the work of El Niño de la Pintura, the "Spanish Banksy", in Granada, or Miró's surrealist sculptures. While you're in the capital, take a street art tour or graffiti workshop with Cool Tour Spain (*www.cooltourspain.com*). Street Art Barcelona will lead you to the city's best works (*www. streetartbcn.com*) and Free Tour Valencia (*freetourvalencia. com*) will show you around art-festooned El Carmen. Look out for works by Escif.

←

Personnage Gothique, Oiseau-Eclair (1976) in the garden of the Fundació Pilar i Joan Miró

 INSIDER TIP
Pick Up Your Paint Brush

Why not try your hand at creating your own Spanish masterpiece on a painting holiday? Paint Andalucía coaches aspiring artists in the little village of Torrox (*paint-andalucia.com*).

Mi Casa Es Tu Casa

Get intimate insights into some of Spain's most revered artists by visiting their homes. Find the source of Salvador Dalí's Surrealist inspiration at his whitewashed cottage in Cadaqués *(p166)*. For Goya, head to the 18th-century farmhouse in Fuendetodos where he was born *(p189)*, while Picasso's birthplace in Málaga is just a stone's throw from the wonderful Picasso Museum *(p507)*.

→

The Museo Casa Natal de Picasso in Málaga, the artist's home town

Adrenaline Adventures

Looking to get your adrenaline pumping? As Europe's second-most-mountainous country, climbing and canyoning are natural sports here. Paddle in Spain offers a range of thrills, including whitewater rafting and paragliding *(www.paddle inspain.com)*. And if you like the view from above, skydive with Skydive Spain *(www. skydivespain.com)*.

Whitewater rafting through rapids on a river in Lleida, a province in Catalonia

SPAIN FOR
OUTDOOR
ACTIVITIES

Blessed with a spectacular coastline and magnificent mountains, every corner of Spain offers a wealth of outdoor activities. Snorkel in the Med, surf Atlantic rollers, snowboard in the Sierra Nevada, go canyoning in the Pyrenees or walk the famed Camino de Santiago: the choice is yours.

Walk This Way

From gentle coastal trails to the remote paths of the Parque Nacional de los Picos de Europa *(p248)*, a host of dramatic and well-marked hikes pepper the country. There are more than a hundred long-distance GR (Gran Recorrido) routes, including the stunning GR11 which tracks the whole breadth of the Pyrenees, the GR92 which runs down the Catalan coast and the GR7 which stretches all the way from Tarifa to Andorra. Then, of course, there is the Camino de Santiago *(p232)*. Follow the snaking route, stopping off at Northern Spain's most religious sites until you reach Santiago de Compostela's imposing cathedral *(p228)*.

→

Walking through verdant countryside on the Camino de Santiago

Hit the Slopes

It may seem surprising for a country renowned for its sun and sand, but snowbunnies are spoilt for choice when it comes to Spanish ski resorts. Most are located in the Pyrenees, including chichi Baqueira-Beret *(p161)*, family-favourite La Molina and budget-friendly El Formigal *(p182)*. But the highest resort is in Andalucía's Sierra Nevada *(p515)*, where you can ski in the morning and take a dip in the Med in the afternoon. Atudem offers a comprehensive list of resorts *(www.atudem.es)*.

→

A group of skiers taking a selfie on the slopes of the Sierra Nevada

Water You Waiting For?

Framed by the Mediterranean and the Atlantic, Spain rewards exploration in a gleaming yacht with billowing sails. But if this all sounds far too gentle, why not brave the swell in the Basque Country? Learn to ride the waves with Mundaka Surf Shop *(mundaka surfshop.com/surf-school)*.

←

Mastering the waves off Mundaka on the Costa Vasca

Wild Things

Spain's national parks and nature reserves shelter a wide range of wildlife. The Parque Nacional de Doñana *(p476)* is home to the Iberian lynx; the Pyrenees and the Cantabrian mountains shelter brown bears; and the Parc Nacional d'Aigüestortes *(p163)* is a refuge for the bearded vulture. Venture out of the towns and see how many of these elusive feathered and furry friends you can spot.

→

A brown bear standing among the trees in a forest

Eat the Streets

Visiting a local market is a great introduction to Spanish cuisine. Jewel-like fruit and vegetables sit beside huge legs of jamon serrano. Some ancient market halls have been transformed into foodie hubs, full of enticing counter bars and stalls. Our favourites are Madrid's Mercado de San Miguel *(p306)* and the Mercat Colón in Valencia *(www.mercadocolon.es)*.

A stall selling jamon serrano in Madrid's Mercado de San Miguel

SPAIN FOR
FOODIES

The salty tang of crispy barbecued sardines; sampling tapas on a jasmine-scented square; setting your tastebuds alight in a Michelin-starred restaurant: Spain offers a whole host of foodie experiences. Get ready to discover delicious regional dishes, mouthwatering markets and cook-it-yourself courses.

EAT

Enjoy Spain's luxurious fine dining restaurants.

Dani García
🅐C6 🏨Hotel Puente Romano, Marbella
🌐grupodanigarcia.com

€€€

DiverXO
🅐C4 🏨NH Eurobuilding, Madrid
🌐diverxo.com

€€€

Culler de Pau
🅐A2 🏨O Grove, Pontevedra
🌐cullerdepau.com

€€€

Cookery Courses

Want to recreate your favourite Spanish dishes? Take a cookery course. Gourmet Madrid *(www.gourmetmadrid.com)* runs classes, Barcelona Slow Travel *(www.barcelonaslowtravel.com)* offers a range of courses and Cooking Olé in Seville *(www.cookingole.com)* shows you how to prepare authentic dishes.

→

Shopping for produce at the market as part of a cookery course

Fine Dining

Spain's fine-dining scene is interstellar - its restaurants have been awarded more than 220 Michelin stars, and El Celler de Can Roca is rated the second best eatery in the world *(p159)*. Catalonia is also renowned for being the home of Ferran Adrià, the godfather of molecular gastronomy. Although his infamous restaurant El Bulli has closed, his influence is still felt on menus everywhere, particularly in the Basque Country. Andoni Aduriz, an El Bulli alumni, has crafted an avant-garde take on traditional Basque cuisine at Mugaritz in San Sebastián *(www.mugaritz.com).*

→

The tree-filled internal courtyard of El Celler de Can Roca

Tapas vs Pintxos

The bar counters of the Basque lands are heaped high with *pintxos* - slices of baguette, covered with anything from *tortilla* (potato omelette) to foie gras. *Pintxos* are the Basque answer to tapas - small plates of *croquetas* (croquettes), *patatas bravas* (fried potatoes in a spicy sauce) and more. Sample both to decide whether tapas or *pintxos* come out on top.

←

Dainty *pintxos*, topped with a mousse and *jamón ibérico* (Iberian ham)

Regional Staples

Everywhere you go in Spain, you'll find distinctive local flavours. Expect hearty stews in the mountains of central Spain and oodles of fresh seafood along the coasts. Tuck into *fabada* - a succulent bean stew - in Asturias, some *pescaíto frito* (fried fish) in Andalucía or *caldereta de langosta* (spiny lobster stew) in Menorca. Seek out paella in Valencia and *pintxos* in the Basque Country.

→

A heaped plate of *pescaíto frito*, served with slices of lime

For Architecture Buffs

There's so much more to Spain's cityscapes than Barcelona's Modernista marvels (*p78*). Golden Salamanca (*p372*) is replete with handsome Renaissance buildings, including one of the oldest universities in the world. In Santiago de Compostela (*p226*), the magnificent cathedral is the culmination of the famous pilgrims' route. The billowing titanium curves of the Guggenheim put Bilbao on the map even before you take the ground-breaking art collection it houses into account (*p266*). Meanwhile, the seductive Andalucían cities of Córdoba (*p482*) and Granada (*p492*) are home to the Mezquita and the Alhambra - testaments to the artistry of the architects of al-Andalus.

→

Strolling through the Plaza Mayor in Salamanca, past the colonnade

SPAIN'S
CAPTIVATING CITIES

Think of Spanish cities and Madrid and Barcelona surely come to mind - but there are so many more begging to be explored. Gourmets should make for San Sebastián, romantics will delight in Seville or Córdoba and elegant little Girona is a delight for those hoping to get off the beaten track.

For Night Owls

In a country that comes alive after dark, a buzzing nightlife is an important factor when deciding where to go. If you're looking for glitzy clubs, then make for Marbella (*p504*) or Eivissa (*p544*) or, for something more traditional, check out Seville's flamenco clubs (*p461*) or feel the *duende* in the caves of Granada (*p492*). Valencia has the most diverse nightlife, offering sleek cocktail bars, reggae nights and jazz jams (*p196*).

←

Punters milling around outside a restaurant in Marbella after dark

Did You Know?

One of the reasons that Spaniards eat late is that Franco moved the clocks forward to match Nazi Germany.

For Foodies

Few cities in Spain equal San Sebastián when it comes to food (p268). Tour the *pintxos* bars with Mimo (www.mimo.eus), or dine at one of the Michelin-starred eateries, such as Arzak (p271). Valencia, the home of paella, will also keep tummies content (p198). Granada (p492), meanwhile, is the perfect city for taking a *tapeo* with Granada Tapas Tours (www.granadatapastours.com).

← A stall piled high with delectable tapas in Valencia's Mercado Central, a Modernista gem

For Shopaholics

The Spanish capital is a shopping mecca: window-shop in Salamanca's upmarket boutiques or scour Malasaña's vintage stores for treasure (p342). In Barcelona, too, you'll find everything from chic homeware to Aladdin's-cave-like thrift stores. Head to Palma (p536) for gourmet goodies, or Seville (p449) for ruffled flamenco dresses and delicate *mantons* (shawls). Don't underestimate pint-sized Gijón (p252), which is chock-a-block with boutiques.

→ Espadrille store La Manual Alpargatera on Carrer d'Avinyó in Barcelona

PEDRO ALMODÓVAR

Pedro Almodóvar is one of the most highly acclaimed film-makers of modern times. Born in La Mancha in 1949, he became part of *la movida* – the post-Franco countercultural movement that galvanized the arts in Spain *(p342)*. *Women on the Edge of a Nervous Breakdown* (1988) brought him international fame but his 1999 film *All About My Mother* is considered his masterpiece.

SPAIN
ON SCREEN

With its awe-inspiring landscapes and exhilarating cities, it's little wonder that Spain has captured the imagination of so many great television and film-makers. Catch a Spanish film at an open-air cinema screening or follow the trail of your favourite show or movie to see the sights behind the sets.

TOP 5 FILMS SHOT IN SPAIN

Pan's Labyrinth (2006)
Guillermo del Toro's film is set in Franco's Spain.

Vicky Cristina Barcelona (2008)
This romantic comedy is by Woody Allen.

Volver (2006)
This Almodóvar hit was filmed in La Mancha.

A Fistful of Dollars (1964)
Sergio Leone's first spaghetti western.

Exodus: Gods and Kings (2014)
Ridley Scott's biblical epic was filmed in the Canary Islands.

Backyard Cinema

On sultry summer nights, pop-up screens show old favourites and new releases in the great outdoors. Barcelona has the vast Sala Montjuïc *(www.salamontjuic.org)*, while Madrid claims the country's largest drive-in cinema – the Autocine Madrid RACE *(autocinesmadrid.es)* – and the gorgeous Cibeles de Cine, where you can catch classics under the glass roof if the weather's bad *(www.centrocentro.org)*. Elsewhere, Cinema Paradiso shows films in Ibiza's swankiest spots *(cinemaparadisoibiza.com)*.

An outdoor film screening in Ibiza, run by Cinema Paradiso ↑

Location, Location, Location

Photogenic Barcelona *(p70)* has served as the set for many films and the city's tourist office offers movie-themed walking routes *(www. barcelonamovie.com)*. Almodóvar used the Catalonian city as the stage for *All About My Mother* (1999), but Madrid *(p288)* is the setting for many of his quirky films, including *Talk To Her* (2002). See the capital through his lens with Insider's Madrid *(www.insiderstravel.io)*. Spain has also starred on the small screen, in TV epic *Game of Thrones* (2011–2019). The Bárdenas Reales *(p281)* served as the Dothraki Sea and Girona *(p158)* as King's Landing.

←

A rock formation in the Bárdenas Reales, a set for *Game of Thrones*

Film-ivals

San Sebastián hosts one of the world's most glamorous film festivals *(p269)*. Alongside the star-studded premieres, there are plenty of opportunities to watch a screening. Elsewhere, Sitges *(p169)* has the Festival Internacional de Cinema Fantàstic de Catalunya *(sitgesfilmfestival.com)* and Barcelona L'Alternativa, a celebration of independent film *(alternativa.cccb.org)*.

←

Spanish actors Penélope Cruz and Javier Bardem at the San Sebastián Film Festival

→

Oasys – Parque Temático del Desierto de Tabernas

Spain's Wild West

Step into a real-life *Westworld* or embrace your inner John Wayne in Andalucía's arid Tabernas Desert, which seems to be populated only by cacti *(p519)*. Dress up as a cowboy, watch a staged shoot-out and have a drink in a saloon bar, with swinging doors, as you discover the surprising set for scores of 1960s and 1970s spaghetti westerns. The two-dimensional buildings and fake tumbleweed once used for *The Good, The Bad and The Ugly* (1966) and *A Fistful of Dollars* (1964) now populate imaginative theme parks – Oasys – Parque Temático del Desierto de Tabernas and Fort Bravo *(p519)*.

Authors on the Road

Washington Irving's *Tales of the Alhambra* (1832) was one of the first travelogues set in Spain. As you walk under the orange trees and filigree-like arches of Granada *(p492)*, judge for yourself whether his self-assessment – "how unworthy is my scribbling of the place" – holds true. Hemingway, known as "Don Ernesto", came to Spain in his early twenties and was immediately captivated. His first novel – *The Sun Also Rises* (1926) – captures the energy of the running of the bulls in Pamplona *(p284)*.

🔍 HIDDEN GEM
You're All Write

After spending some time in Spain, you'll no doubt feel inspired by the epic scenery and buzzing cities. So why not document your travels with a writing class? Ask for an invitation to the Madrid Writers' Club so that you can attend one of their workshops *(www.madridwritersclub.com)*.

Orange trees bearing fruit in front of Granada's cathedral ↑

SPAIN
ON PAGE

The bibliophile will rejoice in Spain. There's plenty for readers to celebrate, with literary festivals, heaving book markets and the chance to explore the places that inspired some of your favourite authors, including the tilting windmills that captured Cervantes' imagination.

Market My Words

The stalls lining Madrid's Calle de Claudio Moyano are Spain's answer to the *bouquinistes* found in Paris. Lined with stalls selling new and second-hand books, it's the perfect place to spend a lazy Sunday morning browsing the pages. Bookworms should visit Barcelona on 23 April, when Sant Jordi – the city's patron saint – is celebrated with the exchange of books and roses. On this day, laden book stalls and brimming flower vendors jostle for space in the streets.

←

A stall selling books during the Sant Jordi celebrations in Barcelona

TOP 5 | SPANISH BOOKS

Don Quixote (1605)
Cervantes' novel immortalized this chivalric nobleman.

The Family of Pascual Duarte (1942)
The protagonist of Cela's novel has no remorse.

The Shadow of the Wind (2001)
A boy discovers a mysterious novel.

Nada (1945)
La Foret's debut follows orphan Andrea.

La Habitació de Nona (2017)
Cubas' short stories present women in adverse situations.

Writers' Pads

Playwright Lope de Vega's home is located in Madrid's Barrio de las Letras. The Casa-Museo de Lope de Vega *(p331)* is just a stone's throw from the tomb of Lope de Vega's arch-rival, Cervantes. Cervantes fans can visit his home in Valladolid *(p392)* and the Museo Casa Natal de Cervantes in Alcalá de Henares *(p365)*.

→

Seated statues in front of the Museo Casa Natal de Cervantes

Literary Festivals

Spain hosts scores of literary festivals. One of the most prestigious is the Hay Festival in Segovia *(p376)*, a four-day celebration of the arts *(www.hayfestival.com)*. Early June sees the biggest – the Feria del Libro Madrid *(www.feria libromadrid.com)*. Theatre fans shouldn't miss Me Vuelves Lorca *(www.me vuelveslorca.com)*, set in an outdoor amphitheatre.

→

Author Fernando Aramburu at the Feria del Libro Madrid

Cocktail Hour

Masters of mixology can be found in all the major cities. In Madrid, Museo Chicote serves up El Chicote – vermouth, gin, Curaçao and Grand Marnier (*museochicote.com*). Behind it is Bar Cock (*www.barcock. com*), a wood-panelled gin joint, famed during *la movida* (*p342*). In Barcelona, the gin-and-tonic craze shows no signs of abating: try one at the XIX bar (*www.xixbar.com*).

A bartender pouring a drink at Boca Chica, a cocktail bar in Barcelona

SPAIN
RAISE A GLASS

Spain's outstanding wines have long been famed, particularly those of La Rioja, but there are plenty of other enticing tipples to try. Celebrate with some cava – the Catalan answer to champagne – savour a full-bodied brandy or sample sherry in its homeland of Andalucía. Don't miss these must-drinks.

Eat, Drink and Be Sherry

There's nothing quite like a glass of ice-cold sherry on a sultry summer evening. The name comes from the English pronunciation of Jerez, and Jerez de la Frontera (*p503*), Sanlúcar de Barrameda (*p502*) and Puerto de Santa María are home to several centuries-old *bodegas*. Founded in 1730, Bodegas Fundador is the oldest and has a vast store, known as "La Mezquita" because of its Moorish arches. Book a tour to learn about how the fortified wine is made or indulge in a paired lunch, where every dish comes with a different sherry (*www.grupoemperadorspain.com*).

MODERN SHERRY

In the 17th century, wars across Europe led sherry sales to plummet. To try to salvage some of this stock, producers began to add new wine to the old. This became known as the solera system. Three distinct types of sherry emerged – *oloroso*, which is dark and nutty, pale and dry *fino* and *manzanilla*, which is bone dry, but has a distinctive salty tang.

Barrels of sherry at Bodegas Osborne, Puerto de Santa María ↑

Get a Grape

Spain is the world's third-largest wine producer, with more than a million acres of vineyards. The most famous Spanish variety is grown in La Rioja, where you'll find stunning wineries such as Ysios, whose undulating design mimics both the surrounding mountains and a row of barrels *(p278)*. For the ultimate La Rioja experience, book a room at Marqués de Riscal *(p278)* – a hotel offering wine-related spa treatments.

→

Harvesting red grapes at a vineyard in Bargota, Navarra

Bubbly Personality

Catalonia has produced cava – the sparkling white wine – since the late 19th century, when the red vines of Penedès were devastated by the phylloxera plague. Sant Sadurní d'Anoia is at the centre of the industry and is home to the Castellroig and Codorníu wineries *(p168)*, where you can cycle through the vines.

←

Toasting with a glass of cava at the Castellroig winery

Don't Worry, Be Hoppy

Barcelona's Eixample district has so many microbreweries that it's been called "Beerxample". We love Kraftank *(www.kraftankbarcelona.com)* and BeirCaB *(www.biercab.com)*. Valencia, too, has plenty of options, including Olhöps *(www.beerhouse.olhops.com)*. Craft beer is also championed in the capital. Madrid's breweries and beer bars include Bee Beer *(www.beebeer.es)* and Chinaski *(www.chinaskilavapies.com)*, which has a cool technicolour interior.

→

Bottles of Dos Bous Cervezas Artesanas craft beer

Baroque Cities

The sumptuous Palacio Real *(p298)* and Palacio Real de la Granja de San Ildefonso *(p388)* exemplify the dramatic Baroque style, and Salamanca *(p372)* bristles with lavish Churrigueresque constructions – the most ornate expression of Spanish Baroque. The sandstone buildings that surround the magnificent Plaza Mayor glow in the sun, earning Salamanca the nickname La Dorada – "The Golden City".

→

The manicured gardens that frame Palacio Real de la Granja de San Ildefonso

SPAIN FOR
ARCHITECTURE

As you travel through Spain, you'll be astounded by the array of different architectural styles represented here. Whether it's the Romanesque chapels in the Pyrenees or the titanium sails of Gehry's Guggenheim Museum in Bilbao, Spain's buildings map the country's illustrious history.

 TOP 3 CONTEMPORARY CONSTRUCTIONS

Museo Guggenheim Bilbao
Frank Gehry's "titanium flower" was completed in 1997 *(p266)*.

Metropol Parasol, Seville
This wooden structure (2011) designed by Jürgen Mayer is made up of six mushroom-shaped pavilions *(p464)*.

Ciutat de les Arts i de les Ciències, Valencia
Santiago Calatrava designed Valencia's futuristic City of Arts and Sciences, which unites a host of cultural institutions *(p199)*.

Majestic Modernisme

Also known as Catalan Art Nouveau, Modernisme has shaped Barcelona's skyline and the city is home to the greatest concentration of Modernista architecture in the world. Gaudí's fairy-tale constructions are the most famous, such as Casa Batlló *(p116)*, La Pedrera *(p118)* and Sagrada Família *(p110)*. For more Modernista marvels see p78.

→

The undulating roof and internal courtyard of La Pedrera

Romanesque Valley

Originating in Italy in the late 10th century, Romanesque architecture quickly spread first to France and, from there, to Spain. To see some of the most remarkable examples, take a drive through the Vall de Boí *(p161)*. Topped with lofty bell towers, the Romanesque churches in this valley are adorned with intricate ironwork and skilful replicas of the original frescoes. To admire the real ones, head to Barcelona's Museu Nacional d'Art de Catalunya *(p133)*.

$\rightarrow$

The Romanesque church in the town of Taüll in the Vall de Boí

Gothic Glory

Flying buttresses, pointed arches and rib vaults characterize Gothic architecture. Seek out the pair of flamboyant spires atop Burgos Cathedral *(p382)* or head to León Cathedral *(p370)* - known as the "House of Light" thanks to its huge windows. But Girona's *(p158)* and Seville's cathedrals are the country's biggest Gothic buildings *(p452)*.

$\leftarrow$

The majestic León Cathedral, a great example of the Gothic style

Moorish Marvels

Characterized by its horseshoe arches and elaborate stucco work, Spain's Moorish architecture transports you to the Islamic world. To travel across the continents, check out the *azulejo*-bedecked Real Alcázar in Seville *(p454)*, walk beneath the red-and-white arches of Córdoba's Mezquita *(p484)* or explore the sumptuous rooms of the Alhambra *(p494)*. For a truly unforgettable experience, tour the Alhambra at night, when the moon is reflected in the patios' mirror-still pools.

$\rightarrow$

The horseshoe arches in the Mezquita, Córdoba's Great Mosque

Shoot Some Hoops

Here in Spain, basketball is almost - but not quite - as popular as football. Top teams include Real Madrid *(www.realmadrid.com/en/basketball)*, who won the 2018 Euroleague, arch-rivals FC Barcelona *(www.fcbarcelona.com/basketball)*, and the Basque team Saski Baskonia *(www.baskonia.com)*, who have a dedicated fan base.

Spain's Laura Nicholls makes a block during the 2018 FIBA World Cup

SPAIN FOR
SPORTS FANS

The home of Nadal, Alonso and Garcia, Spain has produced countless sports stars - and little wonder. From the tennis court to the football pitch, games here are played in the sun and cheered on by passionate crowds. So why not join the locals at the next match or even have a go yourself?

A Tale of Two Cities

Nothing in Spain - not food, religion nor politics - elicits the same passion as football. This is most evident during El Clásico, when Spain's most famous football teams - arch-rivals Real Madrid *(www.realmadrid.com)* and FC Barcelona *(p138)* - meet on the pitch. Catching a match - whether in a stadium or in a packed bar full of frenetic fans - is an unmissable Spanish experience.

→

Players from Real Madrid and FC Barcelona battle for the ball during a match

Acing It

The legendary Rafael Nadal has boosted the popularity of tennis across Spain, and you can catch the quick-footed Mallorcan leaping across the clay at the Madrid or Barcelona Opens. "Rafa" got you inspired? Then pick up a racket yourself. There are plenty of tennis resorts across the country, but our favourite is La Manga Club *(lamangaclub.com)*. One of Europe's top sports resorts, La Manga's 28-court tennis centre has hosted Davis Cup matches and runs an intensive coaching programme. If you'd prefer a casual knockaround, tourist information offices can provide lists of local courts.

→

Spanish tennis player Jaume Munar in action during the Barcelona Open

Par-Tee Time

Spain is Europe's most popular golfing destination and has more than 500 courses, including Real Club Valderrama *(www.valderrama.com)*, La Reserva Club *(www.lareservaclubsoto grande.com)*, Real Club de Golf Las Brisas *(www.realclubdegolflasbrisas.com)*, Son Gual *(www.son-gual.com)* and Alcanada *(www.golf-alcanada.com)*. Try to make par at any one of these courses on a holiday with Golf Breaks *(www.golfbreaks.com)*.

←

A palm-tree-fringed green at the Real Club de Golf Las Brisas in Marbella

Wheelie Good Fun

The Vuelta de España is one of Europe's most prestigious cycle races and is an inspiring spectacle *(www.lavuelta.es)*. If you prefer to cycle yourself, there are scores of bike rental outlets or you could attempt the notoriously difficult Los Machucos in Cantabria, which rises 921 m (3,022 ft) and has gradients of 28 per cent.

→

The peloton hurtling through Madrid during the Vuelta de España

Glitz and Glamour

On some of Spain's beaches, the only thing sparkling more than the water is the bathers' jewels. Marbella's beaches *(p504)* are lined with beach clubs and *chiringuitos* (beachside bars) and arty Cadaqués *(p166)* has oodles of chichi appeal with its galleries and boutiques. Sitges *(p169)* – an LGBTQ+ favourite – is packed with cocktail bars offering deckchair service, Ibiza sizzles and Formentera's sands have become a boho oasis for celebrities *(p552)*.

→
A luxury cabana at RnR, one of Ibiza's beach clubs

SPAIN FOR
BEACH LIFE

With more than 8,000 km (5,000 miles) of coastline, Spain offers a sandy stretch for everyone. Whether you're looking for endless golden sands or a secret cove for a romantic sunset stroll, somewhere to party or a fun-fuelled family beach, Spain delivers in buckets and spades.

Family Fun

There are plenty of kid-friendly resorts on Mallorca, including Playa d'Alcúdia *(p542)*, which is arranged around a huge, shallow bay. Menorca *(p548)* offers similarly sheltered sands along its southern coast, as well as wilder coves on the north, which are perfect for kayaking. Teens might also enjoy surfing along the Costa Verde *(p250)* or kite-surfing in Tarifa *(p503)*.

Party Sands

One of the biggest party islands in the world, Ibiza's reputation for beachside revelry is hard to beat. The party carries on all summer long at Platja de Ses Salines (p545), which is flanked by beach clubs and bars. A clubbers' favourite is Platja d'en Bossa, near Eivissa (p544), while Sant Antoni (p546) is another huge party resort. If you like to mix partying with some big-city attractions, swap the Balearic islands for Barcelona (p70) or Valencia (p196) on the mainland, which both boast a fantastic, fun-filled beach scene in the summer months.

←
Party time at the Bora Bora Beach Club on Ibiza's Platja d'en Bossa

TOP 5 SPANISH COSTAS

Costa Brava
The "rugged coast" has ochre cliffs clad in pines that plunge down to miniature coves (p172).

Costa de la Luz
This Andalucían coast boasts sandy beaches and small family-friendly resorts (p503).

Costa del Sol
The best known *costa* is home to popular resorts like Torremolinos and glitzy Marbella (p522).

Costa Verde
Spain's wild, northern coast has some of its most beautiful cliff-backed beaches (p250).

Costa Blanca
The "white coast" offers endless stretches of sand, a handful of big resorts, such as Alicante, and a string of smaller towns (p214).

Hidden Beaches

Even on Spain's most popular *costas*, you can always find a secret beach or two. The rugged Costa Brava (p172) is home to tiny *calas* (coves), including the Cala Estreta. There are dozens of secluded spots on Menorca (p548), too, such as the Cala Turqueta and the Cala Tortuga.

↑ The paradisal turquoise waters of the Cala Turqueta, Menorca

↑ Kids building a sand castle together on a beach in Mallorca

Club Life

Think of Spain's nightlife and Ibiza is probably the first thing that comes to mind. The island attracts the party set during the sultry summer months, and they dance to the latest tunes at Amnesia *(www.amnesia.es)* or Privilege *(privilegeibiza.com)*. If you're visiting during the colder months, the big cities offer nightclubs hot enough to keep you warm. Fabrik and Kapital *(www.grupo-kapital.com)* headline Madrid's scene, while Café del Mar *(cafedelmar-barcelona.com)* and Pacha *(pachabarcelona.es)* keep Barcelona grooving. But Valencia's vast range of night-time offerings eclipses them all: find out more on p42.

→

A flower power party at Pacha in Ibiza, and *(inset)* DJ Gavid Guetta spins discs

SPAIN
AFTER DARK

The fact that there's a specific Spanish word – *madrugada* – for the small hours between midnight and dawn says everything about the country's nightlife. Start your evening late, lingering over plates of tapas and goblets of gin in a dimly lit bar, before seeing where the night takes you.

Go Flamenco

Finding authentic flamenco *(p461)* can be surprisingly difficult and some *tablaos* lack *duende* (spirit). Avoid the tourist traps and head for Corral de la Moreria *(www.corraldela moreria.com)*, Tablao Cordobés *(tablaocordobes.es)* or El Arenal *(tablaoelarenal.com)*. Jerez de la Frontera has several *peñas* – clubs run by aficionados – but our favourite is Peña La Buleria *(Calle Empedrada 20; 856 05 37 72)*. Got itchy feet? Put on your dancing shoes and take a class at the Museo del Baile Flamenco *(p460)*.

←

A *bailaora* and *bailaor* dancing flamenco, accompanied by a guitar

💬 INSIDER TIP
Start Late

Restaurants in Spain rarely open before 8pm, but you can snack on tapas if you get peckish earlier. If you want to get into the Spanish rhythm, have a siesta, then join the locals for a *paseo* (evening stroll).

Spain Live

From the stirring sound of flamenco to the traditional tunes of the Basque lands, you'll rarely experience silence in Spain and there's a huge range of beats for music lovers to experience. If you yearn for dimly lit jazz bars, spend a mellow night at Madrid's Café Central *(www. cafecentralmadrid.com)*. Indie and rock fans should seek out Seville's Fun Club, which has been hosting up-and-coming bands since the 1980s *(www. funclubsevilla.com)*. Don your jeans, grab a beer and wind your way to the stage. For a more extravagant night, attend a classical concert at the Palau de la Música Catalana *(p88)*.

↑ Listening to live jazz at the Café Central in Madrid

Active Fun

After spending time inside, kids will need to let off some steam. Fortunately, Spain is criss-crossed by *vías verdes* ("greenways"), a network of 115 converted train lines perfect for biking. The country also has 15 national parks in which youngsters can run amok and active kids and teens can try out adrenaline-pumping activities, such as climbing, white-water rafting and canyoning *(p38)*. In the colder months, head to the Pyrenees or the Sierra Nevada for winter sports galore, such as skiing, snowboarding and snow-shoeing. In summer, spend time enjoying the beaches, which offer every activity under the sun, from canoeing to kite-surfing, snorkelling to sailing *(p54)*.

Kids hiking in the Serra de Tramuntana, a mountain range in Mallorca

SPAIN FOR
FAMILIES

Beautiful beaches and expansive nature reserves, outdoor activities and sports aplenty, castles and ancient ruins that inspire inquisitive minds: there are plenty of reasons Spain continues to attract families year after year.

Rainy-Day Activities

If rain stops play, the obvious place to head is a museum. Located in seven Spanish cities, including Barcelona (p132), CaixaForum hosts fun-filled family events, including concerts, painting workshops and film screenings. Another good indoor option is a family cooking class, where kids can learn how to make some of the tasty local dishes that they've enjoyed on their trip. In Barcelona, try Barcelona Cooking (www.barcelonacooking. net); in Seville, contact A Taste of Spain (www. atasteofspain.com).

Admiring Buenaventura (1922) in the Museo Carmen Thyssen Málaga

Children carefully making pastry during a family-friendly cookery class

Theme Parks

Thrill-seekers will love PortAventura (p170), Spain's biggest theme park, which has plenty of hair-raising rides. The fastest is Dragon Khan, which speeds along at more than 110 km/h (68 mph). Step inside your favourite movies at Parque Warner, near Madrid, which brings characters to life in imaginative attractions, including a Superman ride that will make you feel like you're flying like a bird or a plane, and a haunted house where Scooby Doo serves as your furry sidekick (www.parquewarner.com). There is more family fun to be had at Terra Mítica in Benidorm (www.terramitica park.com), Seville's Isla Mágica (p467).

A twirling swing ride at Isla Mágica, a theme park in Seville

---

TOP 5 FAMILY-FRIENDLY FESTIVALS

Cabalgata de los Reyes Magos
The Three Kings parade through towns, throwing sweets to children.

Carnival
Kids all over Spain wear fancy dress to school.

Sant Jordi
Catalonia is overtaken by booksellers and there are lots of special family-friendly events.

Fiesta de San Juan
The feast of St John the Baptist is celebrated with fireworks.

Las Fallas
Giant papier-mâché creations are burned on 19 March in one of Spain's biggest, noisiest and fieriest festivals.

A YEAR IN
SPAIN

JANUARY

Cabalgata de los Reyes Magos *(5 Jan)*. The Three Kings throw sweets to children.

△ **La Tamborrada** *(19–20 Jan)*. San Sebastián resounds with the beats of hundreds of drums.

Canary Islands International Music Festival *(Jan/Feb)*. Classical music fills the air.

FEBRUARY

ARCOmadrid *(Feb/Mar)*. Madrid hosts a week-long contemporary art fair.

△ **Carnival** *(Feb/Mar)*. Every town erupts in colourful celebrations. Cádiz's offering is the best.

Festival de Flamenco de Jerez *(Feb/Mar)*. Performances, workshops and even flash mobs dedicated to flamenco in Jerez de la Frontera.

MAY

Feria del Caballo *(mid-May)*. Jerez de la Frontera's horse fair features fine horses and women in frilly flamenco dresses.

△ **WOMAD** *(mid-May)*. Free concerts are held around Cáceres in this miniature version of the world music festival.

JUNE

△ **Primavera Sound** *(early Jun)*. One of Europe's biggest indie music festivals shakes up Barcelona.

Fiesta de San Juan *(23 Jun)*. Street parties, fireworks and bonfires are found everywhere.

International Festival of Music and Dance *(Jun–Jul)*. Classical music and ballet staged in the Alhambra and the Generalife in Granada.

SEPTEMBER

Bienal de Arte Flamenco *(Sep, even years only)*. Top flamenco artists fight it out with their footwork in Seville.

San Sebastián Film Festival *(mid- to late Sep)*. Film-makers gather in the Basque city for this long-running festival and film competition.

△ **Festes de la Mercé** *(mid- to late Sep)*. Human towers, free concerts and folk events in Barcelona.

OCTOBER

△ **Día de la Hispanidad** *(12 Oct)*. Spain's national holiday marks Columbus's landing in the Americas in 1492, with the biggest celebrations taking place in Zaragoza.

Fiestas de Santa Teresa *(15 Oct)*. Parades of giants, concerts and fairs in honour of the patron saint of Ávila.

MARCH

Fiestas *(mid-Mar)*. Castellón de la Plana is taken over by parades in honour of Mary Magdalene.

△ **Las Fallas** *(15–19 Mar)*. Hilarious papier-mâché figures are paraded through Valencia before being burned on massive pyres on 19 March, while fireworks explode across the sky.

Semana Santa *(Mar/Apr)*. Solemn processions by hooded devotees are held throughout Spain.

APRIL

Moors and Christians *(21–24 Apr)*. This colourful costumed event in Alcoi celebrates the Christian victory over the Moors in 1276.

Sant Jordi *(23 Apr)*. Books and roses are exchanged in Barcelona in honour of St George, the patron saint of Catalonia.

△ **Feria de Abril** *(2 weeks after Easter)*. Seville's exuberant Andalucían fiesta features crowds dancing *sevillanas*, free-flowing sherry and fairground rides.

JULY

Guitar Festival *(early Jul)*. Córdoba celebrates the stringed instrument in performances ranging from classical to flamenco.

△ **Sónar** *(mid-Jul)*. A frenetic festival of electronic music and technology pulsates in Barcelona.

Grec Festival *(late Jul–Aug)*. This Spanish and international theatre, music and dance festival is held in Barcelona.

AUGUST

Copa del Rey MAPFRE *(end Jul/first week Aug)*. This sailing regatta, presided over by King Felipe VI, takes over Palma.

Semanas Grandes *(mid-Aug)*. Traditional Basque music, dance and sports are celebrated in Bilbao and San Sebastián in the "Great Weeks".

△ **La Tomatina** *(late Aug)*. Participants pelt tons of ripe tomatoes at one another during this infamous event which takes place every year in Buñol.

DECEMBER

Nochebuena *(24 Dec)*. The family gathers for a feast on Christmas Eve, before heading to Midnight Mass.

Santos Inocentes *(28 Dec)*. People play tricks on each other during Spain's version of April Fools' Day.

△ **Nochevieja** *(31 Dec)*. You'll find New Year's Eve's biggest fireworks display and most riotous celebrations in Madrid's Puerta del Sol.

NOVEMBER

△ **All Saints' Day** *(1 Nov)*. Spanish families visit the graves of their loved ones and ornament them with extravagant floral decorations.

National Flamenco Competition *(2 weeks in mid-Nov)*. Córdoba hosts song, dance and guitar performances.

A BRIEF
HISTORY

Spain's history is beleaguered by power struggles. Foreign influences can be felt everywhere from Segovia's Roman aqueduct to the Moorish Alhambra and the spectre of Franco's dictatorship still looms large. Today, Spain is an inclusive democracy, where this disparate past is celebrated.

Prehistoric Spain

Tribes of early humans first settled on the Iberian Peninsula in around 800,000 BC. In 5000 BC, these hunter-gatherers were usurped by Neolithic farmers. Next, merchants arrived from across the Mediterranean, starting with the Phoenicians in around 1100 BC. Some 500 years later, the Greeks settled in the northeast and the southeast was occupied by the Carthaginians in 228 BC. During this time, Celts assimilated with the Iberian tribes, resulting in the Celtiberians. This melting pot of cultures coexisted harmoniously until the Romans invaded.

Did You Know?

The Roman name Hispania means "Nearer Iberia".

Timeline of events

800,000 BC
Homo erectus arrives in the Iberian Peninsula.

5000 BC
Farming begins in the Iberian Peninsula.

1100 BC
Phoenicians arrive and found what is now Cádiz.

218 BC
The Second Punic War begins and Rome starts to take control of the peninsula.

19 BC
Augustus consolidates Roman control of what became known as Hispania, ending 200 years of war.

Hispania

The Iberian population fiercely fought their Roman invaders, and it took the Romans over 200 years to subdue the peninsula. The new conquerors named the land Hispania and divided it into three provinces: Tarraconensis, Lusitania and Baetica. In time, they built cities with typical Roman infrastructures and in AD 74 Emperor Vespasian granted the people of Hispania the right to trade, travel and vote. After centuries of prosperity and development, the fall of the Western Roman Empire in 476 left Hispania in the hands of the Visigoths, a nomadic Germanic tribe.

Al-Andalus

North African Arabs and Berbers known as the Moors took advantage of the Visigoths' lack of political organization in 711 and conquered the peninsula. At its height, al-Andalus – as they called their new territory – included part of southern France. During the subsequent 700 years, the Moors made great strides in the fields of mathematics, science, art, agriculture and architecture. A rich and powerful caliphate was established in Córdoba and the city became the epicentre of these al-Andalusian advances.

1 A map showing the Roman settlements in the Spanish region of Cantabria.

2 Vibrant prehistoric paintings in the Cuevas de Altamira.

3 The sun rises over the Alhambra, a beautiful Moorish construction.

4 Detail of a pillar in Granada's Baños del Alcázar Califales.

415
The Visigoths establish their court in Barcelona.

711
The Moors take control of the peninsula from the Visigoths.

716
First recorded use of "al-Andalus" on coinage.

AD 74
Emperor Vespasian grants Latin status to all towns in Hispania, completing the assimilation of the territory into the empire.

476
Western Roman Empire falls, leaving Hispania under the control of the Visigoths.

1

2

The Reconquista and Inquisition

The reconquest *(reconquista)* of Muslim Spain by Christian fighters started almost as soon as the Moors took control. The resistance won its first battle in Covadonga in 722, but it took another 700 years for them to win the war. By the 11th century, the peninsula was split into the Christian north – comprising the five kingdoms of León, Castile, Navarra, Aragón and Catalonia – and the Muslim south. When the Christians captured Seville in 1248, Granada became the last remaining Moorish enclave in the area.

The marriage of Isabel I of Castile and Fernando II of Aragón in 1469 saw their two kingdoms united in diplomatic and religious matters – acting as the blueprint for the unification of the Iberian territories that would eventually become Spain. In their united kingdom, the "Catholic Monarchs", as they came to be known, instigated the Spanish Inquisition *(p304)* – a brutal religious purge which sought to spread Catholicism and rid the country of the Protestants, Jews and Muslims that had previously coexisted here. Their reign also saw the completion of the *reconquista*, when Granada was taken in 1492.

SANTIAGO

One of the 12 apostles, St James (Santiago in Spanish) is the patron saint of Spain and his remains are supposedly held in the cathedral at Santiago de Compostela. It is said that St James miraculously appeared to fight for the Christian army at the Battle of Clavijo in 844 and was subsequently known as Santiago Matamoros (St James the Moor-slayer), an emblem of the *reconquista*.

Timeline of events

1037
León and Castile are united for the first time under Fernando I.

1094
The legendary Castilian fighter El Cid captures Valencia, inspiring the *Poema de Mio Cid*.

1143
Portugal becomes a separate Christian kingdom.

1248
Seville is reconquered from the Moors.

1469
Marriage of Fernando and Isabel unites Castile and Aragón.

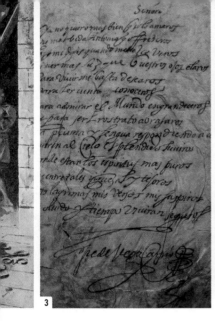

The Colonial Age

Towards the end of 1492, Christopher Columbus – the explorer and colonist – landed in the Americas. During the ensuing years, *conquistadors* travelled to Central and South America, decimating Indigenous populations and establishing colonies for the Spanish Crown. They returned with crops, such as potatoes, maize and cocoa, as well as vast wealth. In the 16th century, huge quantities of gold and silver were plundered from the Americas, and Carlos I, and then his son Felipe II, used some of these riches to fight Protestantism in Europe. Most famously, in 1588, Felipe II launched the doomed Spanish Armada, which aimed to overthrow England's Protestant Queen Elizabeth I.

This wealth also led to the Siglo de Oro (Golden Age) – a time of prolific artistic and literary achievements, led by painters such as El Greco and Velázquez, writers like Cervantes, and the dramatists Lope de Vega and Calderón de la Barca. But this brilliance occurred against a backdrop of colonial exploitation and ruinous wars with the Low Countries and France. Spain was gradually losing its influence in Europe and the reigning house of Habsburg entered irreversible decline.

[1] Alfonso II of Aragon and I of Catalonia and Alfonso VIII of Castile in the Siege of Cuenca, 1177.

[2] A man is tortured during the Inquisition.

[3] A sonnet written by 16th-century poet Lope de Vega.

[4] English naval officers playing a game of bowls before fighting the Spanish Armada.

[5] A painting of the Spanish Armada.

1512
Navarra is annexed, leading to the full unification of Spain.

1605
Publication of the first of two parts of Cervantes' *Don Quixote*.

1648
Holland achieves independence from Spain by the Treaty of Westphalia.

1540
Father Bartolomé de las Casas writes a book denouncing the oppression of Indigenous people.

1492
Fall of Granada; Columbus sets sail for the Americas.

2

3

The Rise of Republicanism

When Carlos II died without an heir, the Habsburgs and Bourbons fought over the Spanish crown. The latter were victorious, but Napoleon invaded in 1807, sparking the Peninsular War. Peace was short lived, with the Carlist Wars beleaguering the country between 1833 and 1876. Spain's First Republic was declared in 1873, but lasted little over a year. In 1874, the monarchy was restored, but corruption fostered anarchism. The country's increasing instability was briefly checked by Primo de Rivera, who seized power in 1923, but he lost the support of the king and army in 1930 and resigned. Following a public vote, Alfonso XIII was also forced to abdicate and the Second Republic was declared in 1931.

Franco's Spain

The Second Republic implemented liberal measures but the Confederación Española de Derechas Autónomas – a conservative party – won the 1933 elections. In response, anarchists and socialists rose up in 1934. Another election in 1936 saw the liberal Popular Front narrowly defeat the right-wing National Front.

① Felipe V and his family. ↑

② The bombing of the Gran Teatre del Liceu by anarchists in 1893.

③ The proclamation of the Second Republic.

④ International Women's Day march in 2019.

Did You Know?

Despite lasting only a year, the First Republic saw four separate presidents.

Timeline of events

1700

Death of Carlos II brings Habsburg line to an end. Felipe V, the first Bourbon king, ascends the throne.

1873

The First Republic is declared.

1936

Nationalists rise up against the government and the Spanish Civil War begins.

1833–9

First Carlist War takes place.

1931

The Second Republic is declared, with a coalition between Socialists and Republicans.

Political tensions came to a head and Civil War broke out. The Nationalists, led by General Franco, took control of swathes of Spain, but were halted outside Madrid. Support from Hitler and Mussolini helped them to take the capital in 1939, and Franco installed himself as a dictator. Under Franco, Spain was a fascist state, ruled by a single party. All cultural diversity was suppressed in an attempt to make the country homogenized, and the legal use of Basque, Catalan and Galician was banned.

Spain Today

Franco named Juan Carlos, Alfonso XIII's grandson, as his heir. He inherited Franco's absolute power, but chose not to exercise it, instead installing himself as a constitutional monarch and considerable power was devolved to the regions. In 2017, Catalonia held an unauthorized referendum for unilateral independence. Separatists hailed the victory as a landslide, despite the fact that it was illegal. The resulting factionalism bolstered the far-right Vox party in the 2019 election, but the socialist Partido Socialista Obrero Español proved victorious.

↑ A Nationalist propaganda poster, displayed during the Spanish Civil War

1975
Death of Franco results in third Bourbon restoration as Juan Carlos is proclaimed king.

1939
Francisco Franco declares victory and installs himself as a military dictator over Spain.

1986
Spain joins the European Community (now the European Union) and NATO.

2014
Felipe VI is crowned king.

2019
On 8 March, International Women's Day, over 5 million women walk out of work to march through the streets.

EXPERIENCE

Málaga's waterfront promenade

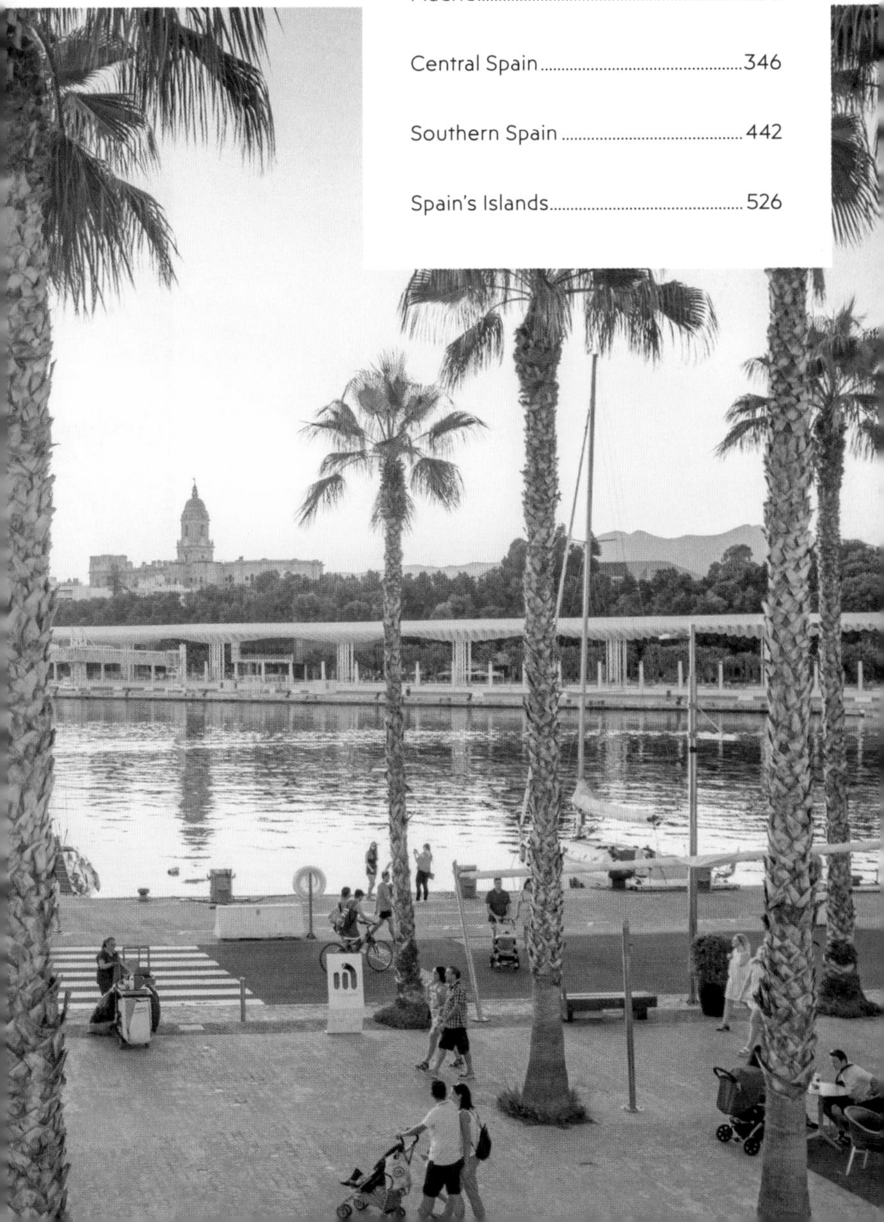

BARCELONA

Gaudí's sculpted air ducts on the roof of La Pedrera

EXPLORE
BARCELONA

This section divides Barcelona into three
sightseeing areas, as shown on this map,
plus an area beyond the centre.

SANTS

LA NOA
ESQUERRA DE
L'EIXAMPLE

GRAN VIA DE LES CORTS CATALANES

PLAÇA
D'ESPANYA

GRAN VIA DE LES

SANT ANTONI

AVINGUDA DEL PARAL·LEL

EL RAVAL

Museu Nacional
d'Art de Catalunya

MONTJUÏC
p126

Fundació
Joan Miró

Estadi Olímpic
de Montjuïc

Parc de Montjuïc

Castell de
Montjuïc

RONDA DEL LITORAL

SPAIN

TRAVESSERA   DE   GRACIA

GRÀCIA

AVINGUDA DIAGONAL

EIXAMPLE

PASSEIG   DE   SANT   JOAN

PASSEIG   DE   GRACIA

RAMBLA DE CATALUNYA

EIXAMPLE
p106

Casa Batlló

AVINGUDA DE GAUDI

Sagrada
Família

AVINGUDA DIAGONAL

CORTS CATALANES

GRAN VIA DE LES CORTS CATALANES

PLAÇA DE
LES GLORIES
CATALANES

PLAÇA DE
CATALUNYA

RONDA DE SANT PERE

LA RAMBLA

Arc del
Triomf

AVINGUDA MERIDIANA

OLD TOWN
p80

**BARRI
GÒTIC**

Barcelona
Cathedral

LA RAMBLA

Museu
Picasso

Born
Cultural
Centre

EL POBLENOU

PLAÇA
REIAL

LA RIBERA

*Parc de la
Ciutadella*

PLAÇA
D'ANTONI
LOPEZ

Estació
de França

Zoo de
Barcelona

Museu Marítim
and Drassanes

PLAÇA DEL
PORTAL
DE LA PAU

PORT VELL

*Dàrsena
Nacional*

Marina
Port Vell

PASSEIG JOAN DE BORBÓ

Parc de la
Barceloneta

Port
Olímpic

BARCELONETA

*Platja
Barceloneta*

*Platja
Sant Sebastià*

Mediterranean Sea

0 metres   500

0 yards   500

N

GETTING TO KNOW
BARCELONA

From the Gothic buildings in the Old Town to the Modernista mansions in Eixample, sizzling Barceloneta beach to hilly Montjuïc, the capital of Catalonia is Spain's most dynamic and stylish city. Becoming familiar with each area will help when planning your trip to this multifaceted metropolis.

PAGE 80

OLD TOWN

Barcelona's medieval maze of crooked streets and secret squares winds inland from the old harbour, Port Vell. It's the perfect place to saunter along narrow alleys, hunt for antiques or just savour a coffee on a street-side table. Crowned by an enormous Gothic cathedral, the Old Town is home to many of the city's best-loved sights, including the tree-shaded promenade of La Rambla. Lined with a host of enticing shops, charming cafés and tiny tapas bars, and thronged with locals, tourists and performance artists, this far-reaching street is the city's beating heart.

Best for
Medieval buildings and quirky museums

Home to
Barcelona Cathedral, La Rambla, Palau de la Música Catalana, Museu Picasso, Parc de la Ciutadella

Experience
A boat ride along the seafront

EIXAMPLE

Laid out in the late 19th century, after the medieval walls were finally dismantled, Eixample is an elegant grid of broad avenues lined with graceful mansions. The area contains the world's greatest concentration of Modernista architecture, with Gaudí's masterpiece – the Sagrada Família – looming over them all. Inside some of these fantastical buildings, you'll find the city's fanciest boutiques and restaurants. Towards the end of Carrer de Casanova is "Gaixample" – several blocks that make up the heart of Barcelona's lively LGBTQ+ scene, with specialist bookshops and chic clubs.

Best for
Modernisme and LGBTQ+ life

Home to
Sagrada Família, Casa Batlló, La Pedrera

Experience
A summer jazz concert on the roof of La Pedrera

→

MONTJUÏC

The journey up to Montjuïc is rewarding in itself as you stroll through leafy parks, ride the funicular or sway in a cable car, looking down on the city below. But these views are no match for those seen from the top of this steep hill. This tranquil spot, crowned by a castle, is the perfect place to indulge in a picnic or take a walk in the shadow of the imposing fortress. But it's the museums that steal the show here. With Catalan treasures, contemporary art and even a reproduced Spanish village, Montjuïc is a cultural treasure trove.

Best for
Strolling and picnicking

Home to
Green spaces

Experience
The mesmerizing spectacle of water, light and music at the Font Mágica (Magic Fountain)

BEYOND THE CENTRE

Before they became suburbs of Barcelona, the settlements around the city had their own distinct identities and many retain their small-town atmosphere. It's easy to feel a million miles from the cosmopolitan Catalan city here. Those who venture outside the city centre are rewarded with a myriad of sights, including the legendary Camp Nou – Europe's biggest football stadium – and Gaudí's ginger-bread-like Park Güell. Traversed by hiking paths, the peak of Tibidabo is home to one of the area's less well-known attractions – a charmingly old-fashioned funfair.

Best for
Football and funfairs

Home to
Camp Nou, Park Güell

Experience
Peace and quiet at the Monestir de Santa Maria de Pedralbes

Driving the Cadafalch

With neo-Gothic spikes and sculptures, Josep Puig i Cadafalch's architecture recalls Catalonia's glory years in the Middle Ages, when it ruled a vast Mediterranean empire. Check out the imposing façade of Casa Terrades, which has needle-thin turrets (p121). Cadafalch also designed Casa Amatller (p121), the home of wealthy chocolatier Antoni Amatller i Costa, to resemble a Gothic palace covered in sculptures of animals making and eating chocolate. Take a tour of the residence, climbing the grand staircase to the family's private apartments, before dipping a *carquinyoli* (almond biscuit) into a steaming cup of hot chocolate.

→

The whimsical exterior of Cadalfalch's Casa Terrades, with its soaring spires

BARCELONA FOR
MODERNISTA MARVELS

Modernisme – sometimes called Catalan Art Nouveau – transformed Barcelona's skyline between the late 19th and early 20th centuries. Although Gaudí is the best-known proponent of the style, Lluís Domènech i Montaner and Josep Puig i Cadafalch also left their marks on the city.

Oh My Gaudí!

From the vast, as yet unfinished, spires of the Sagrada Família (p110) to the luxuriant gardens of the Park Güell (p140), guarded by a pair of fairy-tale pavilions, Gaudí is everywhere you look in Barcelona. As well as these large-scale public works, he designed several imaginative private homes for wealthy patrons, many of which offer visiting experiences beyond the norm. Sip a glass of cava to the sound of a string quartet on the otherworldly roof of Palau Güell (p97), take an augmented reality tour of Casa Batlló (p116) or join Gaudí himself – or Mrs Ramoneta, the family's maid – on a kids' tour of La Pedrera, with an actor (p118).

→

Overlooking the city from Gaudí's multicoloured tiled bench, Park Güell

Climbing the Montaner

Lluís Domènech i Montaner is often described as the father of Modernisme. He designed two of Barcelona's most glorious buildings – the Palau de la Música Catalana (p88) and Hospital de la Santa Creu i de Sant Pau (p120). Guided tours are available for both of these buildings, but catching a concert under the stained glass in the Palau de la Música Catalana or in the grand gardens of what is now the Sant Pau Recinte Modernista is an absolutely unforgettable experience.

←

Statues of muses on a mosaicked wall in the Palau de la Música Catalana

DRINK

Els 4 Gats
Picasso's favourite watering hole has grand Modernista proportions.

📍G6 🏠Carrer de Montsió 🌐4gats.com

London Bar
Enjoy a tipple under this tiny bar's sweeping signage. Delectable tapas accompanies glistening glasses here.

📍F7 🏠Carrer Nou de la Rambla 34 🌐london bar-bar.negocio.site

Café de l'Òpera
Once La Mallorquina chocolate shop, this café has mirrors decorated with characters from different operas.

📍F7 🏠La Rambla 74 🌐cafeoperabcn.com

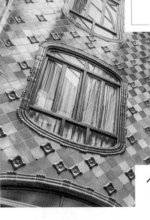

↑ The blue-tiled light well in Gaudí's Casa Batlló

Ruta del Modernisme

As well as covering the big-name sights – and entitling you to discounts – this self-guided walking tour will lead you to the city's hidden Modernista gems (www.rutadelmodernisme.com). Pick up a guide from any of Barcelona's tourist offices and follow the red plaques to some of the 120 buildings. Browse the wooden shelves of the charming Farmàcia Bolós (Rambla de Catalunya 77), after snapping a picture of its stained-glass doorway, or admire the cathedral-like Casa Martí before enjoying a tipple in the tiled Els 4 Gats on the ground floor.

OLD TOWN

Barcelona's Ciutat Vella (Old Town) is where
the city itself came into being. Settled by the
prehistoric Laietani, the area stretching between
the Besòs and Llobregat river deltas was chosen
by the Romans around 15 BC to be the site of their
new *colonia* (town): Barcino. They surrounded the
town with defensive walls, ruins of which can still
be seen today. The Roman forum, on the Plaça de
Sant Jaume, was replaced by the medieval Palau
de la Generalitat in 1596, the seat of Catalonia's
government, and the Ajuntament (Casa de la Ciutat),
the city's town hall. Close by are the 4th-century
former royal palace and the Gothic cathedral, dedicated to Saint Eulàlia, the city's first patron saint.

As the medieval town grew wealthy from trade
across the Mediterranean, it expanded out into El
Born and, later, rural El Raval. In the 18th century,
Barceloneta was developed into a fishing quarter.
The medieval walls surrounded the city until the
mid-19th century, when they were torn down for
an urban expansion project which saw the creation
of neighbouring Eixample.

Today, the Old Town remains the beating heart
of the Catalan capital, particularly its main artery
La Rambla, a magnet for locals and tourists alike,
and one of the most vibrant streets in Europe.

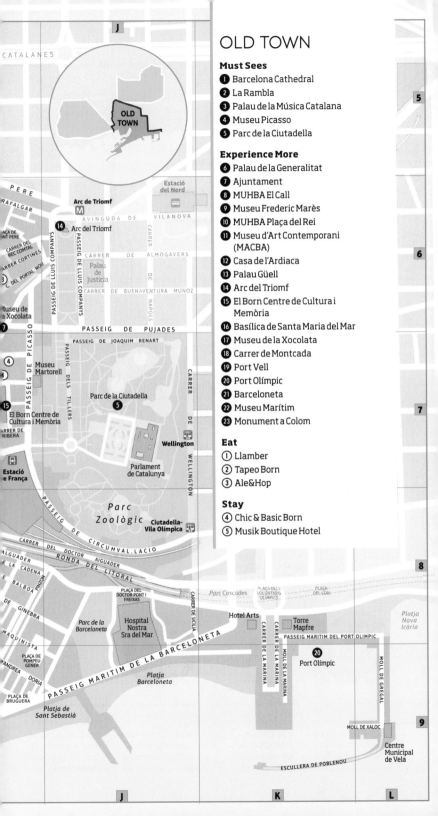

OLD TOWN

Must Sees

1 Barcelona Cathedral
2 La Rambla
3 Palau de la Música Catalana
4 Museu Picasso
5 Parc de la Ciutadella

Experience More

6 Palau de la Generalitat
7 Ajuntament
8 MUHBA El Call
9 Museu Frederic Marès
10 MUHBA Plaça del Rei
11 Museu d'Art Contemporani (MACBA)
12 Casa de l'Ardiaca
13 Palau Güell
14 Arc del Triomf
15 El Born Centre de Cultura i Memòria
16 Basílica de Santa Maria del Mar
17 Museu de la Xocolata
18 Carrer de Montcada
19 Port Vell
20 Port Olímpic
21 Barceloneta
22 Museu Marítim
23 Monument a Colom

Eat

① Llamber
② Tapeo Born
③ Ale&Hop

Stay

④ Chic & Basic Born
⑤ Musik Boutique Hotel

BARCELONA CATHEDRAL

Twin octagonal bell towers, dating from 1386 to 1393

🅶 G6 🏠 Plaça de la Seu Ⓜ Jaume I 🚌 17, 19, 45 🕐 Cathedral: 10:30am–2pm & 3–5:30pm Mon–Fri; 10:30am–5pm Sat; Sacristy Museum: 9am–7pm daily 🌐 catedralbcn.org

With its intricate façade and inviting interior, Barcelona Cathedral is a beguiling sight. Treading beneath the nave's soaring vaulting, you may feel as if you are stepping back in time.

One of the city's few churches spared from destruction in the Civil War, this compact Gothic cathedral was begun in 1298 under Jaime (Jaume) II, on the foundations of a site dating back to Visigothic times, but was not finished until the early 20th century. This interruption has lent Barcelona Cathedral a distinct look compared to the rest of the Barri Gòtic. The cathedral is dedicated to St Eulàlia, the city's patron saint, whose white marble sarcophagus is located in the crypt. Take your time to explore the exceptional interior, as well as the lofty roof terrace and shady cloisters. Visit before 12:30pm or after 5:30pm to skip the entry fee, though a ticket is always required for access to the museum, terrace and choir stalls.

The Catalan-style Gothic interior, with a single wide nave that has 28 side chapels

Beautifully carved choir stalls, which date from the 15th century

The Capella del Santíssim Sagrament

Timeline

877
△ St Eulàlia's remains are brought here from Santa Maria del Mar.

1046–58
△ Romanesque cathedral built under Ramon Berenguer I.

1298
△ Start of the construction of the present Gothic building, which was consecrated in 1339.

1889
Main façade completed, based on plans dating from 1408 by architect Charles Galters.

The crypt, where St Eulàlia's tomb is found

1 The cathedral's central spire was finally completed in 1913.

2 The shady Gothic cloisters are especially popular with visitors.

3 The cathedral's crypt is home to the alabaster sarcophagus of St Eulàlia.

The Capella de Sant Benet, a chapel dedicated to the founder of the Benedictine Order and patron saint of Europe, is home to a magnificent altarpiece.

Cloisters, with a fountain decorated with a statue of St George

Porta de Santa Eulàlia, the entrance to the cloisters

The Sacristy Museum, which houses a small treasury

Capella de Santa Llúcia

↑ The distinctive Barcelona Cathedral, set in the city's Old Town

Did You Know?

Thirteen geese live in the cloisters, representing St Eulàlia's age at her martyrdom.

2 🍴 🖥 🛍

LA RAMBLA

📍F7 Ⓜ Drassanes, Liceu, Catalunya 🚈 **Catalunya**

The historic avenue of La Rambla splits the Old Town in half as it stretches from Plaça de Catalunya to Port Vell *(p102)*. Newsstands, flower stalls, tarot readers, musicians and mime artists line the wide, tree-shaded central walkway around the clock, but La Rambla is particularly frenetic in the evenings and at weekends.

The name of this long avenue, known as Les Rambles in Catalan, comes from the Arabic *ramla*, meaning "the dried-up bed of a seasonal river". The 13th-century city wall followed the left bank of such a river that flowed from the Collserola hills to the sea. Convents, monasteries and the university were built on the opposite bank in the 16th century. As time passed, the riverbed was filled in and those buildings demolished, but they are remembered in the names of the five consecutive Rambles that make up the great avenue.

The first of these, Rambla de Canaletes, is named after an extravagant fountain; and Rambla dels Estudis after a university established here in the 16th century. Along the latter, you'll find the Palau Moja. Pop inside the Baroque first-floor salon to learn more about Catalan culture. Next comes Rambla de Sant Josep, where a monastery dedicated to the saint was demolished to make room for the market better known as "La Boqueria" – the place where goat *(boc)* is sold. Don't miss the Palau de le Virreina, which hosts free exhibitions. Rambla des Caputxins and Rambla de Santa Mònica also recall a long-gone monastery and convent.

→
A street performer, dressed as a golden monster, striking a pose on La Rambla

EAT

Mercat de Sant Josep
"La Boqueria" is Barcelona's most colourful food market. Seek out Bar Quiosc Modern for its seafood.

🏠 Plaça de la Boqueria
🕐 Sun 🌐 boqueria. barcelona

€€€

***

Rocambolesc
The Roca brothers, who are regularly voted the best chefs in the world, are behind the ice-creams served here.

🏠 La Rambla 51-59
🌐 rocambolesc.com

€€€

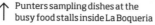

↑ Punters sampling dishes at the busy food stalls inside La Boqueria

Did You Know?

The poet Lorca said La Rambla was "the only street in the world that I wish would never end".

↑ An aerial view of people strolling down the tree-lined La Rambla

Did You Know?

The Palau's concert hall is the only one in Europe to be lit by natural light.

PALAU DE LA MÚSICA CATALANA

📍H6 🏠Carrer Palau de la Música 4-6 Ⓜ Urquinaona 🕐Aug: 9am-6pm daily; Sep-Jul: 10am-3:30pm daily (Easter & Jul: 10am-6pm); and for concerts 🌐palaumusica.cat

This is a monument to music, a Modernista celebration of tilework, sculpture and stained glass. Designed by Lluís Domènech i Montaner (1850–1923), it was completed in 1908. Its red-brick façade is elaborate, but it's the main auditorium that is truly inspiring.

The Palace of Catalan Music was built for the Orfeó Català in 1891, a choral society that played an important role in the Catalan cultural resistance known as the "Renaixença". The building's façade is richly decorated with colourful murals, as well as an enormous sculptural group depicting "Catalan Song" and Sant Jordi, the Catalan patron saint.

Inside, the main auditorium is one of the most beautiful in the world, lit by an inverted dome of stained glass portraying angelic choristers. Sculptures of Wagner and Clavé adorn the proscenium arch above the stage, which features a charming group of dancing muses. An underground concert hall and an outdoor square for summer concerts were later added, consolidating the Palau's reputation as Barcelona's most loved music venue.

 PICTURE PERFECT
Pillar of Culture

Book a tour in advance to gain access to the site's balcony. It's the ideal spot to snap the gorgeous stained-glass skylight framed by the auditorium. The colourful tiled pillars are also worth a close-up shot.

↑ Interior of the Palau's sublime concert hall, beneath its inverted stained-glass dome

THE SARDANA

Catalonia's national dance is more complicated than it appears. The success of the Sardana depends on all of the dancers accurately counting the complicated short- and long-step skips and jumps, which accounts for their serious faces. Music is provided by a *cobla*, an 11-person band consisting of a leader playing a three-holed flute *(flabiol)* and a little drum *(tabal)*, five woodwind players and five brass players. When the music starts, dancers join hands and form circles. The Sardana is performed during most local fiestas and the Palau de la Música Catalana stages performances sometimes.

↑ American jazz singer Madeleine Peyroux performing in the Palau

→ The ornate, pillared façade of the Palau, lit up at dusk

← A sculpture of the composer Lluís Millet standing at the Palau

Visitors wandering through stone archways inside the Museu Picasso →

MUSEU PICASSO

⊙ H7 ⊙ Carrer Montcada 15-23 Ⓜ Jaume I ⊙ Jan-Oct: 10am-5pm Mon, 9am-8:30pm Tue-Sun; Nov & Dec: 9am-7pm Tue-Sun ⊎ museupicasso. bcn.cat

One of Barcelona's most popular attractions, the Picasso Museum is housed in five adjoining medieval palaces: Berenguer d'Aguilar, Baró de Castellet, Meca, Mauri and Finestres. The collection focuses largely on Picasso's early work, showing the development of the young painter and the influence of the city that was his home for many years.

The core of the Picasso Museum's collection is a large donation made in 1963 by the artist's secretary and great friend, Jaume Sabartés. Given that Picasso had publicly sworn that he wouldn't set foot in Spain while Franco lived, it was known as the Sabartés Collection for many years (as a museum using the artist's own name would have been met with censorship). Following Sabartes' death in 1968, Picasso himself donated further paintings, including early examples. These were later complemented by graphic works, left in his will, and 141 ceramic pieces given by his widow, Jacqueline.

The setting of the museum itself makes for a unique experience. Visitors are able to wander through stone archways, into pretty courtyards and up well-preserved staircases as they take in the artworks.

The strength of the 4,200-piece collection, which includes sketches, paintings, sculptures and ceramics, is Picasso's early works. These show how, even at the ages of 15 and 16, he had prodigious talent, while the haunting paintings of his Blue Period evoke the misery and hopelessness of beggars and prostitutes he encountered on Barcelona's streets. The highlight of the museum's collection, however, is Picasso's extraordinary suite of 58 paintings, which he created in response to Velázquez's masterpiece, *Las Meninas* (1656).

← A portrait of Picasso in his later years

PABLO PICASSO IN BARCELONA

Picasso (1881-1973) was born in Málaga and was almost 14 when he came to Barcelona. He enrolled in the city's art academy, and was a precocious talent among his contemporaries. Amid the prostitutes of Carrer d'Avinyò Picasso found inspiration for his *Les Demoiselles d'Avignon* (1906-7). He left Barcelona for Paris in his early twenties and initially returned several times, but after the Civil War his opposition to Franco kept him in France.

↑ One of the paintings in Picasso's *Las Meninas* series (1947)

Did You Know?

As a young student, Antoni Gaudí helped Josep Fontseré build the triumphal arch on the Cascada.

 5

PARC DE LA CIUTADELLA

◉ J7 ⌂ Passeig de Picasso 21 Ⓜ Barceloneta, Ciutadella-Vila Olímpica, Arc de Triomf, Jaume I

With a boating lake, orange groves and palm trees, this park is the perfect place to escape the hustle and bustle of the city. It was once the site of a massive star-shaped citadel, built for Felipe V, which became a notorious prison under Napoleon. But in 1878 it was pulled down and the park given to the people.

 ①

Castell dels Tres Dragons

⊘ To the public 🖰 museu ciencies.cat

At the entrance to the Parc de la Ciutadella is the Castell dels Tres Dragons (Castle of the Three Dragons), named after a play by Frederic Soler. A fine example of Modernista architecture *(p78)*, it was built by Lluís Domènech i Montaner for the 1888 Universal Exhibition and the combination of visible iron supports and exposed red brickwork were radical innovations at the time.

Part of the Museu de Ciències Naturals, the Castell is currently closed for renovations.

 ②

Cascada

Located in the northwest corner of the park, opposite the lake, the cascade was the first thing to be built in the newly established park. When it was initially built in 1881, it was very plain in design but the triumphal arch, modelled on Rome's Trevi Fountain, was added in time for the 1888 Universal Exhibition. The golden figure of Aurora, who represents dawn in Roman mythology, riding four frisky horses crowns this arch. And beneath it is a statue of Venus, goddess of love, standing on an open clam with her arms raised aloft. It is from this figure that the water seems to tumble down a mossy bank.

 ③

Museu Martorell

⊘ To the public 🖰 museu ciencies.cat

Part of the Museu de Ciències Naturals, the Museu Martorell opened in 1882 and was the first building in Barcelona to be constructed expressly for the purpose of housing a public museum.

The building is currently closed to the public for extensive renovations and is slated to reopen in 2023.

Castell dels
Tres Dragons

Hivernacle

Museu
Martorell

Umbracle

Jardins
Fonseré
i Mestré

LA
RIBERA

Estació
de França

Cascada

Parc de la
Ciutadella

The Boating
Lake

Plaça
de Joan
Fiveller

Parlament de
Catalunya

ZOO DE
BARCELONA

Wellington

Ciutadella-
Vila Olímpica

Ciutadella-
Vila Olímpica

0 metres 200
0 yards 200

N

↑ Cyclists taking a break
in front of the arch that
crowns the Cascada

Hivernacle and Umbracle

Beside the Museu Martorell, you'll find the Hivernacle (conservatory) and Umbracle (palm house), which both date from 1884 and were designed for the 1888 Universal Exhibition. The Hivernacle is decorated with wrought iron motifs of palms and other plants. The Umbracle was designed to house the more delicate plants. Both buildings are sadly neglected and plans for their restoration have long been on hold.

The Boating Lake

Although it's not nearly as dramatic as the cascade, the boating lake is a similarly iconic element of the park. The lake is fringed by palm trees and willows that overhang the water's edge. The only interruptions to the peaceful scene are the little green boats.

TOP 3
PARK ACTIVITIES

Rowing a Boat
On a sunny day, why not hire a rowing boat, and head out on the lake? The boats are particularly popular on Sunday afternoons, so arrive early to beat the crowds.

Cycling
Hire a bicycle from Happy Rental Bike to cover as much ground as possible (www.happyrentalbike.com).

Dancing
Groups of people swing or tap dance on the bandstand every Sunday afternoon.

← Spending a sunny day on the park's tree-fringed boating lake

EXPERIENCE MORE

6

Palau de la Generalitat

📍G7 🏛Plaça de Sant Jaume 4 Ⓜ Jaume I 🕐10am-1:30pm 2nd & 4th Sat & Sun of the month; 10am-8pm 23 Apr, 11 & 24 Sep (passport required) 🌐president.cat

The Renaissance Generalitat has been the seat of the Governor of Catalonia since the early 15th century. Above the entrance is a statue of Sant Jordi (St George), the patron saint of Catalonia, and the Dragon.

Inside are the Gothic chapel of Sant Jordi, designed by Marc Safont, and Pere Blai's Italianate Saló de Sant Jordi. Don't miss the *Pati dels Tarongers* (the Orange Tree Patio), by Pau Mateu, which has a bell tower built by Pere Ferrer in 1568.

The Catalan president has offices here as well as in the Casa dels Canonges. The two buildings are connected by a bridge across Carrer del Bisbe, built in 1928 and modelled on the Bridge of Sighs in Venice.

7

Ajuntament

📍G7 🏛Plaça de Sant Jaume 1 Ⓜ Jaume I, Liceu 🕐10am-1:30pm Sun & public hols; 10am-8pm 2nd Sat in Feb, 23 Apr & 30 May; or by appt 🌐ajuntament.barcelona.cat

The magnificent 14th-century city hall faces the Palau de la Generalitat. Flanking the entrance are statues of Jaime I, who granted the city rights to elect councillors in 1249, and Joan Fiveller, who levied taxes on court members in the 1500s.

Inside is the huge council chamber, the 14th-century Saló de Cent, built for the city's 100 councillors. The Saló de les Cròniques, on the first floor, was commissioned for the 1929 International Exhibition and decorated by Josep Maria Sert with murals of momentous events in Catalan history.

8

MUHBA El Call

📍G7 🏛Placeta de Manuel Ribé s/n Ⓜ Jaume I, Liceu 🕐11am-2pm Wed & Fri, 11am-7pm Sat & Sun 🌐ajuntament.barcelona.cat/museuhistoria

One of the numerous branches of the Museu d'Història de Barcelona, this information centre occupies a modern building constructed over

> **BARCELONA'S EARLY JEWISH COMMUNITY**
>
> From the 11th to the 13th centuries, Jews dominated Barcelona's commerce and culture, training as doctors and founding the first seat of learning. But in 1243, violent anti-Semitism led to the Jews being consigned to a ghetto, El Call. Jews were heavily taxed by the monarch, but in return they also received privileges, as they handled most of Catalonia's lucrative trade with North Africa. But in 1401, Martin I declared the ghetto to be illegal and the population fled.

The magnificent Sant Jordi chapel, inside the Palau de la Generalitat

MUHBA Plaça del Rei, facing onto one of Barcelona's oldest squares

what was once the medieval home of Yusef Bonhiac, a Jewish weaver. The touch screen information panels and exhibitions give an excellent overview of the Call (the former Jewish quarter) and the lives of its inhabitants.

Museu Frederic Marès

⦿ G6 ⌂ Plaça de Sant Iu 5 Ⓜ Jaume I ⓖ 10am-7pm Tue-Sat, 11am-8pm Sun & hols Ⓦ barcelona.cat/ museufredericmares

The sculptor Frederic Marès i Deulovol (1893–1991) was also a traveller and collector, and this museum is a monument to his eclectic taste. Part of the Royal Palace complex, the building was home to all sorts of dignitaries before Marès occupied a small apartment here.

Opened by the sculptor in 1948, the museum has a collection of Romanesque and Gothic religious art. On the ground and first floors there are stone sculptures, while exhibits on the three floors above range from clocks and antique cameras to pipes and postcards.

MUHBA Plaça del Rei

⦿ G6 ⌂ Plaça del Rei Ⓜ Jaume I ⓖ 10am-7pm Tue-Sat, 10am-8pm Sun ⏰ 1 Jan, 1 May, 24 Jun, 25 Dec Ⓦ ajuntament. barcelona.cat/museu historia

The Palau Reial (Royal Palace) was the residence of the count-kings of Barcelona from its foundation in the 13th century. The complex includes the Capella Reial de Santa Àgata (royal chapel) and the 14th-century Gothic Saló del Tinell, a vast room with arches spanning 17 m (56 ft). This is where Isabel and Fernando received Columbus on his return from America. It is also where the Holy Inquisition sat, believing that the walls would move if lies were told.

The palace is now part of the Museu d'Història de Barcelona, but its main attraction lies underground. Entire streets of old Barcino are accessible via a lift and walkways suspended over the ruins of Roman Barcelona. Found when the Casa Clariana-Padellàs, the Gothic building from which you enter,

was moved here stone by stone in 1931, these are some of the world's most extensive and complete subterranean Roman ruins.

STAY

Chic & Basic Born
A good bet for style on a budget, this 19th-century townhouse features small but cleverly designed rooms.

⦿ H7 ⌂ Calle Princesa 50 Ⓦ chic andbasic.com

Musik Boutique Hotel
Located in a beautifully restored 18th-century building, this boutique hotel offers outstanding services.

⦿ H6 ⌂ Carrer de Sant Pere més Baix 62 Ⓦ musikboutique hotel.com

← Visitors exploring the airy interior of the Museu d'Art Contemporani

Museu d'Art Contemporani (MACBA)

📍F5 🏛Plaça dels Àngels 1 Ⓜ️Universitat, Catalunya ⏰11am-8pm Mon & Wed-Sat, 10am-3pm Sun & public hols 🔒1 Jan, 25 Dec 🌐macba.cat

This dramatic, glass-fronted building, with its light and airy galleries, was designed by the American architect Richard Meier to house the city's collection of contemporary art.

The permanent collection of predominantly Spanish painting, sculpture and installation from the 1950s onwards is complemented by temporary exhibitions by foreign artists like US painter Susana Solano and South African photo-journalist David Goldblatt.

Next to the MACBA, a remodelled 18th-century hospice, the Casa de la Caritat, houses the **Centre de Cultura Contemporània**, a lively arts centre that hosts major arts festivals and regular exhibitions, shows and other events.

Centre de Cultura Contemporània

🏛Montalegre 5 ⏰11am-8pm Tue-Sun & public hols 🌐cccb.org

Casa de l'Ardiaca

📍G6 🏛Carrer de Santa Llúcia 1 Ⓜ️Jaume I ⏰10am-2pm & 3-7:30pm Mon-Fri 🔒Public hols 🌐ajuntament.barcelona. cat.barcelona.cat/arxiu municipal/arxiuhistoric

Standing beside what was originally the Bishop's Gate in the Roman city wall, the Casa de l'Ardiaca (Archdeacon's House) was built in the 12th century. Its present appearance, however, dates from around 1500 when it was remodelled and a colonnade was added to the exterior. In 1870 this was extended to form the Flamboyant Gothic patio around a fountain. On Corpus Christi (60 days after Easter Sunday), the *"l'ou com balla"* (dancing egg) is celebrated here. The fountain is decorated with flowers and fruits and an egg is laid under the water. Instead of falling, the egg turns, seeming to pirouette.

The Modernista architect Lluís Domènech i Montaner added the marble letterbox, carved with three swallows and a tortoise, beside the Renaissance portal. Upstairs is the Arxiu Històric de la Ciutat (City Archives). Visitors are only allowed into the courtyard and the entrance hall, which occasionally hosts art exhibitions.

💬 INSIDER TIP
Les Nits de Palau Güell

On Thursday nights in summer, the Palau Güell hosts concerts on its unique roof. After you've enjoyed the music with a glass of cava, you can take a tour of the building.

Palau Güell

☉ F7 **⌂** Carrer Nou de la Rambla 3-5 **Ⓜ** Liceu **🕐** 10am–2:30pm & 3:30–8pm Tue–Sun (to 6pm Nov–Mar) **🔒** 1, 6 & 19–25 Jan, 25 & 26 Dec **🌐** palauguell.cat

Gaudí's first major work in Barcelona's city centre was this house, commissioned by his wealthy patron Eusebi Güell. He made it known that, even if he was investing in an inexperienced architect, there would be no limit to the budget at Gaudí's disposal. Gaudí took Güell at his word, as can be seen in the quality of the materials used for what was a disproportionately grand building for a private residence. The stonework is clad with marble and, inside, high-quality woods are used.

Despite the expense of the build, from the street there is little hint of the colour and playfulness to come in Gaudí's later work, except in the spire-like chimneys behind the parapet on

ANTONI GAUDÍ (1852–1926)

Born in Reus (Tarragona) into a family of artisans, Antoni Gaudí i Cornet was the leading exponent of Catalan Modernisme. Following a stint as a blacksmith's apprentice, he studied at Barcelona's School of Architecture. Inspired by a nationalistic search for a romantic medieval past, his work was supremely original. His first major achievement was the Casa Vicens (1888) at No 24 Carrer de les Carolines, but his most celebrated building is the extravagant church of the Sagrada Família *(p110)*, to which he solely devoted his life from 1914. He gave all his money to the project and often went from house to house begging for more. On 7 June 1926, when Gaudí was knocked over by a tram, no one knew who he was and he was taken to the Hospital de Santa Creu *(p120)*. He died three days later. His funeral was a huge event, and most of Barcelona's citizens turned out to pay their respects to the man who had transformed their city.

the roof. The austere façade is symmetrical and characterized mostly by straight lines, both horizontal and vertical. The only indication of Gaudí's later preference for curves is in the two doorways, which are each formed by a parabolic (U-shaped) arch.

Inside is far more dramatic and typical of Gaudí's mature designs. It's easy to see how the architect would later design the Sagrada Família when standing in the central room on the main floor. Something between a sitting room and a covered courtyard, this room rises three floors (of

a six-floor building) and is spanned by a cupola.

Ever the perfectionist, Gaudí designed the Palau Güell's furniture, lights, stained glass and other fittings, as he would do for his future projects.

The house was finished in 1889 and was used by Güell not only as a luxurious family home, but as a place to host important guests, stage chamber concerts and hold political meetings.

Antoni Gaudí's unique chimneys atop the ↓ Neo-Gothic Palau Güell

GAUDÍ'S CITY

Barcelona bears the indelible mark of Catalonia's most famous son, Antoni Gaudí i Cornet, who transformed the city's skyline into an architectural masterpiece. Drawing on Persian and Japanese arts, Mudéjar architecture and the natural world, Gaudí reinvented the already adventurous art and architectural style known as Catalan Modernisme (p78). A highly dexterous architect, Gaudí designed, or collaborated on designs, in almost every known medium. He combined bare, undecorated materials – wood, rough-hewn stone, rubble and brickwork – with meticulous craftwork in wrought iron, stained glass and elaborate mosaics. Every Gaudí creation is unique, but they are united by their skill and romanticism.

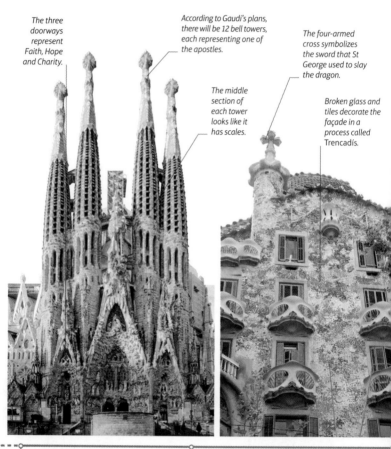

The three doorways represent Faith, Hope and Charity.

According to Gaudí's plans, there will be 12 bell towers, each representing one of the apostles.

The four-armed cross symbolizes the sword that St George used to slay the dragon.

The middle section of each tower looks like it has scales.

Broken glass and tiles decorate the façade in a process called Trencadís.

Gaudí Highlights

Sagrada Família

△ When Gaudí took over the construction of the Sagrada Família (p110) in 1883, it became his lifelong obsession. An extreme expression of devotion, his soaring interior and the Nativity façade reference both biblical events and the natural world. Although he never lived to see its completion, it is still built to his vision.

Casa Batlló

△ Industrialist Josep Batlló gave Gaudí complete creative freedom to reform this late-19th-century house. Completed in 1906, Casa Batlló (p116) is an evocation of artistic joy. The façade acted as an exuberant and marine-inspired canvas, while the roof ripples like a dragon in flight. Inside, light pours in through effervescent stained glass, while the central patio ensures natural light reaches every room.

↑ Gaudí's famous salamander, covered in brightly coloured mosaics, at Park Güell

Gaudí's predilection for curved lines is evident in La Pedrera's wavy façade.

Bizarrely decorated chimneys became one of the trademarks of Gaudí's later work.

The twisting wrought-iron balconies were designed by Josep Maria Jujol.

The influence of nature on Gaudí is seen in the mushroom-shaped dome.

One of the pavilions is topped with a four-armed cross like Casa Batlló.

The stone façade of the pavilion is crowned by a mosaic-covered roof.

La Pedrera

▲ The last private residence to be designed by Gaudí, rough-hewn La Pedrera *(p118)* raised eyebrows in its time due to its undulating stone façade, abstract roof sculptures and opera-mask-like balconies. The entrance doors, designed to facilitate both people and vehicles, are made up of smaller panes of glass in irregular shapes, based on animals and plants, with larger, more luminous pieces at the top.

Park Güell

▲ Created during Gaudí's naturalist phase, Park Güell *(p140)* is emblematic of the architect's fanciful style. The stone-built pavilions, with their brightly tiled gingerbread roofs, are like something from a fairy tale. One of these lodges was designed to be the Casa del Guarda (Caretaker's House). Initially conceived to be a garden city for Barcelona's wealthy families, only two plots were purchased.

Did You Know?

The Arc del Triomf is topped by the 50 shields of each Spanish province.

14

Arc del Triomf

📍J6 🏛Passeig de Lluís Companys Ⓜ Arc de Triomf

The main gateway to the 1888 Universal Exhibition, which filled the Parc de la Ciutadella, was designed by Josep Vilaseca i Casanovas. It is built of brick in Mudéjar style, with sculpted allegories of crafts, industry and business. The frieze by Josep Reynés on the main façade represents the city welcoming foreign visitors and the frieze facing the park shows the city presenting medals to the exhibition participants. Reliefs on one side symbolize agriculture and industry, and commerce and art on the other. Visitors can climb to the viewing terrace

at the top of the arch during the 48h Open House Barcelona festival, usually held at the end of October.

15 🏛🖥📷

El Born Centre de Cultura i Memòria

📍H7 🏛Plaça Comercial 12 Ⓜ Jaume I, Barceloneta ⏰10am–8pm Tue–Sun (Nov–Feb: to 7pm Tue–Sun) 🌐elbornculturaimemoria. barcelona.cat

This covered market, with its ornate ironwork and crystal roof, was Barcelona's main wholesale market until the early 1970s, when it outgrew its location.

While the market was being remodelled, extensive ruins of the 18th-century city were discovered beneath its foundations. These ruins are now the focal point of the El Born cultural centre, set off by exhibitions, talks and screenings.

The street names in the vicinity reflect what went on in Barcelona's former mercantile hub: Flassaders was where you would go for a woven blanket and Vidriería was once lit up

EAT

The El Born district is teeming with tapas bars. Here are a few of the best.

Llamber
📍H7 🏛Carrer de la Fusina 5 🌐Llamber.com

€€€

Tapeo Born
📍H7 🏛Carrer de Montcada 29 🌐tapeoborn.cat

€€€

Ale&Hop
📍H6 🏛Carrer de les Basses de Sant Pere 10 📞93 126 90 94

€€€

with glass-blowers' torches. A few of these establishments remain, but they are now outnumbered by chic fashion and interiors boutiques.

The pink brick façade of the Arc del Triomf, on Passeig de Lluís Companys ↑

↑ The Gothic-style Basílica de Santa Maria del Mar, a prominent landmark in the Ribera district

Much of this area was razed after Barcelona fell to the French-Spanish forces during the War of Succession. This key event is remembered each year on 11 September, with activities focused on a monument dedicated to those who died in 1714, located near the market.

16 Basílica de Santa Maria del Mar

🅠 H7 🅐 Plaça Sta Maria 1 Ⓜ Jaume I 🕐 9am–noon & 5–8:30pm Mon–Sat, 10am–2pm & 5–8pm Sun 🌐 santa mariadelmarbarcelona.org

This is the city's only example of a church entirely in the Catalan Gothic style. Work began in 1329 and it took just 55 years to build, with money donated by merchants and shipbuilders. The speed gave it a unity of style. The west front has a 15th-century rose window of the Coronation of the Virgin. More stained glass, from the 15th to 18th centuries, lights the nave and aisles.

The interior is noted for its simplicity and great acoustics, as demonstrated during the concerts held here. Unfortunately, the choir and furnishings were burned in the Civil War (p67). For an amazing view, take a guided tour of the church's rooftop. Visits are at 1:15pm, 2pm, 3pm and 5:15pm daily.

17 Museu de la Xocolata

🅠 H6 🅐 Carrer del Comerç 36 Ⓜ Jaume I, Arc de Triomf 🕐 10am–7pm Mon–Sat (15 Jun–15 Sep: to 8pm), 10am–3pm Sun & public hols 🚫 1 & 6 Jan, 25 & 26 Dec 🌐 museuxocolata.cat

Founded by Barcelona's chocolate- and pastry-makers' union, this museum celebrates the history of one of the most universally loved foodstuffs, from the discovery of cocoa in South America to the invention of the first chocolate machine in Barcelona. This confectionery tale is told through old posters, photographs and footage. The real thing is displayed in a homage to the art of the *mona*, which was a traditional Easter cake that evolved over the centuries into an edible sculpture. Every year, pâtissiers compete to create the most imaginative piece, decorating their chocolate versions of well-known buildings or folk figures with jewels, feathers and other materials. The

museum shop sells – you guessed it – all manner of chocolate goods.

18 Carrer de Montcada

🅠 H7 Ⓜ Jaume I

The most authentic medieval street in the city is a narrow lane, overshadowed by gargoyles and roofs that almost touch overhead. The Gothic palaces that line it date back to Catalonia's expansion in the 13th century. Almost all of the buildings were modified over the years, particularly during the 17th century. Only Casa Cervelló-Guidice at No 25 retains its original façade.

The **Museu Etnològic i de Cultures del Món** (Museum of Ethnology and World Cultures), in the 16th-century palaces at No 12, imaginatively displays more than 700 exhibits from around the world.

Located at No 22 is one of the city's best-known cava bars, El Xampanyet.

Museu Etnològic i de Cultures del Món

🎫 📞 93 256 23 00 🕐 May–Sep: 10am–8pm Tue–Sun; Oct–Apr: 10am–7pm Tue–Sat, 10am–8pm Sun

↑ Walking past the 17th-century buildings on Carrer de Montcada

⑲ Port Vell

📍 G8 Ⓜ Barceloneta

The city's leisure port is at the foot of La Rambla (p86), just beyond the old customs house, which was built in 1902 at the Portal de la Pau, the former maritime entrance to the city. To the south, the Moll de Barcelona, with a World Trade Centre, serves as the passenger pier for visiting cruise ships. In front of the customs house, La Rambla is linked to the yacht clubs on the Moll d'Espanya by Rambla de Mar – a futuristic swing bridge and pedestrian jetty, designed in 1994. The Moll d'Espanya (*moll* meaning quay, wharf or pier) has a shopping and restaurant complex, the Maremagnum.

The Moll de la Fusta (Timber Wharf) is overlooked by Javier Mariscal's *Gambrinus* – a sculpture of a giant, smiling prawn. At the end of the wharf stands

 GREAT VIEW
Golondrinas

Board a *golondrina* ("swallow") - a small double-decker boat - for a sightseeing trip around Port Vell. The tours last from 40 minutes to an hour and go out beside the steep, castle-topped hill of Montjuïc towards the industrial port. It's a great way to see the city.

El Cap de Barcelona (Barcelona Head), a 20-m (66-ft) sculpture by Pop artist Roy Lichtenstein.

Beyond, the 19th-century warehouses are all that's left of the original port buildings. One has been converted into the **Museu d'Història de Catalunya**, which explores Catalonia's history and culture.

Museu d'Història de Catalunya

 🅰 Plaça de Pau Vila 3 🕐 10am–7pm Tue–Sat (to 8pm Wed & to 2:30pm Sun) 🆆 mhcat.cat

⑳ Port Olímpic

📍 K9 Ⓜ Ciutadella-Vila Olímpica

The most dramatic project for the 1992 Olympics was the demolition of the old industrial waterfront and the laying out of 4 km (2 miles) of promenade and sandy beaches. Suddenly Barcelona seemed like a seaside resort. At the heart of the project was a 0.6 sq km (¼ sq mile) new estate of 2,000 apartments and parks called Nova Icària. The area is still popularly known as the Vila Olímpica because the buildings originally housed the Olympic athletes.

On the seafront there are twin 44-floor blocks, two of Barcelona's tallest skyscrapers, one occupied by offices and the other by the Hotel Arts. They stand beside a bustling marina, which was also built in 1992. The marina hosts several good restaurants and bars.

㉑ Barceloneta

📍 H9 Ⓜ Barceloneta

Barcelona's fishing "village", which lies on a triangular tongue of land jutting into the sea just below the city centre, is known for its fish restaurants and port-side cafés.

Barceloneta was built by the architect and military engineer Juan Martín de Cermeño in 1753 to rehouse people made homeless by the construction of the Ciutadella fortress (p92). Since then it has largely housed fishermen though it is now full of short-let holiday flats. Laid out on a grid system crammed with narrow houses of two or three floors, the area has a friendly air.

In the small Plaça de la Barceloneta is the Baroque church of Sant Miquel del Port, also by Cermeño. The large central square is dominated by a modern covered market.

The modern Rambla de Mar bridge on the waterfront at Port Vell

Did You Know?

Hotel W, on Barceloneta beach, is known as *"La Vela"* (The Sail).

Today, the remnants of Barceloneta's fishing fleet are based in the industrial docks by a small clock tower. On the opposite side of this harbour is the Torre de Sant Sebastià, terminus of the cable car that runs across the port to Montjuïc. Ricardo Bofill's Hotel W presides over Barceloneta beach.

22

Museu Marítim

📍 F8 🏛 Avinguda de les Drassanes Ⓜ Drassanes 🕐 10am–8pm daily (24 & 31 Dec: to 3pm) 🚫 1 & 6 Jan, 25 & 26 Dec 🖥 mmb.cat

The great galleys that made Spain a major seafaring power were built in the sheds of the Drassanes (shipyards), which now house the maritime museum. These royal dry docks are the largest and most complete surviving medieval complex of their kind in the world. They were founded in the mid-13th century, when dynastic marriages uniting the kingdoms of Sicily and Aragón meant that better maritime communications between the two became a priority. Three of the yards' four original corner towers still survive.

Among the vessels to slip from the Drassanes' vaulted halls was the *Real*, flagship of Don Juan of Austria, the illegitimate son of Carlos I (the Holy Roman Emperor Charles V), who led the Christian fleet to victory against the Turks at Lepanto in 1571. The museum's showpiece is a full-scale replica decorated in red and gold.

The renovated halls of the Museu Marítim now host temporary exhibitions with a maritime theme, as well as displaying some historic boats. Three times a month, the charming Jardins de Baluard, a walled garden just behind the museum, is open to the public. Here, you can admire Barcelona's only surviving medieval city gate. The admission ticket also includes a visit to the Santa Eulàlia, a restored century-old schooner, which is moored a short walk away in the Port Vell.

23

Monument a Colom

📍 F8 🏛 Plaça del Portal de la Pau 📞 93 302 52 24 Ⓜ Drassanes 🕐 8:30am–8:30pm daily (26 Dec & 6 Jan: to 2:30pm) 🚫 1 Jan & 25 Dec

The Columbus Monument atop the Portal de la Pau (the "Gate of Peace") was designed by Gaietà Buigas for the 1888 Universal Exhibition.

The 60-m (197-ft) cast-iron monument marks the spot where Christopher Columbus stepped ashore in 1493 after returning from his voyage to the Americas.

There is a statue of the explorer atop the column and the pointing gesture of Columbus is not towards the Americas (as is often surmised), but is simply a dramatic pose.

TOP 5 BARCELONA FIESTAS

La Mercè
Our Lady of Mercy is honoured on 24 September.

Els Tres Tombs
On 17 January horsemen ride three times through the city's streets.

Dia de Sant Ponç
Stalls along Carrer Hospital sell herbs, honey and candied fruit on 11 May.

La Diada
11 September is Catalonia's special day.

Festa Major
Each district tries to outdo the beauty of its neighbours' decorations.

↑ The towering Monument a Colom in Barcelona

A SHORT WALK
BARRI GÒTIC

Distance 1 km (0.5 miles) **Nearest metro**
Jaume I **Time** 15 minutes

The Barri Gòtic (Gothic Quarter) is the true heart of
Barcelona. The oldest part of the city, it was the site chosen
by the Romans in the reign of Augustus (27 BC–AD 14) on
which to found a new *colonia* (town), and has been the
location of the city's administrative buildings ever
since. The Roman forum was on the Plaça de Sant
Jaume, where the medieval Palau de la
Generalitat, Catalonia's parliament, and
the Ajuntament, Barcelona's town hall,
now stand. A walk around the area also
takes in the Gothic cathedral and royal
palace, where Columbus was received by
Fernando and Isabel on his return from
his voyage to the Americas in 1492.

Built on the Roman city wall,
Casa de l'Ardiaca, *the Gothic-
Renaissance archdeacon's
residence, now houses the
city's historical archives (p96).*

*The façade and spire are 20th-century
additions to the original Gothic*
Cathedral (p84). *Among the treasures
inside are medieval Catalan paintings.*

The seat of Catalonia's governor, the **Palau
de la Generalitat** (p94) *has superb Gothic
features, including a stone staircase rising
to an open-air, arcaded gallery.*

To La Rambla

The **Ajuntament**,
*Barcelona's town hall,
may have a Neo-
Classical façade, but
this was only a later
addition to the original
Gothic building,
which was built in the
14th century (p94).*

SANT SEVER

CARRER DEL BISBE

PIET

SANT DOMÈNEC DEL CALL

SANT HONORAT

PLAÇA DE
SANT JAUME

C. DE FERRAN

CARRER DE LA CIUTAT

↑ The intricate 20th-century
façade and spire of
Barcelona Cathedral

0 metres   100

0 yards   100

N

Locator Map
For more detail see p82

↑ Walking under the arches in the internal courtyard of the Museu Frederic Marès

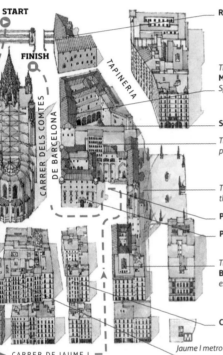

START

FINISH

Roman city wall

The star attraction of the **Museu Frederic Marès** is its extensive collection of Spanish sculptures (p95).

Saló del Tinell

The **MUHBA Plaça del Rei**, the former royal palace, has a dramatic exterior (p95).

The **Capella Reial de Santa Àgata** is one of the highlights of the MUHBA Plaça del Rei.

Plaça del Rei

Palau del Lloctinent

This section of **MUHBA (Museu d'Història de Barcelona)** features the world's most extensive subterranean Roman ruins.

Cereria Subirà candle shop

Jaume I metro

The **Centre Excursionista de Catalunya** displays in its entrance courtyard Roman columns from the Temple of Augustus, whose site is marked by a millstone in the street outside.

CARRER DE JAUME I →

Did You Know?

The Temple of Augustus was discovered during building work in the 19th century.

EIXAMPLE

Barcelona claims to have the greatest collection of Art Nouveau buildings of any city in Europe. The style, known in Catalonia as Modernisme, flourished after 1854, when the government decided to pull down the medieval walls to allow the city to develop into what had previously been a military zone. The designs of the civil engineer Ildefons Cerdà i Sunyer (1815–76) were chosen for the new expansion *(eixample)* inland. These plans called for a rigid grid system of streets, but at each intersection the corners were chamfered, with their corners cut off at a 45° angle, to allow the buildings there to overlook the junctions or squares. The few exceptions to this grid system include the Diagonal, a main avenue running from the area of Pedralbes down to the sea, and the Avinguda de Gaudí, which links the Sagrada Família to the Hospital de la Santa Creu i de Sant Pau by Modernista architect Lluís Domènech i Montaner. The wealth of Barcelona's 19th-century commercial elite, and their passion for all things new, allowed them to give free rein to the age's most innovative architects in designing their residences, creating a unique cityscape.

In the late 20th century, a multitude of shops, bars, discos and restaurants catering to the LGBTQ+ community sprang up in an area of the Eixample, earning it the nickname "Gaixample".

EIXAMPLE

Must Sees
1. Sagrada Família
2. Casa Batlló
3. La Pedrera

Experience More
4. Fundació Antoni Tàpies
5. Sant Pau Recinte Modernista
6. Casa Terrades
7. Illa de la Discòrdia
8. Museu del Modernisme Català
9. Museu de la Música
10. Fundación Mapfre Casa Garriga Nogués
11. Museu Egipci

Eat
① El Nacional
② Mordisco
③ Moments

Drink
④ Garage Bar Co
⑤ Alma Hotel Garden
⑥ Jekyll & Hyde

Stay
⑦ Hotel Constanza
⑧ Cotton House Hotel

①

SAGRADA FAMÍLIA

📍K3 🏛Carrer de Sardenya Ⓜ Sagrada Família 🚌19, 43, 51 🕐9am-3pm Mon-Thu, 9am-6pm Fri-Sun; timed tickets only, book online 🌐sagradafamilia.org

Europe's most unconventional church, the Temple Expiatori de la Sagrada Família is an emblem of a city. Crammed with symbolism inspired by nature and completely original, it is Gaudí's greatest work and a symbol of Modernisme.

Architect Francisco de Paula del Villar i Lozano (1828–1901) was initially commissioned by the Associació Espiritual de Devots de Sant Josep in 1877 to build a Christian temple in Barcelona. Envisioning a Gothic-style building, he drew up plans for a three-nave church. In 1883, a year after work had begun on a Neo-Gothic church on the site, the task of completing the Sagrada Família was given to the 31-year-old Gaudí (p97), who changed everything, extemporizing as he went along. He designed it, like a medieval cathedral, to be considered like a book in stone, with each element representing a biblical event or aspect of Christian faith. It became his life's work and he lived like a recluse on the site for 14 years. At his death (he is buried in the crypt), only one tower on the Nativity façade had been completed, but work resumed after the Civil War and several more have since been finished according to his original plans. Work continues today, financed by ticket sales and donations.

> **Crammed with symbolism inspired by nature and completely original, it is Gaudí's greatest work and a symbol of Modernisme.**

↑ People attending a Mass in the Sagrada Família's soaring nave

Timeline

1866
△ Josep Maria Bocabella founded the Associació Espiritual de Devots de Sant Josep, with the aim of building a temple.

1887
△ The vicarage is completed. This building becomes Gaudí's work space and is where he spent his last days.

1954
△ Work begins on the Passion façade, 62 years after it began on the Nativity façade.

2017
△ On the 135th anniversary of the laying of the foundation stone, 70 per cent of the basilica was finished.

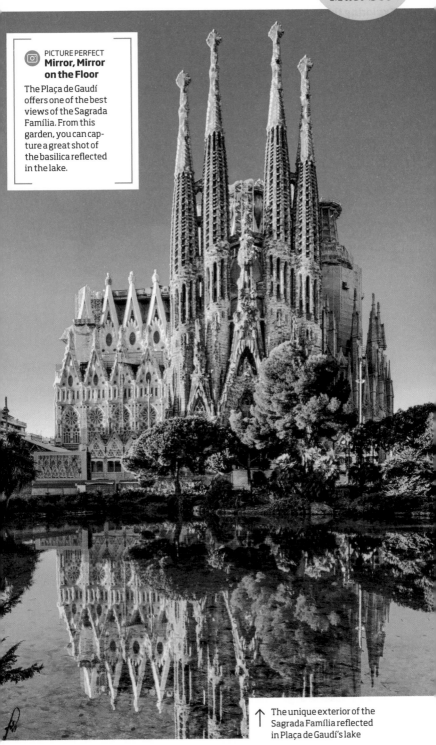

PICTURE PERFECT
Mirror, Mirror on the Floor

The Plaça de Gaudí offers one of the best views of the Sagrada Família. From this garden, you can capture a great shot of the basilica reflected in the lake.

↑ The unique exterior of the Sagrada Família reflected in Plaça de Gaudí's lake

Exploring the Sagrada Família

Gaudí's masterpiece seemingly climbs closer to the heavens as the years progress, its mosaic-covered towers reaching towards the clouds. Of the three decorated façades, the Nativity (p114) and Passion (p115) have been completed, while the Glory is still a work in progress.

The interior of the basilica more than matches the mesmerizing exterior. Soaring pillars form a canopy-like roof and jewel-hued stained glass creates pools of light on the floor of the nave, giving the effect of walking across a magical forest's floor. The experience culminates at the main altar, which is drenched in natural light. It's a profound expression of the architect's devotion, and a challenge to even the firmest of non-believers to remain unmoved.

After touring the nave and climbing one of the towers, explore the museum in the crypt. Charting Gaudí's career and the development of the basilica, it ends at the foot of his tomb.

2030

The date that the basilica is set to be completed.

Spiral staircases

Towers with lift

Eight of the 12 decorated bell towers, one for each apostle, have been built.

The apse was the first part of the church Gaudí completed. Stairs lead down from here to the crypt below.

The altar canopy was designed by Gaudí.

The crypt, where Gaudí is buried, was begun by the original architect, Francesc de Paula Villar i Lozano, in 1882.

GREAT VIEW
Get Low

Lie down on the floor of the nave and look up at the ceiling for a unique view of Gaudí's fantastical creation. Does it look like a vibrant coral reef or the inside of a colourful kaleidoscope?

The Passion façade was crafted from 1986 to 2000. A controversial work, its sculpted figures are angular and often sinister.

① Stained-glass windows bathe the nave in multi-coloured pools of light.

② Spiral staircases lead you to the top of the bell towers, where you'll be rewarded by amazing views of the city.

③ The nave's roof is held up by soaring pillars that branch out at the top to form a canopy.

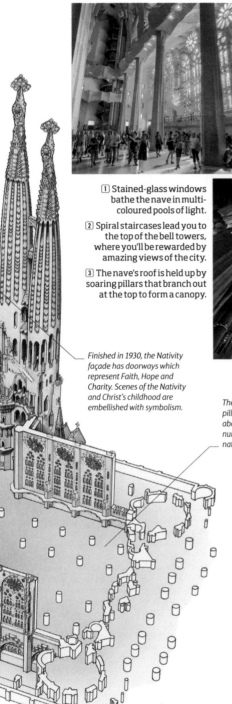

Finished in 1930, the Nativity façade has doorways which represent Faith, Hope and Charity. Scenes of the Nativity and Christ's childhood are embellished with symbolism.

The nave contains a forest of fluted pillars that support four galleries above the side aisles; a large number of skylights let in both natural and artificial light.

←

Illustration depicting the magnificent Sagrada Família, still under construction

THE FINISHED CHURCH

Gaudí's initial ambitions have been fulfilled over the years, using various new technologies to achieve his vision. Still to come is the central tower, which is to be encircled by four large towers representing the Evangelists. Four towers on the Glory (south) façade will match the existing four on the Passion (west) and Nativity (east) façades. An ambulatory - like an inside-out cloister - will skirt the outside of the building.

↑ The soaring bell towers on the honeycomb-like Nativity façade

NATIVITY FAÇADE

Finished according to Gaudí's instructions before his death, the lavish ornamentation on the eastern façade centres around three doors dedicated to Hope (left), Faith (right) and Charity, in the middle.

Hope Doorway

Above this door you'll see Joseph and the child Jesus watched over by Mary's parents, St Ann and St Joachim. The lintel of the door is composed of a woodcutter's two-handled saw and various other tools – all indicative of Joseph's profession.

The spire above the doorway is in the form of an elongated boulder, which is an allusion to the holy Catalan mountain of Montserrat (p154). At the base of this

↑ Stone depiction of the shepherds above the Charity doorway

> ## Did You Know?
>
> The chameleons on this façade represent change, while the turtle signifies stability.

boulder sits Joseph in a boat; he bears a resemblance to Gaudí himself and is very likely a posthumous homage.

Faith Doorway

The heart of Jesus can be seen set into the lintel above this doorway. The scene on the lower left is the Visitation by Mary to Elizabeth, her cousin and mother of John the Baptist. On the right, Jesus wields a hammer and chisel in his father's workshop.

As it rises, the stonework forms an intricate pinnacle recording the fundamentals of Catholicism, including a lamp with three wicks for the Trinity, bunches of grapes and ears of wheat for the Eucharist, and a hand set with an eye, showing God's omniscience.

Charity Doorway

These double doors are separated by a column

recording Jesus's genealogy. The three Magi are on the lower left of the door, with the shepherds opposite them. Out of the Nativity emerges the spiky tail of a many-pointed star, surrounded by a children's choir. Above the star is the Annunciation and the Coronation of the Virgin Mary by Jesus, and on top of that is a pelican sitting on a crown next to a glass egg bearing the JHS monogram of Jesus.

GLORY FAÇADE

The southern façade is set to be the most monumental of the four and, based on Gaudí's plans, will represent the road to God. A large staircase decorated with demons and tombs will lead to the façade, signifying death. The seven pillars supporting the struc-ture will depict the seven sins at the bottom, and the seven virtues at the top, and the seven doors signify the sacraments that open the way to God. Clouds will rise up the bell towers to a glorious image of God.

PASSION FAÇADE

The Passion façade narrates Christ's final days leading up to the Crucifixion. Designed by Josep Maria Subirachs, whose boxy forms are very unlike the organic shapes on the Gaudí-designed Nativity façade, the Passion façade has divided critics since its completion.

Christ's Passion

The Passion façade depicts the sufferings and execution of Jesus, and its style reflects its subject matter. The statuary has attracted criticism for its angular, "dehumanized" carving, but Gaudí would probably have approved. He is known to have favoured an Expressionist style to give the story of Christ's Passion maximum impact. A great porch, whose roof is held up by six inclined buttress-like swamp tree roots, shades the 12 groups of sculptures. The first scene, in the bottom left-hand corner, is the Last Supper at which Jesus (standing) announces his impending betrayal. Next to this is the arrest in the Garden of Gethsemane. The kiss of betrayal by Judas follows. The numbers of the cryptogram to the side of Jesus add up to 33 in every direction: his age at the time of his death.

↑ Bronze door carved with the gospel on the Passion façade

The Flagellation

In the flagellation (between the central doors) Jesus is shown tied to a column at the top of a flight of three steps representing the three days of the Passion. Peter denying Christ is indicated by the cock that will crow three times in fulfilment of Jesus's prophecy. Behind is a labyrinth, a metaphor for Jesus's fate.

The sculptural group on the bottom right shows Christ bound and crowned with thorns. Pilate, overlooked by the Roman eagle, is seen washing his hands, freeing himself of responsibility for Jesus's death. Above, the "Three Marys" weep as Simon the Cyrene is told by the Romans to pick up the cross.

🔍 HIDDEN GEM
School Spirit

To the right of the Passion façade you'll find the Escoles de Gaudí, which the architect designed to be a school. Today, the undulating brick roof shelters a re-creation of Gaudí's office, with displays exploring his craft and aesthetic.

The Holy Shroud

The central sculpture depicts an event not described in the Bible. Veronica holds up her head cloth, which she has offered to Jesus to wipe the blood and sweat from his face. It has been returned, impressed with his likeness.

Next comes a Roman centurion on horseback piercing the side of Jesus with his sword. Above him, three soldiers beneath the cross cast lots for Jesus's tunic. The largest sculpture (top centre) shows Christ hanging from a horizontal cross. At his feet is a skull referring to the place of the Crucifixion, Golgotha. Above him is the veil of the Temple of Jerusalem. The final scene is the burial of Jesus. The figure of Nicodemus, who is anointing the body, is thought to be a self-portrait.

→ Haunting sculptural figures on the Passion façade depicting Peter's betrayal of Jesus

2 🏛️

CASA BATLLÓ

📍G4 🏠 Passeig de Gràcia 43 Ⓜ Passeig de Gràcia 🕐 9am–6:30pm daily (night visits: 6–8pm daily) 🌐 casabatllo.es

With its reworked façade in stunning organic forms and its fantastic chimneys and rooftop, Casa Batlló remains as bold and convention-defying today as it did when it was finished in 1906.

Unlike Gaudí's other works, this block of flats on the prestigious Passeig de Gràcia involved the conversion of an existing structure. Commissioned by Josep Batlló i Casanovas – Gaudí's design has been said to symbolize the legend of St George killing the dragon, whose scaly back arches above the main façade. The spindly columns across the first-floor windows have since been compared to tibias (lower leg bones), earning Casa Batlló the nickname "House of Bones". Inside, highlights include the blue-hued light-well, the skeleton-like attics and the mushroom-shaped fireplace. It was designated a UNESCO World Heritage Site in 2005.

Did You Know?

Salvador Dalí said that the curving walls and windows represent "waves on a stormy day".

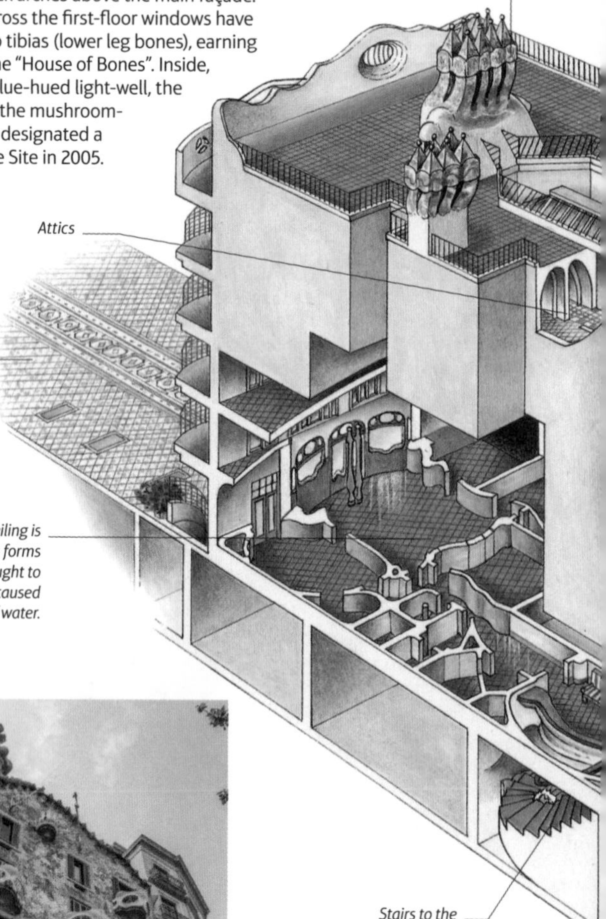

The tightly packed and abstractly patterned chimneys, which have become Gaudí's trademark

Attics

Patio and rear façade, with its cast-iron balconies and superbly colourful trencadís work at the top

The dining room's ceiling is rippled with bulbous forms that are thought to represent the splash caused by a drop of water.

Stairs to the main floor

← The exterior of Casa Batlló, tiled in green and blue

1 The closely packed brick arches of the attics are plastered and painted white, giving the sensation of being inside the skeleton of a large animal.

2 One side of the main drawing room is formed by stained-glass windows looking out over the Passeig de Gràcia.

3 The house is topped by close-packed, spectacularly patterned chimneys.

The light-well, which provides maximum light to interior windows

The Dragon's Back, an incredible narrow, colourfully tiled cap above the façade

Dragon's belly room

The mask-like iron balconies

A damaged ceramic cross, which Gaudí refused to send for repair as he liked the cracked effect

The house is covered in trencadís *decorations (made up of broken tiles).*

← The fantastic layout of Gaudí's 20th-century Casa Batlló

Main drawing room

Fireplace room, which was Josep Batlló's office and has a mushroom-shaped fireplace

117

↑ People walking among the sculptural chimneys on La Pedrera's undulating roof

LA PEDRERA

📍G3 🏠Passeig de Gràcia 92 Ⓜ Diagonal 🕐9am–6:30pm daily (night visits: 9–11pm Thu–Sun) 🚫25 Dec 🌐lapedrera.com

There isn't a single straight line anywhere in La Pedrera, Gaudí's extraordinary apartment building – the façade ripples like water as does the rooftop terrace. With its tiled chimneys and undulating walkways, the rooftop terrace has become one of the city's most popular attractions.

Sometimes called Casa Milà, La Pedrera was Gaudí's last work before he devoted himself entirely to the Sagrada Família (p110). Built between 1906 and 1912 for Pere Milà, a wealthy industrialist, La Pedrera completely departed from the construction principles of the time and, as a result, it was strongly attacked by Barcelona's intellectuals. On its completion, it was greeted with equal parts of horror and amusement, and quickly nicknamed "'La Pedrera", meaning "the quarry", for its wavy façade of undressed stone.

Today, visitors can see a restored apartment, as well as the two circular courtyards, before exploring the Gaudí Exhibition on the top floor. The culmination of the visit is the stunning roof terrace, where jazz concerts are held in the summer among the peculiar air ducts and chimneys.

INSIDER TIP
Light Bulb Moment

Book a night tour to see La Pedrera come to life during a spectacular sound and light show held on the roof. After the show, you can enjoy a glass of cava and a plate of traditional sweets.

1 The intricate ironwork balconies, by Josep Maria Jujol, look like seaweed against La Pedrera's wave-like walls of white undressed stone.

2 In the "Whale Attic", the Gaudí Exhibition displays the architect's drawings and models to explain the aesthetics of his designs.

3 The many sculpted air ducts and chimneys on the roof have been dubbed both the "garden of warriors" and *"espanta-bruixes"* ("witch-scarers").

EXPERIENCE MORE

4

Fundació Antoni Tàpies

📍 G4 🏠 Carrer d'Aragó 255 Ⓜ Passeig de Gràcia 🕐 10am-7pm Thu-Sat (to 3pm Sun) 🚫 1 & 6 Jan, 25 & 26 Dec 🌐 fundacio tapies.org

Antoni Tàpies (1923–2012) was one of Spain's foremost contemporary artists. Inspired by Surrealism, his abstract work was executed in a variety of materials, which included concrete and metal.

A wide variety of his work is housed here in Barcelona's first domestic building built with iron. Lluís Domènech i Montaner's 1880 design is best viewed from across the street, where you can appreciate Tàpies' whimsical tangled wire sculpture *Núvol i Cadira* (Cloud and Chair) on the roof.

Inside, only a few of the artist's paintings, graphics and sculptures can be shown at one time, although the exhibits rotate regularly. In addition to Tàpies own work, the building holds excellent temporary exhibitions, a study centre and library.

5

Sant Pau Recinte Modernista

📍 L2 🏠 Carrer de Sant Antoni Maria Claret 167 Ⓜ Hospital de Sant Pau 🕐 10am-2:30pm Mon-Fri (to 5pm Sat & Sun) 🚫 25 Dec 🌐 santpaubarcelona.org

By the turn of the 20th century, Barcelona's main hospital, the medieval Hospital de la Santa Creu, could no longer meet the demand of the growing city. The banker Pau Gil left an enormous bequest for the creation of a new hospital, stating in his will that it should be dedicated to Sant Pau. In 1901, Lluís Domènech i Montaner designed the new building, which would bear the combined name of the Hospital de la Santa Creu i Sant Pau.

Montaner's concept, which became the largest Modernista construction, consisted of 26 Mudéjar-style pavilions, decorated with ceramic garlands and sculptures. Montaner believed that patients would recover better in beautiful surroundings, so the buildings are sat in extensive gardens. All connecting corridors are hidden underground. The building functioned as a hospital until

Summer Songs

Every Friday in June, the Sant Pau Recinte Modernista hosts concerts in its gardens. You can listen to a range of different musicians in the atmospheric evening light, surrounded by the glowing Modernista buildings.

2009. It is now called Sant Pau Recinte Modernista and offers tours and concerts.

6

Casa Terrades

📍 H3 🏠 Avinguda Diagonal 416 Ⓜ Diagonal 🕐 To the public 🌐 casa delespunxes.com

This six-sided apartment block by Puig i Cadafalch gets its nickname, "Casa de les Punxes" (House of the Spikes), from the spires on its six corner turrets, which are shaped like witches' hats. Built between 1903 and 1905, it is a mixture of medieval and Renaissance styles. The towers and gables are

inspired by Gothic architecture, but the deeply carved stone exterior is typically Modernista.

The building currently serves as a co-working space and is closed to the public.

Illa de la Discòrdia

G4 **Passeig de Gràcia, between Carrer d'Aragó and Carrer del Consell de Cent** **M Passeig de Gràcia**

The most famous group of Modernista buildings in Barcelona amply illustrate the range of styles involved in the movement. The block in which they stand has been dubbed the Illa de la Discòrdia, "Block of Discord", owing to the visual argument between the buildings. The three most famous houses, on Passeig de Gràcia, were remodelled from existing houses early in the 20th century.

No 35 is **Casa Lleó Morera** (1902–6), the first residential work of Lluís Domènech i Montaner. The house is currently closed to the public, but you can still admire the façade.

At No 41 is **Casa Amatller**, designed by Puig i Cadafalch in 1898. Its façade is a harmonious blend of styles, featuring Moorish and Gothic windows. The stepped gable roof is

↑ The exquisite stained-glass gallery on the first floor of Casa Lleó Morera

dotted with tiles. Inside the wrought-iron main doors is a fine stone staircase beneath a stained-glass roof. The Amatller family apartments have been restored to their former glory and are now open to the public. After taking a tour, you can savour a steaming cup of Amatller hot chocolate.

The third, and most impressive, house is Gaudí's Casa Batlló *(p116)*.

Casa Lleó Morera

To the public **casalleomorera.com**

Casa Amatller

By guided tour only **amatller.org**

↑ The Sant Pau Recinte Modernista complex of elaborate buildings

---

EAT

El Nacional
A different speciality is served at each counter here.

G4 **Passeig de Gràcia 24 bis** **elnacionalbcn.com**

€€€

Mordisco
Modern interpretations of classic Catalan cuisine are served in a light-drenched atrium.

G3 **Passatge de la Concepció 10** **mordisco.com**

€€€

Moments
Chef Raül Balam has earned two Michelin stars for his inventive take on Catalan cuisine.

G4 **Passeig de Gràcia 38-40** **Mon & Sun** **mandarinoriental.com**

€€€

↑ Furniture gallery at Museu del Modernisme Català, and *(inset)* Modernista glass

of musical instruments (more than 2,000 of them), gathered from around the world and displayed in red velvet cases.

Museu del Modernisme Català

⑧

🔲F4 🏠Carrer de Balmes 48 Ⓜ️Passeig de Gràcia 🕐Hours vary, check website 📅Aug 🌐mmbcn.cat

In a grand Modernista mansion designed by Enric Sagnier, this museum houses a private collection of Modernista furnishings, paintings, sculptures and decorative arts gathered by local antique dealers over the last half century.

The top floor displays the furniture collection, and has a gallery dedicated to pieces by Gaudí, including a delightful kissing chair.

Elsewhere, there are Modernista posters, many sculptures by Josep Llimona and paintings by Ramon Casas, who was one of the founders of the Els 4 Gats tavern *(p79)*, where Picasso's first exhibition was held. The museum hosts workshops and concerts, as well as family activities.

Museu de la Música

⑨

🔲K5 🏠L'Auditori, Carrer de Lepant 150 Ⓜ️Marina 🕐10am–6pm Tue, Wed & Fri, 10am–9pm Thu, 10am–7pm Sat & Sun 🌐ajuntament. barcelona.cat/museu musica

Barcelona's fascinating Museum of Music is located in the L'Auditori concert hall. It contains a vast collection

TOP 5 GAIXAMPLE EXPERIENCES

Night Barcelona
A buzzing bar that is open nightly *(www. nightbarcelona.net)*.

Plata Bar
This cocktail bar is always packed *(www.platabar.com)*.

Axel Hotel
The world's first hotel chain aimed at LGBTQ+ travellers *(www.axelhotels.com)*.

dDivine
Mediterranean food is accompanied by a drag show at this pink-lit restaurant *(www.ddivine.com)*.

Odd Kiosk
The world's first LGBTQ+ news kiosk has a curated selection of art and fashion magazines, plus a coffee stand *(Corner of C/Valencia and C/Enric Granados)*.

> **The museum's highlight is the collection of classical guitars, with pieces made by Antonio de Torres, considered the world's pre-eminent guitar-maker.**

Displays are complemented by audiovisuals, interactive screens and listening stations. The museum's highlight is the collection of classical guitars, with pieces made by Antonio de Torres, considered the world's pre-eminent guitar-maker. The visit culminates with a chance to try out some of the instruments. There is also a programme of other activities, from concerts to family-friendly workshops.

Museu Egipci

G4 **Carrer de València 284** **93 488 01 88** **Passeig de Gràcia** **11am–2pm & 4–7pm Mon–Fri, 10am–3pm & 4–7pm Sat, 10am–2pm Sun**

This private collection of Ancient Egyptian art is one of the finest anywhere, with more than 1,000 artifacts dating back several millennia.

The exhibition begins with a section devoted to the Egyptian pharaohs, who were worshipped as gods. One of the most popular sections features sarcophagi, which range from the earliest, simply decorated terracotta versions to huge painted caskets. They are displayed with canopic jars, used to hold the intestines of mummified bodies. These jars were often decorated with the symbols of the four sons of Horus, who were believed to protect the contents.

There is also a fine collection of intricate jewellery, pottery, weapons and even a bed. Note that the information available in English is limited, so it is worth downloading the museum's own app (available on the website). The museum offers an extensive calendar of exciting activities, from sleepovers, where kids settle in sleeping bags among the exhibits, to breakfast talks.

DRINK

Garage Bar Co
One of the city's top craft breweries offers around 30 beers on tap.

F4 **Carrer de Consell de Cent 261** **garagebeer.co**

Alma Hotel Garden
Sip on cocktails and listen to birdsong at this inviting garden bar.

G3 **Carrer de Mallorca 269** **almahotels.com**

Jekyll & Hyde
Enjoy a morning coffee or have a cocktail here.

J3 **Carrer de Provença 369** **633 74 00 96**

STAY

Hotel Constanza
This boutique hotel's rooms are painted ochre and blue. There's a rooftop terrace.

H5 **Carrer del Bruc 33** **hotelconstanza.com**

€€€

Cotton House Hotel
A 5-star hotel with white-on-white "cotton rooms" and suites filled with antiques. In summer, cool off in the rooftop plunge pool.

H5 **Gran Via de les Corts Catalanes 670** **hotelcottonhouse.com**

€€€

← Admiring an ancient Egyptian sarcophagus at the Museu Egipci

A SHORT WALK
QUADRAT D'OR

Distance 1.5 km (1 mile) **Nearest metro**
Passeig de Gràcia, Diagonal **Time** 20 minutes

The hundred or so city blocks centring on the Passeig de Gràcia are known as the Quadrat d'Or, or "Golden Square", because they contain so many of Barcelona's best Modernista buildings *(p78)*. This was the area within the Eixample favoured by the wealthy bourgeoisie, who embraced the new artistic and architectural style with enthusiasm. Take a stroll through the area to discover beautiful private residences, as well as ornamented commercial buildings. Most remarkable is the Illa de la Discòrdia, a single block containing houses by Modernisme's most illustrious exponents. Many interiors can be visited, revealing a feast of stained glass, ceramics and ironwork.

Diagonal metro

CARRER DE PROVENÇA

The Eixample's main avenue, **Passeig de Gràcia** *is a showcase of highly original buildings and smart shops.*

CARRER DE MALLORCA

PASSEIG DE GRACIA

Topped by Tàpies' sculpture Cloud and Chair, *the* **Fundació Antoni Tàpies** (p120) *was designed by Domènech i Montaner in 1879.*

CARRER DE VALÈNCIA

↑ Looking through a stained-glass door at Casa Lleó Morera

Casa Amatller

In the **Illa de la Discòrdia,** *three of Barcelona's most famous Modernista houses vie for attention (p121). All were created between 1900 and 1910.*

Ⓜ

Museu del Perfum

Casa Ramon Mulleras

0 metres   100   N
0 yards   100

Casa Lleó Morera

Ⓢ **START**

Gaudí's **Casa Batlló** (p116)

Passeig de Gràcia metro

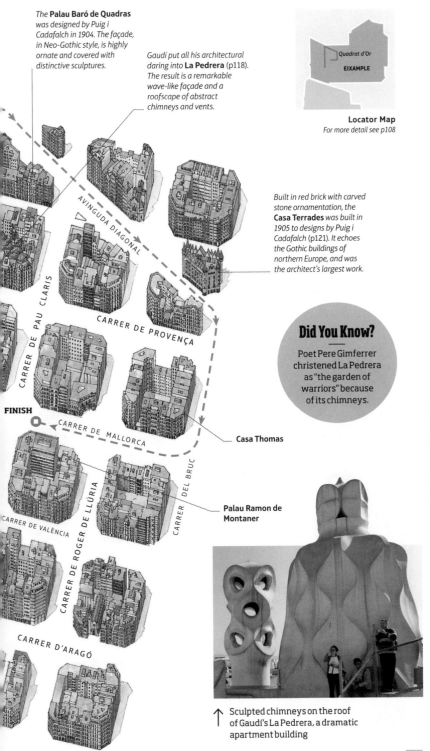

The **Palau Baró de Quadras** was designed by Puig i Cadafalch in 1904. The façade, in Neo-Gothic style, is highly ornate and covered with distinctive sculptures.

Gaudí put all his architectural daring into **La Pedrera** (p118). The result is a remarkable wave-like façade and a roofscape of abstract chimneys and vents.

Locator Map
For more detail see p108

Built in red brick with carved stone ornamentation, the **Casa Terrades** was built in 1905 to designs by Puig i Cadafalch (p121). It echoes the Gothic buildings of northern Europe, and was the architect's largest work.

AVINGUDA DIAGONAL

CARRER DE PAU CLARIS

CARRER DE PROVENÇA

FINISH

CARRER DE MALLORCA

Casa Thomas

Did You Know?

Poet Pere Gimferrer christened La Pedrera as "the garden of warriors" because of its chimneys.

CARRER DEL BRUC

CARRER DE VALÈNCIA

CARRER DE ROGER DE LLÚRIA

Palau Ramon de Montaner

CARRER D'ARAGÓ

↑ Sculpted chimneys on the roof of Gaudí's La Pedrera, a dramatic apartment building

MONTJUÏC

There was probably a Celtiberian settlement on this 213-m- (699-ft-) high hill before the Romans built a temple to Jupiter here, on what they called Mons Jovis (the Hill of Jove), which may have given Montjuïc its name. But another theory suggests that the hill was once home to a Jewish cemetery and that the name Montjuïc developed from it being called "the Mount of the Jews".

Naturally wooded, the slopes of Montjuïc were for years used to grow food and graze cattle to feed the Old Town. The absence of a water supply meant that there were few buildings on Montjuïc until a castle was erected on its summit in 1640. This garrison famously shelled parts of Barcelona in 1842 to end an insurgency against Isabella II. The hill finally came into its own as the site of the 1929 International Exhibition. With great energy and flair, buildings were erected all over the north side, with the grand Avinguda de la Reina María Cristina, lined with huge exhibition halls, leading onto the base of the hill from the Plaça d'Espanya. One of these buildings was a stadium intended to host an alternative 1936 Olympics, in opposition to the Nazi-hosted competition in Berlin, but the event was cancelled on the outbreak of the Spanish Civil War. It seems fitting, then, that the last great surge of building on Montjuïc was for the 1992 Olympic Games, which left Barcelona with world-class sports facilities.

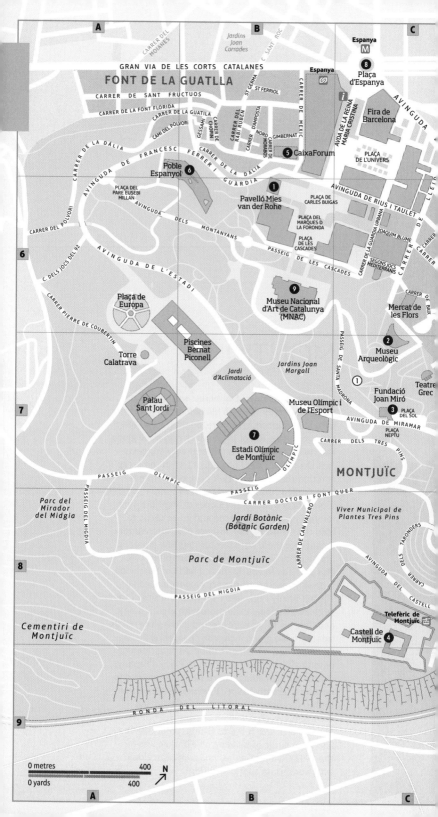

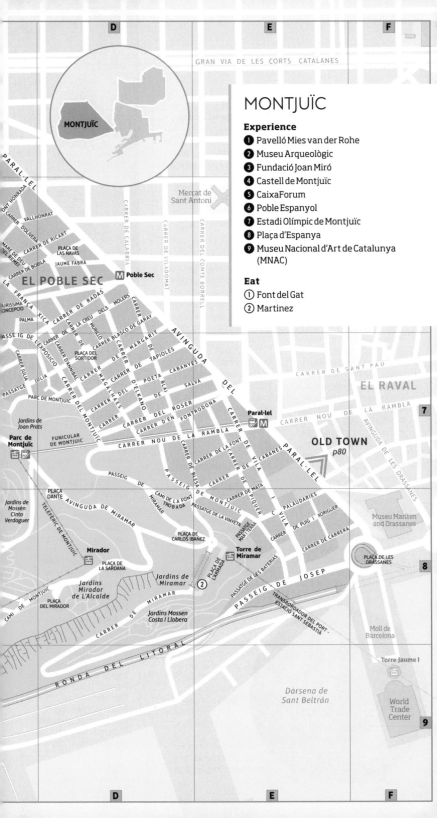

MONTJUÏC

Experience

1. Pavelló Mies van der Rohe
2. Museu Arqueològic
3. Fundació Joan Miró
4. Castell de Montjuïc
5. CaixaForum
6. Poble Espanyol
7. Estadi Olímpic de Montjuïc
8. Plaça d'Espanya
9. Museu Nacional d'Art de Catalunya (MNAC)

Eat

1. Font del Gat
2. Martinez

EXPERIENCE

1

Pavelló Mies van der Rohe

📍 B6 📍 Avinguda de Francesc Ferrer i Guàrdia 7 Ⓜ Espanya 🚋 13, 150 🕐 10am–8pm daily (Nov–Feb: to 6pm) 🚫 1 Jan, 25 Dec 🌐 miesbcn.com

Designed by Ludwig Mies van der Rohe (1886–1969), director of the avant-garde Bauhaus school, and his close collaborator Lilly Reich (1885–1947) for the International Exhibition of 1929, the German Pavilion's modern and simple lines must have shocked its first visitors. The pavilion is characterized by fluid, glassy spaces, in which the boundaries between inside and outside were blurred, and made use of materials like marble and onyx. This was enhanced by highly polished façades and extensive use of tinted glass. Two pools are set into the pavilion's surroundings, one of which is overlooked by a bronze statue entitled *Alba* (Dawn) by Georg Kolbe.

Unlike other pavilions at the exhibition, it was conceived as a place of rest and tranquillity for visitors rather than as a gallery. Nothing was displayed within its walls except the *Barcelona Chair*, now an icon of Modernisme, which has a

PICTURE PERFECT
Dawn Chorus

The best place to get the perfect shot of *Alba* is to stand at the opposite end of the pool, where you can get a picture of the statue reflected not just in the water, but also in the glass façade of the pavilion.

stainless-steel frame and a leather seat. The original was made of ivory-coloured pigskin, and was designed specifically for the Spanish royal family to rest in after they had explored the exhibition's pavilions.

The pavilion was intended to be a temporary structure, and was dismantled after the exhibition, but then painstakingly rebuilt in the 1980s using the same materials.

2

Museu Arqueològic

📍 C7 📍 Passeig de Santa Madrona 39–41 Ⓜ Espanya, Poble Sec 🕐 9:30am–7pm Tue–Sat, 10am–2:30pm Sun & public hols 🚫 1 Jan, 25 & 26 Dec 🌐 macbarcelona.cat

Housed in the Renaissance-inspired 1929 Palace of Graphic Arts, this museum shows artifacts from prehistory to the Visigothic period (AD 415–711). Highlights are finds from the Greco-Roman town of Empúries (*p167*), Iberian silver treasure and Visigothic jewellery.

← Silver libation bowl with wolf detail, at the Museu Arqueològic

TOP 5 **FUNDACIÓ JOAN MIRÓ WORKS**

Chapel of Sant Joan d'Horta (1917)
An early landscape, which is painted in vivid Fauvist colours.

Painting (The White Glove) (1925)
A poetic, abstract work that demonstrates the influence that the Surrealists had on him.

Morning Star (1940)
Part of the celebrated *Constellations* series.

Poem (III) (1968)
Miró claimed that he tried to "paint colours like words that shape poems".

Tapestry of the Foundation (1979)
This tapestry, which features a dancing woman under the moon and stars, was created especially for this space.

↑ Beautiful manicured gardens enclosed by the Castell de Montjuïc

 3 ⊘

Fundació Joan Miró

📍C7 ⊠Parc de Montjuïc
Ⓜ Espanya, then bus 150, 55
or Paral·lel, then Montjuïc
funicular 🕐Apr–Oct: 10am–
8pm Tue–Sat (to 6pm Sun);
Nov–Mar 10am–6pm Tue–
Sat (to 3pm Sun) 🚫1 Jan, 25
& 26 Dec 🌐 fmirobcn.org

In 1975, after the return of democracy to Spain, Joan Miró asked the architect Josep Lluís Sert to design this stunning white building to house a collection of his paintings, sculptures and tapestries.

This is the largest and most comprehensive collection of Miró's work anywhere, donated by the artist himself, and all beautifully displayed in light and airy galleries designed to maximize the natural light.

The works are arranged in roughly chronological order, which gives visitors the chance to see how Miró's style developed over the decades. There are some charming early cityscapes in glowing colours that were inspired by Fauvism, followed by more abstract works from the 1920s, when

Miró was living in Paris and was influenced by André Breton's Surrealist movement. *Morning Star* (1940), part of Miró's poetic *Constellations* series, was painted partly as a response to the Spanish Civil War. The *Constellations* were an escape: at the same time, he was working on the dark and disturbing *Barcelona Series* (1939–44), a set of 50 black-and-white lithographs.

The museum also hosts excellent temporary exhibitions and there is a charming sculpture garden, with some beautiful works such as the *Solarbird* (1968).

 4 ⊘

Castell de Montjuïc

📍C8 ⊠Parc de Montjuïc
Ⓜ Paral·lel, then funicular
& cable car 🚌150 from
Plaça d'Espanya 🕐10am–
8pm daily (Nov–Feb: to 6pm)
🌐 ajuntament.barcelona.
cat/castelldemontjuic

The summit of Montjuïc is occupied by an 18th-century fortress built by the Bourbon family. After the Civil War it became a prison, where the Catalan leader Lluís Companys was executed in 1940. It is now a peace museum.

JOAN MIRÓ

Joan Miró (1893–1983) studied at the fine art school at La Llotja. From 1919, he spent much of his time in Paris. Though opposed to Franco, he returned to Spain in 1940 and lived in Mallorca, where he died. An admirer of primitive Catalan art and Gaudí's Modernisme, Miró remained a Catalan painter but developed a Surrealist style, with vivid colours and fantastical forms suggesting dream-like situations.

↑ Charming houses – some occupied by artisans – at Poble Espanyol

5
CaixaForum

📍B5 🏛Avinguda de Francesc Ferrer i Guàrdia 6-8 Ⓜ️Espanya 🚌13, 50 🕐10am-8pm daily; 24 & 31 Dec, 5 Jan: 10am-6pm 🚫1 & 6 Jan, 25 Dec 🌐caixaforum.org/es/barcelona

This handsome Modernista textile mill, designed by Puig i Cadafalch in 1911, now houses a glossy cultural centre run by the Caixa savings bank.

The Barcelona outpost of the CaixaForum offers a dynamic programme of activities, including screenings, performances and workshops for all ages. It is also the main venue for major visiting art exhibitions and hosts some of the best temporary art shows in Barcelona.

Additionally, the centre houses a collection of contemporary art, and displays a rotating selection of its more than 800 pieces, by artists such as Donald Judd and Gerhard Richter. In the vestibule, you can admire Lucio Fontana's neon cloud, and a mural by Sol LeWitt created specifically for this venue.

6
Poble Espanyol

📍B5 🏛Avinguda de Francesc Ferrer i Guàrdia 13 Ⓜ️Espanya 🚌13, 23, 150 🕐9am-midnight Tue-Thu & Sun (to 8pm Mon) 🌐poble-espanyol.com

The popular Poble Espanyol (Spanish Village) was built for the 1929 International Exhibition to display Spanish architectural styles and crafts. Building styles from all over Spain are illustrated by 116 houses arranged on streets radiating from a main square.

Resident artisans produce crafts including hand-blown glass, ceramics, Toledo damascene and Catalan canvas sandals. There are many bars, restaurants, nightclubs and a flamenco *tablao* to explore here.

7
Estadi Olímpic de Montjuïc

📍B7 🏛Passeig Olímpic 17-19 Ⓜ️Espanya, Poble Sec 🚌13, 35 & 150 🕐Museum: 10am-6pm Tue-Sat, 10am-2:30pm Sun 🌐estadiolimpic.cat; museuolimpicbcn.cat

This Neo-Classical stadium was built by Pere Domènech i Roura in 1927 for the 1929 International Exhibition, as part of Barcelona's bid to host an alternative to the 1936 Berlin Olympics. Its façade has been preserved, but the interior was refitted for the 1992 Olympics and now hosts concerts and sporting competitions. See the website for the programme of events.

Nearby are the Palau Sant Jordi indoor stadium, by Arata Isozaki, swimming pools by Ricardo Bofill and the Museu Olímpic i de l'Esport. The museum's interactive exhibits feature sports idols and sports from different civilizations.

The grand Museu Nacional d'Art de Catalunya (MNAC) and *(inset)* its ornate dome paintings

⑧ Plaça d'Espanya

📍C5 🅐Avinguda de la Gran Via de les Corts Catalanes Ⓜ️Espanya

This square centres around a fountain built by Josep Maria Jujol. On one side of the square is the Avinguda de la Reina Maria Cristina, flanked by two brick campaniles. This avenue leads up to Carles Buigas's *Font Màgica* (Magic Fountain). In the evening, from Wednesday to Sunday (October to May: Thursday to Saturday), its jets are programmed to a multicoloured music and light show.

---

⑨
Museu Nacional d'Art de Catalunya (MNAC)

📍B6 🅐Parc de Montjuïc, Palau Nacional Ⓜ️Espanya 🚌55, 150 🕐10am–8pm Tue–Sat (Oct–Apr: to 6pm), 10am–3pm Sun & public hols 🚫1 Jan, 1 May, 25 Dec 🌐museunacional.cat

The handsome Palau Nacional was built for the 1929 International Exhibition, but in 1934 it was used to house an art collection that has since become the most important in the city. The resulting museum offers a rare opportunity to view more than a millennium worth of Catalan art in one location.

The museum has a superb collection of Romanesque items, centred around a series of magnificent 12th-century frescoes taken from Catalan Pyrenean churches. These are beautifully displayed in purpose-built galleries that evoke the tiny mountain churches from which they originally came. The most remarkable is the mural group from Sant Climent in the Vall de Boí *(p161)*, which includes an impressive depiction of Christ in Majesty (Pantocrator).

The expansive Gothic collection covers the whole of Spain but particularly Catalonia, and includes artworks by outstanding Catalan artists such as Jaume Huguet and Bernat Martorell. The museum has also been enriched by a substantial endowment of notable Baroque and Renaissance works from the

GREAT VIEW
Roof with a View

Don't miss the amazing bird's-eye views of the city from the Museu Nacional d'Art de Catalunya's rooftop terraces. Look out for the Sagrada Família. Access is included in the museum admission.

Thyssen-Bornemisza collection, which includes paintings by Tiepolo and Fra Angelico among others.

A fine collection of modern art includes Modernista furniture by Gaudí *(p97)*, and paintings by Picasso, Ramon Casas and Salvador Dalí.

A SHORT WALK
MONTJUÏC

Distance 3 km (2 miles) **Nearest metro**
Espanya **Time** 45 minutes

Sat high on a hill, Montjuïc is a spectacular vantage point from which to view the city. On a walk through the area, you'll find a wealth of art galleries and museums, an amusement park and an open-air theatre. The most interesting buildings lie around the Palau Nacional, where Europe's greatest Romanesque art collection is housed. Montjuïc is approached from the Plaça d'Espanya between brick pillars based on the campanile of St Mark's in Venice, which give a foretaste of the eclecticism of building styles. The Poble Espanyol illustrates the traditional architecture of Spain's regions, while the Fundació Joan Miró is boldly modern.

*A steel, glass, stone and onyx pavilion, the **Pavelló Mies van der Rohe** was built in the Bauhaus style as the German contribution to the 1929 International Exhibition (p130).*

*Containing replicas of buildings from many regions, the **Poble Espanyol** provides a fascinating glimpse of vernacular styles (p132).*

START

AVINGUDA DE FRANCESC FERRER I GUARDIA

AVINGUDA DELS MONTANYANS

FINISH

PASSE

AVINGUDA DE L'ESTADI

0 metres 100
0 yards 100

N

*Displayed in the Palau Nacional, the **Museu Nacional d'Art de Catalunya (MNAC)** includes Europe's finest collection of early medieval frescoes (p133).*

↑ Walking under an arch on a street in the Poble Espanyol

↑ People watching the dramatic Font Màgica, in front of the MNAC

Locator Map
For more detail see p128

Fountains and cascades descend in terraces from the Palau Nacional. Below them is the **Font Màgica** *(p133). This marvel of engineering was built for the 1929 International Exhibition.*

Did You Know?

The Ibero-American Exposition was held in Seville at the same time as Barcelona's Exhibition.

Mercat de les Flors Theatre

The **Museu Arqueològic** *displays important finds from prehistoric cultures in Catalonia and the Balearic Islands (p130).*

Teatre Grec *is an open-air theatre set among gardens.*

Miró created the **Fundació Joan Miró** *as a centre for the study of modern art (p131). In addition to Miró's works in various media, the modern building by Josep Lluís Sert is of architectural interest.*

The Montjuïc branch of the **Museu Etnològic i de Cultures del Món** *displays artifacts from Oceania, Africa, Asia and Latin America.*

BEYOND THE CENTRE

Must Sees

1. Camp Nou
2. Park Güell

Experience More

3. CosmoCaixa - Museu de la Ciència
4. Parc de Joan Miró
5. Monestir de Santa Maria de Pedralbes
6. Museu de Ciències Naturals de Barcelona
7. Tibidabo
8. Torre de Collserola

A period of radical redevelopment of Barcelona's outskirts in the late 1980s and early 1990s gave it a wealth of new buildings, parks and squares, and restored a treasure trove of Modernista architecture. The city's main station, Sants, was rebuilt and the neighbouring Parc de l'Espanya Industrial and Parc de Joan Miró were created, containing lakes, modern sculpture and futuristic architecture. In the west of the city, where the streets start to climb steeply, the historic royal palace and monastery of Pedralbes and Gaudí's famous Park Güell were restored, and the Torre de Collserola, built for the 1992 Olympics, gave *Barcelonins* the chance to see it all from above.

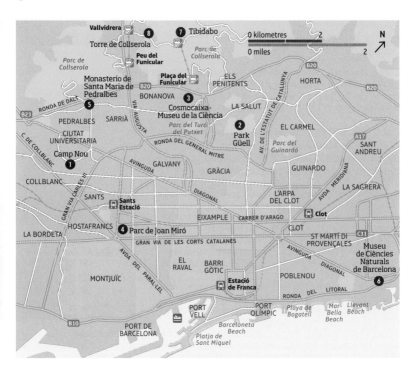

99,354
The seating capacity of the stadium.

① 🛡️ 🅼 🍽️ 📺 🛍️

CAMP NOU

🏠 Avenida de Aristides Maillol 🅼 Maria Cristina, Collblanc 🕐 Mid-Apr-mid-Oct, Christmas & Easter hols: 9:30am-7:30pm daily; mid-Oct-mid-Apr: 10am-6:30pm Mon-Sat, 10am-2:30pm Sun; reduced hours on public hols & match days 🗓️ 1 Jan, 25 Dec 🌐 fcbarcelona.cat

Camp Nou, Europe's largest football stadium, is home to the city's famous football club, FC Barcelona (known locally as Barça). Founded in 1899, it is one of the world's richest soccer clubs, and has more than 140,000 members.

Blau-grana (blue-burgundy), the colours of Barça's strip, hold an important place in the city's heart. The club's flags were used as an expression of local nationalist feelings during the Franco dictatorship, when the Catalan flag was banned.

The stadium is a magnificent, sweeping structure, built in 1957 to a design by Francesc Mitjans and Josep Soteras. An extension was added in 1982 and it can now comfortably seat nearly 100,000 fans.

The Barça Stadium Experience includes a visit to the club's popular museum, where FC Barcelona's many trophies are displayed. This is a glossy interactive experience, with touch-screen panels detailing the club's history and their many victories. After exploring the museum, visitors are taken on a tour of the stadium – from the changing rooms to the impossibly green pitch, the site of so many hotly contested matches.

↑ The László Kubala memorial in front of the stadium

BARCELONA VS REAL MADRID

"Més que un club" is the motto of FC Barcelona: "More than a club". The football team has long been a symbol of the struggle of Catalan nationalism against the central government in Madrid. To fail to win La Liga Santander is one thing. To come in behind Real Madrid is a disaster. Each season the big question is which of the two teams will win the title. In a memorable episode in 1941, Barça won 3-0 at home. At the return match in Madrid, the crowd was so hostile that the police and referee "advised" Barça to prevent trouble. Demoralized by the intimidation, they lost 11-1.

↑ An aerial view of Camp Nou packed with fans on a match day

← Walking down the colourful tunnel that takes players to the pitch

→ Admiring trophies in the Barça museum at Camp Nou

2 (icons)

PARK GÜELL

Carrer d'Olot 7, Vallcarca **Lesseps, Vallcarca** **24, 32, 92, H6** **Park Güell: 9:30am–7:30pm daily (timed tickets only); Casa-Museu Gaudí: Apr–Sep: 9am–8pm daily; Oct–Mar: 10am–6pm daily** **Casa-Museu Gaudí: 1 Jan** **Park Güell: parkguell.cat; Casa-Museu Gaudí: sagradafamilia.org/casa-museu-gaudi**

A UNESCO World Heritage Site, the Park Güell is Antoni Gaudí's most colourful creation. Conceived as a garden city, but never completed, it is now a stunning park that spills down Carmel Hill. Several of Gaudí's creations survive, including a pair of fairy-tale pavilions, a tiled salamander and the world's longest bench.

Gaudí was commissioned in the 1890s by Count Eusebi Güell to design a garden city on 20 hectares (50 acres) of his family estate, but the planned public buildings and 60 houses didn't come to fruition. What we see today was completed between 1910 and 1914, and the park opened in 1922. The "Monumental Area", home to most of Gaudí's surviving creations, requires a ticket, but the green expanses around the edge of this area are free to explore.

Two pavilions at the entrance are by Gaudí, but the Casa-Museu Gaudí, a gingerbread-style house where Gaudí lived from 1906 to 1926, was built by Francesc Berenguer.

Inside the Monumental Area is the Room of a Hundred Columns, a cavernous hall of 84 crooked pillars, which was intended as the marketplace. Above it is the Gran Plaça Circular, an open space with a snaking balcony of coloured mosaics that offers stunning views of the city.

> **PICTURE PERFECT**
> **Double Threat**
>
> The Park Güell gives you two options for that ultimate Barcelona photograph: the mosaic-covered salamander that has become the park's emblem and the views from the Gran Plaça Circular.

1

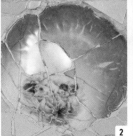

① Gaudí designed one of the entrance pavilions to be the Casa del Guarda (Caretaker's House). It now houses a museum; the other is a shop.

② The Casa-Museu Gaudí has a beautiful garden with architectural features, such as these mosaics.

③ At the top of the stairs to the Gran Plaça Circular is Gaudí's salamander.

2

3

↑ The Gran Plaça Circular, sitting on top of the Room of a Hundred Columns

↑ People observing the Flooded Forest at CosmoCaixa

EXPERIENCE MORE

3

CosmoCaixa - Museu de la Ciència

🏠 Carrer Isaac Newton 26 📞 93 212 60 50 🚇 Avinguda del Tibidabo 🚌 17, 22, 58, 196 🕐 10am–8pm daily (to 6pm 24 & 31 Dec, 5 Jan) 🚫 1 & 6 Jan, 25 Dec

This excellent science museum is located in a Modernista building, designed by Josep Domènech i Estapà in 1909, and offers a huge range of engaging, family-friendly interactive activities. The highlight of the museum is the Flooded Forest, which gives an insight into the Amazonian rainforest, both above and below the waterline, via a walkway that descends five storeys.

Areas designed for young children include "Toca, Toca", where kids are introduced to insects and reptiles from across the Mediterranean; and "Clik", offering a range of technology-led activities that teach kids about science. These activities, along with showings at the planetarium, must be booked in advance. The museum also runs a programme of exhibitions.

4

Parc de Joan Miró

🏠 Carrer d'Aragó 1 🚇 Tarragona

Barcelona's 19th-century slaughterhouse (escorxador) was transformed in the 1980s into this unusual park, hence its alternative name, Parc de l'Escorxador. It has two levels. The lower level is popular with youngsters because of its open areas, fringed with shady paths, while the upper level is paved and dominated by a 1983 sculpture by Joan Miró (p131) entitled Dona i Ocell (Woman and Bird). Standing in the middle of a pool, its surface is coated with glazed tiles.

🔍 HIDDEN GEM
Urban Jungle

A couple of blocks from the Parc de Joan Miró, the Parc de l'Espanya Industrial provides an interesting contrast to its grassy neighbour. Youngsters will love Andrés Nagel's sculpture of a huge metal dragon, which serves as a slide.

5

Monestir de Santa Maria de Pedralbes

🏠 Baixada del Monestir 9 🚇 Reina Elisenda or bus 22, 63, 75, 78 🕐 Apr-Sep: 10am–2pm Tue-Fri, 10am–7pm Sat, 10am–8pm Sun; Oct-Mar: 10am–2pm Tue-Fri, 10am–5pm Sat & Sun by appt 🚫 1 Jan, Good Friday, 1 May, 24 Jun, 25 Dec 🌐 monestir pedralbes.barcelona

Approached through an arch, the monastery of Pedralbes still feels like an enclosed community, even though the nuns of the Order of St Clare moved to an adjoining building in 1983. The monastery was founded in 1326 by Elisenda de Montcada de Piños, fourth wife of Jaime II of Catalonia and Aragón. Her tomb lies between the church and the cloister. On the church side, her effigy is dressed in royal robes; on the other, as a nun.

The monastery encircles the cloister, with a dormitory, refectory, chapterhouse, abbey and day cells. The most important room is the Capella de Sant Miquel, with murals of the Passion and the Life of the Virgin by Ferrer Bassa (1346).

Museu de Ciències Naturals de Barcelona

📍 Plaça Leonardo da Vinci 4-5, Parc del Fòrum Ⓜ El Maresme Fòrum 🚌 H16 🕐 Mar-Sep: 10am-7pm Tue-Sat, 10am-8pm Sun; Oct-Feb: 10am-6pm Tue-Fri, 10am-7pm Sat, 10am-8pm Sun 🕐 1 Jan, 1 May, 24 Jun, 25 Dec 🌐 museuciencies.cat

The city's science museum has a collection that is more than 100 years old. Exhibited across two floors are 3 million specimens in zoology, mineralogy, palaeontology and botany.

The museum is housed in the Parc del Fòrum in a modern, innovative building designed by architects Herzog & de Meuron. The permanent Planet Life exhibition is a fascinating journey through the history of life on earth. The Biography of the Earth section illustrates the evolution of life, while Earth Today details the variety of life forms sharing the planet. Independent "Islands of Science" are spaced throughout Planet Life, focusing on topics such as genetics.

---

❼ Tibidabo

📍 Plaça del Tibidabo 3-4 🚋 Avda Tibidabo, then bus 196 & funicular or Peu del Funicular, then bus 111 🚌 111, T2A from Plaça de Catalunya 🕐 Parc d'Atraccions: check website 🌐 tibidabo.cat

The heights of Tibidabo are reached by a funicular railway. Its name, inspired by views of the city from the mountain, comes from the Latin *tibi dabo* (I shall give you) – a reference to

→

Looking through a telescope on the viewing deck of the Torre de Collserola

the Temptation of Christ when Satan took him up a mountain and offered him the world spread at his feet.

The hugely popular Parc d'Atraccions first opened in 1908. While the old rides retain their charm, more modern additions include the thrilling Dragon Khan roller coaster. The hilltop location at 517 m (1,696 ft) adds to the thrill.

Tibidabo is crowned by the Temple Expiatori del Sagrat Cor (Church of the Sacred Heart), built by Enric Sagnier between 1902 and 1911. A lift takes you up to the feet of an enormous figure of Christ.

---

❽ Torre de Collserola

📍 Carretera de Vallvidrera al Tibidabo 🚋 Peu del Funicular, then Funicular de Vallvidrera & bus 111 🕐 Hours vary, check website 🌐 torrede collserola.com

The city's ultimate ride is at the Torre de Collserola. A glass-sided lift swiftly reaches the top of this 288-m- (944-ft-) tall communications tower standing on the summit of a 445-m (1,460-ft) hill. The tower was designed by English architect Norman Foster for the 1992 Olympic Games. Needle-like in form, it is a

TOP 5 **BARCELONA BEACHES**

Sant Miquel
Overlooked by Rebecca Horn's sculpture, this is a popular and easy-to-access beach.

Barceloneta
Next to Sant Miquel, this beach is home to "Espai de Mar", which offers a whole host of activities (p102).

Bogatell
One of the longest and busiest stretches of sand, particularly popular with families.

Mar Bella
Barcelona's unofficial gay beach, it has *xiringuitos* (beach bars) with DJs and cocktails.

Llevant
Uncrowded Llevant is a favourite with locals and offers lots of watersport options.

tubular steel mast on a concrete pillar. There are 13 levels. The top level has an observatory with a powerful telescope, and a public viewing platform with a 360-degree view of Barcelona, the sea and the mountains.

EASTERN SPAIN

Boats moored in a cove near Blanes on the Costa Brava

EXPLORE EASTERN SPAIN

This section divides Eastern Spain into three colour-coded sightseeing areas, as shown on this map. Find out more about each area on the following pages.

ARAGÓN
p174

VALENCIA AND MURCIA
p192

GETTING TO KNOW
EASTERN SPAIN

With the cold snowy peaks of the Pyrenees, the warm, turquoise waters of the Mediterrean coast and hills of terraced olive trees, Eastern Spain is a medley of magnificent natural beauty. This, coupled with its wealth of historical towns and buildings, keeps visitors enchanted.

CATALONIA

PAGE 150

Sitting at Spain's northeastern extremity, Catalonia includes a long stretch of the Pyrenees, as well as a substantial Mediterranean coastline. Skiers descend upon the snow-covered slopes of Baqueira-Beret, while sun-worshippers flock to the rugged Costa Brava. For history buffs, the region's captivating story is written on its architecture, from Tarragona's Roman monuments to Gaudí's Catalan Modernisme. Naturalists will be itching to discover the wetland wildlife of the Delta de l'Ebre and track down the rare butterflies that brighten the remote valleys of the Pyrenees.

Best for
Unspoiled coastline and medieval towns

Home to
Monestir de Montserrat, Monestir de Poblet, Girona

Experience
The echoing harmonies of the Monestir de Montserrat's choir

ARAGÓN

Stretching from the Pyrenees almost halfway down the length of Spain, Aragón is prime hiking territory, home to the expansive Parque Nacional de Ordesa. But it's not just the natural scenery that's impressive here. The urban landscape is home to a host of attractions, with Roman ruins in Zaragoza and many unspoiled medieval towns. Aragón is particularly famous for its magnificent Mudéjar architecture, left behind by the Moors that stayed in the region after the *reconquista*. These impressive structures, with elaborate brickwork and patterned ceramic decoration, are yours to explore.

Best for
Roman ruins and Mudéjar architecture

Home to
Parque Nacional de Ordesa, Zaragoza

Experience
Watching bearded vultures in the Parque Nacional de Ordesa

VALENCIA AND MURCIA

The two *autonomías* of Valencia and Murcia sweep down a large chunk of Spain's eastern coastline. Here, historic towns and cities have been joined together by modern package holiday resorts, such as Benidorm. Despite these developments, Valencia, in particular, has kept its cool, with funky street art adorning the old quarter and futuristic buildings popping up on the waterfront. Inland, the scenery ranges from picturesque valleys and verdant hills in the north to the semi-desert terrain around Lorca in southern Murcia.

Best for
Cool coastal cities

Home to
Valencia

Experience
Taking part in the riotous Tomatina or Las Fallas festivals

CATALONIA

It was at Empúries, on Catalonia's Costa Brava ("wild coast"), that the Romans first set foot on the land that they would name Hispania. But the Phoenicians and Greeks were here first. After the fall of the Roman empire and a period of Visigothic then Moorish rule, it was conquered by the Franks in the early 9th century. It later enjoyed independence as the County of Barcelona before being incorporated into the Crown of Aragón as the autonomous Principality of Catalonia. This regional autonomy survived the union of Castile and Aragón in 1492, persisting until 1714, when Felipe V centralized the Spanish government in Castile.

In the second half of the 19th century, the independence movement re-emerged, but any progress towards the re-establishment of Catalan autonomy came to a brutal stop when Franco came to power in the 1930s.

Following Franco's death, full autonomy was restored to Catalonia and its Generalitat in 1979. Since then, the independence movement has gathered significant momentum, reaching a head in 2017 when a referendum (declared illegal by the Spanish government) saw Catalans vote to become an independent republic. Political leaders were sent to prison or went into exile, but the Socialist government which took power in 2018 has displayed a more conciliatory approach than its predecessors.

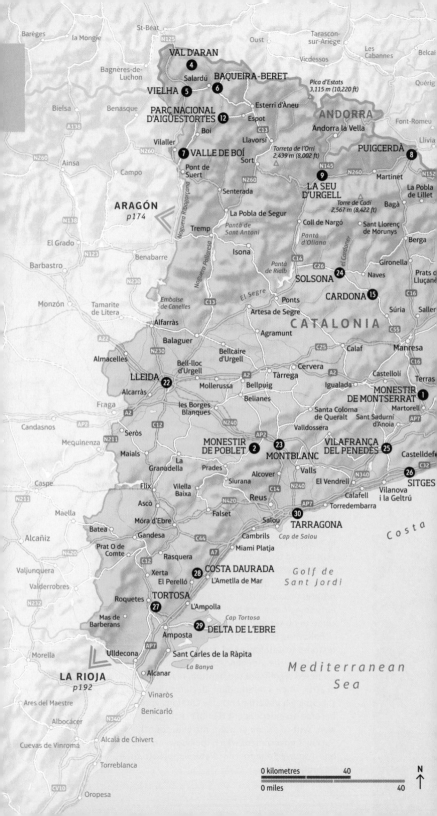

CATALONIA

Must Sees

1 Monestir de Montserrat
2 Monestir de Poblet
3 Girona

Experience More

4 Vall d'Aran
5 Vielha
6 Baqueira-Beret
7 Valle de Boí
8 Puigcerdà
9 La Seu d'Urgell
10 Sant Joan de les Abadesses
11 Ripoll
12 Parc Nacional d'Aigüestortes
13 Olot
14 Figueres
15 Cardona
16 Besalú
17 Tossa de Mar
18 Cadaqués
19 Peratallada
20 Empúries
21 Vic
22 Lleida
23 Montblanc
24 Solsona
25 Vilafranca del Penedès
26 Sitges
27 Tortosa
28 Costa Daurada
29 Delta de L'Ebre
30 Tarragona

MONESTIR DE MONTSERRAT

🅰F3 🄰Parc Natural de la Muntanya de Montserrat,
Barcelona 🄰Aeri de Montserrat, then cable car; Monistrol-
Enllaç, then La Cremallera rack railway 🚌From Barcelona
🄲Basilica: 7am–7pm daily; museum: 10am–5:45pm Sat &
Sun 🆆montserratvisita.com

The "Serrated Mountain", with its highest peak rising
to 1,236 m (4,055 ft), is a grand setting for Catalonia's
holiest place. Here, the Monastery of Montserrat is
surrounded by chapels and hermits' caves.

The monastery has a long history, and a chapel on the
site was first mentioned in documents dating from the
9th century. The present-day monastery was founded in
the 11th century but in 1811, when the French attacked
Catalonia in the War of Independence, it was destroyed
and the monks killed. Rebuilt and repopulated in
1844, it was a beacon of Catalan culture during
the Franco years. Today Benedictine monks
live here and the site has a hallowed
atmosphere. One of the most magical
experiences is listening to the
Escolania boys' choir singing in
the basilica. You can catch their
echoing voices at 1pm Monday
to Friday, 6:45pm Monday to
Thursday and noon and
6:45pm on Sundays.

Gothic cloister

*The museum has a
collection of 19th- and
20th-century Catalan
paintings. It also
displays liturgical items
from the Holy Land.*

*Plaça de Santa Maria's
focal points are two
wings of the Gothic
cloister built in 1476.
The modern monastery
was designed by
Françesc Folguera.*

Inner courtyard

Monestir de Montserrat,
in its dramatic setting ↑
below the mountain

The mountain towering behind the Monestir de Montserrat ↑

Agapit Vallmitjana sculpted Christ and the apostles on the basilica's Neo-Renaissance façade in 1900.

The Black Virgin (La Moreneta) looks down from behind the altar. Protected behind glass, her wooden orb protrudes for pilgrims to touch.

The domed basilica

↑ The awe-inspiring interior of the domed basilica

The rack railway (La Cremallera), follows a rail line built in 1880.

Cable car to Aeri de Montserrat station

THE VIRGIN OF MONTSERRAT

The small wooden statue of La Moreneta ("the dark one") is said to have been made by St Luke and brought here by St Peter in AD 50. Centuries later, the statue is believed to have been hidden from the Moors in the nearby Santa Cova (Holy Cave). Carbon dating suggests, however, that the statue was carved around the 12th century. In 1881 La Moreneta became patroness of Catalonia.

The Monestir de Poblet, surrounded by golden vines ↑

2 🏷️ 🅼🏷️ 🖥️

MONESTIR DE POBLET

🅰️F3 📍Off N240, 10 km (6 miles) from Montblanc, Tarragona 🚉L'Espluga de Francolí, then taxi 🚌Tarragona 🕙10am–12:30pm & 3–5:30pm daily 📅1 Jan, 6 Jul, 25 & 26 Dec 🌐poblet.cat

The largest monastery in the "Cistercian triangle", the Monastery of Santa Maria de Poblet is a haven of tranquillity and a resting place of kings. At sunset, it almost seems to glow in heavenly light.

The Monestir de Poblet was the first and most important of three Cistercian monasteries that helped to consolidate power in Catalonia after it had been recaptured from the Moors by Ramon Berenguer IV. Despite this former importance, Poblet was abandoned and fell into disrepair as a result of the Ecclesiastical Confiscations Act of 1835. Restoration, now largely complete, began in 1930 and monks returned in 1940.

THE CISTERCIAN TRIANGLE

Built in the 12th century, the monasteries of Poblet, Vallbona de les Monges and Santes Creus are captivating examples of Gothic architecture, and each has served as the final resting place of Catalan royalty at one point or another. A 100-km (60-mile) drive will take you around all three. No longer used by a religious order, Santes Creus offers the opportunity to explore the private quarters of a Cistercian monastery.

The vast 87-m (285-ft) dormitory dates from the 13th century.

Wine cellar

The 12th-century refectory is a vaulted hall with an octagonal fountain and a pulpit.

Royal doorway

Museum

Timeline

1150
Santes Creus and Poblet monasteries are founded.

1156
Monastery at Vallbona de les Monges is founded.

1196
△ Alfonso II is the first king to be buried here.

1336–87
Reign of Pere the Ceremonious, who designates Poblet a royal pantheon.

1479
Juan II, last king of Aragón is buried here.

1835
Monestir de Poblet is ravaged in the disentailment of monasteries.

1940
Monks return.

1952
▽ Royal remains are returned to the tombs.

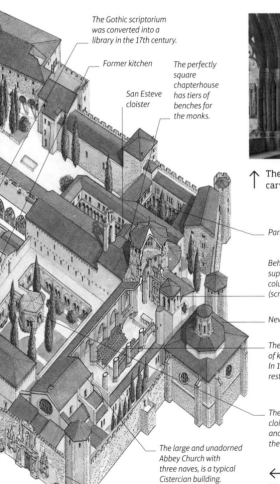

The Gothic scriptorium was converted into a library in the 17th century.

Former kitchen

San Esteve cloister

The perfectly square chapterhouse has tiers of benches for the monks.

↑ The cloisters, with capitals carved with scrollwork

Parlour cloister

Behind the stone altar, supported by Romanesque columns, an alabaster reredos (screen) fills the apse.

New sacristy

The tombs in the pantheon of kings were begun in 1359. In 1950 the sculptures were restored by Frederic Marès.

The evocative, vaulted cloisters were built in the 12th and 13th centuries and were the centre of monastic life.

The large and unadorned Abbey Church with three naves, is a typical Cistercian building.

Baroque church façade

← The many buildings that make up the Monestir de Poblet

3

GIRONA

 G2 Girona Rambla de la Llibertat 1; www.girona.cat/turisme

This handsome city puts on its best face beside the Riu Onyar, where colourful buildings rise above the water. These were built in the 19th century to replace sections of the city wall damaged during an 1809 siege by French troops. Most of the rest of the ramparts are intact and make up the Passeig Arqueològic (Archaeological Walk), which runs around the city. Take a walk along these historic walls before exploring the city's many sights.

The museum's most famous item is a large, well-preserved 11th- to 12th-century tapestry, called *The Creation*. There are also Romanesque paintings.

---

①

Museu d'Història dels Jueus

Carrer de la Força 8
Jul & Aug: 10am-7pm Mon-Sat, 10am-2pm Sun; Sep-Jun: 10am-2pm Mon & Sun, 10am-6pm Tue-Sat
1 & 6 Jan, 25 & 26 Dec

Amid the maze of alleyways in the Old Town is the former Jewish quarter of El Call. One of the West's most important Jewish areas during medieval times, it is now home to the Museu d'Història dels Jueus, which gives a history of Girona's Jews, who were expelled in the late 15th century.

②

Cathedral

Plaça de la Catedral
10am-7pm Mon-Sat, noon-7pm Sun catedraldegirona.cat

The style of Girona cathedral's solid west face is pure Catalan Baroque; the cloister and tower, Romanesque; but the rest of the building is Gothic. The single nave is the widest in the world. Behind the altar is a marble throne known as "Charlemagne's Chair" after the Frankish king whose troops took Girona in AD 785. Admission tickets also allow entry to the Basilica de Sant Feliu.

③

Museu d'Art

Pujada de la Catedral 12
May-Sep: 10am-7pm Tue-Sat, 10am-2pm Sun; Oct-Apr: 10am-6pm Tue-Sat, 10am-2pm Sun 1 & 6 Jan, 24-26 & 31 Dec museuart.cat

This former episcopal palace is one of Catalonia's best art galleries, with works ranging from the Romanesque period to the 20th century, including ecclesiastical items. Highlights are 10th-century carvings, a silver-clad altar from Sant Pere de Rodes and a 12th-century beam from Cruïlles.

Colourful apartment buildings lining the Riu Onyar in Girona

Museu d'Història de Girona

🅐 Carrer de la Força 27
🕐 May-Sep: 10:30am-6:30pm Tue-Sat (to 1:30pm Sun); Oct-Apr: 10:30am-5:30pm Tue-Sat (to 1:30pm Sun)

Housed in a former convent, this museum details Girona's history from its founding by the Romans to the present day.

---

⑤ Monestir de Sant Pere de Galligants

🅐 Carrer de Santa Llúcia 8
🕐 Jun-Sep: 10am-7pm Tue-Sat (to 2pm Sun); Oct-May: 10am-6pm Tue-Sat (to 2pm Sun) 🆆 macgirona.cat

This Romanesque church provides a beautiful setting for the city's archaeological museum. Its stone capitals depict scenes from the New Testament, mythical beasts and geometric patterns.

---

⑥ Basílica de Sant Feliu

🅐 Pujada de Sant Feliu 29
📞 972 427 189 🕐 10am-5:30pm Mon-Sat (from 1pm Sun)

Begun in the 14th century, this basilica was built over the tombs of St Felix and St Narcissus.

---

⑦ Museu del Cinema

🅐 Carrer de la Sèquia 1
🕐 Hours vary, check website 🆆 museudel cinema.girona.cat

A film buff's paradise, the Museu del Cinema offers a wide range of exhibitions. The Tomàs Mallol collection is particularly impressive. It includes around 20,000 objects that tell the history of the still image as well as motion pictures.

EAT

El Celler de Can Roca
This three-Michelin-starred restaurant serves traditional dishes with a twist.

🅐 Can Sunyer 48
🕐 Sun-Mon, Tue lunch 🆆 celler canroca.com

€€€

⑧ Banys Àrabs

🅐 Carrer Ferran el Catòlic s/n
🕐 Hours vary, check website
🗓 1 & 6 Jan, 25 & 26 Dec
🆆 banysarabs.cat

Despite their name, the Banys Àrabs were built under the Christian King Alfons I in the late 12th century, about 300 years after the Moors had left the area. The baths' most striking feature is the octagonal pool, with a domed ceiling.

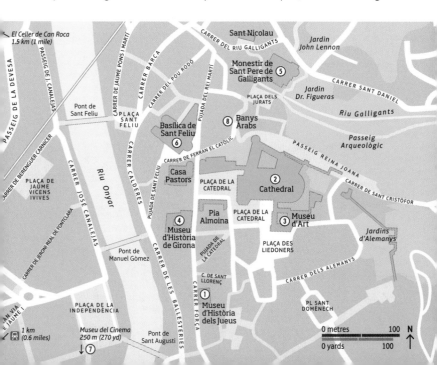

EXPERIENCE MORE

4

Vall d'Aran

F2 **Lleida** **Vielha**
**Carrer Sarriulèra 10,
Vielha; www.visit
valdaran.com**

This Valley of Valleys – *aran* means "valley" – is a beautiful haven of forests and flower-filled meadows, surrounded by towering mountain peaks.

The Vall d'Aran was formed by the Riu Garona, which rises in the area and flows out to France. With no proper link to the outside world until 1924, when a road was built over the Bonaigua Pass, the valley was cut off from the rest of Spain for most of the winter. Snow still blocks the narrow pass from November to April, but today access is easy through the Túnel de Vielha from El Pont de Suert (toll required).

The fact that the Vall d'Aran faces north means that it has a climate similar to that found on the Atlantic coast. Abundant rare wild flowers and butterflies flourish in the perfect conditions that are created by the damp breezes and shady slopes. It is also a noted habitat for many species of white and yellow narcissus. Several tiny villages have grown up beside the Riu Garona, often around Romanesque churches, notably at Bossòst, Salardú, Escunhau and Arties. The valley is also ideal for skiing and is popular with walkers.

5

Vielha

F2 **Lleida** **Carrer
Sarriulèra 10; 973 64 01 10**

The capital of the Vall d'Aran is located on the banks of the Riu Garona and preserves relics of its medieval past. The Romanesque church of Sant Miquel has an octagonal bell tower, a tall, pointed roof and a superb wooden 12th-century crucifix, the *Mig Aran Christ*. It once formed part of a larger carving, since lost, which represented the Descent from the Cross. The **Musèu dera Val d'Aran** is a museum devoted to Aranese history and folklore.

**BUTTERFLIES OF
THE VALL D'ARAN**

A massive variety of butterflies and moths is found high in the mountains and valleys of the Pyrenees. In particular, the isolated Vall d'Aran is the home of several unique and rare subspecies, such as the grizzled skipper (*prygus malvae*), clouded apollo (*parnassius mnemosyne*) and chequered skipper (*carterocephalus palaemon*). The best time of year to see the butterflies is between May and July.

Musèu dera Val d'Aran

⊘ Carrer Major 26
🕙 Summer: 10am–1pm & 5–8pm daily; winter: 10am–1pm & 5–8pm Tue-Sat, 10am–1pm Sun 🔒 Public hols
🌐 visitmuseum.gencat.cat/en/museu-dera-val-d-aran

Skiers tackling the slopes at the ski resort of Baqueira-Beret in the Spanish Pyrenees

Did You Know?

Baqueira-Beret is a favourite holiday destination of the Spanish royal family.

 6

Baqueira-Beret

A F2 **Q** Lleida **⊜** **i** www. baqueira.es

This ski resort is one of Spain's best and most popular. There is reliable winter snow cover and a choice of over 100 pistes at altitudes from 1,520 m to 2,470 m (4,987 ft to 8,104 ft).

Baqueira and Beret were once separate mountain villages before skiing became popular, but they now form a single resort. The Romans took full advantage of the thermal springs located in nearby Tredos; nowadays the springs are also enjoyed by tired skiers looking to relax after a day on the slopes.

←

Vall d'Aran nestled on the hillside, surrounded by snowcapped mountains

 7

Vall de Boí

A F2 **Q** Lleida **R** La Pobla de Segur **⊜** Pont de Suert **i** Passeig Sant Feliu 43, Barruera; www.vallboi.cat

This small valley on the edge of the Parc Nacional d'Aigüestortes is dotted with tiny villages, many of which are built around Catalan Romanesque churches.

Dating from the 11th and 12th centuries, these churches are distinguished by their tall belfries, such as the Església de Santa Eulàlia at Erill-la-Vall, which has six floors.

The two churches at Taüll, Sant Climent and Santa Maria contain wonderful frescoes. Between 1919 and 1923 the originals were taken from the churches to Barcelona's Museu Nacional d'Art de Catalunya (p133) for safekeeping and replicas now stand in their place. It is possible to climb the towers of Sant Climent for superb views of the surrounding countryside.

Other churches in the area worth visiting include those at Coll, for its fine ironwork, Barruera and Durro, which has another massive bell tower.

At the head of the valley is the hamlet of Caldes de Boí, which is popular for its

STAY

Hotel El Ciervo

Right in the centre of Vielha, this homely hotel offers unpretentious luxury. Close to the Baqueira-Beret ski resort, it's the perfect place to relax after an exhausting day on the slopes.

A F3 **Q** Plaza de San Orencio 3, Vielha **w** hotelelciervo.net

Hostal Sa Rascassa

If big hotels aren't your thing, choose this Costa Brava boutique for a rural Spanish stay. Book early to nab one of the five twin rooms above the elegant restaurant.

A G2 **Q** Cala d'Aiguafreda 3, Begur **w** hostal sarascassa.com

Hotel Costabella

With its excellent transport links and proximity to main roads, this hotel is a good base for exploring Catalonia. Its modern rooms are complemented by a steaming sauna and outdoor pool.

A G2 **Q** Avinguda de França 61, Girona **w** hotelcostabella.com

thermal springs, and the nearby ski station, Boí-Taüll, the highest ski resort in the Pyrenees. It is also a good base for exploring the Parc Nacional d'Aigüestortes (p163), the entrance to which is only 5 km (3 miles) from here.

8

Puigcerdà

🅰 F2 🅰 Girona
🅸 Plaça Santa Maria;
www.puigcerda.cat

Located practically on the French border, Puigcerdà was founded in 1177 by Alfonso II as the capital of Cerdanya, which shares a past and its culture with the neighbouring French region of Cerdagne. The only Spanish settlement that can claim to be closer to France is Llívia, a Spanish enclave that lies 6 km (4 miles) inside the border.

Puig is Catalan for "hill" and Puigcerdà buzzes with skiers in the winter season and hikers in summer. Although the town sits on a relatively small hill compared with the encircling mountains, which rise to 2,900 m (9,500 ft), it nevertheless has a fine view right down the beautiful Cerdanya Valley, watered by the trout-filled Riu Segre. This is the largest valley in the Pyrenees. At its edge is the nature reserve of Cadí-Moixeró, which has a population of alpine choughs.

 INSIDER TIP
Open Andorra's Box

La Seu d'Urgell is only 10 km (6 miles) from the Andorran border. Take a trip to this tiny principality to shop – it's tax-free – or discover its rural charms. Don't forget your passport.

9

La Seu d'Urgell

🅰 F2 🅰 Lleida 🚍 🅸 Carrer Major 8; 973 35 15 11

This ancient Pyrenean town was made a bishopric by the Visigoths in the 6th century. Feuds between the bishops of Urgell and the Counts of Foix over land ownership led to the emergence of Andorra in the 13th century. The 12th-century cathedral has an admired Romanesque statue of Santa Maria d'Urgell. The **Museu Diocesà** contains medieval art and manuscripts, including a 10th-century copy of St Beatus of Liébana's Commentary on the Apocalypse.

Museu Diocesà

🖾 🅰 Plaça del Deganat
🕐 Hours vary, check website 🕐 Public hols 🔳 visit museum.gencat.cat/en/museu-diocesa-d-urgelll

10

Sant Joan de les Abadesses

🅰 F2 🅰 Girona 🚍🅸 Plaça de l'Abadía 9; www.sant joandelesabadesses.cat

A fine 12th-century Gothic bridge arches over the Riu Ter to this unassuming market town, whose main attraction is its monastery.

Founded in AD 885, it was a gift from Guifré, the first count of Barcelona, to his daughter, the first abbess. The church is unadorned except for a superb wooden calvary, *The Descent from the Cross*, dating from 1150. Part of this scene, a thief, was burned in the Civil War and replaced with such skill that it is hard to tell which is new. The monastery's museum has Baroque and Renaissance altarpieces.

To the north is Camprodon, a small town full of grand houses, and shops selling *embutits* (charcuterie).

The heart of Puigcerdà town, with views out over the Cerdanya Valley ↑

The rugged terrain of the Parc Nacional d'Aigüestortes ↑

⑪ Ripoll

🏛 F2 🚉 Girona 🚌🚆
ℹ Plaça Abat Oliba; www.visit.ripoll.cat

Once a tiny mountain base from which raids against the Moors were made, Ripoll is now best known for the Monestir de Santa Maria, built in AD 888. The town has been called "the cradle of Catalonia", as the monastery was both the power base of Guifré el Pélos (Wilfred the Hairy), founder of the 500-year dynasty of the House of Barcelona. He is buried here.

In the late 12th century, the huge west portal gained a series of intricate carvings, which are perhaps the finest Romanesque carvings in Spain. They depict historical and biblical scenes.

⑫ Parc Nacional d'Aigüestortes

🏛 F2 🚉 Lleida 🚆 La Pobla de Segur 🚌 Pont de Suert, La Pobla de Segur
ℹ Carrer de les Graieres 2, Boí, 973 69 61 89; Carrer Sant Maurici 5, Espot, 973 62 40 36; www.parcs naturals.gencat.cat

The pristine mountain scenery of Catalonia's only national park is among the most dramatic seen in the Pyrenees.

Established in 1955, the park covers an area of 102 sq km (40 sq miles). The main access towns are Espot, to the east, and Caldes de Boí, to the west. Dotted around the park are waterfalls and the clear waters of around 150 lakes. The finest scenery is around Sant Maurici lake, which lies beneath the twin shards of the Serra dels Encantats (Mountains of the Enchanted). From here, there are many walks, particularly along the string of lakes that lead north to the towering

peaks of Agulles d'Amitges. To the south is the dramatic vista of Estany Negre, the highest and deepest tarn in the park.

Early summer in the lower valleys is marked by a mass of pink and red rhododendrons, while later in the year wild lilies bloom in the forests. The park is also home to a variety of wildlife. Chamois live on mountain screes and in the meadows, beavers and otters can be seen by the lakes, while bearded vultures nest on mountain ledges.

THE CATALAN LANGUAGE

Catalan has recovered from the ban it suffered under Franco's dictatorship and has supplanted Castilian (Spanish) as the language in everyday use in Catalonia. Spoken by more than 9.5 million people, it is a Romance language akin to the Provençal of France. Previously it was suppressed by Felipe V in 1717 and only officially resurfaced in the 19th century, when the Jocs Florals (medieval poetry contests) were revived during the rebirth of Catalan literature.

⑬
Olot

🅐 G2 🅐 Girona 🚌 🛈 Carrer Francesc Fàbregas 6; www.turismeolot.com

This small market town is at the centre of a landscape pockmarked with the conical hills of extinct volcanoes. But it was an earthquake in 1474 which last disturbed the town, destroying its medieval past. Visitors can learn more about the history of the town at the **Museu dels Volcans**.

During the 19th century, the region's extraordinary light inspired landscape artists known as the "Olot School" of art. See examples in the **Museu Comarcal de la Garrotxa**, which is housed in an 18th-century hospice. The town's other star attraction is the **Museu dels Sants.** Here, you can see skillful statues of saints and carefully crafted Biblical scenes, before watching craftsmen in the workshop.

Museu dels Volcans
🅐 Avda de Santa Coloma 47 🕙 10am–1pm & 3–6pm

Tue–Fri, 10am–2pm & 3–6pm Sat, 10am–2pm Sun
🌐 museus.olot.cat

Museu Comarcal de la Garrotxa
♿ 🅐 Carrer de l'Hospici 8 🕙 10am–1pm & 3–6pm Mon–Fri, 11am–2pm & 4–7pm Sat, 11am–2pm Sun 🌐 museus.olot.cat

Museu dels Sants
♿ 🅐 Carrer de Joaquim Vayreda 9 🕙 10am–1pm & 3–6pm Tue–Fri, 11am–2pm & 4–7pm Sat, 11am–2pm Sun 🌐 museus.olot.cat

---

⑭
Figueres

🅐 G2 🅐 Girona 🚆 🚌 🛈 Plaça de l'Escorxador 2; www.turismefigueres.com

Figueres is in the north of the Empordà (Ampurdán) region,

←
A beautiful sculpture of a winged saint in Olot's Museu dels Sants

the fertile plain that sweeps inland from the Gulf of Roses. As you would expect from these fruitful surroundings, every Thursday, the market here fills with fruit and vegetables from the area.

The **Museu del Joguet** (Toy Museum) is on the Rambla, Figueres' main street. Inside

---

THE ART OF DALÍ

Born in Figueres in 1904, Salvador Dalí mounted his first exhibition at the age of 15. After studying at the Escuela de Bellas Artes in Madrid, and dabbling with Cubism, Futurism and Meta-physical painting, Dalí embraced Surrealism in 1929, becoming the movement's best-known painter. Never far from controversy, Dalí became famous for his hallucinatory images, which he described as "hand-painted dream photographs". He died in Figueres in 1989.

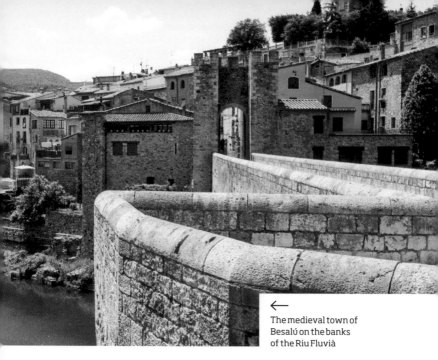

← The medieval town of Besalú on the banks of the Riu Fluvià

A magnificent medieval town, with a striking approach across a fortified bridge over the Riu Fluvià, Besalú has two fine churches.

are exhibits from all over Catalonia. At the lower end of the Rambla is a statue of Narcís Monturiol i Estarriol (1819–85), claimed to be the inventor of the submarine.

A much better known local is Salvador Dalí, who founded the **Teatre-Museu Dalí**. This is the most visited museum in Spain after Madrid's Museo del Prado (p316). The galleries occupy an old theatre. Inside, works by Dalí are displayed alongside other artists. Look out for Rainy Taxi – a Cadillac being sprayed by a fountain.

Museu del Joguet
⌖ ⌂ Carrer Sant Pere 1
🕐 Hours vary, check website
Ⓦ mjc.cat

Teatre-Museu Dalí
⌖ ⌂ Plaça Gala-Salvador Dalí 🕐 Hours vary, check website ⌚ 1 Jan, 25 Dec
Ⓦ salvador-dali.org

Cardona

Ⓐ F2 ⌂ Barcelona 🚌
ℹ Avinguda Rastrillo; www.cardonaturisme.cat

Sited on a hill, surrounded by the Riu Cardener, the town of Cardona is best known for its Montanya de Sal (Salt Mountain), a huge salt deposit, which has been mined since Roman times. This almost translucent material has been crafted into statues and crucifixes by Cardona's artists for centuries.

For the best views of the Montanya de Sal, and the town itself, head up to the **Castell de Cardona**. The 13th-century castle of the dukes of Cardona, constables to the crown of Aragón, is set on the top of a hill. Rebuilt in the 18th century, it is now a parador. Beside the castle is

an early 11th-century church, the Església de Sant Vicenç, where the dukes are buried.

Castell de Cardona
⌖ ⌖ ⌖ ⌂ Castell de Cardona s/n 🕐 By guided tour only, check website for details
Ⓦ cardonaturisme.cat

Besalú

Ⓐ G2 ⌂ Girona 🚌 ℹ Carrer del Pont 1; www.besalu.cat

A magnificent medieval town, with a striking approach across a fortified bridge over the Riu Fluvià, Besalú has two fine churches. These are the Romanesque Sant Vicenç and Sant Pere, the sole remnants of Besalú's Benedictine monastery, founded in AD 948.

In 1964 a mikvah, a ritual Jewish bath, was discovered. It was built in 1264 and is one of only three of that period to survive in Europe.

After exploring the town, head 14 km (8 miles) south to the sky-blue lake of Banyoles for a scenic picnic.

17
Tossa de Mar

⚑G3 ⚐Girona 🚌
ℹ️ Avinguda Pelegrí 25;
www.infotossa.com

The Roman town of Turissa is one of the prettiest along the Costa Brava. Above the New Town is the Vila Vella (Old Town), a protected national monument. In the Old Town, the **Museu Municipal** has a collection of local archaeological finds and modern art.

Museu Municipal

♿ 🏛️ Plaça Pintor Roig i Soler 1 🕐 May-Sep: 10:30am-6:30pm Mon-Sat (to 1:30pm Sun); Oct-Apr: 10:30am-5:30pm Tue-Sat(to 1:30pm Sun) 🖥️ visit museum.gencat.cat/en/museu-municipal-de-tossa-de-mar

18
Cadaqués

⚑G2 ⚐Girona 🚌
ℹ️ Carrer Cotxe 1; www.visitcadaques.org

Sitting at the tip of the remote Cap de Creus headland, this whitewashed town is simply enchanting. Stroll through the Old Town and note the slate pavements, which are best preserved on Carrer des Call. Within these twisting streets is the **Museu de Cadaqués**, which has temporary exhibitions about the town's history and its visual arts.

In the 1960s, Cadaqués was dubbed the "St Tropez of Spain", because of the young crowd that sought out Salvador Dalí in nearby Portlligat. The house where he lived from 1930 until his death in 1989 is known as the **Casa-Museu Salvador Dalí**. Here, you can see the painter's workshop, library and swimming pool.

Museu de Cadaqués

♿ 🏛️ Carrer d'en Narcís Monturiol 15 📞 972 25 88 77 🕐 Hours vary, call ahead

Casa-Museu Salvador Dalí

♿🕐 🏛️ Portlligat
🕐 Advanced booking is required to visit; Hours vary, check website 🕐 1 Jan, mid-Jan-mid-Feb, 3 Jun, 7 Oct, 25 Dec 🖥️ salvador-dali.org

Did You Know?

"Peratallada" means "cut stone", and the village is known for its stone architecture.

19
Peratallada

⚑G2 ⚐Girona ℹ️ Plaça del Castell 3; www.visit peratallada.cat

This tiny village is stunning and only a short inland trip from the Costa Brava. With Pals and Palau Sator it forms part of the "Golden Triangle" of medieval villages.

Its mountaintop position gives some dramatic views of the area. A labyrinth of cobbled streets winds up to the well-conserved castle and lookout tower, whose written records date from the 11th century. Attackers were fended off by constructing a sturdy wall, enclosing the entire village, which even

← The medieval walled Vila Vella of Tossa de Mar, overlooking the bay

today limits the nucleus from further expansion, ensuring it retains its medieval character.

Empúries

A G2 **A** Girona **E** L'Escala **O** From 10am; closing time varies with season, check website **W** mac.cat

Three settlements were built here between the 6th and 3rd centuries BC: the Old Town (Palaiapolis); the New Town (Neapolis); and the Roman Town. The Old Town was founded by the Greeks in 600 BC as a trading port. It was built on what was a small island, and is now the site of the hamlet of Sant Martí de Empúries. In 550 BC, this was replaced by a town on the shore which the Greeks named Emporion, meaning "trading place". In 218 BC, the Romans landed at Empúries and built a city next to the New Town.

A nearby museum exhibits some of the site's finds, but the best examples are displayed in Barcelona's Museu Arqueològic (p130).

Vic

A F2 **A** Barcelona **A** **B** **A** Plaça del Pes; www.victurisme.cat

Coincide a visit to this rural town with market day (Tuesday, Saturday and Sunday), when the local sausages (embotits) are piled high in the Plaça Major, along with other produce from the surrounding plains.

In the 3rd century BC Vic was the capital of an ancient Iberian tribe, the Ausetans. The town was then colonized by the Romans – the remains of a Roman temple survive today. Since the 6th century AD, the town has been a bishop's see. In the 11th century, Abbot Oliba commissioned the El Cloquer tower, around which the cathedral was built in the 18th century. The interior of the cathedral is covered with vast murals by Josep Maria Sert (1874–1945). They are painted in reds and golds, and represent scenes from the Bible.

Adjacent to the cathedral is the **Museu Episcopal de Vic**, which has one of the best collections of Romanesque artifacts in Catalonia. Its large display of mainly religious art and relics includes bright, simple murals and wooden sculptures from rural churches.

Museu Episcopal de Vic

 A Plaça Bisbe Oliba 3 **O** Apr-Sep: 10am-7pm Tue-Sat, 10am-2pm Sun; Oct-Mar: 10am-1pm & 3-6pm Tue-Fri, 10am-7pm Sat, 10am-2pm Sun **C** 1 & 6 Jan, Easter Sun, 25 & 26 Dec **W** museuepiscopal vic.com

EAT

El Racó del Mar

Close to the beach, this restaurant has a varied seafood menu, with vegetarian and vegan options. It's popular so reserving a table is recommended.

A G2 **A** Passeig Marítim, Empuriabrava **W** elracodelmar.com

€€€

Portal 22

Open kitchens at this chic tapas bar let you see the chefs at work as they prepare classic Spanish dishes.

A F3 **A** Plaça del Portal Nou 22, Valls (Alt Camp) **C** Sun dinner **W** portal22.cat

€€€

Compartir

A trio of Catalonia's top chefs serve imaginative dishes, such as sardines marinated in orange and mint here.

A G2 **A** Riera Sant Vicenç s/n, Cadaqués **W** compartircadaques. com

€€€

← Remains of a gated Roman wall at the ruins of Empúries

㉒ Lleida

F3 **Lleida** **Carrer Major 31 bis;**
www.turismedelleida.cat

Dominating Lleida (Lérida), the capital of Catalonia's only landlocked province, is La Suda, a large fort taken from the Moors in 1149. Within its walls is the old cathedral, La Seu Vella, founded in 1203, which was transformed into barracks by Felipe V in 1707 but still retains its beautiful cloisters and Gothic rose window. After years of neglect, the fort complex was restored and now offers panoramic viewpoints.

A lift descends from the Seu Vella to the Plaça de Sant Joan in the town below. This square is at the midpoint of a busy street sweeping round the foot of the hill. A pedestrianized walk takes visitors past many interesting shops, set in some of Lleida's most striking buildings. The new cathedral, La Seu Nova, is here, as are manorial buildings such as the 13th-century town hall.

↑ The shaded cloisters of Lleida's old cathedral, La Seu Vella

㉓ Montblanc

F3 **Tarragona** **Muralla de Santa Tecla 54; www.mont blancmedieval.cat**

The medieval grandeur of this town lives on within its walls, said to be Catalonia's finest piece of military architecture. At the Sant Jordi gate, St George allegedly slew the dragon. The **Museu Comarcal de la Conca de Barberà** has displays on local crafts.

Museu Comarcal de la Conca de Barberà

Carrer Josa 6 **Summer: 10am–2pm & 4–7pm Tue-Sat, 10am–2pm Sun; winter: 10am–2pm Tue-Fri & Sun, 10am–2pm & 4–7pm Sat** **mccb.cat**

㉔ Solsona

F2 **Lleida** **Carretera de Bassella 1; www.solsonaturisme.com**

Nine towers and three gateways remain of Solsona's fortifications. Inside the walls is an ancient town of noble mansions. The beautiful cathedral is notable for its black stone Virgin. The **Museu Diocesà i Comarcal** contains Romanesque paintings and archaeological finds.

TOP 5 **CAVA VINEYARDS**

Codorníu
A bus from Barcelona travels to this old winery in Sant Sadurní d'Anoia *(www.visitas codorniu.com)*.

Freixenet
The world's largest exporter of Cava offers guided tours *(www. freixenet.es)*.

Gramona
A boutique wine cellar dating back to 1850 *(www.gramona.com)*.

Raventós i Blanc
This winery has made Cava since the 1870s *(www.raventos.com)*.

Alta Alella
A vineyard overlooking the Mediterranean *(www.altaalella.wine)*.

Museu Diocesà i Comarcal

🏠 Plaça Palau 1 🕐 11am–5pm
Fri & Sat, 11am–2pm Sun
🔒 1 & 6 Jan, 25 & 26 Dec
🌐 museusolsona.cat

The sun setting
over Sitges, and
(inset) the Museu
Cau Ferrat ↑

25
Vilafranca del Penedès

🅰F3 🏠 Barcelona 🚊🚌
ℹ️ Carrer Hermenegild
Clascar 2; www.turisme
vilafranca.com

This busy market town is
set in Catalonia's main
wine-producing region. The
Vinseum (Wine Museum),
in a 14th-century palace,
documents the history of
the area's wine trade. Local
bodegas can be visited
for wine tasting.

A must-visit for wine lovers,
8 km (5 miles) to the north
is Sant Sadurní d'Anoia, the
capital of Spain's sparkling
wine, cava. Many of the
wineries have tasting rooms
in the town centre, and others
offer tours of their vineyards.

Vinseum

 🏠 Plaça Jaume I 🕐 10am–
2pm & 4–7pm Tue–Sat,
10am–2pm Sun & public
hols 🌐 vinseum.cat

26
Sitges

🅰F3 🏠 Barcelona 🚊🚌
ℹ️ Plaça Eduard Maristany
2; www.sitgesanytime.com

There are no less than nine
beaches to choose from at this
pretty seaside town. Bars and
restaurants line its main
boulevard, the Passeig Marítim,
and there are many examples
of Modernista architecture
among the apartment blocks.
Modernista artist Santiago
Rusiñol (1861–1931) spent much
time here and bequeathed his
quirky collection of ceramics,
sculptures, painting and
ornate ironwork to the **Museu
Cau Ferrat**. The museum lies
next to the 17th-century
church of Sant Bartomeu i
Santa Tecla, which juts out
proudly on a promontory.

Museu Cau Ferrat

♿🖼 🏠 Carrer Fonollar
📞 938 94 03 64 🕐 10am–
5pm Tue–Sun (to 7pm Oct &
Mar–Jun; to 8pm Jul–Sep;
to 5pm Nov–Feb)

27

Tortosa

Ⓐ F3 Ⓣ Tarragona
ⓘ Rambla Felip Pedrell 3;
www.tortosaturisme.cat

A ruined castle and medieval walls are clues to Tortosa's historical importance. Sited at the lowest crossing point on the Riu Ebre (Ebro River), it has been strategically significant since Iberian times.

The Moors held the city from the 8th century until 1148. The old Moorish castle, known as La Zuda, is all that remains of their defences. It has been renovated as a parador. The Moors also built a mosque in AD 914. Its foundations were used for the Gothic cathedral, on which work began in 1347.

28

Costa Daurada

Ⓐ F3 Ⓣ Tarragona
Ⓡ Ⓔ Calafell, Sant Vicenç de Calders, Salou ⓘ Rambla Felip Pedrell 3, Tarragona; www.costadaurada.info

The long, sandy beaches of the Costa Daurada (Golden Coast) run along the shores of Tarragona province. Cambrils and Salou are the liveliest resorts – the rest are low-key, family holiday spots. The *costa* is home to many attractions.

The **Museu Pau Casals** in Sant Salvador (El Vendrell) is dedicated to the famous cellist. **PortAventura** is one of Europe's largest theme parks and includes Ferrari Land, home to Europe's largest and fastest roller coaster.

Museu Pau Casals

⊛ Ⓐ Avinguda Palfuriana 67
Ⓞ Hours vary, check website
Ⓦ paucasals.org

PortAventura

⊛ Ⓐ Avinguda de l'Alcalde Pere Molas, km 2, Vila-seca
Ⓞ Hours vary, check website
Ⓦ portaventuraworld.com

29

Delta de l'Ebre

Ⓐ F3 Ⓣ Tarragona Ⓡ Aldea
Ⓔ Deltebre, Aldea ⓘ Carrer Sant Miquel 1, Deltebre; www.atraccionatural.cat

The delta of the Riu Ebre is a prosperous rice-growing region and wildlife haven. Some 70 sq km (27 sq miles) have been turned into a nature reserve, the Parc Natural del Delta de l'Ebre. In Deltebre there is an information centre and an interesting **Eco-Museu**, with an aquarium containing species found in the delta.

The main towns in the area are Amposta and Sant Carles

Jimoneca
Head here for a fresh *horchata* (a drink made with tiger nuts, almonds or rice) or an artisan ice cream.

Ⓐ G2 Ⓐ 11 de Setembre 87, Palamós
Ⓦ jijonenca.es

Ceràmica Planas Marquès
Beautiful ceramics, made in the on-site workshop, are sold here.

Ⓐ G2 Ⓐ Av Costa Brava 34, Corçà Ⓦ ceramica planasmarques.com

de la Ràpita, both of which serve as good bases for exploring the reserve.

The best sites for seeing wildlife are along the shore, from the Punta del Fangar in the north to the Punta de la Banya in the south. Everywhere is accessible by car except Illa de Buda. Flamingos and other waterbirds, such as avocets, breed on this island. Take a tour of the Illa de Buda on one of the tourist boats that depart from Riumar or Deltebre to see these critters.

↑ The preserved remains of the Roman amphitheatre at Tarragona

Eco-Museu

 Carrer Doctor Martí Buera 22 ☎ 977 48 96 79 ⏰ 10am–1pm & 3–6pm daily (winter: to 5pm) 🚫 1 & 6 Jan, 25 & 26 Dec

---

30

Tarragona

📍 F3 🏛 Tarragona 🚂🚌🚌 ℹ Carrer Major 39; www. tarragonaturisme.cat

The Romans used Tarragona, now a big industrial port, as a base for the conquest of the peninsula in the 3rd century BC. The Rambla Nova ends on the clifftop Balcó de Europa,

---

💬 **INSIDER TIP**
Special Visits

Events at Tarragona's Roman ruins include theatrical visits and family-friendly activities. Check the Museu Nacional Arqueològic de Tarragona's website for more details *(www. mnat.cat)*.

← A twisting roller coaster towering over Port Aventura's other attractions

in sight of the ruins of the Amfiteatre Romà. Nearby is the Praetorium, a Roman tower converted into a palace in medieval times. It now houses the **Pretori i Circ Romans**, which displays Roman and medieval finds, and gives access to the cavernous passageways of the Roman circus, built in the 1st century AD. Next door is the **Museu Nacional Arqueològic de Tarragona**, which has an extensive collection of bronze tools and beautiful mosaics, including a *Head of Medusa*.

An archaeological walk runs along the Roman wall. Behind the wall lies the 12th-century cathedral, built on the site of a Roman temple. This evolved over many centuries, as seen from the blend of styles of the exterior. Inside is an alabaster altarpiece of St Tecla, carved by Pere Joan in 1434.

To the west of town is a 3rd- to 6th-century Christian cemetery, the Necròpolis Paleocristiana i Conjunt Paleocristià del Francolí.

Pretori i Circ Romans

 Plaça del Rei ☎ 977 22 17 36 ⏰ Apr–May & Sep: 9am–9pm Tue–Sat, 9am–3pm Sun; Jun–Aug: 9am–3pm Mon & Sun, 9am–9pm Tue–Sat; Oct–Mar: 9am–7:30pm Tue–Fri, 9am–7pm Sat, 9am–3pm Sun

TOP 5 **CATALAN FESTES**

Human Towers
Tarragona province is known for its *castelleres* festivals, where teams of men stand on each other's shoulders.

Dance of Death
Men dressed as skeletons dance in Verges, near Girona, on Maundy Thursday.

Sant Jordi
Lovers exchange a rose and a book on 23 April to honour Catalonia's patron saint and the day he died in 1616.

La Patum
Giants, devils and bizarre monsters parade through Berga for Corpus Christi.

Midsummer's Eve
Bonfires and fireworks illuminate Catalonia on 23 June.

Museu Nacional Arqueològic de Tarragona

 Plaça del Rei 5 🚫 Closed for renovation until 2025 🌐 mnat.cat

A DRIVING TOUR
THE COSTA BRAVA

Length 135 km (84 miles) **Stopping-off points** L'Escala; Begur; Palamós; Tossa de Mar **Terrain** Some steep, hilly roads to Begur, but generally easy

The Costa Brava ("wild coast") runs for some 200 km (125 miles) from Blanes northwards to the region of Empordà (Ampurdán), which borders France. This driving tour runs along the coast, from arty Cadaqués to lively Lloret de Mar, and takes in a varied landscape of pine-backed sandy coves, golden beaches and crowded, modern resorts. Wine, olives and fishing were the mainstays of the area before the tourists came in the 1960s and the first part of this route takes in pretty little towns that seem almost untouched by tourism. The busiest resorts – La Platja d'Aro and Tossa de Mar, as well as Lloret de Mar – are to the south, but there are also some unspoiled gems to be discovered on this stretch of the coast, including Sant Feliu de Guíxols and Palamós, which are still working towns behind the summer rush. Take a detour inland to explore medieval villages, such as Peralada, Peratallada and Pals.

↑ Overlooking the sandy beach at Llafranc

*Lounge on one of **Tossa de Mar**'s golden beaches. Locals love the small cove beneath the fortified Old Town (p166).*

*End your drive at **Lloret de Mar**. Although it has more hotels than anywhere else on the coast, there are unspoiled beaches nearby, such as Santa Cristina.*

0 kilometres 10
0 miles 10

N ↗

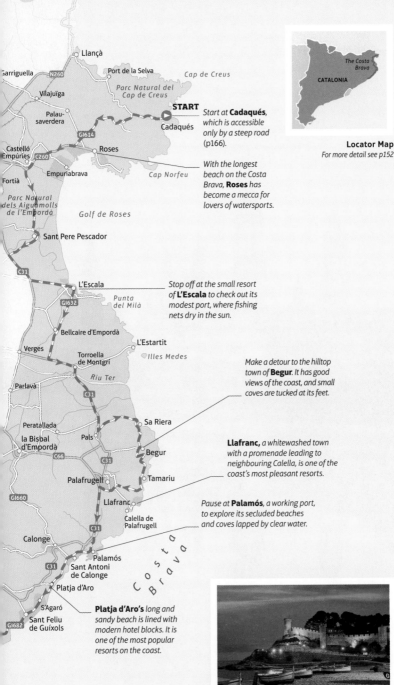

Llançà

Garriguella N260

Vilajuïga

Port de la Selva   *Cap de Creus*

Parc Natural del Cap de Creus

Palau-saverdera

START

GI614   Cadaqués

Start at **Cadaqués**, which is accessible only by a steep road (p166).

Castelló Empúries   C260   Roses

Fortià

Empuriabrava   *Cap Norfeu*

With the longest beach on the Costa Brava, **Roses** has become a mecca for lovers of watersports.

Parc Natural dels Aiguamolls de l'Empordà   *Golf de Roses*

Sant Pere Pescador

C31

L'Escala

GI632   *Punta del Milà*

Stop off at the small resort of **L'Escala** to check out its modest port, where fishing nets dry in the sun.

Bellcaire d'Empordà

Verges

Torroella de Montgrí

L'Estartit

Illes Medes

Parlavà

Riu Ter

C31

Make a detour to the hilltop town of **Begur**. It has good views of the coast, and small coves are tucked at its feet.

Peratallada

la Bisbal d'Empordà   C66

Pals

Sa Riera

C31

Begur

Llafranc, a whitewashed town with a promenade leading to neighbouring Calella, is one of the coast's most pleasant resorts.

Palafrugell

GI660

Tamariu

Llafranc

Calella de Palafrugell

Pause at **Palamós,** a working port, to explore its secluded beaches and coves lapped by clear water.

Calonge

C31

Palamós

Sant Antoni de Calonge

C o s t a   B r a v a

Platja d'Aro

S'Agaró

Sant Feliu de Guíxols   GI682

Platja d'Aro's long and sandy beach is lined with modern hotel blocks. It is one of the most popular resorts on the coast.

Mediterranean Sea

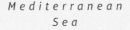

↑ Boats beached on the sand at Tossa de Mar at low tide

Locator Map
For more detail see p152

The Costa Brava

CATALONIA

ARAGÓN

In 1035, Sancho III of Pamplona bequeathed the small Pyrenean county of Aragón to his third son, Ramiro I. By 1104, the kingdom had doubled in size with the additions of Sobrarbe and Ribagorza to the east and conquests to the south.

When Ramon Berenguer IV, count of Barcelona, married Petronilla of Aragón in 1137, the kingdom became united with Catalonia. From the 12th to 15th centuries, Aragón became a powerful federation of states, with the Catalans devoting themselves to commerce and maritime expansion and the Aragonese kings reconquering the rich kingdom of Valencia from the Moors in 1238. After the *reconquista*, Moorish architects and craftsmen were treated more tolerantly here than elsewhere, and they continued their work in the distinctive Mudéjar style. In its heyday, in the 13th century, Aragón's dominions stretched across the Mediterranean as far as Sicily.

By his marriage to Isabel of Castile and León in 1469, Fernando II of Aragón paved the way for the unification of Spain. But the region had a tense relationship with the monarchy – in the 16th century Aragón supported the unsuccessful Habsburg claimant in the War of Succession. Aragón's decline continued into the 19th century, when it was a Carlist stronghold, and it was divided in two by the Nationalists and Republicans during the Civil War. The east was run by the Republicans, while the Nationalists controlled the west. The two areas were only united by Franco's victory. On 23 April 1978, more than 100,000 people marched through the streets of Zaragoza, demanding Aragón's autonomy from Spain.

ARAGÓN

Must Sees

1. Parque Nacional de Ordesa
2. Zaragoza

Experience More

3. Puerto de Somport
4. Aínsa
5. Los Valles
6. Benasque
7. Sos del Rey Católico
8. Jaca
9. Monasterio de San Juan de la Peña
10. Alquézar
11. Castillo de Loarre
12. Agüero
13. Tarazona
14. Graus
15. Huesca
16. Santuario de Torreciudad
17. Monasterio de Veruela
18. Calatayud
19. Daroca
20. Alcañiz
21. Fuendetodos
22. Monasterio de Piedra
23. Valderrobres
24. Teruel
25. Sierra de Gúdar
26. Rincón de Ademuz
27. Albarracín
28. Mora de Rubielos

INSIDER TIP
Tips for Walkers

Several well-marked trails follow the valleys (see website for details). Walking boots are a must and the mountain routes may require climbing gear. Pyrenean weather changes rapidly - beware of ice and snow early and late in the season.

1

PARQUE NACIONAL DE ORDESA

E2 Aragón Change at Sabiñánigo for Torla Sabiñánigo Avenida Ordesa s/n, Torla-Ordesa; www.aragon.es/ordesa

Within its borders the Parque Nacional de Ordesa y Monte Perdido combines the most dramatic elements of Spain's Pyrenean scenery. Made inaccessible by snow in the winter, Ordesa blooms into a paradise for walkers and nature lovers alike once the sun starts shining.

With its core of slate-roofed houses and cobbled streets around the church, the town of Torla-Ordesa is a popular base for visitors to Ordesa. From here you can walk through the Valle de Ordesa, where the Río Arazas cuts through the forest. This valley is one of four glacial canyons – the Añisclo, Pineta and Escuain are the others – that carve the great upland limestone massifs into striking cliffs and chasms.

The 70-m (230-ft) Cola de Caballo ("Horse's Tail") waterfall makes a scenic stopping point near the northern end of the long hike around the Circo Soaso. The falls provide just a taste of the scenery found along the route. Another route takes in the Cañon de Añisclo. A wide path leads along this beautiful, steep-sided gorge, following the wooded course of the turbulent Río Vellos through dramatic limestone scenery.

← The sun setting over the Valle de Ordesa in the Parque Nacional de Ordesa

← A hiker traversing one of the mountainous trails through the park

↑ The town of Torla-Ordesa, at the gateway to the Ordesa and Mount Perdido National Park

PYRENEAN WILDLIFE

Ordesa is home to many unique species of flora and fauna. Trout streams rush along the valley floor and wooded slopes harbour otters, marmots and caper-caillies (large grouse). Gentians and orchids shelter in crevices and edelweiss brave the most hostile crags. Higher up, the Pyrenean chamois is still fairly common but the Ordesa ibex became extinct in 2000. Attempts at cloning have had little success so far. The rocky pinnacles above the valley are the domain of the bearded vulture.

2

ZARAGOZA

E3 Zaragoza 🚆🚌 *i*Plaza del Pilar; ww.zaragoza.es/sede/portal/turismo/

Located on the fertile banks of the Río Ebro, Zaragoza is Spain's fifth-largest city and the capital of Aragón. Damaged during the Peninsular War *(p66)*, the city was largely rebuilt, but the old centre retains some interesting buildings.

1

Roman Walls

Towards the end of the 1st century BC, the Romans founded the city of Caesaraugusta, which became known as Zaragoza. And its name is not the only Roman legacy; among the city's ruins are magnificent city walls. As you walk along them, it's easy to picture the ancient Zaragozans who would have done the same almost 2,000 years ago.

2

Alma Mater Museum

Plaza de la Seo 5 🕐10am-8pm Tue-Sat, 10am-2pm Sun 🌐almamatermuseum.com

Built between 1779 and 1787, the Archbishop's Palace of Zaragoza now houses a museum, displaying works of art by the likes of Goya under the vaulted ceilings.

3

Museo Pablo Gargallo

Plaza San Felipe 3 📞976 72 49 22 🕐10am-2pm & 5-9pm Tue-Sat, 10am-2:30pm Sun & public hols

Housed in a 16th-century building is this museum

> ### Did You Know?
>
> Lord Byron describes Zaragoza during the Peninsular War in *Childe Harold's Pilgrimage.*

dedicated to the Aragonese sculptor Pablo Gargallo (1881–1934). You can see his most celebrated sculptures, such as *The Prophet* and the *Olympic Salute*, as well as drawings and other items here.

4

Mercado de Lanuza

Calle Murallas Romanas 🕐8am-2pm & 5-8pm Mon-Fri, 8:30am-2:30pm Sat 🌐mercadocentralzaragoza.com

Designed in 1895 by local architect Félix Navarro to replace the existing open-air market, this covered hall is an impressive sight, especially its sinuous ironwork in the Art Nouveau style. It still houses food stalls today and is also known as the Mercado Central.

5

Basílica de Nuestra Señora del Pilar

Plaza del Pilar 🕐6:45am-8:30pm Mon-Sat (till 9:30pm Sun) 🌐catedraldezaragoza.es/basilica

Most of the city's main sights are grouped around Plaza del Pilar. The most impressive is the Basílica de Nuestra Señora

⑥

Museo Goya

🏠 Calle Espoz y Mina 23
🕐 10am–2pm & 4–8pm
Tue–Sat, 10am–2pm Sun
🌐 museogoya.ibercaja.es

The Museo Goya exhibits the eclectic collection of a wealthy local art historian, whose special interest was Goya. The top floor contains a collection of Goya's etchings. Works by other artists are also on display.

---

⑦

La Seo

🏠 Plaza de la Seo 📞 976 29 12 31 🕐 Hours vary, call ahead

Zaragoza's cathedral, La Seo, displays a great mix of styles. Part of the exterior is faced with typical Mudéjar brick and ceramic decoration, and inside are a fine Gothic reredos and splendid Flemish tapestries.

⑧

Lonja

🏠 Plaza del Pilar
📞 976 39 72 39 🕐 10am–2pm & 5–8pm Tue–Sat

The commodities exchange was built in the 16th century as a place for merchants to deal their goods. It is now used as an exhibition space.

---

⑨

Aljafería Palace

🏠 Calle de los Diputados
📞 976 28 96 83 🕐 Apr–mid-Oct: 10am–2pm & 4:30–8pm daily; mid-Oct–Mar: 10am–2pm & 4–6:30pm Mon–Sat, 10am–2pm Sun

One of the most important monuments in Zaragoza lies on the busy road to Bilbao. The Aljafería is an 11th-century Moorish palace. A courtyard of lacy arches surrounds a sunken garden and a small mosque.

←

Zaragoza, with the spires of the basilica rising above the river

del Pilar, with its huge church sporting 11 brightly tiled cupolas. Inside, the Santa Capilla (Lady Chapel) by Ventura Rodríguez contains a small statue of the Virgin on a pillar. Her manta (cape) is changed daily, and pilgrims pass behind the chapel to kiss an exposed part of the pillar. The basílica also has frescoes by Goya.

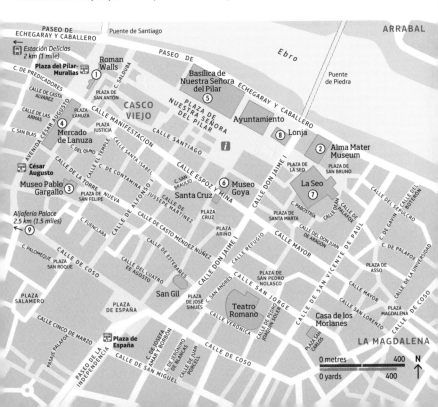

EXPERIENCE MORE

Puerto de Somport

🅰E2 🄰Huesca 🚌To Somport, Astún or Jaca
ℹPlaza del Ayuntamiento 1, Canfranc; closed Sep-Jun: Sun & Mon; www.canfranc.es

Just inside the border with France, the Somport Pass was for centuries a strategic crossing point for the Romans and Moors, and for medieval pilgrims en route to Santiago de Compostela. Today the austere scenery is specked with ski resorts. Astún is modern while El Formigal is a purpose-built resort. Non-skiers can enjoy the scenery around the Panticosa gorge. Sallent de Gállego is popular for rock climbing and fishing.

Aínsa

🅰E2 🄰Huesca 🚌 ℹAvda Ordesa 5; www.ainsa-sobrarbe.es

The capital of the kingdom of Sobrarbe in medieval times, Aínsa has retained its charm. Plaza Mayor, a broad cobbled square, is surrounded by neat terraced arcades of brown stone. On one side is the belfry of the Iglesia de Santa María – consecrated in 1181 – and on the other the restored castle.

Los Valles

🅰E2 🄰Huesca 🚂Jaca 🚌From Jaca to Hecho ℹMuseo de Arte Contemporáneo al Aire Libre, Pallar d'Agustin, Hecho, 974 37 55 05

The delightful valleys of Ansó and Hecho, formed by the Veral and Aragón Subordán rivers respectively, were once isolated due to poor road links, enabling their villages to retain traditional customs and a local dialect called *Cheso*. Now the area's crafts and costumes have made it popular with tourists. The Pyrenean foothills and forests above the valleys are good for walking, fishing and cross-country skiing.

Ansó lies in the prettiest valley, which becomes a shadowy gorge where the Río Veral squeezes between vertical crags. Many of its buildings have stone façades and steep, tiled roofs. The 16th-century church has a museum dedicated to local costume. Pieces of modern sculpture lie scattered beside the tourist information office, from an open-air festival once held here.

Benasque

🅰E2 🄰Huesca ℹCalle de San Pedro s/n; www.turismobenasque.com

Tucked away in the northeast corner of Aragón, at the head of the Esera Valley, the village of Benasque presides over a ruggedly beautiful stretch of Pyrenean scenery. Although the village has expanded greatly to meet the needs of the holiday trade, a sympathetic use of wood and stone has resulted in buildings that complement the existing older houses. It is well worth a stroll through the old centre, which is filled with delightful aristocratic mansions and

---

 PICTURE PERFECT
Peak-a-Boo

For €1, you can climb the tower of Aínsa's Iglesia de Santa Maria. This is the perfect vantage point to snap a dramatic photograph of the Peña Montañesa mountain, framed by the stone window, that looms over the town.

other striking buildings. Look out for the 13th-century Iglesia de Santa María Mayor and the Palacio de los Condes de Ribagorza. The latter has a Renaissance façade.

Above the village rises the Maladeta massif. There are magnificent views from its ski slopes and hiking trails.

For walkers, skiers and climbers, the area around Benasque has a great deal to offer. The neighbouring resort of Aramón Cerler was developed with care from a rustic village into a popular base for skiing and other winter sports.

At Castejón de Sos, 14 km (9 miles) south of Benasque, the road passes through the Congosto de Ventamillo, a scenic rocky gorge.

Sos del Rey Católico

E2 🕸Zaragoza 🚌
ℹ️ Palacio de Sada, Plaza
Hispanidad s/n (closed
Mon); www.oficina
turismosossdelrey
catolico.com

Fernando of Aragón – the so-called "Catholic King" who married Isabel of Castile and León, thereby uniting Spain – was born in this small town in 1452, thus its distinguished royal name.

 The crypt of the Iglesia de San Esteban at Sos del Rey Católico

The Palacio de Sada, the king's reputed birthplace, is among the town's grandest stone mansions. It stands in a small square amid a maze of narrow cobbled streets. At the top of the town are the remnants of a castle and the Iglesia de San Esteban. The church's font and carved capitals are noteworthy, as are the 13th-century frescoes in two of the crypt's apses. From here there are fine views over the surrounding hills.

The Gothic-arched Lonja (commodities exchange) and the 16th-century town hall (*ayuntamiento*) are located on the adjacent main square.

EAT

El Origen
Old meets new at this central Huesca spot, which is committed to Aragonese cuisine. All of the ingredients are responsibly sourced.

🅰️E2 🕸Plaza de la
Justicia 4, Huesca
🔳 elorigenhuesca.com

€€€

Casa Pardina
Tucked away in the village of Alquézar, this friendly restaurant offers a varied menu in a typical Spanish setting - it's draped in olive trees and looks out onto a hillside of tiered houses.

🅰️E2 🕸Calle Medio,
Alquézar 🔳 casa
pardina.com

€€€

La Parilla
With an old-fashioned exterior, this Benasque restaurant offers top-quality food in a charming building.

🅰️E2 🕸Carretera
Francia s/n, Benasque
📞974 55 11 34

€€€

 The hilltop village of Aínsa, surrounded by wooded hills

8

Jaca

E2 **Huesca**
Plaza de San Pedro 11; www.jaca.es

In the 8th century the people in this town bravely repulsed the Moors – an act which is commemorated in the festival of La Victoria – and in 1035 became the first capital of the kingdom of Aragón. Jaca's 11th-century cathedral, one of Spain's oldest, is much altered inside. Traces of its original splendour can be seen on the restored south porch and doorway, where carvings depict biblical scenes. The dim nave and chapels are decorated with ornate vaulting and sculpture. A museum of sacred art, in the cloisters, contains a collection of Romanesque and Gothic frescoes and sculptures from local churches. The streets that surround the cathedral form an attractive quarter.

Jaca's only other significant sight is its 16th-century citadel, a fort decorated with corner turrets. Today the town is often used as a base for exploring the Aragonese Pyrenees.

9

Monasterio de San Juan de la Peña

E2 **Huesca** **Nov-mid-Mar: 10am–2pm daily (to 5pm Sat); mid-Mar-Oct: 10am–2pm, 3:30–7pm daily (to 8pm Jun-Aug)** **1 Jan, 25 Dec** **monasteriosan juan.com**

Partially carved into a cliff, this monastery is said to have been an early guardian of the Holy Grail. In the 11th century it underwent reformation, and was the first monastery to introduce the Latin Mass in Spain. After a fire in the 1600s, the building was abandoned in favour of a newer one further up the hillside. This was later sacked by Napoleon's troops. It now houses an interpretation centre and hotel.

The striking cloister of the Monasterio de San Juan de la Peña, and *(inset)*, its exterior
↓

The church belonging to the old monastery is on two floors. The lower one is a primitive 10th-century rock-hewn crypt while the upper floor contains an 11th-century church with a triple apse hollowed out of the side of the cliff. Here, the Romanesque pantheon contains the stacked tombs of the early Aragonese kings. The exterior cloister is San Juan de la Peña's *pièce de résistance*, the capitals of its columns carved with biblical scenes.

10

Alquézar

E2 **Huesca** **Calle Arrabal s/n; www.alquezar.es**

The Moorish village of Alquézar is popular for its spectacular setting. Its main monument, the stately 16th-century collegiate church, dominates a hill jutting above the strange rock formations of the canyon of the Río Vero. Inside, the church's cloisters have capitals carved with biblical scenes. Next to it is the chapel built after Sancho I recaptured Alquézar from the Moors. Nearby are the ruined walls of the original *alcázar*, which gave the village its name.

The small town of Agüero, sat at the foot of the Mallos rock formation ↑

Castillo de Loarre

🅰 E2 **🏠 Loarre, Huesca**
🚆 Ayerbe **🚌 From Huesca**
🕐 Hours vary, check website **🚫 Nov-Feb: Mon, 1 Jan, 25 Dec**
🌐 castillodeloarre.es

The ramparts of this fortress stand majestically above the road from Ayerbe. The fortress is so closely moulded around the contours of a rock that in poor visibility it could be easily mistaken for a natural outcrop. It was used as a set for Ridley Scott's film *Kingdom of Heaven* (2005). On a clear day, the hill-top setting is stupendous, with views of surrounding orchards and reservoirs.

Inside the curtain walls is a complex founded in the 11th century on the site of what had originally been a Roman settlement. It was later remodelled under Sancho I (Sancho Ramírez) of Aragón, who established a religious community here, placing the complex under the rule of the Order of St Augustine. Within the castle walls is a Romanesque church. Sentry paths, iron ladders and flights of steps ramble precariously around the castle's towers, dungeons and keep.

⑫ Agüero

🅰 E2 **🏠 Huesca**
🌐 aytoaguero.es

The picturesque setting of this attractive village, which is clustered against a dramatic crag of eroded pudding rock known as the Mallos de Agüero, amply rewards a brief detour from the main road. As you wander around the village, the rocks are always visible, providing a wonderful backdrop.

The main reason for visiting Agüero, however, is to see the 12th-century Iglesia de Santiago. This Romanesque church is reached by a long stony track leading uphill just before the village. The capitals of the columns in this unusual triple-naved building are carved with fantastical beasts as well as scenes from the life of Jesus and the Virgin Mary. The beautiful carvings on the doorway display biblical events, including scenes from the Epiphany and Salome dancing ecstatically. The lively, large-eyed figures are attributed to the mason responsible for the superb carvings in the monastery at San Juan de la Peña.

⑬ Tarazona

🅰 E3 🏛 Zaragoza 🚌
ℹ Plaza San Francisco 1;
www.tarazona.es

Mudéjar towers stand high above the earth-coloured, mottled roofs of the ancient bishopric of Tarazona. On the outskirts of the Old Town is the cathedral, all turreted finials and pierced brickwork with Moorish cloister tracery and Gothic tombs.

In the upper town on the other side of the river, more churches, in typical Mudéjar style, can be found amid the maze of narrow hilly streets. More unusual perhaps are the former bullring, now a circular plaza enclosed by houses, and the splendid Renaissance *ayuntamiento* . This town hall, built of golden stone, has a façade carved with mythical giants and a frieze showing Carlos I's homage to Tarazona. The unique Gothic cathedral has a Baroque façade and Mudéjar towers.

Did You Know?

On 27 August, a "harlequin" tries to cross Tarazona's plaza while being pelted with tomatoes.

> Mudéjar towers stand high above the earth-coloured, mottled pantiles of the ancient bishopric of Tarazona.

⑭ Graus

🅰 E2 🏛 Huesca 🚌 ℹ Plaza Mayor 15; www.turismo graus.com

In the heart of Graus's Old Town is the unusual Plaza de España, surrounded by stone arcades and columns. It has brightly frescoed half-timbered houses and a 16th-century city hall. The home of Tomás de Torquemada, the Inquisitor General, is in the narrow streets of the old quarter. During mid-September, these streets serve as the stage for traditional Aragonese dancing during Graus's fiesta.

---

⑮ Huesca

🅰 E2 🏛 Huesca 🚉🚌
ℹ Plaza López Allué; www. huescaturismo.com

Founded in the 1st century BC, the independent state of Osca (Huesca) had a senate and an advanced education system. From the 8th century AD, the area grew into a Moorish stronghold.

Huesca is now the provincial capital. The pleasant Old Town has a Gothic cathedral, with an eroded west front surmounted by an unusual wooden gallery in Mudéjar style. Above the nave is slender-ribbed star vaulting studded with golden bosses. An alabaster altarpiece, by the master sculptor Damià Forment has a series of Crucifixion scenes in relief, highlighted by illumination.

Opposite the cathedral is the fortress-like Renaissance *ayuntamiento*. Inside hangs La Campana de Huesca, a gory 19th-century painting depicting the town's most infamous event: the beheading of a group of troublesome nobles in the 12th century by order of King Ramiro II. The massacre occurred in the former Palacio de los Reyes de Aragón, later the university and now the superb **Museo de Huesca**, containing archaeological finds and a collection of art.

Museo de Huesca

🏛 Plaza de la Universidad 1
🕐 10am–2pm & 5–8pm Tue-Sat, 10am–2pm Sun & public hols 🔒 1 & 6 Jan, 24, 25 & 31 Dec 🌐 museodehuesca.es

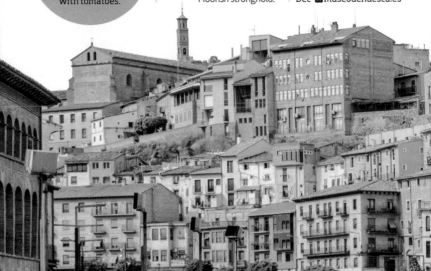

16
Santuario de Torreciudad

🅰E2 🅰Huesca 🚌To El Grado from Barbastro 🕐May-Oct: 10am-7:30pm daily (Jul & Aug: to 8:30pm); Nov-Apr: 10am-2pm & 4-6:30pm Mon-Fri, 10am-7pm Sat & Sun 🔗torre ciudad.org

This shrine was built to honour the founder of the Catholic lay order of Opus Dei – San Jose María Escrivá de Balaguer. It occupies a promontory with picturesque views. The huge church is made of red brick in a stark, modern design.

Inside, there is a surprisingly elaborate altarpiece, sheltering a glittering Romanesque Virgin, which sits in contrast to the bleak, functional nave.

Barbastro, 30 km (18 miles) to the south, has an arcaded *plaza mayor* and a 16th-century cathedral with an altar by Damià Forment.

17 ⚡ Ⓜ
Monasterio de Veruela

🅰E3 🅰Vera de Moncayo, Zaragoza 🚌Vera de Moncayo 🕐Apr-Sep: 10:30am-6pm Tue-Sun; Oct-Mar: 10:30am-8pm Tue-Sun 🔗turismodearagon.com

This Cistercian retreat, set in the green Huecha Valley near the Sierra de Moncayo, is one of the greatest monasteries in Aragón. Founded in the 12th century by French monks, the huge abbey church has a mixture of Romanesque and Gothic features. Worn green and blue Aragonese tiles line the floor of its handsomely vaulted triple nave. The well-preserved cloisters sprout exuberantly decorated beasts, busts and foliage in the Gothic style. The plain, dignified chambers make a suitable venue for art exhibitions in the summer.

In the hills to the west, the Parque Natural de Moncayo rises 2,315 m (7,600 ft). Streams race through the woodland of this nature reserve, which abounds with bird life.

← Attractive buildings towering over Tarazona's tree-lined streets

18

Calatayud

D3 Zaragoza 🚌🚂
🛈 Plaza España 1; www.
calatayud.es/turismo

Nestled in the midst of the
Sistema Ibérico mountain
range, Calatayud's huge
Moorish fortress and minaret-
like church towers are visible
from miles around. Only ruins
are left of the 8th-century
Arab castle of the ruler, Ayub,
which gave the town its name.

The church of Santa María
la Mayor features a Mudéjar
tower and an elaborate
façade in the Plateresque
style. The 17th-century church
of San Juan Real contains
some Goya paintings.

The ruins of the Roman
settlement of Bílbilis are east
of Calatayud, near Huérmeda.

The Mudéjar tower of
the church of San Juan
Real, Calatayud

19

Daroca

🅰E3 🔼Zaragoza 🛈Calle
Mayor 44; 976 80 01 29

An impressive array of battlemented medieval walls
stretches approximately 4 km
(2 miles) around this old Moorish stronghold. Although parts
of the walls have decayed,
some of the 114 towers and
gateways are still a remarkable sight, particularly from
the main road to Zaragoza.

The Colegial de Santa
María, a church in the Plaza
España, houses the Holy
Cloths from the *reconquista*.
After a surprise attack by
the Moors in 1239, priests
celebrating Mass bundled the
consecrated bread into the
linen sheets used for the altar.
Upon being unwrapped, the
cloths were said to be miraculously stained with blood.

The agricultural town of
Monreal del Campo, 42 km
(26 miles) south of Daroca,
has a saffron museum,
celebrating the local crop.

20

Alcañiz

🅰E3 🔼Teruel 🚌 🛈Calle
Mayor 1; www.alcaniz.es

Two buildings rise above the
town of Alcañiz. One is the
castle, once the headquarters
of the Order of Calatrava. This
historic building has been
converted into a parador. The
keep, the Torre del Homenaje,
has a collection of 14th-
century frescoes depicting
the conquest of Valencia by
Jaime I.

The other building is
the Iglesia de Santa María.
This church, on the sloping
Plaza de España, has a Gothic
tower and a Baroque façade.

On the same square are the
elegantly galleried Lonja
(commodities exchange), with
its lacy Gothic arches, and the
town hall (*ayuntamiento*), which
has one Mudéjar and one
Renaissance façade.

FRANCISCO DE
GOYA

Born in Fuendetodos
in 1746, Francisco de
Goya specialized in
designing cartoons for
the tapestry industry
in his early life, and in
decorating churches
such as Zaragoza's
Basílica del Pilar with
vivacious frescoes.
In 1799 he became
painter to Carlos IV,
and depicted the king
and his wife María
Luisa with unflattering
accuracy. The invasion
of Madrid by Napoleon's
troops in 1808 and
its attendant horrors
had a profound and
lasting effect on Goya's
temperament, and his
later works are imbued
with cynical despair
and isolation. He died
in Bordeaux in 1828.

 21

Fuendetodos

🅰 E3 🏠 Zaragoza 🛈 Calle Cortes de Aragón 7; 976 14 38 67

This small village was the birthplace of one of Spain's best-known artists, Francisco de Goya. The **Casa-Museo de Goya** is a cottage said to have been the painter's home. It has been furnished in an early 19th-century style.

In Cariñena, 25 km (16 miles) west of Fuendetodos, *bodegas* offer the opportunity to sample and buy the excellent, full-bodied red wine for which the region is justly renowned.

Casa-Museo de Goya

⌖ 🏠 Calle Zuloaga 3 📞 976 14 38 47 🕐 11am–2pm & 4–7pm Tue–Sun

---

22

Monasterio de Piedra

🅰 E3 🏠 Zaragoza 🚉 Calatayud 🚌 From Zaragoza 🕐 Daily 🌐 monasteriopiedra.com

Built on the site of a Moorish castle conquered by Alfonso II of Aragón and given to Cistercian monks in the 12th century, this monastery was damaged in the 19th century and subsequently rebuilt. Some 12th-century buildings remain, including the chapter-house, refectory and hostel.

In the damp cellars, the monks once distilled herbal liqueur. This was allegedly the first place in Europe where drinking chocolate was made, and there is now an exhibition on all things chocolate here.

The park in which the monastery stands is a nature reserve full of grottoes and waterfalls. A hotel and spa is now located in the old monastery buildings.

> HIDDEN GEM
> ## Memories of War
>
> Lying 14 km (9 miles) east of Fuendetodos is Belchite, site of one of the most horrific battles of the Spanish Civil War, when factions fought for control of the strategic Ebro Valley. Remains of the shell-torn town have been left as a monument to the horrors of war.

↑ Espejo Lake, located in the park of the Monasterio de Piedra

23

Valderrobres

🅰 E3 🏠 Teruel 🚌 🛈 Avenida Cortes de Aragón 7; www.valderrobres.es

Just inside Aragón's border with Catalonia, the town of Valderrobres overlooks the trout-filled Río Matarraña. Dominating the town is the **Castillo de Valderrobres**, formerly a grand palace for Aragonese royalty. Below this hollow structure stands the imposing Gothic Iglesia de Santa María la Mayor, with a huge rose window in Catalan Gothic style. The arcaded plaza in which it stands has a pleasing late 16th-century town hall.

Near Valderrobres is the mountain peak of La Caixa. Located 14 km (9 miles) from the town are the mountain passes of Beceite.

Castillo de Valderrobres

⌖ 🕐 Hours vary, check website 🌐 castillode valderrobres.com

24

Teruel

△E4 △Teruel
**🅸 Plaza de los Amantes 6;
www.turismo.teruel.es**

This industrial city has been the scene of much desperate fighting throughout the centuries, beginning with the Romans, the first to capture and civilize Celtiberian Turba.

During the *reconquista*, Teruel became a strategic frontier prize. In 1171 Alfonso II recaptured Teruel for Christian Spain, but many Moors continued to live peacefully in the city, which they embellished with beautiful Mudéjar towers. The last mosque was closed only at the height of the Inquisition, in 1502.

The old quarter is home to the wedge-shaped Plaza del Torico, with a monument of a small bull, the city's emblem. Within walking distance lie the five remaining Mudéjar towers.

1937

The Civil War's bitterest battle was fought in Teruel during this freezing winter.

THE LOVERS OF TERUEL

According to legend, in 13th-century Teruel, Diego de Marcilla and Isabel de Segura wished to marry but her wealthy family forbade the match because he was poor. Diego was given five years to make his fortune. When he returned to Teruel, laden with wealth, he found Isabel already married. Diego died of a broken heart and Isabel died the following day. The Bodas de Isabel de Segura, a festival in February, re-enacts the events.

Most striking are those of San Salvador and San Martín, both dating back to the 12th century. The latter has multi-patterned brickwork studded with blue and green ceramics. Nearby, the grand Escalinata is also crowned with Mudéjar towers, but this staircase was actually built in 1920.

The cathedral has colourful Mudéjar work, including a lantern dome of glazed tiles, and a tower completed in the 17th century. But the tombs of the famous Lovers of Teruel are beside the Iglesia de San Pedro, rather than the cathedral.

The **Museo Provincial** houses a large collection of ceramics, testifying to an industry for which Teruel has long been known.

Museo Provincial

🅰 Plaza Fray Anselmo Polanco 3 🕙 10am–2pm & 4–7pm Tue–Fri, 10am–2pm Sat & Sun 🆆 museo. deteruel.es

25

Sierra de Gúdar

△E4 △Teruel 🚌 Mora de Rubielos 🚌 Alcalá de la Selva 🅸 Calle Diputación 2, Mora de Rubielos; www.turismo. gudarjavalambre.es

This range of hills, northeast of Teruel, is a region of pine woods, jagged limestone outcrops and scrub-covered slopes. At 2,028 m (6,653 ft), Peñarroya is the highest point. Nearby Valdelinares, Spain's highest village, is a ski station. From the access roads there are panoramic views of the hills. Especially noteworthy are

→ Mudéjar-style towers at the top of the Escalinata staircase in Teruel

→ Stone dwellings clinging to the hillside in the village of Rubielos de Mora

the views from the towns of Linares de Mora and Alcalá de la Selva, which has a castle set against a backdrop of rock faces. Its Gothic-Renaissance church, with shell motifs and twisted columns, shelters the shrine of the Virgen de la Vega.

26

Rincón de Ademuz

E4 Valencia Ademuz Plaza de la Villa 1, Ademuz; www. rincondeademuz.es

This remote enclave south of Teruel belongs to the Comunidad Valenciana (p193), but is effectively an island of territory, stranded between the borders of Aragón and Castilla-La Mancha. The area has not prospered in modern times, but still has an austere charm and peaceful tracts of country scattered with red rocks.

27

Albarracín

E4 Teruel Calle San Antonio 2; www. albarracin.es

A dramatic cliff above the Río Guadalaviar is the ideal setting for this attractive cluster of mellow pink buildings. Standing on a ridge behind the

town are defensive walls and towers from Moorish times.

There is a good view of the town from below the Palacio Episcopal (Bishop's Palace). Inside the neighbouring 16th-century cathedral, which is topped by a belfry, there is a Renaissance carved wooden altarpiece depicting scenes from the life of St Peter. The treasury museum contains 16th-century Brussels tapestries and enamelled chalices.

Some of Albarracín's sturdy beamed and galleried houses have an unusual two-tier structure. The ground floor is limestone, and the overhanging upper storey is covered in rough coral-pink plasterwork. Many have been restored to their medieval form. Just outside the town are the caves of Navazo and Callejón, with their prehistoric rock paintings. Reproductions can be seen in Teruel's Museo Provincial.

28

Mora de Rubielos

E4 Teruel Calle Diputación 2; 978 80 05 29

Dominated by one of the best-preserved castles in Aragón, the municipality of Mora de Rubielos retains the remains of the old walled city, and a medieval Old Town. Most noteworthy are the fine

17th-century town hall and the church of Santa María.

Rubielos de Mora, 14 km (9 miles) to the southeast, is worth exploring for its well-preserved stone and timber buildings. Among the houses is an Augustinian convent with a Gothic reredos.

EAT

Meseguer
Great service and delicious food come together at the chic Meseguer. For the best deals, order from the tasting or set menus.

E3 Avenida Maestrazgo 9, Alcañiz aparthotelmeseguer.es

€€€

Alizia
Delicious local specialities await at this inviting spot in Albarracín. Prior booking is essential.

E4 Calle del Postigo 6, Albarracín alizia.eu

€€€

VALENCIA AND MURCIA

These fertile lands have been occupied for over 50,000 years, with the Greeks, Phoenicians, Carthaginians and Romans all settling here before the Moors arrived in the 8th century. The provinces of Castellón, Valencia and Alicante, which make up the Comunidad Valenciana, were taken from the Moors by Jaime I's Christian army in 1238 as part of the *reconquista (p64)*. Here, Jaime I established the Kingdom of Valencia. Catalan people moved into these areas following the conquest, bringing with them the Catalan language. The Kingdom of Valencia was fully incorporated into the Spanish Crown in 1707 by Filipe V, but the Catalan language remained in the area, developing into a distinct dialect known as *valencià*. This language is widely spoken and is often seen on signposts alongside Castilian Spanish in Valencia.

Murcia, to the south, was also taken from the Moors by Jaime I, in 1266, but it was incorporated into the Crown of Castile in 1304, rather than retaining any degree of independence. From the 16th to 18th centuries, Murcia's urban centre began to grow, eventually bursting out of its old city walls. Many churches were built, which still typify Murcia's cityscape today. The region has seen more than its fair share of natural disasters, with several floods and earthquakes devastating parts of the region over the centuries.

Mediterranean Sea

VALENCIA AND MURCIA

Must See

1 Valencia

Experience More

2 Costa del Azahar
3 Morella
4 El Maestrat
5 Peníscola
6 Castelló de la Plana
7 Vilafamés
8 Coves de Sant Josep
9 Alto Turia
10 Onda
11 Xàtiva
12 Monasterio del Puig
13 Sagunt
14 L'Albufera
15 Gandia
16 Dénia
17 Penyal d'Ifac
18 Xàbia
19 Guadalest
20 Novelda
21 Alcoi
22 Alicante
23 Benidorm
24 Elx
25 Orihuela
26 Illa de Tabarca
27 Torrevieja
28 Murcia
29 Lorca
30 Costa Cálida
31 Mar Menor
32 Caravaca de la Cruz
33 Cartagena

Mediterranean Sea

0 kilometres   50

0 miles   50

N

❶

VALENCIA

🗺E4 🏛Valencia ✈8 km (5 miles) SW 🚂🚌🚇 *i*Plaça de l'Ajuntament 1; www.visitvalencia.com

Spain's third-largest city is sited in the middle of the *huerta*: a fertile plain of orange groves and market gardens, and one of Europe's most intensively farmed regions. With its warm coastal climate, Valencia is known for its exuberant outdoor living. In March the city stages one of Spain's most spectacular fiestas, Las Fallas, in which papier-mâché sculptures are burned in the streets.

INSIDER TIP
Street Art

Valencia is full of thought-provoking graffiti art, including works by the renowned Argentinian street artist Escif. Tours are available that will walk you past the best of them *(www.urban adventures.com)*.

①

Palau de la Generalitat

🏛Plaça de Manises ☎963 42 46 36 ⏰9am–2pm Mon–Fri and by appt

This palace, which is now used by the Valencian regional government, was built between 1482 and 1579 but added to in the 17th and 20th centuries. It surrounds a stone patio from which staircases lead to ornate rooms.

The larger of the two Salas Doradas (Golden Chambers) has a multicoloured coffered ceiling and tiled floor. The walls of the parliament chamber are decorated with frescoes.

Did You Know?

Paella is a serious business here - there's been much debate over the inclusion of chorizo for instance.

②

Colegio del Patriarca

🏛Carrer de la Nau ⏰Tue–Sun, by appt only 🚫Aug 🌐patriarcavalencia.es

This seminary was built in 1584, and the walls and ceiling of the church are covered with frescoes by Bartolomé Matarana. During Friday morning Mass, the painting above the altar, *The Last Supper* by Francisco Ribalta, is lowered to reveal a sculpture of the Crucifixion by an anonymous 15th-century German artist.

③

Torres dels Serrans

🏛Plaça dels Furs ☎963 91 90 70 ⏰10am–7pm Mon–Fri (to 2pm Sat & Sun) 🚫1 Jan, 1 May, 25 Dec

Erected in 1391 as a triumphal arch in the city's walls, this gateway combines defensive and decorative features. Its two towers mix battlements and

←
An aerial view of
Valencia, taken
from the Miguelete

delicate Gothic tracery. The
towers can be closed for safety
reasons during wet weather.
On Sundays, entrance is fee.

④
Catedral

🏠 Plaça de la Reina
📞 963 91 81 27 ⏰ Cathedral
& Museum: 10am-6pm
Mon-Sat, 2-6pm Sun
& public hols (Nov-19 Mar:
10am-5pm Mon-Sat);
Miguelete: 10am-1pm &
4:30-7pm daily

Built originally in 1262, the
cathedral has been added
to over the ages, and its
three doorways are all in
different styles. The oldest is
the Romanesque Puerta del
Palau, but the main entrance
is the Baroque portal, the
Puerta de los Hierros.

A unique court meets on
Thursdays at noon in front of
the Gothic Puerta de los Após-
toles. For about 1,000 years,
the Water Tribunal has settled
disputes between farmers
over irrigation in the *huerta*.

Inside the cathedral, a
chapel holds an agate cup,
claimed to be the Holy Grail
and formerly kept in the
San Juan de la Peña (p184).

The cathedral's bell tower,
the Miguelete, is popular
for the views it offers from
the top. The cathedral also
houses a museum.

⑤
Llotja

🏠 Plaza del Mercado 📞 962
08 41 53 ⏰ 9:30am-7pm
Mon-Sat, 9:30am-3pm Sun

An exquisite Late Gothic hall,
built between 1482 and 1498
as a commodities exchange,
Llotja is one of Valencia's

finest buildings, and now
hosts cultural events. The
outside walls are decorated
with gargoyles and other
grotesque figures. Inside,
the ceiling of the transactions
hall features star-patterned
vaulting, supported by
beautiful spiral columns.

⑥
Museo Nacional de Cerámica Gonzalez Martí

🏠 Carrer del Querol 📞 963
08 54 29 ⏰ 10am-2pm &
4-8pm Tue-Sat, 10am-2pm
Sun ⏰ 1, 6 & 22 Jan, 1 May,
24, 25 & 31 Dec

Spain's Ceramics Museum
is housed in the mansion
of Marqués de Dos Aguas,
an 18th-century fantasy
of plasterwork, with a door
edged by an Ignacio Vergara
carving. The exhibits include

prehistoric, Greek and Roman
ceramics and pieces by Picasso.
Entrance is free on Saturday
afternoons and Sundays.

SHOP

Mercado Central
This huge iron, glass
and tile Art Nouveau
building, with its parrot
and swordfish weather-
vanes, opened in 1928
and is one of the largest
and most attractive
markets in Europe.
Every morning its 300
or so stalls are filled
with a bewildering
variety of food.

🏠 Plaça del Mercat 6
📞 963 82 91 00
⏰ 7am-3pm Mon-Sat

EAT

Here are three top spots in Valencia for paella, the city's speciality.

Restaurante Navarro
 Carrer de l'Arquebisbe Mayoral 5 restaurante navarro.com

€€€€

Casa Carmela
Carrer d'Isabel de Villena 155
 casa-carmela.com

€€€€

La Pepica
Passeig de Neptú 6
lapepica.com

€€€€

---

⑦
Jardín del Turia

 Dawn to dusk daily

Where once there was a river there is now a 10-km- (6-mile-) long strip of gardens, sports fields and playgrounds, crossed by 19 bridges. In a prominent position above the riverbed stands the Palau de la Música, a concert hall built in the 1980s. The centrepiece of the nearby children's play-ground is the giant figure of Gulliver pinned to the ground and covered with steps and slides. Jardín de Cabecera aims to re-create the Túria river's original landscape, with a lake, beach, waterwheel, waterfall and riverside wood.

The best of Valencia's other public gardens stand near the banks of the river. The largest of them, the Jardines del Real – known locally as Los Viveros – occupy the site of a royal palace which was torn down in the Peninsular War. The Jardín Botánico, created in 1802, is planted with 7,000 species of shrubs and trees.

↑ The Basílica de la Virgen de los Desamparados, situated on the Plaza del La Virgen, one of Valencia's pleasant squares

⑧
Basílica de la Virgen de los Desamparados

Plaça de la Verge
📞 963 91 92 14 ⏰ 7:45am-2pm & 4:30-9pm daily

The statue of Valencia's patroness, the Virgin of the Helpless, stands above an altar in this 17th-century church, lavishly adorned with flowers and candles. She is honoured during Las Fallas by La Ofrenda ("the Offering"), a display of flowers in the square outside the church.

---

⑨
Museu de Belles Arts

Carrer de Sant Pius V 9
⏰ 10am-8pm Tue-Sun
🚫 1 Jan, 25 Dec 🌐 museo bellasartesvalencia.gva.es

An important collection of 2,000 paintings and statues dating from the 14th to the 19th centuries is housed in this former seminary, built between 1683 and 1744.

Valencian art dating from the 14th and 15th centuries is represented by a series of golden altarpieces by Alcanyis, Pere Nicolau and Maestro de Bonastre. Velázquez's self-portrait and works by Bosch, El Greco, Murillo, Ribalta, Van Dyck and local Renaissance painter Juan de Juanes hang on the first floor. A large collection of Antonio Muñoz Degrain's hallucinatory coloured paint-ings are gathered together on the top floor, among them the disturbing *Amor de Madre*.

→ The fantastic structure of the Ciutat de les Arts i de les Ciències

⑩
Institut Valencià d'Art Modern

🅰 Carrer de Guillem de Castro 118 🕐 11am-8pm Wed-Sat (to 9pm Fri & 2pm Sun) 🌐 ivam.es

The Valencian Institute of Modern Art is one of Spain's most highly respected spaces for displaying contemporary art. The core of its permanent collection is formed of work by the 20th-century sculptor Julio Gonzalez. All art forms are represented in its temporary exhibitions, with emphasis on photography and photomontage. One of the galleries, Sala Muralles, incorporates a stretch of the old city walls.

💬 HIDDEN GEM
Beach Life

To the east of the city, the beaches of El Cabañal and La Malvarrosa are bordered by a broad and lively esplanade. Both former fishermen's districts retain some quaint, traditional houses, which are tiled on the outside to keep them cool in summer.

⑪
Museu d'Història de València

🅰 Carrer València 42, Mislata 🕐 10am-7pm Tue-Sat, 10am-2pm Sun 🌐 mhv.valencia.es

Valencia's history museum is housed in the 19th-century cistern that used to supply the city with water, now a labyrinth of pillars and arches. The displays tell the story of the city's development, from its foundations by the Romans to the present day. In each section there is a "time machine", a full-sized screen on which a typical scene of daily life is reproduced in the language of the visitor's choice.

---

⑫
Ciutat de les Arts i de les Ciències

🅰 Avinguda del Professor López Piñero 7 ☎ 961 97 46 86 🕐 Hours vary, call to check

The futuristic complex of the City of Arts and Sciences stands at the seaward end of the Jardines del Río Túria. It is made up of five stunning buildings, four of them designed by Valencian architect Santiago Calatrava.

The Palau de les Arts, the final building to be added to the complex, has a concert hall with an open-air theatre. On the other side of the Puente de Monteolivete bridge is L'Hermisfèric, an architectural pun by Calatrava on the theme of vision, consisting of a blinking eye. The "eyeball" is an auditorium equipped as an IMAX cinema and planetarium.

Next to this is the Museu de les Ciències Príncipe Felipe, a science museum contained within a structure of glass and gleaming white steel arches. The displays inside are mainly geared towards visiting school parties. Opposite the museum is L'Umbracle, a giant pergola of parabolic arches covering the complex's car park. The last part of the "city" is an aquarium, designed by architect Felix Candela as a series of lagoons and pavilions linked by bridges and tunnels.

EXPERIENCE MORE

Costa del Azahar

E4 **Castellón**
Castelló de la Plana
Castelló de la Plana
**Plaza de la Hierba s/n,
Castelló de la Plana; www.
turismodecastellon.com**

The "Orange Blossom Coast" of Castellón (Castelló) province is named after the dense citrus groves of the coastal plain. The three principal resorts are Oropesa, Peníscola and Benicàssim, where handsome old villas stand beside modern hotels and other tourist amenities. Alcossebre also has a popular beach. Vinaròs – located at the most northerly point – and Benicarló are key fishing ports supplying prawns and date mussels to local restaurants.

Morella

F3 **Castellón**
**Plaza de San Miguel;
www.morella.net**

Built on a high, isolated outcrop and crowned by a ruined castle, Morella cuts a dramatic profile. If you're up to the steep climb to the castle, it's worth it to walk around the huge stone edifice. Parts have been restored, and there are information points. On the hike up to the castle is the Convent de Sant Francesc.

Walk along Morella's medieval walls, passing through one of the six gates, which lead into a fan-shaped maze of streets and steep, tapering alleys, many of which are shaded by the eaves of ancient houses. The main street is lined with shady porticoes. In the upper part of town is the Basílica de Santa María la Mayor, which is open for a small fee, where you can marvel at its Gothic architecture and the intricate carvings inside. Its standout feature is the unique raised choir loft, reached by a finely carved spiral staircase.

El Maestrat

E3 **Castellón & Teruel**
Morella **Calle Mayor
15, Cantavieja; www.
comarcamaestrazgo.es**

Crusading warlords of the Knights Templar and the Knights of Montesa – known as *maestres* (masters) – gave their name to this lonely upland region. To rule over this frontier land, which straddles the border between Valencia and Aragón, they built fortified settlements in dramatic defensive positions, often on rocky crags. The best preserved of them is Morella. Forcall, not far from Morella, has two 16th-century mansions on its porticoed square.

MORELLA'S MIRACLE

A plaque on the wall of Morella's Calle de la Virgen marks the house in which St Vincent Ferrer is said to have performed a bizarre miracle in the early 15th century. A housewife, distraught at having no meat to offer the visiting saint, cut up her son and put him in the cooking pot. When St Vincent discovered this, he reconstituted the boy - except for one of his little fingers, which his mother had eaten to see if the dish was sufficiently salted.

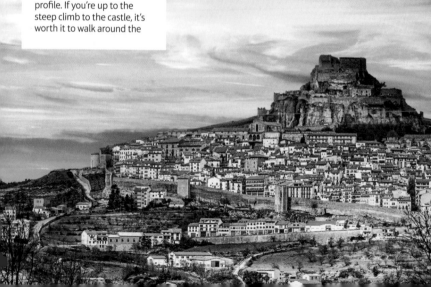

↑ Shops lining the narrow streets of Peníscola's Old Town

To the south, the village of Ares del Maestre is spectacularly sited beneath a 1,318-m- (4,300-ft-) high rock.

Cantavieja is the main town in the Aragonese part of El Maestrat. It has a pretty arcaded square. The walled village of Mirambel, nearby, has been restored to its medieval condition.

There are several spooky but fascinating shrines to the Virgin in El Maestrat, notably the cave of La Balma at Zorita, which can be reached by walking along a rocky ledge.

The scenery in most parts is striking. Fertile valleys alternate with breathtaking cliffs and bare, flat-topped mountains. Tourism is developing very slowly here: there are few places to stay and the roads can be windy and slow.

---

❺

Peníscola

 F3 🚉 **Castellón** 🚌 ℹ **Paseo Marítimo; www.peniscola.es**

The fortified Old Town of Peníscola clusters around the base of a castle, surrounded on three sides by the sea. This labyrinth of narrow winding streets and white houses is enclosed by massive ramparts. These are entered by either the Fosch Gate – reached by a ramp from the Plaza del Caudillo – or through the San Pedro Gate, from the harbour.

The **Castell del Papa Luna** was built on the foundations of an Arab fortress in the late 13th century by the Knights Templar. It later became the residence of Pedro de Luna, cardinal of Aragón. He was elected Pope Benedict XIII during the Great Schism that split the Catholic Church in the 14th century. He was deposed in 1414, but continued to proclaim his right to the papacy until his death as a nonagenarian in 1423.

Castell del Papa Luna

🎟🎫 🏛 Calle Castillo 🕐 9:30am–9:30pm daily 🔒 1 & 6 Jan, 9 Sep, 9 Oct, 25 Dec 🌐 castillode peniscola.dipcas.es

---

 TOP 5 **REGIONAL DISHES**

Paella
Rice dish containing a mix of vegetables, seafood and meat.

Fideuà
Similar to paella, but this one-pot wonder is made with noodles instead of rice.

Esgarraet
In Castellón province, aubergine is added to this dish of red peppers and cod.

Pastel de Carne Murciano
A traditional meat pie topped with patterned filo pastry.

Michirones
A stew of dried beans, meat and stock. Often served as a starter.

← The town of Morella sprawling out beneath a dramatic ruined castle

6
Castelló de la Plana

A E4 **Q** Castellón **Q** **m**
i Plaza de la Hierba s/n;
www.castellonturismo.com

Founded inland, the capital of Castellón province was relocated nearer to the coast in the 13th century. The Plaza Mayor is bordered by the market, the cathedral, the town hall and El Fadrí, a 58-m- (190-ft-) high octagonal bell tower begun in 1590 and finished in 1604.

The **Museo de Bellas Artes** contains artifacts dating from the middle Palaeolithic era, paintings from the 14th to the 19th centuries and modern ceramics from the region. An important collection of paintings attributed to Francisco de Zurbarán is also on display.

In **El Planetari** there are demonstrations of the night sky, solar system and nearest stars, plus temporary exhibits.

Museo de Bellas Artes

Q **Avda Hermanos Bou 28
C 964 72 75 00
O 10am- 2pm & 4-8pm Tue- Sat, 10am- 2pm Sun

El Planetari

Q Paseo Marítimo 1, Grao
C 964 28 29 68 **O** Oct-Jun: 9:30am-2:45pm Tue-Fri, 10:30am-2pm & 4:30- 7:45pm Sat, 10:30am-2pm Sun (Mar-Jun & Oct: also 4:30-7:45pm Tue-Fri); Jul- Sep: 9:30am- 2:30pm & 4:30-8:45pm daily

---

7
Vilafamés

A E4 **Q** Castellón **m**
i Plaza del Ayuntamiento 2; 964 32 99 70

This medieval town climbs from a plain along a rocky ridge to the restored round keep of its castle. The older, upper part of the town is a warren of sloping streets.

Located in the Old Town, a 15th-century Gothic palace houses the **Museo de Arte Contemporáneo de Vilafamés**. The contemporary artworks on display here date from 1959 to the present.

Museo de Arte Contemporáneo de Vilafamés

 Q Casa del Batlle, Calle Diputación 20 **O** 10am- 2pm & 4-6:30pm Tue- Sun **w** macvac.es

El Fadrí towering over Castelló de la Plana's cathedral ↓

EAT

La Vinya
Order from the set menu at homely La Vinya or try out the tapas.

A E4 **Q** Calle La Fuente 17, Vilafamés
C 664 38 67 38

€€€

Asoko
This chic Japanese restaurant uses the local catch to serve up imaginative sushi dishes.

A E4 **Q** Sierra de Espadan 86, Onda
C 964 91 92 93

€€€

8
Coves de Sant Josep

A E4 **Q** Vall d'Uixó, Castellón **m** Vall d'Uixó
O Mar-Oct: 10am-1:30pm & 3:30pm-6pm daily; Nov- Feb: 10am-2pm daily
C 1 & 6 Jan, 25 Dec
w covesdesantjosep.es

The caves of St Joseph were first explored in 1902. The subterranean river that formed them originally has been

charted for almost 3 km (2 miles). However, only part of this distance can be explored on a visit.

Boats take visitors along the serpentine course of the river. You may have to duck to avoid projections of rock on the way. Sometimes the narrow caves open out into large chambers such as the Sala de los Murciélagos (Hall of the Bats – the bats left when the floodlights were added). The water is at its deepest – 12 m (39 ft) – in the Lago Azul (Blue Lake). You can explore a further 250 m (820 ft) along the Galería Seca (Dry Gallery) on foot. The caves are often closed after heavy rain.

Alto Turia

E4 **Valencia** **Chelva**
Plaza Mayor 1, Chelva; www.altoturia.es

The district of Alto Turia encompasses the wooded hills of the upper reaches of the Río Turia. The area's highest peak is Pico del Remedio (1,054 m/3,458 ft), which overlooks Chelva, the district's main town. Chelva is famous for the unusual clock on its church, which shows not only the hour but the day and month as well.

The most attractive and interesting village in Alto Turia is Alpuente, situated above a dry gorge. Between 1031 and 1089, when it was captured by El Cid (p380), Alpuente was the capital of a small *taifa*, a Moorish kingdom. In the 14th century it was still important enough for the kingdom of Valencia's parliament to meet here. The town hall is confined to a small tower over a 14th-century gateway, which was later extended in the 16th century by the addition of a rectangular council chamber.

Requena, to the south, is Valencia's main wine town. Further south, Valencia's other principal river, the Xúquer

(Júcar), carves tremendous gorges near Cortes de Pallas on its way past the Muela de Cortes. This massive, wild plateau and nature reserve is crossed by one small road and a lonely dirt track.

Onda

E4 **Castellón**
Calle Ceramista Peyró; www.onda.es

Onda, home to a thriving ceramics industry, is overlooked by a ruined castle, which houses a museum of local history. However, the main attraction is the **Museo de Ciencias Naturales El Carmen**, a natural history museum belonging to a Carmelite monastery. The clever use of subdued lighting lends dramatic effect to the 10,000 plant and animal specimens that are exhibited here.

Museo de Ciencias Naturales El Carmen
Carretera de Tales
Daily (winter: Fri-Sun only); see website for details **20 Dec-7 Jan**
museodelcarmen.com

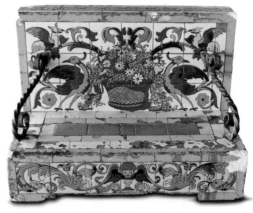

↑ A seat covered with beautiful ceramic tiles, produced in the town of Onda

11

Xàtiva

🅰 E5 🅰 Valencia 🅰 🚐
ℹ Alameda de Jaime I 50;
www.xativaturismo.com

Along the narrow ridge of
Mount Vernissa, above Xàtiva,
run the ruins of the once-grand
Castillo de Xàtiva, with 30
towers. It was largely destroyed
by Felipe V in the War of the
Spanish Succession. Felipe also
set fire to the town, which continues to wreak its revenge
in an extraordinary way – by
hanging Felipe's full-length
portrait upside down in the
Museo de Bellas Artes.
Elsewhere in the museum's
collection, you'll find
masterpieces by Josep

Did You Know?

In the 12th century,
Xàtiva became the first
European city to
produce paper.

de Ribera, who was born in
Xàtiva in 1591, and a valuable
collection of engravings by
Goya entitled *Los Disparates*
(The Follies).

Explore the streets and
squares of the Old Town,
stopping to admire the former
hospital, which has a magnificent Gothic-Renaissance
façade, and the Gothic fountain
in the Plaça de la Trinitat.

The oldest church in Xàtiva
is the Ermita de San Feliú
(Chapel of St Felix) on the
road up to the fortress. It
dates from around 1262
and is hung with a number of
14th- to 16th-century icons.

Castillo de Xàtiva

🌐 🅰 Subida del Castillo
🕐 Apr-Oct: 10am-7pm Tue-
Sun; Nov-Mar: 10am-6pm
Tue-Sun 🔲 xativaturismo.
com/entradas-castillo

Museo de Bellas Artes

🌐 🅰 Plaza Arzobispo
Mayoral 2 📞 962 28 24 55
🕐 Mid-Jun-mid-Sep: 9:30am-
2:30pm Mon-Fri, 10am-
2:30pm Sat & Sun; mid-Sep-
mid-Jun: 10am-2pm & 4-7pm
Mon-Sat, 10am-2pm Sun

SHOP

Momo

A chic clothing shop for
men, women and
children, Momo stocks
stylish outfits for
everyday wear, as
well as some more
extravagant pieces for
special occasions.

🅰 E5 🅰 Calle
Zarandona 1, Murcia
🔲 momo.com.es

Mercadillo

This weekly food
market is held on
Xàtiva's market square
every Tuesday and
Friday. Alongside the
fresh local produce,
you'll find handcrafted
household items.

🅰 E5 🅰 Plaça del
Mercat, Xàtiva
📞 962 27 33 46 🕐 Tue &
Fri morning

↑ The medieval castle of Xàtiva set against a dramatic backdrop

Monasterio del Puig

🅰E4 🄰El Puig, Valencia
🄰🄰El Puig 🄰Tue-Sat by
guided tour only at 10am,
11am, noon, 4pm & 5pm
🅦monasteriodelpuig.org

This Mercedarian monastery was founded by King Jaime I of Aragón, who conquered Valencia from the Moors in the 13th century. The monastery is now home to the Museo de la Imprenta y de la Obra Gráfica (Museum of Printing and Graphic Art), which commemorates the printing of the first book in Spain – in Valencia in 1474.

Sagunt

🅰E4 🄰Valencia 🄰🄰
🄸Plaza Cronista Chabret;
www.aytosagunto.es

In 219 BC, Hannibal, the Carthaginian commander in southern Spain, stormed and sacked Rome's ally Saguntum. All the inhabitants of the town were said to have died in the assault. The incident sparked the Second Punic War, a disaster for the Carthaginians, which ended with Rome's occupation of the peninsula.

Sagunt (Saguntо in Spanish) has reminders of the Roman occupation, including a 1st-century-AD Roman theatre, which is still used as a venue for music and plays.

The ruins of the **Castillo de Sagunt**, sprawling along the hill above the town, mark the original site of Saguntum.

Castillo de Sagunt
📞962 66 62 01 🄰10am–8pm
Tue-Sun

L'Albufera

🅰E4 🄰Valencia 🄰
🄸Carretera del Palmar,
Racó de l'Olla; 963 86 80 50

A freshwater lake on the coast, L'Albufera is a prime wetland habitat for birds. It is cut off from the sea by a wooded sandbar and fringed by a network of paddy fields, which produce a third of Spain's rice.

L'Albufera is fed by the Río Turia and connected to the sea by three channels, which are fitted with sluice gates to control the water level. The lake reaches a maximum depth of

TOP 5 VALENCIAN AND MURCIAN FIESTAS

Le Falles
Papier-mâché monuments are erected in Valencia, 15 to 19 March.

Good Friday
In Lorca, the "blue" and "white" brotherhoods compete in a procession of biblical characters.

Moors and Christians
Two costumed armies fight mock *reconquista* battles at Alcoi from 21 to 24 April.

Misteri d'Elx
A choral play takes place in Elx's Iglesia de Santa María, 11 to 15 August.

La Tomatina
A tomato explosion in Buñol (p203).

2.5 m (8 ft), and is gradually shrinking because of natural silting and the reclamation of land. In the Middle Ages the lake encompassed an area over ten times its present size.

A visitors' centre at Racó de l'Olla, on L'Albufera' eastern bank, provides information on the ecology of the lake.

↑ Bird-watchers hoping to catch a glimpse from the observatory at L'Albufera nature reserve

The exterior of the Palau Ducal, Gandia, and *(inset)* its Golden Gallery

As well as its historic appeal, Gandia, with its golden sands, has a lively beach scene.

Palau Ducal
⊘⊘ ⬛ Carrer Duc Alfons el Vell 1 🕙 10am–2pm & 5–8pm Tue–Sat
🌐 palauducal.com

🅖 Gandia

🄰 E4 🄰 Valencia ⬛⬛
🄸 Avinguda Marqués de Campo; www.visitgandia.com

In 1485, Rodrigo Borja (who became Pope Alexander VI) was granted the title of Duchy of Gandia. He founded the Borgia clan and, together with his children, was later implicated in murder and debauchery. Rodrigo's great-grandson later redeemed the family name by joining the Jesuit order. He was canonized as St Francis Borja by Pope Clement X in 1671.

You can visit the house in which he was born, the **Palau Ducal** (Duke's Palace). Its simple Gothic courtyard belies the ornate chambers within, especially the grand, Baroque Golden Gallery.

🅖 Dénia

🄰 E5 🄰 Alicante ⬛⬛⬛
🄸 Plaza Oculista Baigues 9; www.denia.net

This town takes its name from the Roman goddess Diana – a temple in her honour was excavated here.

It is now a fishing port and holiday resort, and its town centre spreads around the base of a low hill. The **Castillo de Dénia**, once an Arab fortress, on the hill's summit overlooks the harbour. The entrance gate, the Portal de la Vila, survives, but it was altered in the 17th century. The Palacio del Gobernador (Governor's House), within the castle, contains an archaeological museum, which shows the development of Dénia from 200 BC to the 18th century.

North of the harbour is the sandy beach of Las Marinas. To the south, Les Rotes beach is good for snorkelling.

Castillo de Dénia
⊘ ⬛ Carrer Sant Francesc
🄲 966 42 06 56 🕙 Hours vary, call ahead 🚫 1 Jan, 25 Dec

Ibiza Calling

The Penyal d'Ifac affords spectacular views of the Costa Blanca. You'll see the "white coast" unfolding below as you climb but, on a clear day, you'll be rewarded by the sight of Ibiza at the summit.

17
Penyal d'Ifac

🅰E5 🅐Calp, Alicante 🅡Calp 🚌Calp 🅘Avenida de los Ejércitos Españoles, 30, Calp; 965 83 69 20

Known by the Phoenicians as the "Northern Rock", the rocky outcrop of the Penyal d'Ifac seems to rise vertically out of the sea. One of the Costa Blanca's most dramatic sights, this 332-m- (1,089-ft-) tall block of limestone looks virtually unclimbable. However, a short tunnel, built in 1918, allows walkers access (limited from July to August) to the gentler slopes on its seaward side. Allow about 2 hours for the round trip, which starts at the visitors' centre above Calp harbour. The steep walk takes you up slopes covered with juniper and fan palm, with the waves crashing below.

The Penyal d'Ifac is also home to 300 types of wild plant, including several rare species. Migrating birds use it as a landmark, and the salt flats below it are an important habitat for them. The rock was privately owned until 1987, when the regional government acquired it and turned it into a nature reserve.

Situated below the rock is the town of Calp, which is renowned for its beaches.

18
Xàbia

🅰E5 🅐Alicante 🚌 🅘Plaza de la Iglesia 4; www.xabia.org

Once the site of an Iberian settlement, the centre of Xàbia (also known as Jávea) is perched on a hill. The town centre has a uniformed look as many of its buildings are made from the local Tosca sandstone. One of these golden buildings, the 16th-century Iglesia de San Bartolomé, was fortified to serve as a refuge in times of invasion, and missiles could be dropped onto attackers via openings over the door.

Xàbia's centre perches above miles of rocky coastline. Once the haunt of pirates and smugglers, the seafront is now lined with modern developments, but the beaches are still beautiful.

↑ Seascape showing Calp and its beach with the Penyal d'Ifac in the distance

Looking down over the resort of Alicante and out to sea at sunset

19

Guadalest

🅰E5 🚉Alicante 🛈Avenida de Alicante; www.guadalest.es

Despite drawing coach loads of day-trippers, this pretty mountain village remains relatively unspoiled. This is largely because its older part is accessible only on foot by a single entrance: a sloping tunnel cut into the rock on which the castle ruins and the church's distinctive belfry are precariously perched.

Guadalest was founded by the Moors, who carved the surrounding hillsides into terraces and planted them with crops. These are still irrigated by the original ditches constructed by the Moors.

The intriguing **Museo de Microminiaturas** displays a microscopic version of Goya's *Fusilamiento 3 de Mayo* painted on a grain of rice; his *The Naked Maja*, painted on the wing of a fly; and a sculpture of a camel passing through the eye of a needle.

Museo de Microminiaturas

 🏠Plaza San Gregorio 14 ⏰Summer: 10am-9pm daily; winter 10am-6pm daily 🌐miniaturasguadalest.com

20

Novelda

🅰E5 🚉Alicante 🚌🚍 🛈Carrer Mayor 6; www.novelda.es

The industrial town of Novelda is dominated by marble factories, but it is the exquisitely preserved Art Nouveau house, the **Casa-Museo Modernista**, that is of special interest. It was built in 1903 and rescued from demolition in 1970. The building's three floors are furnished in period style. There are few straight lines or functional shapes and almost every inch of wall space has some floral or playful motif.

Casa-Museo Modernista

 🏠Calle Mayor 24 📞965 60 02 28 ⏰10am-2pm Tue-Fri

21

Alcoi

🅰E5 🚉Alicante 🚍🚌 🛈Plaça de Espanya, 14; www.alcoyturismo.com

Sited at the confluence of three rivers and surrounded by high mountains, Alcoi is an industrial city. It is best known for its festival, when mock battles are staged between Moors and Christians *(p205)*, as well as *peladillas* – almonds coated in sugar.

On the slopes above Alcoi is Font Roja, a nature reserve offering pleasant walks, and a shrine marked by a towering statue of the Virgin Mary.

North of Alcoi is the Sierra de Mariola, a mountain range famed for its herbs. The best point of access is the village of Agres. A scenic route runs from here to the summit of Mont Cabrer at 1,390 m (4,560 ft).

22

Alicante

🅰E5 🚉Alicante 🚌🚍🚍🚍 🛈Rambla Méndez Núñez 41; www.alicanteturismo.com

A port and seaside resort built around a natural harbour, Alicante (Alacant) is the main city on the Costa Blanca. Both the Greeks and Romans established settlements here. In the 8th century the Moors refounded the city under the shadow of Mount Benacantil. Its summit is now occupied by the **Castillo de Santa Bárbara**, which dates from the 16th century. Its top battlements offer rewarding views over the whole city.

The focus of the city is the Explanada de España, a palm-lined promenade along the waterfront. The 18th-century **ayuntamiento** is worth visiting for the sumptuous Salón Azul (Blue Room). A metal disc on the marble staircase is used as a reference point in measuring the sea level all around Spain.

Local artist Eusebio Sempere (1924–85) assembled works by Dalí, Miró, Picasso and other 20th-century artists to form the **Museo de Arte Contemporáneo (MACA)**.

Castillo de Santa Bárbara

⊛⊛ ☐ Playa del Postiguet 【 965 14 71 60 ◐ Apr-Sep: 10am-10pm daily; Oct-Mar: 10am-8pm daily ☒ castillo desantabarbara.com

Ayuntamiento

☐ Plaza del Ayuntamiento 1 【 966 90 08 86 ◐ 9am-2pm Mon-Fri

Did You Know?

Benidorm has the third largest number of skyscrapers in Europe, second only to London and Milan.

Museo de Arte Contemporáneo (MACA)

☐ Plaza de Santa María 3 ◐ Summer: 11am-8pm Tue-Sat, 11am-2pm Sun; winter: 10am-2pm Tue-Fri ☒ 1 & 6 Jan, 1 May, 25 Dec & local hols ☒ maca-alicante.es

---

Benidorm

🅰 E5 ☐ Alicante 🚃🚌 🚹 Plaza Canalejas, El Torrejó; www.visitbenidorm.es

With forests of skyscrapers dwarfing its two long beaches, Benidorm is far removed from the fishing village it once was in the early 1950s.

Benidorm has more accommodation than any other resort on the Mediterranean, but its clientele has changed since the 1980s, when its name was synonymous with "lager louts". A huge public park and open-air auditorium used for cultural events, the Parque de l'Aigüera, is emblematic of the face-lift Benidorm has gone through. The town now attracts elderly holiday-makers from the north of Spain and English expats, the latter coming for splendid sandy beaches, reliable sunshine and nightclubs. There's also a lively LGBTQ+ scene.

Benidorm's Old Town is set on a promontory between two beaches. From the Balcón del Mediterráneo, a park ending in a giant fountain, there is a good view of the town. A short way out to sea is the Illa de Benidorm, a wedge-shaped island served by ferries, which is a nature reserve for sea birds.

La Vila Joiosa (Villajoyosa), to the south, is much older than Benidorm. Its most notable sight is a line of brightly painted houses that overhang the riverbed.

The older part of Altea, to the north of Benidorm, is a delightful jumble of white houses, narrow streets and long flights of steps around a blue-domed church.

24

Elx

A E5 **A** Alicante 🚂🚌
i Plaza Parque 3;
www.visitelche.com

The forest of over 300,000 palm trees that surrounds Elx (Elche) on three sides is said to have been planted by the Phoenicians around 300 BC. Part of it has been enclosed as a garden called the **Jardín Huerto del Cura**. Some of the palms found here are dedicated to notable people.

Elx's blue-domed Baroque church, the Basílica de Santa María, was built in the 17th century to house the Misteri d'Elx. Beside it is **La Calahorra**, a Gothic tower. A clock on the roof next to the town hall has two 16th-century mechanical figures, which strike the hours on bells.

Jardín Huerto del Cura

🌳🕐 **A** Porta de la Morera 49 🕐 Daily (hours vary, check website) 🌐 jardin.huerto delcura.com

La Calahorra

A Calle Uberna 14 ☎ 966 65 82 43 🕐 10am-2pm & 3-6pm Tue-Sat, 10am-2pm Sun

↑ A walkway through the palms at the Jardín Huerto del Cura in Elx

25

Orihuela

A E5 **A** Alicante 🚂🚌
i Plaza de la Soledad 1;
www.orihuelaturistica.es

In the 15th century Orihuela was prosperous enough for Fernando and Isabel to stop and collect men and money here on their way to do battle against the Moors at Granada. The Gothic cathedral houses Velázquez's *The Temptation of St Thomas Aquinas* in its museum. Among the exhibits in the **Museo San Juan de Dios,** an archaeological museum, is a processional float with a 17th-century statue of a she-devil, *La Diablesa.*

Museo San Juan de Dios

 A Calle del Hospital ☎ 966 74 31 54 🕐 10am-2pm & 5-8pm Tue-Sun

26

Illa de Tabarca

A E5 **A** Alicante 🚢 From Santa Pola/Alicante
i Santa Pola; 966 69 22 76

The best point of departure for the Illa de Tabarca is Santa Pola. Small and flat, Illa de Tabarca is divided into two parts: a stony, treeless area of level ground known as *el campo* (the countryside), and a walled settlement, which is entered through three gateways. The settlement was laid out on a grid plan in the 18th century, on the orders of Carlos III, to deter pirates.

> 📷 PICTURE PERFECT
> **Port-able Camera**
>
> Despite its diminutive size, the Illa de Tabarca offers plenty of photo opportunities and the island's tiny port is particularly picturesque. Focus on the little boats bobbing on the sea.

27

Torrevieja

A E5 **A** Alicante **i** Paseo Vista Alegre; www.turismo detorrevieja.com

During the 1980s, Torrevieja grew at a prodigious rate as thousands of Europeans purchased homes here. Before tourism, the town's source of income was sea salt and the saltworks are the most productive in Europe. The *habaneras* festival celebrates Cuban music brought back by salt exporters.

28

Murcia

A E5 **A** Murcia 🚂🚌
i Plaza Cardenal Belluga, Ayuntamiento Building; www.turismodemurcia.es

This university city on the Rio Segura was founded in AD 825 by the Moors and centres on the pedestrianized

↑ Murcia's imposing cathedral, fronting the Plaza del Cardenal Belluga

Calle de la Trapería, linking the cathedral and the Plaza Santo Domingo. The **Casino**, a gentlemen's club founded in 1847, stands on this main street. It is entered through an Arab-style patio, fashioned on the royal chambers of the Alhambra. Inside, the huge ballroom has a polished parquet floor and is illuminated by chandeliers.

Work on the cathedral began in 1394 over the foundations of Murcia's central mosque. Though it was consecrated in 1467, the building continued to be augmented over the years. The cathedral has two exquisite side chapels. The first, the Capilla de los Vélez, was built between 1490 and 1507. The second, the Capilla del Junterón, dates from the early 16th century. The cathedral museum displays grand Gothic altarpieces and a frieze from a Roman sarcophagus.

Sculptor Francisco Salzillo (1707–83) was born in Murcia, and the **Museo Salzillo** exhibits nine of his *pasos* – sculptures on platforms.

Step back in time at the **Museo Etnológico de la Huerta de Murcia**, 7 km (4.5 miles) out of town. A traditional, thatched Murcian farmhouse forms part of the museum.

Casino

◈ ◈ 🏠 Calle de la Trapería 18 📞 968 21 53 99 🕐 Aug: 10:30am–2:30pm Mon–Sat; Sep–Jul: 10:30am–7:30pm daily

Museo Salzillo

◈ 🏠 Plaza de San Agustín 3 🕐 15 Jun–15 Sep: 10am–2pm Mon–Fri; 16 Sep–14 Jun: 10am–5pm Mon–Sat, 11am–2pm Sun & public hols 🌐 museosalzillo.es

Museo Etnológico de la Huerta de Murcia

🏠 Avda Principe, Alcantarilla 📞 968 89 38 66 🕐 Jun, Jul, Sep: 9am–8pm Tue–Fri, 10am–2pm & 4–7:30pm Sat, 10am–2pm Sun; Oct–May: 9am–7pm Tue–Fri, 10am–2pm & 4–7:30pm Sat, 10am–2pm Sun 🚫 Aug & public hols

EAT

Cabaña Buenavista

A gastronomical experience - the tasting menu is the best way to sample the international flavours on offer.

🅰 E5 🏠 Urb Buenavista, El Palmar, Murcia 🌐 restaurantela cabaña.es

---

Mano A Mano

A Spanish take on an Italian classic, this pizza place will fill you up for a fraction of what you might expect to pay.

🅰 E5 🏠 Calle Gutiérrez Mellado 9, Murcia 🌐 manoamano-pye.com

Puerto de Mazarrón
on the Costa Cálida,
illuminated as dusk falls ↑

29

Lorca

 D5 Murcia
Plaza de España 7;
www.lorcaturismo.es

The farmland around Lorca is a fertile oasis in one of Europe's most arid areas. Lorca was an important staging post on the Via Heraclea, as witnessed by the Roman milepost standing in a corner of the Plaza San Vicente. During the wars between Moors and Christians in the 13th to 15th centuries, Lorca became a frontier town between Al Andalus and the Castilian territory of Murcia. Its castle dates from this era, although only two of its original 35 towers remain. The castle was badly damaged in the 2011 earthquake but it has since been repaired and there is now a parador inside. After Granada fell, the town lost its importance and, except for one surviving gateway, its walls were demolished.

LORCA EARTHQUAKE 2011

On 11 May 2011 a series of tremors struck Lorca. The worst came at 6:47pm, when a 5.1-magnitude earthquake hit. Tragically, ten people died and many more were injured during the disaster. Many buildings were damaged, including one of the castle's 13th-century towers and the Iglesia de Santiago. It was Spain's worst earthquake since 1956, when a similar incident killed 12 people in Granada.

The central Plaza de España is lined with handsome stone buildings. One side of the square is occupied by the Colegiata de San Patricio (Church of St Patrick), built between 1533 and 1704, and the only church in Spain dedicated to the Irish saint.

30

Costa Cálida

E6 Murcia Murcia
Murcia Plaza Antonio
Cortijos, Águilas; www.
murciaturistica.es

The most popular resorts of Murcia's Costa Cálida – "Warm Coast" – are around the Mar Menor. Between Cabo de Palos and Cabo Tinoso the few small beaches are dwarfed by the surrounding cliffs. The resorts of the southern part of the coast are relatively quiet. There are several fine beaches at Puerto de Mazarrón, while at nearby Bolnuevo the wind

has eroded soft rocks into strange shapes. The growing resort of Águilas marks the southern limit of the coast, at the border with Andalucía.

31

Mar Menor

E5 Murcia San Javier
To Cartagena, then bus
La Manga Gran Vía
Km 0, La Manga; www.
marmenor.es

The high-rise holiday resort of La Manga, built on a long, thin, sandy strip, separates the Mediterranean and the Mar Menor, literally the "Smaller Sea".

Really a large lagoon, the sheltered Mar Menor can be 5° C (9° F) warmer than the Mediterranean in summer. Its fragile ecosystem has long been under threat from over-development and intensive farming, but new laws have finally been introduced to mitigate the damage.

From either La Manga or Santiago de la Ribera you can make a ferry trip to the Isla Perdiguera, one of the five islands in the Mar Menor.

These days the region is very built-up, but it is possible to escape the crowds by heading to the Parque Regional de Calblanque, which has wild dunes and unspoiled beaches.

Caravaca de la Cruz

Ⓐ D5 **Ⓜ Murcia** **𝒊 Calle de las Monjas 17; www.caravaca.org**

A town of ancient churches, Caravaca de la Cruz's fame lies in its castle, which houses the Santuario de la Vera Cruz (Sanctuary of the True Cross). This is where a double-armed cross is said to have appeared miraculously in 1231 – 12 years before the town was seized by Christians. The highlight of the Vera Cruz fiesta is the Race of the Wine Horses, which commemorates the lifting of a Moorish siege of the castle and the appearance of the cross. The cross was dipped in wine, which the thirsty defenders then drank and recovered their fighting strength.

Just to the north of Caravaca de la Cruz, nestled among the foothills on Murcia's western border, is the pretty village of Moratalla. This jumble of steep streets and stone houses sits beneath the remains of a 15th-century castle. Cehegín, east of Caravaca, is a partially preserved 16th- and 17th-century town.

↑ The sacred cross in the Santuario de la Vera Cruz, Caravaca de la Cruz

↑ An exhibit at the Museo Nacional de Arqueología Subacuática, Cartagena

Cartagena

Ⓐ E5 **Ⓜ Murcia** **✈ San Javier** **🚌🚆🚢** **𝒊 Palacio Consistorial, Plaza del Ayuntamiento 1; www.turismo.cartagena.es**

The first settlement founded in the natural harbour of Cartagena was constructed in 223 BC by the Carthaginians. Although the city declined in importance in the Middle Ages, its prestige increased in the 18th century when it became a naval base.

The impressive Roman theatre and its museum, the **Museo del Teatro Romano**, offer an insight into this period in Cartagena's history. Elsewhere, you can walk the Roman street and see a section of the Byzantine Wall, built between AD 589 and 590, in the **Domus del Pórtico Gallery**. Other notable attractions are the **Museo Nacional de Arqueología Subacuática,** housing treasures from Greek and Roman wrecks, the **Museo Arqueológico Municipal**, which has exhibits covering all periods of the city's history, and the **Museo-Refugio de la Guerra Civil,** where visitors can learn about Cartagena's role in the Spanish Civil War.

Museo del Teatro Romano

🏛🏛 **Ⓐ Plaza del Ayuntamiento 9** **🕐 May-Sep: 10am-8pm Tue-Sat, 10am-2pm Sun; Oct-Apr: 10am-6pm Tue-Sat, 10am-2pm Sun** **🌐 teatroromanocartagena.org**

Domus del Pórtico Gallery

Ⓐ Calle Doctor Tapia Martínez **📞 968 50 79 66** **🕐 Hours vary, call ahead**

Museo Nacional de Arqueología Subacuática

🏛 **Ⓐ Paseo Alfonso XII** **🕐 15 Apr-15 Oct: 10am-9pm Tue-Sat, 10am-3pm Sun; 16 Oct-14 Apr: 10am-8pm Tue-Sat, 10am-3pm Sun & public hols** **🌐 museoarqua.mcu.es**

Museo Arqueológico Municipal

🏛 **Ⓐ Calle Ramón y Cajal 45** **🕐 9am-2pm & 5-8pm Tue-Fri, 11am-2pm Sat & Sun** **🌐 museoarqueologico.cartagena.es**

Museo-Refugio de la Guerra Civil

Ⓐ Calle Gisbert 10 **📞 968 50 00 93** **🕐 16 Mar-Jun & 16 Sep-4 Nov: 10am-7pm Tue-Sun; Jul-15 Sep: 10am-8pm daily; 5 Nov-15 Mar: 10am-5:30pm Tue-Sun**

A DRIVING TOUR
THE COSTA BLANCA

Length 180 km (112 miles) **Stopping-off points** Denia; Benidorm; Alicante **Terrain** An easy drive along the well-maintained N332

Less hectic than the Costa del Sol (p522) and with warmer winters than the Costa Brava (p172), the Costa Blanca occupies a prime stretch of Spain's Mediterranean coastline. This driving tour takes you from Gandia – the closest point to Valencia – down the coast to the resort of Torrevieja. Between Gandia and Altea, the beaches are broken by dramatic cliffs and coves, whereas the long stretches of sandy beach from Altea to Alicante have been heavily built up with apartment blocks and hotels. South from Alicante, as far as Torrevieja, the scenery is drier and more barren, relieved only by the wooded sand dunes of Guardamar del Segura.

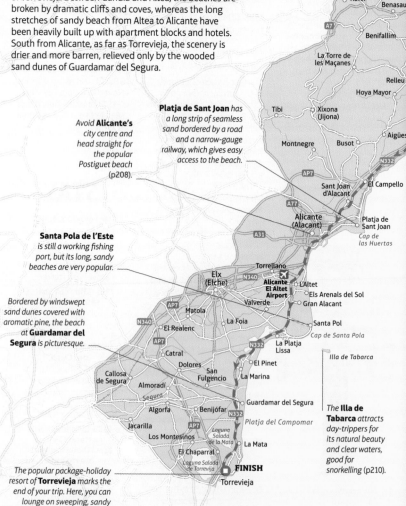

Avoid **Alicante's** city centre and head straight for the popular Postiguet beach (p208).

Platja de Sant Joan has a long strip of seamless sand bordered by a road and a narrow-gauge railway, which gives easy access to the beach.

Santa Pola de l'Este is still a working fishing port, but its long, sandy beaches are very popular.

Bordered by windswept sand dunes covered with aromatic pine, the beach at **Guardamar del Segura** is picturesque.

The popular package-holiday resort of **Torrevieja** marks the end of your trip. Here, you can lounge on sweeping, sandy beaches to the south (p210).

The **Illa de Tabarca** attracts day-trippers for its natural beauty and clear waters, good for snorkelling (p210).

Start at **Gandia**, which marks the southern end of the Costa de Valencia. Here, there are extensive beaches of fine sand (p206).

Stop for a snorkel at **Dénia's** rocky Les Rotes beach (p206).

El Grau
Gandia (Gandía)
START
AP7
Bellreguard
Oliva
N332
AP7
Pego
La Vall d'Ebo
Ondara
Dénia (Denia)
Les Rotes
Cap de Sant Antoni
Beniaia
Pedreguer
Xàbia (Jávea)
Gata de Gorgos
CV734
Cala
Blanca
Cap de la Nau
(Cabo de la Nao)
Fageca
Parcent
Alcalalí
N332
La Granadella
Castell de
Castells
Benissa
Solgros
Tàrbena
Moraira
Guadalest
Punta de Moraira
nimantell
Callosa
d'en Sarrià
Calp (Calpe)
Aitana
,557 m
,108 ft)
Polop
N332
Penyal d'Ifac
(Peñón d'Ifach)
Sella
L'Olla
Altea
Aqualandia
l'Albir
Orxeta
Benidorm
AP7
N332
La Vila Joiosa
(Villajoyosa)
Isla de
Benidorm

Blanca

Costa

Locator Map
For more detail see p194

VALENCIA
AND
MURCIA

The Costa
Blanca

Most of the coastline around **Xàbia** is punctuated by cliffs and coves (p207).

Altea is a resort with an unspoiled, whitewashed Old Town on a hilltop (p209). Beneath it is a long, shingle beach.

Have lunch on **Benidorm's** liveliest beach, Levante, which has been voted one of the ten best beaches in the world (p209).

*Mediterranean
Sea*

0 kilometres   15
0 miles   15
N

Swimming at Cala del Palangre, one of Torrevieja's beaches ↑

Did You Know?

The term "Costa Blanca" was coined by British European Airways to promote its flights.

NORTHERN SPAIN

The winding path to San Juan de Gaztelugatxe on the Costa Vasca

EXPLORE
NORTHERN SPAIN

This section divides Northern Spain into three colour-coded sightseeing areas, as shown on the map below. Find out more about each area on the following pages.

Atlantic Ocean

Ortigueira

Ferrol
Viveiro
Ribadeo
Luarca
Luanco
Gijón

A Coruña
Vilalba
Canero
Avilés

Carballo
Betanzos
Sierra de Meira
Tineo
Oviedo
Villavicios

Santa Comba
ASTURIAS
Infiesto

Arzúa
Lugo
Pola de Lena
Mieres

Santiago de Compostela
GALICIA
p222

A Estrada
Lalín
Chantada

Ribeira
GALICIA
Ponferrada
León

Pontevedra
Carballiño
Monforte de Lemos
Montes de León
Astorga

Vigo
Ourense

Xinzo de Limia
Verín
Benavente

Bragança

Chaves

Barcelos
Braga
Mirandela
Miranda do Douro
Toro

Guimarães
Zamora

Amarante
Vila Real

Porto
Penafiel

Espinho
Lamego
Salamanca

PORTUGAL

Viseu
Ciudad Rodrigo

Aveiro
Guarda

SPAIN

La Rochelle

Saintes

Royan

Soulac-sur-Mer

Bordeaux

Arcachon

Bay of Biscay

FRANCE

Dax

Costa Verde

Biarritz

Orthez

Llanes

Santander

Santoña

Castro-Urdiales

Bermeo

San Sebastian

Arriondas

CANTABRIA

Laredo

Bilbao

Zarautz

Eibar

Hernani

ASTURIAS AND CANTABRIA
p244

Llodio

PAÍS VASCO

Zumárraga

Pyrenees

Vitoria-Gasteiz

Pamplona

NAVARRA

Miranda de Ebro

THE BASQUE COUNTRY, NAVARRA AND LA RIOJA
p260

Embalse de Yesa

CASTILLA Y LEÓN

Burgos

LA RIOJA

Sierra de la Demanda

Calahorra

Palencia

Tudela

Valladolid

Aranda de Duero

Soria

Zaragoza

Peñafiel

ARAGÓN

Medina del Campo

Almazán

Calatayud

Segovia

CASTILE-LA MANCHA

Ávila

MADRID

Guadalajara

0 kilometres 50
0 miles 50

N

GETTING TO KNOW
NORTHERN SPAIN

Countless visitors are drawn to the magnificent landscape of the north, with its sandy Atlantic beaches and intense blue waters, green mountains and verdant valleys. The cities, too, are enthralling: Santiago de Compostela, San Sebastián and Bilbao all give Barcelona and Madrid a run for their money.

GALICIA

PAGE 222

Tucked away in the northwest corner of the peninsula, Galicia is Spain's greenest region, as well as its main seafaring one. Three of its four provinces have an Atlantic coastline and, inevitably, its cuisine is based around the daily catch. Inland, much of Galicia retains a medieval quality; the misty, emerald countryside is dotted with old granite villages and *pazos* – traditional stone manor houses. Those who brave the massive Camino de Santiago pilgrimage will experience this time-warped land at its finest as they journey to Santiago de Compostela, Galicia's capital.

Best for
Verdant landscapes and sparkling-fresh seafood

Home to
Santiago de Compostela

Experience
Joining the pilgrims on the legendary Camino de Santiago

PAGE 244

ASTURIAS AND CANTABRIA

These two provinces are straddled by the Picos de Europa mountain range, whose jagged peaks offer excellent rock-climbing and hiking opportunities. On the coast, you'll find the ancient seaside town of Santillana del Mar and many sandy coves, while Santander and Oviedo are busy university cities with a rich cultural life. Some of the earliest examples of art exist in Cantabria, most notably at Altamira, where the cave drawings and engravings are among the oldest to be found in Europe.

Best for
Outdoor activities and ancient art

Home to
Parque Nacional de los Picos de Europa

Experience
The ancient paintings in the Cueva de Tito Bustillo

PAGE 260

THE BASQUE COUNTRY, NAVARRA AND LA RIOJA

The Basque people are great deep-sea fishers and seafood plays a major role in their imaginative cuisine, regarded by many as the best in Spain. This gourmet paradise is complemented by La Rioja to the south – a fertile region of vegetable gardens and, most famously, vineyards. Navarra, meanwhile, is perhaps best known for an event that takes place in its capital, Pamplona, every July – the running of the bulls.

Best for
World-class cooking and unique traditions

Home to
Bilbao, San Sebastián

Experience
A warm-bodied red from the source, at a vineyard in La Rioja

GALICIA

The oldest evidence of early humans in Galicia dates back around 120,000 years. By the time the Roman conquerors arrived in the 2nd century BC, the area was inhabited by the Celtic Gallaeci, from whom the region takes its name. After the fall of the Western Roman Empire, Galicia existed as an independent kingdom, first under the Suebi people (whose conversion to Christianity saw Galicia officially adopt the religion) and then the Visigoths. Following a brief occupation by the Moors, Galicia was reconquered by Christian forces and subsumed into the Kingdom of Asturias, which was itself later absorbed into the Kingdom of Castile.

The discovery of the supposed tomb of St James the Apostle in the 9th century AD confirmed medieval Santiago de Compostela as Europe's most important religious shrine, after St Peter's in Rome. Pilgrims from beyond the Pyrenees first flocked to this holy site along what became the Camino de Santiago in the 11th century, following the scallop shells that line the route.

The establishment of a central Spanish state in the 15th century saw Galicia's distinct culture and language, *galego*, sidelined. This erosion persisted until the 19th century, when the *Rexurdimento* (revival) of all things Galician began in earnest, particularly the use of *galego* as a literary language. Franco's regime suppressed this resurgence until his death, after which Galicia regained its autonomy in 1981, and its culture was fiercely celebrated once more. Today, *galego* is an everyday language, spoken fluently by over half of Galicians.

GALICIA

Must See
1 Santiago de Compostela

Experience More
2 A Coruña
3 Betanzos
4 Mondoñedo
5 Rías Altas
6 Pontevedra
7 A Toxa
8 Padrón
9 Costa da Morte
10 Vigo
11 A Guarda
12 Tui
13 Verín
14 Baiona
15 Celanova
16 Ourense
17 Lugo
18 Monasterio de Ribas de Sil
19 Monasterior de Oseira
20 Vilar de Donas
21 O Cebreiro

↑ The terracotta roofs of the sprawling Mosteiro de San Martiño Pinario

1

SANTIAGO DE COMPOSTELA

🗺️ A2 ✈️ A Coruña 🚌 10 km (6 miles) north 🚆🚌 ℹ️ Calle Rúa do Vilar 63; www.santiagoturismo.com

Santiago de Compostela was Christendom's third most important place of pilgrimage in the Middle Ages, after Jerusalem and Rome *(p223)*. And, today, more than 200,000 pilgrims journey to the city every year.

1

Museo das Peregrinacións e de Santiago

📍 Praza das Praterías 2 📞 881 867 315 🕐 9:30am-8pm Tue-Fri, 11am-7:30pm Sat, 10:15am-2:45pm Sun 🚫 1 & 6 Jan, 1 May, 16 Aug, 24-25 & 31 Dec

This museum, founded in 1951, has three main focuses. It considers pilgrimage as a general concept, the Camino de Santiago in particular, and the city of Santiago de Compostela – the pilgrimage's end point. It also hosts temporary exhibitions about pilgrimages elsewhere in the world. Entry is free after 2:30pm on Saturdays, all day Sunday and on some holidays throughout the year.

2

Mosteiro de San Martiño Pinario

📍 Praza da Inmaculada 5 🕐 Church: Jun-Oct: 10am-8pm daily; Nov-May: 11am-7pm daily 🌐 espacio culturalsmpinario.com

This huge monastery, the second largest in Spain, dominates Santiago de Compostela's Praza da la Inmaculada. It is now home to a theological school and is not open to the public. Visitors can enter the impressive Baroque church, however, which has a huge double altar and an ornate Plateresque façade with carved figures of saints and bishops.

3

Museo do Pobo Galego

📍 Costa de San Domingos s/n 🕐 11am-6pm Tue-Sat (to 2pm Sun & public hols) 🌐 museodopobo.gal

Housed in a former convent, this museum tells the story of Galicia's history and culture. The building alone is worth

---

📷 PICTURE PERFECT
Spiral Staircase

Within the Museo do Pobo Galego, photographers shouldn't miss the chance to snap a shot of the triple-helix staircase, with its branches twirling elegantly upwards to wrap themselves around a circle of sunlight.

a visit, with its most intriguing features being the triple-helix staircase and the adjoining church, admission to which is included in the price of entry to the museum. Most of the signage around the museum is in *galego* and Castilian only, but there is some English-language information available from reception.

---

④

Hostal dos Reis Católicos

🏠 Praza do Obradoiro 1
🌐 parador.es

Built by the Catholic monarchs in the late 15th century as an inn and hospital for sick pilgrims, this magnificent building sits proudly on the Praza do Obradoiro. Now a parador, it is thought to be one of the oldest hotels in the world. Parts of it remain open to the general public, such as its courtyards. A stand-out feature is its elaborate Plateresque doorway.

⑤

Centro Galego de Arte Contemporánea (CGAC)

🏠 Rúa Valle Inclán 2
🕐 11am-8pm Tue-Sun
🌐 cgac.xunta.gal

This impressive collection of contemporary art is housed in a stark granite building, which was designed by Portuguese architect and Pritzker-prize-winner Álvaro Siza between 1988 and 1993. The museum was established to promote local contemporary artists but, alongside Galician works, you'll find artists from the rest of Spain, Portugal and South America well represented here.

There are some 1,200 works on show, including some pieces that were created specifically for this space. Alongside the permanent collection, the light-flooded gallery also hosts temporary exhibitions and workshops for both adults and children.

Outside, Siza collaborated with the Galician landscape gardener Isabel Aguirre to preserve an orchard, which was once attached to the convent that borders the site. Siza painstakingly designed the building to make it look as though it is part of the wall surrounding this garden. It's a lovely place to sit and relax after exploring the museum, or enjoy great views across the city from the terrace.

EAT

Casa Marcelo
An affordable spot to enjoy a Michelin-starred menu. If you simply can't decide, the chef will be happy to select and prepare a tasting menu for you.

🏠 Rúa Hortas 1
📞 981 55 85 80

€€€

O Curro da Parra
Situated right next to the market, this trendy restaurant uses only fresh local produce to create Galician dishes with gourmet twists.

🏠 Rúa Traversa 20
🌐 ocurrodaparra.com

€€€

Abastos 2.0
Make the most of being near the ocean by sampling the delicious seafood on offer at this small but impressive venue. Tasting menus are available, so you can try as many tapas as possible.

🏠 Praza Abastos, Caestas 13-18 🕐 Sun 🌐 abastos douspuntocero.com

€€€

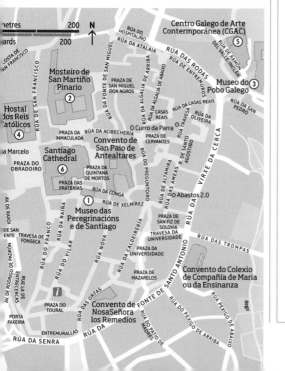

(6) 🏛 Ⓜ

SANTIAGO CATHEDRAL

🏠 Praza do Obradoiro 🕐 Cathedral: 8am-9pm daily;
Museum: 10am-2pm & 4-7pm Tue-Sat, 10am-2pm Sun
📅 1 Jan, 25 Jul, 25 Dec 🌐 catedraldesantiago.es

With its twin Baroque towers soaring high over the
Praza do Obradoiro, this monument to St James is a
majestic sight, as befits the finishing line of the
Camino de Santiago (p232).

Constructed between the 11th and 13th centuries,
the cathedral stands on the site of a 9th-century
basilica built by Alfonso II. The resulting melting
pot of architectural styles only serves to remind
visitors of this building's status as one of the
greatest shrines in Christendom. As you walk
through the famous Pórtico da Gloria, you'll be
greeted by the same interior that met pilgrims
in medieval times.

Did You Know?

The scallop shells
marking the Camino
symbolize the fact that
St James was once
a fisherman.

The twin towers
are 74 m
(243 ft) high.

Statue of St James

The richly sculpted
Baroque Obradoiro
façade was added
in the 18th century.

Pazo de Xelmírez, the
old archbishop's palace

The Pórtico da
Gloria is sculpted
with statues of
the apostles.

Touching the Santo dos
Croques (Saint of Bumps)
with the forehead is said to
impart luck and wisdom.

← A fountain in the shadow
of Santiago Cathedral's
clock tower

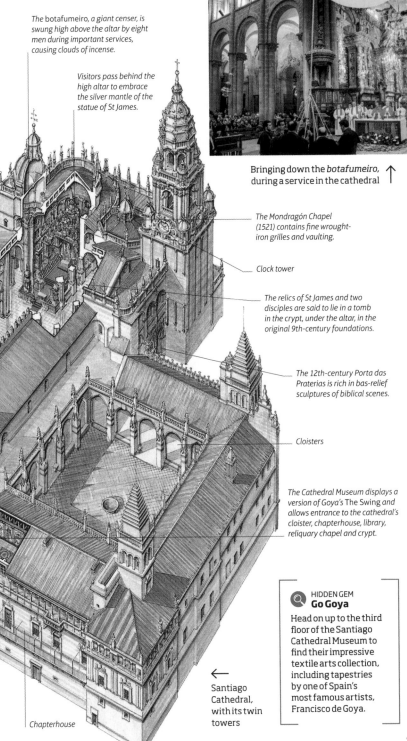

The *botafumeiro*, a giant censer, is swung high above the altar by eight men during important services, causing clouds of incense.

Visitors pass behind the high altar to embrace the silver mantle of the statue of St James.

Bringing down the *botafumeiro*, during a service in the cathedral ↑

The Mondragón Chapel (1521) contains fine wrought-iron grilles and vaulting.

Clock tower

The relics of St James and two disciples are said to lie in a tomb in the crypt, under the altar, in the original 9th-century foundations.

The 12th-century Porta das Praterias is rich in bas-relief sculptures of biblical scenes.

Cloisters

The Cathedral Museum displays a version of Goya's The Swing and allows entrance to the cathedral's cloister, chapterhouse, library, reliquary chapel and crypt.

← Santiago Cathedral, with its twin towers

Chapterhouse

> ### 🔍 HIDDEN GEM
> **Go Goya**
>
> Head on up to the third floor of the Santiago Cathedral Museum to find their impressive textile arts collection, including tapestries by one of Spain's most famous artists, Francisco de Goya.

Must See

A SHORT WALK
SANTIAGO DE COMPOSTELA

Distance 1 km (0.5 miles) **Nearest train station**
Santiago de Compostela **Time** 15 minutes

With its narrow streets and old squares, the city centre is
compact enough to explore on foot. So, if the Camino de
Santiago sounds completely overwhelming, why not take
this gentle stroll through the city to get a tapas-size taste
of the famous pilgrimage instead? The route even finishes
at the Praza do Obradoiro, where the Camino also reaches
its climax. Around this grand square is an ensemble of
historic buildings that has few equals in Europe. The local
granite gives a harmonious unity to the mixture of
architectural styles. And, of course, the hallowed
Santiago Cathedral looms over them all.

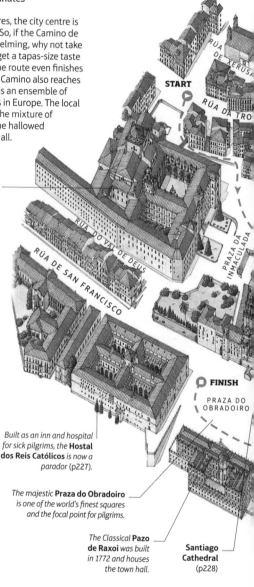

START

RÚA DE XERUS...

RÚA DA TRO...

PRAZA DA INMACULADA

RÚA DO VAL DE DEUS

RÚA DE SAN FRANCISCO

The Baroque church of the **Mosteiro
de San Martiño Pinario** *has a huge
double altar and an ornate Plateresque
façade with carved figures of saints
and bishops (p226).*

FINISH

PRAZA DO
OBRADOIRO

*Built as an inn and hospital
for sick pilgrims, the* **Hostal
dos Reis Católicos** *is now a
parador (p227).*

The majestic **Praza do Obradoiro**
*is one of the world's finest squares
and the focal point for pilgrims.*

The Classical **Pazo
de Raxoi** *was built
in 1772 and houses
the town hall.*

**Santiago
Cathedral**
(p228)

↑ Santiago Cathedral,
dominating the Praza do
Obradoiro, at dusk

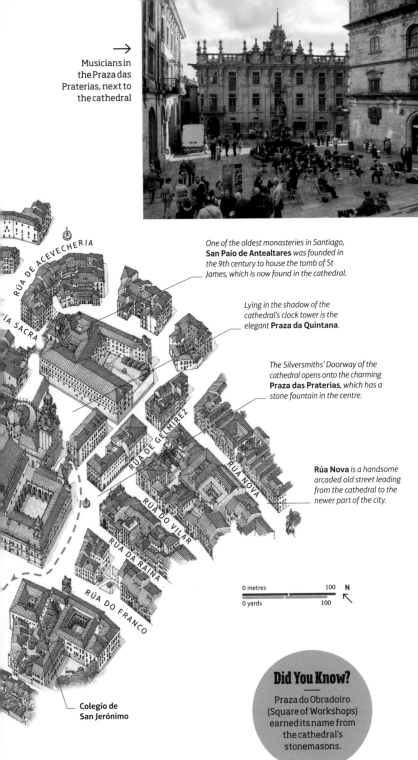

→ Musicians in the Praza das Praterias, next to the cathedral

One of the oldest monasteries in Santiago, **San Paio de Antealtares** was founded in the 9th century to house the tomb of St James, which is now found in the cathedral.

Lying in the shadow of the cathedral's clock tower is the elegant **Praza da Quintana**.

The Silversmiths' Doorway of the cathedral opens onto the charming **Praza das Praterias**, which has a stone fountain in the centre.

Rúa Nova is a handsome arcaded old street leading from the cathedral to the newer part of the city.

RÚA DE ACEVECHERIA

ÍA SACRA

RÚA DE GELMIREZ

RÚA NOVA

RÚA DO VILAR

RÚA DA RAINA

RÚA DO FRANCO

Colegio de San Jerónimo

| 0 metres | 100 | N |
| 0 yards | 100 | |

↙

Did You Know?
—
Praza do Obradoiro (Square of Workshops) earned its name from the cathedral's stonemasons.

A LONG WALK
CAMINO DE SANTIAGO

Distance About 770 km (480 miles) **Walking time** Four weeks **Difficulty** The route begins with a steep climb through the Pyrenees and there are several other challenging parts

According to legend the body of Christ's apostle James was brought to Galicia. In AD 813 the relics were supposedly discovered at Santiago de Compostela, where a cathedral was built in his honour (p228). In the Middle Ages half a million pilgrims a year flocked there from all over Europe, crossing the Pyrenees at Roncesvalles (p286) or via the Somport Pass (p182). They often donned the traditional garb of cape, long staff and curling felt hat adorned with scallop shells, the symbol of the saint. The various routes, marked by the cathedrals, churches and hospitals built along them, are still used by travellers today. Here, we guide you on the French Route.

Atlantic Ocean

*End your walk as pilgrims have for centuries – at the door of **Santiago Cathedral** (p228).*

*You need to walk the last 100 km (62 miles) – from **Sarria** to Santiago de Compostela (p226) – to be eligible for a Compostela Certificate.*

*One of the main pilgrim stops, **León Cathedral** (p370) contains one of Spain's finest collections of stained glass.*

O Cebreiro (p241) has a 9th-century church and some of the ancient pallozas the pilgrims often used for shelter.

Ponferrada's huge Templar castle stands close to the town centre (p384).

*Once a Roman city, **Astorga** (p386) was an important halt on the pilgrim route in the Middle Ages.*

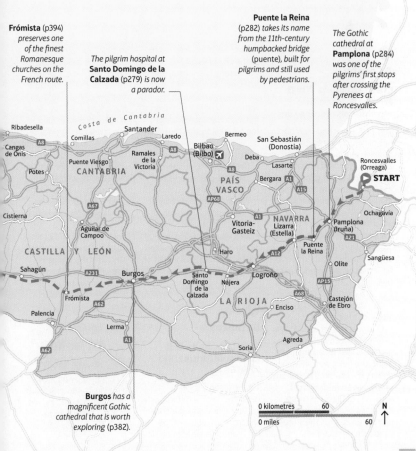

Locator Map
For more detail see p224, p246 and p262

GALICIA

Camino de Santiago

← Walking along pretty Calle del Carmen, on the approach to the centre of Pamplona

Bay of Biscay

Frómista (p394) *preserves one of the finest Romanesque churches on the French route.*

The pilgrim hospital at **Santo Domingo de la Calzada** (p279) *is now a parador.*

Puente la Reina (p282) *takes its name from the 11th-century humpbacked bridge (puente), built for pilgrims and still used by pedestrians.*

The Gothic cathedral at **Pamplona** (p284) *was one of the pilgrims' first stops after crossing the Pyrenees at Roncesvalles.*

Costa de Cantabria

Ribadesella

Comillas Santander Laredo Bermeo San Sebastián (Donostia)

Cangas de Onis

Bilbao (Bilbo) Deba Lasarte

Potes Puente Viesgo Ramales de la Victoria **CANTABRIA**

Roncesvalles (Orreaga) **START**

Cistierna

Bergara

PAÍS VASCO

Ochagavía

Aguilar de Campoo

Vitoria-Gasteiz **NAVARRA** Pamplona (Iruña)

Lizarra (Estella)

CASTILLA Y LEÓN

Sahagún

Burgos Santo Domingo de la Calzada Nájera Logroño

Haro

Puente la Reina Olite

Sangüesa

Frómista

Palencia **LA RIOJA**

Lerma Enciso Castejón de Ebro

Soria Agreda

Burgos *has a magnificent Gothic cathedral that is worth exploring (p382).*

0 kilometres 60

0 miles 60

N ↑

EXPERIENCE MORE

② A Coruña

 A1 A Coruña ✈🚌🚐
🛈 Praza de María Pita;
www.turismocoruna.com

This proud city and busy port has played a sizable role in Spanish maritime history. Felipe II's doomed Armada sailed from here to England in 1588. Today, the sprawling industrial suburbs contrast with the elegant city centre, which is laid out on an isthmus leading to a headland. The Torre de Hércules, Europe's oldest working lighthouse, is a famous local landmark. Built by the Romans and rebuilt in the 18th century, it still flashes across the deep. Climb its 242 steps for a wide ocean view.

On the large, arcaded Praza de María Pita, the city's main square, is the handsome town hall. From here, you can walk down to La Marina, the seafront promenade, which is lined with tiers of glass-enclosed balconies or *galerías*. Built as protection against the strong winds, they explain why

A Coruña is often referred to as the City of Glass.

A Coruña has several fine Romanesque churches, such as the Iglesia de Santiago, with a carving of its saint on horseback situated beneath the tympanum, and the Iglesia de Santa María, with a tympanum carved with the Adoration of the Magi. The latter is one of the best-preserved 12th-century buildings in Galicia.

The quiet Jardín de San Carlos contains the tomb of the Scottish general Sir John Moore, who was killed in 1809 as the British army evacuated the port during Spain's War of Independence from France.

③ Betanzos

 A1 A Coruña 🚉🚌
🛈 Praza de Galicia 1; 981 77 66 66

The handsome town of Betanzos lies in a fertile valley slightly inland. Its broad main square has a replica of the Fountain of Diana at Versailles.

In its steep, narrow streets are fine old houses and Gothic churches. The Iglesia de Santiago, built in the 15th century by the tailors' guild, has a statue of St James on horseback above the door. The Iglesia de San Francisco, dating from 1387, has statues of wild boars and a heraldic emblem of Earl Fernán Pérez de Andrade, whose 14th-century tomb is inside the church. For centuries his family were the overlords of the region.

Around 20 km (12 miles) north of Betanzos is the pretty fishing village of Pontedeume, which features narrow, hilly streets and a medieval bridge.

Did You Know?

Nuestra Señora la Inglesa was rescued from London's St Paul's Cathedral during the Reformation.

A Coruña's elegant town hall, standing on Praza de María Pita

4

Mondoñedo

🅰B1 🚗Lugo 🚌 ℹ️Praza da Catedral 34; 982 50 71 77

This delightful town is set in a fertile inland valley. Stately houses with carved coats of arms and *galerías* line the main square, which is dominated by the cathedral, a building of golden stone crowned by 18th-century Baroque towers. Inside, the high altar holds the fabled *Nuestra Señora la Inglesa* (the English Madonna), a polychrome statue.

The **Museo Diocesano**, entered through the cathedral, contains large 16th-century Flemish panels and important pieces made of silver and ivory, as well as notable works by Zurbarán and El Greco.

Museo Diocesano

🔄 🏠Praza da Catedral 📞982 52 10 06 🕐10:15am-1:50pm & 4:15-6:30pm Tue-Sat, 10:15-11:45am, 12:45-1:50pm & 4:30-7:50pm Sun

5

Rías Altas

🅰B1 🚗Lugo & A Coruña 🚆Ribadeo 🚌Viveiro ℹ️Travesía da Travesía Riveira 4, Foz; 982 13 24 26

The "upper rivers" are a series of inlets found along Galicia's north coast from Ribadeo to A Coruña. These deep *rías* are interspersed with coves and headlands, small resorts and fishing villages, while hills covered with forests of pine and eucalyptus lie inland.

The lovely, winding Ría de Ribadeo forms the border with Asturias's Costa Verde (*p250*). To the west of the river is the small fishing port of Foz, which has two good beaches. Nearby, the medieval Iglesia de San Martín de Mondoñedo, standing alone on a hill, contains carvings of biblical scenes on its transept capitals. Viveiro, a summer holiday resort 37 km (23 miles) away, is a handsome old town surrounded by Renaissance walls and gateways, typically Galician glassed-in balconies, or *galerías*, and a Romanesque church. Near the pretty fishing village of O Barqueiro is the headland of Estaca de Bares, recognizable by its lighthouse and wind turbines.

Westward along the coast, the lovely Ría de Ortigueira leads to the fishing port of the same name, characterized by neat white houses. Around this area there are also many wild and unspoiled beaches. High cliffs rise out of the sea near the village of San Andrés de Teixido, whose church is the focal point for pilgrims on 8 September. According to legend, those who

Nuestra Señora la Inglesa, in the high altar of Mondoñedo's cathedral

EAT

Restaurante O Fado
Tucked away on a peninsula in A Coruña, this restaurant specializes in seafood. The standout dish is the *arroces* - a creamy rice dish.

🅰A1 🏠Estrada Circunvalación, A Coruña 🌐restaurante-o-fado.negocio.site

Bar Puerto
This restaurant right next to Vigo's buzzing port serves seafood bought daily from the local market. The owners pride themselves on their traditional Galician menu.

🅰A2 🏠Rúa República Argentina 15, Vigo 📞986 22 20 44

Restaurante Rocamar
Incredible sea views accompany the equally impressive seafood at this traditionally Galician restaurant in Baiona. The daily catches are always local.

🅰A2 🏠Lugar Baredo s/n, Baiona 🌐restaurante rocamar.com

fail to visit the church in their lifetime will come back to it as an animal in the afterlife. The village of Cedeira, which sits on a quiet bay, is a rich summer resort with neat lawns, modern houses with *galerías*, and a long, curving beach.

6 Pontevedra

A2 **Pontevedra**
Casa da Luz, Praza da Verdura s/n; www.visit-pontevedra.com

Pontevedra lies inland, at the head of a long *ría* backed by green hills. The delightful Old Town is typically Galician and has a network of cobbled alleys and tiny squares with granite calvaries and flower-filled balconies.

On the Praza de la Leña, two 18th-century mansions, along with two other buildings in the adjacent streets, make up the **Museo de Pontevedra**, one of the best museums in Galicia. Its Bronze Age treasures are superb. Among the paintings are 15th-century Spanish primitives, canvases by Zurbarán and Goya, and on the top floor a collection by Alfonso Castelao, a Galician artist and nationalist who forcefully depicted the misery endured by his people during the Spanish Civil War.

The Gothic Ruinas de San Domingos, on the south side of the Old Town, are also part of the Museo de

Pontevedra, with Roman steles and Galician coats of arms and tombs.

Museo de Pontevedra

Calle Pasanteria 2-12
10am-9pm Tue-Sat, 11am-2pm Sun museo.depo.es

Ruinas de San Domingos

 Avenida Montero Rios 1
15 Mar-Oct: 10am-2pm & 4-7:30pm Tue-Sat, 11am-2pm Sun; Nov-14 Mar: email gabinetedidactico.museo@depo.es museo.depo.es

7 A Toxa

A2 **Near O Grove, Pontevedra** **Praza do Corgo, O Grove; 986 73 14 15**

A tiny pine-covered island joined to the mainland by a bridge, A Toxa (La Toja in Castilian) is one of the most stylish resorts in Galicia. The belle époque palace-hotel and a cluster of luxury villas add to the island's grand atmosphere.

A Toxa's best-known landmark is its small church, which is covered with scallop shells. Across the bridge is O Grove (El Grove), a thriving family resort and fishing port on a peninsula, with holiday hotels and flats alongside glorious beaches.

(p232)

> **INSIDER TIP**
> **Some Like it Hot**
>
> If you're a bit of a risk-taker, try some of Padrón's famous green peppers. More often than not, they are mild, but one pepper in every few platefuls will pack a real punch.

8 Padrón

A2 **A Coruña**
Avenida Compostela; 646 59 33 19

Famed for its piquant green peppers, this town was a seaport until it silted up. Legend has it the boat carrying the body of St James to Galicia *(p232)* arrived here. The supposed mooring stone lies below the church's altar.

The leafy avenue beside the church features in the poems of one of Galicia's greatest writers, Rosalia de Castro (1837-85). Trace her steps at the **Museo Rosalia de Castro**.

Museo Rosalia de Castro

A Matanza Jul-Sep: 10am-2pm & 4-8pm Tue-Sat, 10am-1:30pm Sun; Oct-Jun: 10am-1:30pm Tue-Sun museos.xunta.gal/gl/casa-rosalia

The rugged coastline at Cabo Vilán, Costa da Morte ↑

Costa da Morte

⬛A5 ⬛A Coruña ⬛A Coruña, Malpica ⬛Praza de María Pita, A Coruña; www.turismo.gal/que-visitar/xeodestinos/costa-da-morte

From Malpica to Cabo Fisterra the coast is wild and remote. It is called the Costa da Morte – "Coast of Death" – because of the many ships lost in storms or smashed on the rocks by gales over the centuries. There are no coastal towns, only fishing villages specializing in *percebes* (barnacles), destined for the region's restaurants.

The most northerly point of the Costa da Morte, Malpica, has a picturesque fishing port. Moving south, Laxe has good beaches and safe bathing and Camariñas is a picturesque

> **It is called the Costa da Morte – "Coast of Death" – because of the many ships lost in storms or smashed on the rocks by gales over the centuries.**

←

The unique Capela das Cunchas on A Toxa island, covered with scallop shells

fishing village where women make bobbin-lace in the streets. Look out for a group of futuristic wind turbines in nearby Cabo Vilán. Next you reach Corcubión, which exudes a faded elegance, and, lastly, Cabo Fisterra "where the land ends". This cape is a good place to watch the sun go down over the Atlantic.

Vigo

⬛A2 ⬛Pontevedra ⬛⬛⬛ ⬛Cánovas del Castillo 3; www.turismodevigo.org

Galicia's largest town is also the biggest fishing port in Spain. It's in a lovely setting near the mouth of a deep *ría* spanned by a high suspension bridge, and is surrounded by wooded hills. Vigo is not noted for its buildings but does have striking modern sculptures such as Juan José Oliveira's statue of horses in the Praza de España. The oldest part of the town, Barrio del Berbes, is near the port and used to be the sailors' quarter. Its cobbled alleys are full of bars and cafés where you can find some of the finest tapas. The Mercado de la Piedra, better known by its Galician name Mercado de A Pedra, is located near the port and sells super fresh fish at great prices.

STAY

Sercotel Blue Coruna
A sleek hotel close to A Coruña's sights and beaches. Free drinks are offered throughout the afternoon.

A1 ⬛Rúa Juana de Vega 7, A Coruña ⬛hotelbluecoruna.com

€€€

A Maquia
Rural boutique hotel with excellent views of the Ría de Pontevedra. There's a swimming pool, and it's just a short walk to the beach.

A2 ⬛Avenida de Laño 17, Pontevedra ⬛amaquia.com

€€€

Gran Hotel Nagari Boutique & Spa
This five-star hotel in Vigo is great value. You won't want to leave the opulent rooftop pool.

A2 ⬛Plaza de Compostela 21, Vigo ⬛gran hotelnagari.com

€€€

↑ Foundations of a Celtic settlement on the hillside at A Guarda

 11

A Guarda

A2 ◎Pontevedra
🚌 🛈Praza do Reloxo 1;
www.turismoaguarda.es

The little fishing port of A Guarda (La Guardia) is famous for seafood and is particularly well known for its lobsters.

On the slopes of Monte de Santa Tecla are the remains of a Celtic settlement of some 100 round stone dwellings dating from around 600–200 BC. The **Museo de Monte de Santa Tecla** explores the settlement.

FISHING IN SPAIN

The Spanish eat more seafood than any other European nation except Portugal. The country has Europe's largest fishing fleet in terms of catch. Much of this is caught offshore, where octopus, mackerel, clams and lobster are plentiful. But, the stocks in the seas around Spain have become depleted because of overfishing and an oil spill in 2002, forcing trawlers to venture further afield. There are now only about 9,500 boats that land Spain's catch.

About 10 km (6 miles) north, the tiny Baroque Monasterio de Santa María stands by the beach at Oia. Semi-wild horses roam the hills surrounding the town and, in May and June, are rounded up for grooming in a series of day-long fiestas.

Museo de Monte de Santa Tecla

⊛⊛ 🏠A Guarda 📞690 01 70 38 ◎Summer: 10am–8pm Tue–Sun; winter: 11am–5pm Tue–Sun 🚫Jan

---

 12

Tui

A2 ◎Pontevedra 🚇🚌
🛈Praza de San Fernando;
www.tui.gal

Spain's main frontier town with Portugal, Tui (Tuy) stands on a hillside above the Río Miño. Its graceful old streets curve up to an old quarter and the 12th-century hilltop cathedral. The two countries were often at war during the Middle Ages, and as a result the church is built in the style of a fortress, with towers and battlements. It has a cloister and choir stalls and a richly decorated west porch.

Nearby is the Iglesia de San Telmo, dedicated to the patron saint of fishermen, whose Baroque ornamentation shows a Portuguese influence. Near

the cathedral is an iron bridge, the Puente Internacional, built by Gustave Eiffel in 1884 to stretch across the river to Valença do Minho in Portugal.

The Romanesque Iglesia de Santo Domingo, beside the Parque de la Alameda, has ivy-covered cloisters and tombs with carved effigies. The church overlooks the river, which is used in August for the Descent of the Río Miño, a canoe race.

13

Verín

B2 ◎Ourense 🚌
🛈Rúa Irmáns La Salle s/n; 988 41 16 14

Though it stands amid vineyards, Verín's mineral springs have given it a thriving bottled water industry. The town has many old houses with arcades and glass balconies (galerías). The Castelo de Monterrei, built during the wars with Portugal, is 3 km (2 miles) to the west. Inside its three rings of walls are two keeps, an arcaded courtyard and a 13th-century church with a carved portal.

→

The magnificent interior of the Monasterio de San Salvador, Celanova

The castle once housed a monastery and hospital. Now a parador, it can still be visited on a guided tour.

Baiona

A2 **Pontevedra** **Paseo Ribeira; www.turismodebaiona.com**

The *Pinta*, one of the caravels from the fleet of Christopher Columbus, arrived at this small port on 1 March 1493, bringing the first news of the fleet's landing in the Americas. Today Baiona (Bayona) is a popular summer resort, its harbour a mix of pleasure and fishing boats. The 12th- to 17th-century Iglesia Antigua Colegiata de Santa María is Romanesque with Cistercian influences. Symbols on the arches indicate the local guilds that helped build the church.

A royal fortress once stood on Monterreal promontory, to the north of town. Sections of its defensive walls remain, but the interior has been converted into a smart parador. A walk around the battlements offers superb views of the coast.

On the coast a short distance to the south is a huge granite and porcelain statue of the Virgen de la Roca sculpted by Antonio Palacios in 1930. Visitors can climb up inside the statue.

Celanova

A2 **Ourense** **Praza Maior 1; 988 43 22 01**

On the main square of this little town is the massive Monasterio de San Salvador, also known as the Monasterio de San Rosendo, after its founder. Established during the 10th century and later rebuilt, it is mainly Baroque, though one of its two lovely cloisters is Renaissance. The enormous

church of this Benedictine monastery has an ornate altarpiece and Gothic choir stalls. In the garden is the 10th-century Mozarabic Iglesia de San Miguel.

⑯ Ourense

🅰A2 🚉Ourense 🚉🚌
ℹ️ Isabel la Católica 2; 988 36 60 64

The old quarter of Ourense was built around the city's well-known thermal springs, Fonte das Burgas. Even today, these spout water at a temperature of 65° C (150° F). This part of the city is the most interesting, particularly the small area around the arcaded Plaza Mayor. Here the cathedral, founded in AD 572 and rebuilt in the 12th–13th centuries, has a vast gilded reredos by Cornelis de Holanda. On the triple-arched doorway are carved figures reminiscent of the Pórtico da Gloria at Santiago (*p228*). Nearby is the elegant 14th-century cloister, the Claustro de San Francisco.

Another landmark is the 13th-century Puente Romano, a seven-arched bridge that crosses the Río Miño, north of town. Built on Roman foundations, it is now pedestrianized.

The towns of Allariz, 25 km (16 miles) south, and Ribadavia, to the west, have old Jewish quarters with narrow streets, as well as Romanesque churches. Ribadavia is also noted for its Ribeiro wines – a dry white and a port-like red – and has a wine museum.

---

⑰ Lugo

🅰B2 🚉Lugo 🚉🚌 ℹ️Praza do Campo 11; www.turismo gal

Capital of Galicia's largest province, Lugo was also an important centre under the Romans. Attracted to the town by its thermal springs, they built what is now the finest surviving Roman wall in Spain. The wall, which encircles the city, is about 6 m (20 ft) thick and 10 m (33 ft) high, with ten gateways. Six of these give access to the top of the wall, from which there is a good view of the city.

Inside the wall, the Old Town is lively, with pretty squares. In the Praza de Santo Domingo is a black statue of a Roman eagle, built to commemorate Augustus's capture of Lugo from the Celts in the 1st century BC. The large, Romanesque cathedral is modelled on that of Santiago. It features an elegant Baroque cloister and a chapel containing the alabaster statue of Nuestra Señora de los Ojos Grandes (Virgin of the Big Eyes). The **Museo Provincial** exhibits local Celtic and Roman finds, while the **Museo Interactivo da Historia de Lugo** presents the city's history with high-tech exhibits in a modern building.

→
Café tables on the attractive Praza Maior in Ourense

Museo Provincial

 Praza da Soidade
🕐 9am-9pm Mon-Fri,
10:30am-8pm Sat, 11am-
2pm Sun 🌐 museolugo.org

Museo Interactivo da Historia de Lugo

📍 Parque da Milagrosa
🕐 11am-1:30pm & 5-7:30pm
Tue-Sat, 5-8pm Sun
🌐 lugo.es

18

Monasterio de Ribas de Sil

🅰 B2 📍 Ribas de Sil, Ourense
📞 988 01 01 10 🕐 Daily

Near its confluence with the Miño, 28 km (17 miles) from Ourense, the Río Sil carves a deep curving gorge. A hairpin road winds to the top of the gorge, where the Romanesque Gothic Monasterio de Ribas de Sil is set high above the chasm. Converted into a parador, it has an enormous glass wall in one of its three cloisters.

19

Monasterio de Oseira

🅰 A1 📍 Oseira, Ourense
🕐 For tours only at
10:30am, noon, 3:30pm,
4:30pm & 5:30pm Mon-Sat,
12:45pm, 3:30pm, 5pm &
6:30pm Sun 🌐 mosteirode
oseira.org

This monastery stands in a lovely wooded valley near the hamlet of Oseira, named after

---

> **GREAT VIEW**
> ## Gorgeous Panorama
>
> As you climb up to the Monasterio de Ribas de Sil, look down over the Canón do Sil for an awe-inspiring view. Down in the gorge, dams of the Río Sil form two jewel-like reservoirs of dark-green water.

↑ The grand exterior of the Monasterio de Oseira, with its manicured gardens

the bears (*osos*) that once lived in this area.

The grand Baroque building is crowned by a soaring dome, supported by four columns. Look out for the curious statue on the doorway of the Virgin as a nurse, with St Bernard kneeling at her feet. The interior of the 12th- to 13th-century church is typically Cistercian in its simplicity.

20

Vilar de Donas

🅰 B2 📍 Lugo 🛈 Palas de
Rei, Avenida de Compostela
28; 982 38 00 01

This hamlet on the Camino de Santiago (*p232*) has a small church, called San Salvador, just off the main road. Inside are tombs of some of the Knights of the Order of Santiago, as well as some gorgeous frescoes painted by the nuns who lived here until the 15th century.

The Cistercian Monasterio Sobrado de los Monjes, to the northwest of Vilar de Donas, has a medieval kitchen and chapterhouse, and a church with unusual domes.

21

O Cebreiro

🅰 B2 📍 Lugo 🚌 🛈 Plaza
de España 4; 982 36 71 03

In the hills in the east of Galicia is one of the most mystical villages on the Camino de Santiago. Its 9th-century church was supposedly the scene of a miracle in 1300 when the wine was turned into blood and the bread into flesh. Nearby, there are several *pallozas*, round thatched stone huts. Some have been restored, and are now part of the **Museo Etnográfico**.

Museo Etnográfico

📍 Pedrafita do Cebreiro
📞 982 82 87 30 🕐 11am-
6pm Tue-Sat

→ Cross inside the 9th-century church at the village of O Cebreiro

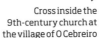

A DRIVING TOUR
RÍAS BAIXAS

Length 270 km (168 miles)
Stopping-off points Vilagarcía
de Arousa; Cambados; Pontevedra;
Hio **Terrain** Winding coastal roads

This southern part of Galicia's west coast consists of four large *rías* or inlets between pine-covered hills. Take a driving tour to discover the area's charms: the beaches are good, the scenery is lovely, the bathing safe and the climate much milder than on the wilder coast to the north. Though areas such as Vilagarcía de Arousa and Panxón have become popular holiday resorts, much of the Rías Baixas (Rías Bajas) coastline is unspoiled, such as the quiet stretch from Muros to Noia. This part of the coastline provides some of Spain's most fertile fishing grounds. Mussel-breeding platforms are positioned in neat rows along the *rías*, looking like half-submerged submarines, and clams are harvested in late summer, so be sure to break up the journey with a super-fresh seafood lunch.

Set off from **Muros**, *a pretty little fortified port.*

A small fishing village with a good beach, **Hio** *is noted for having one of the finest carved calvaries in Galicia.*

The **illas Cíes** *have white sand, clear water and a bird sanctuary.*

Finish your trip in **Panxón**, *where you can soak up the sun on one of its excellent sandy beaches.*

↑ Overlooking the charming
Illas Cíes

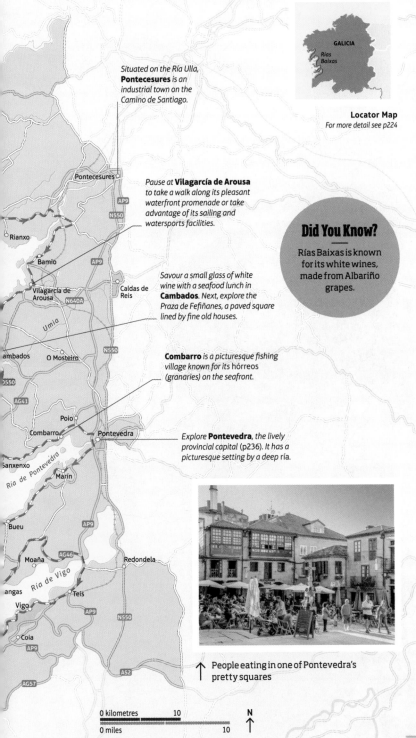

Situated on the Ría Ulla, **Pontecesures** is an industrial town on the Camino de Santiago.

Pause at **Vilagarcía de Arousa** to take a walk along its pleasant waterfront promenade or take advantage of its sailing and watersports facilities.

Did You Know?

Rías Baixas is known for its white wines, made from Albariño grapes.

Savour a small glass of white wine with a seafood lunch in **Cambados**. Next, explore the Praza de Fefiñanes, a paved square lined by fine old houses.

Combarro is a picturesque fishing village known for its hórreos (granaries) on the seafront.

Explore **Pontevedra**, the lively provincial capital (p236). It has a picturesque setting by a deep ría.

↑ People eating in one of Pontevedra's pretty squares

0 kilometres 10

0 miles 10

N ↑

ASTURIAS AND CANTABRIA

Asturias, helped by its mountainous terrain, has a long history of resisting invasion. Although the Romans did conquer the area, they failed to fully subdue its inhabitants. The *reconquista* is said to have begun in Asturias around AD 722, when a Moorish force was defeated by the Christians at Covadonga. The Christian Kingdom of Asturias was founded in the 8th century, eventually stretching from the Basque Country down to what is now northern Portugal as Asturias conquered more and more Moorish-held land. Uniting with the Kingdom of Castile in 1230, the area now known as Asturias was declared a principality in the 14th century, and put under the patronage of the heir to the Spanish throne. To this day, the region's official name is the Principality of Asturias, and Spain's heir is known as the Prince or Princess of Asturias.

Cantabria also fell to the Romans, and came close to defeat by the Moors, who were pushed back after Cantabria entered into an alliance with neighbouring Asturias. In the late 19th century, numerous smaller areas were amalgamated to create the Province of Cantabria. Its capital, Santander, has a long history as a Roman settlement, medieval town, and later a major port of trade with the Americas. However, traces of its illustrious past are scarce due to a huge fire in 1941 that destroyed more than 400 buildings in the Old Town.

ASTURIAS AND CANTABRIA

Must See

1 Parque Nacional de los Picos de Europa

Experience More

2 Taramundi
3 Teverga
4 Castro de Coaña
5 Costa Verde
6 Avilés
7 Gijón
8 Oviedo
9 Potes

10 Valdediós
11 Cangas de Onís
12 Ribadesella
13 Comillas
14 Alto Campoo
15 Valle de Cabuérniga
16 Cuevas de Altamira
17 Puente Viesgo
18 Santander
19 Santillana del Mar
20 Laredo
21 Castro Urdiales

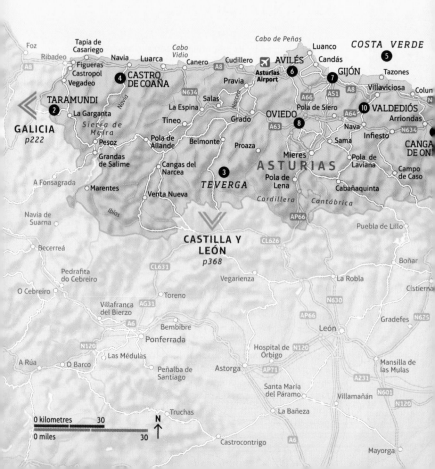

Verdant plains surrounding the Lago de la Ercina, fringed by the Picos de Europa ↑

❶

PARQUE NACIONAL DE LOS PICOS DE EUROPA

🅰C2 🅰Asturias, Cantabria and Castilla y León 🚌Oviedo to Cangas de Onís
🅸Avenida Covadonga 43, Cangas de Onís; www.parquenacionalpicoseuropa.es

Stretching for 647 sq km (250 sq miles), this national park straddles three regions and is crowned by the Picos de Europa. These beautiful mountains were reputedly christened the "Peaks of Europe" by returning sailors for whom this was often the first sight of their homeland.

Encompassing deep winding gorges and verdant valleys, the Parque Nacional de los Picos de Europa is rich walking territory. A dramatic footpath follows the Desfiladero del Río Cares gorge in the heart of the Picos, passing through tunnels and across high bridges. If this sounds too energetic, a cable car makes the 753-m (2,470-ft) ascent from Fuente Dé to a wild rocky plateau pitted with craters and offering a spectacular panorama of the Picos' peaks and valleys. Other highlights include the Naranjo de Bulnes – a tooth-like crest, the sparkling Lago de la Ercina and the town of Covadonga, the site of Pelayo's historic victory.

Did You Know?

Cabrales - the celebrated creamy blue cheese - is made in the park.

Basílica de Santa
María la Real
de Covadonga ←

Riding the
Fuente Dé
cable car to
the peaks ↓

PELAYO THE WARRIOR

A statue *(below)* of this Visigothic nobleman who became king of Asturias guards the basilica at Covadonga. It was close to this site, in AD 722, that Pelayo and a band of men – though vastly out-numbered – are said to have defeated a Moorish army. The victory inspired Christians in the north of Spain to reconquer the pen-insula. The tomb of the warrior is in a cave which has become a shrine.

EXPERIENCE MORE

Taramundi

🅰B1 🏛Asturias
ℹ Calle Solleiro 18;
www.taramundi.es

Situated in the remote Los Oscos region, this small village houses a rural tourism centre which organizes forest tours in four-wheel drive vehicles and has several hotels and holiday cottages to rent. Taramundi has a tradition of wrought-iron craftsmanship. Iron ore was first mined in the area by the Romans. There are approximately 13 forges in and around the village, where artisans can still be seen making traditional knives with decorated wooden handles.

Teverga

🅰B2 🏛Asturias 🚌La Plaza
ℹ Dr García Miranda 14, San Martín de Teverga, Tue–Sun; www.tevergaturismo.com

This area is rich in scenery, wildlife and ancient churches. Near the southern end of the Teverga gorge is La Plaza. Its church, Iglesia de San Pedro de Teverga, is a fine example of Romanesque architecture. West of La Plaza is Villanueva, with its Romanesque Iglesia de Santa María.

Nearby, the high meadows and forests of the Parque Natural de Somiedo are a sanctuary for brown bears. The Senda del Oso walking trail skirts the edge of the park.

Castro de Coaña

🅰B1 🏛Asturias 🚌5 km (3 miles) from Navia 📞985 97 84 01 🕙10:30am–5:30pm Tue–Sun

One of the best-preserved prehistoric sites in the area, Castro de Coaña was later occupied by the Romans. On a hillside in the Navia Valley are the remains of its fortifications and the stone foundations of oval and rectangular dwellings. Inside can be found hollowed-out stones that are thought to have been used for crushing corn. The museum on the site displays many of the finds that have been unearthed at Castro de Coaña.

Costa Verde

🅰B1 🏛Asturias ✈🚆Avilés 🚌Oviedo, Gijón ℹ Avilés, Calle Ruiz Gomez 21; 985 54 43 25

The aptly named "green coast" is a succession of attractive sandy coves and dramatic cliffs, punctuated by fishing villages.

THE BROWN BEAR

The population of Spain's brown bears (*Ursus arctos*) has dwindled from about 1,000 at the beginning of the 20th century to about 300 today. Hunting by man and the destruction of the bear's habitat have caused the decline. But now, protected by nature reserves such as Teverga's Parque Natural de Somiedo, where most of the Asturias's bears are found, together with conservation laws, the bear is increasing in numbers again.

Medieval arcaded streets, lined with colourful buildings, at the centre of Avilés

Inland, there are lush meadows, and pine and eucalyptus forests, backed by mountains.

Two pretty fishing ports, Castropol and Figueras, stand by the eastern shore of the Ría de Ribadeo, forming the border with Galicia. To the east are other picturesque villages such as Tapia de Casariego and Ortiguera, in a small rocky cove. Following the coast, Luarca lies beside a church on a headland, and has a neat little harbour. The village of Cudillero is even more delightful – cafés and restaurants crowd the tiny plaza beside the port and behind, white cottages are scattered over the hillsides.

Further along the coast is Cabo de Peñas where, in the fishing village of Candás, bullfights are held on the sand at low tide on 14 September. East of Gijón, Lastres is impressively located below a cliff, and Isla has a broad open beach. Beyond Ribadesella is the old fortified seaport of Llanes, which has ruined ramparts and good beaches.

Avilés

B1 Asturias
Calle Ruîz Gómez 21; 985 54 43 25

Avilés became the capital of Asturias' steel industry in the 1800s and is still ringed by big factories. The town hides a medieval heart of some character, especially around the Plaza de España. The Iglesia de San Nicolás Bari is decorated with frescoes and has a Renaissance cloister. The Iglesia de Padres Franciscanos contains a fine 14th-century chapel and holds the tomb of the first Governor of the US state of Florida. All around are arcaded streets.

 TOP 5 COSTA VERDE BEACHES

Playa del Silencio
Near Castañeras; there are incredible views of the coastline cliffs.

Playa de Langre
Great beach for surfers, walkers and sunbathers.

Playa de Cuevas del Mar
Near Llanes; the caves are fun to explore.

Playa de San Lorenzo
A good family beach at Gijón, but it gets busy.

Playa de Santa Marina
This long sandy beach at Ribadesella makes for lovely walks.

Limestone peaks, carpeted with forests, rising above Taverga in the valley below

❼

Gijón

🅰C1 🄰Asturias 🚆🚌
ℹ Puerto Deportivo, Espigón Central de Fomento; www.gijon.es

The province's largest city, this industrial port has been much rebuilt since the Civil War when it was bombarded by the Nationalist navy. The city's most famous resident is Gaspar Melchor de Jovellanos, an eminent 18th-century author, reformer and diplomat.

Gijon's Old Town sits on a small headland, overlooking a popular beach. The Old Town centres on the arcaded Plaza Mayor and the 18th-century **Palacio de Revillagigedo (Centro Cultural Cajastur)**, a Neo-Renaissance folly now housing a cultural centre. Even if there isn't an exhibition on, it's worth seeking out for its imposing façade.

Palacio de Revillagigedo (Centro Cultural Cajastur)
🄰Plaza del Marqués 2 📞985 34 69 21 🕓For temporary exhibitions; Jul & Aug: 11am–1:30pm & 4–9pm Tue–Sat, noon–2:30pm Sun & public hols; Sep–Jun: 11:30am–1:30pm & 5–8pm Tue–Sat, noon–2pm Sun & public hols

❽

Oviedo

🅰B1 🄰Asturias
🚆🚌 ℹPlaza de la Constitución 4; www. turismoasturias.es

Oviedo, a university city and the cultural and commercial capital of Asturias, stands on a raised site on a fertile plain. The nearby coal mines have made it an important industrial centre since the 19th century.

In and around Oviedo are many Pre-Romanesque buildings. This style flourished in the 8th–10th centuries and was confined to a small area of the kingdom of Asturias, one of the few enclaves of Spain not invaded by the Moors.

The nucleus of the medieval city is the Plaza Alfonso II, bordered by a number of handsome old palaces. On this square is situated the cathedral with its high tower and asymmetrical west façade. Inside are tombs of Asturian kings and a majestic 16th-century gilded reredos. The cathedral's highlight is the Cámara Santa, a restored 9th-century chapel containing statues of Christ and the apostles. The chapel also has two crosses and a reliquary made of gold, silver and precious stones.

> ## Did You Know?
>
> Legend says that Oviedo was founded by two monks, Maximo and Fromestano, in AD 761.

Also situated in the Plaza Alfonso II is the Iglesia de San Tirso. Originally constructed in the 9th century, subsequent restorations have left the east window as the only surviving Pre-Romanesque feature.

Behind the cathedral is the **Museo Arqueológico de Asturias**, housed in the old Benedictine monastery of San Vicente. It contains local prehistoric, Romanesque and Pre-Romanesque treasures.

The **Museo de Bellas Artes**, in Velarde Palace, has a range of Asturian and Spanish paintings, such as Carreño's portrait of Carlos II and others by Greco, Goya, Dalí, Miró and Picasso.

Two of the most magnificent Pre-Romanesque churches are on Mount Naranco, to the north. Some of the intricate reliefs on the door jambs of **San Miguel de Lillo** show acrobats and animal tamers in a circus. **Santa María del**

↑ Gijón's old port, illuminated by street lamps in the evening

Naranco was originally built as a summer palace for Ramiro I in the 9th century. It is one of the finest examples of Pre-Romanesque architecture.

The early 9th-century church of San Julián de los Prados, on the road leading northeast out of Oviedo, is Spain's largest surviving Pre-Romanesque church and is noted for its frescoes covering the interior.

Museo Arqueológico de Asturias

🏠 Calle San Vicente 3
🕐 9:30am–8pm Wed–Fri, 9:30am–2pm & 5–8pm Sat, 9am–3pm Sun & public hols
🌐 museoarqueologicode asturias.com

Museo de Bellas Artes

🏠 Calle Santa Ana 1 🕐 Jul & Aug: 10:30am–2pm & 4–8pm Tue–Sat, 10:30am–2:30pm Sun; Sep–Jun: 10:30am–2pm & 4:30–8:30pm Tue–Fri, 11:30am–2pm & 5–8pm Sat, 11:30am–2:30pm Sun
🌐 museobbaa.com

San Miguel de Lillo

🏠 Avenida de los Monumentos 🕐 Apr–Sep: 10am–2pm Tue–Sat, 10am–noon Mon & Sun; Oct–Mar: 10am–2:30pm Tue–Sat, 10am–12:30pm Mon & Sun

Santa María del Naranco

♿ 🏠 Avenida de los Monumentos 🕐 Apr–Sep: 9:30am–1pm & 3:30pm–7pm Tue–Sat, 9:30am–1pm Mon & Sun; Oct–Mar: 10am–2:30pm Tue–Sat, 10am–12:30pm Mon & Sun

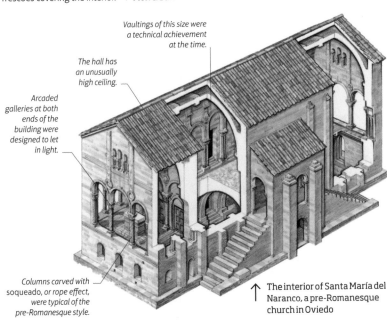

Vaultings of this size were a technical achievement at the time.

The hall has an unusually high ceiling.

Arcaded galleries at both ends of the building were designed to let in light.

Columns carved with soqueado, or rope effect, were typical of the pre-Romanesque style.

↑ The interior of Santa María del Naranco, a pre-Romanesque church in Oviedo

TOP 5 REGIONAL FIESTAS

La Vijanera
This costumed parade has taken place in Silió on the first Sunday in January since pre-Roman times.

La Folía
On the second Sunday after Easter, a statue of the Virgen de la Barquera is put in a decorated boat in San Vicente de la Barquera, while groups of girls, called *picayos*, stand on the shore singing traditional songs.

Fiesta del Pastor
Regional dances are performed on the shores of Lake Enol in the Picos de Europa National Park on 25 July.

Battle of the Flowers
On the last Friday of August, floats adorned with flowers are paraded through Laredo.

Nuestra Señora de Covadonga
Crowds converge on the shrine of Covadonga to pay homage to the patron saint of Asturias on 8 September.

9

Potes

🄰C2 🄰Cantabria 🛈Plaza de la Independencia s/n; 942 73 07 87

A small ancient town, with old balconied houses lining the river, Potes lies to the east of the Parque Nacional de los Picos de Europa *(p248)*. It is situated in the broad Valle de Liébana, whose fertile soil yields prime crops of walnuts, cherries and grapes. A potent spirit called *orujo* is made in the town. The Torre del Infantado, in the main square, is a defensive tower that was built in the 15th century.

Between Potes and the coast runs a spectacular gorge, the Desfiladero de la Hermida, with deep slopes of limestone sparsely covered with oak forests. Halfway up it is stone-built Santa María de Lebeña, a 10th-century Mozarabic church.

West of Potes is the monastery church of Santo Toribio de Liébana, one of the most revered spots in the area. Founded in the 7th century, it became known throughout Spain a century later when it received reputedly the largest fragment of the True Cross. The church is also known for being the home of St Beatus Liébana, the 8th-century monk who wrote the *Commentary on the Apocalypse*. The restored Romanesque monastic buildings are now occupied by Franciscan monks.

10

Valdediós

🄰C1 🄰Asturias 🛈Monasterio de Santa María; 985 90 59 05

Set alone in a field near this hamlet, the tiny 9th-century Iglesia de San Salvador is a jewel of pre-Romanesque art. Its ceiling has vivid Asturian frescoes, and by the portal are recesses where pilgrims slept. The church in the **Monasterio de Santa María** next door is 13th-century Cistercian, with cloisters from the 16th century.

To the north, Villaviciosa lies amid apple orchards. In nearby Amandi, the hilltop Iglesia de San Juan has delicate carvings.

Monasterio de Santa María
📞 985 90 59 05 🕙Apr-Sep: 11am-1:30pm & 4:30-7pm Tue-Sun; Oct-Mar: 11am-1:30pm Tue-Sun

←

Pre-Romanesque Iglesia de San Salvador in Valdedíos, set in a peaceful spot

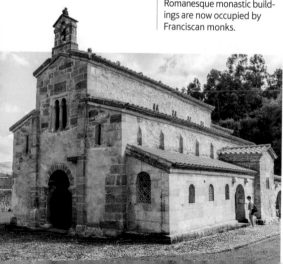

Straddling a broad estuary, Ribadesella is an enchanting little seaside town. On one side is the lively old seaport, which now bustles with tasty tapas bars.

de Covadonga – a Catholic sanctuary set in a cave. Individually, the lakes are called Lago Enol and Lago Ercina. The best way to explore them is by bicycle. Hire a bike and be prepared to work up a sweat.

↑ Sunset over the colourful houses of Ribadesella, looking out over the sea

Cangas de Onís

🅰C2 🏠Asturias 🚌
🛈Avenida Covadonga 1;
www.cangasdeonis.es

Cangas de Onís, one of the gateways to the Picos de Europa, is where Pelayo (p249), the 8th-century Visigothic nobleman and hero of the reconquista, set up his court. The town has a Romanesque bridge and the 8th-century chapel of Santa Cruz.

About 20 km (12 miles) southeast are the Lagos Covadonga. Located in the Picos de Europa, these two glacial lakes are collectively named after the Santa Cueva

Ribadesella

🅰C1 🏠Asturias 🚉🚌
🛈Paseo Princesa Letizia;
www.ribadesella.es

Straddling a broad estuary, Ribadesella is an enchanting little seaside town. On one side is the lively old seaport, which now bustles with tasty tapas bars. While the other side of the estuary is home to a holiday resort. The most important event in the town's calendar is the annual arrival of a multicoloured flotilla of kayaks from Arriondas on the first Saturday in August.

On the edge of town is the **Cueva de Tito Bustillo**. This cave is rich in stalactites but is best known for its many

prehistoric drawings, some dating from around 18,000 BC. The 12 clusters of paintings include red and black pictures of stags and horses. To protect the paintings, only 360 visitors are allowed in per day; tickets should be booked in advance. There is a museum on the site, displaying faithful replicas.

Cueva de Tito Bustillo

♿⏱ 🏠Ribadesella
📞985 18 58 60 🕐Mar–Oct: 11am–5pm Wed–Sun (by guided tour only)

📷 **PICTURE PERFECT**
Descent of the Sella

On the first Saturday in August, a flotilla of kayaks rushes through Ribadesella during a race to the sea. Grab a spot on or by the bridge to watch them go past.

13
Comillas

C1 🏛Cantabria 🚶Plaza
Joaquín del Piélago 1; 942 72
25 91

This pretty resort is known for
its buildings by Modernista
architects. Antonio López y
López, the first Marquis of
Comillas, hired Joan Martorell
to design the Neo-Gothic
Palacio Sobrellano (1881).
Inside, the grand lounge has
ornate wood-carved fireplaces
decorated with Gaudí's
dragons, while the elaborate
dining room features a gold
ceiling of interlaced beams.

Comilla's best-known
building, however, is Gaudí's
El Capricho, now a restaurant.
It was built from 1883 to 1889
and is a Mudéjar-inspired fantasy with a minaret-like tower
covered in green and yellow
tiles. The Universidad Pontificia
is another Modernista building.
It was designed by Joan
Martorell to plans by Lluís
Domènech i Montaner.

The fishing port of San
Vicente de la Barquera, 10 km
(6 miles) to the east is worth
visiting for its arcaded streets
and ramparts.

Palacio Sobrellano
♿🕐 🏛Barrio el Parque 8
📞942 72 03 39 ⏱Apr-Oct:
9:50am-6:30pm daily (mid-
Jun-mid-Sep: 9:50am-7:30pm
daily); Nov-Mar: 9:30am-
3:30pm Tue-Sun

14
Alto Campoo

C2 🏛Cantabria 🚉
🚌Reinosa 🚶Estación de
Montaña, 942 77 92 23 (am
only); Reinosa, www.alto
campoo.com

Sited high in the Cantabrian
mountains, this winter resort
lies below the Pico de Tres
Mares, the "Peak of the Three
Seas", so called because the
rivers rising near it flow into
the Mediterranean, the Atlantic
and the Bay of Biscay. The Río
Ebro, one of Spain's longest
rivers, rises in this area and its
source, at Fontíbre, is a beauty
spot. A road and a chair lift
reach the summit of Tres
Mares for a breathtaking panorama of the Picos de Europa

↑ The market town
of Reinosa, east
of Alto Campoo

↑ El Capricho, a building
designed by Antoni
Gaudí in Comillas

and other mountain chains.
The resort is small, with
22 pistes totalling 32 km
(20 miles) in length, and has
few facilities for après-ski.

Reinosa, some 26 km
(16 miles) to the east of
Alto Campoo, is a handsome
market town with old stone
houses. Further southeast
is Retortillo, a hamlet where
the remains of Julióbriga, a
town built by the Romans as
a bastion against the indigenous Cantabri, can be seen.

The main road south out
of Reinosa leads to Cervatos,
where the former collegiate
church has erotic carvings on
its façade. This novel device
was meant to deter the vil-
lagers from earthly pleasures.

At Arroyuelo and Cadalso,
to the southeast, are two
churches built into rock faces
in the 8th and 9th centuries.

15
Valle de Cabuérniga

C2 🏛Cantabria
🚌Bárcena Mayor
🚶Ayuntamiento de
Cabuérniga; 942 70 60 01

Two exceptionally picturesque
towns, notable for their superb
examples of rural architecture,
draw visitors to the Cabuérniga

Valley. The first of these towns is the once-remote Bárcena Mayor. Although it's now easily reached by road, the town still has a time-warp atmosphere. Its cobbled streets, furnished with old lamps, are lined by pretty houses and cattle barns.

Carmona, which is located approximately 20 km (12 miles) to the northwest of Bárcena Mayor, is the valley's second draw. Its sturdy stone houses with wooden balconies and pantile roofs are typically Cantabrian. Woodcarving, the traditional craft of the region, is still practised in this village, where the locals work outside their houses on a variety of artifacts including bowls, fiddles, *albarcas* (clogs) and chairs. The 13th-century Palacio de los Mier, a manor house in the centre of the village, is being respectfully transformed into a hotel.

The extensive, wild beech woods near Saja, 13 km (8 miles) to the East of Bárcena Mayor, have been designated a nature reserve. Iberian wolves and brown bears have been sighted here and there are also colonies of griffon vultures.

16 (⊗) (⋈)

Cuevas de Altamira

🅰 C1 🏛 Cantabria
🚌 Santillana del Mar
🕘 Museum: 9:30am–6pm Tue-Sat (to 8pm May-Oct), 9:30am-3pm Sun 🔒 1 & 6 Jan, 1 May, 28 Jun, 24, 25 & 31 Dec
🌐 museodealtamira.mcu.es

These caves contain some of the world's finest examples of prehistoric art. The earliest engravings and drawings, discovered in 1879, date back to around 30,000 BC. Public entry to the caves is restricted, but the on-site museum contains a three-dimensional replica based on scientific study of methods and materials used in prehistoric times. Visitors can get some insight into the habitat of its occupants and the beauty of the rock art they created there. There is also a programme of changing exhibitions.

Similar sites that are open to the public can be found at Puente Viesgo *(p258)*, Ribadesella *(p254)* and at Nerja *(p512)* in Andalucía.

(p258), (p254), (p512)

DRINK

Little Bobby Speakeasy
This bar serves cocktails amid quirky decor. Classic films play in the background.

🅰 C1 🏠 Calle Sol 20, Santander
🌐 littlebobby.es

Pub la Lolita
The chilled atmosphere makes this an ideal spot to relax and enjoy a quiet drink.

🅰 C1 🏠 Calle Rio 2, Santillana del Mar

Rvbicón
An easy-going jazz bar where you can enjoy a drink while listening to live music.

🅰 C1 🏠 Calle del Sol 4, Santander
🌐 rubiconbar.es

↑ Prehistoric paintings in the Cuevas de Altamira replica cavern

❶⓱ Puente Viesgo

🅰C2 🏛Cantabria 🚌
ℹCalle Manuel Pérez
Mazo 2; 942 59 81 05

This spa village is best known for **El Monte Castillo**, a complex of caves dotted around the surrounding limestone hills. Late Palaeolithic cave dwellers used the complex as a sanctuary and left drawings of horses, bison and other animals, plus some 50 hand prints. The colours used to create the images were made from minerals in the cave.

To the southeast, in the Pas valley's main town of Vega de Pas, you can buy two Pasiego specialities – *sobaos*, or sponge cakes, and *quesada pasiega*, a sweet which is made from milk, butter and eggs.

El Monte Castillo

❁ 🏛Puente Viesgo
☎942 59 84 25 🕑Mar–Oct: 9:30am–2pm & 3–6:30pm Tue–Sun (mid-Jun–mid-Sep: 10am–2pm & 3–7pm Tue–Sun); Nov–Feb: 9:30am–3:30pm Tue–Fri & Sun, 9:30am–2:30pm & 3:30–5:30pm Sat

⓲ Santander

🅰C1 🏛Cantabria ✈🚆
🚌⛴ ℹJardines de Pereda
s/n; www.turismode
cantabria.com

Cantabria's capital, a busy port, enjoys a splendid site near the mouth of a deep bay. The city has several museums: the **MAS** houses modern and contemporary artworks; the **Museo de Prehistoria y Arqueología** displays finds from caves at Altamira and Puente Viesgo; the **Museo Marítimo** has rare whale skeletons; and the **Centro Botín** hosts artistic workshops and exhibitions.

The town extends along the coast around the Península de la Magdalena, a headland on which sits a summer palace built for Alfonso XIII in 1912.

MAS

 🏛Calle Rubio 6 🕑For renovation; check website
🌐 museosantandermas.es

Museo de Prehistoria y Arqueología

 🏛Calle Bailén s/n ☎942 20 99 22 🕑10am–2pm & 5–8pm Wed–Sun

Museo Marítimo

🏛Calle Severiano Ballesteros s/n ☎942 27 49 62 🕑Oct–May: 10am–6pm Tue–Sun; May–Oct: 10am–7:30pm Tue–Sun

Centro Botín

❁❁❁ 🏛Muelle de Albareda, Jardines de Pereda s/n
🕑10am–9pm Tue–Sun
🚫1 Jan, 25 Dec
🌐centrobotin.org

⓳ Santillana del Mar

🅰C1 🏛Cantabria 🚌 ℹCalle Jesus Otero 20; www.santillana-del-mar.com

Set just inland, belying its name, this town is one of the prettiest in Spain.

> 🔍 HIDDEN GEM
> **Sandy Justa**
>
> Hidden away in a corner of Santillana del Mar is the peaceful Santa Justa beach. A walk along this stretch of sand will take you to the Ermita de Santa Justa - a church tucked into a cove.

→ The futuristic exterior of Santander's Centro Botín arts centre

Its ensemble of 15th- to 18th-century stone houses has survived largely intact.

The town grew up around a monastery, which was an important pilgrimage centre, the Romanesque La Colegiata. The church houses the tomb of the local early medieval martyr St Juliana, and contains a 17th-century painted reredos and a carved south door. In its lovely cloisters, vivid biblical scenes have been sculpted on the capitals. On the town's two main cobbled streets there are houses built by local noblemen. These have either fine wooden galleries or iron balconies, and coats of arms inlaid into their stone façades. One of these mansions, on the enchanting Plaza Mayor, has been turned into a parador, offering a luxurious stay.

To the east of the town centre is the **Museo Diocesano**, which is housed in the restored Convento de Regina Coeli. It has a collection of medieval and Baroque painted carvings of religious figures, and Spanish silverware.

Museo Diocesano
⊕ 🅰 El Cruce 📞 942 84 03 17
🕐 10am–1:30pm & 4–6:30pm
Tue–Sun

↑ Peering down a steep cobbled street in pretty Santillana del Mar

20
Laredo

 D1 🅰 Cantabria 🚉
🛈 Alameda Miramar;
942 61 10 96

Its long, sandy beach has made Laredo one of Cantabria's most popular bathing resorts. The attractive Old Town has narrow streets with balconied houses leading up to the 13th-century Iglesia de Santa María de la Asunción, with its Flemish altar and bronze lecterns. Try to time your visit with the Battle of the Flowers, which takes place in August (*p254*).

21
Castro Urdiales

🅰 D1 🅰 Cantabria
🚌 🛈 Parque Amestoy,
Avenida de la Constitución
s/n; 942 87 15 12

Castro Urdiales, a busy fishing town and popular holiday resort, is built around a picturesque harbour. Above the port, on a high promontory, stands the pinkish Gothic Iglesia de Santa María, as big as a cathedral. Beside it, the restored castle, said to have been built by the Knights Templar, has been converted into a lighthouse. Handsome glass-fronted houses, or *galerías*, line the promenade.

The town's small beach often becomes crowded, but there are bigger ones to the west, such as the Playa de Ostende.

Near the village of Ramales de la Victoria, 40 km (25 miles) south, are prehistoric caves containing etchings and engravings, reached by a very steep mountain road.

EAT

El Marqués
Set on the riverbank, this restaurant offers an à la carte menu, as well as a huge variety of tapas. Seafood is their speciality.

 C2 🅰 Calle Manuel
Pérez Mazo 0, Puente
Viesgo 📞 942 59 86 94

€€€

La Vinoteca
This restaurant serves a lot of Spanish dishes, but often with unique Mediterranean influences.

 C1 🅰 Calle Hernan
Cortes 38, Santander
📞 942 07 57 41

€€€

THE BASQUE COUNTRY, NAVARRA AND LA RIOJA

The Basque people are thought to be one of the oldest races in Europe. Occupying a region that straddles the border of what is now France and Spain for millennia, they are most likely descended from early Iberian farming peoples. Their isolation in mountainous regions has prevented them from complete assimilation with the Roman descendants of France and Spain, even to this day. Their distinct culture is different to anything else found in Europe and their language, *euskara*, isn't related to any known dialect, alive or dead, in the world. Attempts to suppress the Basque culture have long been resisted, most recently by the armed separatist group ETA, who fought violently for Basque independence until their dissolution in 2018.

Navarra was once an independent kingdom containing areas from modern Navarra, the Basque Country and La Rioja, but it came under the control of the Crown of Aragon in the early 16th century. The modern autonomous region came into being following Spain's transition to democracy in the 1970s and 1980s.

La Rioja was controlled by the Romans, the Visigoths and the Moors of Al-Andalus before its reconquest by the Christians in the 10th century. Today it is world famous as a producer of the fine eponymous wine.

THE BASQUE COUNTRY, NAVARRA AND LA RIOJA

Bay of Biscay

THE BASQUE COUNTRY,
NAVARRA AND LA RIOJA

Biarritz

FRANCE

Lekeitio
Ondárroa
Deba
Zarautz
SAN
SEBASTIÁN 2
HONDARRIBIA
Irun 4
Rentería
LAS CINCO VILLAS
DEL VALLE
DE BIDASOA 26
Dantxarinea
Mauléon-
Licharre
Tardets-
Sorholus
Ste-Enggrace

oibar
Eibar
Bergara
Azpeitia
SANTUARIO
DE LOIOLA 6
Hernani
Zugarramurdi
ELIZONDO 24
Valcarlos
RONCESVALLES 28
Orhy
2,021 m (6,630 ft)
Pyrenees

OÑATI 8
Zumárraga
Tolosa
Leitza
Almandoz
Zubiri
Ochagavía
Izaba
(Isaba)

londragón
Arrasate)
Beasain
Ordizia
N1
Betelu
Lekunberri
(Anue)
Olague
VALLE DE
RONCAL
Roncal

Arantzazu
N1
Etxarri-
Aranatz
Irurtzun
N135
RONCAL 27

Altsasu (Alsasua)
Salvatierra
A10
AP15
PAMPLONA 23
Aoiz
Navascués
Ansó

ómaniz
NA120
NAVARRA
Sigüés

Acedo
ESTELLA 21
PUENTE LA
REINA 20
MONASTERIO
DE LEYRE 29
Lumbier
Yesa
CASTILLO
DE JAVIER 30
Puente la
Reina

Los Arcos
A12
NA132
Artajona
SANGÜESA 25
Santa María

LOGROÑO 15
Sesma
Tafalla
OLITE 22
UJUÉ 18
ARAGÓN
p174
Agüero

varrete
Lodosa
Peralta
Carcastillo
Ardisa

Ausejo
AP68
Calahorra
Caparroso
MONASTERIO
DE LA OLIVA 16
Sádaba

El Villar de Arnedo
Rincón de Soto
Ejea de los
Caballeros
Erla

LA RIOJA
Arnedo
Alfaro
Castejón
Valareña

ENCISO 17
Fitero
Cintruénigo
TUDELA 19
Valareña

Cornago
Cervera del
Río Alhama
Monteagudo
Cortes
Castejón de
Valdejasa

CASTILLA
Y LEÓN
p368
Tarazona
Tauste
Gallur
Alagón
Villanueva
de Gállego

Matalebreras
Ágreda
Borja

Soria
N122
Sierra del
Moncayo
Tierga

Almenar de Soria
N234
Villarroya
de la Sierra

Gomara
Torrelapaja

lmazán

↑ Charming medieval houses along the river in Bilbao's Casco Viejo (Old Town)

❶

BILBAO

D2 Vizcaya 🚄🚌🚃 *i* Plaza Circular 1; www.bilbaoturismo.net

An important port and the largest city in the Basque Country, Bilbao (Bilbo) rivals Madrid and Barcelona, with its unique culture, illustrious history and fabulous museums, housed in ground-breaking buildings. The city's development gathered pace in the mid-19th century, when iron ore was first extracted from deposits northwest of the city. But, since the dawn of the 21st century, the old steelworks, shipyards and factories have been transformed into exciting public spaces.

①
Museo de Bellas Artes

Plaza del Museo 2
🕐 Jun–Sep: 11am–8pm Mon–Sat (to 3pm Sun); Oct–May: 11am–8pm Wed–Mon
W museobilbao.com

Located in the Doña Casilda Iturrizar park is the Museo de Bellas Artes (Museum of Fine Art), one of Spain's best art museums. It displays art ranging from 12th-century Basque and Catalan pieces to works by modern artists of international fame, including Vasarely, Kokoschka, Bacon, Delaunay and Léger. There are paintings by local Basque artists too.

After 6pm, entry to the museum is free. Guided tours are in Spanish or Basque only.

→ A visitor admiring the works in the city's Museo de Bellas Artes

②
Euskal Museoa Bilbao Museo Vasco

Plaza Miguel de Unamuno 4 🕐 10am–7pm Mon & Wed–Sat, 10am–2pm Sun 🚫 Public hols
W euskalmuseoa.eus

Housed in a 17th-century building within the city's medieval heart, the Museo Vasco's permanent collection presents Basque art, folk artifacts and photographs of Basque life. Not to be missed is the Idol of Mikeldi, an animal-like carving dating from the 3rd to 2nd century BC, which sits in the cloister.

---

③
Palacio de Congresos y de la Música Euskalduna Jauregia

Avenida Abandoibarra 4
🕐 For concerts
W euskalduna.eus

This striking building sits at the site of the old shipyard. In tribute to the city's industrial past, it resembles a ship. The Palacio is home to the ABAO Bilbao Opera and the Bilbao Symphony Orchestra. Inside is an auditorium, congress halls and an exhibition hall. There are free guided tours in Spanish – and occasionally in the Basque language – on Saturdays. Tours in other languages can be arranged at any time for a fee.

Azkuna Zentroa

🏛 Plaza Arriquibar 4
🕐 9am-9pm daily
🌐 azkunazentroa.eus

In 2010, a century-old wine exchange that had stood empty for over 30 years was converted into this stunning cultural centre.

🏔 GREAT VIEW
Fun-icular

Those keen to escape Bilbao's bustle should make for a funicular railway west of the city. The Funicular de Artxada ascends to the village of La Reineta, and offers a stunning panorama across the dockyards.

Originally known as the Alhóndiga Bilbao, its name was changed in 2015 to honour the city's mayor Iñaki Azkuna, who had died the previous year. The centre features design shops and restaurants, a library, a fabulous pool and a rooftop terrace, with a bar.

Itsasmuseum Bilbao

🏛 Ramón de la Sota Kaia 1
🕐 11am-7pm Tue-Sun
🌐 itsasmuseum.eus

Bilbao's maritime history is expertly displayed at this museum, located on the city's old docks. Exhibitions both inside and outside the museum recount the history of Bilbao Estuary, one of the city's most important lifelines. Visitors can download a free app to their smartphone in order to access additional information during their visit, including an audio guide. Buy tickets in advance and bear in mind that the museum does not accept cash. Admission is free on Tuesdays.

EAT

Mercado de la Ribera
A stylish restaurant sits alongside *pintxos* bars.

🏛 Erribera Kalea 20
🌐 lariberabilbao.com

€€€

Bikandi Etxea
Expect traditional Basque dishes here.

🏛 Paseo Campo Volantin 4
🌐 bikandi-etxea. negocio.site

€€€

Casa Rufo
This gem lies beneath a forgettable exterior – try the steak.

🏛 Calle Hurtado de Amezaga 5
🌐 casarufo.com

€€€

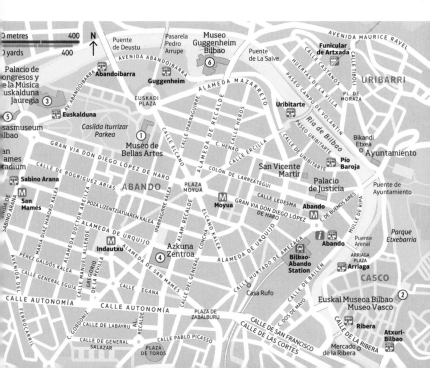

⑥ 🏛 Ⓜ 🍴 🖥 🛍

MUSEO GUGGENHEIM BILBAO

📍 Avenida Abandoibarra 2 Ⓜ Moyua 🚌 1, 10, 11, 13, 18, 27, 38, 48, 71 🕐 11am–7pm Tue–Sun (daily Jul & Aug) 🌐 guggenheim-bilbao.eus

The Museo Guggenheim Bilbao is the jewel in the city's cultural crown. The building itself is a star attraction: a mind-boggling array of silvery curves by the American architect Frank Gehry, alleged to resemble a ship or a flower. Inside, the collection is just as impressive.

The Guggenheim Bilbao's collection represents an intriguingly broad spectrum of modern and contemporary art, and includes works by Abstract Impressionists such as Willem de Kooning and Mark Rothko. As well as this stellar permanent collection, the museum regularly hosts intriguing temporary exhibitions, and often shows works from the permanent collections of its sister institutions – the Guggenheim museums in New York and Venice.

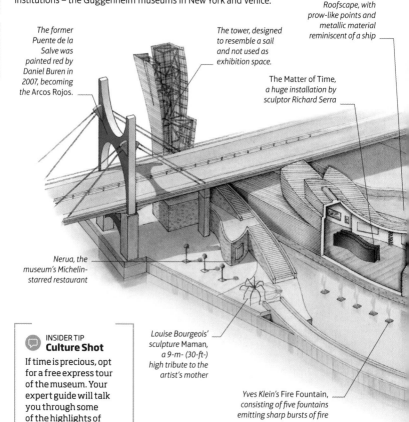

Roofscape, with prow-like points and metallic material reminiscent of a ship

The former Puente de la Salve was painted red by Daniel Buren in 2007, becoming the Arcos Rojos.

The tower, designed to resemble a sail and not used as exhibition space.

The Matter of Time, a huge installation by sculptor Richard Serra

Nerua, the museum's Michelin-starred restaurant

Louise Bourgeois' sculpture Maman, a 9-m- (30-ft-) high tribute to the artist's mother

Yves Klein's Fire Fountain, consisting of five fountains emitting sharp bursts of fire

💬 **INSIDER TIP**
Culture Shot

If time is precious, opt for a free express tour of the museum. Your expert guide will talk you through some of the highlights of the collection at breakneck speed.

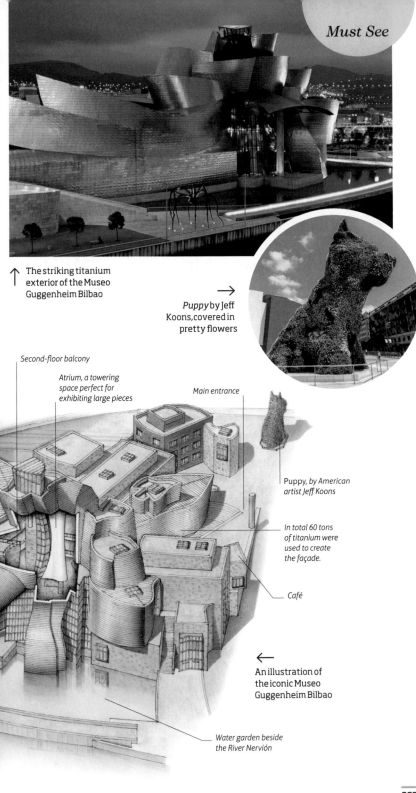

↑ The striking titanium exterior of the Museo Guggenheim Bilbao

→ *Puppy* by Jeff Koons, covered in pretty flowers

Second-floor balcony

Atrium, a towering space perfect for exhibiting large pieces

Main entrance

Puppy, *by American artist Jeff Koons*

In total 60 tons of titanium were used to create the façade.

Café

← An illustration of the iconic Museo Guggenheim Bilbao

Water garden beside the River Nervión

2

SAN SEBASTIÁN

D2 **Guipúzcoa** **Hondarribia (22 km/14 miles)**
Alameda del Bulevard 8; www.sansebastianturismo.com

Gloriously situated on a neat, shell-shaped bay, San Sebastián (Donostia) developed in the late 19th century into Spain's most elegant and fashionable seaside resort. It still has many luxury shops and one of Spain's grandest hotels, the María Cristina, but San Sebastián is now renowned for its great summer arts festivals and delicious Basque cuisine.

1

Plaza de la Constitución

Wedged between the bay and the Río Urumea is San Sebastián's fascinating Old Town (Parte Vieja). At its heart is the Plaza de la Constitución, a handsome, arcaded square. The square was once used as a bullring, and the numbers on the balconies date from this time, when organizers would sell a ticket for each numbered place. From this square you can explore the Old Town's alleys, which are packed with restaurants and tapas bars, and really come alive at night. Overflowing stalls at the local fish market are a testament to this fishing city's past.

2

Monte Urgull

This mountain rises behind the Old Town. It's a bit of a hike to the summit, but is well worth the climb for the spectacular views. The summit is also home to a large statue of Christ and the ruined Castillo de Santa Cruz de la Mota, with old cannons.

3

Basílica de Santa María

 Calle 31 de Agosto 46
 943 48 11 66 10:15am-1:15pm & 4:45-7:45pm daily

This 18th-century church's façade features an impressive vaulted niche. Built where a Roman church once stood, it's

→
Crowds gathering in front of the Basílica de Santa María

← The pretty curve of San Sebastián, with the town lit up at nighttime

considered the oldest church in the city. Don't miss the museum of religious artifacts.

④

Isla de Santa Clara

🅐 Banía de la Concha 🚢
🅞 Jun-Oct 🅝 Nov-May 🅦 san sebastianturismoa.eus

Located in the middle of the Banía de Concha, about 1 km (0.5 miles) from Playa de Ondarreta, is the Isla de Santa Clara. In 1597, those who were infected by the plague were brought here from the city centre. Today, it's a popular summer escape, with a small beach, a saltwater swimming pool and a bar. Look out for sea birds and, if you're lucky, you might spot whales and dolphins from the shore.

Did You Know?

After the Siege of San Sebastián in 1813, British troops burned the city to the ground.

SAN SEBASTIÁN FILM FESTIVAL

This festival, founded in 1953, is one of the five leading European annual film festivals. It is held in late September, and draws more than 200,000 spectators. Visiting celebrities are rife, with the likes of Quentin Tarantino, Ethan Coen and Bertrand Tavernier among their ranks. The special Donostia Prize is awarded as a tribute to the career of a star or director: past winners have included Meryl Streep and Ian McKellen. Prizes also go to individual new films. An early winner was Hitchcock's *Vertigo*. Find out more at www.sansebastian festival.com.

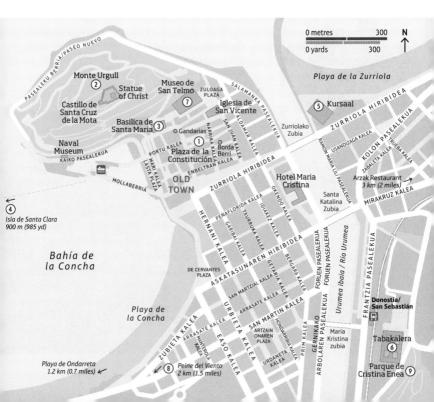

Kursaal

🏠 Avenida de Zurriola 1
🌐 kursaal.eus

This cultural centre is housed in an iconic building, made up of cubes. Designed by Rafael Moneo, and opened in 1999, the current Kursaal was built on the site of the former Gran Kursaal, San Sebastián's old casino and event space that was demolished in 1972. The project was hugely expensive, but the two massive cubes have come to be viewed as icons of the city. They contain large auditoriums, home for most of the year to conferences and concerts, including frequent appearances by the Basque National Orchestra, and temporary art exhibitions in the Kubo-Kutxa Gallery. Kursaal is also used as a venue for the San Sebastián Film Festival (p269).

Tabakalera

🏠 Andre Zigarrogileak Plaza 1 🕐 9am-10pm Mon-Fri (from 10am Sat, Sun & public hols) 🌐 tabakalera.eus

Based in a former tobacco factory, San Sebastián's International Centre for Contemporary Culture is set across five floors connected by an exquisite old wooden staircase. The top floor has a roof terrace that offers an excellent view of the city. Entry to the building is free, and includes access to its temporary exhibitions, details of which can be found on the website. Free tours are also offered, although visitors need to register in advance.

Particularly popular with locals, the Tabakalera is an impressive cultural hub. It has its own media centre and cinema, plus a large library offering work stations with free WiFi. There is also a four-star hotel at the site: One Shot Tabakalera House.

The striking exterior of the Kursaal, and (inset) a workspace within the centre

Museo de San Telmo

🏠 Plaza Zuloaga 1 🕐 10am-8pm Tue-Sun 🚫 1 & 20 Jan, 25 Dec 🌐 santelmo museoa.eus

This is a large museum below Monte Urgull that is dedicated to the history of Basque culture. Housed in a 16th-century monastery, modern extensions have since been added, carefully designed to blend subtly with the original structure. In the cloister is a

TOP 3 BEACHES IN SAN SEBASTIÁN

La Concha
This beautifully picturesque sandy beach is considered one of the best in Europe.

Ondarreta
Close to La Concha, this strand is often quieter and better for families.

Zurriola
This spot is great for a paddle in the sea, and absolutely perfect for keen surfers.

 Peine del Viento, or "Comb of the Wind", sculptures along the coastline

EAT

Arzak

Head to this three-Michelin-starred restaurant for fresh ingredients and Basque cooking. A tasting menu is available.

Avenida Alcade José Elosegui 273 **arzak.es**

Borda Berri

Located in the Old Town, this rustic restaurant serves traditional Basque *pintxos* (snacks). It's popular with tourists and locals alike so you may need to queue for a table - but it's well worth the wait.

Calle Fermin Calbeton 12 **943 43 03 42**

Gandarias

Nestled in the heart of the Old Town, this bar-restaurant offers a real taste of authentic Basque cuisine. There's a varied menu of *pintxos* and other dishes.

Calle 31 de Agosto 23 **restaurante gandarias.com**

collection of Basque funerary columns dating from the 15th to 17th centuries. The museum, which has been in operation since 1900 and had been housed on two previous, smaller sites, was inaugurated here in 1932.

The museum also contains displays of furniture, tools and other artifacts, and paintings by local Basque artists: 19th-century works by Antonio Ortiz Echagüe, modern paintings by Ignacio Zuloaga, portraits by Vicente López and masterpieces by El Greco. The chapel holds 11 golden murals by the Catalan artist Josep Maria Sert, depicting Basque legends, culture and the region's seafaring life. The scenes almost seem to glow, making for an arresting sight.

Guided tours of both the permanent and temporary museums are available at a charge and must be booked in advance; normal entry to the museum is free every Tuesday.

⑧
Peine del Viento

Ondarreta Beach

These three steel sculptures, called the "Comb of the Wind", are a collaboration between two San Sebastián creatives – sculptor Eduardo Chillida and architect Luis Peña Ganchegui. Their setting is made all the more dramatic by the waves that crash against the rocks, sending water soaring into the sky around the visitors who have come to view them.

⑨
Parque de Cristina Enea

Paseo Duque de Mandas
May-Sep: 7am-10pm daily (Oct-Apr: to 9pm)
cristinaenea.eus

This urban park was designed by Pierre Ducasse following a

commission from the Duke of Mandas who wanted to create the park for his wife, Cristina Brunetti de los Cobos. It's a calm, relaxing place – an ideal spot for a break from the city, where visitors can unwind and wander around. Here, you can walk beneath the shade of towering red sequoias and a magnificent Lebanese cedar. As well as the lush lawns and beds, there are ducks and even peacocks at the site.

←

A stained-glass ceiling showing the Oak of Gernika at Casa de Juntas

charcoal drawings of animals made by cave dwellers around 11,000 BC, discovered in 1917. For conservation reasons the caves are closed to the public, but there is an impressive 3D simulation in the nearby hermitage and replicas of the drawings are projected on the walls of the entrance. Guided visits last 90 minutes and must be booked in advance.

Museo de la Paz de Gernika
⊛⊛ 🚻 Foru Plaza 1
🕐 Hours vary, check website
🚫 Jan 🌐 museodelapaz.org

Casa de Juntas
⊛ 🚻 Calle Allende Salazar
📞 946 25 11 38 🕐 10am–2pm & 4–6pm daily 🚫 1 & 6 Jan, 16 Aug, 24, 25 & 31 Dec

Cuevas de Santimamiñe
⊛⊛ 🚻 Kortézubi 📞 944 65 16 57 🕐 May–Oct: 10am–5:30pm daily; Nov–Apr: 10am–1pm Tue–Sun

EXPERIENCE MORE

Gernika-Lumo

🅰️D2 🚩 Vizcaya 🚉🚌
ℹ️ Artekalea 8; www.gernika-lumo.net

This little town will always be remembered for being the target of the world's first saturation bombing raid, carried out by Nazi aircraft at Franco's request on 26 April 1937. Picasso's powerful painting of the bombing hangs in Madrid (p322), but the town's **Museo de la Paz de Gernika** examines the event and its aftermath.

It is important to remember that Gernika-Lumo had an illustrious history before this infamous event. For centuries, Basque leaders met in democratic assembly under an oak on a hillside here. Known as the *Gernikako Arbola*, or Oak of Gernika, the tree's 300-year-old petrified trunk has become a site of pilgrimage for the Basque people.

The **Casa de Juntas**, nearby, is a former chapel where the parliament of the province of Vizcaya reconvened in 1979, when the Basque provinces regained their autonomy. A stained-glass ceiling depicts Basque citizens debating under the *Gernikako Arbola*. The Europa Park, next door, has peace sculptures by Henry Moore and Eduardo Chillida.

Five km (3 miles) northeast of Gernika are the **Cuevas de Santimamiñe**. On the walls of a small chamber are

Hondarribia

🅰️D2 🚩 Guipúzcoa 🚌🚌
ℹ️ Arma Plaza 9; www.bidasoaturismo.com

Hondarribia (Fuenterrabía), the historic town at the mouth of the Río Bidasoa, was attacked by the French over many centuries. The upper town is protected by 15th-century walls and entered via their original gateway, the handsome Puerta de Santa María. They enclose alleys of old houses with carved eaves, balconies and coats of arms.

> This little town will always be remembered for being the target of the world's first saturation bombing raid, carried out by Nazi aircraft at Franco's request.

Did You Know?

Minke whales can sometimes be spotted along the Costa Vasca.

The streets cluster round the church of Nuestra Señora de la Asunción y del Manzano, with its massive buttresses, tall Baroque tower and, inside, a gold reredos. At the town's highest point is the 10th-century castle, now a parador.

Hondarribia has seafront cafés in La Marina, its fishermen's quarter, and beaches stretching to the north.

5

Costa Vasca

 D1 ☐ Vizcaya & Guipúzcoa 🚌 Bilbao 🚈 Bilbao 🛈 Muelle de Ereaga, s/n, Getxo; 944 91 08 00

This 176-km- (110-mile-) long coastline is heavily indented: rugged cliffs alternate with inlets and coves, backed by wooded hills.

Eastwards on the coast is Bakio, a large fishing village. Beyond it the BI-3101 winds high above the sea past the tiny island hermitage, San Juan de Gaztelugatxe, and Matxitxaco, a headland lighthouse. It passes Bermeo, a port with a fishery museum – the **Museo del Pescador**.

At Lekeitio, Basque houses line the seafront below the 15th-century church of Santa María. One long beach sweeps round the village of Saturrarán and the old port of Ondarroa.

In Zumaia is the **Espacio Cultural Ignacio Zuloaga**, the former home of the well-known Basque painter who lived here from 1870 to 1945. Studies of Basque rural and maritime life are on display. Getaria, along the coast, is spread steeply around a fishing port, and has lively cafés.

Museo del Pescador

⊘ ☐ Torre de Ercilla, Bermeo 📞 946 88 11 71 🕐 10am–2pm & 4–7pm Tue–Sat, 10am–2pm Sun 🚫 Public hols

Espacio Cultural Ignacio Zuloaga

⊘ ⊙ ☐ Santiago Auzoa 3, Zumaia 📞 677 07 84 45 🕐 Jul & Aug: 4–8pm Wed & Fri; other times by appt

↑ The rugged rocky coastline of the Costa Vasca

6

Santuario de Loiola

D2 **Loiola, Guipúzcoa**
8am–2pm & 3:30–7pm daily **santuariode loyola.org**

Saint Ignatius of Loiola (San Ignacio de Loyola), founder of the Jesuits, was born in the 1490s in the Santa Casa (holy house), a stone manor near Azpeitia. In the 1600s it was enclosed by the Basílica de San Ignacio, and the rooms in which the aristocratic Loiola family lived were converted into chapels. The Chapel of the Conversion is where Ignatius, as a young soldier, rested while he recovered from a war injury and had a profound religious experience.

A diorama depicts episodes in the saint's life: dedicating his life to Christ at the Monastery of Montserrat (*p154*); writing his *Spiritual Exercises* in a cave at Manresa; his imprisonment by the Inquisition; and his pilgrimage to the Holy Land. The basilica, built from 1681 to 1738, has a Churrigueresque dome and a circular nave with rich carvings.

THE FOUNDING OF THE JESUIT ORDER

The Society of Jesus was founded in Rome in 1539 by Saint Ignatius and a group of priests who were dedicated to helping the poor. Pope Paul III soon approved the order's establishment, appointing Ignatius as Superior General. The order, which grew very wealthy, vowed military obedience to the pope and became his most powerful weapon against the Reformation. Today, there are approximately 20,000 Jesuits working, mainly in education, in 112 countries.

7

Torre Palacio de los Varona

D2 **Villanañe, Álava**
945 35 30 35 **11am–2pm & 4–7pm Tue–Sat, 11am–2pm Sun (winter: Sat & Sun only)**

The small town of Villanañe hosts a beautiful example of medieval civil architecture, the tower and mansion of the Verona family. Set on a hill, this imposing structure is the the best-preserved 14th-century fortified military building in the region. It now houses a museum displaying original furniture. The upper rooms are decorated with colourful 17th-century wallpaper, which replaced the tapestries that previously hung on the walls. Some of the floors are wood, while others are tiled with tiles, decorated with scenes from *Don Quixote*.

On the A2622 Pobes–Tuesta road are the Salinas de Añana, a group of saltpans fed by mineral springs. The nearby village of Tuesta has a Romanesque church, where the capitals are carved with historical scenes. There is also a medieval wood sculpture of St Sebastián.

The basilica of the Santuario de Loiola and *(inset)* detail of its Churrigueresque cupola ↑

Oñati

△D2 ⊡Guipúzcoa ⊞
⨯ Calle San Juan 14;
www.oñatiturismo.eus

This historic town in the Udana Valley has a distinguished past. In the First Carlist War (1833–9) it was a seat of the court of Don Carlos, brother of King Fernando VII and pretender to the throne. Its **Universidad de Sancti Spriritus**, built in about 1540, was for centuries the only one in the Basque Country. It has a Renaissance façade, decorated with statues of saints, and an elegant patio.

In the Plaza de los Fueros is the Gothic Iglesia de San Miguel, containing the tomb of Bishop Zuázola de Ávila, the founder of the university.

A mountain road ascends 9 km (6 miles) to the Santuario de Arantzazu, below the peak of Aitzgorri. In 1469 it is believed that a shepherd saw the Virgin here. Over the door of the church, built in the 1950s, are sculptures of the apostles by Jorge Oteiza.

Universidad de Sancti Spiritus

⊛⊗ **△ Avenida de la Universidad Vasca** ⊠ **943 78 34 53** ⊙ **Daily for guided tours (phone Oñati tourist information in advance)**

↑ Galleried courtyard of the former Universidad de Sancti Spiritus in Oñati

---

EAT

Bar Benigno
Great *pintxos* and tapas – all homemade by the friendly owners – are on offer at this laid-back spot in Haro.

△D2 △ Calle Navarra 1, Haro ⊠ **629 12 58 52**

€€€

9

Haro

△D2 △ La Rioja ⊞⊞
⨯ Plaza de la Paz;
www.haroturismo.org

Set among extensive vineyards on the Río Ebro, the graceful town of Haro is the capital of the Rioja Alta wine region. The town's main monument is a baroque basilica devoted to its patron saint, Nuestra Señora de la Vega – there's a Gothic figure of her on the high altar, but the hilltop Iglesia de Santo Tomás is also of note. Check out the Plateresque portal, which was designed as an altar and depicts scenes from the cross.

But Haro's real highlight is its wine. The clay soil and the climate – the town is sheltered by a sierra to the north – create perfect vine-growing conditions.

Sample the area's famous grapes at one of the town's many *bodegas*. Several of them offer tours and tastings (book in advance; a small fee may apply). But you can also savour a glass – or two – at one of the charming cafés in the Old Town, which offer local wines and tapas at low prices and a convivial atmosphere.

The town is so enamoured by its grapes that it is celebrated in its annual fiesta at the end of June (*p280*).

→ Bronze statue depicting stages of the wine-making process, Haro

Bodega Ysios near Laguardia, one of many *bodegas* found in this wine-producing region

⑩ Laguardia

 D2 Álava 🛈 Calle Mayor 52; 945 60 08 45

This little wine town is the capital of La Rioja Alavesa, a part of southern Álava province where Rioja wines have been produced for centuries. It is a fertile, vine-clad plain, sheltered by high hills to the north. There are fine panoramic views from the road that climbs up to the Herrera pass. Laguardia is a medieval hill town, its encircling ramparts, towers and fortified gateways visible from afar. Along its steep, narrow cobbled streets there are many *bodegas* (wine cellars),

📷 PICTURE PERFECT
Through the Keyhole

Pose in front of the intricate double doorway to Laguardia's Santa María de los Reyes church. If you turn up the contrast, you'll capture the vibrant detail on its colourful sculptures.

→
Plaza de la Virgen Blanca, with the Iglesia de San Miguel at the far end, Vitoria

offering wine tastings and tours throughout the year. It is usually necessary to make a booking in advance. In Plaza Mayor, the main square, you can see the old 16th-century town hall and the newer 19th-century building that serves as the current town hall. The Gothic Iglesia de Santa María de los Reyes is well worth a visit, with its austere façade and a richly embellished inner portal that has retained its original colouring. Another church worth seeing is the Iglesia de San Juan Bautista, a 12th-century building built as a temple-fortress.

The majority of the church was built in the Gothic style in the 13th and 14th centuries, and modifications in the 16th century reduced its fortress-like appearance. It now houses a museum of liturgical objects.

A walkable distance from Laguardia is the Poblado de la Hoya, a prehistoric excavation sight that explores the history of the Celtiberian peoples that once lived in the area.

⑪ Vitoria

 D2 Álava 🚌🚲🚗 🛈 Plaza de España 1; www. vitoria-gasteiz.org/turismo

Vitoria (Gasteiz), the seat of the Basque government, was founded on the site of an ancient Basque town, Gasteiz. Vitoria's oldest part, El Campillo, was rebuilt in 1200 after a fire. The city later grew rich on the iron and wool trades.

The Old Town focuses on the Plaza de la Virgen Blanca, with its monument to a battle fought nearby in 1813, when the British Duke of Wellington defeated the French. Around the plaza are old houses with *miradores* (glazed balconies).

Presiding over the plaza is the Gothic Iglesia de San Miguel. An outside niche contains a statue of the Virgen Blanca (White Virgin), Vitoria's patron

saint. A big festival takes place before her feast day (5 August). On the wall of San Miguel facing the Plaza del Machete there is a recess with a replica of the machete on which the city's rulers swore to uphold the laws or be slain.

The Old Town has several Renaissance palaces, including the 16th-century Palacio de Escoriaza-Esquibel, with its Plateresque patio. Around it is a charming area of alleys linked by steep steps.

The city has two cathedrals. The oldest is the Gothic Catedral de Santa María, with a sculpted west porch. Close by, in Calle Correría, a street of old houses, is El Portalón, a merchant's house and hostel from the 15th century. The building, which is full of Basque Country furniture and art, is now a restaurant.

Among the city's later architectural gems are an arcaded street, Los Arquillos, and the adjoining Plaza de España, also arcaded. They were built in the late 18th century to link the Old Town with the new quarter then being built. South of the Old Town is the Neo-Gothic Catedral Nueva de María Inmaculada, begun in 1907 and finished in 1973.

Located in the centre of Vitoria's Old Town is **Artium**, the Basque Museum of Contemporary Art. It occupies a striking white building and contains one of Spain's largest collections of modern and contemporary art, which is displayed over three large rooms. The focus of the permanent collection is mainly on Spanish artists like Dalí, Miró, Tàpies and Chillida.

The **Museo de Arqueología y Naipes** has 1,500 pieces, including prehistoric artifacts and Roman sculptures found at Álava. Visitors can experience multimedia projections and sound effects. The grandson of Heraclio Fournier, who founded a playing cards factory in Vitoria in 1868, also displays his collection of more than 6,000 items in this museum. The oldest exhibits are late 14th-century Italian cards. Among the many sets of tarot cards are some designed by Salvador Dalí in the 1980s.

BASQUE CULTURE

The Basques may be Europe's oldest race, thought to have descended from Cro-Magnon people who lived in the Pyrenees 40,000 years ago. The dolmens and carved stones of their ancestors are evidence of the Basques' pagan roots. Long isolated in their mountain valleys, the Basques preserved their unique language, myths and art for millennia. Many families still live in the chalet-style stone *caseríos*, or farmhouses, built by their forebears. Their music and high-bounding dances are unlike those of any other culture, and their cuisine is varied and imaginative. The *fueros*, or ancient Basque laws and rights, were suppressed under General Franco, but since the arrival of democracy in 1975 the Basques have had their own parliament and police force, having won great autonomy over their own affairs.

Artium
♿♨ 🏠 Calle de Francia 24
🕐 11am–2pm & 5–8pm Tue–Fri, 11am–8pm Sat & Sun
🌐 artium.eus

Museo de Arqueología y Naipes (BIBAT)
🏠 Palacio de Bendaña, Calle Cuchillería 54
📞 945 20 37 00 🕐 10am–2pm & 4–6:30pm Tue-Sat, 11am–2pm Sun

Did You Know?

Vitoria's mascot is *El Caminante* – a statue of a slender man walking through the Plaza del Arca.

DRINK

La Rioja is home to some of the country's most famous wineries. Here are our favourites.

Marqués de Riscal
🅐D2 🅐Calle Torrea 1, Elciego 🆆marques deriscal.com

Bodegas Franco-Españolas
🅐D2 🅐Calle Cabo Noval 2, Logroño 🆆franco espanolas.com

Bodegas Ruiz de Viñaspre
🅐D2 🅐Camino de la Hoya s/n, Laguardia 🆆bodegaruizde vinaspre.com

Bodegas Ysios
🅐D2 🅐Camino de la Hoya s/n, Laguardia 🆆bodegasysios.com

Vivanco
🅐D2 🅐Carretera Nacional 232, Briones 🆆vivancocultura devino.es

---

San Millán de la Cogolla

🅐D2 🅐La Rioja 🚌From Logroño 🚹Paseo de San Julián 4, Nájera; www. najeraturismo.es

People only really visit this village for its twin monasteries. The first of these is the **Monasterio de San Millán de Suso**, which stands on a hillside above San Millán de la Cogolla ("Suso" means upper). It was built in the 10th century on the site of a community founded by St Emilian, a shepherd hermit, in AD 537. The pink-sanstone church contains the tomb of St Emilian and the graves of seven ifants who, according to legend, were kidnapped and beheaded by the Moors.

The **Monasterio de San Millán de Yuso** ("Yuso" means lower) is in the valley below. It was built between the 16th and 18th centuries. Look out for the ivory plaques in the treasury. They were once part of two 11th-century jewelled reliquaries, which were plundered by French troops in 1813.

Monasterio de San Millán de Suso
⊛🚫 🅒Book ahead 🆆monasteriodeyuso.org

Monasterio de San Millán de Yuso
⊛🚫 🅒Easter-Sep: 10am-1:30pm & 4-6:30pm Tue-Sun; Oct-Easter: 10am-1pm & 3:30-5:30pm Tue-Sat 🆆monasteriodeyuso.org

---

Nájera

🅐D2 🅐La Rioja 🚉 🚹Paseo de San Julián 4; www.najeraturismo.es

The Old Town of Nájera was the capital of La Rioja and Navarra until 1076, when La Rioja was incorporated into Castile. The royal families of Navarra, León and Castile are buried in the **Monasterio de Santa María la Real**. This monastery was founded in the 11th century by Don García Sánchez III beside a sandstone cliff; a statue of the Virgin was found here in a cave. Today, a 13th-century Madonna stands in the cave.

Monasterio de Santa María la Real
⊛ 🅒Plaza Santa María 1, Nájera 🅒Apr-Oct: 10am-1:30pm & 4-7pm Tue-Sat, 10am-1:30pm & 4-6pm Sun; Nov-Mar: 10am-1:30pm & 4-5:30pm daily 🆆santa marialareal.net

 The narrow Calle Laurel in Logroño, popular for its tapas

 Santo Domingo de la Calzada

🏛D2 📍La Rioja 🚌 ℹ️Calle Mayor 33; 941 34 12 38

This town on the Camino de Santiago (*p232*) is named after the 11th-century saint who built bridges and *calzadas* (roads) to help pilgrims. Santo Domingo also founded a hospital, which now serves as a parador.

Miracles performed by the saint are recorded in carvings on his tomb in the town's part-Romanesque, part-Gothic cathedral, and in paintings on the wall of the choir. The most obvious and bizarre record is a sumptuously decorated cage set in a wall in which, for centuries, a live cock and hen have been kept. The cathedral has a carved walnut reredos at the high altar, the last work, in 1541, of the artist Damià Forment. The restored 14th-century ramparts of the town are also worth seeing.

15 **Logroño**

🏛D2 📍La Rioja 🚌 ℹ️Escuelas Trevijano, Calle Portales 50; www. lariojaturismo.com

The capital of La Rioja is a tidy, modern city of wide boulevards and smart shops. It is the commercial centre of a fertile plain where quality vegetables are produced, in addition to Rioja wines. In Logroño's pleasant old quarter on the Río Ebro is the Gothic cathedral, with twin towers. Above the south portal of the nearby Iglesia de Santiago el Real, which houses an image of the patron saint Our Lady of Hope, is an equestrian statue of St James (Santiago).

About 50 km (30 miles) south of Logroño, the N111 twists and turns through the dramatic Iregua Valley to the Sierra de Cameros.

THE COCK AND HEN OF SANTO DOMINGO

A live cock and hen are kept in the cathedral of Santo Domingo de la Calzada as a tribute to the saint's miraculous life-giving powers. Centuries ago, it is said, a German pilgrim refused the advances of a local girl, who then denounced him as a thief. He was hanged as a consequence, but later his parents found him alive on the gallows. They rushed to a judge, who said, dismissively, "Nonsense, he's no more alive than this roast chicken on my plate." Whereupon, the chicken stood up on the plate and crowed.

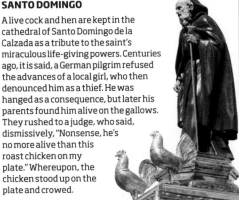

 The Monasterio de San Millán de Yuso, superbly set in the Cárdenas Valley

TOP
4
REGIONAL
FIESTAS

Fiesta del Santo
From 10 to 15 May, Santo Domingo de la Calzada celebrate their patron saint with colourful dances and fun processions.

Wine Battle
On 29 June, people in white clothes squirt each other with wine from drinking bottles in Haro (p275), capital of the Rioja Alta region.

Danza de los Zancos
Dancers on stilts hurtle down the steps from Anguiano's church to the main square between 21 and 23 July and the last Saturday and Sunday of September. No one knows why.

La Virgen Blanca
In Vitoria on 4 August, to honour the Virgin Mary, a dummy holding an umbrella is lowered from San Miguel church to a house below – from which a man in similar dress emerges.

16

Monasterio de La Oliva

E2 **Carcastillo, Navarra** **From Pamplona** **Daily** **monasteriodelaoliva.org**

French Cistercian monks built this small monastery on a remote plain in the 1100s. The church is adorned with rose windows and has a 17th-century tower. The serene cloister, dating from the 14th and 15th centuries, adjoins a 12th-century chapterhouse.

Today, the monks survive by selling local honey and cheese, their own wine, and by accepting paying guests.

17

Enciso

D2 **La Rioja** **From Logroño** **Plaza Mayor; 941 39 60 80**

Near this remote hill village west of Calahorra is Spain's "Jurassic Park". Signposts point to the *huellas de dinosaurios* (dinosaur footprints). Embedded in rocks overhanging a stream are the prints of many giant, three-toed feet, up to 30 cm (1 ft) long. They were made around

> An unspoiled hill village, Ujué commands a high spur at the end of a winding road. The village is a charming maze of cobbled alleys and steep steps.

150 million years ago, when dinosaurs moved between the marshes of the Ebro Valley, at that time a sea, and these hills. Prints can also be seen at other locations in the area.

Arnedillo, 10 km (6 miles) to the north of Enciso, is a spa with thermal baths once used by Fernando VI. In Autol, to the east, there are two unusual limestone peaks.

18

Ujué

E2 **Navarra** **Plaza Municipal; www.ujue.info**

An unspoiled hill village, Ujué commands a high spur at the end of a winding road. The village is a charming maze of cobbled alleys and steep steps.

The impressive and austere Iglesia de Santa María is in Gothic style, featuring a Romanesque chancel and an

A street in Tudela, with sand-coloured houses and the cathedral tower behind

exterior lookout gallery. The ruined fortifications around the church offer extensive views of the Pyrenees.

On the Sunday after 25 April, pilgrims in black capes visit the Virgin of Ujué, whose image is displayed in the church.

---

⑲

Tudela

🅐E2 🄽Navarra 🚉🚌
🛈Plaza Fueros 5; 948 84 80 58

Navarra's second city is the great commercial centre of the vast agricultural lands of the Ebro Valley, known as the Ribera. Much of Tudela consists of modern developments, but its origins are ancient. Spanning the Ebro is a 13th-century bridge with

Dinosaur statue marking the spot where these creatures once roamed in Enciso

17 irregular arches. The Old Town has two well-preserved Jewish districts.

The Plaza de los Fueros is old Tudela's main square. It is surrounded by houses with wrought-iron balconies. On some of their façades are paintings of bullfights, a reminder that the plaza was formerly used as a bullring.

The cathedral, begun in 1194, exemplifies the religious toleration under which Tudela was governed after the Reconquest. It is Early Gothic, with a carved portal depicting the Last Judgment and a Romanesque cloister. Beside the cathedral is a 9th-century chapel.

To the north is the Bárdenas Reales, an arid area of limestone cliffs and crags. This desert-like landscape is the result of hot summers, cold winters and long dry periods interrupted by heavy rain.

About 20 km (12 miles) west of Tudela is the spa town of Fitero, with the 12th-century Monasterio de Santa María.

THE KINGDOM OF NAVARRA

Navarra emerged as an independent Christian kingdom in the 10th century, after Sancho I Garcés became king of Pamplona. It became a formidable force as Sancho III the Great expanded the kingdom, and at his death, in 1035, Navarra stretched all the way from Ribagorza in Aragón to Valladolid. But the kingdom's autonomy was not to last. In 1234, Navarra passed by marriage to a line of French rulers. But, one, Carlos de Viana *(below)*, wrote *The Chronicle of the Kings of Navarra* in 1455, which lauded his predecessors. In 1512 Navarra was annexed by Fernando II of Castile and became part of Spain as we know it, but it kept its own laws and currency until the 1800s.

↑ The pilgrims' bridge over the Río Arga at Puente la Reina, and *(inset)* cycling on the bridge

20

Puente la Reina

🅰D2 🄰Navarra 🄘Puente de los Peregrinos 1; 948 34 13 01 (closed Jan & Feb)

Few towns along the Camino de Santiago *(p232)* evoke the past as vividly as Puente la Reina. The town takes its name from the humpbacked pedestrian bridge over the Río Arga. The bridge was built for pilgrims during the 11th century by royal command.

On Puente la Reina's narrow main street is the Iglesia de Santiago, which has a gilded statue by the west door showing the saint as a pilgrim. On the edge of town is the Iglesia del Crucifijo, another pilgrim church which was built in the 12th century by the Knights Templar. Contained within the church is a Y-shaped wooden crucifix of a sorrowful Christ with arms upraised, which is

believed to have been a gift from a German pilgrim in the 14th century.

Isolated in the fields about 5 km (3 miles) to the east is the 12th-century Iglesia de Santa María de Eunate. This octagonal Romanesque church is fringed by a remarkable cloister, with many arches, which may have given the church its name – in Basque *ehun atea* means "one hundred doors".

West of Puente la Reina is the showpiece hill village of Cirauqui. It is also charming, if rather over-restored. Chic little balconied houses line tortuously twisting alleys linked by steps. The Iglesia de San Román, built in the 13th century on top of the hill, has a sculpted west door.

21

Estella

🅰D2 🄰Navarra 🄫 🄘Calle de San Nicolás 1; www.visitnavarra.es

King Sancho Ramírez, who founded Estella (Lizarra) in the 11th century, ensured that the Camino de Santiago passed through the town and throughout the Middle ages it was the centre of the royal court of Navarra and a major stop on the pilgrimage.

The most important monuments in Estella are sited on the edge of town, across the bridge over the Río Ega. Steps climb steeply from the arcaded Plaza de San Martín to the remarkable Iglesia de San Pedro de la Rúa, built on top of a cliff from the 12th to 14th centuries. The carved capitals are all that now remain of the Romanesque cloister, which was destroyed when a castle overlooking the church was

On Puente la Reina's narrow main street is the Iglesia de Santiago, which has a gilded statue by the west door showing the saint as a pilgrim.

blown up in 1592. The Palacio de los Reyes de Navarra (now a museum), on the other side of the Plaza de San Martín, is a rare example of civil Romanesque architecture.

In the town centre, on Plaza de los Fueros, Iglesia de San Juan Bautista has a Romanesque porch. The north portal of the Iglesia de San Miguel has Romanesque carvings of St Michael slaying a dragon.

The Monasterio de Nuestra Señora de Iranche, 3 km (2 miles) southwest of Estella, was a Benedictine monastery which sheltered pilgrims on their way to Santiago. The church is mainly Transitional Gothic in style, but it has Romanesque apses and a cloister in Plateresque style. It is capped by a remarkable dome. A *bodega* next to the monastery provides pilgrims with wine from a tap in a wall.

A small road branches off the NA120 north of Estella and leads to the Monasterio de Iranzu, built in the 12th to 14th centuries. The austerity of its church and cloisters is typically Cistercian.

㉒

Olite

ⒶD2 **Ⓐ**Navarra **🚍🚌**
ℹPlaza de Teobaldos 10;
www.olite.es

The historic town of Olite was founded by the Romans and later chosen as a royal residence by the kings of Navarra. Parts of the town's Roman walls can be seen but Olite is known as "the Gothic town" and abounds with examples of the architectural style.

In the 15th century, Carlos III set about constructing the monumental **Palacio Real de Olite**, regarded as a gem of Navarrese Gothic style. The palace was heavily fortified, but was brilliantly decorated inside with *azulejos* (ceramic tiles) and marquetry ceilings. The walkways were planted with vines and orange trees,

and there was an aviary and a lions' den. Further diversion came from the tournaments held in the grounds, which monarchs could watch from the "windy tower". The palace was burned down in the War of Independence to prevent it falling into French hands, but it was meticulously rebuilt in 1937. Today, part of the palace houses a parador but non-guests can still explore the palace's courtyards, passages, large halls, royal chambers, battlements and turrets. Adjoining the castle is a 13th-century former royal chapel, the Iglesia de Santa María, with its richly carved Gothic portal.

Elewhere in Olite, the delightful jumble of steep, narrow streets and little squares shelter churches, delightful Baroque houses and, as you would expect from the Navarra wine region, scores of traditional *bodegas*.

Palacio Real de Olite

⊗ⓂⒶPlaza de Carlos III
📞948 74 12 73 **🕐**10am–7pm daily (Jul & Aug: to 8pm)

↑ The vast battlements and towers of the 15th-century Palacio Real de Olite

←

Bars, shops and cafés on Calle Mercaderes, looking towards the cathedral in Pamplona

The Museo Diocesano, housed in the cathedral's 14th-century kitchen and refectory, has displays of Gothic altarpieces, polychrome wood statues from all over Navarra, and a French 13th-century reliquary of the Holy Sepulchre.

West of the cathedral is the Old Town, cut through with many alleys. The Neo-Classical **Palacio del Gobierno de Navarra** lies in the Plaza del Castillo and is the seat of the Navarrese government. Outside, a statue of 1903 shows a symbolic woman upholding the *fueros* (historic laws) of Navarra. North of the palace is the medieval Iglesia de San Saturnino, built on the site where St Saturninus is believed to have baptized some 40,000 pagan townspeople, and the Baroque *ayuntamiento*.

Beneath the Old Town wall, housed in a 16th-century hospital with a Plateresque doorway, is the **Museo de Navarra**. This is a museum of regional archaeology, history and art. Exhibits include Roman mosaics and an 11th-century, Islam-inspired ivory casket. There are murals painted during the 14th–16th centuries, a portrait by Goya and a collection of paintings by Basque artists.

㉓

Pamplona

A D2 **A** Navarra ► 🚌 **i** Calle San Saturnino 2; www.turismode pamplona.es

The old fortress city of Pamplona (Iruña) is said to have been founded by the Roman general Pompey. In the 9th century it became the capital of Navarra. But the city is best known for the fiesta of San Fermín, with its bull-running, held in July.

From the old city walls (*murallas*) you can get a good overview of Pamplona. The nearby cathedral, which is built in ochre-coloured stone, looks down on a loop in the Río Arga. It was built on the foundations of its 12th-century predecessor, and is mainly Gothic in style, with twin towers and an 18th-century façade. Inside there

are lovely choir stalls and the alabaster tomb of Carlos III and Queen Leonor.

The southern entrance to the cloister is the beautifully carved, medieval Puerta de la Preciosa. The cathedral priests would gather here to sing an antiphon (hymn) to La Preciosa (Precious Virgin) before the night service.

RUNNING OF THE BULLS

The *encierro* (running of the bulls) is a traditional Spanish event where a number of bulls are released into the streets, and people, often dressed all in white with red scarves around their waists and necks, try to outrun them. By far the most famous run is in Pamplona, which takes place during the San Fermín festival. Animal rights groups regularly protest against the event, as the bulls are often hurt or killed during or following the run.

To the southeast is the city's massive 16th-century citadel, which was erected in Felipe II's reign. It is designed with five bastions in a star shape. Beyond it are the spacious boulevards of the new town, and the city's university.

Palacio del Gobierno de Navarra

⊛ 🚹 Avenida Carlos III 2
☎ 848 42 70 00 ◐ By appointment only

Museo de Navarra

⊛ 🚹 Cuesta de Santo Domingo s/n ☎ 848 42 64 93
◑ 9:30am–2pm & 5–7pm Tue–Sat, 11am–2pm Sun & public hols ◪ 1 Jan, 6 & 7 Jul, 25 Dec

---

Elizondo

🅰 E2 🄰 Navarra 🚌
🚹 Palacio de Arizkunenea (closed Mon–Thu in winter); www.baztan.eus

This rural village lies in the middle of a beautiful valley, straddling the banks of the Baztán river. Named "beside the church", Elizondo centres around the eclectic Iglesia de Santiago. Despite its Baroque appearance, this church was built in the 20th century.

The town of Zugarramurdi, further up the valley, is infused with the fragrance of herbs. Its most famous site is the Cuevas de Brujas. Witch sabbaths were said to have taken place here, and in 1609 the Inquisition tried 40 women from Zugarramurdi, accusing them of witchcraft. The site's museum tells their story.

Sangüesa

🅰 E2 🄰 Navarra 🚌 🚹 Calle Mayor 2 (closed Mon in winter); www.sanguesa.es

Since medieval times this small town on the Río Aragón has been a popular stop on the Camino de Santiago *(p232)*. The richly sculpted south portal of the Iglesia de Santa María la Real is a 12th- and 13th-century treasure of Romanesque art. It features several figures and details depicting the *Last Judgment* and society in the 13th century. The 12th- to 13th-century Gothic Iglesia de San Francisco and the Gothic Iglesia de Santiago are also worth seeing. The latter is decorated with symbols of the Camino, including scallop shells and walking sticks.

North of Sangüesa there are two deep, narrow gorges. The most impressive is the Hoz de Arbayún, whose limestone cliffs are inhabited by colonies of vultures. It is best seen from the NA178 north of Domeño. The Hoz de Lumbier can be seen from a point on the A21.

GREAT VIEW
Reading La Rhune

The mountain of La Rhune stands high above the Valle de Bidasoa, straddling the border with France. Set off from Bera and follow the trail to its summit, where you will be rewarded by panoramic views of the Pyrenees.

Las Cinco Villas del Valle de Bidasoa

🅰 E2 🄰 Navarra
🚌 Pamplona, San Sebastián
🌐 baztan-bidasoa.com

In the Bidasoa valley are five towns that owe their unique character to their proximity with France. The largest is Bera (Vera), home to the celebrated writer Pío Baroja. Heading south, you'll come to Lesaka, where the houses have distinctive wooden balconies. Continue further south to reach Igantzi (Yanci), the smallest of the towns.

Although Arantza is the most remote town, Etxalar (Echalar) seems the most frozen in time.

↓ Basque houses in the picturesque town of Etxalar, Valle de Bidasoa

↑ Larra Belagua Forest, carpeted in autumn leaves, in the Valle de Roncal

27

Valle de Roncal

 E2 Navarra From Pamplona Paseo Julian Gayarre s/n, Roncal; www.vallederoncal.es

Running perpendicular to the Pyrenees, this valley is mountainous part of Navarra and is home to the province's

TOP 5 PINTXO DISHES

La Gilda
Anchovy wrapped around *guindilla* peppers served with olives on either side.

Tortilla
Spanish omelette made with potato and onion.

Pintxo Pimiento Anchoa y Ajo
A piece of bread topped with red pepper, anchovy and garlic.

Stuffed peppers
Sweet *piquillo* peppers stuffed with salted cod.

Asparagus
White asparagus served with different sauces is a Navarran delicacy.

loftiest peak – Mesa de los Tres Reyes, or Table of Three Kings. As you would expect from this landscape, the Valle de Roncal's relies on farming – the village of Roncal is well known for its cheeses – and mountain pursuits.

The ski resort of Isaba, the largest town in the valley, has an interesting museum of local history and life. A spectacular road winds from Isaba to the tree-lined village of Ochagavia in the parallel Valle de Salazar. To the north, the Selva de Irati, one of Europe's largest woodlands, spreads over the Pyrenees into France, below snowy Monte Ori at 2,017 m (6,617 ft).

28

Roncesvalles

 E2 Navarra Antiguo Molino s/n; www.roncesvalles.es

Roncesvalles (Orreaga), on the Spanish side of a pass through the Pyrenees, is a major halt on the Camino de Santiago *(p232)*. Before it became associated with the pilgrim's way, Roncesvalles was the site of a major battle in AD 778, in which the Basques of Navarra slaughtered the rearguard of Charlemagne's army as it marched homeward.

This event is described in the 12th-century French epic poem *The Song of Roland*.

The 13th-century Colegiata Real, which has served travellers down the centuries, has a silver-plated Virgin and Child below a high canopy. In its chapterhouse is the white tomb of Sancho VII the Strong (1170–1234), which is looked down upon by a stained-glass window of his great victory, the battle of Las Navas de Tolosa. Exhibits displayed in the church museum include "Charlemagne's chessboard", an enamelled reliquary which is so called because of its chequered design.

The impressive hilltop → Castillo de Javier, birthplace of St Francis Xavier

Monasterio de Leyre

⬛E2 🏠Yesa, Navarra
🚌Yesa ⏰Mar-Oct: 10am-
7pm daily; Nov-Feb: 10am-
6pm daily ⛔1 & 6 Jan, 25 Dec
🌐monasteriodeleyre.com

The monastery of San Salvador de Leyre is situated high above a reservoir, alone amid grand scenery, backed by limestone cliffs. The abbey has been here since the 11th century, when it was a great spiritual and political centre. Sancho III and his successors made it the royal pantheon of Navarra. The monastery began to decline in the 12th century. It was abandoned from 1836 until 1954, when it was restored by the Benedictines, who turned part of it into a hotel. To see the monastery, you must join one of the tours run every morning and afternoon. Time your visit to coincide with the monks' Gregorian chant (p397) at 7:30am, 9am, 7pm or 9:10pm.

The large 11th-century church has a Gothic vault and three lofty apses. On its west portal are weather-worn carvings of strange beasts, as well as biblical figures. The Romanesque crypt has unusually short columns with chunky capitals.

↑ Monks walking in the grounds of the Monasterio de Leyre

Castillo de Javier

⬛E2 🏠Javier, Navarra
🚌From Pamplona 📞948
88 40 24 ⏰Mar-Oct: 10am-
6:30pm daily; Nov: 10am-
5:30pm daily; Dec-Feb:
10am-4pm daily ⛔1 Jan,
24, 25 & 31 Dec

St Francis Xavier, patron saint of Navarra, was born in this 13th-century castle in 1506. It is now a Jesuit spiritual centre, but there is a museum in the keep devoted to his life. In the oratory is a macabre mural of grinning skeletons.

EAT

Bar Gaucho

Take a table outside at this bar and enjoy heaped *pintxos*.

⬛D2 🏠Calle Espoz y
Mina 7, Plaza del Castillo,
Pamplona 🌐cafe
bargaucho.com

€€€

La Mandarra de la Ramos

A vibrant *pintxos* bar; hanging Iberian hams give a Spanish feel.

⬛D2 🏠Calle San
Nicolas 9 Bajo,
Pamplona
🌐lamandarrade
laramos.com

€€€

Casa Sabina

This eatery in Roncesvalles offers a "pilgrim's menu".

⬛E2 🏠Carretera Francia
s/n, Roncesvalles
🌐casasabina.
roncesvalles.es

€€€

MADRID

The striking Edificio Metrópolis on the Gran Vía

EXPLORE
MADRID

This section divides Madrid into two sightseeing areas, as shown on this map, plus an area beyond the centre.

UNIVERSIDAD

Cuartel del Conde Duque

Museo de Historia de Madrid

MALASAÑA

Templo de Debod

Torre de Madrid

Edificio España

Parque de la Montaña

Museo Cerralbo

Monumento a Cervantes

Estación del Norte (Príncipe Pío)

Palacio del Senado

Monasterio de la Encarnación

Monasterio de las Descalzas Reales

CENTRO

Real Acaden de Bellas Ar

Jardines del Palacio Real

Palacio Real

PLAZA DE ORIENTE

PLAZA DE ISABEL II

Teatro Real

WEST MADRID
p294

PUERTA DEL SOL

Jardines del Campo del Moro

AUSTRIAS

PLAZA MAYOR

Casa de Correos

SOL

Parque de Atenas

Catedral de la Almudena

Mercado de San Miguel

Palacio de Santa Cruz

Mercado de la Cebada

San Francisco el Grande

LAVAPIÉS

Parque de la Cornisa

Real Fabrica de Tabacos

EMBAJADORES

ARGANZUELA

SPAIN

Museo Sorolla

Museo de
Arte Público

Palacio de
Amboage

Fundación
Carlos de Amberes

Fundación
Juan March

GAR

SALAMANCA

Museo del
Romanticismo

Audiencia
Nacional

Mercado de
la Paz

JUSTICIA

Jardines del
Descubrimiento

Museo
de Cera

Biblioteca
Nacional de España

CHUECA

Museo
Arqueológico
Nacional

RECOLETOS

Palacio de
Linares

Puerta de
Alcalá

Banco de
España

Palacio de
Comunicaciones

Museo Nacional
de Artes Decorativas

Teatro de la
Zarzuela

Museo
Naval

Parque
del Retiro

Congreso de
los Diputados

Museo
Thyssen-
Bornemisza

Salón de Reinos

Teatro
Español

Basílica Jesús
de Mendinaceli

CORTES

Museo
del Prado

EAST MADRID
p312

Real Academia
de la Historia

El Angel Caido

Cine Doré

CaixaForum

Real Jardín
Botánico

Viveras
Municipales

Palacio de
Fernán Nuñez

Ministerio de
Agricultura

Convento
Santa Isabel

Museo Nacional
Centro de
Arte Reina Sofía

Museo
Nacional de
Antropología

Estación de
Atocha

Real Fábrica
de Tapices

PACÍFICO

CALLE P. MÉNDEZ ÁLVARO

ATOCHA

ADELFAS

| 0 metres | | 400 |
| 0 yards | | 400 |

N

GETTING TO KNOW
MADRID

A patchwork of architecturally and culturally distinct neighbourhoods, Spain's capital has a number of great Habsburg and Bourbon monuments at its core, along with three great art museums. Above the Gran Vía you'll find the lively *barrios* of Malasaña and Chueca, with upmarket Salamanca running north.

PAGE 294

WEST MADRID

Also known as "Madrid de los Austrias" (after the Habsburg monarchs), the zone from the leafy Jardines del Campo del Moro to the Puerta del Sol includes palatial buildings, revered restaurants and pretty pedestrianized streets. The spiritual heart of the city – as well as the country – West Madrid exudes alfresco living. Here, *Madrileños* spend afternoons mingling on the Plaza Mayor and sipping steaming cups of coffee on sun-filled terrace-cafés. A flood of cosmopolitan hotels makes this a lively, as well as convenient, base but West Madrid still retains its authentic charm.

Best for
City strolls

Home to
Palacio Real, Plaza Mayor

Experience
Sipping a café con leche on the grand Plaza de Oriente, overlooked by the palace

EAST MADRID

PAGE 312

The city's Golden Triangle of Art – a trio of world-class museums – lies along the Paseo del Prado. On one side of this axis is the aptly named Barrio de las Letras ("Literary Neighbourhood"), where an artistic atmosphere pervades every aspect of life and cobbled pavements are adorned with literary quotations. Here, you can walk in the footsteps of Madrid's literary giants and take advantage of the lively bar scene. On the other side of the Paseo del Prado, you'll find the city's most impressive green lung – the Parque del Retiro – the perfect place to take a break from urban life.

Best for
World-class art

Home to
Museo del Prado, Museo Thyssen-Bornemisza, Museo Nacional Centro de Arte Reina Sofía, Parque del Retiro

Experience
Checking out a contemporary art exhibition in the Parque del Retiro's Palacio de Cristal

BEYOND THE CENTRE

PAGE 336

Outside the centre, you'll find some of Madrid's most atmospheric neighbourhoods, from sophisticated Salamanca to earthier Malasaña and La Latina. Exquisite boutiques stand shoulder to shoulder on Salamanca's orderly grid of streets, while vintage stalls jostle for space at El Rastro's flea market. Rainbow flags fly in Chueca – Madrid's principal LGBTQ+ area – while Malasaña derives much of its hipster ambiance from the nearby university community. As the home of *la movida*, this is the place to come after dark.

Best for
Lively nightlife and vintage shopping

Home to
Museo Lázaro Galdiano

Experience
The Sunday morning vermouth crowd in one of La Latina's squares

WEST MADRID

When Felipe II chose Madrid as his capital in 1561, it was a small Castilian town of little real significance. In the following years, it was to grow into the nerve centre of a mighty empire.

According to tradition, it was the Moorish chieftain Muhammad ben Abd al Rahman who established a fortress above the Río Manzanares. Magerit, as it was called in Arabic, fell to Alfonso VI of Castile between 1083 and 1086. Narrow streets with houses and medieval churches began to grow up on the higher ground behind the old Arab *alcázar* (fortress). When this burned down in 1734, it became the site of the present Bourbon palace, the Palacio Real.

The population had scarcely reached 20,000 when Madrid was chosen as capital, but by the end of the 16th century it had more than trebled. The 16th-century city is known as the "Madrid de los Austrias", after the reigning Habsburg dynasty. During this period royal monasteries were endowed and churches and private palaces were built. In the 17th century, the Plaza Mayor was added and the Puerta del Sol, the "Gate of the Sun", became the spiritual and geographical heart not only of Madrid but all of Spain.

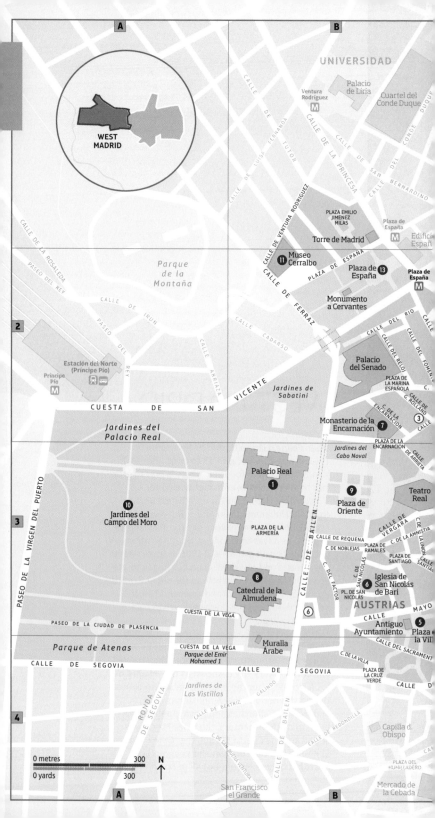

WEST MADRID

Must Sees

1 Palacio Real
2 Plaza Mayor

Experience More

3 Colegiata de San Isidro
4 Puerta del Sol
5 Plaza de la Villa
6 Iglesia de San Nicolás de Bari
7 Monasterio de la Encarnación
8 Catedral de la Almudena
9 Plaza de Oriente
10 Jardines del Campo del Moro
11 Museo Cerralbo
12 Monasterio de las Descalzas Reales

13 Plaza de España
14 Real Academia de Bellas Artes de San Fernando
15 Gran Vía

Eat

① Botín
② Mercado de San Miguel
③ La Bola

Drink

④ Casa Labra
⑤ Casa Revuelta
⑥ El Anciano Rey de los Vinos
⑦ Taberna Malaspina

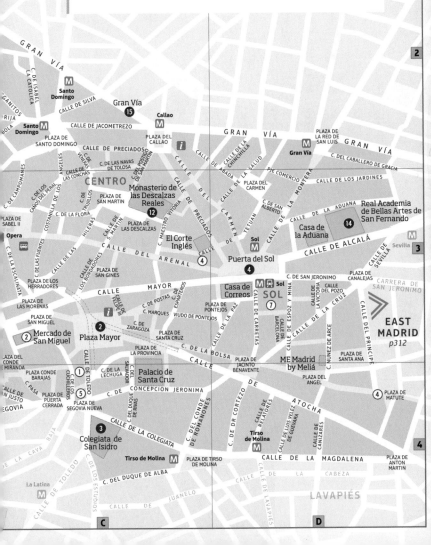

INSIDER TIP
Changing of the Guard

Every Wednesday and Saturday, soldiers march on the Plaza de la Armería, in front of the palace, to the sound of fifes, drums and horses' hoofs. Get there early to get the best spot.

The sun bathing the limestone north façade of the Palacio Real ↑

① ⟨✏⟩ ⟨M3⟩ ⟨▭⟩

PALACIO REAL

⊙ B3 ⌂ Calle de Bailén Ⓜ Ópera, Príncipe Pío, Plaza de España 🚌 3, 25, 39, 46, 75, 138, 148 ⊙ Palace: Apr–Sep: 10am–8pm daily; Oct–Mar: 10am–6pm daily; Changing of the Guard: 11am–2pm Wed & Sat (every 30 min) 🚫 For official functions, some public hols 🅦 patrimonionacional.es

Madrid's vast and lavish Royal Palace was built to impress. The site, on a high bluff over the Río Manzanares, had been occupied for centuries by a royal fortress, but after a fire in 1734, Felipe V commissioned a truly palatial replacement.

This splendid Royal Palace stands on the site of the original Moorish fortress. After the *reconquista* of Madrid in 1085, this *alcázar* served as a residence for visiting royals. But, following extensive modifications in 1561, it became the residence of Felipe II until the completion of El Escorial (*p358*) in 1584.

A fire on Christmas Eve 1734, during the reign of Felipe V, all but destroyed the castle. This suited Spain's first Bourbon king well – Felipe's idea of a royal palace was the Versailles of his childhood, and so he commissioned a new royal palace decorated in the French style.

Most of the limestone building is the work of Giovanni Battista Sachetti, with later modifications by other architects. So vast was the plan that construction lasted from 1738 to 1755, by which time Felipe V was dead. His son, Carlos III, became the first royal resident and the palace was the home of the Spanish royal family until Alfonso XIII went into exile in 1931.

> **Felipe's idea of a royal palace was the Versailles of his childhood, and so he commissioned a new royal palace decorated in the French style.**

↑ The landscaped gardens in the Plaza de Oriente, next to the palace

↑ The painted ceiling crowning the central staircase of the Palacio Real

1561
▽ King Felipe II moves his court to Madrid.

1738
▽ Construction of the palace begins under the orders of King Felipe V.

1764
King Carlos III moves into the newly built palace.

Timeline

800s
△ 9th-century *alcázar* is built.

1734
The old *alcázar* burns down.

1931
△ King Alfonso XIII – the last monarch to live in the palace – decides on voluntary exile.

↑ Crystal chandeliers illuminating the long
table in the dining room

Inside the Palace

Unsurprisingly, the interior of the Palacio Real matches the grandeur of its façade. It is remarkable both for its size and for the exuberant furnishings found in many of the rooms, including luxurious carpets, massive tapestries and glittering silverware. Take a guided tour or carve your own route through some of the 2,800 rooms to see this decor and some fascinating treasures from the royal collection, including glittering suits of armour, masterpieces by Goya and finely tuned violins.

Did You Know?

The Palacio Real is the largest castle in Europe by floor area.

Visitors climbing the
Palacio Real's grand ↑
marble staircase

Palace Rooms

Entrance Rooms

The first port of call is the Salón de los Alabarderos (Hall of the Palace Guards), decorated with a fresco by Tiépolo. Adjoining it is the Salón de Columnas (Hall of Columns), which served as the banquet hall until the new dining hall was incorporated in the 19th century. Today it is used for receptions and functions. Next, visitors enter the Rococo Salón del Trono (Throne Room). Completed in 1772, it has two rock crystal chandeliers, numerous candelabra and mirrors, and walls of crimson velvet with silver embroidery. The twin thrones are recent (1977), while the bronze lions that guard them date from 1651. The room is still used for functions, such as the royal reception on the Día de la Hispanidad or the yearly reception for the diplomatic corps posted in Madrid.

Carlos III Rooms

▷ Leading off from the Salón del Trono are the king's private chambers. He would take his meals in the Sala de Gasparini – lonely affairs considering the queen had her own dining room. In the Cámara de Gasparini, with its stucco ceiling and embroidered silk walls, the king would be dressed in the presence of courtiers.

Dining Room

This 400-sq-m (4,300-sq-ft) banquet hall was formed in 1879 when the queen's private chambers were joined together, during the reign of Alfonso XII. It is richly adorned with gold plate decoration on the ceiling and walls, frescoes, chandeliers, Flemish tapestries, Chinese vases and embroidered curtains. The table can accommodate up to 160 diners. The room immediately off the dining hall is devoted to commemorative medals, and also contains the elaborate centrepiece used during banquets. Other rooms contain silverware, china, crystal and an extraordinary collection of musical instruments.

Chapel Rooms

Built in 1749-57, the chapel is still used for religious services, and also for musical soirées. While the decor is luxurious, it is the dome, with its murals by Giaquinto, that immediately catches the eye. Next, visitors pass through the Salón de Paso and into María Cristina's chambers. During the reign of Alfonso XII these four small rooms served as an American-style billiards room, Oriental-style smoking room, the Salón de Estucos (queen's bedroom) and the Gabinete de Maderas de Indias, used as an office.

Royal Armoury

◁ Returning to the Plaza de la Armería, near the ticket office, you come to the Real Armería (Royal Armoury), which is housed in a pavilion built in 1897 after the original armoury was destroyed by fire. It contains weapons and royal suits of armour. On display is an elaborate suit of armour which once belonged to Carlos I. The armoury could be considered as Madrid's first museum because it has been open to the public since Felipe II inherited the collection from his father.

2 🍴 🍵 🛍️

PLAZA MAYOR

📍C3 Ⓜ Ópera, Sol, Tirso de Molina

At the very heart of Madrid life for centuries, the Plaza Mayor has seen it all, from *autos-da-fé (p304)* to coronations to Christmas markets. In an ongoing tradition, residents of this grand arcaded square have long rented out balcony space to *Madrileños* wanting ringside seats to the city's big events.

The splendid rectangular square, lined with pinnacles and dormer windows, was started in 1617 and built in just two years, replacing slum houses. Its architect, Juan Gómez de Mora, was successor to Juan de Herrera, designer of Felipe II's austere monastery-palace, El Escorial *(p358)*. Gómez de Mora echoed the style of his master, softening it slightly. The square was later reformed by Juan de Villanueva. The fanciest part of the arcaded construction is the Casa de la Panadería – the bakery. Its façade, now crudely reinvented, is decorated with allegorical paintings. The equestrian statue in the centre is of Felipe III, who ordered the square's construction. Today the square is lined with cafés that spill out onto the cobbles, and hosts a bustling collectors' market on Sundays, as well as occassional pageants and rock concerts.

→

The elaborately painted façade of the Casa de la Panadería, with its balconied windows

A HISTORIC SQUARE

Plaza Mayor has been witness to a number of historical events. The canonization of Madrid's patron, San Isidro, took place here in 1622, and the square was Carlos III's first stop after arriving from Italy in 1760. But what lives on most in popular culture is the 1621 execution of Rodrigo Calderón, secretary to Felipe III, here. Although hated by the Madrid populace, Calderón bore himself with such dignity on the day of his death that the phrase "proud as Rodrigo on the scaffold" survives today.

↑ The square at dusk, seen through one of its gates

237

The number of
decorative balconies
that surround the
Plaza Mayor.

↑ One of the many cafés on
Plaza Mayor, spilling out
onto the square's cobbles

↑ Francisco Rizi's *Auto-da-fé* painting of a trial held in the Plaza Mayor

THE SPANISH INQUISITION

The Spanish Inquisition was set up by King Fernando and Queen Isabel in 1478 to create a single, monolithic Catholic ideology in Spain. Protestant heretics and alleged "false converts" to Catholicism from the Jewish and Muslim faiths were tried, to ensure the religious unity of Spain.

AN UNFAIR TRIAL

Beginning with a papal bull, the Inquisition was run like a court, presided over by the Inquisitor-General. However, the defendants were denied counsel, not told the charges facing them and tortured to obtain confessions. Punishment ranged from imprisonment to beheading, hanging or burning at the stake. A formidable system of control, it gave Spain's Protestant enemies abroad a major propaganda weapon. The Inquisition lasted into the 18th century.

AUTO-DA-FÉ IN THE PLAZA MAYOR

The above painting by Francisco Rizi (1683) depicts a trial, or *auto-da-fé* – literally, "show of faith" – held in Madrid's main square on 30 June 1680. Unlike papal inquisitions elsewhere in Europe, this trial was presided over by the reigning monarch, Carlos II, accompanied by his queen. The painting shows a convicted defendant, forced to wear a red *sanbenito* robe, being led away to prison after refusing his last chance to repent and convert. Those who didn't confess were sentenced by day, and then executed.

> 💬 INSIDER TIP
> ## Walk on the Wild Side
>
> Sandemans offers 3-hour walking tours that take you to the sites where the Inquisition played out *(www.neweurope tours.eu)*. Starting and finishing in the Plaza Mayor, you'll be taken back to dark days of trials and torture, exorcisms and executions.

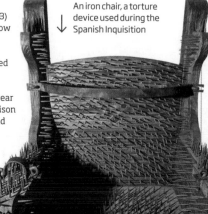
↓ An iron chair, a torture device used during the Spanish Inquisition

EXPERIENCE MORE

❸
Colegiata de San Isidro

📍 C4 🏛 Calle de Toledo 37
📞 91 369 23 10 Ⓜ La Latina,
Tirso de Molina 🕐 Summer:
7:30am–1pm & 7-9pm daily;
winter: 7:30am–1pm &
6-9pm daily

The Baroque-style Colegiata de San Isidro was built for the Jesuits in the mid-17th century. This twin-towered church was Madrid's cathedral until La Almudena (p307) was completed in 1993. After Carlos III expelled the Jesuits from Spain in 1767, it was rededicated to Madrid's patron saint, St Isidore. Two years later the saint's remains were moved here from the Iglesia de San Andrés.

❹
Puerta del Sol

📍 D3 Ⓜ Sol

One of the city's most popular meeting places, the Puerta del Sol is crowded and noisy with chatter. The square marks the site of the original eastern entrance to the city, once occupied by a gatehouse and castle. These disappeared long ago and a succession of churches came in their place. In the late 19th century the area was turned into a square and became the centre of café society.

Today the "square" is shaped like a half-moon, with a modern glass train station in front of the statue of Carlos III. The southern side of the square is edged by an austere red-brick building, home to the regional government. The buildings opposite it are arranged in a semicircle and contain modern shops and cafés. Originally the city's post office, it was built in the 1760s under Carlos III. In 1847 it became the headquarters of the Ministry of the Interior. The clock tower, which gives the building much of its identity, was added in 1866. During the Franco regime, the police cells under the building were the site of human rights abuses. In 1963, Julián Grimau, a member of the underground Communist

Party, allegedly fell from an upstairs window and miraculously survived, only to be executed soon afterwards.

The Puerta del Sol itself has witnessed many important historical events. On 2 May 1808 the uprising against the occupying French forces began here, but the crowd was crushed. In 1912 the liberal prime minister José Canalejas was assassinated in the square and, in 1931, the Second Republic was proclaimed from the balcony of the Ministry of the Interior.

On New Year's Eve, crowds fill the square to eat a grape on each stroke of the clock, a tradition supposed to bring good luck for the year.

> ### Did You Know?
>
> The statue of the bear and the madrona tree on the Puerta del Sol is the symbol of Madrid.

↑ Huge crowds gathering in the Puerta del Sol in the early evening

❺
Plaza de la Villa

🔲 B3 Ⓜ Ópera, Sol

The much-restored Plaza de la Villa is one of the most atmospheric spots in Madrid. Some of the city's most historic secular buildings are situated around this square.

The oldest building is the early 15th-century Torre de los Lujanes, with its Gothic portal and Mudéjar-style horseshoe arches. The Casa de Cisneros was built in 1537 for the nephew of Cardinal Cisneros, founder of the University of Alcalá *(p364)*. The main façade, on the Calle de Sacramento, is a fine example of the Plateresque style.

Linked to this building, by an enclosed bridge, is the old *ayuntamiento*. Designed in the 1640s by Juan Gómez de Mora, architect of the Plaza Mayor, it exhibits the same combination of steep roofs with dormer windows, steeple-like towers at the corners and an austere façade of brick and stone. Before construction was finished – over 30 years later – the building had acquired handsome Baroque doorways. A balcony was later added by Juan de Villanueva, the architect of the Prado *(p316)*, so that the royal family could watch Corpus Christi processions passing by.

❻
Iglesia de San Nicolás de Bari

🔲 B3 🏛 Plaza de San Nicolás 6 📞 91 559 40 64 Ⓜ Ópera 🕐 8:30am–1pm & 7–8:30pm Mon, 8:30–9:30am & 6:30–8:30pm Tue–Sat, 10am–1:45pm & 6:30–8:45pm Sun & public hols

The first mention of the church of San Nicolás is in a document of 1202. Its brick tower, with horseshoe arches, is the oldest surviving ecclesiastical structure in Madrid. It is thought to be 12th-century Mudéjar in style, and may have originally been the minaret of a Moorish mosque.

❼
Monasterio de la Encarnación

🔲 B2 🏛 Plaza de la Encarnación 1 Ⓜ Ópera, Santo Domingo 🕐 10am–2pm & 4–6:30pm Tue–Sat, 10am–3pm Sun & public hols 🚫 Easter, 17–20 Apr, 1 May, 24, 25 & 31 Dec 🌐 patrimonionacional.es

Standing in a delightful tree-shaded square, this tranquil Augustinian convent was founded in 1611 for Margaret of Austria, wife of Felipe III.

EAT

El Sobrino de Botín
The world's oldest restaurant, set in rustic dining rooms, is justly lauded for its excellent *cochinillo* (roast suckling pig).

🔲 C4 🏛 Calle Cuchilleros 17 🌐 botin.es

€€€

Mercado de San Miguel
An elegant century-old glass and iron construction houses this gastro food court.

🔲 C3 🏛 Plaza de San Miguel s/n 🌐 mercadodesan miguel.es

€€€

La Bola
Once a meeting place for the literary set, this Madrid institution has been serving traditional dishes since 1870.

🔲 B2 🏛 Calle de la Bola 5 🌐 labola.es

€€€

Still inhabited by nuns, the convent has blue and white Talavera tiles, wooden doors, exposed beams and portraits of royal benefactors. Inside is a collection of 17th-century art, with paintings by José de Ribera and Vincente Carducho.

The convent's main attraction is the reliquary chamber with a ceiling painted by Carducho. A phial containing the dried blood of St Pantaleon can be found here. According to a popular myth, the blood liquefies each year on 27 July, the anniversary of the saint's death. Should the blood fail to liquefy, it is said that disaster will befall Madrid.

Catedral de la Almudena

⑨B3 ⑥Calle de Bailén 10 ⑩Ópera ⑥Sep-Jun: 10:30am-2pm & 5-8pm Mon-Fri, 10:30am-8pm Sat & Sun (10am-9pm Jul & Aug); Museum & Dome: 10am-2:30pm Mon-Sat ⑩catedraldelaalmudena.es

Dedicated to the city's patron, the cathedral was begun in

←

The old *ayuntamiento*, or Town Hall, on Madrid's Plaza de la Villa

1883 and completed over a century later. The Neo-Gothic grey and white façade is similar to that of the Palacio Real opposite *(p298)*. The crypt houses a 16th-century image of the Virgen de la Almudena, while the dome offers grand views of the city. The first royal wedding also took place here between Prince Felipe (now King Felipe VI) and Letizia Ortiz in May 2004.

Plaza de Oriente

⑨B3 ⑩Ópera

While king of Spain, Joseph Bonaparte carved out this stirrup-shaped space from the jumble of buildings to the east of the Palacio Real, providing the view of the palace seen today. The square was once an important meeting place for state occasions; kings, queens and dictators all made public appearances on the palace balcony. The statues of kings that stand here were originally intended for the palace roof, but proved too heavy. The equestrian statue of Felipe IV in the centre of the square is by Italian sculptor Pietro Tacca, and is based on drawings by Velázquez. Across the square is the imposing Teatro Real, or Teatro de la Ópera, inaugurated in 1850 by Isabel II.

↑ Visitors admiring the altar inside the Catedral de la Almudena

⑩

Jardines del Campo del Moro

⑨A3 ⑥Paseo de la Virgen del Puerto s/n ⑩Ópera, Príncipe Pío ⑥10am-midnight daily ⑥1 & 6 Jan, 1 & 15 May, 12 Oct, 9 Nov, 24, 25 & 31 Dec and for official functions ⑩patrimonionacional.es

Jardines del Campo del Moro (the "Field of the Moor") is a pleasing park, rising steeply from the Río Manzanares to offer one of the finest views of the Palacio Real.

The park has a varied history. In 1109 a Moorish army led by Ali ben Yusuf camped here, hence the name. It went on to become a jousting ground for Christian knights. In the late 19th century it was used as a lavish playground for royal children. Around the same time it was landscaped in what is described as English style, with winding paths, grass and woodland, fountains and statues. It was reopened to the public in 1931 under the Second Republic, then closed again under Franco, and not reopened until 1978.

←

The exquisite staircase inside the Museo Cerralbo, lined with beautiful artifacts

The stairway has a fresco of Felipe IV's family looking down, as if from a balcony, and a fine ceiling by Claudio Coello and his pupils. It leads up to a first-floor cloister, ringed with chapels containing works of art relating to the lives of the former nuns. The main chapel houses Doña Juana's tomb. The Sala de Tapices has a series of tapestries, one woven in 1627 for Felipe II's daughter, Isabel Clara Eugenia. Another, *The Triumph of the Eucharist,* is based on cartoons by Rubens.

Museo Cerralbo

♥ B2 ⌂ Calle de Ventura Rodríguez 17 Ⓜ Plaza de España, Ventura Rodríguez ⏲ 9:30am-3pm Tue-Sat (also 5-8pm Thu), 10am-3pm Sun ⌧ Mon, 1 & 6 Jan, 1 May & some public hols ⬤ culturaydeporte.gob.es/mcerralbo

This 19th-century mansion is a monument to Enrique de Aguilera y Gamboa, the 17th Marquis of Cerralbo. A compulsive collector of art and artifacts, he bequeathed his lifetime's collection to the nation in 1922, stipulating that the exhibits be arranged exactly as he left them. They range from Iberian pottery to 18th-century marble busts.

One of the star exhibits is El Greco's magnificent *The Ecstasy of Saint Francis of Assisi.* There are also paintings by Ribera, Zurbarán, Cano and Goya.

The focal point of the main floor is the ballroom, lavishly decorated with mirrors. A large collection of weaponry is on display on this floor.

Monasterio de las Descalzas Reales

♥ C3 ⌂ Plaza de las Descalzas 3 Ⓜ Sol, Callao ⏲ 10am-2pm & 4-6:30pm Tue-Sat, 10am-3pm Sun & public hols ⌧ 1 & 6 Jan, Easter, 1 May, 24, 25 & 31 Dec ⬤ patrimonionacional.es

Around 1560, Felipe II's sister, Doña Juana, decided to convert the original medieval palace that stood here into a convent for nuns. Her status accounts for the huge collection of art and enormous wealth of the Convent of Las Descalzas Reales (Royal Barefooted).

> △ GREAT VIEW
> ## Staircase to Heaven
>
> Inside the Museo Cerralbo, no angle is more striking than the view up the staircase, resplendent with a large coat of arms framed by two 17th-century tapestries.

13

Plaza de España

♥ B2 Ⓜ Plaza de España

One of Madrid's busiest traffic intersections is the Plaza de España, which slopes down towards the Palacio Real *(p298)* and the Sabatini Gardens.

The square acquired its present appearance during the Franco period, with the construction, on the northern side, of the massive Edificio España between 1947 and 1953. Across the square is the Torre de Madrid (1957), known as *La Jirafa* (The Giraffe), which, for a while, was the tallest concrete structure in the world. The most attractive part of the square is its centre, occupied by a massive stone obelisk built in 1928. In front of it is a statue of the author Cervantes *(p364).* Below him, Don Quixote *(p419)* rides his horse Rocinante while the plump Sancho Panza trots alongside on his donkey. On the left-hand side is Dulcinea, Don Quixote's sweetheart.

Work is ongoing to remodel the square, and will see the addition of 1,000 trees and pedestrianized areas by 2021.

Real Academia de Bellas Artes de San Fernando

⊙ D3 **⌂** Calle de Alcalá 13
Ⓜ Banco de España, Gran Vía, Sevilla, Sol
⊙ 10am–3pm Tue–Sun
🗙 Aug & some public hols
ⓦ realacademiabellasartes
sanfernando.com

Former students of this fine arts academy, which is housed in an 18th-century building by José Benito de Churriguera, include Dalí and Picasso. Its art gallery's collection includes drawings by Raphael and Titian and, among the old masters, are huge paintings by Van Dyck and Rubens. Spanish artists from the 16th to the 19th centuries are also well represented. One of the highlights is Zurbarán's *Fray Pedro Machado*, typical of the artist's paintings of monks.

An entire room is devoted to Goya, a former director of the academy. On show here are his paintings of a relaxed Manuel Godoy, the *Burial of the Sardine*, the grim *Madhouse* and a self-portrait painted in 1815.

↓ Traffic passing the Edificio Metrópolis on the Gran Vía

⑮ Gran Vía

⊙ C2 **Ⓜ** Plaza de España, Santo Domingo, Callao, Gran Vía

A main traffic artery of the modern city, the Gran Vía was inaugurated in 1910, and its construction spanned several decades. Nowadays, the road is at the centre of city life and, following a restoration programme, has become an architectural showpiece.

The most interesting buildings are clustered at the Alcalá end, starting with the Corinthian columns, high-level statuary and tiled dome of the Edificio Metrópolis (p334).

A temple with Art Nouveau mosaics on its upper levels crowns No 1 Gran Vía. One striking feature of the buildings at this end of the street is colonnaded galleries on the upper floors, imitating medieval Aragonese and Catalan architecture. Another is the fine wrought-iron balconies and carved stone details, such as the gargoyle-like caryatids at No 12.

On the Red de San Luis, an intersection of four major roads, is the Telefónica building, the first skyscraper to be erected in the capital, built between 1926 and 1929.

DRINK

West Madrid has more than its fair share of *tabernas*, where beer, sherry and other tipples are served alongside hearty bar snacks. Here are some of our favourite local watering holes.

Casa Labra
⊙ C3 **⌂** Calle de Tetuán 12
ⓦ casalabra.es

———

Casa Revuelta
⊙ C4 **⌂** Calle de Latoneros 3
☎ 913 66 33 32

———

El Anciano Rey de los Vinos
⊙ B3 **⌂** Calle de Bailén 19
ⓦ elancianorey delosvinos.es

———

Taberna Malaspina
⊙ D3 **⌂** Calle de Cádiz 9
☎ 915 23 40 24

A SHORT WALK

WEST MADRID

Distance 2 km (1 mile) **Nearest metro** Tirso de Molina, Sol **Time** 30 minutes

Stretching from the charming Plaza de la Villa to the busy Puerta del Sol, the compact heart of West Madrid is steeped in history and full of interesting sights. As you walk through the area, you'll feel poignant points in the city's history seeping through the streets. This is no more apparent than in the Plaza Mayor, which you'll cross more than once. Trials and executions under the orders of the Inquisition *(p304)* were held in this porticoed square. Despite this gruesome past, it is West Madrid's finest piece of architecture, a legacy of the Habsburgs *(p295)*. Other buildings of note are the Colegiata de San Isidro and the Palacio de Santa Cruz. Although the route is short in length, take your time, stopping to sit in one of the area's numerous cafés and browsing among the stalls of the Mercado de San Miguel.

The beautiful **Plaza Mayor** *(p302) competes with the Puerta del Sol as the focus of West Madrid. The arcades at the base of the three-storey buildings are filled with cafés and craft shops.*

The **Mercado de San Miguel** *is housed in a 19th-century building with wrought-iron columns (p306). It's a great place to stop for a snack.*

PLAZA COMMANDANTE MORENAS

CALLE MAYOR

CORDON

PUÑONROSTRO

CUCHILLEROS

START

Old Town Hall (ayuntamiento)

Casa de Cisneros

A statue of Álvaro de Bazán stands in the centre of the **Plaza de la Villa** *(p306).*

0 metres   100   N
0 yards   100

Arco de Cuchilleros

The **Basílica Pontificia de San Miguel** *is an imposing 18th-century church with a beautiful façade and a graceful interior. It is one of very few churches in Spain inspired by the Italian Baroque style.*

← People visiting the Mercado de San Miguel for a bite to eat at dusk

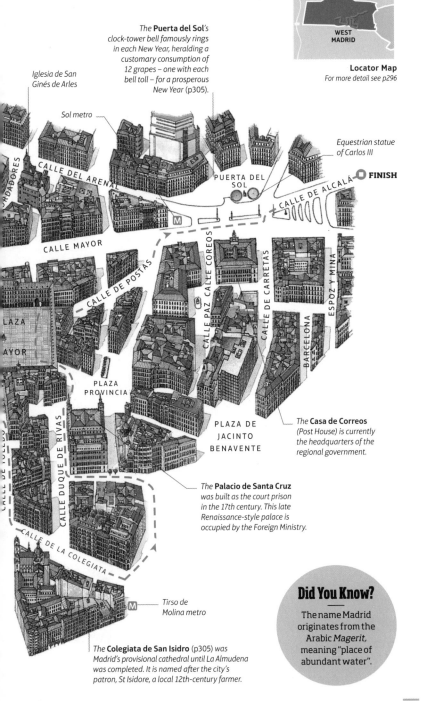

The **Puerta del Sol**'s clock-tower bell famously rings in each New Year, heralding a customary consumption of 12 grapes – one with each bell toll – for a prosperous New Year (p305).

Iglesia de San Ginés de Arles

Sol metro

Equestrian statue of Carlos III

CALLE DEL ARENAL

RDADORES

PUERTA DEL SOL

CALLE DE ALCALÁ

○ **FINISH**

CALLE MAYOR

CALLE DE POSTAS

CALLE DE PAZ

CALLE CORREOS

CALLE DE CARRETAS

ESPOZ Y MINA

BARCELONA

LAZA

AYOR

PLAZA PROVINCIA

CALLE DUQUE DE RIVAS

PLAZA DE JACINTO BENAVENTE

The **Casa de Correos** (Post House) is currently the headquarters of the regional government.

The **Palacio de Santa Cruz** was built as the court prison in the 17th century. This late Renaissance-style palace is occupied by the Foreign Ministry.

CALLE DE LA COLEGIATA

Tirso de Molina metro

The **Colegiata de San Isidro** (p305) was Madrid's provisional cathedral until La Almudena was completed. It is named after the city's patron, St Isidore, a local 12th-century farmer.

Locator Map
For more detail see p296

WEST MADRID

Did You Know?

The name Madrid originates from the Arabic *Magerit*, meaning "place of abundant water".

EAST MADRID

To the east of the city centre, there once lay an idyllic district of market gardens known as the Prado, the "Meadow". In the 16th century a monastery was built and later the Habsburgs extended it to form a palace, of which only fragments now remain; the palace gardens are now the popular Parque del Retiro.

This development attracted intellectuals to this corner of the city and the Huertas district, which had once been farmland, soon became the haunt of Spain's most famous writers of the time. During the 17th century, the Barrio de las Letras (Writers' Quarter) played host to everyone from Miguel de Cervantes to Lope de Vega.

The Bourbon monarchs chose this eastern area to expand and embellish the city in the 18th century. They built grand squares with fountains, a triumphal gateway, and, in 1785, work began on a Neo-Classical building that was set to house a museum of natural history. This ambition never came to fruition and the Museo del Prado opened here instead in 1819, housing works from the former Spanish Royal Collection. In the 20th century, the Prado was joined by the Museo Nacional Centro de Arte Reina Sofía, a collection of modern Spanish and international art, and the Museo Thyssen-Bornemisza, displaying works from across the centuries, to form the "Golden Triangle of Art".

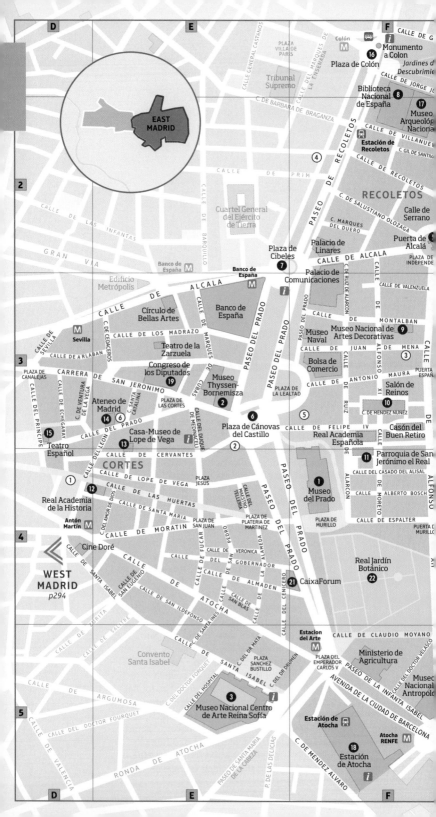

EAST MADRID

D E F

2

RECOLETOS

CORTES

WEST MADRID
p294

16 Monumento a Colon
Plaza de Colón
Jardines d Descubrimie
Biblioteca Nacional de España 8
Museo Arqueológ Naciona 17
Estación de Recoletos
Calle de Serrano
Puerta de Alcalá

Tribunal Supremo

Cuartel General del Ejército de Tierra

Edificio Metrópolis

Plaza de Cibeles 7
Palacio de Linares
Palacio de Comunicaciones

Banco de España

Círculo de Bellas Artes
Teatro de la Zarzuela
Congreso de los Diputados 19
Museo Thyssen-Bornemisza 2
Museo Naval
Museo Nacional de Artes Decorativas 9
Bolsa de Comercio
Salón de Reinos 10
Casón del Buen Retiro
Real Academia Española

Ateneo de Madrid 14 6
Casa-Museo de Lope de Vega 13
Plaza de Cánovas del Castillo 2

Teatro Español 15

Real Academia de la Historia
Museo del Prado 1

Cine Doré
CaixaForum 21
Real Jardín Botánico 22

Convento Santa Isabel

Estacion del Arte
Ministerio de Agricultura
Museo Nacional Antropolo

Museo Nacional Centro de Arte Reina Sofía 3

Estación de Atocha
Atocha RENFE

Estación de Atocha 18

EAST MADRID

Must Sees
1. Museo del Prado
2. Museo Thyssen-Bornemisza
3. Museo Nacional Centro de Arte Reina Sofía
4. Parque del Retiro

Experience More
5. Puerta de Alcalá
6. Plaza de Cánovas del Castillo
7. Plaza de Cibeles
8. Biblioteca Nacional de España
9. Museo Nacional de Artes Decorativas
10. Salón de Reinos
11. Parroquia de San Jerónimo el Real
12. Real Academia de la Historia
13. Casa-Museo de Lope de Vega
14. Ateneo de Madrid
15. Teatro Español
16. Plaza de Colón
17. Museo Arqueológico Nacional
18. Estación de Atocha
19. Congreso de los Diputados
20. Calle de Serrano
21. CaixaForum
22. Real Jardín Botánico

Eat
1. Taberna El Sur de Huertas
2. Estado Puro
3. Viridiana

Drink
4. Café Gijón

Stay
5. Mandarin Oriental Ritz
6. Hotel One Shot Prado 23

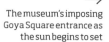

❶ 🤿 🎨 🍽 🖥 🛍

MUSEO DEL PRADO

📍F4 🚇Paseo del Prado Ⓜ Estación del Arte, Banco de España 🚌9, 10, 14, 19, 27, 34, 37, 45 🕙10am-8pm Mon-Sat, 10am-7pm Sun & public hols; 10am-2pm 6 Jan, 24 & 31 Dec 🚫1 Jan, 1 May, 25 Dec 🌐museodelprado.es

A must for any art fan, the Prado Museum contains the world's greatest assembly of Spanish painting – especially works by Velázquez and Goya – ranging from the 12th to 19th centuries. But that's not all – it also houses impressive foreign collections, particularly of Italian and Flemish works.

The Neo-Classical main building of the Museo Nacional del Prado, as it's formally known, was designed in 1785 by Juan de Villanueva on the orders of Carlos III. It was built to house the Natural History Cabinet, a museum of natural history, but it was under Carlos III's grandson, Fernando VII, that it opened as the Royal Museum of Paintings and Sculptures in 1819. The collection initially comprised 311 Spanish paintings, but the current collection of over 20,000 works reflects the historical power of the Spanish Crown. The Low Countries and parts of Italy were under Spanish domination for centuries and are well represented in the collection, while the 18th century was an era of French influence. The Prado is worthy of repeated visits, but if you go only once, see the Spanish works of the 17th century.

Upon the deposition of Isabella II in 1868, the museum was nationalized and the collection grew beyond its original building. The expansion has been ongoing since 1918. In 2007, a new building was constructed over the adjacent church's cloister to house temporary exhibitions. Norman Foster and Carlos Rubio Carvajal's redesign of the Salón de Reinos, a building nearby, was chosen in 2016 as the museum's next expansion.

ART AT WAR

As tensions peaked and the Spanish Civil War commenced, the League of Nations recommended the removal of some of the Museo del Prado's most precious treasures. Museum staff sent 353 paintings, 168 drawings and the Dauphin's Treasure first to Valencia, then on to Girona, before they finally arrived safely in Geneva. Although the Spanish Civil War ended in 1939, the advent of World War II meant that the art had to travel back to the Prado - across French territory - under the cover of darkness.

→ The museum's imposing Goya Square entrance as the sun begins to set

💬 **INSIDER TIP**
Be Late

If you're on a budget, head to the Prado two hours before it closes, when admission is free. You'll have a lot to cover in a short time, but it's the perfect way to get an arty fix on the cheap.

↑ Art enthusiasts viewing paintings in one of the Prado's light-filled galleries

← Admiring the museum's collection of Greek and Roman statues

↑ Visitors taking in *The Clothed Maja*, an early
19th-century work by Goya

Exploring the Collection

The museum's extensive permanent collection is arranged
chronologically over three main floors. Classical sculpture
is on the ground floor, Velázquez on the first floor, and the
extensive Goya collection across the Murillo side of all three
floors. The permanent collection is accessed via the Velázquez
and Goya entrances. Visitors to the temporary exhibitions
should use the Jerónimos entrance.

Did You Know?

Goya was accused of
obscenity for his naked
version of *The Clothed
Maja*, exhibited beside
it in the Prado.

The large interior
of one of the Prado's
many galleries ↓

The Collection

Spanish Painting

Right up to the 19th century, Spanish painting focused on religious and royal themes, offering a sharp focus that seems to have suited Spanish painters. What is often considered as a truly Spanish style - with its highly wrought emotion and deepening sombreness - first started to emerge in the 16th century in the paintings of the Mannerists, of which the Prado has an impressive collection. The 17th century is best represented by the work of Diego Velázquez.

Flemish and Dutch Painting

▷ Spain's long connection with the Low Countries naturally resulted in an intense admiration for the so-called Flemish primitives. Most notable are nearly 100 canvases by the 17th-century Flemish painter Peter Paul Rubens, including *The Adoration of the Magi (right)*. The most significant Dutch painting on display is Rembrandt's *Artemisia*.

Italian Painting

▷ Botticelli's dramatic wooden panels telling *The Story of Nastagio degli Onesti*, a vision of a knight condemned to kill his own beloved, were commissioned by two rich Florentine families and are a sinister high point. Raphael contributes the superb *The Holy Family with a Lamb (right)*, while *Christ Washing the Disciples' Feet*, an early masterpiece by Tintoretto, reveals the painter's brilliant handling of perspective. Titian, who served as court painter to Carlos I, and Caravaggio are also represented.

French Painting

Marriages between French and Spanish royalty in the 17th century, culminating in the 18th-century Bourbon accession to the throne, brought French art to Spain. The Prado has eight works attributed to Poussin, among them his serene *St Cecilia* and *Landscape with St Jerome*. The magnificent *Landscape with the Embarkation of St Paula Romana at Ostia* is the best work here by Claude Lorrain. Among the 18th-century artists featured are Antoine Watteau and Jean Ranc. *Felipe V* is the work of the royal portraitist Louis-Michel van Loo.

German Painting

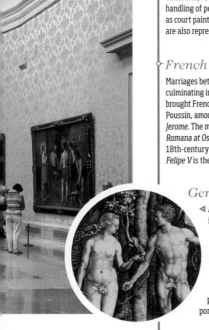

◁ Although German art is not especially well represented in the Prado's collection, there are a number of paintings by Albrecht Dürer, including his classical depictions of Adam and Eve *(left)*. His lively *Self-Portrait* of 1498, painted at the tender age of 26, is undoubtedly the highlight of the small but valuable German collection in the museum. Lucas Cranach is also featured and works by the late 18th-century painter Anton Raffael Mengs include some magnificent portraits of Carlos III.

② 🏃 🎿 🍴 🖥 🛍

MUSEO THYSSEN-BORNEMISZA

📍E3 🏛Paseo del Prado 8 Ⓜ Banco de España, Sevilla 🚌1, 2, 5, 9, 10, 14 and many others 🕐Jun-mid-Sep: 10am-7pm Tue-Sun, 10am-4pm Mon for temp exhibs; mid-Sep-May: noon-4pm Mon, 10am-7pm Tue-Sun 🚫1 Jan, 1 May & 25 Dec 🌐museothyssen.org

Regarded by many critics as the most important privately assembled art collection in the world, the Museo Thyssen-Bornemisza illustrates the history of Western art, from European primitives through to 20th-century works. The museum's collection, consisting of more than 1,000 paintings, includes masterpieces by Goya, Van Gogh and Picasso.

This magnificent museum is based on the collection assembled by Baron Heinrich Thyssen-Bornemisza and his son, Hans Heinrich. In 1992 it was installed in Madrid's 18th-century Villahermosa Palace, and was sold to the nation the following year. A collection of mainly Impressionist art acquired by Carmen Thyssen, Hans Heinrich's wife, opened to the public in 2004. The museum's galleries are arranged around a central courtyard. The top floor exhibits early Italian art through to 17th century works, while the first floor continues with 17th-century Dutch art and German Expressionism. The ground floor displays 20th-century paintings.

Did You Know?

Baron Thyssen-Bornemisza originally housed his collection in his mansion in Lugano, Switzerland.

↑ *Venus y Cupido,* an expressive piece by
Flemish painter Peter Paul Rubens

TOP 5 MUSEUM HIGHLIGHTS

Portrait of Giovanna degli Albizzi Tornabuoni (1489–90)
A symbolic painting by Domenico Ghirlandaio.

Les Vessenots in Auvers (1890)
A painting of old country cottages by Van Gogh.

Venus y Cupido (1606–11)
Peter Paul Rubens' depiction of a reflection of ideal beauty.

The Grand Canal From San Vio, Venice (c 1723–24)
This Canaletto painting is prized for its topographic accuracy.

Swaying Dancer (1877–79)
Degas conveys the ballerina's movement.

← A pink-hued gallery, and *(inset)* Museo Thyssen-Bornemisza's exterior

MUSEO NACIONAL CENTRO DE ARTE REINA SOFÍA

Q E5 **⌂** Calle de Santa Isabel 52 **Ⓜ** Estación del Arte
🚌 6, 14, 19, 27, 45, 55, 86 **⏰** 10am–8pm Mon, Wed–Sat,
10am–2:30pm Sun **🕐** Tue, 1 & 6 Jan, 1 & 15 May, 9 Nov, 24,
25 & 31 Dec, some public hols **🌐** museoreinasofia.es

Perhaps most famous for Picasso's *Guernica*, this museum of 20th-century art holds other major works by influential artists, including pieces by Miró and Dalí. The museum has been at the cutting-edge since it opened in 1992 and continues to reinvent itself.

Housed in Madrid's former General Hospital, the museum's collection is as exciting and impressive as its building. Built in the late 18th century and designed by José de Hermosilla and Francisco Sabatini, the hospital was shut down in 1965, but survived demolition as it was declared a national monument in 1977 due to its history and unique architecture. Restoration of the building began under the direction of Antonio Fernández Alba, and in April 1986 the Reina Sofía Art Centre opened. The distinct steel and glass elevator towers, designed by Spanish architects José Luis Iñiguez de Onzoño and Antonio Vázquez de Castro in collaboration with British architect Ian Ritchie, were added in 1988. The collection was finally inaugurated as a permanent collection – now commonly referred to as simply the Museo Reina Sofía – in 1992. The latest major extension, designed by Jean Nouvel, was added in 2005. Named after its architect, this stunning building increased the museum's exhibition space and includes Collection 3: From Revolt to Postmodernity, a library, a café and auditoriums which host various events such as film screenings and concerts.

Did You Know?

Jean Nouvel was awarded the Pritzker Prize, architecture's highest honour, in 2008.

← *Wheat & Steak*, a sculpture by Spanish artist Antoni Miralda

INSIDER TIP
Free Time

Entry to the museum is free after 6pm every-day apart from Tuesday and Sunday. If you'd rather take your time, visit after 1:30pm on Sunday, when you'll have until 4:15pm to explore.

↑ Roy Lichtenstein's *Brushstroke* in Nouvel's extension, and *(inset)* the original building

Exploring the Collection

The 20th century has undoubtedly been the most brilliant period in the history of Spanish art since the 17th century. Many facets of the Spanish artistic genius are on show in the Museo Reina Sofía. Sculpture, paintings and even work by the Surrealist film-maker Luis Buñuel provide a skilfully arranged tour through an eventful century. The permanent collection, in the Sabatini Building, is arranged around an open courtyard. Collection 1, on the second floor, displays works dating from 1900 to 1945, and includes rooms dedicated to important movements such as Cubism and Surrealism; Collection 2, on the fourth floor, has works dating from 1945 to 1968, including representatives of Pop Art, Minimalism and more recent tendencies. Collection 3: From Revolt to Postmodernity is dedicated to art from the 1960s to the 1980s.

↑ A crowd gathering in front of Picasso's spectacular *Guernica*

Did You Know?

The museum is named after Queen Sofía of Spain, mother of the current King Felipe VI.

PICASSO'S GUERNICA

The most well-known single work of the 20th century, this Civil War protest painting was commissioned by the Spanish Republican government in 1937 for a Paris exhibition. Picasso found his inspiration in the mass air attack of the same year on the Basque town of Gernika-Lumo (*p272*), by German pilots flying for the Nationalist air force. The painting hung in a New York gallery until 1981, reflecting the artist's wish that it should not return to Spain until democracy was re-established. It was moved here from the Prado (*p316*) in 1992.

The Beginnings of Modern Spanish Art

▷ Following the storm of creativity that culminated with Goya in the 19th century, Spanish painting went through an unremarkable period. A few artists managed to break the mould, hinting at the dawn of a new era of artistic brilliance; the museum displays the brooding works of Gutiérrez Solana, whose favourite subjects are the people of Madrid. Influenced by the Spanish masters, his paintings include *La Tertulia del Café de Pombo* (1920, *right*).

Pablo Picasso

The works on display span five decades in the life of Pablo Picasso. The first image visitors notice is the haunting *Woman in Blue* (1901), one of Picasso's earliest works from his so-called "blue" period. In Room 206 is the most-visited piece in the collection - the vast *Guernica* (1937). Aside from its unquestionable artistic merits, the canvas has a deep historical significance for Spaniards.

Miró, Dalí and the Surrealists

Joan Miró turned his hand to many styles. His Surrealist experiments of the 1920s provide evidence of his love of the vivid colours and bold shapes of Catalan folk art. His fellow Catalan, Salvador Dalí, is especially well known as a member of the Surrealist movement, which depended on access to subconscious images without censorship by the rational mind. Other prominent Surrealists whose work is displayed here include Benjamín Palencia, Oscar Domínguez and Luis Buñuel. Dalí's Surrealist masterpiece, *The Great Masturbator* (1929), hangs in contrast to the realistic *Girl at the Window* (1925). Like many of his contemporaries, Dalí embraced widely differing styles during his career.

Julio González

◁ A friend and contemporary of Gargallo and Picasso, Julio González is known as the father of modern Spanish sculpture, chiefly because of his pioneering use of iron as a raw material. Look out for González' humorous self-portrait entitled *Tête dite "Lapin"*, or *Head called "Rabbit"* (1930, *left*).

The Paris School

The turbulent history of Spain in the 20th century resulted in a steady stream of talented Spanish artists leaving their homeland. Many of them, including Picasso, Dalí, Juan Gris and Miró, passed through Paris - some staying for a few months, others for years. Artists of other nationalities also congregated in the French capital, and all of these artists were part of the Paris School. It is possible to see the mutual influence of this closely knit, yet constantly evolving, group of young artists.

Franco and Beyond

The Civil War (1936-9) had an enormous effect on the development of Spanish art. Under Franco, the state enforced rigid censorship. In the rooms of the fourth floor, the Museo Reina Sofía displays pieces of modern art from the 20th century. Works span the period from the end of World War II in 1945 through to 1968, and the development of different movements is marked. Artists on show include Robert Delaunay, Max Ernst, Francis Bacon and Georges Braque. Later works by Picasso and Miró can also be found here, as can pieces by sculptors Julio López-Hernández and Jorge Oteiza.

↑ *Green-Blue* by Gerhard Richter and *Untitled* by Bruce Nauman.

PARQUE DEL RETIRO

◉ G4 ⌂ Plaza de la Independencia 7 ☏ 91 530 00 41 Ⓜ Retiro, Ibiza, Estación del Arte ◷ Apr-Sep: 6am-midnight daily; Oct-Mar: 6am-10pm daily

Strolling the manicured pathways of the Retiro was once the preserve of kings and queens, but nowadays it is a blissful pastime for *Madrileños* and visitors of the pleasure garden. At dusk, as the temperature drops, it feels as though half the city turns out to see and be seen.

The Retiro, which is situated in Madrid's smart Jerónimos district, takes its name from Felipe IV's royal palace complex, which once stood here. Today, all that is left of the palace is the Casón del Buen Retiro – now the Prado's library (p316) – and the Salón de Reinos (p330), both located just outside the park.

Used privately by the royal family from 1632, the park became the scene of elaborate pageants, bullfights and mock naval battles. In the 18th century it was partially opened to the public, provided visitors were formally dressed, and in 1869 it was fully opened.

A short stroll from the park's northern entrance down the tree-lined avenue leads to the bustling *estanque* (pleasure lake). This is a hub for much of the park's activity, and rowing boats can be hired here. On one side of the lake is a half-moon colonnade in front of which an equestrian statue of Alfonso XII rides high on a column. Opposite, portrait painters and fortune-tellers ply their trade.

To the south of the lake are two ornate palaces. The Neo-Classical Palacio de Velázquez and the Palacio de Cristal (Crystal Palace) were built by Ricardo Velázquez Bosco in 1883 and 1887 respectively and regularly hold contemporary art exhibitions.

The gardens are also home to many elegant marble monuments and statues. Among them is *El Ángel Caído* (Fallen Angel), which is a late 19th-century sculpture by Ricardo Bellver that crowns one of the park's fountains. It is one of perhaps three statues of the devil in the world.

PICTURE PERFECT
Those in Glass Houses

The intricate iron architecture of the Palacio de Cristal can be perfectly captured reflected in the lake. Get the best shot of the east-facing structure at sunrise, when the light reflects off the hundreds of glass panels.

① Visitors can seek shade beneath the colonnade encircling Alfonso XII's monument.

② The park's turquoise pleasure lake is an especially popular spot to take a rest.

③ As well as rolling parkland, the Parque del Retiro is also home to a parterre garden of formal French design.

The Palacio de Cristal at sunset, in the southern part of the Parque del Retiro ↑

The Puerta de Alcalá, fronted by a carpet of yellow flowers

EXPERIENCE MORE

⑤

Puerta de Alcalá

⑨ F2 ⑧ Plaza de la Independencia Ⓜ Retiro

This grand ceremonial gateway was designed by Francesco Sabatini in 1769 to replace a smaller Baroque gateway, which had been built by Felipe III for his wife, Margarita de Austria. Constructed from granite in Neo-Classical style, with a lofty pediment and sculpted angels, Sabatini's gateway took nine years to build. Visit at night when it is floodlit to fully appreciate its grandeur.

---

⑥

Plaza de Cánovas del Castillo

⑨ E3 Ⓜ Banco de España

This busy roundabout is named after Antonio Cánovas del Castillo, one of the leading statesmen of 19th-century Spain, who was assassinated in 1897. Dominating the plaza is the Fuente de Neptuno – a fountain with a statue depicting Neptune in his chariot. The statue was designed in 1777 by Ventura Rodríguez as part of Carlos III's scheme to beautify eastern Madrid.

---

⑦

Plaza de Cibeles

⑨ E2 Ⓜ Banco de España

The Plaza de Cibeles is one of Madrid's best-known landmarks. The Fuente de Cibeles stands in the middle of the busy traffic island at the junction of the Paseo del Prado and the Calle de Alcalá. This sculpted fountain is named after Cybele, the Greco-Roman goddess of nature, and shows her sitting in her lion-drawn chariot. Designed by José Hermosilla and Ventura Rodríguez in the late 18th century, it is considered a symbol of Madrid.

Around the square rise four important buildings. The most notable are the town hall and the Palacio de Comunicaciones, home to a cultural centre, **CentroCentro**. Built from 1905 to 1917, its appearance – white, with high pinnacles – is often likened to a wedding cake. On the northeast side is the stone façade of the Palacio de Linares, built by the Marquis of Linares at the time of the second Bourbon restoration of 1875. Once threatened with demolition, the palace was reprieved and converted into the **Casa de América**, which

---

GREAT VIEW
Panorama Drama

A ticketed lift will sweep you up to the eighth floor of CentroCentro (inside the Palacio de Comunicaciones on the Plaza de Cibeles) for the most impressive panoramic view of the city.

8

Biblioteca Nacional de España

F1 🏛 Paseo de Recoletos 20-22 Ⓜ Colón, Serrano 🕐 9am-9pm Mon-Fri, 9am-2pm Sat, museum and exhibitions only Sun 🚫 Public hols 🌐 bne.es

King Felipe V of Spain founded the National Library in 1712. Since then, it has been mandatory for printers to submit a copy of every book printed in Spain. Currently it holds some 28 million publications, plus a large number of maps, musical scores and audiovisual records. Jewels include a first-edition *Don Quixote* and two hand-written codes by da Vinci.

A museum looks at the history of the library as well as the evolution of writing. The library also holds regular exhibitions, talks and concerts.

9

Museo Nacional de Artes Decorativas

F3 🏛 Calle de Montalbán 12 Ⓜ Retiro, Banco de España 🕐 9:30am-3pm Tue-Sat (Thu also 5-8pm, except Jul & Aug), 10am-3pm Sun 🚫 Public hols 🌐 mnartesdecorativas.mecd.es

Housed in the 19th-century Palacio de Santoña near the Parque del Retiro, the National

hosts art exhibitions by Latin American artists and theatrical performances and lectures.

In the northwest corner of the Plaza de Cibeles, surrounded by gardens, is the heavily guarded Army Headquarters, housed in the buildings of the former Palacio de Buenavista. Commissioned by the Duchess of Alba in 1777, construction was twice delayed by fire. On the opposite corner is the Banco de España, constructed between 1884 and 1891. Its design was inspired by the Venetian Renaissance style, with delicate ironwork on the roof and windows. Renovation work has returned the bank to its late 19th-century glory.

CentroCentro
🕐 10am-8pm Tue-Sun 🚫 Mon 🌐 centrocentro.org

Casa de América
🕐 9am-3pm & 4-8pm Mon-Fri 🚫 Aug & public hols 🌐 casamerica.es

Museum of Decorative Arts contains an interesting collection of furniture and *objets d'art*. The exhibits are mainly from Spain and date back as far as Phoenician times. There are also some excellent ceramics from Talavera de la Reina (*p417*) and ornaments from the Far East.

→ The beautiful Fuente de Cibeles on the Plaza de Cibeles

Salón de Reinos

 F3 Calle de Méndez Núñez 1 Retiro, Banco de España
For refurbishment

The Salón de Reinos (Hall of Kingdoms) is one of the two remaining parts of the 17th-century Palacio del Buen Retiro and gets its name from the shields of the 24 kingdoms of the Spanish monarchy, which are part of the decor supervised by court painter Velázquez. In the time of Felipe IV, the Salón was used for diplomatic receptions and official ceremonies.

Parroquia de San Jerónimo el Real

F4 Calle del Moreto 4 91 420 30 78 Banco de España Oct-Jun: 10am-1pm & 5-8pm daily; Jul-Sep: 10am-1pm & 6-8:30pm daily

Built in the 16th century for Queen Isabel, but since remodelled, San Jerónimo is Madrid's royal church. From the 17th century it became virtually a part of the Retiro

palace which once stood here (p326). The church was originally attached to the Hieronymite monastery. The cloister and part of the atrium now form part of a building at the Prado Museum.

The marriage of Alfonso XIII and Victoria Eugenia of Battenberg took place here in 1906, as did King Juan Carlos I's coronation in 1975.

Real Academia de la Historia

D4 Calle del León 21 Antón Martín To the public rah.es

The Royal Academy of History, aptly located in the so-called Barrio de las Letras (Writers' Quarter) is an austere brick building built by Juan de Villanueva in 1788.

In 1898, the intellectual and bibliophile Marcelino Menéndez Pelayo became director of the academy, living here until his death in 1912. The academy retains significant libraries and its collections of antiquities include more than 200,000 books, brochures and manuscripts.

The building is closed to the public and can only be viewed from the outside.

EAT

Taberna El Sur de Huertas
This friendly taberna serves traditional homemade dishes.
E4 Calle de las Huertas 24 919 20 56 86
€€€

Viridiana
Chef Abraham García reinvents classic dishes at this unpretentious restaurant.
F3 Calle Juan de Mena 14 restauranteviridiana.com
€€€

Casa Alberto
This taberna serves classic Madrilenian dishes in a room decorated with pictures of bullfighters.
D4 Calle de las Huertas 18 Sun D, Mon casaalberto.es
€€€

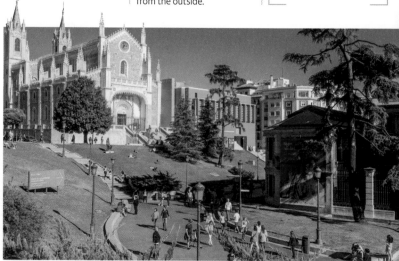

Casa-Museo de Lope de Vega

▣ E3 ▢ Calle de Cervantes 11 Ⓜ Antón Martín, Sevilla ◷ By appt only: 10am-6pm Tue-Sun ▣ 1 & 6 Jan, 1 & 15 May, 24, 25 & 31 Dec ◱ casa museolopedevega.org

Félix Lope de Vega, a leading 17th-century writer, moved into this house in 1610. Here he wrote over two-thirds of his plays, thought to total almost 1,000. Meticulously restored in 1935 using some of Lope de Vega's own furniture, the house gives a great feeling of Castilian life in the early 17th century. A dark chapel with no external windows occupies the centre, separated from the writer's bedroom by only a barred window. The small garden at the rear is planted with the flowers and fruit trees mentioned by the writer in his works. He died here in 1635.

Ateneo de Madrid

▣ E3 ▢ Calle del Prado 21 Ⓜ Antón Martín, Sevilla ◷ By appt only: 10am-1pm Mon-Fri ◱ ateneode madrid.com

Formally founded in 1835, this learned association is similar to a club in atmosphere. It is housed in a Modernist building with a grand stairway and panelled hall hung with the portraits of famous fellows.

Although closed down during past periods of repression, the institution has remained a mainstay of liberal thought in Spain. Many leading Socialists are members, along with writers and other intellectuals.

←

The Parroquia de San Jerónimo el Real, next to the Museo del Prado

↑ The Neo-Classical façade of the Teatro Español, on the Plaza de Santa Ana

Teatro Español

▣ D3 ▢ Calle del Príncipe 25 Ⓜ Sol, Sevilla ◔ Performances from 7pm Tue-Sun ◱ teatroespanol.es

Dominating the Plaza de Santa Ana is the Teatro Español, one of Madrid's oldest and most beautiful theatres.

From 1583, many of Spain's finest plays, by leading dramatists of the time such as Lope de Rueda, were first performed in the Corral del Príncipe, which originally stood on this site. In 1802 a large fire barely left the façade standing and reconstruction saw it replaced by the Teatro Español.

The Neo-Classical façade, with pilasters and medallions, is by Juan de Villanueva. Engraved on it are the names of great Spanish dramatists, including that of celebrated writer Federico García Lorca.

Hour-long guided tours are available (at noon on random days, check the website), which take in the stage, the king's box and private rooms.

→

Roman mosaics depicting the seasons and months at the Museo Arqueológico Nacional

 16

Plaza de Colón

📍F1 Ⓜ Serrano, Colón

This large square, overlooked by huge 1970s tower blocks, is dedicated to 15th-century navigator Christopher Columbus (Colón in Spanish).

On the south side of the square is a palace housing the National Library and the Archaeological Museum. The Post-Modernist skyscraper of the Heron Corporation towers over the plaza from the far side of the Paseo de la Castellana.

The highlight of the square, however, is the pair of monuments dedicated to Columbus. The prettiest, and oldest, is a Neo-Gothic spire erected in 1885, with Columbus at its top, pointing west. Carved reliefs on the plinth depict his landings.

A plinth that once supported another statue of the Genovese navigator has since been reclaimed and now plays host to rotating art installations. Since 2018, it has been occupied by Jaume Plensa's Julia. This 12-m (39-ft) statue of a woman's head is made from polyester resin and white marble dust. The installation that will take its place in 2022 is yet to be announced.

Across the square is the other, more modern monument – four large concrete shapes inscribed with quotations about Columbus's journeys.

 17

Museo Arqueológico Nacional

📍F2 🏛 Calle de Serrano 13 Ⓜ Serrano, Retiro, Colón 🚌1, 9, 19, 51, 74 🕐9:30am-8pm Tue-Sat, 9:30am-3pm Sun 🕐 Some public hols 🌐man.es

Founded by Isabel II in 1867, Madrid's archaeological museum houses a collection that consists mainly of material uncovered during excavations all over Spain, as well as pieces from Egypt, ancient Greece and the Etruscan civilization.

Highlights of the earliest finds include an exhibition on the ancient civilization of El Argar in Andalucía, and a display of jewellery uncovered at the Roman settlement of Numantia, near Soria (p398).

Other exhibited pieces are devoted to the period between Roman and Mudéjar Spain. Iberian culture is also represented, with two notable funerary sculptures – La Dama de Elche

and La Dama de Baza. The Roman period is illustrated with some impressive mosaics, including one from the 3rd century AD. The underside of this 1,800-year-old work shows a combat between gladiators, Simmachius and Maternus; the upper register displays Simmachius' victory. Outstanding pieces from the Visigothic period include splendid 7th-century gold votive crowns from Toledo province.

On show from the Islamic era is well-preserved pottery uncovered from Medina Azahara in Andalucía (p510). Romanesque exhibits at the museum include an ivory crucifix carved in 1063 for Fernando I of Castilla-León, and the Madonna and Child from Sahagún, considered a masterpiece of Spanish art.

💬 INSIDER TIP
Free For All

The Plaza de Colón is home to the Teatro Fernán Gómez Centro Cultural de la Villa, which has free art exhibitions, puppet shows and zarzuela (light opera) performances (www. teatrofernangomez.com).

Estación de Atocha

F5 **Plaza del Emperador Carlos V** **Atocha RENFE** **5am–1am daily** **renfe.com**

Madrid's first railway service, from Atocha to Aranjuez, was inaugurated in 1851. Forty years later Atocha station was replaced by a new building, which was extended in the 1980s. The older part, built of glass and wrought iron, now houses an indoor palm garden, planted with over 500 species.

Congreso de los Diputados

E3 **Plaza de las Cortes 1** **Sevilla** **By appt only: 9am–2:30pm & 4–6:30pm Mon–Thu, 9am–1:30pm Fri** **Aug** **congreso.es**

This imposing yet attractive building is home to the Spanish parliament, the Cortes. Built in the mid-19th century, it is characterized by Classical columns, heavy pediments and guardian bronze lions. It was here, in 1981, that Colonel Tejero of the Civil Guard held the deputies at gunpoint on national television, as he tried to spark off a military coup. His failure was seen as an indication that democracy was now firmly established in Spain.

Calle de Serrano

F2 **Serrano**

Running north from the Plaza de la Independencia to the Plaza del Ecuador, Calle de Serrano is lined with shops housed in old-fashioned mansion blocks. Top Spanish designers, such as Adolfo Domínguez and Purificación García, have boutiques towards the north. Branches of the Italian shops Versace, Gucci

and Armani can be found on the Calle de José Ortega y Gasset. Lower down the Calle de Serrano, towards Serrano metro station, are two branches of the department store El Corte Inglés. On the Calle de Claudio Coello, which runs parallel with Serrano, there are lavish antique shops, in keeping with the area's upmarket atmosphere. Under Juan Bravo's bridge is the Museo de Arte Público de Madrid, an open-air sculpture museum.

CaixaForum

F4 **Paseo del Prado 36** **Estación del Arte** **10am–8pm daily** **1 & 6 Jan, 25 Dec** **lacaixa.es/obrasocial**

This cultural centre hosts modern art and photography exhibitions, educational workshops, conferences, music and poetry festivals, and concerts. Set in a former electric power station and built in 2007 by Swiss architects Herzog & de Meuron, this eye-catching building appears as if it's levitating above ground. The industrial interior is a work of art in itself, and there is a beautiful vertical garden right next to the building. It also has a top-floor café and restaurant.

Real Jardín Botánico

F4 **Plaza de Murillo 2** **Banco de España, Estación del Arte** **10am–dusk daily** **1 Jan, 25 Dec** **rjb.csic.es**

South of the Prado (p316) are the Royal Botanical Gardens. Inspired by Carlos III, they were designed in 1781 by Gómez Ortega, Francesco Sabatini and Juan de Villanueva, architect of the Prado. Interest in the plants of South America and the Philippines took hold during the Spanish Enlightenment, and the neatly laid out beds offer a huge variety of flora, ranging from trees to herbs.

↑ A vibrant display of tulips at the Real Jardín Botánico, the perfect place to relax

A SHORT WALK
PASEO DEL PRADO

Distance 2.5 km (1.5 miles) **Nearest metro** Banco de España **Time** 40 minutes

In the late 18th century, before the museums and lavish hotels of East Madrid took shape, the Paseo del Prado was laid out and soon became a fashionable spot for strolling. Combine this original attraction with visits to the Paseo's museums and art galleries to make the most of the area. Take a detour to visit the Museo Thyssen-Bornemisza and the Museo del Prado (just south of the Plaza de Cánovas del Castillo). You'll pass grand monuments built under Carlos III along the route, including the Puerta de Alcalá, the Fuente de Neptuno and the Fuente de Cibeles. Surprisingly, they stand in the middle of busy roundabouts.

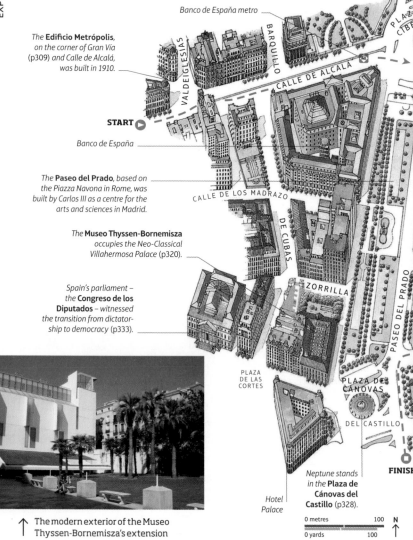

Banco de España metro

The **Edificio Metrópolis**, on the corner of Gran Vía (p309) and Calle de Alcalá, was built in 1910.

VALDEIGLESIAS

BARQUILLO

PLAZA DE CIBE

CALLE DE ALCALÁ

START

Banco de España

The **Paseo del Prado**, based on the Piazza Navona in Rome, was built by Carlos III as a centre for the arts and sciences in Madrid.

CALLE DE LOS MADRAZO

The **Museo Thyssen-Bornemisza** occupies the Neo-Classical Villahermosa Palace (p320).

DE CUBAS

Spain's parliament – the **Congreso de los Diputados** – witnessed the transition from dictatorship to democracy (p333).

ZORRILLA

PASEO DEL PRADO

PLAZA DE LAS CORTES

PLAZA DE CÁNOVAS

DEL CASTILLO

FINISH

Neptune stands in the **Plaza de Cánovas del Castillo** (p328).

Hotel Palace

0 metres   100
0 yards   100

N

↑ The modern exterior of the Museo Thyssen-Bornemisza's extension

A fountain with a statue of the Roman goddess Cybele stands in the **Plaza de Cibeles** (p328).

Sculpted from granite, the **Puerta de Alcalá** is especially beautiful when floodlit at night (p328).

Palacio del Marques de Linares

Palacio de Comunicaciones and City Hall

Locator Map
For more detail see p314

↑ The statue of Cybele decorating the fountain in the Plaza de Cibeles

The **Museo Nacional de Artes Decorativas**, *near the Retiro, was founded in 1912 as a showcase for the Spanish manufacturing industry* (p329).

The former army museum of the Palacio del Buen Retiro, the **Salón de Reinos** (p330), *forms part of the Museo del Prado.*

The **Casón del Buen Retiro** is an annex of the Museo del Prado (p316).

With its Belle Époque interior, the **Hotel Mandarin Oriental Ritz** *is one of the most elegant hotels in Spain* (p329).

The **Monumento del Dos de Mayo** *commemorates the War of Independence against the French.*

A bicycle outside a pretty shop in hip Malasaña

BEYOND THE CENTRE

Some of Madrid's most interesting districts are found outside the centre. Affluent Salamanca is named after the aristocrat, José de Salamanca y Mayol, who built the elegant mansions here in the 1860s. In stark contrast, Chueca, to the west, was originally home to tile-makers and blacksmiths but was transformed into an artistic area in the early 1980s, when it starred in the street films of Pedro Almodóvar. Meanwhile, Malasaña was the principal site of the 1808 uprising against the French, but became a hipster hangout in the 1960s.

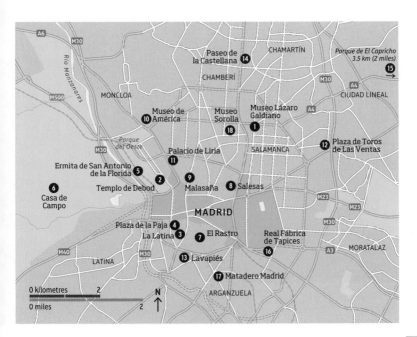

1 🖉 🏛

MUSEO LÁZARO GALDIANO

🏠 Calle de Serrano 122 Ⓜ Rubén Darío, Gregorio Marañón 🚌 7, 9, 12, 14, 16, 19, 27, 40, 51, 61, 145, 150 🕐 9:30am-3pm Tue-Sun 🚫 Public hols 🖥 flg.es

Reflecting the broad and exquisite tastes of its founder, Lázaro Galdiano, this museum displays works by Europe's top names in the fields of fine and applied art. Take a stroll through the imposing Italianate mansion, wondering at the treasures.

This art museum is housed in the former mansion of the editor and financier José Lázaro Galdiano. In 1903, he married Argentine heiress Paula Florido and they built the home to celebrate – and to show off their growing art collection. By the time Lázaro Galdiano died, some 13,000 items were housed here. His private pieces were bequeathed to the nation in 1947.

The collection ranges from the 6th century BC to the 20th century and contains items of exceptional quality, from less familiar Goya portraits to a mass of fob watches, including one worn by Carlos I. Among the most beautiful objects are a series of Limoges enamels and *The Saviour*, a portrait attributed to a student of Leonardo da Vinci. The museum features paintings by English artists Constable, Gainsborough, Reynolds and Turner, as well as 17th-century works by the likes of Spanish painters Zurbarán, Ribera, Murillo and El Greco.

Did You Know?

Goya was rejected from Madrid's Real Academia de Bellas Artes de San Fernando in 1763 and 1766.

Interior of the museum, adorned with paintings and sculptures on display →

← Michelangelo Naccherino's *Christ at the Column* sculpture

↑ The pleasant red-brick exterior of the Museo Lázaro Galdiano

TOP 5 MUSEUM HIGHLIGHTS

The Witches' Sabbath
Goya's painting, dating from 1798, is based on a legend from Aragón and depicts a witches' Sabbath around the devil (represented by the scapegoat).

Christ at the Column
This life-size marble statue was sculpted by Michelangelo Naccherino in 1764.

St John the Baptist
Hieronymus Bosch's contemplative St John (painted c1485–1510) reclines in an almost pastoral landscape punctuated by grotesque plants.

Crosier Head
This beautiful gilded object was made in Limoges in the 13th century for the top of a bishop's staff (crosier).

Tartessic Ewer
This Tartessic bronze jug, from the mid-6th century BC, is one of the museum's oldest items.

EXPERIENCE MORE

2

Templo de Debod

🏛 Calle Ferraz 1 Ⓜ Ventura Rodríguez, Plaza de España ⏰ Summer: 10am–7pm Tue–Sun; winter: 10am–8pm Tue–Sun 🚫 Public hols & afternoons in Aug 🌐 madrid.es/templodebod

The Egyptian temple of Debod, built in the 2nd century BC, was rescued from the area flooded by the Aswan Dam and given to Spain as a tribute to Spanish engineers involved in the project. The temple is carved with shallow reliefs, and stands in a line with two of its original three gates on high ground above the Río Manzanares, in the gardens of the Parque del Oeste. From the park there are views over the Casa de Campo to the Guadarrama mountains.

3

La Latina

Ⓜ La Latina

The district of La Latina runs along the city's southern hillside from the Plaza Puerta de Moros, southwards through the streets where the Rastro is held. To the east it merges with Lavapiés. La Latina's steep streets are lined with tall, narrow houses, renovated to form an attractive neighbourhood. There are old-fashioned and trendy bars around the Plaza del Humilladero as well as in the Lavapiés district.

4

Plaza de la Paja

Ⓜ La Latina

Once the focus of medieval Madrid, the area around the Plaza de la Paja – which means "Straw Square" – is still extremely atmospheric. Many interesting buildings are located on the square. Climbing upwards from the Calle de Segovia, a glimpse

Did You Know?

La Latina is considered to be the heart of *castizo* Madrid - the traditional working-class city.

left along the Calle Príncipe Anglona yields a view of the Mudéjar-style brick tower of the Iglesia de San Pedro, dating from the 14th century. Up past the fountain, the Plaza de la Paja ends with the harsh stone walls of the Capilla del Obispo, or Bishop's Chapel, originally belonging to the adjoining Palacio Vargas. The superb Plateresque altarpiece is by Francisco Giralte. Up to the left, the Baroque, cherub-covered dome of the Iglesia de San Andrés stands out.

Nearby is a small cluster of interlinked squares, ending in the Plaza Puerta de Moros. From here, a right turn leads to the domed bulk of San Francisco el Grande, an impressive landmark.

5

Ermita de San Antonio de la Florida

🏛 Glorieta San Antonio de la Florida 5 Ⓜ Príncipe Pío ⏰ 9:30am–8pm Tue–Sun 🚫 Public hols 🌐 esmadrid.com

Goya fans should not miss a visit to the Neo-Classical Ermita de San Antonio de la

 Egyptian temple of Debod, with two of its original gateways

Florida, built during the reign of Carlos IV. The present church is on the site of two previous ones and is dedicated to St Anthony. It is named after the pastureland of la Florida, on which the first church was built.

Goya took four months, in 1798, to paint the cupola. It depicts the resurrection of a murdered man who rises in order to prove the innocence of the falsely accused father of St Anthony. The characters in it are everyday people of the late 18th century. It is considered by many art critics to be among Goya's finest works.

Goya's tomb is housed in the chapel. His remains were brought here from Bordeaux, where he died in exile in 1828.

6
Casa de Campo

🏛 Paseo Puerta del Angel 1 Ⓜ Batán, Lago, Príncipe Pío, Casa de Campo 🚗 To cars 🌐 esmadrid.com

This former royal hunting ground, stretching over 1,740 ha (4,300 acres), lies in south-western Madrid. Its amenities make it a popular daytime recreation area. Attractions include a boating lake, a zoo and an amusement park – the Parque de Atracciones. If you want to exercise, you can make use of the swimming pool and jogging track. In the summer the park is also used as a venue for rock concerts.

7
El Rastro

🏛 Calle Ribera de Curtidores Ⓜ La Latina, Tirso de Molina 🕘 9am–3pm Sun & public hols

Madrid's celebrated flea market, established in the Middle Ages, has its hub in the Plaza de Cascorro and sprawls downhill towards the Río Manzanares. The main street is the Calle Ribera de Curtidores, or "Tanners' Riverbank", once the centre of the slaughter-house and tanning industry.

Although some claim that the Rastro has changed a great deal since its heyday during the 19th century, plenty of *Madrileños* still come here. Tourists come in search of a bargain from the stalls, which sell a huge range of wares – anything from new furniture to second-hand clothes. The lively crowds in the Rastro make it an ideal way to spend a Sunday morning. It is also worth making a stop at the Galerías Piquer *(Calle Ribera de Curtidores 29)* and the Plaza General Vara del Rey.

The Calle de Embajadores is the market's other main street. It runs down past the Baroque façade of the Iglesia de San

Cayetano, designed by José Churriguera and Pedro de Ribera. Further along the street is the former Real Fábrica de Tabacos (the Royal Tobacco Factory), begun as a state enterprise in 1809.

↑ A market stall crammed with decorative household goods at El Rastro flea market

Salesas

Ⓜ Colón, Chueca

Stretching from Chueca towards Salamanca, this trendy neighbourhood is full of art galleries, concept stores, stylish boutiques, cafés and delis. Take a stroll down the delightful Calle de Fernando VI to see the Modernist Longoria Palace, the 18th-century Convento de las Salesas Reales and the Neo-Classical Parroquia de Santa Bárbara.

Malasaña

Ⓜ Tribunal, Bilbao

A feeling of the authentic old Madrid pervades this district of narrow, sloping streets and tall houses. For some years it was the centre of *la movida*, the frenzied nightlife which began after the death of Franco. Today, it is one of the capital's hippest neighbourhoods, full of vintage shops and laid-back bars.

A walk along the Calle de San Andrés leads to the

TupperWare, a popular nightspot in the Malasaña quarter ↓

fashionable area, Plaza del Dos de Mayo. In the centre is a monument to artillery officers Daoíz and Velarde, who defended the barracks that stood here at the time of the uprising against the French in 1808.

The **Museo de Historia de Madrid** on Calle de Fuencarral is worth visiting just for its Baroque doorway by Pedro de Ribera – arguably the finest in Madrid. Housed in the former hospice of St Ferdinand, the museum was inaugurated in 1929. The museum offers an overview of the arts, industries, lifestyles and customs of *Madrileños* from 1561.

On Calle de la Puebla is the Iglesia de San Antonio de los Alemanes. The church was founded by Felipe III in the 17th century as a hospital for Portuguese immigrants, and was later given over for use by

German émigrés. Inside, the walls are decorated with 18th-century frescoes by Giordano.

Nearby is the neighbourhood of Conde Duque, a lively area with a great cultural scene.

Museo de Historia de Madrid
🏛 Calle de Fuencarral 78
🕙 10am-8pm Tue-Sun
🌐 madrid.es/museodehistoria

Museo de América

🏛 Avenida de los Reyes Católicos 6 Ⓜ Moncloa
🕙 9:30am-3pm Tue-Sat (to 7pm Thu), 10am-3pm Sun 🗓 Some public hols
🌐 esmadrid.com

This museum houses artifacts related to Spain's colonization of parts of the Americas. Many of the exhibits, which range

from prehistoric times to the present, were brought back to Europe by those who travelled to the Americas (p65).

The collection is arranged on the first and second floors, and

Palacio de Liria's drawing room, and *(inset)* the exterior ↑

STAY

STAY

Hotel Único
Located in Madrid's main fashion district, the Hotel Único has elegant rooms, glorious marble-mosaic floors and a fabulous Michelin-starred restaurant.

 Calle de Claudio Coello 67 Ⓦunico hotelmadrid.com

€€€

Hotel Abalú
A cool little boutique hotel, Hotel Abalú is well priced, flamboyantly designed and within striking distance of Malasaña's many bars and eateries.

 Calle del Pez 19 Ⓦhotelabalu.com

€€€

individual rooms are given a cultural theme such as society and religion. There is documentation of the Atlantic voyages and examples of the objects which they found. The highlight of the museum is perhaps a war helmet belonging to the Tlingit people of North America. It depicts a wolf, the lineage motif and protector spirit, and it was worn as a symbol of power and strength during battle. Also worth seeing are the solid gold funereal ornaments from Colombia, the Treasure of the Quimbayas (AD 500–1000), and the collection of contemporary folk art from some of Spain's former American colonies.

⓫ Ⓜ

Palacio de Liria

 Calle la Princesa 20
Ⓜ Ventura Rodríguez
Ⓒ For tours only: 10:15am-noon Mon, 10:15am-noon & 4:15-6:30pm Tue-Sun
Ⓦ esmadrid.com

The lavish but much-restored Palacio de Liria was completed by Ventura Rodríguez in 1780. Once the residence of the Alba family, and still owned by the duke, it can be visited by a maximum of 15 people at one time and by appointment only.

The palace houses the Albas' outstanding collection of art, and Flemish tapestries. There are paintings by Titian, Rubens and Rembrandt. Spanish art is particularly well represented, with major works by Goya, such as his 1795 portrait of the Duchess of Alba, as well as examples of work by El Greco, Zurbarán and Velázquez.

Behind the palace is the Cuartel del Conde-Duque, the former barracks of the Count-Duke Olivares, Felipe IV's minister. The huge square buildings, set around a central courtyard, were built in 1720 by Pedro de Ribera, who adorned them with a Baroque façade. The barracks now house a cultural centre that hosts music and dance performances and temporary exhibitions.

12
Plaza de Toros de Las Ventas

🏠 Calle Alcalá 237 Ⓜ Ventas
🕐 Bullring: for tours by appt; Museo Taurino: 10am–3pm daily
🌐 lasventastour.com

Whatever your opinion of bullfighting, Las Ventas is undoubtedly one of the most beautiful bullrings in Spain. Built in 1929 in Neo-Mudéjar style, it replaced the city's original bullring that stood near the Puerta de Alcalá. With its horseshoe arches around the outer galleries and the elaborate tilework decoration, it's a dramatic venue for the *corridas* held during the bullfighting season, from May to October.

Adjoining the bullring is the Museo Taurino, which displays memorabilia such as portraits and sculptures of famous matadors, as well as their elaborate costumes.

13
Lavapiés

Ⓜ Embajadores, Antón Martín

Multicultural Lavapiés is a diverse district. It is home to traditional tavernas and Indian restaurants, contemporary art galleries and medieval sights. Don't miss La Tabacalera de Lavapiés, a cultural centre hosting edgy art exhibitions, live music and community events. Another highlight is the Cine Doré, an independent cinema with a stunning façade.

14
Paseo de la Castellana

Ⓜ Santiago Bernabéu, Cuzco, Plaza de Castilla, Gregorio Marañón, Colón

The busy traffic artery which cuts through eastern Madrid has several parts. The Plaza de Colón marks the start of the Paseo de la Castellana. This northernmost section has modern architecture, including the Nuevos Ministerios building. East of the square is the Estadio Bernabéu, home of Real Madrid Football Club (*p52*). At the north end, in Plaza de Castilla, are the two Puerta de Europa buildings, built at an angle as if leaning towards each other.

The southernmost portion – the Paseo del Prado (*p334*) – is situated 5km (3 miles) south of the Paseo de la Castellana and starts just north of the Estación de Atocha (*p333*). The oldest section was built by Carlos III as part of his embellishment of eastern Madrid. At the Plaza de Cibeles, the avenue becomes the Paseo de Recoletos, which features stylish cafés.

15
Parque de El Capricho

🏠 Paseo de la Alameda de Osuna s/n ☎ 915 88 01 14
Ⓜ El Capricho 🕐 Apr–Sep: 9am–9pm Sat, Sun & public hols; Oct–Mar: 9am–6:30pm Sat, Sun & public hols

This remote park is one of the most unique and charming examples of a landscape garden in Spain. Built in the

Romantic style on the whim of a duchess in the late 18th century, it displays both Italian and French influences. It is abundant with greenery, particularly in spring. Other interesting places include an artificial canal that leads to a lake with ducks and swans, the reed-covered boathouse known as the Casa de Cañas, the Casino del Baile (Dance Casino), a temple, a modest palace with a ballroom, and underground bunkers from the Spanish Civil War.

16
Real Fábrica de Tapices

🏠 Calle Fuenterrabía 2
Ⓜ Menéndez Pelayo
🕐 10am–2pm Mon–Fri
🚫 Public hols & Aug
🌐 realfabricadetapices.com

Founded by Felipe V in 1721, the Royal Tapestry Factory is the sole survivor of several factories which were opened by the Bourbons during the 18th century. In 1889 the factory was relocated to this building just south of the Parque del Retiro.

Visitors can see the making of the carpets and tapestries by hand. Goya and his brother-in-law Francisco Bayeu created drawings, or cartoons, which were the models for tapestries made for the royal family. A number of the cartoons are displayed in the museum here;

←

The Temple of Bacchus surrounded by greenery, Parque de El Capricho

→ Relaxing outside the Matadero Madrid cultural centre, once a slaughterhouse

others can be seen in the Museo del Prado (p316). Some of the tapestries can be seen at the Palacio Real de El Pardo (p362) and at El Escorial (p358). Nowadays one of the factory's main tasks is making and repairing the carpets decorating Madrid's Hotel Ritz.

17

Matadero Madrid

🏠 Plaza de Legazpi 8
Ⓜ Legazpi ⏰ 9am-10pm daily 🖥 mataderomadrid.org

From its inauspicious beginnings as a slaughterhouse (matadero) sat on the side of the Manzanares river, this complex of hangars has been part of a stunning transformation of the area south of the centre.

The buildings bear grisly reminders of their original function in the shape of tiled signs indicating "poultry slaughter", "throat-cutting" and so on, but the architecture – Madrid's characteristic Neo-Mudéjar style of elaborate brickwork – is far from gloomy.

It is now a cultural centre, and each hangar is dedicated to a different discipline – music, cinema, literature and more. There are regular exhibitions, performances and workshops,

but it is also worth a visit just to stroll around, soaking up the lively atmosphere and making the most of its well-priced canteen, which has organic and locally produced food, or the terrace-bar at its heart.

18

Museo Sorolla

🏠 Paseo del General Martínez Campos 37 Ⓜ Rubén Darío, Iglesia, Gregorio Marañón ⏰ 9:30am-8pm Tue-Sat, 10am-3pm Sun 🚫 Some public hols 🖥 culturay deporte.gob.es/msorolla/el-museo

The former studio-mansion of Valencian Impressionist painter Joaquín Sorolla has been left virtually as it was when he died in 1923.

Although Sorolla is perhaps best known for his brilliantly lit Mediterranean beach scenes, the changing styles of his paintings are well represented in the museum, with examples of his gentle portraiture and a series of works representing people from different parts of Spain. Also on display are objects that were amassed during Sorolla's lifetime. The house, built in 1910, has an Andalucían-style garden designed by Sorolla himself.

EAT

La Tasquita de Enfrente
There's no menu here - you're offered a choice of Spanish recipes with a modern twist, based on fresh local produce.

🏠 Calle de la Ballesta 6
🖥 latasquitade enfrente.com

€€€

Ástor
This small family-friendly restaurant offers a traditional but trendy menu.

🏠 Calle del Almendro 9
🖥 astor.es

€€€

Santceloni
The late great chef Santi Santamaria's legacy lives on in this Michelin-starred restaurant.

🏠 Paseo de la Castellana 57
🖥 restaurante santceloni.com

€€€

CENTRAL SPAIN

Toledo's Alcázar, presiding over the city below

EXPLORE
CENTRAL
SPAIN

This guide divides Central Spain into four
colour-coded sightseeing areas, as shown
on this map. Find out more about each area
on the following pages.

ASTURIAS

Mieres

Cordiller

Ponferrada

Montes de
León

Astorga

Benavente

Miranda do
Douro

Embalse
de Ricobayo

Mirandela

Zamora

Penafiel

Porto

Vila Real

Embalse de
Almendra

Lamego

PORTUGAL

Salamanca

Aveiro

Viseu

Ciudad Rodrigo

Guarda

Béj

Covilhã

Fogueira da Foz

Colmbra

Coria

Plasencia

Pombal

Castelo Branco

Navalmo
de la Ma

Embalse de
Alcántara

Alcántara

Sierra de
San Pedro

Cáceres

Trujillo

EXTREMADURA
p426

SPAIN

Villanueva d
la Serena

Badajoz

Mérida

La Serena

Almendralejo

Castue

Villafranca
de los Barros

Jerez de los
Caballeros

Zafra

Azuaga

Sierra
Morena

GETTING TO KNOW
CENTRAL SPAIN

Much of Spain's central plateau, the *meseta*, is covered with wheat fields or dry, dusty plains, but this empty appearance belies the fact that this region served as the stage for many events in the country's rich history. Roman ruins, Gothic cathedrals and imposing castles are testament to the past.

PAGE 354

COMUNIDAD DE MADRID

It's hard to imagine, as you sit on a sun-bathed café terrace in Madrid, that you are a short train ride away from snow-tipped peaks. A playground for *Madrileños*, Comunidad de Madrid is capped with sierras that are perfect for hiking, skiing or simply taking a break from the capital. Pretty little towns, such as Chinchón, Aranjuez and Alcalá de Henares, and a couple of splendid palaces, including the imposing El Escorial, await those who prefer a slower pace of life.

Best for
Mountain hiking and royal palaces

Home to
El Escorial

Experience
Horse-riding across the sierras

CASTILLA Y LEÓN

A land of fanciful palaces and imposing cathedrals, Castilla y León is perhaps the region where visitors can best experience Spanish history writ large. From pretty Segovia, with its castle that seems straight out of a Disney film, to the ecclesiastical architecture of Burgos and León, the awe-inspiring city walls of Ávila to the handsome university town of Salamanca, this area encapsulates the diversity of Spain's historic urban landscape. Beyond the cities, vast, uninterrupterd plains stretch into the horizon, errupting into a vivid carpet of red poppies every spring.

Best for
Castles and cathedrals

Home to
León Cathedral, Salamanca, Segovia, Burgos

Experience
The echoing chants of the monks of the Monasterio de Santo Domingo de Silos

→

CASTILLA-LA MANCHA

La Mancha's empty beauty – its windmills and medieval castles silhouetted above the sierras – was immortalized by Cervantes in Don Quixote's epic adventures. But this is no no-man's-land. Rimming the plains are olive groves, limestone mountains and swathes of brimming vines in the world's largest expanse of vineyards. In the autumn, as the grapes are harvested, the fields around Consuegra and Albacete turn mauve as the saffron crocus blooms. The towns, too, have their charms, especially Cuenca, with its Casas Colgadas (hanging houses) perched precariously over the gorge.

Best for
Following in the footsteps of Don Quixote

Home to
Toledo, Cuenca

Experience
A tour of La Mancha's vineyards

EXTREMADURA

Of all the Spanish regions, Extremadura is one of the least accessible, but consequently one of the most unspoiled. Green sierras run southwards through rolling hills strewn with boulders, while forests and reservoirs shelter rare wildlife. The towns, with their atmospheric old quarters and storks nesting on spires and bell towers, exude a romantic, slow-paced charm. Trujillo and Cáceres – built with the wealth returned to the area by its many *conquistador* sons – remain frozen in time and it'll come as no surprise that they often serve as sets for period films.

Best for
Roman ruins and medieval towns

Home to
Mérida, Real Monasterio de Nuestra Señora de Guadalupe, Cáceres

Experience
Wildlife-watching in the Parque Nacional de Monfragüe

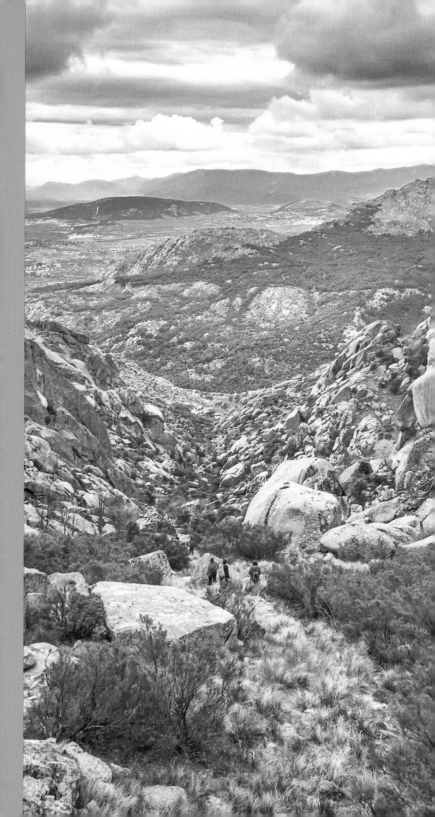

COMUNIDAD DE MADRID

During Roman occupation, when Hispania was made up of three provinces, most of this region was in the Citerior Tarraconese province, with the southwest belonging to Lusitania. Due to its location close to the River Henares, the region become an important merchant route and was crossed by two important Roman roads. The resulting trade caused the city of Complutum (now Alcalá de Henares) to flourish.

The Moors built the fortress of Mayrit (Madrid) in the 9th century, but it was taken by the Christian Castilian monarch Alfonso VI in 1083 as part of the *reconquista*. In 1561, Felipe II moved his royal court from Toledo to Madrid, reportedly because it was "neutral territory", and the city became the de facto Spanish capital as a result. Felipe built a royal palace, El Escorial, in the foothills of the mountains, and Madrid began to thrive as a result of its new-found status, with a growing population and increasing cultural and economic significance.

During the Spanish Civil War, the region witnessed much bloodshed as a Republican stronghold trying to resist Franco's Nationalist army. Unable to take the region by sheer force, Franco's forces besieged Madrid, which fell on 28 April 1939. Franco declared victory in the Civil War soon after.

COMUNIDAD DE MADRID

Must See

❶ El Escorial

Experience More

❷ Sierra Norte
❸ Monasterio de Santa María de El Paular
❹ Sierra Centro de Guadarrama
❺ Buitrago del Lozoya
❻ Patones
❼ Nuevo Baztán
❽ Palacio de El Pardo
❾ Manzanares el Real
❿ Palacio Real de Aranjuez
⓫ Alcalá de Henares
⓬ Chinchón

1 ⬡ ⬡ ⬡ ⬡

EL ESCORIAL

🗺 C3 🏛 Avenida de Juan de Borbón y Battemberg 🚉 From Estación del Arte, Sol or Chamartín 🚌 661, 664 🕐 Apr-Sep: 10am-7pm Tue-Sun; Oct-Mar: 10am-6pm Tue-Sun 🚫 1 May, 8 Sep, 24, 25 & 31 Dec 🌐 patrimonionacional.es

Felipe II's imposing grey palace stands out against the foothills of the Sierra de Guadarrama. It was built between 1563 and 1584, and its unornamented severity sparked an influential architectural style in Spain.

Officially called San Lorenzo de El Escorial, the palace was conceived as a mausoleum rather than a splendid residence. When architect Juan Bautista de Toledo died in 1567, he was replaced by Juan de Herrera, royal inspector of monuments. His former role may be why El Escorial was built in the plain architectural style known as *desornamentado*, literally, "unadorned". But inside this sober façade are some of the most important works of art in the royal Habsburg collections, displayed in the palace's museums, chapterhouses, church, royal pantheon and library.

↑ The palace library, with its ceiling decorated with 16th-century frescoes

Did You Know?

El Escorial is laid out to a gridiron shape in honour of St Lawrence, who was burned to death on a grill.

Architectural museum

Sala de Batallas

Bourbon Palace

The Alfonso XII College, founded by monks in 1875 as a boarding school

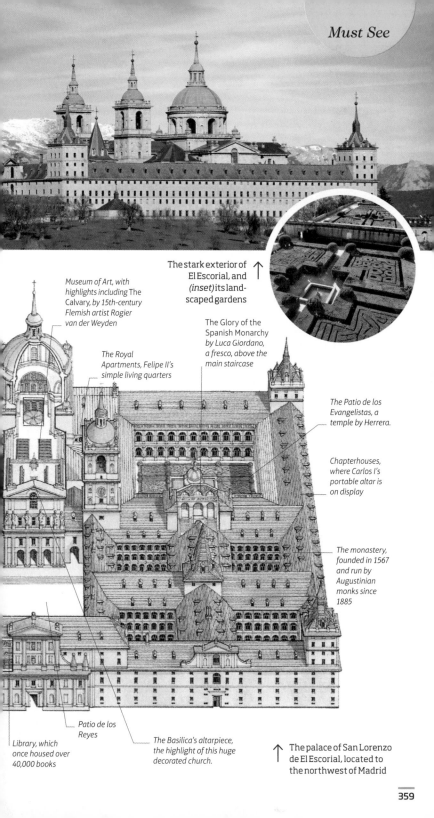

The stark exterior of El Escorial, and *(inset)* its land-scaped gardens ↑

Museum of Art, with highlights including The Calvary, by 15th-century Flemish artist Rogier van der Weyden

The Royal Apartments, Felipe II's simple living quarters

The Glory of the Spanish Monarchy by Luca Giordano, a fresco, above the main staircase

The Patio de los Evangelistas, a temple by Herrera.

Chapterhouses, where Carlos I's portable altar is on display

The monastery, founded in 1567 and run by Augustinian monks since 1885

Patio de los Reyes

Library, which once housed over 40,000 books

The Basilica's altarpiece, the highlight of this huge decorated church.

The palace of San Lorenzo de El Escorial, located to the northwest of Madrid ↑

Autumn colours displayed in the beech forest at Montejo, Sierra Norte

EXPERIENCE MORE

Sierra Norte

🅐D3 🏛Madrid 🚌Montejo de la Sierra 🛈Calle Real 64, Montejo; 9:30am-3pm daily; www.sierradelrincon.org

The black slate hamlets of the Sierra Norte, which were once known as the Sierra Pobre (Poor Sierra), are located in the most attractively rural part of Madrid province.

At Montejo de la Sierra an information centre organizes the rental of traditional houses, horse-riding excursions and visits to the nearby nature reserve of the Hayedo de Montejo de la Sierra. Made a World Heritage Site in 2017, this is one of the most southern beech woods in Europe, and a relic of an era when climatic conditions here were more suitable for the beech.

The drier southern hills slope down to the Embalse de Puentes Viejas, a reservoir where summer chalets cluster around artificial beaches. On the eastern edge of the sierra is the village of Patones, which is thought to have escaped invasion by the Moors and Napoleon's troops because of its isolated location.

Monasterio de Santa María de El Paular

🅐C3 🏛Southwest of Rascafría on M604, Madrid 🚌Rascafría 🕙11am-2pm & 4-7pm daily (Nov-mid-Apr: to 6pm) 🚫Some public hols 🌐monasteriopaular.com

Founded in 1390 as Castile's first Carthusian monastery, Santa María de El Paular stands on the site of a medieval royal hunting lodge. Although it is mainly Gothic in style, Plate-resque and Renaissance features were added later. The monastery was abandoned in 1836, and it fell into disrepair until its restoration in the 1950s. The complex now comprises a working Benedictine monastery, church and private hotel.

The church's delicate alabaster altarpiece, attributed to Flemish craftsmen, dates from the 15th century. Its panels depict scenes from the life of Jesus. The lavish Baroque *camarín* (chamber), behind the altar, was designed by Francisco de Hurtado in 1718. The cloister has impressive paintings by Vicente Carducho.

Every Sunday, the monks sing an hour-long Gregorian chant. If they are not busy, they will show you the cloister's Mudéjar brick vaulting and double sun-clock.

The monastery is a good starting point for exploring the towns of Rascafría and Lozoya. To the southwest is the nature reserve Lagunas de Peñalara.

The walled town of Buitrago del Lozoya, standing next to the Río Lozoya

It has a well-preserved stretch of the original Roman road, as well as several picnic spots and marked walking routes.

 4

Sierra Centro de Guadarrama

C3 Madrid Puerto de Navacerrada, Cercedilla Navacerrada, Cercedilla Cuartel 1, Navacerrada, Cercedilla; www.sierra guadarrama.info

The granite slopes of the Sierra de Guadarrama are planted with pines and specked with holiday chalets. Villages such as Navacerrada and Cercedilla are popular resorts for skiing, mountain-biking, rock climbing and horse-riding. Keen walkers can follow marked routes from Navacerrada.

The Valle de la Fuenfría, a nature reserve of wild forests, is best reached via Cercedilla.

 5

Buitrago del Lozoya

C3 Madrid Calle Tahona 19; www.ayto-buitragodellozoya.es

Set above a meander in the Río Lozoya is the walled town of Buitrago del Lozoya. The 14th-century **Castillo de Buitrago del Lozoya** is in ruins, although the gatehouse, arches and parts of the original wall have survived, and there is an artillery exhibition on the site.

In the newer part of town is the **Museo Picasso**. The prints, drawings and ceramics were collected by the artist's friend, Eugenio Arias.

Castillo de Buitrago del Lozoya

Plaza del Castillo s/n 11:30am–1:45pm & 4–5:45pm Tue–Fri (to 6:45pm Sat), 11:30am–4pm Sun

Museo Picasso

Plaza de Picasso 1 11am–1:45pm & 4–6pm Tue–Fri, 10am–2pm & 4–7pm Sat, 10am–2pm Sun & hols madrid.org/museopicasso

EAT

Casa José
Set in a mansion in Aranjuez, Casa José serves dishes such as leek with a broccoli foam and sea anemone.

D4 Calle de los Abastos 32, Aranjuez casajose.es

€€€

Montia
This Michelin-starred restaurant serves creative dishes made using organic products.

C3 Calle de Calvario 4, San Lorenzo de El Escorial montia.es

€€€

El Rumba
Expect wonderful charcoal-grilled meats and a sprinkling of modern dishes here.

C3 Plaza del Dr Gereda 1, Navacerrada elrumba.com

€€€

⑥ Patones

🅰 C3 🄰 Madrid
🚉 Patones de Abajo
🚌 65 from Avenida de
Juan Prieto 🆆 esmadrid.
com

The quiet town of Patones consists of an upper and lower town: Patones de Arriba (upper) and Patones de Abajo (lower). Patones de Arriba is known as the more historic of the two, with cobbled streets and slate buildings hugging the mountain slope. Before the 16th century, it used to be a part of the town of Uceda, but the local Patón family decided to split from the town and elect their own king. The independent kingdom existed until the 18th century. In the 20th century, the inhabitants of Patones de Arriba gradually descended down the mountain to the plains below, and established the lower town Patones de Abajo. Today, the lower town is still where most residents live.

One of the best ways to discover charming Patones is to follow the marked trails through the town, which allow you to explore everything, from its architecture to the mouthwatering food. At each stop, there is a sign (complete with interactive QR codes) that explains the site's history.

⑦ Nuevo Baztán

🅰 D3 🄰 R3, km 92, Madrid
🚌 261 from Plaza de la
Iglesia 3 🆆 turismo.
ayto-nuevobaztan.es

Founded in the 1700 with the arrival of the Bourbons, the historical town of Nuevo Baztán was built as a model town, incorporating architectural trends that were flourishing in France at that time. Its construction was financed by the Goyeneche family, who named it after their hometown in Navarre (Baztán).

The town centres around the Goyeneche's palace complex, which was designed by José de Churriguera and typifies his style. The complex includes the palace itself, a church, and glass and textile factories.

Start your visit at the palace's old wine cellar, which now houses the tourist information centre and also hosts an interesting exhibition on the history of the town. Then, take a tour of the palace. Visit the famed red marble altar of Iglesia de San Francisco Javier next door, before

Did You Know?

El Cid (1961), starring Charles Heston and Sophia Loren, was shot at Manzanares.

strolling through the wide streets and symmetrical plazas around.

⑧
Palacio Real de El Pardo

🅰 C3 🄰 El Pardo, northwest of Madrid off the A6, Madrid
🚌 601 from Moncloa
🕙 10am-7pm Tue-Sun 🚫 For royal visits & public hols
🆆 patrimonionacional.es

This royal hunting lodge and palace, just outside Madrid's city limits, lists General Franco among its former residents. A tour takes you round the moated palace's Habsburg wing and the identical 18th-century extension, designed by Francesco Sabatini.

The Bourbon interior is heavy with frescoes, gilt mouldings and tapestries. Today the palace hosts heads of state and royal guests. Surrounding the

↑ Iberian wild goats grazing on La Pedriza, Manzanares el Real

palace and the 18th-century village of El Pardo is a vast forest of holm oak, popular for picnicking.

9

Manzanares el Real

⬛C3 ⬛Madrid 🚌 ℹ️Plaza del Pueblo 1; www.manzanareselreal.org

The skyline of Manzanares el Real is dominated by its restored 15th-century castle. Although the castle has some traditionally military features, such as double machicolations and turrets, it was used mainly as a residence by the Dukes of Infantado. Below the castle is a 16th-century church, a Renaissance portico and fine capitals.

Behind the town, bordering the foothills of the Sierra de Guadarrama, is the geological feature La Pedriza, a mass of granite screes and ravines, which is very popular with climbers. It now forms part of an attractive nature reserve.

The town of Colmenar Viejo, 12 km (7.5 miles) southeast of Manzanares, has a notable church called Basílica de la Asunción de Nuestra Señora.

←
Serene setting of Patones de Arriba, with the church in the distance

STAY

Condesa de Chinchón

A small, great-value hotel with attractive rooms and antique furniture, set around a pretty courtyard.

⬛D4 ⬛Calle de los Huertos 26, Chinchón
🌐condesade chinchon.com

€€€

Hotel Posada Don Jaime

This historic hotel has traditionally decorated rooms, a lovely, plant-filled terrace and a plunge pool open in summer months.

⬛C3 ⬛Calle de San Antón 24, San Lorenzo de El Escorial
🌐posadadonjaime.es

€€€

10

Palacio Real de Aranjuez

🅰D4 🅰Plaza de Parejas, Aranjuez, Madrid 🚇🚌 🕐Apr-Sep: 10am-7pm Tue-Sun; Oct-Mar: 10am-4pm Tue-Fri (to 6pm Sat & Sun) 🚫Some public hols 🌐patrimonionacional.es

The Royal Summer Palace and Gardens of Aranjuez grew up around a medieval hunting lodge standing beside a natural weir, the meeting point of the Tagus and Jarama rivers.

Today's palace of brick and white stone was built in the 18th century and later redecorated by the Bourbons. A guided tour takes you through numerous Baroque rooms, among them the Chinese Porcelain Room, the Hall of Mirrors and the Smoking Room, modelled on the Alhambra in Granada. It is worth visiting Aranjuez to walk in the 3 sq km (1 sq mile) of shady royal gardens which inspired Joaquín Rodrigo's *Concierto de Aranjuez*. The Parterre Garden and the Island Garden survive from the original 16th-century palace.

Between the palace and the Tagus River is the 18th-century Prince's Garden, decorated with sculptures, fountains and lofty trees from the Americas.

The Plaza de Cervantes in Alcalá de Henares, bordered by plane trees

In the garden is the Casa de Marinos (Sailors' House), a museum housing the launches once used by the royal family for trips along the river. At the far end of the garden is the Casa del Labrador (Labourer's Cottage), a decorative royal pavilion built by Carlos IV.

Aranjuez's restaurants are famed for their asparagus and strawberries. In summer, a 19th-century steam train, built specifically to carry strawberries, runs between here and the capital.

MIGUEL DE CERVANTES

Miguel de Cervantes Saavedra, Spain's greatest literary figure, was born in Alcalá de Henares in 1547. After fighting in the naval Battle of Lepanto (1571), he was held captive by the Turks for more than five years. In 1605, when he was almost 60 years old, the first of two parts of his comic masterpiece *Don Quixote (p419)* was published to popular acclaim. He continued writing novels and plays until his death in Madrid on 23 April 1616, the same date that Shakespeare died.

11

Alcalá de Henares

🅰D3 🅰Madrid 🚇🚌 ℹPlaza de los Santos Niños s/n; www.turismoalcala.es

At the heart of a modern industrial city is one of Spain's most renowned university quarters. Founded in 1499 by Cardinal Cisneros, Alcalá's university became one of the foremost places of learning in 16th-century Europe. The most historic college, San Ildefonso, survives. Former students include Lope de Vega. In 1517 the university produced Europe's first polyglot Bible, with text in Latin, Greek, Hebrew and Chaldean.

The centre of the city is mostly medieval, with winding cobbled streets and many historic buildings. But rather than these buildings themselves, Alcalá is famed for the many white storks that nest atop them.

Beneath the messy nests you'll find Alcalá's cathedral, built between 1497 and 1514, the **Museo Casa Natal de**

> Chinchón is arguably Madrid province's most picturesque town. The 15th- to 16th-century, typically Castilian, porticoed Plaza Mayor has a splendidly theatrical air.

Cervantes, birthplace of the 17th-century author, and the restored 19th-century Neo-Moorish Palacio de Laredo.

Museo Casa Natal de Cervantes

🏠 Calle Mayor 48 🕙 10am–6pm Tue–Sun 🚫 Some public hols 🌐 museocasanatalde cervantes.org

---

Chinchón

🅰 D4 🏠 Madrid 🚌
ℹ Plaza Mayor 6; www.
ciudad-chinchon.com

Chinchón is arguably Madrid province's most picturesque town. The 15th- to 16th-century, typically Castilian, porticoed Plaza Mayor has a splendidly theatrical air. Lined with outdoor restaurants and cafés, it is the nerve centre of the town. The square comes alive for the Easter Passion Play, acted out by the townspeople, and during the August bullfights.

The 16th-century church, perched above the square, has an altar painting by Goya, whose brother was a priest here. Just off the square is the 18th-century Augustinian monastery, which has been converted into a parador with a peaceful patio garden. A ruined 15th-century castle is located on a hill to the west of town. Although it is closed to the public, there are fine views of Chinchón and the countryside from outside it.

Chinchón is a popular weekend destination for *Madrileños*, who come here to sample the excellent chorizo and locally produced *anís* in the town's many taverns.

DRINK

Terraza Los Huertos
Named for the kitchen garden of the convent that once stood here, Los Huertos is a sunny spot for an afternoon *caña* (beer), with a glassed area and tables outside.

🅰 D4 🏠 Calle de los Huertos 3, Chinchón
📞 918 94 00 02

Habana Café
On warm summer nights, the place to be seen sipping a cocktail is the terrace of elegantly kitsch Habana Café, a stone's throw from the royal palace.

🅰 D4 🏠 Carretera de Andalucía 11, Aranjuez
📞 678 50 95 96

The tranquil cloisters of the Monasterio de Santo Domingo de Silos

CASTILLA Y LEÓN

The territories of the two rival medieval kingdoms of Castile and León, occupying the northern half of the great plateau in the centre of Spain, now form the country's largest region, or *comunidad autónoma*.

Castile and León were first brought together under one crown in 1037 by Fernando I, and the powerful kingdom became one of the driving forces of the *reconquista*, seizing territory from the Moors. El Cid, the legendary Christian hero, was born near Burgos. The two kingdoms were divided again on the death of Alfonso VII in 1157 and were only consolidated into one kingdom in 1230. Alfonso IX of León had bequeathed his kingdom to his two eldest daughters, Sancha and Dulce, on his death, but his son, Fernando III of Castile, successfully contested the will and formed the united kingdom of Castilla y León.

This kingdom became the cradle of the nation. Through the marriage of Isabel I of Castile to Fernando II of Aragón in 1469, Catalonia became part of the domain and Isabel and Fernando's reign saw the beginnings of a united Christian Spain, with the conquest of Moorish Granada in 1492.

In the 16th century, wealth poured into the area as a result of the wool trade and spoils seized from the Americas. These newfound riches financed the building of great monuments to Castilla y León's eminence, including Burgos' exuberantly decorated Gothic cathedral, León Cathedral, with its wonderful stained glass, and Salamanca's respected university.

CASTILLA Y LEÓN

Must Sees
1. León Cathedral
2. Salamanca
3. Segovia
4. Burgos

Experience More
5. El Bierzo
6. Ponferrada
7. Villafranca del Bierzo
8. Astorga
9. Cueva de Valporquero
10. Ciudad Rodrigo
11. Puebla de Sanabria
12. Sierra de Gredos
13. Palacio Real de la Granja de San Ildefonso
14. Zamora
15. Sepúlveda
16. Ávila
17. Pedraza de la Sierra
18. Castillo de Coca
19. Valladolid
20. Medina del Campo
21. Tordesillas
22. Frómista
23. Palencia
24. Medina de Rioseco
25. Briviesca
26. Aguilar de Campoo
27. Covarrubias
28. Monasterio de Santo Domingo de Silos
29. Peñaranda de Duero
30. Lerma
31. Soria
32. El Burgo de Osma
33. Medinaceli

① ⊗ ⊗

LEÓN CATHEDRAL

⚑ C2 ☗ Plaza de Regla, León ☗☗ 🕓 Cathedral: Oct-Apr: 9:30am-1:30pm & 4-8pm Mon-Sat, 9:30-10:30am & 4-8pm Sun; May-Sep: hours vary, check website; Museum: hours vary, check website 🖐 catedraldeleon.org

Santa María de León Cathedral is one of Spain's greatest religious landmarks, expressing the devotion of the people who built it and inspiring awe even today. The highlight of this Gothic cathedral is its vibrant stained glass, which depicts local life over the centuries.

The present structure of golden sandstone, built on the site of King Ordoño II's 10th-century palace, was begun in the mid-13th century and completed less than 100 years later. The façade is covered with splendid 13th-century Gothic carvings. Among these, above the Puerta de la Virgen Blanca, is one depicting a scene from the Last Judgment. The plan of the building is a Latin cross.

It combines a slender but very high nave, measuring 90 m (295 ft) by 40 m (130 ft) at its widest, with huge panels of stained glass that flood the interior with light. To best appreciate the dazzling colours of the stained glass, visit on a sunny day. There is also a museum in the cathedral, where Pedro de Campaña's panel, *The Adoration of the Magi*, is one of the many treasures on display.

LEÓN'S STAINED GLASS

León Cathedral's great glory is its superb glass-work. The 125 large windows and 57 round ones date from the 13th to the 20th centuries and cover a huge range of subjects. *La Cacería*, on the north wall, depicts a hunting scene, while the rose window in the Capilla del Nacimiento shows pilgrims worshipping at the tomb of St James in Santiago de Compostela in Galicia *(p228)*. Learn more about the scenes on a guided tour.

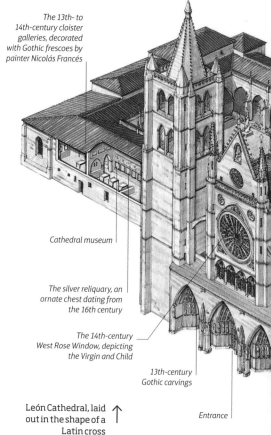

The 13th- to 14th-century cloister galleries, decorated with Gothic frescoes by painter Nicolás Francés

Cathedral museum

The silver reliquary, an ornate chest dating from the 16th century

The 14th-century West Rose Window, depicting the Virgin and Child

13th-century Gothic carvings

Entrance

León Cathedral, laid out in the shape of a Latin cross ↑

TOP 4 OTHER SIGHTS IN LEÓN

Colegiata de San Isidoro
This beautiful church is the final resting place of many monarchs.

Museo de León
An intriguing local history museum – look out for the Cristo de Carrizo crucifix.

Plaza Mayor
The alleyways around this square are dotted with bars and cafés.

MUSAC
A radical contemporary art museum.

1 The cathedral rises from the café-lined Plaza Regla.

2 Visitors can admire the Renaissance retrochoir, with its alabaster sculptures.

3 The high nave is ornamented with vaulting and stained glass.

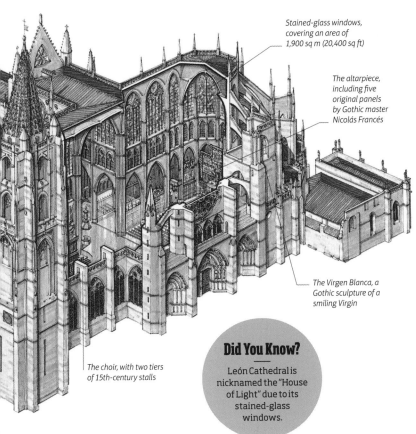

Stained-glass windows, covering an area of 1,900 sq m (20,400 sq ft)

The altarpiece, including five original panels by Gothic master Nicolás Francés

The Virgen Blanca, a Gothic sculpture of a smiling Virgin

The choir, with two tiers of 15th-century stalls

Did You Know?

León Cathedral is nicknamed the "House of Light" due to its stained-glass windows.

↑ Salamanca's town hall on the wide Plaza Mayor, blazing with lights

②

SALAMANCA

△B3 **⌂**Salamanca **✈**15 km (9 miles) east **🚆🚌** **ℹ**Plaza Mayor 32; www.salamanca.es

Founded as an Iberian settlement in pre-Roman times, Salamanca fell to Hannibal in 217 BC. The city later enjoyed more illustrious times, and is now Spain's finest showcase of Renaissance and Plateresque architecture. Pre-eminent among its artists and master craftsmen of later years were the Churriguera brothers. Their work can be seen in many of Salamanca's golden sandstone buildings, notably in the Plaza Mayor. Other major sights are the two cathedrals and the 13th-century university, one of Europe's oldest and most distinguished.

①

Plaza Mayor

This magnificent square was built by Felipe V to thank the city for its support during the War of the Spanish Succession (1701–14). Designed by the Churriguera brothers in 1729 and completed in 1755, it was once used for bullfights, but nowadays is a delightful place to stroll or shop. Within the harmonious blend of arcaded buildings and cafés are the Baroque town hall and, opposite, the Royal Pavilion, from where the royal family used to watch events in the square. The Plaza Mayor is surrounded by warm golden sandstone buildings, and is especially resplendent at dusk.

②

Catedral Vieja and Catedral Nueva

⌂Calle Cardenal Pla y Deniel **◷**10am–8pm daily (Oct–Mar: to 6pm) **🌐**catedral salamanca.org

The new cathedral (built during the 16th–18th centuries) did not replace the old, but was built beside it. It combines a mix of styles – it's mainly Gothic, with Renaissance and Baroque additions. The west front has elaborate Late Gothic stonework.

The 12th- to 13th-century Romanesque old cathedral is entered through the new one. The highlight is a 53-panel altarpiece, painted in lustrous

> ### Did You Know?
>
> An astronaut, carved in 1992, can be seen beside the doors of the Catedral Nueva.

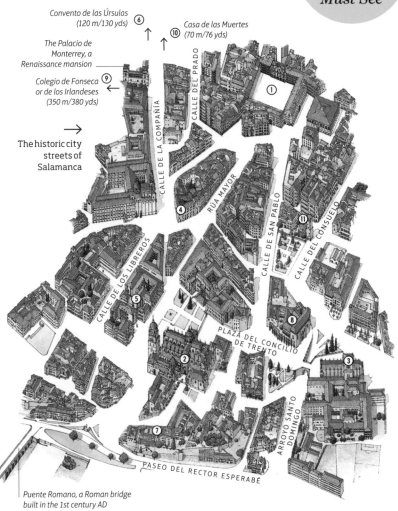

Convento de las Úrsulas
(120 m/130 yds) ⑥

Casa de las Muertes
(70 m/76 yds) ⑩

The Palacio de
Monterrey, a
Renaissance mansion

Colegio de Fonseca ⑨
or de los Irlandeses
(350 m/380 yds)

→
The historic city
streets of
Salamanca

CALLE DE LA COMPAÑÍA

CALLE DEL PRADO

RÚA MAYOR

CALLE DE SAN PABLO

CALLE DEL CONSUELO

CALLE DE LOS LIBREROS

PLAZA DEL CONCILIO
DE TRENTO

ARROYO SANTO
DOMINGO

PASEO DEL RECTOR ESPERABÉ

Puente Romano, a Roman bridge
built in the 1st century AD

colours by Nicolás Florentino. It frames a statue of Salamanca's patron saint, the 12th-century Virgen de la Vega, crafted in Limoges enamel. In the vault above is a fresco depicting vivid scenes from the Last Judgment, also by Florentino.

The 15th-century Capilla de Anaya (Anaya Chapel) contains the superb 15th-century alabaster tomb of Diego de Anaya, who was an archbishop of Salamanca.

Guided tours of the churches are mandatory, and audio guides are available in six different languages.

↑ A richly decorated altarpiece depicting the life of Christ, found in the Catedral Vieja

③
Iglesia-Convento de San Esteban

🏛 Plaza del Concilio de Trento s/n 📞 923 21 50 00 🕐 10am-2pm & 4-6pm Tue-Sat, 10am-2pm Sun 🚫 Public hols

This Dominican monastery was built between 1524 and 1610. Start at the on-site church, which has an ornamented Plateresque façade. The relief on the central panel, completed by Juan Antonio Ceroni in 1610, depicts the stoning of St Stephen, to whom the monastery is dedicated. The frieze above shows children and horses.

The interior is equally stunning. The ornate altarpiece, comprised of twisted gilt columns decorated with vines, is the work of José Churriguera and dates from 1693. Below it is one of Claudio Coello's last paintings, another representation of the martyrdom of St Stephen.

The double-galleried Claustro de los Reyes, completed in Plateresque style in 1591, has capitals that are carved with the heads of the prophets. The lower storey is a processional cloister and offers plenty of space, while

> **This mansion's name - Casa de las Conchas (House of the Shells) - derives from the many stone scallop shells that cover its walls. They are a symbol of the Order of Santiago.**

the smaller upper storey is intended for more personal communion with religion. Don't miss the on-site museum, which details monastic life.

___

④
Casa de las Conchas

🏛 Calle de la Compañía 2 📞 923 26 93 17 🕐 9am-9pm Mon-Fri, 9am-2pm Sat

This mansion's name – Casa de las Conchas (House of the Shells) – derives from the many stone scallop shells that cover its walls. They are a symbol of the Order of Santiago, one of whose knights, Rodrigo Arias Maldonado, built the mansion in the early 1500s. He also adorned it with his family's coat of arms. It now houses a public library.

⑤
Universidad

🏛 Calle Libreros 🕐 Apr-mid-Sep: 10am-8pm Mon-Sat, 10am-2pm Sun & public hols; mid-Sep-Mar: 10am-7pm Mon-Sat 🚫 1 & 6 Jan, 25 Dec and for official functions 🌐 usal.es

The university was founded by Alfonso IX of León in 1218, making it the oldest in Spain. Opposite the 16th-century façade of the Patio de las Escuelas (Schools Square) is a statue of Fray Luis de León, who taught theology here; visit his lecture room, preserved as it was when he taught. The Escuelas Menores building houses a huge zodiac fresco, *The Salamanca Sky*.

___

⑥
Convento de las Úrsulas

🏛 Calle de las Úrsulas 2 📞 923 21 98 77 🕐 10am-2pm Tue-Sun 🚫 Last Sun of month

In the church of this convent is the carved tomb of its founder, Alonso de Fonseca, the powerful 16th-century Archbishop of Santiago and Toledo. The on-site museum includes fine paintings by Luis de Morales.

↑ A splendid stained-glass artwork within the Casa Lis Museo Art Nouveau y Art Deco

Casa Lis Museo Art Nouveau y Art Deco

🏠 Calle Gibraltar 14 🕐 11am–2pm & 4-7pm Mon-Fri, 11am–7pm Sat & Sun 🌐 museocasalis.org

This collection of early-20th-century decorative art, housed in a 19th-century building, has paintings, jewellery and furniture from all over Europe. Individual rooms are devoted to porcelain and Limoges enamel, and stained-glass work by Lalique. The museum is free on Thursday mornings.

⑧ 🧭

Convento de las Dueñas

🏠 Plaza del Concilio de Trento 1 📞 923 21 54 42 🕐 10:30am–12:45pm & 4:30-7:30pm Mon-Sat 🚫 Public hols

The main feature of this Dominican convent is its Renaissance double cloister, whose tranquil gardens seem strangely at odds with the grotesques carved on the capitals. The cloister also preserves tiled Moorish arches.

←

The extraordinary façade of the Iglesia-Convento de San Esteban

Colegio de Fonseca or de los Irlandeses

🏠 Calle de Fonseca 4 📞 923 29 45 70 🕐 9am–2pm Mon-Fri

Alonso de Fonseca built this Renaissance palace in 1521, and his coat of arms appears over the entrance. The building became a seminary for Irish priests at the end of the 19th century – hence its name – and the interior Italianate courtyard has a chapel. Today it is used as a hotel, restaurant and university premises.

⑩

Casa de las Muertes

🏠 Calle Bordadores 🕐 Casa-Museo de Unamuno: 10am–2pm Mon-Fri 🚫 Casa de las Muertes: to the public

The House of the Dead takes its name from the small skulls that embellish its façade. Grotesques and other figures also feature, and there is a cornice decorated with cherubs. The façade is an accomplished example of the early Plateresque style.

Author and philosopher Miguel de Unamuno died in the adjacent house in 1936. The Casa-Museo de Unamuno contains information about his life.

Torre del Clavero

🏠 Plaza de Colón 🚫 To the public

This tower is the last vestige of a palace that once stood here. It was built around 1480 and is named after a former resident, the key warden (clavero) of the Order of Alcántara. Its turrets are adorned with the coats of arms of its founders, and Mudéjar trelliswork.

EAT

La Cocina de Toño

This Michelin-starred establishment serves nouveau Castilian cuisine with a Basque twist. Stand at the bar for excellent tapas if you don't fancy a full meal.

🏠 Gran Vía 20 🌐 lacocinadetoño.es

€€€

iPan iVino

Featuring the best wine menu in the city, this colourful bar opposite the Palacio de la Salina serves creative tapas.

🏠 Calle Felipe Espino 10 🌐 ipanivino.com

€€€

Zazu Bistro

A stylish restaurant located in the heart of Salamanca. It pays tribute to Mediterranean cuisine, with nods to classic French and Italian recipes. In summer, you can dine on the terrace.

🏠 Plaza Libertad 8 🌐 restaurantezazu.com

€€€

 3

SEGOVIA

 **C3** 🏛️🚌 *i* **Plaza del Azoguejo, 1; 921 46 67 20;
www.turismodesegovia.com**

Segovia is the most spectacularly sited city in Spain,
set high on a rocky spur and surrounded by the Río
Eresma and Río Clamores. It is often compared to a
ship – the Alcázar on its sharp crag forming the prow,
the pinnacles of the cathedral rising like masts, and
the aqueduct trailing behind like a rudder. The view
of it from the valley below at sunset is magical.

①
Museo de Segovia

🏠 Casa del Sol, Calle
Socorro 11 📞 921 46 06 13
🕐 Jul-Sep: 10am-2pm &
4-7pm Tue-Sat, 10am-2pm
Sun; Oct-Jun: 10am-2pm &
5-8pm Tue-Sat, 10am-
2pm Sun

This archaeological museum
contains 15,000-year-old
Stone Age engravings, as well
as historic tools, arms, pottery
and metalwork. There are
Roman coins, wall fragments
from Arab houses and a collection of belt buckles. Also
worth seeing are two huge
Celtic stone bulls that were
excavated in the Calle Mayor.
It is thought they may have
been divine protectors of

people or livestock. In the
nearby province of Ávila, such
icons are linked with burials.

 ②
Convento de
San Juan de la Cruz

🏠 Alameda de la Fuencisla
📞 921 43 13 49 🕐 4-7pm
Mon, 10am-1:30pm & 4-7pm
Tue-Sun (Jun-Sep: till 8pm)

In a secluded Eresma valley,
St John of the Cross founded
this convent in the 16th century and was the prior from
1588 to 1591. The mystical
poet was also co-founder,
along with Santa Teresa, of a
barefooted *(descalzos)* order
of Carmelites that ran to the
strictest of disciplines.

 ③
Casa de los Picos

Just inside the city walls is the
Casa de los Picos, a mansion
whose 15th-century façade is
adorned with diamond-shaped
stones. The building houses
an art gallery and school.

 ④
Museo Zuloaga

🏠 Plaza de Colmenares 4
📞 921 46 33 34 🕐 10am-
2pm & 4-7pm Mon-Fri,
10am-2pm Sat & Sun

Set in the Iglesia de San Juan
de los Caballeros, this museum
exhibits the works of the
Zuloaga family, including paintings by Ignacio Zuloaga and
ceramics by Daniel Zuloaga.

 ⑤
Monasterio de
Santa María del Parral

🏠 Subida al Parral 📞 921 43
12 98 🕐 11am & 5pm Wed-
Sun (booking is advised)

Just north of the city walls is
Segovia's largest monastery.
The Monasterio de Santa
María del Parral has four
cloisters and a Plateresque
altarpiece. The tombs of its

←

Segovia's two-tiered Roman aqueduct, built in the 1st century AD

benefactor, the Marqués de Villena, and his wife, María, are also in the 15th-century Plateresque style.

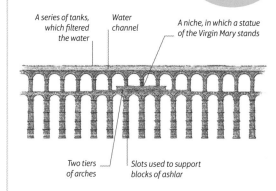

A series of tanks, which filtered the water

Water channel

A niche, in which a statue of the Virgin Mary stands

Two tiers of arches

Slots used to support blocks of ashlar

⑥
Cathedral

🏛 **Plaza Mayor** 📞 **921 46 22 05** 🕐 **9:30am–6:30pm Mon-Sat (from 10am Sun)**

Dating from 1525, this Gothic structure replaced the old cathedral, which was destroyed in 1520 during the revolt of the Castilian towns. The old cloister, however, survived and was rebuilt alongside architect Juan Gil de Hontañón's austere but elegant design. The flying buttresses, pinnacles, tower and dome form an impressive silhouette, while the interior is light and elegantly vaulted, with stained-glass windows.

Inside there is a high altar designed by Sabatini, the Italian architect, in 1768. Lining the nave and apse are 18 chapels, most enclosed by ironwork grilles. The most interesting is the Chapel of the Pietà, which took its name from the sculpture by Juan de Juni. The cloister, filled with pointed arches, is accessed through a Gothic arch by Juan Guas in the Chapel of Christ's Solace. The cloister leads to the chapter-house museum, which houses 17th-century Brussels tapestries, coins, paintings, sculptures, silver, furniture and books.

⑦
Aqueduct

🏛 **Plaza del Azoguejo 1**

In use until the late 19th century, this aqueduct was

↑ An illustration showing Segovia's Roman aqueduct in detail

built at the end of the 1st century AD by the Romans, who turned ancient Segovia into an important military base. Two tiers of arches, which reached a total of 728 m (2,400 ft) in length, were needed to cope with the ground's gradient. In terms of height, the arches stretched to a maximum of 29 m (95 ft). With this elaborate feat of engineering, water from the Río Frío flowed into the city, filtered through a series of tanks along the way.

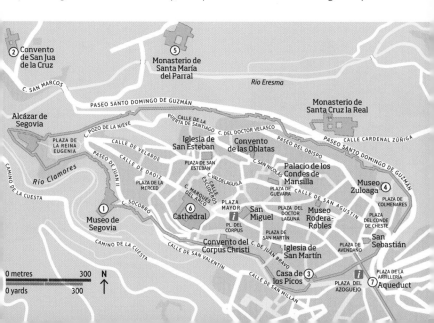

② Convento de San Jua de la Cruz
⑤ Monasterio de Santa María del Parral
Río Eresma
Alcázar de Segovia
PASEO SANTO DOMINGO DE GUZMÁN
Monasterio de Santa Cruz la Real
C. SAN MARCOS
PLAZA DE LA REINA EUGENIA
POZO DE LA NIEVE
PUERTA DE SANTIAGO
CALLE DE LA
C. DEL DOCTOR VELASCO
PASEO DEL OBISPO
PASEO CALLE CARDENAL ZÚÑIGA
PASEO SANTO DOMINGO DE GUZMÁN
Río Clamores
CALLE DE VELARDE
CALLE DE DAOIZ
PASEO DE JUAN II
Iglesia de San Esteban
PLAZA DE SAN ESTEBAN
C. SAN NICOLÁS
Convento de las Oblatas
Palacio de los Condes de Mansilla
Museo Zuloaga ④
PLAZA DE COLMENARES
CAMINO DE LA CUESTA
PLAZA DE LA MERCED
C. VALDELAGUILA
C. MARQUÉS DEL ARCO
C. SOCORRO
PLAZA MAYOR
San Miguel
PLAZA DE GUEVARA
CALLE DE SAN AGUSTÍN
PLAZA DEL DOCTOR LAGUNA
Museo Rodera-Robles
PLAZA DEL CONDE DE CHESTE
① Museo de Segovia
Cathedral
PL. DEL CORPUS
PLAZA DE SAN MARTÍN
San Sebastián
CAMINO DE LA CUESTA
CALLE DE SAN VALENTÍN
Convento del Corpus Christi
C. DE JUAN BRAVO
Iglesia de San Martín
PLAZA DE AVENDAÑO
PLAZA DE LA ARTILLERÍA
Casa de los Picos ③
CALLE DE SAN MILLÁN
PLAZA DEL AZOGUEJO
⑦ Aqueduct

0 metres 300
0 yards 300
N ↑

EXPERIENCE Castilla y León

ALCÁZAR DE SEGOVIA

📍 Plaza de la Reina Victoria Eugenia 🕐 Apr-Sep: 10am-8pm daily;
Oct-Mar: 10am-6pm daily 🚫 1 & 6 Jan, 24 & 25 Dec 🌐 alcazardesegovia.com

Rising sheer above crags with a multitude of gabled
roofs, turrets and crenellations, the Alcázar de Segovia
appears like the archetypal fairy-tale castle. It contains
a museum of weaponry and a series of elaborately
decorated rooms.

The layout of Segovia's royal castle is determined by the contours
of the rocky outcrop on which it stands. Although first records
date from the 12th century, it was mostly built between 1410
and 1455, and had to be largely rebuilt following a fire in 1862.
Its rooms are decorated with armour, paintings and furniture
that enhance its medieval atmosphere. In 1764 Carlos III
founded the Royal School of Artillery here. Two of the school's
pupils, Daoíz and Velarde, became heroes in the 1808 uprising
of *Madrileños* against the French.

Did You Know?

The castle served as
Joyous Gard, the home
of Sir Lancelot du Lac
in the 1967 musical
film *Camelot*.

🔺 GREAT VIEW
Juan's Tower

For breathtaking views
of Segovia and the
Guadarrama mountains,
climb the narrow stairs
to the top of the Torre de
Juan II, built during the
15th-century reign of
Enrique IV and named
after his father.

→
Alcázar de Segovia,
perched on an outcrop

Bartizan turrets

*Torre de Juan II,
which acted as
the dungeon*

↑ The imposing exterior
of the castle, nestled in
the hills above Segovia

*The barbican,
which contained
the portcullis and
guards' watchrooms*

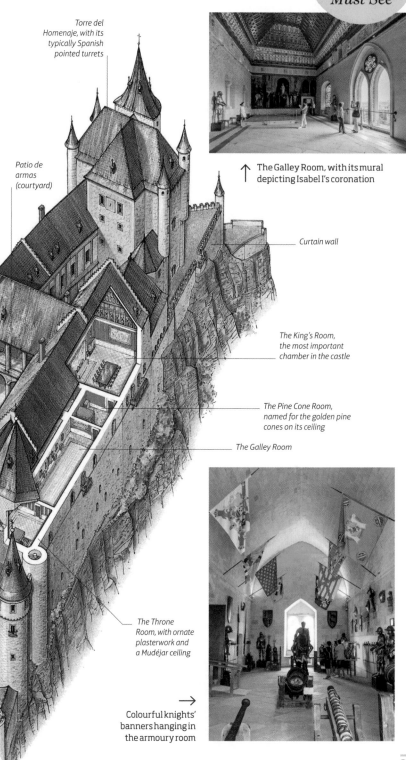

Torre del Homenaje, with its typically Spanish pointed turrets

Patio de armas (courtyard)

↑ The Galley Room, with its mural depicting Isabel I's coronation

Curtain wall

The King's Room, the most important chamber in the castle

The Pine Cone Room, named for the golden pine cones on its ceiling

The Galley Room

The Throne Room, with ornate plasterwork and a Mudéjar ceiling

→ Colourful knights' banners hanging in the armoury room

④

BURGOS

🗺D2 🚉Burgos 🚌🚍 ℹPlaza de Alonso Martínez 7; www. turismoburgos.org

Founded in AD 884, Burgos has played a significant role in Spanish history. It was the capital of the united kingdoms of Castile and León from 1073 until after the fall of Granada in 1492. The city grew rich from the wool trade during the 15th and 16th centuries, financing great art and architecture. Franco chose Burgos as his Civil War headquarters.

Iglesia de San Esteban

**🏠Calle San Esteban 1
🕐Jul-Sep: 10am-2pm & 4-7pm Tue-Sat, 10am-2pm Sun**

This Gothic church replaced a Romanesque church that once stood on this site. It is no longer used for worship but houses the Museo del Retablo, a collection of 18 historic altarpieces that were taken from churches across the region, and brought here to be restored and displayed. Religious paintings, crucifixes and chalices make up a second collection.

②

Iglesia de Santa Águeda

🏠Calle Santa Agueda 12

Also known as the Iglesia de Santa Gadea, this church sits

on the site where El Cid made King Alfonso VI swear that he had played no part in the murder of his elder brother, King Sancho II, in 1072. The incident is re-enacted by actors on summer evenings.

Real Monasterio de las Huelgas

**🏠Calle de los Compases
📞947 20 16 30 🕐10am-2pm & 4-6:30pm Tue-Sat, 10am-3pm Sun 🚫Some public hols**

This 12th-century Cistercian convent was founded by Alfonso VIII. Inside is the Museo de Ricas Telas, displaying ancient fabrics from the convent's royal tombs.

EL CID

Rodrigo Díaz de Vivar was born in Vivar del Cid, north of Burgos, in 1043. He was banished from Castile after becoming embroiled in the fratricidal squabbles of the king's sons, Sancho II and Alfonso VI. He fought for the Moors, then changed side again to capture Valencia for the Christians in 1094, and ruled the city until his death. For his heroism he was named El Cid, from the Arabic *Sidi* (Lord). His tomb lies in Burgos Cathedral.

↑ The nighttime skyline of Burgos, dominated by the city's cathedral

④

Iglesia de San Lorenzo

📍 Calle San Lorenzo 8

Located besides the city's cathedral (p382), this church dedicated to St Lawrence is worth visiting for its superb Baroque ceiling.

---

⑤

Arco de Santa María

📍 Plaza Rey San Fernando 9

The bridge of Santa María leads into the old quarter of Burgos through the restored Arco de Santa María, a gateway carved with statues of various local worthies.

---

⑥

Casa del Cordón

📍 Plaza de la Libertad

The Casa del Cordón is a 15th-century palace that now houses a bank. It's recognizable by the Franciscan cord motif carved over the portal. A plaque declares that this is where the Catholic Monarchs welcomed Columbus in 1497, on his return from the second of his famous voyages to the Americas.

⑦

Museo de Burgos

📍 Calle Miranda, 13 🕐 Jul-Sep: 10am-2pm & 5-8pm Tue-Sat, 10am-2pm Sun; Oct-Jun: 10am-2pm & 4-7pm Tue-Sat, 10am-2pm Sun 🚫 1 & 6 Jan, 11 & 29 Jun, 1 Nov, 24, 25 & 31 Dec 🌐 museodeburgos.com

The Casa de Miranda, a Renaissace palace, houses the Museo de Burgos. The archaeological section displays finds from the Roman city of Clunia.

---

⑧

Museo de la Evolución Humana

📍 Paseo Sierra de Atapuerca 🕐 10am-2:30pm & 4:30-8pm Tue-Fri, 10am-8pm Sat, Sun & public hols 🌐 museo evolucionhumana.com

This huge museum exhibits fossils dating from some 780,000 years ago. A combined entrance ticket includes transport and entrance to Yacimientos de Atapuerca, the site of Europe's earliest human settlement.

STAY

AC Hotel Burgos

This stylish hotel is set right in the heart of the city. Fuel up at the restaurant's sumptuous breakfast buffet before exploring the sights. There's also a hotel bar to round off the day.

📍 Paseo de la Audiencia 7 🌐 marriott.co.uk hotels/travel/rgsbu-ac-hotel-burgos

€€€

NH Collection Palacio de Burgos

Centrally located, this 16th-century former convent offers spacious rooms, a charming Gothic cloister and an excellent restaurant.

📍 Calle de la Merced 13 🌐 nh-hotels.com/burgos/palacio

€€€

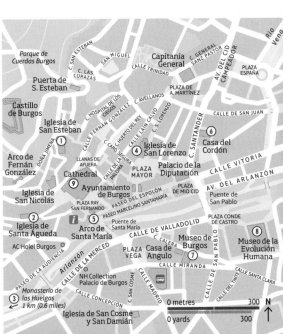

BURGOS CATHEDRAL

📍 Plaza de Santa María 🕐 10am–7pm daily 🌐 catedraldeburgos.info

The lacy, steel-grey spires of Santa Iglesia Catedral Basílica Metropolitana de Burgos soar above the city. Spain's third largest cathedral, it is best known for being the final resting place of Burgos' most famous son – El Cid (p380).

Burgos' cathedral was founded in 1221 by Bishop Don Mauricio under Fernando III. The ground plan – a Latin cross – measures 84 m (276 ft) by 59 m (194 ft). Its construction was carried out in stages over three centuries and involved many of the greatest architects and artists in Europe. The style of the cathedral is almost entirely Gothic, and shows influences from Germany, France and the Low Countries. The architects cleverly adapted the building to its sloping site, incorporating stairways inside and out.

Did You Know?

The three doors of the Puerta de Santa María represent forgiveness, the assumption and the immaculate conception.

↑ The intricate, crocketed spires of the cathedral stretching into the sky at dusk

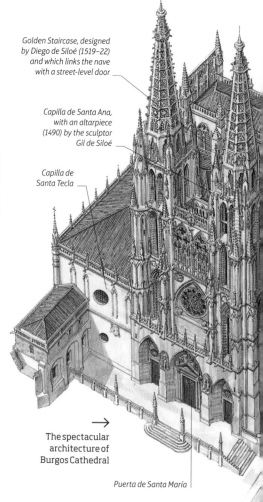

Golden Staircase, designed by Diego de Siloé (1519–22) and which links the nave with a street-level door

Capilla de Santa Ana, with an altarpiece (1490) by the sculptor Gil de Siloé

Capilla de Santa Tecla

→ The spectacular architecture of Burgos Cathedral

Puerta de Santa María

Must See

Constables' Chapel, where the tombs of the High Constable of Castile and his wife are found

Retrochoir, with several reliefs carved by Philippe de Bigarny

Lantern

Tomb of El Cid

↑ Visitors exploring the cathedral's graceful vaulted cloisters

Capilla de San Juan Bautista and museum

↑ An altarpiece from the Capilla de Santa Ana

Sacristy (1765), which was rebuilt in Baroque style

Interpretation Centre

The Crossing, a star-ribbed dome beneath which is the tomb of El Cid and his wife

Puerta del Sarmental, the main entrance for tourists

Capilla de la Visitación

Reception and Information Centre

Capilla de la Presentación (1519–24), a funerary chapel with a star-shaped, traceried vault

Capilla del Santísimo Cristo

EXPERIENCE MORE

❺

El Bierzo

🅰B2 🚉León 🚌Ponferrada 🚆Ponferrada ℹCalle de Gil y Carrasco, Ponferrada; www.turismodelbierzo.es

This northwestern region of León province was at one time the bed of an ancient lake. Sheltered by hills from the worst extremes of Central Spain's climate, its sun-soaked, alluvial soils make for fertile orchards and vineyards. Over the centuries, the area has also yielded rich mineral pickings including coal, iron and gold. Nowadays, El Bierzo is a popular destination for walkers, with many routes and picnic spots.

In the eastern section, you can trace the course of the old Camino de Santiago (p232) through the Montes de León, past the pilgrim church and medieval bridge of Molinaseca. Turning off the road at the remote village of El Acebo, you pass through a deep valley where there are signs pointing to the **Herrería de Compludo**, a water-powered 7th-century ironworks. The equipment still works and is demonstrated regularly.

The Lago de Carucedo, to the southwest of Ponferrada, is an ancient artificial lake. It acted as a reservoir in Roman times, a by-product of a vast gold-mining operation. Using enslaved labourers, millions of tonnes of alluvium were washed from the hills of Las Médulas by a complex system of canals and sluice gates. The ore was then panned, and the gold dust collected on sheep's wool. It is estimated that more than 500 tonnes of precious metal were extracted between the 1st and 4th centuries AD. These ancient workings lie within a memorable landscape of wind-eroded crags, and hills pierced by tunnels and colonized by gnarled chestnut trees. The goldmines of **Las Médulas** are now a UNESCO World Heritage Site. You can best appreciate the area from a viewpoint at Orellán, which is reached via a rough, steep track.

North of the A6 highway lies the Sierra de Ancares, a wild region of rounded, slate mountains marking the borders with Galicia and Asturias. Part of it forms a nature reserve, Reserva Nacional de los Ancares Leoneses. The heathland is home to deer, wolves and brown bears.

Several villages in the hills contain *pallozas* – primitive, pre-Roman stone dwellings. One of the most striking collections can be found in isolated Campo del Agua, in the west.

→

Craggy, tree-clad hills around the ancient gold mines near Las Médulas

Herrería de Compludo

⊗ 🅓Compludo 📞987 424 236 🕐10am–2pm & 4–8pm Wed–Sun & public hols

Las Médulas

⊗⊗ 🕐11am–2pm & 4–8pm daily (Oct–Mar: to 6pm) 🚫Public hols 🌐espaciolas medulas.es

❻

Ponferrada

🅰B2 🚉León 🚌🚆 ℹCalle Gil y Carrasco 4; www. ponferrada.org/turismo

A medieval bridge reinforced with iron (pons ferrata), erected for the benefit of pilgrims on their way to Santiago de Compostela, gave this town its name. Today, prosperous from both iron and coal deposits, Ponferrada has expanded into a sizable town.

Most of the town's attractions are confined to the small old quarter. Ponferrada's majestic castle was constructed between the 12th and 14th centuries by the Knights Templar to protect pilgrims. During the

←

The medieval Knights Templar castle, a major landmark at Ponferrada

Middle Ages it was one of the largest fortresses standing in northwest Spain.

Standing on the main square is the Baroque *ayuntamiento*. One entrance to the square, one of the gateways of the medieval wall, is straddled by a tall clock tower. Nearby is the Renaissance Basílica de la Virgen de la Encina. The older Iglesia de Santo Tomás de las Ollas is hidden away in the town's village-like northern suburbs. Mozarabic, Romanesque and Baroque elements combine in the architecture of this simple church. The 10th-century apse has beautiful horseshoe arches. Ask at the nearest house for the key. The neighbour will open it for you.

A drive through the idyllic Valle de Silencio (Valley of

Silence), south of Ponferrada, follows a poplar-lined stream past several bucolic villages. The last and most beautiful of these is Peñalba de Santiago. Its 10th-century Mozarabic church has horseshoe arches above its double portal.

Villafranca del Bierzo

Ⓐ B2 **Ⓐ León** **▨** **ℹ Avenida Díez Ovelar 10; www. villafrancadelbierzo.org**

Emblazoned mansions line the ancient streets of this town. The solid, early 16th-century, drum-towered castle is still inhabited. Near the Plaza Mayor a number of imposing churches and convents, such as San Nicolás el Real, compete for attention. Particularly worth seeing are the sculptures adorning the north portal of the **Iglesia de Santiago Apóstol**. At the church's Puerta del Perdón (Door of Mercy), pilgrims who were too weak to make the final gruelling hike across the hills of Galicia could obtain dispensation. Also sample the local speciality, cherries in *aguardiente*, a spirit.

One of the finest views over El Bierzo is from Corullón, to the south. This village with grey stone houses is set above the broad, fertile basin of the

Río Burbia where vines flourish. Two churches, the late 11th-century San Miguel and the Romanesque San Esteban, are worth a visit. Don't miss the Benedictine monastery at Carracedo del Monasterio. Founded in 990, it was once the most powerful religious community in El Bierzo.

Iglesia de Santiago Apóstol
Ⓐ Calle Camino Santiago 18
Ⓞ Jul–mid-Sep: 10:30am–1:30pm & 5–8pm Tue–Sun
Ⓒ Mid-Sep–Jun

↑ The 17th-century façade of San Nicolás el Real in Villafranca del Bierzo

HIDDEN GEM
Wireless Technology

Radio fans will enjoy Ponferrada's Museo de la Radio (Calle Gil y Carrasco 7), which displays over 200 old sets belonging to Luis del Olmo (b 1937), a celebrated radio presenter in Spain. It's fascinating to see how radio has developed over the years.

A Gaudí masterpiece of turrets and spires, the Palacio de Gaudí at Astorga

STAY

Hostal Puerta del Alcázar

In front of the city walls, this budget hotel is fairly basic but it's set in an unbeatable location. The terrace has views over the cathedral.

 C3 ⓐ Calle San Segundo 38, Ávila ⓦ puertadelalcazar.com

€€€

Parador de Zamora

Suits of armour and tapestries adorn the interior at this parador set in a medieval palace. But there are also modern touches, including a big outdoor pool.

ⓐ B3 ⓐ Plaza Viriato 5, Zamora ⓦ parador.es

€€€

 8

Astorga

ⓐ B2 ⓐ León 🚊🚌 ⓘ Plaza Eduardo de Castro 5; www.aytoastorga.es

The Roman town of Asturica Augusta was a strategic halt on the Vía de la Plata (Silver Road), a Roman road linking Andalucía and northwest Spain. Later it came to form a stage on the pilgrimage route to Santiago (p232).

Soaring above the ramparts in the upper town are Astorga's two principal monuments, the cathedral and the Palacio Episcopal. The cathedral was built between the 15th and 18th centuries and displays a variety of architectural styles ranging from its Gothic apse to the effusive Baroque of its two towers, which are carved with various biblical scenes. The gilt altarpiece by Gaspar Becerra is a masterpiece of the Spanish Renaissance. Among the many fine exhibits in the cathedral's museum are the 10th-century carved casket of Alfonso III the Great, the jewelled Reliquary of the True Cross and a lavish silver

monstrance studded with enormous emeralds.

Opposite the cathedral is a fairy-tale building of multiple turrets and quasi-Gothic windows. The unconventional Palacio Episcopal is now known as the **Palacio de Gaudí**. It was designed by the Modernista architect (p51) for the incumbent bishop, a fellow Catalan, after a fire in 1887 had destroyed the previous building. Its bizarre appearance as well as its phenomenal cost so horrified the diocese that no subsequent bishops ever lived in it.

Today it houses an assembly of medieval religious art devoted to the history of Astorga and the Camino de Santiago. Roman relics, including coins found in the Plaza Romana, are evidence of Astorga's importance as a Roman settlement. The interior is decorated with ceramic tiles and stained glass.

Palacio de Gaudí

⊛ ⓐ Plaza Eduardo de Castro 15 ⓞ May–Oct: 10am–2pm & 4–8pm daily; Nov–Apr: 10:30am–2pm & 4–6:30pm Tue–Sun ⓞ 1 & 6 Jan, 25 Dec ⓦ palaciodegaudi.es

---

9

Cueva de Valporquero

ⓐ C2 ⓐ León ⓞ Mid-Oct–Dec & Mar–mid-May: 10am–5pm Thu–Sun & public hols; mid-May–mid-Oct: 10am–5pm daily ⓦ cuevade valporquero.es

This complex of limestone caves – technically a single cave with three separate entrances – is directly beneath the village of Valporquero de Torío. The caves were formed in the Miocene period between 5 and 25 million years ago.

THE MARAGATOS

Astorga is the main town of the Maragatos, a group of unknown origin, thought to be descended from 8th-century Berber migrants. By marrying only among themselves, they managed to preserve their customs through the years and keep themselves apart from the rest of society. But the demise of their traditional trade of mule-driving changed their way of life and the Maragatos have adapted to contemporary life, although their gastronomy and craftwork still survive.

TRADITIONAL MARAGATO COSTUME

Severe weather conditions in the surrounding mountains make the caverns inaccessible between December and Easter. Less than half of the huge system, which stretches 3,100 m (10,200 ft) under the ground, is open to the public. Guided tours take parties through an impressive series of galleries in which lighting picks out the beautiful limestone concretions. Iron and sulphur oxides have tinted the rocks many subtle shades of red, grey and black. The vast Gran Rotonda, covering an area of 5,600 sq m (18,350 sq ft) and reaching a height of 20 m (65 ft), is the most stunning.

As the interior is cold, and the surface often slippery, it is advisable to wear warm clothes and sturdy shoes.

10

Ciudad Rodrigo

B3 **Salamanca**
Plaza Mayor 27; 923 49 84 00

Despite its lonely setting – stranded on the country's western marches miles from anywhere – this lovely old town, with its golden stone buildings, is well worth a detour. Its frontier location inevitably gave rise to

fortification, and its robust 14th-century castle is now an atmospheric parador. The prosperous 15th and 16th centuries were Ciudad Rodrigo's heyday. During the War of Independence, the city, then occupied by the French, was besieged for two years before falling to the Duke of Wellington's forces.

The cathedral's belfry still bears the marks of shellfire from the siege. The exterior has a shapely curved balustrade and accomplished portal carvings. Inside, it is worth seeing the cloisters and the choir stalls, carved with lively scenes by Rodrigo Alemán. Within the adjacent

16th-century Capilla de Cerralbo (open to tourists only in summer) is a 17th-century altarpiece. Off the chapel's south side is the arcaded Plaza del Buen Alcalde.

11

Puebla de Sanabria

B2 **Zamora**
Muralla Mariquillo; www.pueblasanabria.com

This attractive old village lies beyond the undulating broom and oak scrub of the Sierra de la Culebra. A steep cobbled street leads past stone and slate houses with huge, overhanging eaves and walls bearing coats of arms, to a hilltop church and castle.

The village has become the centre of a popular inland holiday resort based around the largest glacial lake in Spain, the Lago de Sanabria, now a nature park. Among the many activities available are fishing, walking and water sports.

Most routes beckon visitors to Ribadelago, but the road to the quaint hill village of San Martín de Castañeda gives better views. There's a small visitors' centre for the nature reserve in San Martín's restored monastery. The village is very traditional – you may see cattle yoked to carts, and locals dancing the jota.

↑ Holiday-makers bathing in Lago de Sanabria at Peubla de Sanabria

Sierra de Gredos

C4 ⬛ Ávila ⬛ Arenas de San Pedro ⬛ Calle de la Triste Condesa 1, Arenas de San Pedro; www.turismo arenas.es

This great mountain range has abundant wildlife. Tourism here isn't a recent phenomenon – Spain's first parador opened in Gredos in 1928 and some parts of the sierra have been developed to cater for week-enders who come here to ski, fish, hunt or hike. Despite this, there are many traditional vil-lages off the beaten track.

Did You Know?

Pico Almanzor in the Sierra de Gredos is 2,502 m (8,500 ft) tall.

The slopes on the south side of the range, extending into Extremadura, are fertile and sheltered, with pinewoods, and apple and olive trees. The northern slopes, in contrast, have a covering of scrub and a scattering of granite boulders.

A single main road, the N502, crosses the centre of the range via the Puerto del Pico, a pass at 1,352 m (4,435 ft), leading to Arenas de San Pedro, the largest town of the Sierra de Gredos. Situated on this road is the castle of Mombeltrán, built at the end of the 14th century.

Near Ramacastañas, south of the town of Arenas de San Pedro, are the limestone cav-erns of the Cuevas del Águila.

The sierra's highest summit, the Pico Almanzor dominates the west. Around it lies the Reserva Nacional de Gredos, protecting the mountain's wildlife. Near El Tiemblo, in the east, stand the Toros de Guisando, four stone statues resembling bulls, believed to be of Celtiberian origin.

💬 INSIDER TIP
Water Show

Time your visit to Palacio Real de la Granja de San Ildefonso with its fountains. Three times a year, on 30 May, 25 July and 25 August, all of the jets are set in motion at once, and between May and July four fountains run every Wednesday and Saturday at 5:30pm and Sunday at 1pm.

Palacio Real de la Granja de San Ildefonso

C3 ⬛ Plazuela de la Calandria 29, Segovia ⬛ From Madrid or Segovia ⬛ Apr-Sep: 10am-8pm Tue-Sun; Oct-Mar: (to 6pm Tue-Sun) ⬛ 1, 6 & 23 Jan, 1 May, 24, 25 & 31 Dec ⬛ turismo realsitiodesanildefonso.com

This royal pleasure palace, a project launched by Felipe V

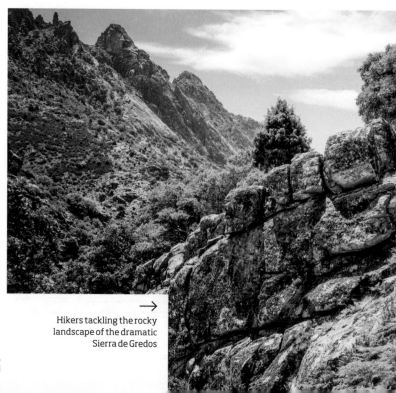

→ Hikers tackling the rocky landscape of the dramatic Sierra de Gredos

in 1720, is set against the Sierra de Guadarrama, on the site of the old Convento de Jerónimos.

A guided tour meanders through countless impressive salons decorated with ornate objets d'art and Classical frescoes against settings of marble, gilt and velvet. Huge glittering chandeliers, produced locally, hang from the ceiling. In the private apartments there are superb tapestries. The church is decorated in lavish high Baroque style, and the Royal Mausoleum contains the tomb of Felipe V and his queen.

Out in the gardens, stately chestnut trees, manicured hedges and statues frame a complex series of pools that are enhanced with fountains.

The Real Fábrica de Cristales de La Granja (Royal Glass Factory), 11 km (7 miles) southeast, is also worth a visit. Founded in 1727 by Felipe V of Spain, it still produces high-quality pieces of crystal, and it includes a glass museum with glass-blowing demonstrations.

Zamora

AB3 **Q**Zamora **Q**
i Plaza de Arias Gonzalo; www.zamora-turismo.com

In Roman times, Zamora was on the Vía de la Plata (p386), and during the *reconquista* was fought over fiercely. The city has expanded beyond its original boundaries, but the old quarter contains a wealth of Romanesque churches.

The ruins of the city walls, built by Alfonso III in 893, are pierced by the Portillo de la Traición (Traitor's Gate), through which the murderer of Sancho II passed in 1072. The parador is in a 16th-century palace with a Renaissance courtyard.

Two other palaces, the Palacio de los Momos and the Palacio del Cordón, have ornately carved façades and windows. Zamora's most important monument is its cathedral, a 12th-century structure built in Romanesque style but with a number of later Gothic additions. The building's most eye-catching feature is its striking, scaly, hemispherical dome. Inside, there are superb iron grilles and Mudéjar pulpits surround Juan de Bruselas' 15th-century choir stalls. The allegorical carvings of nuns and monks on the misericords and arm-rests were once considered risqué. The museum, off the cloisters, has a collection of 15th- and 16th-century Flemish tapestries.

Another reason for visiting Zamora is for its lively Easter Week celebrations, when elaborate *pasos* (sculpted floats) are paraded in the streets.

DRINK

Cinco Sentidos
This cosy café is the perfect place to take a break in Ponferrada. It sells "healthy" treats, so you won't feel guilty for ordering a snack.

AB2 **Q**Calle Juan de Lama 13, Ponferrada
C 665 209 907

Cafeteria Hotel Gaudí
As you might expect from the name, this hotel café offers great views of Astorga's Palacio de Gaudí.

AB2 **Q**Glorieta Eduardo de Castro 6, Astorga **C** 987 61 56 54

La Fundición
Set close to the Palacio Real de la Granja de San Ildefonso, this bar-restaurant serves drinks plus delicious dishes.

AC3 **Q**Plazuela de la Calandria 1, Real Sitio de San Ildefonso
C 921 472 406

⑮

Sepúlveda

🅰C3 🄰Segovia 🛈Plaza del Trigo 6; Jul-Sep: Tue-Sun, Oct-Jun: Wed-Sun; www. turismosepulveda.es

On a slope above the Río Duratón, this picturesque town offers views of the Sierra de Guadarrama. Parts of its medieval walls and castle survive. Of its several Romanesque churches, the Iglesia del Salvador, behind the main square, is notable for possessing one of the oldest atria in Spain (1093).

Winding through a canyon haunted by griffon vultures is the Río Duratón, 7 km (4 miles) west of Sepúlveda. This extensive area of striking beauty has been designated the Parque Natural de las Hoces del Duratón.

Ayllón, 45 km (28 miles) northeast of Sepúlveda, has

Did You Know?

Relics of Santa Teresa de Ávila are found in Paris, Lisbon, Rome and all over Spain.

an arcaded main square and the Plateresque Palacio de Juan de Contreras of 1497.

---

⑯

Ávila

🅰C3 🄰Ávila 🚉🚌 🛈Avenida de Madrid 39; www.avilaturismo.com

At 1,131 m (3,710 ft) above sea level, Ávila de los Caballeros ("of the Knights") is the highest provincial capital in Spain. In winter access roads can be blocked with snow.

The centre of the city is encircled by the finest-preserved medieval **walls** in Europe, which you can walk along. Built in the 11th century, the walls are over 2 km (1 mile) long, and are punctuated by 88 sturdy turrets, on which you might spot storks nesting. The ground falls away very steeply from the walls on three sides, but the ground to the east is relatively flat, and therefore had to be fortified more heavily. This section of the wall is guarded by the most impressive of the city's nine gateways, the Puerta de San Vicente.

The apse of the cathedral also forms part of the walls. The cathedral's war-like (and unfinished) exterior

is decorated with beasts and scaly wild men, while the interior is formed of an unusual mottled red and white stone. Finer points to note are the carvings on the retrochoir and, in the apse, the tomb of a 15th-century bishop known as El Tostado, "the Tanned One", because of his dark complexion.

Many churches and convents in Ávila are linked to St Teresa, who was born in the city. The Convento de Santa Teresa was built on the site of her home within the walls and she also lived for over 20 years in the Monasterio de la Encarnación outside the walls. There is even a local sweetmeat, *yemas de Santa Teresa*, named after her.

The Basílica de San Vicente, also just outside the eastern walls, is Ávila's most important Romanesque church, distinguished by its ornamented belfry. It was begun in the 11th century but has some Gothic features which were added later. The west doorway is often compared to the Pórtico da Gloria of Santiago Cathedral (p228). Inside, the carved tomb of St Vincent and his sisters depicts their hideous martyrdom in detail. Another Romanesque-Gothic church worth seeing is the Iglesia de San Pedro.

River flowing through the Parque Natural de las Hoces del Duratón, Sepúlveda

Some way from the centre is the Real Monasterio de Santo Tomás, which boasts three cloisters. The middle one, carved with the yoke and arrow emblem of the Catholic Monarchs, is the most beautiful. The last cloister leads to a museum displaying chalices and processional crosses. The church contains the tomb of Prince Juan, the only son of Fernando and Isabel. In the sacristy lies another historic figure: Tomás de Torquemada, head of the Inquisition.

In Ávila, you may see groups of *tunas* – students dressed in traditional costume walking the town's streets while singing and playing guitars.

Walls

⬦ ⏱ 10am–8pm Tue–Sun
🅦 muralladeavila.com

⓱

Pedraza de la Sierra

🅐 C3 🅓 Segovia
🅘 Calle Real 3; 921 50 86 66; Wed–Sun

The aristocratic little town of Pedraza de la Sierra is perched high over rolling countryside. Within its medieval walls, old streets

lead to the porticoed Plaza Mayor. The huge castle, standing on a rocky outcrop, was owned by Basque artist Ignacio Zuloaga (1870–1945). The castle museum shows some of his works. On the first and second Saturdays in July, concerts are held in the Plaza Mayor.

⓲

Castillo de Coca

🅐 C3 🅓 Coca, Segovia
🅒 617 57 35 54 ⏱ Hours vary, check website
🗓 15 days in Jan, 1st Tue of each month

Built in the late 15th century for the influential Fonseca family, Coca castle is one of Castilla y León's most memorable fortresses. Unlike the region's other castles, it was used more as a residential palace than a defensive fortress, although its turrets and battlements are a fine example of Mudéjar military architecture. The complex moated structure comprises three concentric walls around a massive keep. It is now a forestry school, which features a display of Romanesque woodcarvings.

The 14th-century castle of Arévalo in Ávila province, located 26 km (16 miles) southwest, is where Isabel I spent her childhood. The porticoed Plaza de la Villa is surrounded by several attractive half-timbered houses.

↑ Massive defensive walls of the 15th-century Castillo de Coca

19

Valladolid

🅰C3 🚉Valladolid 🚌
ℹ️Glass Pavilion, Acera
de Recoletos; www.info.
valladolid.es

Located at the confluence
of the Río Esgueva and
Río Pisuerga, Valladolid is a
sprawling and industrialized
city, but it still has some of
Spain's best Renaissance
art and architecture.

The city has had many
famous inhabitants. Fernando
and Isabel were married in
the Palacio Vivero in the city in
1469 and, following the completion of the *reconquista* in
1492, they made Valladolid
their capital. Columbus died
here, alone and forgotten, in
1506. Felipe II was born in the
Palacio de los Pimentel in 1527
and José Zorrilla, who popu-
larized the legendary Don Juan
in his 1844 play, was born here
in 1817. But perhaps the city's
most famous inhabitant is the
author of *Don Quixote*, who
lived in the **Casa de Cervantes**
from 1603 to 1606.

Valladolid's has many
beautiful churches. The Iglesia
de San Pablo's façade is
embellished with angels and
coats of arms in Plateresque

The immense Mudéjar
exterior of the Castillo de la
Mota at Medina del Campo

→

style. Santa María la Antigua
has Romanesque belfry and
the Iglesia de Las Angustias
houses Juan de Juni's fine
sculpture of the Virgen de los
Cuchillos (Virgin of the Knives).

Work started on the
unfinished **cathedral** in
1580 by Felipe II's favourite
architect, Juan de Herrera,
but lost momentum over the
centuries. Churrigueresque
flourishes on the façade
contrast to the sombre interior,
whose only flamboyance is
a Juan de Juni altarpiece. The
Museo Diocesano inside, however, contains some fine
religious art and sculpture.

Housed in the 15th-century
Colegio de San Gregorio, the
Museo Nacional de Escultura
houses mainly religious
sculptures from the 13th to
18th centuries. They include
Juan de Juni's emotive depiction of the burial of Christ and
Recumbent Christ by Gregorio
Fernández. An Alonso
Berruguete altarpiece and
walnut choir stalls by Diego
de Siloé are among the other
fine works to be found here.
The building, too, is impressive,
particularly the Plateresque
staircase, the chapel by Juan
Güas, and the patio of twisted
columns and delicate basket
arches. The façade is a fine
example of Isabelline sculpture,
portraying a melee of naked
children scrambling about in
thorn trees.

Inside the former Monastery
of San Benito, the **Patio
Herreriano Museo de Arte
Contemporáneo Español**
holds a private collection of
contemporary Spanish art.
Among the 800 works are

←

Wooden sculpture at
the Museo Nacional de
Escultura in Valladolid

masterpieces by Joan Miró,
Eduardo Chillida, Antoni
Tàpies and Miquel Barceló.

Casa de Cervantes
⊕ 🅰Calle Rastro s/n
🕐9:30am-3pm Tue-Sat
(from 10am Sun)
🚫Public hols 🌐museo
casacervantes.mcu.es

Cathedral
⊕⊗ 🅰Calle Arribas 1
🕐10am-1:30pm & 4:30-7pm
Tue-Fri, 10am-2pm Sat & Sun
🌐catedral-valladolid.com

Museo Nacional
de Escultura
⊕ 🅰Calle Cadenas de San
Gregorio 1 🕐10am-2pm &
4-7:30pm Tue-Sun 🌐museo
escultura.mcu.es

📷 PICTURE PERFECT
Life in Squares

Valladolid's Plaza Mayor
is one of Spain's most
splendid, but unlike
most others, it is not
normally thronging
with tourists. The
porticoed terraces and
elegant buildings make
for lovely shots.

Patio Herreriano Museo de Arte Contemporáneo Español

⟨⟩ ⌂Calle Jorge Guillén 6 ⏲11am-2pm & 5-8pm Tue-Fri, 11am-8pm Sat, 11am-3pm Sun 🚫1 Jan, 25 Dec 🌐museopatioherreriano.org

 20

Medina del Campo

🄰C3 ⌂Valladolid 🚆🚌 ℹPlaza Mayor 48; www.medinadelcampo.es

Medina became wealthy in medieval times on the proceeds of huge sheep fairs and is still an important agricultural centre. The Gothic-Mudéjar **Castillo de la Mota**, on its outskirts, began as a Moorish castle but was rebuilt in 1440. The town transferred the castle's ownership to the Crown in 1475. Isabel I and her daughter Juana "la Loca" ("the Mad") both stayed here. Later, it served as a prison – Cesare Borja was incarcerated here from 1506 to 1508. In a corner of the Plaza Mayor stands the house where Isabel died in 1504.

Towering over the plains, some 25 km (16 miles) to

the south of Medina del Campo, are the walls of Madrigal de las Altas Torres, which owes its name to the hundreds of bastions that marked the old wall; only 23 remain. In 1451 Isabel was born here in a palace that later became the Monasterio de las Agustinas in 1527.

Castillo de la Mota

⟨⟩⟨⟩ ⏲Summer: 11am-2pm & 4-7pm Mon-Sat, 11am-2pm Sun; winter: 11am-2pm & 4-6pm Mon-Sat, 11am-2pm Sun 🌐castillodelamota.es

 21

Tordesillas

🄰C3 ⌂Valladolid 🚌 ℹCasas del Tratado; Tue-Fri; www.tordesillas.net

This pleasant town is known for being where the historic treaty between Spain and Portugal was signed in 1494, which divided the lands of the Americas. A fateful oversight by the Spanish map-makers left the immense prize of Brazil to Portugal.

The **Real Monasterio de Santa Clara** was constructed

EAT

Restaurante Alcaravea

The menu offered at this warm, ochre-walled restaurant features local recipes that have been followed in Ávila for generations.

🄰C3 ⌂Plaza de la Catedral 15, Ávila ☎920 22 66 00

€€€

La Parrilla de San Lorenzo

This traditional grill is located in the basement of a Valladolid monastery filled with antiques.

🄰C3 ⌂Calle Pedro Niño 1, Valladolid 🌐laparrilladesanlorenzo.es

€€€

by Alfonso XI around 1340 and then converted by his son Pedro the Cruel into a stunning residence for his mistress, María de Padilla. Pining for her native Andalucía, she had the convent decorated with fine Moorish arches, baths and tiles.

Located in the old quarter, the **Iglesia de San Antolín** now houses religious art, with paintings as well as a collection of liturgical objects.

Real Monasterio de Santa Clara

⟨⟩ ⌂Calle Alonso Castillo Solorzano ⏲10am-2pm Tue-Fri, 10am-2pm & 4-6:30pm Sat, 10:30am-3pm Sun 🌐patrimonionacional.es

Iglesia de San Antolín

⟨⟩ ⌂Calle Postigo ☎983 77 09 80 ⏲11:30am-1:30pm & 4:30-6:30pm Tue-Sun

EXPERIENCE Castilla y León

㉒
Frómista

🅰C2 🏛Palencia 🚉🚌
🛈 Carretera de Astudillo;
www.fromista.es

This town on the road to
Santiago de Compostela
(p232) is the site of one of
Spain's purest Romanesque
churches. The Iglesia de San
Martín is the highlight of the
town, partly due to restoration work in 1904, leaving the
church, dating from 1066,
entirely Romanesque in style.
The presence of pagan and
Roman motifs suggests it may
have pre-Christian origins.
Nearby, the Iglesia de San

Pedro has Renaissance and
Gothic sculptures.

Carrión de los Condes,
20 km (12 miles) to the northwest of Frómista, is also on
the Camino de Santiago. The
frieze on the door of the
Iglesia de Santiago depicts
not religious figures but local
artisans. There are carvings
of bulls on the façade of
the 12th-century Iglesia
de Santa María del Camino.
The Monasterio de San Zoilo
has a Gothic cloister and
now operates as a hotel.

Located at Gañinas, 20 km
(12 miles) to the northwest
(just south of Saldaña), is the
Villa Romana La Olmeda. It
contains a number of mosaics,
including a notable hunting
scene. Finds are displayed in
the archaeological museum
in the Iglesia de San Pedro
in Saldaña.

The Villa Romana
La Olmeda, and
(inset) a detail
of the intricate
↓ mosaic floor

Villa Romana La Olmeda
♿♿ 🏛Pedrosa de la Vega
📞979 11 99 97 🕙10:30am-
6:30pm Tue-Sun 🚫1 & 6 Jan,
24, 25 & 31 Dec

㉓
Palencia

🅰C2 🏛Palencia 🚉🚌
🛈 Calle Mayor 31; www.
palenciaturismo.es

In medieval times, Palencia
was a royal residence and the
site of Spain's first university,
founded in 1208. The city

> 🔍 HIDDEN GEM
> **El Cid's City**
>
> Palencia's cathedral isn't
> the only sacred building
> worth visiting. The
> Iglesia de San Miguel
> blends Romanesque and
> Gothic architecture, and
> sits on the bank of the
> River Carrión. It is here
> that El Cid is said to have
> married Jimena Díaz.

> **The ancient buildings on Medina de Rioseco's main street, the Calle de la Rúa, are supported on wooden pillars, forming charming shady porticoes.**

gradually diminished in importance following its involvement in the failed revolt of the Castilian towns over Carlos I's regent in 1520.

Although Palencia has since expanded considerably on profits from coal and wheat, its centre, by the old stone bridge over the Río Carrión, remains almost village-like.

The city's main sight is the cathedral, known as *La Bella Desconocida* (the Unknown Beauty). It is especially worth a visit for its superb works of art, many the result of Bishop Fonseca's generous patronage. The retrochoir, exquisitely sculpted by Gil de Siloé and Simon of Cologne, and the two altarpieces, are also note-worthy. The altarpiece above the high altar was carved by Philippe de Bigarny early in the 16th century. The inset panels are by Juan de Flandes,

Isabel I's court painter. Behind the high altar is the Chapel of the Holy Sacrament, with an altarpiece dating from 1529 by Valmaseda. In this chapel, high on a ledge to the left, is the colourful tomb of Doña Urraca of Navarra. Below the retrochoir, a Plateresque staircase leads down to the fine Visigothic crypt.

Baños de Cerrato, 12 km (7 miles) to the south, boasts the tiny Visigothic Iglesia de San Juan Bautista, founded in 661. It is held to be the oldest intact church in Spain. Carved capitals and horseshoe arches decorate the interior.

Medina de Rioseco

🅰C3 🄰Valladolid 🚌
ℹ️ Paseo de San Francisco; Tue–Sun; www.medina derioseco.com

During the Middle Ages this town grew wealthy from the profitable wool trade, enabling it to commission leading artists, mainly of the Valladolid school, to decorate its churches. The dazzling star vaulting and superb woodwork of the Iglesia de Santa María de Mediavilla, in the centre of town, are evidence of this. Inside, the Los Benavente Chapel is a tour de force, with a colourful stucco ceiling by Jerónimo del Corral (1554), and an altarpiece by Juan de Juni.

The interior of the Iglesia de Santiago is stunning, with a triple altarpiece designed by the Churriguera brothers of Salamanca.

The ancient buildings on Medina de Rioseco's main street, the Calle de la Rúa, are supported on wooden pillars, forming charming shady porticoes.

TOP 4 LOCAL FIESTAS

El Colacho
On the Sunday after Corpus Christi, babies born during the pre-vious year are laid on mattresses in the streets of Castrillo de Murcia. El Colacho – a man dressed as the Devil – then jumps over them to free them from illnesses.

St Agatha's Day
In Zamarramala, two women are elected as town leaders on the Sunday closest to 5 February – the day of the patron saint of married women – and ceremonially burn a stuffed figure of a man.

Good Friday
A procession of coloured sculptures, depicting scenes from the Passion, takes place in Valladolid.

Fire-walking
On 23 June in San Pedro Manrique, men walk barefoot over burning embers; it is said only local people can do it without being burned.

↑ Altarpiece of the Iglesia de Santa Maria de Mediavilla

25

Briviesca

 D2 Burgos 🚌
Calle Santa María
Encimera 1; turismo.
briviesca.es

The walled town of Briviesca, in the northeast of Burgos province, has an arcaded main square and several mansions. The best known of its churches is the Convento de Santa Clara, with its 16th-century walnut reredos carved with religious scenes. In 1387 Juan I of Aragón created the title Príncipe de Asturias for his son, Enrique, in the town. The Santuario de Santa Casilda, outside Briviesca, has a collection of votive objects.

GREAT VIEW
Parador Paramour

Head up to the parador outside Cervera de Pisuerga, 25 km (15 miles) northwest of Aguilar de Campoo, for a drink. Although the building itself is unremarkable, the view over the Reserva Nacional de Fuentes Carrionas is spectacular (www.parador.es).

Oña, 25 km (15 miles) north of Briviesca, is a pretty town where a Benedictine monastery was founded in 1011. Overlooking a fertile valley, 20 km (12 miles) further northeast, is the little hilltop town of Frías. Its castle overlooks cobbled streets and pretty old houses. Crossing the Río Ebro is a fortified medieval bridge, still with its central gate tower.

At Medina de Pomar, 30 km (20 miles) north of Oña, there is a 15th-century castle, once the seat of the Velasco family. Inside are the ruins of a palace with fine Mudéjar stucco decoration and Arabic inscriptions.

26

Aguilar de Campoo

 C2 Palencia 🚌
Paseo de la Cascajera 10; 10am–1pm & 4–7pm daily; www.aguilardecampoo.com

Situated between the parched plains of Central Spain and the lush foothills of the Cantabrian Mountains is the old fortified town of Aguilar de Campoo. In the centre of its ancient porticoed main square is the bell tower of the Colegiata

↑ Bunting strung out across a street, Medina de Pomar

de San Miguel. In this church is a mausoleum containing the tomb of the Marquises of Aguilar. Ask at the priest's house for the key.

Other places of interest are the Ermita de Santa Cecilia, and the restored Romanesque-Gothic Monasterio de Santa María la Real, which has a friendly posada (inn).

Some 6 km (4 miles) south, at Olleros de Pisuerga, is a church built in a cave. From the parador at Cervera de Pisuerga, there are tours of the Reserva Nacional de Fuentes Carrionas. This is a rugged region overlooked by Curavacas, a 2,540-m (8,333-ft) peak.

27

Covarrubias

 D2 Burgos Calle
Monseñor Vargas; 947 40
64 61; 10am–1pm Tue–Fri,
10am–2:40pm & 4–6pm Sat,
10am–2:40pm Sun

Named after the reddish caves situated on its outskirts, Covarrubias stands on the banks of the Río Arlanza.

At regular intervals throughout the day, the monks of Santo Domingo de Silos sing services in plainchant, an unaccompanied singing of Latin texts in unison. The origins of chant date back to the beginnings of Christianity, but it was Pope Gregory I (AD 590-604) who codified this manner of worship. It is an ancient and austere form of music which has found a new appeal with modern audiences. In 1994 a recording of the monks became a surprise hit all over the world.

Medieval walls surround the charming old centre with its arcaded half-timbered houses. The distinguished collegiate church (closed Tue) shows the historical importance of Covarrubias: here is the tomb of Fernán González, first independent Count of Castile, and one of the great figures in Castilian history. By uniting several fiefs against the Moors in the 10th century, he started the rise in Castilian power that ensured the resulting kingdom of Castile would play a leading role in the unification of Spain. The church museum contains a beautiful Flemish triptych of the Adoration of the Magi, attributed to the school of Gil de Siloé, and a 17th-century organ.

A short distance east along the Río Arlanza lies the ruins of the 11th-century Romanesque monastery of San Pedro de Arlanza. At Quintanilla de las Viñas,

24 km (15 miles) north of Covarrubias, is a ruined 7th-century Visigothic church. Look out for the reliefs on the columns of the triumphal arch, which depict sun and moon symbols. This suggests that they may be pagan.

28

Monasterio de Santo Domingo de Silos

🅰 D2 🏛 Santo Domingo de Silos, Burgos 🚌 From Burgos 🕐 10am-1pm & 4:30-6pm Tue-Sun 🚫 Public hols 🌐 abadia desilos.es

St Dominic gave his name to the monastery he built in 1041 over the ruins of an abbey destroyed by the Moors. It is a place of spiritual and artistic pilgrimage – its tranquil setting has inspired countless poets.

Others come to admire the beautiful Romanesque cloisters, whose capitals are sculpted in a variety of designs, both symbolic and realistic. The carvings on the corner piers depict various scenes from the Bible and the ceilings are coffered in Moorish style. The body of St Dominic rests in a silver urn, supported by three Romanesque lions, in a chapel in the north gallery. The old pharmacy, which is located just off the cloisters, has a display of jars from Talavera de la Reina (p417).

The Benedictine community holds regular services in Gregorian chant in the Neo-Classical church by Ventura Rodríguez. The monastery offers accommodation for male guests.

To the southwest lies the Garganta de la Yecla (Yecla Gorge), where a path leads to a narrow fissure cut by the river. A suggested walk allows you to cross footbridges over waterfalls and pools. To the northeast, the peaks and wildlife reserve of the Sierra de la Demanda extend over into La Rioja.

→

Cloisters of the Monasterio de Santo Domingo de Silos, and *(inset)* its serene setting

㉙ Peñaranda de Duero

Ⓐ D3 **Ⓐ Burgos** **🚌**
🛈 Calle Trinquete 7;
10am–2pm & 4–7pm Tue–
Sat, 10am–2pm Sun; www.
penarandadeduero.es

The castle of Peñaranda was built during the *reconquista* by the Castilians, who had driven the Moors back south of the Río Duero. From its hilltop site, there are views down to one of the most charming villages in old Castile, where pantiled houses cluster around a huge church. The main square is lined with porticoed, timber-framed buildings. The door of the **Palacio de Avellaneda** is framed by various heraldic devices, and inside is a patio with decorated ceilings. On Calle de la Botica is a 17th-century pharmacy.

In Aranda de Duero, 18 km (10 miles) to the west, the Iglesia de Santa María has an Isabelline façade.

Palacio de Avellaneda

Ⓢ **Ⓐ Plaza Condes de Miranda 1** **📞 947 55 20 13** **🕐 10am–2pm & 4–8pm Tue–Sun**

Did You Know?

William Randolph Hearst wanted to rebuild the Palacio de Avellaneda in the US.

㉚ Lerma

Ⓐ C2 **Ⓐ Burgos** **🚍🚌**
🛈 Calle Audiencia 6; Aug:
9am–2pm daily, Sep–Jul:
9am–2pm Tue–Sun; www.
citlerma.com

The grandiose appearance of this town is largely due to the ambition of the notorious first Duke of Lerma, Felipe III's favourite and a corrupt minister from 1598 to 1618. He misused vast quantities of Spain's new-found wealth, acquired from the Americas, on new buildings in his home town – all strictly Classical in style. At the top of the town, the Palacio Ducal, built in 1605 as his residence, has been transformed into a parador.

There are good views over the Río Arlanza from the archways near to the Convento de Santa Clara and also from the Colegiata de San Pedro church, which has a bronze statue of the Duke's uncle, Don Cristóbal de Rojas, Archbishop of Seville.

㉛ Soria

Ⓐ D3 **Ⓐ Soria** **🚍🚌** **🛈 Calle Medinaceli 2; www.turismo soria.es**

Castilla y León's smallest provincial capital stands on

↑ Roman pottery exhibited at the Museo Numantino in Soria

the banks of the Río Duero. Soria's stylish, modern parador is named after the poet Antonio Machado (1875–1939), who wrote in praise of the town and the surrounding plains. Many of the older buildings are gone, but among those remaining are the imposing Palacio de los Condes de Gómara, and the Concatedral de San Pedro, both built in the 16th century.

The **Museo Numantino**, opposite the municipal gardens, displays a variety of finds from the nearby Roman ruins of Numantia and Tiermes. Across the Duero is the ruined monastery of San Juan de Duero, with a 13th-century cloister of interlacing arches.

North of Soria are the ruins of Numantia, whose inhabitants endured a year-long Roman siege in 133 BC

 The triumphal Roman arch in Medinaceli, lit up at night

before defiantly burning the town and themselves. To the northwest is the Sierra de Urbión, a range of pine-clad hills with a lake, the Laguna Negra de Urbión.

Museo Numantino

 🏛 Paseo del Espolón 8 📞 975 22 13 97 🕙 10am-2pm & 4-8pm Tue-Sat, 10am-2pm Sun

---

㉜

El Burgo de Osma

🅰 D3 🏛 Soria 🚌 ℹ Plaza Mayor 9; 10am-2pm & 4-7pm Wed-Sun; www.burgodeosma.com

The most interesting sight in this small, attractive city is the cathedral. Although it is mostly Gothic (dating from 1232), the tower is Baroque (1739). Its treasures include a Juan de Juni altarpiece and the tomb of the founder, San Pedro de Osma. The museum here has a valuable collection of illuminated manuscripts and codices.

Porticoed buildings line the streets and the Plaza Mayor, and storks nest on the Baroque Hospital de San Agustín.

Overlooking the Río Duero at Gormaz, 12 km (7 miles) south, is a massive castle that has 28 towers. There are also medieval fortresses still standing at Berlanga de Duero, 20 km (12 miles) further southeast, and at Calatañazor, 25 km (16 miles) northeast of El Burgo de Osma, near to where the Moorish leader al Mansur was killed in 1002.

 Pantiled houses at Peñaranda de Duero, clustered around the village church

㉝

Medinaceli

🅰 D3 🏛 Soria 🚌 ℹ Campo de San Nicolás 13; www.medinaceli.es

Situated at the confluence of the rivers Jalón and Arbujuelo, Medinaceli was the site of the Celtiberian town known as Ocilis. Only a triumphal arch remains of Roman Ocilis, perched on a high ridge over the Río Jalón. Built in the 1st century AD, it is the only one in Spain with three arches. It has been adopted as the symbol for ancient monuments on Spanish road signs.

On the Madrid–Zaragoza road is the 12th-century Cistercian **Monasterio de Santa María de Huerta**. It includes a 13th-century Gothic cloister and the superb, crypt-like Monks' Refectory, with pointed arched windows.

Monasterio de Santa María de Huerta

 🕙 10am-1pm & 4-6pm daily 🔒 24 Aug 🖥 monasterio huerta.org

A DRIVING TOUR

SIERRA DE FRANCIA
AND SIERRA DE BÉJAR

Length 72 km (45 miles) **Stopping-off points** Candelario, Miranda del Castañar
and La Alberca all have good eating places, and are renowned for their hams and
sausages **Terrain** Narrow, winding roads climb up steep mountains

These attractive schist hills buttress the
western edges of the Sierra de Gredos
(p388). Narrow roads wind their way through
picturesque chestnut, olive and almond
groves, and quaint rural villages of wood
and stone. The highest point of the range

is La Peña de Francia, which, at 1,732 m
(5,700 ft), is easily recognizable from miles
around. The views from the peak, and from
the roads leading up to it, offer a breathtaking
panorama of the surrounding empty plains
and rolling hills.

Start off from **La Peña de Francia**.
*Atop the windswept peak is a 15th-century
Dominican monastery.*

*The narrow streets
of **Miranda del
Castañar** are lined
with ancient houses
with wide eaves.*

Nava de Francia

San Martín
del Castañar

Garcibuey

Las Casas de
Conde

START

La Peña
de Francia

Francio

SA203

Mogarraz

Francia

SA220

La Alberca

Monforte de
la Sierra

Miranda del
Castañar

SA201

Batuecas

Las
Batuecas

Madroñal

Cepeda

SA225

*Stop off in
La Alberca
to buy some
local honey,
hams and
handicrafts.*

Herguijuela
de la Sierra

Sotoserrano

Francia

Alagón

Las Mestas

*The road to **Las Batuecas**
careers down into a green
valley, past the monastery
where Luis Buñuel made his
film* Tierra sin Pan *(Land
without Bread).*

Rebollosa

EX204

SA225

Alagón

→
Walking along a forested
path in Las Batuecas, a
valley in the Sierra de Francia

CASTILLA Y LEÓN

Sierra de Francia and Sierra de Béjar

Locator Map
For more detail see p368

↑ The fortified town of Miranda del Castañar, surrounded by forest

Surrounded by vineyards and orchards, **Santibáñez de la Sierra** *has thriving wine and fruit industries.*

Did You Know?

The Sierra de Francia is home to one of the highest shrines to the Virgin Mary in the world.

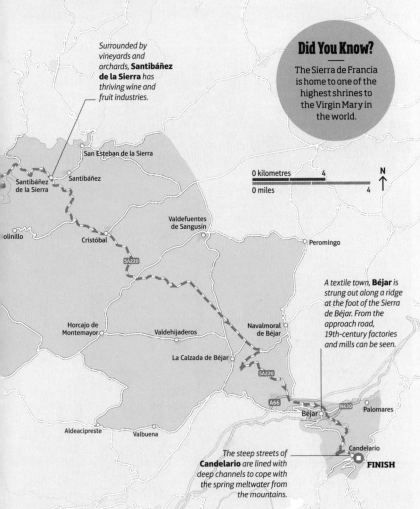

San Esteban de la Sierra

Santibáñez de la Sierra

Santibáñez

...olinillo

Cristóbal

SA220

Valdefuentes de Sangusín

Peromingo

0 kilometres   4

0 miles   4

N ↑

A textile town, **Béjar** *is strung out along a ridge at the foot of the Sierra de Béjar. From the approach road, 19th-century factories and mills can be seen.*

Horcajo de Montemayor

Valdehijaderos

Navalmoral de Béjar

La Calzada de Béjar

SA220

A66

Béjar   **N630**

Palomares

Aldeacipreste

Valbuena

The steep streets of **Candelario** *are lined with deep channels to cope with the spring meltwater from the mountains.*

Candelario

FINISH

CASTILLA-LA MANCHA

True to its name, Castilla-La Mancha is a region speckled with castles. Most of these fortresses were built between the 9th and 12th centuries, when the region was a battleground between the Christians and the Moors, while others mark the 14th- and 15th-century frontiers between the kingdoms of Aragón and Castile. The region is also famed for its windmills, immortalized by Miguel de Cervantes in his 1605 epic *Don Quixote.*

The region's seemingly empty plains were the stage for a rich history of religious tolerance. Toledo, now the capital of the *comunidad autónoma,* was once the capital of Visigothic Spain. Captured by the Moors in AD 711, the city became a literary and ecclesiastical centre as part of al-Andalus. Muslims, Christians and Jews peacefully coexisted here, even after it became the first major Moorish city to fall to the Christians in 1085.

Carlos I established his court at Toledo in 1518, and it became the imperial capital of the Holy Roman Empire. This eminence lasted until the court moved to Madrid in 1561, triggering a lengthy period of stagnation. But this lack of development has led to the preservation of Toledo, and the rest of Castilla-La Mancha, making it the perfect place to see the Spain of yesteryear.

CASTILLA-LA MANCHA

EXTREMADURA p426

0 kilometres 50

0 miles 50

N

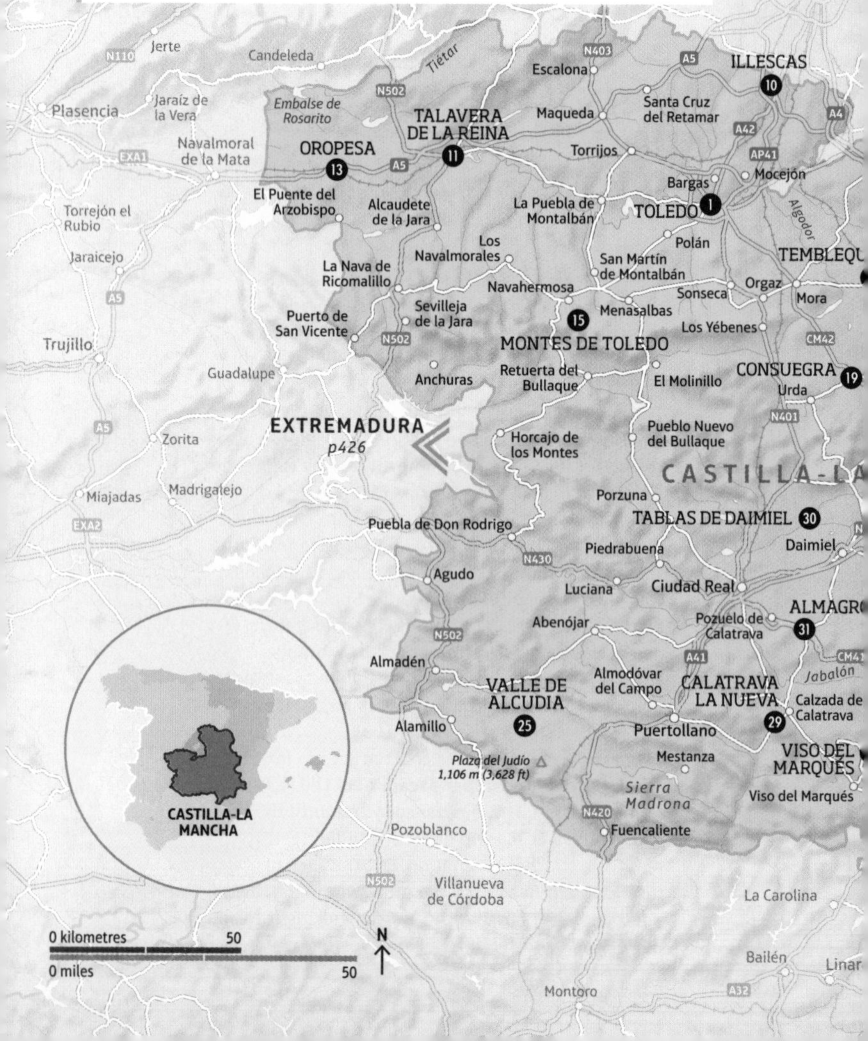

1

TOLEDO

A C4 **⌂** Toledo **🚌🚆** **i** Plaza del Consistorio 1;
www.toledo-turismo.com

Picturesquely sited on a hill above the River Tagus is the richly historic centre of Toledo. Home to reminders of its Roman, Visigothic and Moorish past, as well as its time as a melting pot of Christian, Muslim and Jewish cultures, it's an atmospheric area to explore. Nowadays, these monument are floodlit after dark, causing the city to resemble one of the moon-lit landscapes painted by Toledo's most famous inhabitant – El Greco, who came to live here in the 16th century.

Did You Know?

Toledo was known as the "city of three cultures" because of its Christian, Muslim and Jewish citizens.

The Iglesia de San Román houses a museum dedicated to the Visigoths.

①

Alcázar

⌂ Calle Unión s/n **📞** 925 23 88 00 **⏱** 11am-5pm Tue-Sun

Carlos V's fortified palace stands on the site of former Roman, Visigothic and Moorish fortresses. Its severe, square profile suffered damage by fire three times before being almost completely destroyed in 1936, when the Nationalists survived a 70-day siege by the

Republicans. Restoration followed the original plans, and the siege headquarters have been preserved as a monument to Nationalist heroism. The former National Museo del Ejército was transferred from Madrid to this building, making the Alcázar the main army museum in Spain.

The Alcázar is also home to the Borbón-Lorenzana Library, which contains 100,000 books and manuscripts from the 16th to 19th centuries.

To Monasterio de San Juan de los Reyes (600 m/ 655 yds) and Sinagoga de Santa María la Blanca (450 m/490 yds)

To Sinagoga del Tránsito (250 m/275 yds)and Museo del Greco (200 m/220 yds)

INSIDER TIP
Overnight Stay

To visit all of Toledo's main sights you will need at least two days, but it is possible to walk around the medieval and Jewish quarters in a long morning. To avoid heavy crowds, go midweek and stay for a night, when the historic city is at its most atmospheric.

← The rambling city of Toledo as night falls

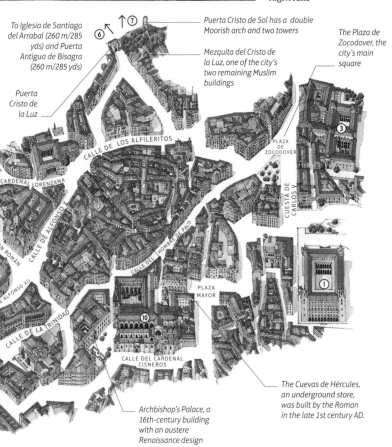

To Iglesia de Santiago del Arrabal (260 m/285 yds) and Puerta Antigua de Bisagra (260 m/285 yds)

Puerta Cristo de la Luz

Puerta Cristo de Sol has a double Moorish arch and two towers

Mezquita del Cristo de la Luz, one of the city's two remaining Muslim buildings

The Plaza de Zocodover, the city's main square

CALLE DE LOS ALFILERITOS

CARDENAL LORENZANA

CALLE DE ALFONSO

AN ROMAN

DE ALFONSO XII

CALLE DE LA TRINIDAD

CALLE DEL HOMBRE DE PALO

PLAZA DE ZOCODOVER

CUESTA DE CARLOS V

PLAZA MAYOR

CALLE DEL CARDENAL CISNEROS

Archbishop's Palace, a 16th-century building with an austere Renaissance design

The Cuevas de Hércules, an underground store, was built by the Roman in the late 1st century AD.

↑ The gilded interior of Toledo's Iglesia de Santo Tomé, a church thought to date from the 11th century

Iglesia de Santo Tomé

📍Plaza del Conde 4 🕐Mar-mid-Oct: 10am-6:45pm daily; mid-Oct-Feb: 10am-5:45pm daily 🌐santotome.org

The main attraction of this church is El Greco's masterpiece, *The Burial of the Count of Orgaz*. This count paid for much of the 14th-century building that stands today. The painting, commissioned in his memory by a parish priest, depicts the miraculous appearance of St Augustine and St Stephen at his burial, to raise his body to heaven. It is remarkable for its contrast of glowing and sombre colours. In the foreground, allegedly, are the artist and his son (both looking out), as well as Cervantes. The church is thought to date back to the 11th century, and its tower is a fine example of Mudéjar architecture. Nearby is the Pastelería Santo Tomé, a good place to buy locally made marzipan.

Museo de Santa Cruz

📍Calle Miguel de Cervantes 3 🕐9:30am-6:30pm Mon-Sat, 10am-2pm Sun 🌐cultura.castillalamancha.es

This museum is housed in a 16th-century hospital, which has some Renaissance features, including the main doorway, staircase and cloister. The four main wings, laid out in the shape of a cross, are dedicated to the fine arts. The collection holds medieval and Renaissance tapestries, paintings and sculptures. There are also works by El Greco, including one of his last paintings, *The Virgin of the Immaculate Conception* (1613). Decorative arts on display include two typically Toledan crafts: armour and damascened swords, made by inlaying steel with gold wire.

Sinagoga del Tránsito, Museo Sefardí

📍Calle Samuel Leví 🕐Mar-Oct: 9:30am-7:30pm Tue-Sat, 10am-3pm Sun; Nov-Feb: 9:30am-6pm Tue-Sat, 10am-3pm Sun 🕐Public hols 🌐museosefardi.mcu.es

The most elaborate Mudéjar interior in the city is hidden behind the humble façade of this former synagogue, built in the 14th century by Samuel Ha-Leví, the Jewish treasurer to Pedro the Cruel. The interlaced frieze of the lofty prayer hall fuses Islamic, Gothic and Hebrew geometric motifs below a wonderful coffered ceiling. The synagogue houses a museum of Sephardi (Spanish Jewish) culture, with items on display from both before and after the Jews' expulsion from Spain in the late 15th century.

Monasterio de San Juan de los Reyes

📍Calle de los Reyes Católicos 17 🕐Mar-mid-Oct: 10am-6:45pm daily; mid-Oct-Feb: 10am-5:45pm daily 🕐1 Jan, 25 Dec 🌐sanjuandelosreyes.org

A brilliant mix of architectural styles, this monastery was commissioned by the Catholic Monarchs in honour of their victory at the battle of Toro in 1476. It was originally intended to be their burial place, but they were actually laid to rest in Granada (p492). Largely designed by Juan Guas, the church's main Isabelline structure was completed in 1496. Although badly damaged by Napoleon's troops in 1808, it has been restored to its

→

Horseshoe-shaped arches within the Sinagoga de Santa María la Blanca

STAY

Hotel Santa Isabel
Housed in the 14th-century home of a local noble, this hotel is good-value and has a roof terrace with stunning views over the city.

📍Calle de Santa Isabel 24 🌐hotelsantaisabeltoledo.es

original splendour with features such as a Gothic cloister (1510) with a multi-coloured Mudéjar ceiling.

Iglesia de Santiago del Arrabal

📍Plaza de Santiago Arrabal 4 📞925 22 06 36 🕐For Mass

This is one of Toledo's most beautiful Mudéjar monuments. It can be easily identified by its tower, which dates from the 12th-century *reconquista*. The church, which was built slightly later, has a beautiful woodwork ceiling and an ornate Mudéjar pulpit, but only the exterior of the building can be visited.

Puerta Antigua de Bisagra

When Alfonso VI conquered Toledo in 1085, he entered it through this gateway, alongside El Cid *(p380)*. It is the only gateway in the city to have kept its original 10th-century military architecture. The huge towers are topped by a 12th-century Arab gatehouse.

EL GRECO

Born in Crete in 1541, El Greco ("the Greek") came to Toledo in 1577 to paint the altarpiece in the convent of Santo Domingo el Antiguo. Enchanted by the city, he remained, painting other religious works, and came to be closely identified with Toledo. He died in the city in 1614.

Museo del Greco

📍Paseo del Tránsito 🕐Mar-Oct: 9:30am-7:30pm Tue-Sat, 10am-3pm Sun; Nov-Feb: 9:30am-6pm Tue-Sat, 10am-3pm Sun 🌐museodelgreco.mcu.es

Located in a house near to the one in which El Greco lived, this museum has a wide collection of his works. Canvases on display include *View of Toledo*, a detailed depiction of the city, and the superb series *Christ and the Apostles*. On the ground floor is a domestic chapel with a fine Mudéjar ceiling and an excellent collection of art by other painters associated with Toledo.

Sinagoga de Santa María la Blanca

📍Calle de los Reyes Católicos 4 🕐Mar-mid-Oct: 10am-6:45pm daily; mid-Oct-Feb: 10am-5:45pm daily 🚫1 Jan, 25 Dec 🌐toledomonumental.com

The oldest and largest of the city's original synagogues dates back to the 12th century. In 1391 a massacre of Jews took place on this site. In 1405 it was taken over as a church after the expulsion of the Jews, but restoration has returned it to its original state – carved stone capitals stand out against white horseshoe arches and plasterwork.

EXPERIENCE Castilla-La Mancha

TOLEDO CATHEDRAL

🏛 Calle Cardenal Cisneros 1   🕐 10am–6pm Mon–Sat, 2–6pm Sun   🌐 catedralprimada.es

The splendour of Toledo's massive cathedral reflects its history as the spiritual heart of the Church in Spain and the seat of the Primate Archdiocese over all of Spain's Catholic churches. This illustrious past is particularly apparent during the saying of Mozarabic Mass, which dates back to Visigothic times.

The Catedral Primada Santa María de Toledo is interesting from an architectural point of view. It was built on the site of a 7th-century church. Work began in 1226 and spanned three centuries, until the completion of the last vaults in 1493. This long period of construction explains the cathedral's mixture of styles: pure French Gothic – complete with flying buttresses – on the exterior; with Spanish decorative styles, such as Mudéjar and Plateresque work, used in the interior.

Sacristy, which contains many works of art

The belfry, containing a heavy bell known as La Gorda ("the Fat One")

The cloister, built in the 14th century

Did You Know?

The monstrance contains the first gold brought back by Columbus from the Americas.

The Puerta del Mollete, the main entrance to the cathedral

A 16th-century silver and gold monstrance (a vessel containing a holy object) is housed in the Treasury.

The Capilla Mozárabe, with a Renaissance ironwork grille

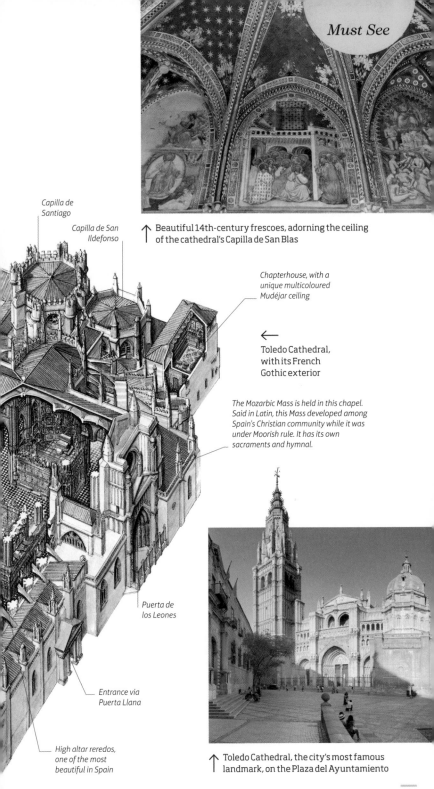

↑ Beautiful 14th-century frescoes, adorning the ceiling of the cathedral's Capilla de San Blas

Capilla de Santiago

Capilla de San Ildefonso

Chapterhouse, with a unique multicoloured Mudéjar ceiling

← Toledo Cathedral, with its French Gothic exterior

The Mozarbic Mass is held in this chapel. Said in Latin, this Mass developed among Spain's Christian community while it was under Moorish rule. It has its own sacraments and hymnal.

Puerta de los Leones

Entrance via Puerta Llana

High altar reredos, one of the most beautiful in Spain

↑ Toledo Cathedral, the city's most famous landmark, on the Plaza del Ayuntamiento

→ Casas Colgadas in Cuenca, perched dramatically at the edge of a ravine

2

CUENCA

🗺D4 🚌Cuenca 🚉🚌 ℹCalle Alfonso VIII 2; www.cuenca.es

Sitting on a rocky outcrop, Cuenca's enchanting Old Town seems like something out of a stage set, with its Casas Colgadas (Hanging Houses) perched over the gorge below. Wander through the city's atmospheric streets and you'll be transported back to times gone by.

Cuenca's picturesque Old Town is built astride a steeply sided spur, which drops precipitously on either side to the deep gorges of the Júcar and Huécar rivers. At its heart is the Plaza Mayor, a café-lined, arcaded square that hums with activity. Around the Moorish town's narrow, winding streets grew the Gothic and Renaissance city, its monuments built with the profits of the wool and textile trade.

Perhaps the biggest draw for visitors is the cathedral, which is one of the most original works of Spanish Gothic, with Anglo-Norman influences. One of the charming Casas Colgadas, which jut out over the Huécar ravine, has been converted into the excellent Museo de Arte Abstracto Español. Here, you'll find works by the movement's leading artists, including Tàpies and Chillida.

↑ Colourful medieval houses within Cuenca's Old Town

> **HIDDEN GEM**
> **Museo Tesoro**
>
> Adjoining Cuenca's cathedral is the Treasure Museum, a glittering site housing a wonderful collection of ecclesiastical pieces, jewellery and artworks. Look out for the two religious works by El Greco (p409).

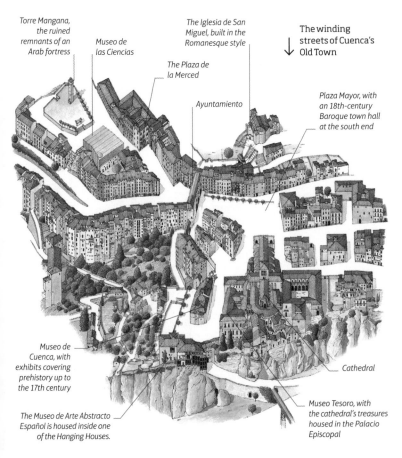

Torre Mangana, the ruined remnants of an Arab fortress

Museo de las Ciencias

The Iglesia de San Miguel, built in the Romanesque style

The winding streets of Cuenca's Old Town ↓

The Plaza de la Merced

Ayuntamiento

Plaza Mayor, with an 18th-century Baroque town hall at the south end

Museo de Cuenca, with exhibits covering prehistory up to the 17th century

Cathedral

The Museo de Arte Abstracto Español is housed inside one of the Hanging Houses.

Museo Tesoro, with the cathedral's treasures housed in the Palacio Episcopal

EXPERIENCE MORE

❸
Sigüenza

 D3 Guadalajara
i Calle Serrano Sanz 9;
www.siguenza.es

The highlight of this hillside
town is the Catedral de
Santa María de Sigüenza.
This cathedral is Romanesque,
with later additions such
as the Gothic-Plateresque
cloisters. In one of the chapels
is the Tomb of El Doncel, built
for Martín Vázquez de Arce,
Isabel of Castile's page. He
was killed in battle against the
Moors in 1486. The sacristy
has a notable ceiling carved
with flowers and cherubs.

PICTURE PERFECT
Street Scene

Walk halfway up
Sigüenza's Calle Mayor,
and then turn around
for a perfectly framed
photo of the porticoed
buildings on the Plaza
Mayor, along with the
town's cathedral.

---

❹
Atienza

 D3 Guadalajara
i Héctor Vázquez 2;
Sat & Sun; www.turismo
atienza.es

Rising high above the valley
it once protected, Atienza
contains vestiges of its medieval past. Crowning the hill is
a ruined 12th-century castle,
and the arcaded Plaza Mayor
and the Plaza del Trigo are
joined by an original gateway.
The **Museo de San Gil**, a
religious art museum, is in the
church of the same name. The
Iglesia de Santa María del Rey,
at the foot of the hill, displays
a Baroque altarpiece.

Campisábalos, located to
the west, has a 12th-century
Romanesque church. The
Hayedo de Tejera Negra,
further west, is a nature
reserve of beech woods.

Sigüenza's cathedral,
and *(inset)* the tomb of
El Doncel, topped by a
statue of him ↓

Museo de San Gil

⊗ Calle San Gil 📞 949
39 90 41 🕐 10:30am–2pm
Sat & Sun (by appt weekdays)

---

❺
La Alcarria

 D3 Guadalajara
Guadalajara **i** Palacio
Ducal, Plaza de la Hora,
Pastrana; www.turismo
castillalamancha.es

This vast stretch of undulating
olive groves and fields east of
Guadalajara is still evocative of
Camilo José Cela's book *Journey
to the Alcarria*. Driving through
the rolling hills, it seems that
little has changed since this
account of Spanish rural life

was written in the 1940s. The region is noted for its fauna and flora, and the regional cuisine benefits from the good-quality honey and La Alcarria's special breed of lamb.

Towards the centre of the Alcarria are three immense, adjoining reservoirs called the Mar de Castilla (Sea of Castile). The first reservoir was built in 1946, and holiday homes have sprung up close to the shores and on the outskirts of villages.

The historic ducal town of Pastrana, 45 km (28 miles) southeast of Guadalajara, is one of the prettiest towns in the Alcarria. The town developed alongside the Palacio Mendoza, and by the 17th century was larger and more affluent than Guadalajara. The Iglesia Colegiata de la Asunción contains four 15th-century Flemish tapestries and paintings from El Greco's school.

Brihuega, 30 km (19 miles) northeast of Guadalajara, has a pleasant old centre with porticoed squares. The country's oldest bull-running events are held here in the valleys and gullies that surround the town.

↑ The nave inside the Virgen de la Hoz chapel at the village of Ventosa, near Molina de Aragón

---

Molina de Aragón

▲D3 ⬛Guadalajara 🚌
🛈 Calle de las Tiendas 62; www.turismomolinade aragon.com

Molina's attractive medieval quarter is at the foot of a hill next to the Río Gallo. The town was disputed during the *reconquista* and captured from the Moors by Alfonso I of Aragón in 1129. Many monuments were destroyed during the War of Independence, but the 11th-century hilltop castle preserves seven original towers. It is possible to visit the Romanesque-Gothic Iglesia de Santa Clara.

West of Molina is the Virgen de la Hoz chapel, set in a rust-red ravine. Further southwest

is a nature reserve, the Parque Natural del Alto Tajo.

---

❼ Guadalajara

▲D3 ⬛Guadalajara
🚌🚆 🛈 Plaza Aviación Militar Española; www.guadalajara.es

Guadalajara's history is largely lost within the modern city, although traces of some of its Renaissance splendour survive. The **Palacio de los Duques del Infantado**, built between the 14th and 17th centuries by the powerful Mendoza dynasty, is an outstanding example of Gothic-Mudéjar architecture. The main façade and patio are adorned with carving. The restored palace now houses the Museo Provincial.

The 15th-century Iglesia de San Francisco is home to the mausoleum of the Mendoza family; it cannot, however, be visited. But you can see the Iglesia de Santiago, with its Gothic-Plateresque chapel by Alonso de Covarrubias.

Palacio de los Duques del Infantado

🏛Plaza de España 13
📞949 21 33 01 🕐Jun-Sep: 10am-2pm Tue-Sun; Oct-Apr: 10am-2pm & 4-7pm Tue-Sat, 10am-2pm Sun

---

↑ The Monasterio de Uclés facing onto the pretty Plaza Pelayo Quintero

Monasterio de Uclés

⚑D4 ⌂Uclés, Cuenca ⏲By appt only 🗓1 & 6 Jan, 25 Dec 🌐monasterio ucles.com

The small village of Uclés is dominated by its impressive castle-monastery, nicknamed "El Escorial de La Mancha" for the similarity of its church's profile to that of El Escorial (p358). Originally an impregnable medieval fortress, Uclés became the monastery seat of the Order of Santiago from 1174, because of its central location. The

← Roman statue discovered at the archaeological site in Segóbriga

austere building you see today is mainly Renaissance but overlaid with Baroque detail. It has a magnificent carved wooden ceiling and staircase.

Segóbriga

⚑D4 ⌂Saelices, Cuenca, CM-310, km 58 ⏲Apr-Sep: 10am-3pm & 4-7:30pm Tue-Sun; Oct-Mar: 10am-6pm Tue-Sun 🌐cultura. castillalamancha.es

The small ruined Roman city of Segóbriga is located in open, countryside. Many parts of the city can be explored. The 1st-century AD theatre – which has a capacity of 2,000 people – is sometimes used for performances today. Segóbriga also had a necropolis, an amphitheatre, a temple to Diana and public baths. The quarries which supplied the stone to build the city can also be seen.

Nearby, a small museum has some of the site's finds, although the best statues are displayed in the Museo de Cuenca (p413).

Illescas

⚑C4 ⌂Toledo 🚆🚌 🛈Plaza Mercado 14; www.illescas.es

Illescas was the summer location for Felipe II's court. While there is little to see of its Old Town, the **Museo del Greco del Santuario de la Caridad**, near the Iglesia de Santa María, has an important art collection, including five late works by El Greco (p409). The subjects of three of these are the Nativity, the Annunciation and the Coronation of the Virgin.

Museo del Greco del Santuario de la Caridad

 ⌂Calle Cardenal Cisneros 2 ⏲By appt only 🌐elgreco illescas.com

Talavera de la Reina

⚑C4 ⌂Toledo 🚆🚌 🛈Calle Ronda del Cañillo 22; www.turismo talavera.org

A ruined 15th-century bridge across the Tagus marks the entrance to the old part of this busy market town. From the bridge you can walk past the surviving part of the Moorish and medieval wall to the 12th-century collegiate church.

Talavera's ceramic workshops still produce the blue and yellow azulejos (tiles) which have been a trademark of the town since the 16th century. A wonderful selection of azulejos can be seen in the large Ermita de la Virgen del Prado by the river. Many of the interior walls have superb 16th- to 20th-century tile friezes of religious scenes.

Housed in a 17th-century convent, the Museo Ruiz de Luna houses the private Talavera pottery collection and personal works of ceramicist Juan Ruiz de Luna.

Serranía de Cuenca

D4 Cuenca Cuenca Calle Alfonso VIII 2, Cuenca; www.turismo castillalamancha.es

North and east of Cuenca stretches the vast *serranía*, a mountainous area of forests and pastures dissected by deep gorges. Its two most popular beauty spots are the Ciudad Encantada (Enchanted City), where the limestone has been eroded into spectacular shapes, and the moss-clad waterfalls and rock pools of the Nacimiento del Río Cuervo (Source of the River Cuervo).

The main river flowing through the area, the Júcar, carves a gorge near Villalba de la Sierra. The viewpoint of the Ventano del Diablo gives the best view of the gorge.

Between Beteta and Priego, to the north, is another spectacular river canyon, the Hoz de Beteta, where the Río Guadiela has cut through the surrounding cliffs. A small road leads to the 18th-century royal spa of Solán de Cabras.

In the emptier eastern and southern tracts is Cañete, a pretty, fortified old town with a parish church displaying 16th-century paintings.

Oropesa

C4 Toledo Calle Hospital 25; www.oropesa detoledo.org

Oropesa's former medieval and Renaissance splendour has left a charming old quarter at the centre of today's small farming town. A circular Ruta Monumental starts from the massive, mainly 15th-century castle on the top of the hill. A Renaissance extension was added to the castle in the 16th century by the wealthy and influential Álvarez family. Part of the castle has been converted into a parador. The Ruta Monumental continues around the town, taking in other notable buidings.

EAT

Álvarez
Expect the likes of croquettes, stews and roast lamb at this Albacete spot.

D4 Calle de Carmen 42, Albacete restau rantealvarez.com

€€€

Tierra
Enjoy gourmet fare in this Michelin-starred restaurant near Oropesa. The name "land" refers to the area's quality produce.

C4 Carretera de Oropesa a Puente del Arzobispo km 9, Torrico tierra-valde palacios.com

€€€

↑ Eroded rock formations in the Ciudad Encantada park at Serranía de Cuenca

The entrance to Plaza Mayor, Tembleque's main square

 14

Tembleque

A D4 **⌂** Toledo **i** Plaza Mayor 1; www.turismo castillalamancha.es

The stone Plaza Mayor at Tembleque dates from the 17th century. It is decorated with the red cross of the Knights Hospitallers, the military order which once ruled the town.

Ocaña, 30 km (20 miles) north of Tembleque, centres on the huge yet elegant, late 18th-century Plaza Mayor, one of the largest town squares in Spain, after Madrid and Salamanca.

 15

Montes de Toledo

A C4 **⌂** Toledo **⊟** Pueblo Nuevo del Bullaque **i** Parque Nacional de Cabañeros; www. montesdetoledo.net

To the southwest of Toledo a range of low mountains sweeps towards Extremadura. In medieval times the Montes de Toledo were owned by bishops and the kings. They cover some 1,000 sq km (386 sq miles).

The Parque Nacional de Cabañeros is formed of wood-land and pastures used for grazing sheep. The easiest

access to the park is from Pueblo Nuevo del Bullaque. From here you can take a tour in a Land Rover and, if you're lucky, you may spot wild boar, deer and imperial eagles. In the pasturelands stand *chozos*, conical refuges for shepherds.

In the eastern foothills of the Montes de Toledo is Orgaz, with a parish church which contains works by El Greco. Nearby villages, such as Los Yébenes and Ventas con Peña Aguilera, are known for their leather goods and restaurants serving game.

On the plains stands the small church of Santa María de Melque, believed to date back to the 8th century. Close by is the Templar castle of Montalbán, a vast but ruined 12th-century fortress.

 16

Belmonte

A D4 **⌂** Cuenca **⊟** **i** Avenida Luis Pinedo; www.turismo castillalamancha.es

This tranquil town is noteworthy for being the birthplace of the poet Fray Luis de León and for its story-

book castle. The magnificent 15th-century **Castillo de Belmonte** is one of the best preserved in the region. It was built by Juan Pacheco, Marquis of Villena, after Enrique IV gave him the town in 1456. Inside it has decorative carved coffered ceilings, and Mudéjar plaster-work. The collegiate church is especially remarkable for its richly decorated chapels and Gothic choir stalls, which were brought here from Cuenca Cathedral *(p412)*. There is also outstanding ironwork, a Renaissance reredos and the font at which the poet Fray Luis de León (1527–91) was baptized.

There are two villages near Belmonte that also flourished under the Marquis of Villena: Villaescusa de Haro and San Clemente. The church at

→

Windmills on the ridge above Consuegra, overlooking the plains of La Mancha

Villaescusa de Haro, 6 km (4 miles) to the northeast, has an outstanding 16th-century reredos, while San Clemente, some 40 km (25 miles) south-east of Belmonte, clusters around two near-perfect Renaissance squares.

Castillo de Belmonte
⊛ 🏠 Calle Eugenia de Montijo s/n 🕐 Hours vary, check website 🌐 castillo debelmonte.com

---

El Toboso

🗺 D4 🏠 Toledo 🛈 Calle Daoíz y Velarde 3; Tue–Sun; www.eltoboso.es

Of all the villages of La Mancha claiming links to Don Quixote, El Toboso has the clearest ties. It was chosen by Cervantes as the birthplace of Dulcinea, Don Quixote's sweetheart. Here, you can visit the **Casa de Dulcinea**, the home of Doña Ana Martínez Zarco, on whom Dulcinea was allegedly based.

Casa de Dulcinea
⊛ 🏠 Calle Don Quijote 1 📞 925 19 72 88 🕐 10am–2pm & 3–6:30pm Tue–Sun

---

Consuegra

🗺 D4 🏠 Toledo 🚌 🛈 Avenida Castilla-La Mancha; 925 47 57 31

Consuegra's 11 windmills and restored castle stand on a ridge, overlooking the plains of La Mancha. One windmill is set in motion every year during the town's festival to

---

DON QUIXOTE'S LA MANCHA
Cervantes *(p364)* doesn't specify where his hero was born, but several places are mentioned in the novel. Don Quixote is knighted in an inn in Puerto Lápice, believing it to be a castle. His sweet-heart, Dulcinea, lives in the village of El Toboso. The windmills he tilts at, imagining them to be giants, are thought to be those at Campo de Criptana. And another adventure takes place in the Cueva de Montesinos *(p421)*.

celebrate the autumn harvest of saffron. During the fiesta, pickers compete to see who can strip petals from the saffron crocus the fastest.

About 4 km (2 miles) from Consuegra, on the road to Urda, is a Roman dam. An old restaurant at Puerto Lápice, off the A4 20 km (13 miles) south of Consuegra, claims to be the inn in which Don Quixote was "knighted" by the landlord.

Campo de Criptana

🗺 D4 🏠 Ciudad Real 🚍 🛈 Molino Poyatos, Sierra de los Molinos; Tue–Sun; www.campodecriptana.es

Ten windmills stand on a hill-crest in the town of Campo de Criptana. Three are 16th-century and have their original machinery intact. One is the tourist information office, and three others are museums.

More windmills are located above the towns of Alcázar de San Juan and Mota del Cuervo, a good place to purchase *queso manchego*, local sheep's cheese.

Alarcón

D4 Cuenca Calle Posadas 6; www.descubre alarcon.es

The fortified village of Alarcón guards a narrow loop of the Río Júcar from on top of a rock. As you drive through its defences, you may have the impression of entering a film set for a medieval epic.

The village dates back to the 8th century. It became a key military base for the *reconquista* (*p64*) and was recaptured from the Moors by Alfonso VIII in 1184 following a nine-month siege. Alarcón has dramatic walls and three defensive precincts. The small, triangular castle, high above the river, has been turned into a parador.

The Iglesia de Santa María is a Renaissance church with a fine portico and an altarpiece

 GREAT VIEW
Arch Hero

A grand vista of Alarcón's castle is to be had when you look through the arch next to the Torre de Armas on the road that leads up to the town. It frames the fortress.

attributed to the Berruguete school. The nearby Iglesia de Santísima Trinidad is in Gothic-Plateresque style.

Alcalá del Júcar

E4 Albacete Avenida de los Robles 1; www.turismo alcaladeljucar.com

Where the Río Júcar runs through the chalk hills to the northeast of Albacete, it cuts a deep, winding gorge, the Hoz de Júcar, along which you can drive for a stretch. Alcalá del Júcar is dramatically sited on the side of a spur of rock jutting out into the gorge. The town is a warren of steep alleys and flights of steps. At the top of the town, houses have been extended by digging into the rock; some have even become tunnels cut from one side of the spur to the other.

Albacete

D4 Albacete Plaza del Altozano; www. albaceteturistico.es

This provincial capital , known for its daggers and jackknives, is not without its attractions.

The excellent **Museo de Albacete** is located in a pleasant park and has exhibits ranging from Iberian sculptures and unique Roman amber and ivory dolls to 20th-century paintings. The cathedral, begun in 1515 and devoted to San Juan Bautista, has Renaissance altarpieces.

Museo de Albacete
Parque Abelardo Sánchez 967 22 83 07 Jul-mid-Sep: 10am-2pm Tue-Sat, 9:30am-2pm Sun; mid-Sep-Jun: 10am-2pm & 4:30-7pm Tue-Sat, 9:30am-2pm Sun

---

Lagunas de Ruidera

D4 Ciudad Real Ruidera Avenida Castilla la Mancha 47, Ruidera; Sep-Jun: Wed-Sun, Jul-Aug: daily; www. lagunasderuidera.es

Nicknamed "The Mirrors of La Mancha", the 15 interconnected lakes which make up the Parque Natural de las Lagunas de Ruidera stretch for 39 km (24 miles) through a valley. They allegedly take their name from a story in *Don Quixote (p419)* in which a certain Mistress Ruidera, her

A distant view of the castle of Alarcón, standing at a bend in the Río Júcar

daughters and her nieces are said to have been turned into lakes by a magician.

La Mancha's lakes have recovered well from the recent years' falling water table, and are especially worth visiting for their wealth of wildlife, which includes great and little bustards, herons and many types of duck. The wildlife has increasingly come under threat due to the number of tourists, and the development of holiday chalets on the lakes' shores. Near one of the lakes, the Laguna de San Pedro, is the Cueva de Montesinos, a deep, explorable cave which was also used as the setting for an episode in *Don Quixote*.

Villanueva de los Infantes

D5 **Ciudad Real**
Calle Cervantes 16; www. villanuevadelosinfantes.es

Villanueva's Old Town, which centres on the graceful Neo-Classical Plaza Mayor, is one of

the most attractive in La Mancha. Many buildings on the square have wooden balconies and arcades. Also on the square is the Iglesia de San Andrés, which has a Renaissance façade. Inside are a Baroque altarpiece and organ, as well as the tomb of the 17th-century author Francisco de Quevedo. He lived and died in the Convento de los Dominicos.

Valle de Alcudia

C5 **Ciudad Real**
Fuencaliente **Plaza Mayor 41; 926 47 02 88; Tue-Sun**

Alcudia's lush lowlands, which border the Sierra Morena foothills to the south, are among Central Spain's most unspoiled countryside. The area is used largely as pastureland. In late autumn it is filled with sheep, whose milk makes the farmhouse cheese for which the valley is known.

The mountain village of Fuencaliente has thermal baths that open in the summer. Further north, Almadén is the site of a large mercury mine with a museum. The town of Chillón, to the northwest, has a Late Gothic church.

> **Alcudia's lush lowlands, which border the Sierra Morena foothills to the south, are among Central Spain's most unspoiled countryside.**

Alcaraz

D5 **Albacete** **Calle Mayor 3; 10:30am–1:30pm & 5–7pm Tue-Sun; www. alcaraz.es**

An important Arab and Christian stronghold, Alcaraz's military power waned after the *reconquista*. But many buildings dating from the height of the city's power are preserved in its historic Old Town. Standing in the Renaissance Plaza Monumental are the "twin towers" of Tardón and Trinidad, and an 18th-century commodity exchange, the Lonja del Corregidor, with Plateresque decoration. The square is surrounded by lively, narrow streets. On the outskirts of the town are the castle ruins and surviving arch of a Gothic aqueduct. Alcaraz makes a good base for touring the sierras of Alcaraz and Segura.

The "twin towers" of Tardón and Trinidad on Alcaraz's main square

La Endiablada
Men dressed as devils process through the streets of Almonacid del Marquesado on 2 and 3 Feb.

Romería del Cristo del Sahúco
On Whit Monday, in Peñas de San Pedro, a coffin bearing a figure of Christ is carried 15 km (9 miles) by men dressed in white.

La Caballada
Horsemen follow the route taken by the 12th-century muleteers of Atienza (Guadalajara) on Whit Sunday.

Corpus Christi
Toledo hosts Spain's most dramatic Corpus Christi procession.

27

Valdepeñas

D5 Ciudad Real Plaza de España; www.valdepenas.es

Valdepeñas is the capital of La Mancha's vast wine region, the world's largest expanse of vineyards, producing vast quantities of red wine. This largely modern town comes alive for its wine festival in September. In the network of older streets around the café-lined Plaza de España are the Iglesia de la Asunción and the municipal museum.

Valdepeñas has over 30 *bodegas*, 10 of which can be visited. One of them has been converted into the **Museo del Vino**, illustrating the various stages of wine production.

Museo del Vino
 Calle Princesa 39 10am-2pm & 5-8pm Tue-Sat, 11am-2pm Sun museodelvinovaldepenas.es

---

28

Viso del Marqués

D5 Ciudad Real Calle Real 39; www.visodelmarques.es

Set in Viso del Marqués, **Palacio del Marqués de Santa Cruz** is a grand Renaissance mansion commissioned in 1564 by the Marquis of Santa Cruz (Álvaro Bazán y Guzmán), the admiral of the fleet that defeated the Turks at Lepanto in 1571. One of the main features of the house is a Classical patio. Inside, the main rooms are decorated with Italian frescoes.

Palacio del Marqués de Santa Cruz
Plaza del Pradillo 12 926 33 75 18 Jul & Aug: 9am-2pm Tue-Sun; Sep-Jun: 9am-1pm & 4-6pm Tue-Fri, 10am-1pm & 4-6pm Sat, 9:30am-2pm Sun

---

29

Calatrava la Nueva

C5 Aldea del Rey, Ciudad Real Apr-Sep: 11am-2pm & 5:30-8:30pm Tue-Sat, 10am-2pm & 5-9pm Sun; Oct-Mar: 11am-2pm & 4-6pm Tue-Sat, 10am-6pm Sun castillodecalatrava.org

Standing in a magnificent hilltop setting, the ruined castle of Calatrava la Nueva is reached by a stretch of original medieval road.

The castle was founded in 1217 by the Knights of Calatrava, Spain's first military-religious order. The complex is of huge proportions, with a double patio and a church with a triple nave illuminated by a beautiful rose window. After the *reconquista*, the building continued to be used as a monastery until it was damaged in a fire in 1802.

Opposite the castle are the ruins of a Muslim frontier fortress, Salvatierra, which was captured from the Moors by the Order of Calatrava in the 12th century.

→ The beautiful courtyard of the Palacio del Viso in Viso del Marqués

↑ Walkway at Tablas de Daimiel, and *(inset)* aquatic birds on the water

30 ⓂⒷ

Tablas de Daimiel

🅰C4 🅰Ciudad Real
🚌Daimiel 🚩Calle Santa
Teresa s/n, Daimiel; Tue-
Sun; www.lastablasde
daimiel.com

The marshy wetlands of the Tablas de Daimiel, northeast of Ciudad Real, are the feeding and nesting grounds of a huge range of aquatic and migratory birds, making it perfect bird-watching territory. The wetlands were designated as national parkland in 1973, and since became an ecological *cause célèbre* due to the growing threat from the area's lowering water table. They are now fully recovered.

One corner of the park is open to the public, with walking routes to islets and observation towers. Breeding birds here include great crested grebes and mallards. Otters and red foxes are also found in the park.

31

Almagro

🅰C5 🅰Ciudad Real 🚉🚌
🚩Calle San Agustín 21;
www.ciudad-almagro.com

Almagro was disputed during the *reconquista*, until the Order of Calatrava captured it and built the castle of Calatrava la Nueva to the southwest of the town. The rich architectural heritage of the atmospheric Old Town is partly the legacy of the Fugger brothers, the Habsburgs' bankers, who settled in nearby Almadén during the 16th century.

The town's main attraction is its colonnaded stone plaza, with enclosed, green balconies. On one side is a 17th-century courtyard-theatre, the Corral de Comedias – where a drama festival is held for the spectacular Festival de Teatro Clásico each summer.

Other monuments worth seeing include the Fuggers' Renaissance warehouse and former university, and also the castle, which has been converted into a parador.

DRINK

Enjoy a tasting at one of these La Mancha vineyards.

Bodega Finca Antigua
🅰D4 🅰Carretera
Quintanar 5, km 11,
Los Hinojosos
🌐fincaantigua.com

Finca Loranque
🅰C4 🅰Finca Loranque
s/n, Bargas 🕒Sun
🌐fincaloranque.com

Finca La Estancada
🅰D4 🅰Carretera
Nacional 412, km 103,
Tarancón 🌐fincala
estancada.com

Pago del Vicario
🅰C4 🅰Carretera
Nacional 400, km 16,
Las Casas 🌐pagodel
vicario.com

Casa del Valle
🅰D4 🅰Carretera
Nacional 4004, km
47.700, Yepes 🌐eventos
casadelvalle.es

A DRIVING TOUR
SIERRA DE ALCARAZ

Length 280 km (175 miles) **Stopping-off points** Liétor; Letur; Yeste **Terrain** Mountainous climbs, but the roads are in good condition

Where the Sierras of Segura and Alcaraz push northwards into the southeastern plains of La Mancha, they form spectacular mountains, broken up by dramatic gorges and fertile valleys. This circular route takes in picturesque villages, including Letur, Ayna, Yeste and Liétor, that specialize in crafts, such as basketry, pottery and metalwork, and are firmly off the well-beaten tourist trail.

N322

Alcaraz   Peñascosa

Vianos

Paterna del Madera

Salobre

Bogarra

Sierra   del   Alcaraz

N322

Bienservida

Riópar

CM412

*The **Río Mundo** begins as a waterfall, inside the Cueva de Los Chorros, and tumbles down a dramatic cliff face into a bubbling spring at the bottom.*

Mundo

Villaverde de Guadalimar

Source of the Río Mundo

Calar del Mundo

Tus

Ardal
1,435 m
(4,708 ft) △   Yeste

↑ The tumbling waterfall at the source of the Río Mundo

*The village of **Yeste**, which stands at the foot of the Sierra de Ardal, is crowned by a hilltop Arab castle. It was reconquered under Fernando III, and was later ruled by the Order of Santiago.*

↑ Ayna's red-roofed buildings, shrouded in low-hanging clouds

Locator Map
For more detail see p404

Set off from the village of **Ayna**, which is set deep in a gorge of the Río Mundo. There are spectacular views over the countryside from the Mirador del Diablo.

First stop is **Liétor**. Worth visiting in this small hillside village are the Gothic Ermita de Belén and the Iglesia de Santiago, with a trompe l'oeil altarpiece.

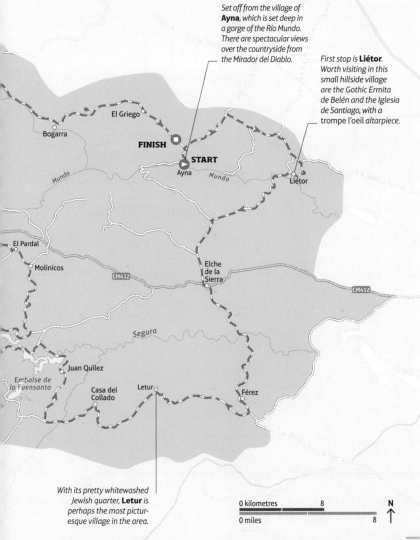

With its pretty whitewashed Jewish quarter, **Letur** is perhaps the most picturesque village in the area.

0 kilometres   8

0 miles   8

N ↑

EXTREMADURA

Extremadura once formed part of the Roman province of Lusitania, and Mérida, its capital, was a major centre during that time. Evidence of this is still writ large in the city's extraordinary set of Roman remains, including a forum, a circus and a magnificent amphitheatre, as well as elsewhere in the region, such as the Roman bridge at Alcántara.

Extremadura's climate, however, made it an inhospitable region, and over the centuries it became one of Spain's poorest. It may have been these conditions that pushed some of its inhabitants to seek their fortune overseas, and Extremadura is famously the birthplace of many conquistadors and emigrants to the Americas in the 15th and 16th centuries. The riches they acquired on the other side of the world financed a surge of building. The Real Monasterio de Nuestra Señora de Guadalupe, in the eastern hills, is perhaps the most splendid monument to the region's colonial ties. The old town of Cáceres, with its noble mansions, and Trujillo's many palaces and grand churches are a testament to the wealth of that time.

The castles and stout walls of Alburquerque and Olivenza, meanwhile, mark frontiers embattled throughout history, notably during the *reconquista* of those regions in the 13th century and the 19th-century battles with neighbouring Portugal (Olivenza was part of Portugal from 1297 to 1801 and the country still claims sovereignty over the town). Today, Extremadura remains one of Spain's poorest and least densely populated regions. Somewhat overlooked by international tourism, its economy is bolstered by producing tobacco and cultivating pork for Spain's famous *jamón ibérico*.

EXTREMADURA

Must Sees

1. Mérida
2. Real Monasterio de Nuestra Señora de Guadalupe
3. Cáceres

Experience More

4. Las Hurdes
5. Sierra de Gata
6. Hervás
7. Coria
8. Plasencia
9. Badajoz
10. Parque Nacional de Monfragüe
11. Arroyo de la Luz
12. Alcántara
13. Valencia de Alcántara
14. Monasterio de San Jerónimo de Yuste
15. Trujillo
16. Tentudía
17. Jerez de los Caballeros
18. Olivenza
19. Cancho Roano
20. Zafra
21. Llerena

❶

MÉRIDA

🅰B5 🏛**Badajoz** 🚊🚌 ℹ**Plaza Margarita Xirgú; www.turismomerida.org**

Founded by Augustus in 25 BC, Augusta Emerita (as Mérida was originally named) grew into the cultural and economic capital of Rome's westernmost province, Lusitania, but lost its eminence under the Moors. Though a small city, Mérida is a UNESCO World Heritage Site thanks to its large number of Roman monuments.

①

Museo Nacional de Arte Romano

🏛**Calle José Ramón Mélida**
🕐**Apr–Sep: 9:30am–8pm Tue–Sat, 10am–3pm Sun; Oct–Mar: 9:30am–6:30pm Tue–Sat, 10am–3pm Sun**
🌐**mecd.gob.es/mnromano**

The red-brick Museo Nacional de Arte Romano was designed by Rafael Moneo to be harmonious with the area's Roman remains. The semicircular arches of its main hall, for example, are built to the same height as the city's Los Milagros aqueduct. Over three floors, the gallery exhibits ceramics, mosaics, coins and statuary. There is also an excavated stretch of the famed Via de la Plata Roman road.

②

Anfiteatro

🏛**Plaza Margarita Xirgú s/n** 🕐**Hours vary, check website** 🗓**1 Jan, 24 & 25 Dec** 🌐**consorciomerida.org**

According to inscriptions on its grandstand, Mérida's amphitheatre dates back to 8 BC, 17 years after Augustus founded the city as a colony for honourably discharged soldiers. Entertainment for these veterans included gladiatorial fights and other grisly battles. The central pit is still clearly visible, as is a large section of a seating area that once held over 15,000 people. Also intact is the tribune, from which various nobles would enjoy the show.

③

Teatro Romano

🏛**Plaza Margarita Xirgú s/n**
🕐**Hours vary, check website**
🗓**1 Jan, 24 & 25 Dec**
🌐**consorciomerida.org**

The city's centrepiece is the Teatro Romano, built between 16 and 15 BC and designed to seat 6,000 people. Its stage is

---

GREAT VIEW
Riverside Stroll

Cross the Rio Guadiana via the perfectly preserved Puente Romano. From here there's a good view of the walls of the Alcazaba, one of Spain's oldest Moorish buildings (AD 835).

← The vast central pit of Mérida's Anfiteatro, overlooked by seats

up with earth, with only the "Seven Chairs" – where Moorish kings would sit – still visible.

The theatre was excavated in 1910 and, in summer, the stage is used for the city's drama festival. Entry tickets include admission to the adjacent Anfiteatro.

④

Templo de Diana

🏛 Calle Romero Leal s/n
🕐 Hours vary, check website
🚫 1 Jan, 24 & 25 Dec
🌐 consorciomerida.org

Mérida's Roman forum was one of the first buildings erected by Augustus and dates to 25 BC. Around 24 years later, the rectangular temple was erected, with towering Corinthian columns made from granite. For centuries the temple was thought to be dedicated to Diana, and although it has since been confirmed that it was only ever dedicated to the emperor himself, the name has endured. The structure of the temple has remained mostly intact, and is one of the most impressive Roman monuments anywhere in the world, but the forum has seen change. While the area was under Moorish rule, part of the governor's palace was built here, and later, in the 15th century, a small palace was built on the site, part of which remains.

the most stunning feature, with a tall, double-level *scenae frons* (backdrop), made from marble and supported by Corinthian columns. The theatre was abandoned for centuries, during which time it filled

> **For centuries the temple was thought to be dedicated to Diana, and although it has since been confirmed that it was only ever dedicated to the emperor himself, the name has endured.**

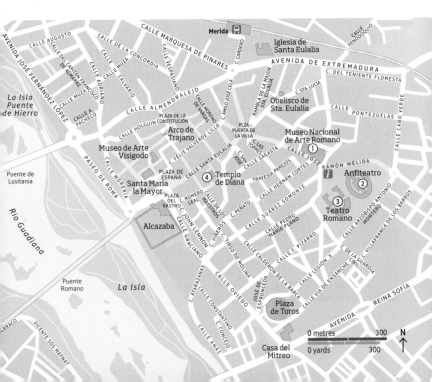

REAL MONASTERIO DE NUESTRA SEÑORA DE GUADALUPE

**🅰C4 🏠Cáceres ⬛ 🕐By guided tour only, 9am–2pm & 3–7pm daily
🆆monasterioguadalupe.com**

With its turreted towers and wooded valley setting, the Royal Monastery of Santa María of Guadalupe has a fairy-tale air. According to legend, this is the site where a 13th-century shepherd found a wooden image of the Virgin Mary.

A chapel was built on the site of the shepherd's discovery and was dedicated to Our Lady of Guadalupe – the river near to where the statue was found. The monastery became a royal sanctuary in the 14th century, when Alfonso XI invoked Santa Maria de Guadalupe before his victory at the Battle of Río Salado (1340). The monastery grew to splendour under royal patronage, acquiring schools of grammar and medicine, three hospitals, an important pharmacy and one of the largest libraries in Spain. But the monastery's most impressive aspect is the magnificent Baroque sacristy, nicknamed "the Spanish Sistine Chapel" because of Zurbarán's portraits of monks hanging on the highly decorated walls. For many, the chance to kiss the tiny Virgin's dress in the *camarín* (chamber) behind the altar is the highlight of the tour.

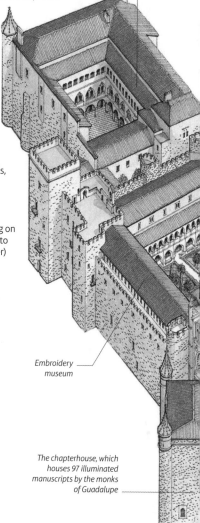

Gothic cloister

Embroidery museum

The chapterhouse, which houses 97 illuminated manuscripts by the monks of Guadalupe

↑ The 16th-century reliquaries chapel, with its spectacular gilded decoration

Timeline

1340
△ Monastery is founded.

1402
Spain's first dissection is performed here.

c 1700
The Gothic cloister is built.

1808
△ Napoleon sacks the monastery.

1993
The monastery is declared a UNESCO World Heritage Site.

→ Stone steps leading to the front entrance of the monastery

Painting and sculpture museum

The Virgin of Guadalupe, kept in the camarín and worshipped by pilgrims from around the world

The sacristy, which contains Zurbarán's painting Father Gonzalo de Illescas at Work *(1639)*

Church

↑ The Real Monasterio de Nuestra Señora de Guadalupe

Did You Know?

The Virgin of Guadalupe's face is black because of smoke from the smouldering lamps.

433

Did You Know?

Storks nest in the Old Town - hence the name given to one house, the Casa de las Ciguenas.

③
CÁCERES

🅰B4 🏛Cáceres 🚉🚌 ℹ Plaza Mayor; www.ayto-caceres.es/turismo

Mansions and palaces line the twisting streets of Cáceres; their towers, topped with characterful gargoyles, reaching skywards. Take a walk through the atmospheric streets of one of the country's best-preserved Renaissance cities to see Spain at its most grand.

After Alfonso IX of León conquered Cáceres in 1229, its growing prosperity as a free-trade town attracted merchants, and later aristocracy, to settle here. The new inhabitants outdid each other with stately homes and palaces fortified by watchtowers, most of which Isabel and Fernando, the reigning monarchs (p64), ordered to be demolished in 1476 to halt their continual jostling for power. Today's serene Renaissance town dates from the late 15th and 16th centuries, after which economic decline set in. Untouched by the wars of the 19th and 20th centuries (largely thanks to the surviving 16th-century defensive walls), Cáceres became Spain's first listed heritage city in 1949.

> **Untouched by the wars of the 19th and 20th centuries (largely thanks to the surviving 16th-century defensive walls), Cáceres became Spain's first listed heritage city in 1949.**

Iglesia de Santa María, a Gothic-Renaissance church with a beautiful cedarwood reredos and a 15th-century crucifix

Casa y Torre de Carvajal, a typical Renaissance mansion with a round Arab tower

Arco de la Estrella, a low-arched gateway that was built by Manuel Churriguera in 1726

↑ The close-packed, winding streets of Cáceres

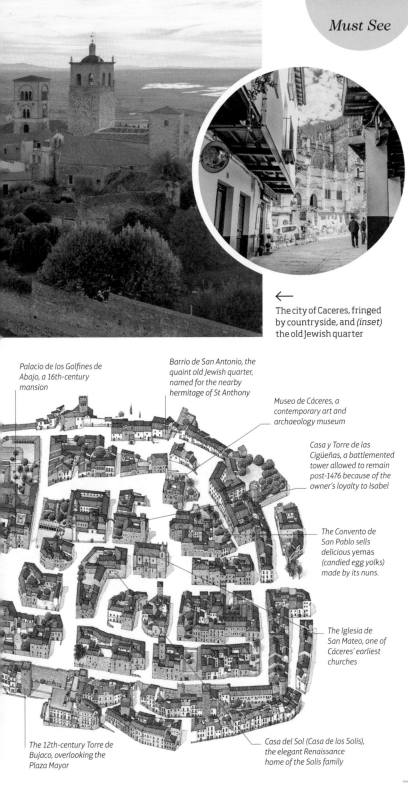

← The city of Caceres, fringed
by countryside, and *(inset)*
the old Jewish quarter

*Palacio de los Golfines de
Abajo, a 16th-century
mansion*

*Barrio de San Antonio, the
quaint old Jewish quarter,
named for the nearby
hermitage of St Anthony*

*Museo de Cáceres, a
contemporary art and
archaeology museum*

*Casa y Torre de las
Cigüeñas, a battlemented
tower allowed to remain
post-1476 because of the
owner's loyalty to Isabel*

*The Convento de
San Pablo sells
delicious yemas
(candied egg yolks)
made by its nuns.*

*The Iglesia de
San Mateo, one of
Cáceres' earliest
churches*

*The 12th-century Torre de
Bujaco, overlooking the
Plaza Mayor*

*Casa del Sol (Casa de los Solís),
the elegant Renaissance
home of the Solís family*

EXPERIENCE MORE

4
Las Hurdes

B4 🏛Cáceres
🚌Pinofranqueado,
Nuñomoral, Caminomorisco
ℹ️Caminomorisco;
www.todohurdes.com

The harship faced by Las
Hurdes' people was captured
in the 1932 Luis Buñuel film
*Tierra sin Pan (Land without
Bread)*. The area's poverty
disappeared with the arrival
of roads in the 1950s, but the
black slopes, riverbeds and
hill terraces remain. As a
result, Las Hurdes is great for
trekking, with a multitude of
mountain viewpoints, including
the Melero Meander. From
Pinofranqueado, roads climb
past picturesque "black" villages like Batuequilla, Fragosa
and El Gasco, which sits under
an extinct volcano. The Lower
Hurdes area and the main
access route (EX204) are
dotted with camp sites.

5
Sierra de Gata

C4 🏛Cáceres 🚌Cáceres
ℹ️San Martín de Trevejo;
www.sierradegata.org

There are 21 hamlets in the
Sierra de Gata, scattered
between olive groves,
orchards and fields. The area
has retained its charm by
conserving hunters' paths
for woodland walking, and
its local crafts, most notably
lace-making. In Valverde del
Fresno, Eljas and San Martín
de Trevejo, the local dialect,
a fala, is still spoken. On the
higher slopes, Gata and
Villamiel have remains of
medieval fortresses. The old
granite houses have family
crests on the front and distinctive outside staircases.

6
Hervás

B4 🏛Cáceres ℹ️Calle
Braulio Navas 6; www.
turismodehervas.com

Sitting at the top of the Valle
del Ambroz, Hervás is known
for its medieval Jewish quarter,
with its whitewashed, half-
timbered houses. The tiny
streets, dotted with taverns
and workshops, slope down
towards the Río Ambroz. Just
off the main plaza is the **Museo
Pérez Comendador-Leroux**,
named after the town's 20th-
century sculptor and his wife,
whose work is exhibited here.

The next town up towards
the Béjar pass is **Baños de
Montemayor**, whose name
comes from its sulphurous
Roman baths.

Museo Pérez Comendador-Leroux

⊗ 🏠 Calle Asensio Neila 5
🕐 Hours vary, check website
🌐 mpcl.net

Baños de Montemayor

⊗ 🏠 Avenida Las Termas 57
🌐 balneariomontemayor.com

❼
Coria

🅰 B4 🏠 Cáceres 🚌
🚌 Plaza de San Pedro 1;
www.turismo.coria.org

Coria's walled Old Town, perched above the Río Alagón, boasts a Gothic-Renaissance cathedral with rich Plateresque carving, and the 16th-century Convento de la Madre de Dios, with a fine Renaissance cloister.

Forming part of the town walls are an imposing castle tower and four gates, two dating back to Roman times.

←
The Melero Meander created by the Alagón River, in Las Hurdes

The gates are closed for the fiesta of San Juan in June for bull-running. Below the Old Town is the Puente Seco, or Puente Viejo, a Roman bridge.

❽
Plasencia

🅰 B4 🏠 Cáceres 🚋🚌
🚌 Santa Clara 4; www.plasencia.es

Plasencia's golden-grey walls, rising above a curve in the banks of the Río Jerte, tell of the town's past as a military bastion. Today Plasencia is best known for its Tuesday market, dating from the 12th century.

A short walk away are the town's two cathedrals, built back-to-back. The 15th- to 16th-century Catedral Nueva has a Baroque organ and carved wooden choir stalls. The Romanesque Catedral Vieja, next to it, has a museum with a late 14th-century Bible.

❾
Badajoz

🅰 B5 🏠 Badajoz ✈🚋🚌
🚌 Pasaje de San Juan Bautista; www.turismo badajoz.es

Badajoz was a major centre under the Moors, but centuries of conflict robbed it of its former glories. Today, it is known for its Carnival.

The Alcazaba houses the **Museo Arqueológico**, which has over 15,000 pieces from around the province, as far back as Palaeolithic times. But the town's stand-out museum is **MEIAC**, exhibiting contemporary Spanish and Latin American art.

Museo Arqueológico

🏠 Plaza José Álvarez Saez de Buruaga 📞 924 00 19 08
🕐 9am–3pm Tue–Sun

MEIAC

🏠 Calle Museo s/n 🕐 10am–2pm & 5:30–8pm Tue–Sat, 10am–2pm Sun 🌐 meiac.es

↑ The stunning altarpiece inside the Catedral Nueva at Plasencia

EAT

Parador de Zafra
Zafra's 15th-century castle is now the place to taste tapas.

🅰 B5 🏠 Plaza Corazon de Maria 7, Zafra
🌐 parador.es

€€€

Corral del Rey
A cosy Trujillo restaurant specializing in roast meats and fish.

🅰 B4 🏠 Plazuela Corral del Rey 2, Trujillo
🌐 corraldelrey trujillo.com

€€€

Atrio
Enjoy Michelin-starred dishes at this sophisticated Cáceres restaurant.

🅰 B4 🏠 Plaza de San Mateo 1, Cáceres
🌐 restauranteatrio.com

€€€

 ←
Cattle grazing beside
the river in the Parque
Nacional de Monfragüe

12
Alcántara

B4 Cáceres
Avenida de Mérida 21;
www.turismoalcantara.es

Alcántara has two important
sights – the drystone Roman
bridge, with its arch and a
temple, and the Convento de
San Benito. This was built as the
headquarters of the Knights of
the Order of Alcántara during
the 16th century and was sacked by Napoleon. Its surviving
treasures are in the Iglesia
de Santa María de Almocovar.

 10
Parque Nacional de
Monfragüe

B4 Cáceres Villarreal
de San Carlos Villarreal
de San Carlos 16; www.
turismoextremadura.com

To the south of Plasencia,
rolling hills drop from scrubby
peaks through wild olive and
cork woods to the dammed

Tagus and Tiétar river valleys.
This is the Parque Nacional de
Monfragüe, which is full of
wildlife. The many species of
bird which breed here include
the black-winged kite, black
vulture and, most notably, the
black stork. Mammals living
here include the lynx, red deer
and wild boar. At Villarreal de
San Carlos, a hamlet founded
in the 18th century, there is
parking and an information
centre. An ideal time to visit
the park is September, when
many migrating birds stop off
here. Monfragüe was granted
UNESCO Biosphere Reserve
status in 2003 and became
a National Park in 2007.

13
Valencia de Alcántara

B4 Cáceres Calle
de Hernán Cortés; www.
valenciadealcantara.es

The Gothic quarter of this
town features fountains and
orange trees. The Castillo de
Piedrabuena, in nearby San
Vicente de Alcántara, was built
by the Knights of the Order
of Alcántara. On the outskirts
are more than 40 dolmens,
or megalithic burial sites.

11
Arroyo de la Luz

B4 Cáceres Plaza
de la Constitución 21;
www.arroyodelaluz.es

The town of Arroyo de la Luz
is home to one of the artistic
masterpieces of Extremadura.
Its Iglesia de la Asunción
contains a spectacular altarpiece, completed in 1565,
which incorporates 20
paintings by the mystical religious painter Luis de Morales.
Nearby, Los Barruecos
Natural Park is home to
Europe's largest white-stork
colony, their nests often built
on top of gigantic granite
stones. There are some good
picnic spots in the surrounding countryside.

14
Monasterio de San
Jerónimo de Yuste

C4 Cuacos de Yuste,
Cáceres Apr-Sep: 10am-
7pm Tue-Sun; Oct-Mar:
10am-4pm Tue-Fri (to 6pm
Sat & Sun) patrimonio
nacional.es

Yuste's Hieronymite monastery,
where Carlos I retired from

→
The atmospheric Plaza
Mayor, Trujillo's main
square, floodlit at night

public life in 1557 and died a year later, is remarkable for its simplicity and its setting in the wooded valley of La Vera. The church's Gothic and Plateresque cloisters and the austere palace are open to visitors.

From here, a single-track road leads to the village of Garganta la Olla, with its half-timbered architecture and the bright-blue Casa de las Muñecas building.

⑮
Trujillo

↑ Bust of Carlos I in the Monasterio de San Jerónimo de Yuste

Ⓐ B4 Ⓐ Cáceres 🚌 ⓘ Plaza Mayor; www.turismo trujillo.com

When the Plaza Mayor of the medieval hilltop town of Trujillo is floodlit at night, it is one of the most beautiful squares in Spain. By day, there is much to visit, including the Iglesia de Santa María la Mayor, on one of the town's winding streets, which contains various sarcophagi.

Trujillo was the birthplace of several conquistadors, most notably Francisco Pizarro, who conquered Peru, of whom there is a statue in the main square. His brother, Hernando Pizarro, founded the Palacio

del Marqués de la Conquista, one of several palaces and convents built with wealth acquired in the Americas. It has an elaborate corner window with carved stone heads of the Pizarro brothers and their Inca wives. The beautiful 16th-century **Palacio Juan Pizarro**

de Orellana was built by descendants of Francisco de Orellana, the navigator of Ecuador and the Amazon.

In late April or early May, gourmets flock here for the four-day cheese fair.

Palacio Juan Pizarro de Orellana

🏠 Plaza de Don Juan Tena (access via the convent) ☎ 927 32 26 77 🕐 10am–1pm & 4–6pm Mon–Fri, 11am–2pm & 4:30–7pm Sat & Sun

---

△ GREAT VIEW
Capture the Castle

Trujillo's 11th-century Islamic fortress sits on a hill about the town. Before you explore the castle, which acted as Casterly Rock in *Game of Thrones*, look out over the Plaza Mayor. You'll see the grand buildings framing the square, as well as Trujillo's verdant surroundings.

HIDDEN GEM
Calera's Cloisters

Calera de León, which is just 6 km (4 miles) north of Tentudía, has a Renaissance convent. Founded by the Order of Santiago, the Convento de Santiago has a Gothic church and a unique cloister on two floors. Take a walk around the atmospheric courtyard – it's always peaceful.

16 ⌖ ⌖
Tentudía

🅐 B5 🏰 Badajoz 🚌 Calera de León 🛈 Plaza de España 12, Calera de León; www. turismoextremadura.com

Fortified towns and churches founded by the medieval military orders stand among the wooded hills of Tentudía. Here, on a hilltop, is the tiny **Monasterio de Tentudía**. Founded in the 13th century by the Order of Santiago, the monastery contains a superb Mudéjar-style cloister, and reredos with *azulejos* (tiles) from Seville.

Monasterio de Tentudía
⌖ 🏰 Carretera Calera de León-Badajoz, km 9 🕐 May-Oct: 11am-6pm Tue-Sun; Nov-Apr: 10am-5pm Tue-Sun

17
Jerez de los Caballeros

🅐 B5 🏰 Badajoz 🚌 🛈 Plaza de San Agustín 1; www. jerezcaballeros.es

The hillside profile of Jerez, broken by three Baroque church towers, is one of Extremadura's prettiest. This small town is also historically important – Vasco Núñez de Balboa, who "discovered" the Pacific, was born here. In the castle, now laid out as gardens, knights of the Order of Knights Templar were beheaded in the Torre Sangrienta (Bloody Tower) in 1312.

The old quarters of the town grew up around three churches: San Bartolomé, its façade studded with glazed ceramics; San Miguel, whose brick tower dominates the Plaza de España; and Santa María de la Encarnación. The latter is the oldest, and is attributed to the Visigoths.

Fregenal de la Sierra, 25 km (16 miles) to the south, is an attractive old town with a bullring inside a 13th-century Templar castle, and the restored 16th-century convent of San Francisco. The Palace of the Condes de Torrepilares *(Calle Iglesia de Santa Ana)* is a superb example of civil architecture.

18
Olivenza

🅐 B5 🏰 Badajoz 🚌 🛈 Plaza San Juan de Dios; 924 49 01 51

A Portuguese enclave until 1801, Olivenza has a lively atmosphere. Within the walled town are the medieval castle, housing the **Museo Etnográfico González Santana**, a museum of rural life, and three churches. Next to the castle, Santa María del Castillo has a family tree of the Virgin Mary. Santa María Magdalena is a fine example of the 16th-century Portuguese Manueline style. The 16th-century Santa Casa de Misericordia has blue and white tiled friezes – in one, God offers Adam and Eve 18th-century coats to cover their nakedness.

Just off the main square, the Casa Fuentes bakery sells *Técula Mécula* cake, an almond-flavoured tart.

Museo Etnográfico González Santana
⌖ 🏰 Plaza de Santa María 🕐 10am-2pm & 5-8pm Tue-Sat, 10am-2pm Sun 🌐 museodeolivenza.com

Cancho Roano

A B5 **A** Carretera Zalamea-Quintana, km 3 (Badajoz)
C 629 23 52 79 **O** Summer: 10am–2pm & 5–8pm Mon-Sat, 10am–2pm Sun; winter: 10am–2pm & 4–6pm Mon-Sat, 10am–2pm Sun
D Some public hols

This sanctuary-palace, which is believed to have been built under the civilization of Tartessus (700 BC), was discovered in the 1960s. Excavations on this small site (begun in 1978) have revealed a moated temple that was rebuilt three times – many of the walls and slate floors are still intact. Each temple was constructed on a grander scale than the previous one and then burned in the face of invasion during the 6th century BC.

Don't expect to see loads of precious historic artifacts here, though. Most of the items unearthed from the site during excavations are on display in the archaeological museum at Badajoz (p437).

Nearby Zalamea de la Serena is a small town made up of whitewashed houses with red tiled roofs. Seek out the Roman funereal monument that stands next to the church.

The town comes alive during the August fiestas, when the townsfolk act out the classic 17th-century play, The Mayor of Zalamea, by Calderón de la Barca, which was supposedly based on a local character. The drama explores the themes of honour and the rights of the military.

While visiting the town, look out for torta de la Serena. This strong, creamy cheese, made of sheep's milk, is sold in Zalamea de la Serena's many quaint shops.

 ←

Santa María de la Encarnación, perched above the town of Jerez de los Caballeros

↑ The arcaded Plaza Grande at Zafra, shaded by palm trees

20 Zafra

A B5 **A** Badajoz **R** **E**
i Plaza de España 8;
www.visitazafra.com

At the heart of this graceful town, nicknamed "little Seville" because of its similarity to the capital of Andalucía, are two arcaded squares. The Plaza Grande, the larger of the two, near the Iglesia de la Candelaria, was built in the 15th century. The older square is Plaza Chica, which used to be the market-place. On Calle Sevilla is the 15th-century Convento de Santa Clara. Nearby is the Alcázar de los Duques de Feria, now a parador, with a patio of Herreriano style.

21 Llerena

A B5 **A** Badajoz **R** **E** **i** Calle Aurora 3; www.llerena.org

Extremadura's southeastern gateway to Andalucía, the town of Llerena is an attractive mixture of Mudéjar and Baroque buildings. In the pretty square, which is lined with palm trees, stands the arcaded, whitewash-and-stone church of Nuestra Señora de la Granada. Its sumptuous interior reflects the town's former importance as a seat of the Inquisition (p304). At one end of the square is a fountain designed by Zurbarán, who lived here for 15 years. Also worth seeing is the 16th-century Convento de Santa Clara, on a street leading out of the main square.

At Azuaga, 30 km (20 miles) to the east, is the Iglesia de la Consolación. This 16th-century building has some remarkable Renaissance and Mudéjar tiles.

DRINK

Queseria Bar La Bendita
True to its name, this tapas bar specializes in queso (cheese). Set in one of Zafra's many atmospheric square, it's the perfect place for an evening tipple and nibble before seeing where the night will take you.

Q B5 **A** Plaza Chica 14a, Zafra **W** labendita. negocio.site

SOUTHERN SPAIN

One of Seville's ubiquitous orange trees against a peach-hued wall

EXPLORE
SOUTHERN SPAIN

This section divides Southern Spain into two colour-coded sightseeing areas, as shown on this map. Find out more about each area on the following pages.

Villafranca de los Barros

Jerez de los Caballeros

Zafra

EXTREMADURA

Pozoblanco

Azuaga

PORTUGAL

Sierra Morena

Espiel

Sierra de Aracena

Jabugo

Córdoba

El Ronquillo

Palma del Río

Fernán Núñez

Tharsis

Lora del Río

Valverde del Camino

Itálica

Carmona

Écija

Aguilar

Seville

Herrera

Huelva

Moguer

SEVILLE
p448

Marchena

El Arahal

Estepa

El Rocío

Los Palacios y Villafranca

Morón de la Frontera

Osuna

Anteque

Torre de la Higuera

Olvera

Golfo de Cádiz

Chipiona

Villamartín

Ronda

Coín

Costa de la Luz

Puerto Real

Cádiz

Medina Sidonia

Alhaurín el Grande

San Fernando

Estepona

Vejer de la Frontera

San Roque

Atlantic Ocean

Algeciras

Gibraltar (UK)

Tarifa

Estrecho de Gibraltar

| 0 kilometres | 50 |
| 0 miles | 50 |

N
↑

MOROCCO

CASTILLA-LA MANCHA

Mota del Cuervo

Alcázar de
San Juan

Villarrobledo

La Roda

Daimiel

Tomelloso

Albacete

Ciudad Real

Manzanares

Valdepeñas

Puertollano

Hellín

*Serranía de
Cuenca*

*Sierra
Morena*

Beas de
Segura

La Carolina

Bailén

Linares

Villacarrillo

Andújar

Úbeda

VALENCIA AND
MURCIA

ANDALUCÍA
p472

Baeza

Quesada

Torredonjimeno

Huéscar

Lorca

Pozo Alcón

Baena

Alcaudete

Cúllar

Cabra

Baza

Albox

Águilas

Diezma

Guadix

Los Lobos

Pinos-
Puente

Archidona

Granada

Mojácar

Sierra Nevada

Tabernas

Carboneras

Lanjarón

Berja

Málaga

Nerja

Motril

Almería

San José

Torremolinos

Adra

El Ejido

Costa del Sol

SPAIN

*Mediterranean
Sea*

GETTING TO KNOW
SOUTHERN SPAIN

The autonomous region of Andalucía dominates Southern Spain, with its dramatic landscape of deserts, wetlands, mountains and, of course, the beaches of the Costa del Sol. Three inland cities between them share the greatest of Spain's Moorish monuments: Granada, Córdoba and Seville.

SEVILLE

PAGE 448

One of the world's most romantic cities, Seville is a bewitching labyrinth of perfumed streets, geranium-filled courtyards and plazas lined with rows of orange trees. Barrio Santa Cruz echoes with the sound of carriages ferrying visitors across the cobbled streets, while Triana, across the Guadalquivir river, is Seville at its most authentic. Here, you'll find *Sevillano* artisans crafting ceramics, guitars and extravagant polka-dot gowns, just as their families have for generations. After dark, music drifts from packed flamenco *tablaos* and people spill from clamorous bars.

Best for
Flamboyant flamenco and Moorish marvels

Home to
Seville Cathedral and La Giralda, Real Alcázar, Parque María Luisa

Experience
Duende at a soulful flamenco show in Triana

PAGE 472

ANDALUCÍA

It's hard not to be swept up in the passion that embodies Spain's most populous *comunidad autónoma*. Crimson-clad *bailaoras* twirl their skirts as fiery musicians sing about their homeland and heartbreak in the dingy caves where flamenco originated. Lively fiestas are held all year round, with people drinking sherry on balconies while watching colourful floats parade through the streets below. Even the buildings seem to embody this feeling: in the Alhambra's honeycomb-like details, and the Mezquita's hallowed arches, but also in the quiet beauty of Andalucía's *pueblos blancos* (white towns).

Best for
Graceful architecture and whitewashed houses

Home to
Parque Nacional de Doñana, Cádiz, Ronda, Córdoba, Úbeda, Baeza, Granada

Experience
A night-time visit to the Generalife, when the gardens are illuminated by the moon

SEVILLE

Seville was one of the first Spanish cities to fall to the Moors. It became part of the Caliphate of Córdoba in AD 712 after the Moorish Abbadid dynasty had defeated Roderic, the Visigothic king known as "the last king of the Goths", at the Battle of Guadalete. As part of this affluent Islamic *taifa* (state), the city became a centre of chivalric pursuits, such as poetry, with its last Abbadid ruler, al-Mu'tamid, becoming known as the "poet king". But this decadence attracted the contempt of the Almoravids, a group of conservative Berber Muslims, who took control of the caliphate in 1091. The Almoravids attempted to rule from afar, leaving themselves vulnerable to attack, and they were supplanted by a different Berber incursion – the Almohads in 1147. The Almohads made Seville their capital and undertook a programme of public building works, including the construction of La Giralda, a towering minaret attached to the mosque. In 1248, when the city was conquered by the Christian king Ferdinand III of Castile, the mosque became a cathedral.

Under Christian rule, Seville became a trading outpost and grew affluent from trade with England, Flanders and Genoa. In 1503, the city was granted exclusive rights as the port of entry and exit for all goods amassed from the Americas. The city was hit hard by the economic crisis that plagued Europe in the 17th century and Seville languished for many of the following years, with Napoleon's forces taking control in 1810. After the French were forced to retreat by Anglo-Spanish counterattacks in 1812, Seville was regenerated. The city's cultural importance was showcased in the Ibero-American Exposition of 1929 and again, almost a century later, in the Expo '92.

SEVILLE

Must Sees

① Seville Cathedral and La Giralda
② Real Alcázar
③ Parque María Luisa

Experience More

④ Museo de Bellas Artes
⑤ Iglesia de la Magdalena
⑥ Plaza de Toros de la Maestranza
⑦ Hospital de la Caridad
⑧ Torre del Oro
⑨ Calle de las Sierpes
⑩ Ayuntamiento
⑪ Hospital de los Venerables
⑫ Archivo de Indias
⑬ Palacio de Lebrija
⑭ Casa de Pilatos
⑮ Metropol Parasol
⑯ Basílica de la Macarena
⑰ Iglesia de San Pedro
⑱ Palacio de las Dueñas
⑲ Convento de Santa Paula
⑳ Palacio de San Telmo
㉑ Universidad
㉒ Triana
㉓ Isla de la Cartuja
㉔ Torre Sevilla
㉕ Torre de los Perdigones

Eat

① Casa Robles
② Casa Plácido

Stay

③ Las Casas del Rey de Baeza
④ Patio de la Alameda

Shop

⑤ Botellas y Latas
⑥ Rompemoldes

SEVILLE CATHEDRAL AND LA GIRALDA

📍E4 🚇Avenida de la Constitución Ⓜ Puerta Jerez 🚌Archivo de Indias 🚍C1, C2, C3, C4, 5, 41, 42 🕐10:45am–5pm Mon–Sat, 2:30–6pm Sun 🚫Religious hols, including 1 & 6 Jan, 25 Dec 🌐catedraldesevilla.es

Seville's cathedral is an arresting sight not only for its size (it's the world's largest Gothic cathedral) but also for its mighty Moorish bell tower – La Giralda. A visit here is a great introduction to Seville's Muslim and Christian heritage.

Officially named Santa María de la Séde, Seville's cathedral occupies the site of a great mosque built by the Almohads in the late 12th century, which had been based on the Koutoubia Mosque of Marrakesh. Eclipsed by the Christian construction, La Giralda and the Patio de los Naranjos are the only lasting legacy of the original Moorish structure. Work on the Gothic cathedral, the largest in Europe, began in 1401 and took just over a century to complete. As well as enjoying the cathedral's Gothic immensity and the works of art in its chapels and sacristy, visitors flock here to ascend the ramped La Giralda for stunning city views.

Did You Know?

The bronze weathervane *(giraldillo)* crowning the tower gave La Giralda its name.

THE RISE OF LA GIRALDA

The tower was built as a minaret for the mosque in 1198. But, in the 14th century, after Ferdinand III had successfully taken the city from the Moors in 1248, the bronze spheres at its top were replaced by Christian symbols. A new belfry was planned in 1557, but built to a more ornate design by Hernán Ruiz in 1568.

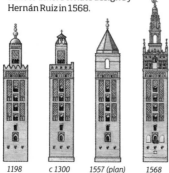

| 1198 | c 1300 | 1557 (plan) | 1568 |

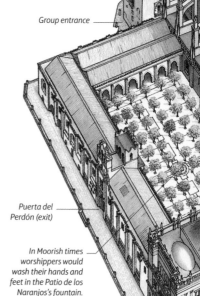

La Giralda

Group entrance

Puerta del Perdón (exit)

In Moorish times worshippers would wash their hands and feet in the Patio de los Naranjos's fountain.

Roman pillars from Itálica (p508) surround the steps.

↑ The tree- and café-lined Calle Mateos Gago, leading to La Giralda

Santa María de la Sede, the cathedral's patron saint, sits at the high altar below a waterfall of gold.

The Sacristía Mayor houses many works of art, including paintings by Murillo.

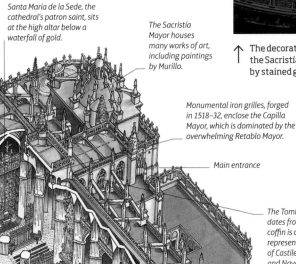

↑ The decorated dome of the Sacristía Mayor, lit by stained glass

Monumental iron grilles, forged in 1518–32, enclose the Capilla Mayor, which is dominated by the overwhelming Retablo Mayor.

Main entrance

The Tomb of Columbus dates from the 1890s. His coffin is carried by bearers representing the kingdoms of Castile, León, Aragón and Navarra.

← Seville Cathedral and La Giralda

Puerta de la Asunción is Gothic in style, though the portal was not completed until 1833.

Puerta del Bautismo

Iglesia del Sagrario, a large 17th-century chapel

> 💬 **INSIDER TIP**
> **Step Out of Line**
>
> As one of Seville's biggest sights, the cathedral attracts hordes of visitors. To skip the queue at the ticket office, buy a combined ticket at the church of El Salvador, in the nearby plaza of the same name.

2 ⊗

REAL ALCÁZAR

9 E4 **🏠** Patio de Banderas **Ⓜ** Puerta Jerez **🚊** Archivo de Indias **🚌** C5 **🕐** 9:30am–7pm daily (to 5pm mid-Sep–Mar); for night visits with theatre, check website (book in advance) **📅** 1 & 6 Jan, Good Fri, 25 Dec **🌐** alcazarsevilla.org

Home to Spanish kings for almost seven centuries, the Real Alcázar is one of the most beautiful buildings in the world. Set in a huge paradise garden, it is a celebration of Mudéjar architecture.

In 1364 Pedro I ordered the construction of a royal residence within the palaces which had been built by the city's Almohad rulers in the 12th century. Craftsmen from Granada and Toledo created a jewel box of Mudéjar patios and halls, the Palacio de Pedro I, now at the heart of Seville's Real Alcázar. Later monarchs added their own distinguishing marks: Isabel I dispatched navigators to the Americas from her Casa de la Contratación, while Carlos I had grandiose apartments built. More recently, in 2014, the Alcázar was used as a location for the hit TV series *Game of Thrones*.

The Salón de Embajadores' dome is made of carved and gilded wood.

Azulejos and complex plasterwork decorate the Salón de Embajadores.

Jardín de Troya

The Patio de las Doncellas (Patio of the Maidens) boasts plasterwork by the top craftsmen of Granada.

The gardens are laid out with terraces, fountains and pavilions.

Tapestries and 16th-century azulejos decorate the vaulted halls of the apartments and chapel of Carlos I.

AZULEJOS

Colourful ceramic tiles are a striking feature of Seville. The craft was introduced to Spain by the Moors, who created fantastic mosaics in sophisticated geometric patterns for palace walls – *azulejo* derives from the Arabic for "little stone". New techniques were introduced in the 16th century and the tiles became mass produced.

Patio del Crucero lies above the old baths

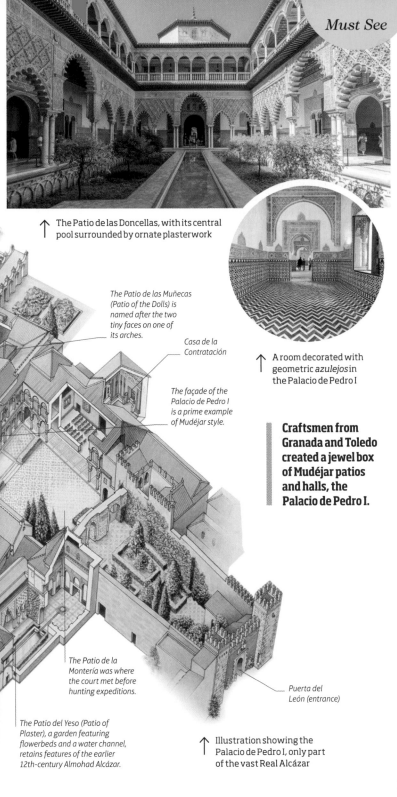

↑ The Patio de las Doncellas, with its central pool surrounded by ornate plasterwork

The Patio de las Muñecas (Patio of the Dolls) is named after the two tiny faces on one of its arches.

Casa de la Contratación

↑ A room decorated with geometric *azulejos* in the Palacio de Pedro I

The façade of the Palacio de Pedro I is a prime example of Mudéjar style.

Craftsmen from Granada and Toledo created a jewel box of Mudéjar patios and halls, the Palacio de Pedro I.

The Patio de la Montería was where the court met before hunting expeditions.

Puerta del León (entrance)

The Patio del Yeso (Patio of Plaster), a garden featuring flowerbeds and a water channel, retains features of the earlier 12th-century Almohad Alcázar.

↑ Illustration showing the Palacio de Pedro I, only part of the vast Real Alcázar

PARQUE MARÍA LUISA

⦿E5 🅰Paseo de las Delicias s/n Ⓜ🚊Prado de San Sebastián ⏱Museo de Artes y Costumbres Populares: Jul-Aug: 9am-3pm Tue-Sun; Sep-Jun: 9am-9pm Tue- Sat, 9am-3pm Sun; Museo Arqueológico: closed for renovations until 2025 📅1 & 6 Jan, 1 May, 24, 25 & 31 Dec 🌐museosdeandalucia.es

Sprinkling fountains, blooming flowers and cool, tree-shaded avenues all help to make Parque María Luisa a refreshing retreat from the heat and dust of the city. Take a stroll through Seville's green lung.

Princess Maria Luisa donated part of the grounds of the Palacio de San Telmo to the city for this park in 1893. Landscaped by Jean Forestier, director of the Bois de Boulogne in Paris, the park was the leafy setting for the 1929 Ibero-American Exposition. The legacies of this extravaganza are the Plaza de España, decorated with regional scenes on ceramic tiles, and the Plaza de América, both the work of Aníbal González. On the latter, in the Pabellón Mudéjar, the Museo de Artes y Costumbres Populares displays traditional Andalucían folk arts. The Neo-Renaissance Pabellón de las Bellas Artes houses the Museo Arqueológico, exhibiting artifacts from Itálica (p508).

📷 PICTURE PERFECT
Plaza-rama

The horseshoe-shaped Plaza de España, curling around an ornamental water feature, is tiled with ceramics representing every region of Spain. To perfectly sum up your trip, pose in front of the *azulejos* that reflect the provinces that you've visited. It's the perfect photographic souvenir.

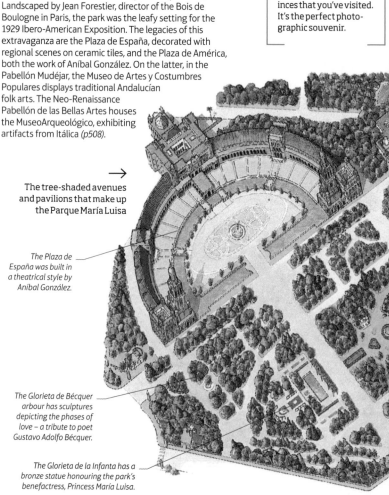

→
The tree-shaded avenues and pavilions that make up the Parque María Luisa

The Plaza de España was built in a theatrical style by Aníbal González.

The Glorieta de Bécquer arbour has sculptures depicting the phases of love – a tribute to poet Gustavo Adolfo Bécquer.

The Glorieta de la Infanta has a bronze statue honouring the park's benefactress, Princess María Luisa.

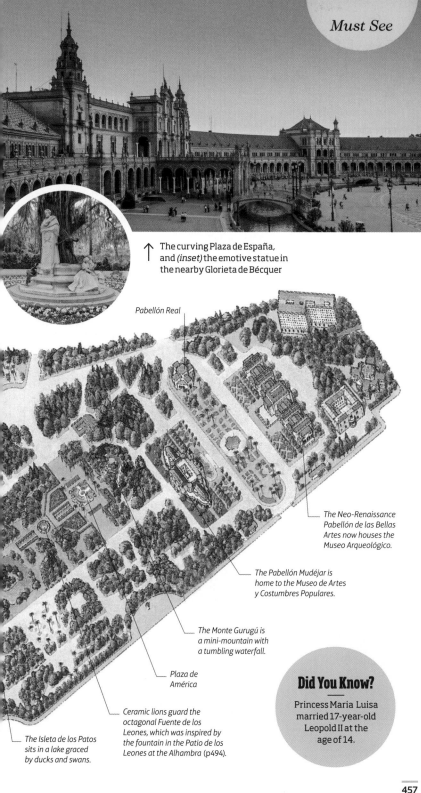

↑ The curving Plaza de España, and *(inset)* the emotive statue in the nearby Glorieta de Bécquer

Pabellón Real

The Neo-Renaissance Pabellón de las Bellas Artes now houses the Museo Arqueológico.

The Pabellón Mudéjar is home to the Museo de Artes y Costumbres Populares.

The Monte Gurugú is a mini-mountain with a tumbling waterfall.

Plaza de América

Ceramic lions guard the octagonal Fuente de los Leones, which was inspired by the fountain in the Patio de los Leones at the Alhambra (p494).

The Isleta de los Patos sits in a lake graced by ducks and swans.

Did You Know?

Princess Maria Luisa married 17-year-old Leopold II at the age of 14.

EXPERIENCE MORE

4

Museo de Bellas Artes

📍D3 🏛Plaza del Museo 9
🚌C3, C4, C5, 6, 13, 14, 43
🕐Hours vary, check
website 🚫1 & 6 Jan,
1 May, 24, 25 & 31 Dec
🌐museosdeandalucia.es

The Convento de la Merced
Calzada houses one of the
best fine art museums in
Spain. Completed in 1612 by
Juan de Oviedo, the building is
designed around three patios.
The Patio Mayor is the largest
of these, remodelled by the
architect Leonardo de Figueroa
in 1724. The convent church
is noteworthy for its Baroque
domed ceiling, painted by
Domingo Martínez.

The museum's collection
of Spanish art and sculpture,
which spans from the medieval
to the modern, focuses on the
work of the Seville School.
Among the star attractions is
Murillo's *Virgen de la Servilleta*
(1665–8), which is said to be
painted on a napkin *(servilleta)*.
It now hangs in the restored
convent church.

The boisterous *La Inmaculada*
(1672) by Juan de Valdés
Leal is in a gallery devoted
to the artist's forceful religious
paintings. Several fine works
by Zurbarán include *San Hugo
en el Refectorio* (1655), which
was painted for the monastery at La Cartuja *(p492)*.

5

Iglesia de la Magdalena

📍D3 🏛Calle San Pablo 10
🚇Plaza Nueva 🚌3, 21, 40,
41, 43, C5 📞95 422 96 03
🕐For services daily

Completed in 1709, this
immense Baroque church
by Leonardo de Figueroa
is gradually being restored
to its former glory. In its
southwest corner stands
the Capilla de la Quinta
Angustia, a Mudéjar

chapel with three cupolas.
This chapel survived from
an earlier church where the
great Seville School painter
Bartolomé Murillo, the creator
of *La Servilleta*, was baptized
in 1618. The font that was used
for his baptism is now in the
baptistry of the present building. The church's west front
is topped by a belfry, which is
painted in vivid colours.

Among the religious works
in the church are a painting
by Francisco de Zurbarán,
St Dominic in Soria, housed in
the Capilla Sacramental (to
the right of the south door),
and frescoes by Lucas Valdés
over the sanctuary. On the
wall of the north transept
there is a cautionary fresco of
a medieval *auto-da-fé (p304)*.

→
The Museo de
Bellas Artes and
(inset) the exterior

6

Plaza de Toros de la Maestranza

⊙ D4 ⌂ Paseo de Cristóbal Colón 12 Ⓜ Puerta Jerez 🚂 Archivo de Indias 🚌 3, 21, 40, 41, C5 🕐 10am–4pm Wed–Sun ⊘ 25 Dec, from 3pm bullfight days 🌐 realmaestranza.com

Seville's famous bullring was built between 1761 and 1881 and holds up to 14,000 spectators. Whatever your opinion is of bullfighting, this immense building is interesting. Guided tours start from the entrance on Paseo de Cristóbal Colón. On the west side is the Puerta del Príncipe (Prince's Gate), through which the triumphant matadors are carried aloft by admirers from the crowd.

Just beyond the *enfermería* (emergency hospital) is a museum of portraits, posters and costumes, including a purple cape painted by Pablo Picasso. The tour continues on to the chapel where matadors pray for success, and then to the stables where the horses of the *picadores* (lance-carrying horsemen) are kept.

7

Hospital de la Caridad

⊙ D4 ⌂ Calle Temprado 3 📞 95 422 32 32 Ⓜ🚂 Puerta Jerez 🚌 3, 21, 40, 41, C4, C5 🕐 10am–7:30pm Mon–Sat, 10am–12:30pm & 2–7:30pm Sun

This charity hospital was founded in 1674 and it is still used today as a sanctuary for elderly and infirm people. In the gardens stands a statue of its benefactor, Miguel de Mañara, whose dissolute life before he joined a brotherhood is said to have inspired the story of Don Juan.

The hospital centres around two square patios decorated with plants, 18th-century Dutch tiles, and fountains with Italian statues of Charity and

Mercy. At their northern end, a passage to the right leads to another patio, containing a 13th-century arch which survives from the city's shipyards.

The façade of the hospital church, with its whitewashed walls, reddish stonework and framed *azulejos*, provides a glorious example of Sevillian Baroque. Inside the church there are a number of original canvases. Directly above the entrance is the ghoulish *Finis Gloriae Mundi* (The End of the World's Glory) by Juan de Valdés Leal, and opposite hangs his morbid *In Ictu Oculi* (In the Blink of an Eye).

8

Torre del Oro

⊙ D4 ⌂ Paseo de Cristóbal Colón 📞 95 422 24 19 Ⓜ🚂 Puerta Jerez 🚌 3, 6, 21, 40, 41, C3, C4 🕐 9:30am–6:45pm Mon–Fri, 10:30am–6:45pm Sat & Sun ⊘ Public hols

In Moorish Seville, the Tower of Gold formed part of the walled defences, linking up with the Real Alcázar *(p454)*. It was built in 1220, with a companion tower on the opposite bank. A metal chain stretched between them to prevent hostile ships from sailing upriver. The gold in its name may be the gilded

↑ Torre del Oro at dusk, standing beside the River Guadalquivir

azulejos that once clad its walls, or treasures from the Americas unloaded here, or the gold reflection it casts on the water. The tower has had many uses, such as a chapel and a prison, but it is now the Museo Marítimo.

EAT

Casa Robles
Enjoy the cathedral views from the terrace of this prize-winning gastronomic spot.

⊙ E4 ⌂ Calle Álvarez Quintero 58 🌐 casa robles.es

€€€

Casa Plácido
This tapas bar is bedecked with traditional tiles, posters and hanging hams.

⊙ E4 ⌂ Calle del Mesón del Moro 11 🌐 casa placido.es

€€€

↑ Window-shopping on Calle de las Sierpes, the main shopping street

⑨ Calle de las Sierpes

◉ E3 🚌 10, 11, 12, 13, 14, 15, 20, 21, 23, 24, 25, 26, 27, 30, 31, 32, 33, 34, 35, 40, 41, 42, 43 🚇 Plaza Nueva

The city's main shopping promenade, the "Street of the Snakes", runs north from Plaza de San Francisco. Long-established stores selling hats, fans and traditional *mantillas* (lace headdresses) stand alongside clothes and souvenir shops. The parallel streets of Cuna and Tetuán also offer some enjoyable window-shopping.

At the southern end of Calle de las Sierpes, on the wall of the Banco Central Hispano, a plaque marks the site of the Cárcel Real (Royal Prison), where the famous Spanish writer Miguel de Cervantes (1547–1616) was incarcerated. Halfway up the road walking north, Calle Jovellanos to the left leads to the 17th-century Capillita de San José.

Continuing north from here, at the junction with Calle Pedro Caravaca, you can take a look back into the anachronistic, upholstered world of the Real Círculo de Labradores, a private men's club founded in 1856.

Right at the end of the street is La Campana, Seville's best-known *pastelería* (cake shop).

---

⑩ Ayuntamiento

◉ E3 🏠 Plaza Nueva 1 📞 95 501 00 10 🚇 Plaza Nueva ⏰ By guided tour only: 7pm & 8pm Mon–Thu, 10am Sat 🌐 sevilla.org

Seville's City Hall stands between the Plaza de San Francisco, where *autos-da-fé* (public trials of heretics) were held, and the Plaza Nueva.

Building was completed between 1527 and 1534. The side bordering the Plaza de San Francisco is a fine example of ornate Plateresque style favoured by the architect Diego de Riaño. The west front is Neo-Classical, built in 1891. Sculpted ceilings survive in the vestibule and the lower Casa Consistorial (Council Meeting Room), containing Velázquez's *Imposition of the Chasuble on St Ildefonso*. The upper Casa Consistorial has a dazzling coffered ceiling and paintings by Zurbarán and Valdés Leal.

> 💬 INSIDER TIP
> **Go Flamenco**
>
> Take a class at the Museo del Baile Flamenco (*www.museodelbaile flamenco.com*). The museum occupies a restored 18th-century house on a small street between the Plaza del Alfalfa and the cathedral and intends to give visitors an introduction to the art form. As well as the flamenco school, you can check out the exhibits and watch live performances.

> Long-established stores selling hats, fans and traditional *mantillas* (lace headdresses) stand alongside clothes and souvenir shops.

FLAMENCO, THE SOUL OF ANDALUCÍA

More than just a dance, flamenco is a rousing artistic expression of the joys and sorrows of life. There is no strict choreography – dancers improvise from basic movements. Although there are interpretations all over Spain, it is a uniquely Andalucían art form. Head to one of Seville's *tablaos* to experience it.

A fan is a typical prop

The proud yet graceful posture of the bailaora is suggestive of a restrained passion.

Traditional dress

THE BAILAORA AND THE BAILAOR

The *bailaora* (female dancer) is renowned for amazing footwork as well as intensive dance moments. Eva Yerbabuena and Sara Baras are both famous for their personal styles. Both lead their own acclaimed flamenco companies. Another flamenco star is Juana Amaya. The *bailaor* (male dancer) plays a less important role than the *bailaora*. However, many have achieved fame, including Antonio Canales. He has introduced a new beat through his original foot movements.

THE MUSIC AND RHYTHM

Although the dancer often steals the show, it is through the music that they feel the *duende* ("magic spirit"). The guitar has a major role in flamenco, traditionally accompanying the singer. Flamenco guitars have a lighter, shallower construction than the modern classical guitar and a thickened plate below the sound hole, used to tap rhythms. Although the unmistakable rhythm of flamenco is created by the guitar, the beat created by hand-clapping and by the dancer's feet in heeled shoes is just as important. The *bailaoras* may also beat a rhythm with castanets. Graceful hand movements, accompanying the castanets, are used to express the dancer's feelings of the moment – whether pain, sorrow or happiness.

↑ A *bailaora*, wearing a traditional red dress and holding a fan

↑ A troupe of dancers and musicians performing flamenco in the early 20th century

---

TOP 3 SEVILLE TABLAOS

La Carbonería
Catch a performance in this covered courtyard *(Calle de los Céspedes 21; 95 422 99 45)*.

Casa de la Memoria
A small theatre set in a gorgeous patio, with performances most nights *(www.casa delamemoria.es)*.

Los Gallos
A little more formal, but authentic nonetheless *(www.tablao losgallos.com)*.

Hospital de los Venerables

Q E4 **A** Plaza de los Venerables 8 **C** 697 898 659 **Archivo de Indias** **O** 10am–2pm Tue, Wed & Thu, 10am–7pm Fri, 10am–2pm & 4–7pm Sat, 10am–2pm Sun **O** 1 Jan, Good Friday, 25 Dec

Construction of this home for elderly priests began in 1675 and was completed around 20 years later by Leonardo de Figueroa. It has now been restored as a cultural centre by FOCUS (Fundación Fondo de Cultura de Sevilla).

Stairs from the central, sunken patio lead to the upper floors, which, along with the infirmary and cellar, are used as exhibition galleries.

The Hospital church, which is a showcase of Baroque splendours, has frescoes by both Juan de Valdés Leal and his son Lucas Valdés. Other highlights of the church include sculptures of St Peter and St Ferdinand by Pedro Roldán, flanking the east door; and *The Apotheosis of St Ferdinand* by Lucas Valdés, top centre in the reredos of the main altar. Its frieze (inscribed in Greek) advises to "Fear God and Honour the Priest".

The sacristy's ceiling has an effective trompe l'oeil depicting *The Triumph of the Cross* by Juan de Valdés Leal.

---

12 Archivo de Indias

Q E4 **A** Avda de la Constitución **C** 95 450 05 28 **M** Puerta Jerez **C5** **Archivo de Indias** **O** 9:30am–5pm Tue–Sat, 10am–2pm Sun **O** Public hols

The Archive of the Indies illustrates Seville's role in the colonization and exploitation of the Americas. Built between 1584 and 1598 to designs by Juan de Herrera, co-architect of El Escorial (*p358*), it was originally a *lonja* (exchange), where merchants traded. In 1785, Carlos III had all Spanish documents relating to the "Indies" collected under one roof. Among the archive's 86 million handwritten pages are letters from Columbus, Cortés and Cervantes.

Upstairs, the library rooms contain displays of drawings, maps and facsimile documents.

HIDDEN GEM
Uncovered City

In Calle Santo Tomás, off the southeastern corner of the Plaza del Triunfo, is a building used by the Archivo de Indias. Dating from 1770, it was once a barn where tithes collected by the Church were stored. Parts of the Moorish city walls were found during the renovation of the building.

Palacio de Lebrija

Q E3 **A** Calle Cuna 8 **27, 32** **O** 10am–7pm Fri & Sat, 10am–3pm Sun **W** palacio delebrija.com

The home of the family of the Countess Lebrija since 1901, this mansion illustrates palatial life in Seville. The ground floor houses Roman and medieval exhibits, while the first floor (visited by guided tour) features a library and halls lined with Moorish-inspired *azulejos*. The house itself dates from the

15th century and has some Mudéjar features, including the arches around the main patio. Many of its Roman treasures were taken from the ruins at Itálica *(p508)*, including the mosaic floor in the main patio. The geometric ceiling above the staircase came from the palace of the Dukes of Arcos in Marchena, near Seville.

Ancient roman glassware, coins and later examples of marble from Medina Azahara *(p510)* are displayed in rooms off the main patio.

Casa de Pilatos

F3 **Plaza de Pilatos**
C3, C4, C5, 21, 24, 27
Apr-Oct: 9am-7pm daily; Nov-Mar: 9am-6pm daily
fundacionmedinaceli.org

Enraptured by the architectural and decorative wonders of High Renaissance Italy and the Holy Land, the first Marquis of Tarifa built the Casa de Pilatos. So called because it was thought to resemble Pontius Pilate's home in Jerusalem, today it is the residence of the Dukes of Medinaceli and is one of the finest palaces in Seville.

Visitors enter through a marble portal, commissioned by the Marquis in 1529 from Genoese craftsmen. Across the arcaded Apeadero (carriage yard) is the Patio Principal. This courtyard is essentially Mudéjar in style and decorated with *azulejos* and intricate plaster-work. In its corners are Roman statues, depicting Minerva, a dancing muse and Ceres, and a Greek statue of Athena, dating from the 5th century.

In its centre is a fountain that was imported from Genoa. To the right, through the Salón del Pretorio with

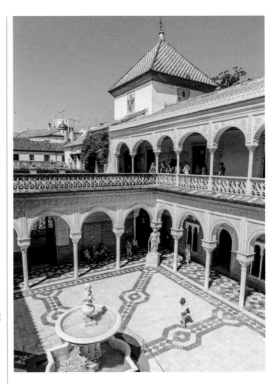

← The ornately decorated church of the Hospital de los Venerables

its coffered ceiling and marquetry, is the Corredor de Zaquizamí. The antiquities on display in adjacent rooms include a bas-relief of *Leda and the Swan* and two Roman reliefs commemorating the Battle of Actium of 31 BC.

Coming back to the Patio Principal, you turn right into the Salón de Descanso de los Jueces. Beyond is a rib-vaulted Gothic chapel, with Mudéjar plasterwork walls and ceiling. On the altar is a copy of a 4th-century sculpture in the Vatican, *The Good Shepherd*. Left, through the Gabinete de Pilatos, with its small central fountain, is the Jardín Grande.

Returning once more to the main patio, behind the statue of Ceres, a tiled stair-case leads to the upper floor. It is roofed with a wonderful *media naranja* (half-orange) cupola built in 1537. There are Mudéjar ceilings in some rooms, which are full of family portraits and antiques.

↑ Genoese fountain in the Patio Principal of Casa de Pilatos

→ The undulating form of the Metropol Parasol, shading the cafés and shops below

Metropol Parasol

☷E3 ☖Plaza de la Encarnación 🚌C5, 10, 11, 12, 15, 16, 20, 24, 27, 32 **☉Observation deck & walkways:** 9:30am-10:30pm daily; Museum: 10am-8pm Tue-Sat (to 2pm Sun & public hols) **☷setasdesevilla.com**

Known locally as *"Las Setas"* ("The Mushrooms"), this ultramodern structure with a latticed canopy was built from

2005 to 2011, and includes a museum, market, bars and restaurants. The main draw is the observation deck.

Basílica de la Macarena

☷E1 ☖Calle Bécquer 1 📞95 490 18 00 🚌C1-5, 2, 10, 13, 14 **☉**9am-2pm, 6-9pm daily (from 9:30am Sun) **☖**Easter Fri

Built in 1949 by Gómez Millán, the Basílica de la Macarena is Neo-Baroque in style and was intended as a new home for the much-loved Virgen de la Esperanza Macarena. It backs onto the 13th-century Iglesia de San Gil, where the image was housed until a fire in 1936.

The image of the Virgin, standing above the main altar amid waterfalls of gold and silver, has been attributed to Luisa Roldán (1656–1703), the most

talented female artist of the Seville School.The Virgin's magnificent processional gowns and jewels are in the Treasury museum.

Iglesia de San Pedro

☷E3 ☖Plaza San Pedro 📞95 421 68 58 🚌10, 11, 12, 15, 16, 20, 24, 27, 32, C5 **☉**9am-noon & 7-8:30pm Mon-Sat, 9am-1:30pm & 7-8:30pm Sun

This church features a mix of architectural styles; Mudéjar elements survive in the lobed brickwork of its tower, which is surmounted by a Baroque belfry. The vault of one of its chapels is decorated with exquisite geometric patterns of bricks.

Behind the Iglesia de San Pedro, at Calle Doña María Coronel 5, cakes are sold from a revolving drum in the wall of the 14th-century Convento de Santa Inés.

> **GREAT VIEW**
> **Fun Guy**
>
> Although striking from the ground, the Metropol Parasol offers the best view from its observation deck. Take the lift to the top and look out over the modern, wavy roof onto the historic city, counting the bell towers below.

Behind the Iglesia de San Pedro, at Calle Doña María Coronel 5, cakes are sold from a revolving drum in the wall of the 14th-century Convento de Santa Inés.

 18

Palacio de las Dueñas

📍E2 🏛Calle Dueñas 5 🚌C5, 10, 11, 12, 15, 16, 20, 24, 27, 32 🕐10am–3pm Mon–Thu, 10am–6pm Fri–Sun & public hols 🚫1 & 6 Jan, 25 Dec 🌐lasduenas.es

Built in Renaissance style with Mudéjar and Gothic influences, this 15th-century palace is the official Seville residence of the Dukes of Alba. Its courtyards offer a peaceful oasis from the bustle of the streets. The house's grand rooms are filled with period furniture, but family photos and personal

letters are also scattered about, plus a room is dedicated to the history of the Feria de Abril.

 19

Convento de Santa Paula

📍F2 🏛Calle Santa Paula 11 🚌C1, C2, C3, C4, C5, 10, 11 🕐9:30am–1:30pm & 5–6:45pm daily 🌐santa paula.es

Founded in 1475, Santa Paula is a working convent and home to about 30 nuns. The museum consists of two galleries filled with religious artifacts and paintings. The nave of the convent church has a wooden roof, dating from 1623. Among the statues in the church are St John the Evangelist and St John the Baptist, both the work of Juan Martínez Montañés.

 20

Palacio de San Telmo

📍E5 🏛Avenida de Roma ☎955 50 10 10 Ⓜ🚏Puerta de Jerez 🚌C3, C4, C5, 3, 5, 6, 41 🕐By reservation Thu pm, Sat am & pm

This imposing palace was built in 1682 as a university to train ships' pilots, navigators and high-ranking officers. In 1849 it became the residence of the Dukes of Monpensier and until 1893 its grounds included what is now Parque María Luisa. Today it is the presidential headquarters of the Junta de Andalucía (the regional government).

The most striking feature of the Palacio de San Telmo is the Churrigueresque portal by Leonardo de Figueroa, completed in 1734. Surrounding the Ionic columns are allegorical figures representing the Sciences and Arts.

Opposite is Seville's most famous hotel, the Alfonso XIII, dating from the 1920s. Non-residents are welcome to visit the bar and the restaurant.

TOP 3 SEVILLE FIESTAS

Holy Week
Over 100 gilded *pasos* (floats bearing religious images) are borne through the streets between Palm Sunday and Easter Day.

Feria de Abril
Two weeks after Easter, various groups meet in *casetas* (entertainment booths) to drink and dance to the rhythm of *Sevillanas*. Riders on horseback and mantilla-crowned women in carriages parade their flamenco attire.

Corpus Christi
The *Seises*, boys dressed in Baroque costume, dance before the main altar of the cathedral on this day in May or June.

 21

Universidad

📍E5 🏛Calle San Fernando 4 Ⓜ Puerta de Jerez 🚏Puerta de Jerez or Prado de San Sebastían 🚌C1, C2, C3, C4, 5, 21, 22, 25, 26, 28, 29, 30, 31, 34, 37, 38 🕐8am–9pm Mon–Fri 🚫Public hols 🌐us.es

The former Real Fábrica de Tabacos (Royal Tobacco Factory) is now part of Seville University. In the 19th century, three-quarters of Europe's cigars were manufactured in this building, rolled by 10,000 *cigarreras* (female cigar-makers). These women were the inspiration for French author Mérimée's *Carmen*.

Built in 1728–71, the factory complex is the third-largest building in Spain. The moat and watchtowers are evidence of the importance given to protecting the king's lucrative tobacco monopoly.

Located in the heart of Triana, the 17th-century Iglesia de Nuestra Señora de la O is easily spotted by its colourful tiled belfry. Step inside to see more beautiful ceramics, along with some impressive Baroque sculptures.

Triana

C4 **Plaza de Cuba, Parque de los Príncipes**
C1, C2, C3

This close-knit area, named after the Roman Emperor Trajan, was once Seville's Romany quarter. Triana remains a traditional working-class district, with compact, flower-filled streets. For centuries it has been famous for its potteries and associations with flamenco. Worth a visit is the museum dedicated to this fine craft at Centro Cerámica Triana *(Calle Callao 16)*, formerly the factory of the Cerámica Santa Ana shop. Among other displays, you can admire tiles decorated by the famous Aníbal González, before seeing the kilns used in production (some dating from the 16th century), plus tools and materials.

A good way to approach Triana is across the Puente de Isabel II, leading to the Plaza del Altozano. The Museo de la Inquisición, in Castillo de San Jorge, is largely tasteful and avoids sensational images, concluding with a presentation on human rights today.

Nearby is one of the characteristic streets of the area, the Calle Rodrigo de Triana, named after the Andalucían sailor who was first to sight the shores of the Americas on Columbus's voyage of 1492.

The Iglesia de Santa Ana, founded in the 13th century, is Triana's most popular church. In the baptistry is the famous font, believed to pass on the gift of flamenco song to the children of the faithful.

Isla de la Cartuja

C1 **C1, C2**

The site of Expo '92, this area has since been transformed into a sprawling complex of exhibition halls, museums and entertainment and leisure spaces.

The 15th-century Monasterio de Santa María de las Cuevas, inhabited by monks until 1836, now houses the **Centro Andaluz de Arte Contemporáneo**, which

A monument paying tribute to flamenco at the centre of the Triana quarter

contains works by Andalucían artists, plus Spanish and international art. Free jazz jam sessions take place in the patio of the café on Sundays.

The centrepiece of Expo '92, the Lago de España, is part of the **Isla Mágica** theme park. This re-creates the journeys and exploits of the explorers who left Seville in the 16th century for the Americas. Isla Mágica also has a fun-filled water park, the Agua Mágica.

Centro Andaluz de Arte Contemporáneo

◈ 🅰 Avenida Américo Vespucio 2 🕐 11am–9pm Tue–Sat, 10am–3:30pm Sun & public hols 🔽 caac.es

Isla Mágica

◈ 🅰 Pabellón de España s/n 🕐 Hours vary, check website 🔽 Nov–mid-Apr 🔽 islamagica.es

---

Torre Sevilla

📍 B3 🅰 Calle Gonzalo Jiménez de Quesada 2 🚌 C1, C2, C3, 5, 6, 43

Designed by the Argentine architect César Pelli, this 40-storey tower was the subject of much controversy while in its planning stages. Despite UNESCO voting against its construction, due to its obstruction of the skyline, the Torre Sevilla now presides over the Guadalquivir River, offering commanding panoramic views.

Opened in 2015, it is the tallest building in Andalucía and houses a five-star hotel on the top 19 floors. The remaining floors are primarily devoted to office space.

For a good view of the tower itself, visit the adjacent shopping centre's garden roof.

Torre de los Perdigones

📍 E1 🅰 Torre de los Perdigones, Calle Resolana 44 🚌 C1, C2, C3, C4, C5, 2, 13, 14 🔽 torredelos perdigones.com

With a height of 45 m (148 ft), this tower was built in 1885 as a foundry. Today, the tower is home to a restaurant and a camera obscura. Make a reservation for dinner and enjoy romantic nighttime views over the city.

↑ The modern Torre Sevilla, soaring 180.5 m (591 ft) into the sky

---

SHOP

Botellas y Latas
Gourmet shop overflowing with regional products such as artisan cheeses, Iberian ham, sausages, choice patés, preserves, olive oil, wine and beers.

📍 E2 🅰 Calle Regina 15 📞 954 29 31 22

Rompemoldes
A complex of workshops where artists and craftsmen work, exhibit and sell to the public. Find ceramics, jewellery, clothing, sculptures, decorative pieces and paintings. Hours vary according to each individual space.

📍 F2 🅰 Calle San Luís 70 🔽 rompemoldes.com

A SHORT WALK
EL ARENAL

Distance 1.5 km (1 mile) **Nearest metro**
Puerta Jerez **Time** 25 minutes

Once the bustling home of Seville's port, ammunition works and artillery headquarters, El Arenal is now set by the city's bullring, the majestic Plaza de Toros de la Maestranza. El Arenal is a popular nightlife hub year-round, but during the bullfighting season the area's bars and restaurants are especially packed. The riverfront is dominated by one of Seville's best-known monuments, the Moorish Torre del Oro, while the long, tree-lined promenade beside the Paseo de Cristóbal Colón is perfect for a slow, romantic walk along the Guadalquivir.

The **Plaza de Toros de la Maestranza**, Seville's 18th-century bullring, has a Baroque façade in white and ochre (p459).

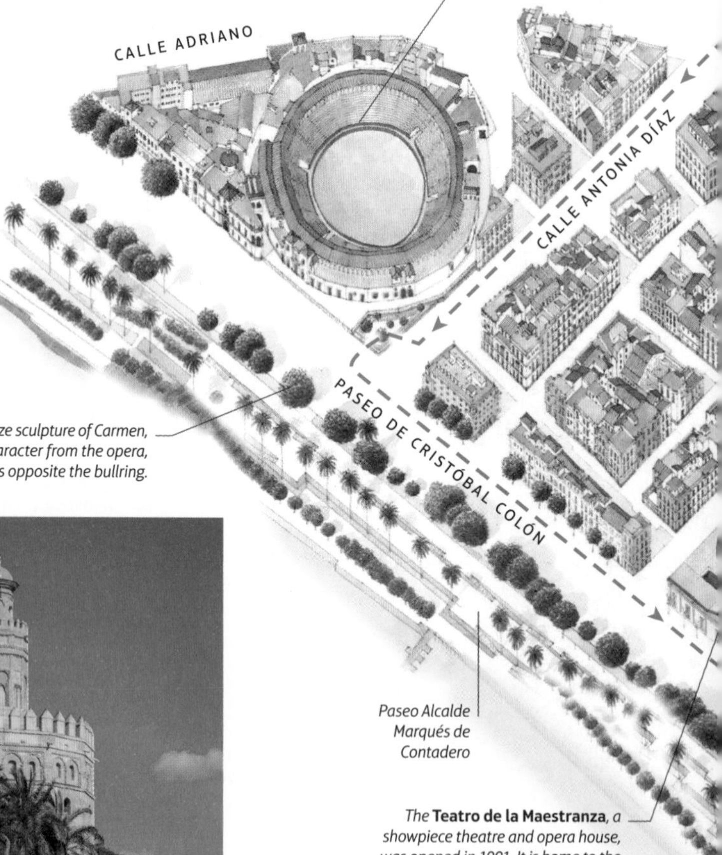

CALLE ADRIANO

CALLE ANTONIA DÍAZ

PASEO DE CRISTÓBAL COLÓN

A bronze sculpture of Carmen, the character from the opera, stands opposite the bullring.

Paseo Alcalde Marqués de Contadero

The **Teatro de la Maestranza**, a showpiece theatre and opera house, was opened in 1991. It is home to the Orquesta Sinfónica de Sevilla.

←
Cycling by the Torre del Oro, a Moorish tower on the bank of the Guadalquivir

→ The striking exterior of the Plaza de Toros de la Maestranza, Seville's bullring

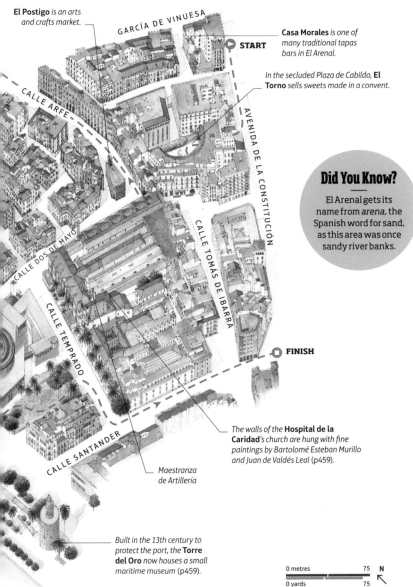

El Postigo *is an arts and crafts market.*

GARCÍA DE VINUESA

Casa Morales *is one of many traditional tapas bars in El Arenal.*

O START

In the secluded Plaza de Cabildo, **El Torno** *sells sweets made in a convent.*

CALLE ARFE

AVENIDA DE LA CONSTITUCIÓN

Did You Know?

El Arenal gets its name from *arena*, the Spanish word for sand, as this area was once sandy river banks.

CALLE DOS DE MAYO

CALLE TOMÁS DE IBARRA

CALLE TEMPRADO

O FINISH

The walls of the **Hospital de la Caridad**'s *church are hung with fine paintings by Bartolomé Esteban Murillo and Juan de Valdés Leal (p459).*

CALLE SANTANDER

Maestranza de Artillería

Built in the 13th century to protect the port, the **Torre del Oro** *now houses a small maritime museum (p459).*

| 0 metres | 75 |
| 0 yards | 75 |

N

A SHORT WALK
SANTA CRUZ

Distance 1 km (0.5 miles) **Nearest metro**
Puerta Jerez **Time** 15 minutes

The compact maze of narrow streets to the east of Seville Cathedral and the Real Alcázar represents Seville at its most romantic. As well as the expected souvenir shops, tapas bars and strolling guitarists, there are plenty of picturesque alleys, hidden plazas and flower-decked patios to reward the casual wanderer. Once a Jewish ghetto, its restored buildings, with characteristic window grilles, are now a harmonious mix of upmarket residences and tourist accommodation. Good bars and restaurants make the area well worth an evening visit.

Calle Mateos Gago is shaded by orange trees and filled with souvenir shops, cafés and tapas bars.

*The 18th-century **Palacio Arzobispal** is still used by Seville's clergy.*

*In the centre of the **Plaza Virgen de los Reyes** is a 20th-century fountain by José Lafita.*

MATE

Convento de la Encarnación

PLAZA DEL TRIUNFO

AVENIDA DE LA CONSTITUCIÓN

JOAQUIN ROMERO MURU

*The huge Gothic **Cathedral** and **La Giralda**, its Moorish bell tower, are Seville's most popular sights (p452).*

START

Did You Know?

Santa Cruz as we know it was set to be demolished for the 1929 Ibero-American Exposition.

SANTO TOMÁS

MIGUEL MANARA

*The **Plaza del Triunfo** has a Baroque column celebrating the city's survival of the great earthquake of 1755. In the centre is a modern statue of the Virgin Mary (Immaculate Conception).*

*Built in the 16th century as a merchants' exchange, the **Archivo de Indias** now houses documents relating to the Spanish colonization of the Americas (p462).*

0 metres 50
0 yards 50
N ↑

↑ Outdoor café tables in the pretty Plaza Santa Cruz

MESÓN DEL MORO

RODRIGO CARO

XIMÉNEZ ENCISCO

JAMERDANA

REINOSO

GLORIA

PL DOÑA ELVIRA

SUSONA

PIMIENTA

VIDA

SANTA TERESA

LOPE DE RUEDA

STA CRUZ

CALLEJÓN DE AGUA

FINISH

Plaza Santa Cruz *is adorned by an ornate iron cross from 1692.*

The **Hospital de los Venerables** *was a home for elderly priests in the 17th century (p462).*

Callejón del Agua *(Water Street) is a whitewashed alleyway offering glimpses into enchanting plant-filled patios.*

The **Real Alcázar** *is a rewarding combination of exquisite Mudéjar craftsmanship, regal grandeur and landscaped gardens (p454).*

→ A beautiful tree-shaded building on the Callejón del Agua

ANDALUCÍA

Waves of settlers each brought new ideas and customs with them to Andalucía. Starting as early as 206 BC, the Romans built cities in this southern province, which they called Baetica, including Córdoba, Itálica and Cástulo – once the greatest city on the peninsula. It was in Andalucía, too, that the Moors lingered longest and left their most impressive buildings, the Mezquita and Alhambra.

By 1251, Fernando III of Castille had wrestled all of southern Spain from Moorish control, apart from Granada, which remained a Muslim kingdom until its capture by Isabel I of Castile and Fernando II of Aragón in 1492. Andalucía prospered after the *reconquista*: Columbus set sail from Palos de la Frontera in 1492 and the region's ports became gateways to the wealth of the Americas.

But this prosperity was not to last. In 1609, the *Moriscos* (Christianized Muslims) were expelled from Spain and Andalucía forfeited a substantial proportion of its agricultural workforce as a result. In the 18th century, Seville and Cádiz lost their trading monopolies over the Americas and, in 1713, Spain ceded Gibraltar to the British following the Spanish War of Succession.

During the Civil War, Andalucía was a Republican stronghold and suffered greatly at the hands of Franco's victorious Nationalist forces. It is estimated that over 50,000 people were executed in the province, including 17,000 people in Malaga alone.

Nowadays, Andalucía is the most populated of Spain's 17 autonomous communities, and its one of Spain's most visited regions.

ANDALUCÍA

Must Sees

1 Parque Nacional
de Doñana
2 Cádiz
3 Ronda
4 Córdoba
5 Úbeda
6 Baeza
7 Granada

Experience More

8 Huelva
9 Sierra de Aracena
10 Monasterio de la Rábida
11 Palos de la Frontera
12 El Rocío
13 Sanlúcar de Barrameda
14 Jerez de la Frontera
15 Costa de la Luz

16 Gibraltar
17 Algeciras
18 Marbella
19 Arcos de la Frontera
20 El Torcal
21 Garganta del Chorro
22 Antequera
23 Málaga
24 Palma del Río

- 25 Itálica
- 26 Osuna
- 27 Sierra Morena
- 28 Carmona
- 29 Medina Azahara
- 30 Écija
- 31 Priego de Córdoba
- 32 Montilla
- 33 Lanjarón
- 34 Nerja
- 35 Almuñécar
- 36 Montefrío
- 37 Guadix
- 38 Laujar de Andarax
- 39 Castillo de La Calahorra
- 40 Jaén
- 41 Sierra Nevada
- 42 Parque Natural de Cazorla
- 43 Mojácar
- 44 Cástulo
- 45 Vélez Blanco
- 46 Andújar
- 47 Almería
- 48 Tabernas
- 49 Parque Natural de Cabo de Gata

→ Greater flamingo fishing on a marsh in the Parque Nacional de Doñana at dusk

PARQUE NACIONAL DE DOÑANA

🅰B6 🅰Huelva & Seville 🛈Carretera A-483, km 1, La Rocina; Carretera A-483 Almonte-Matalascañas, km 27.5, Palacio del Acebrón; Carretera A-483 del Rocío a Matalascañas, km 12, El Acebuche; www.donanareservas.com

Doñana National Park is ranked among Europe's greatest wetlands. Together with its adjoining protected areas, the park covers in excess of 500 sq km (193 sq miles) of marshes and sand dunes, and is home to an abundance of wildlife.

The area used to be a hunting ground belonging to the Dukes of Medina Sidonia. As the land was never suitable for human settlers, wildlife was able to flourish and, in 1969, this large area became officially protected. In addition to a wealth of endemic species, such as fallow deer *(Dama dama)*, red deer *(Cervus elaphus)* and the imperial eagle *(Aquila adalberti)*, thousands of migratory birds, including the squacco heron *(Ardeola ralloides)* and the

greater flamingo *(Phoenicopterus ruber)*, stop here in winter when the marshes become flooded again, after months of drought.

Softly rounded dunes, up to 30 m (100 ft) high, fringe the park's coastal edge. Monte de Doñana, the wooded area behind these sand dunes, provides shelter for lynx, deer and boar and the number of visitors to the park's interior is strictly controlled. The only way to access the area is on a tour.

THE LYNX'S LAST REFUGE

The lynx is one of Europe's rarest mammals and is only glimpsed with patience. In Doñana about 125 individual Iberian lynx *(Lynx pardinus)* have found refuge. They have yellow-brown fur with dark brown spots and pointed ears with black tufts. Research is under way into this shy, nocturnal animal, which tends to stay hidden in scrub. It feeds mainly on rabbits and ducks, but might catch an unguarded fawn.

←
A squacco heron, with a bright blue bill during the breeding season

A spiny thrift *(Armeria pungens)* growing on
↓ Doñana's dunes

 INSIDER TIP
Walk this Way

The park has three self-guided paths: La Rocina to Charco de la Boca is 3.5 km (2 miles) long, Charco del Acebrón is a 1.5-km (1-mile) route and there is a 1.5-km (1-mile) circuit around Laguna del Acebuche.

The seafront of Cadíz, with the cathedral towering behind ↑

② CÁDIZ

🅰 B6 📍 Cádiz 🚌 ℹ Avenida Cuatro de Diciembre de 1977 32D; www.cadizturismo.com

Jutting out of the Bay of Cádiz, and almost entirely surrounded by water, Cádiz lays claim to being Europe's oldest city. Legend names Hercules as its founder, although history credits the Phoenicians with establishing the town of Gadir, as Cádiz was known, in 1100 BC. In 1812 Cádiz briefly became Spain's capital when the nation's first constitution was declared here.

Today the joy of visiting this city is to wander along the waterfront with its neat gardens and open squares before exploring the narrow alleys of the Old Town. The pride of the city is its Carnival – a riotous explosion of festivities, fancy dress, singing and drinking.

① Catedral

🅰 Plaza de la Catedral s/n
🕐 Hours vary, check website
🌐 catedraldecadiz.com

Known as the Catedral Nueva (New Cathedral) and built on the site of an older one, this Baroque and Neo-Classical church is one of Spain's largest. Its treasures are stored in the Casa de la Contaduria.

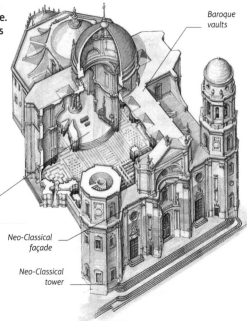

Baroque vaults

The presbytery altar, partly sponsored by Isabel II

Neo-Classical façade

Neo-Classical tower

→ Cádiz Cathedral, with a splendid cupola built by Juan Daura

Did You Know?

Lord Byron dubbed Cádiz the "Siren of the Ocean".

 ②

Museo de Cádiz

🏛 Plaza de Mina 📞 856 10 50 23 🕐 Mid-Jun–mid-Sep: 9am–3pm Tue–Sun (mid-Sep–mid-Jun: to 9pm)

This museum charts the history of Cádiz and houses

the largest art gallery in Andalucía. On the third floor is a collec-tion of puppets made for village fiestas.

③

Torre Tavira

🏛 Calle Marqués del Real Tesoro 10 🕐 May–Sep: 10am–8pm daily (Oct–Apr: to 6pm) 🚫 1 & 6 Jan, 25 Dec 🌐 torretavira.com

The city's official 18th-century watchtower is now a camera obscura, offering great views.

④

Oratorio de San Felipe Neri

🏛 Calle Santa Inés s/n 📞 662 64 22 33 🕐 9am–3pm Tue–Fri, 10am–3pm Sat (to 2pm Sun) 🚫 Public hols

In 1812, as Napoleon tightened his grip on Spain, a provisional government assembled at this 18th-century church to try to lay the foundations of Spain's first constitutional monarchy.

EAT

Freiduría Cervecería Las Flores

A simple spot specializing in shellfish, which can be cooked in front of you.

🏛 Plaza Topete 4 📞 956 22 61 12

€€€

Balandro

Set overlooking the Bay of Cadíz, this restaurant offers a good selection of meat dishes.

🏛 Alameda Apodaca 22 🌐 restaurante balandro.com

€€€

El Faro

An atmospheric seafood restaurant in the port district – try one of the various tasting menus.

🏛 Calle de San Félix 15 🌐 elfarodecadiz.com

€€€

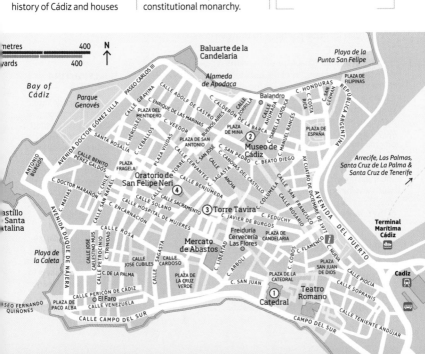

③

RONDA

🄰 C6 🄰 Málaga 🚌🚐 𝑖 Paseo de Blas Infante s/n; www.turismoderonda.es

One of the most spectacularly located cities in Spain, Ronda sits on a huge rocky outcrop, straddling a precipitous limestone cleft. This dramatic setting seems appropriate for a place which has historically sheltered outlaws and rebels, including author Ernest Hemingway and actor and director Orson Welles. Today, Ronda's rich history and spectacular location continue to draw visitors.

Because of its impregnable position on the region's rocky landscape, Ronda was one of the last Moorish bastions, finally falling to the Christians in 1485. On the south side perches La Ciudad, a classic Moorish *pueblo blanco* (white town) of cobbled alleys, window grilles and dazzling whitewash. Most historic sights are in this part of the city, including the Palacio Mondragón, which features an arcaded patio adorned with original Moorish mosaics and plasterwork (although much of the rest of the palace was rebuilt following the *reconquista*). Located in El Mercadillo, the newer district, is one of the oldest and most important bullrings in Spain – the Plaza de Toros, which was inaugurated in 1785. In September, aficionados travel from all over the country for the singular atmosphere of the Corrida Goyesca while millions watch it on television.

> **Because of its impregnable position on the region's rocky landscape, this town was one of the last Moorish bastions, finally falling to the Christians in 1485.**

BULLFIGHTING AT RONDA

Ronda's Plaza de Toros is the spiritual home of bullfighting. The sport is an integral part of southern Spanish life, but it is highly controversial due to the prolonged nature of the kill purely for entertainment. If you decide to attend a *corrida*, try to see a big-name matador, who is likely to make a "clean" kill (p589).

Must See

↑ Old and new Ronda, linked across the gorge by the Puente Nuevo

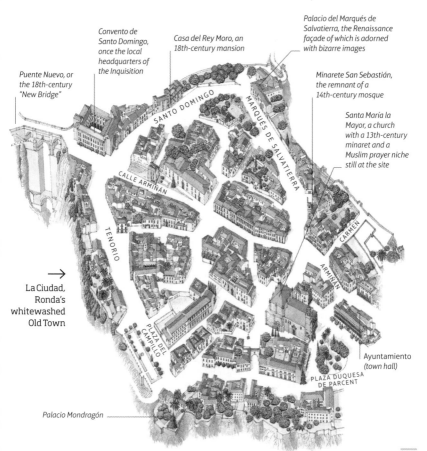

Convento de Santo Domingo, once the local headquarters of the Inquisition

Casa del Rey Moro, an 18th-century mansion

Palacio del Marqués de Salvatierra, the Renaissance façade of which is adorned with bizarre images

Puente Nuevo, or the 18th-century "New Bridge"

Minarete San Sebastián, the remnant of a 14th-century mosque

Santa María la Mayor, a church with a 13th-century minaret and a Muslim prayer niche still at the site

SANTO DOMINGO

MARQUÉS DE SALVATIERRA

CALLE ARMIÑAN

CARMEN

ARMIÑAN

TENORIO

→ La Ciudad, Ronda's whitewashed Old Town

PLAZA DEL CAMPILLO

Ayuntamiento (town hall)

PLAZA DUQUESA DE PARCENT

Palacio Mondragón

Córdoba's Punte Romano, stretching across the Río Guadalquivir

④

CÓRDOBA

 C5   Córdoba   Plaza del Triunfo s/n; www.turismodecordoba.org

This city has had a long and illustrious history. Under the Romans Córdoba was famed as the birthplace of philosopher Seneca and in the 10th century Abd al Rahman III made the city the capital of his powerful caliphate. Today, Córdoba is still as awe-inspiring.

①

Museo Arqueológico

Plaza Jerónimo Páez 7   957 35 55 17   Mid-Jun-mid-Sep: 9am-3pm Tue-Sun; mid-Sep-mid-Jun: 9am-9pm Tue-Sat, 9am-3pm Sun

Located in a Renaissance mansion, this excellent museum displays the remains of a Roman theatre found beneath the building, including mosaics and pottery, as well as impressive finds from the Moorish era. Highlights include a 10th-century bronze stag found at Medina Azahara (p510). Also on display is a marble sculpted head of the Emperor Augustus, dating to the 1st century AD, which was found in the area.

②

Alcázar de los Reyes Cristianos

Calle Caballerizas Reales s/n   957 42 01 51   Mid-Jun-mid-Sep: 8:30am-2:30pm Tue-Sat, 9:30am-2:30pm Sun; mid-Sep-mid-Jun: 8:30am-8:45pm Tue-Fri, 8:30am-4:30pm Sat, 8:45am-3:15pm Sun

This palace-fortress was built in 1328 for Alfonso XI. Fernando II and Isabel stayed here during their campaign to conquer Granada from the Moors. Later it was used by the Inquisition (p304), and then as a prison. The gardens are particularly lovely with their ponds and fountains. They stay open into the evenings in July and August.

③

Sinagoga

Calle Judíos 20   957 74 90 15   Mid-Jun-mid-Sep: 9am-3:30pm Tue-Sun & public hols; mid-Sep-mid-Jun: 9am-8:30pm Tue-Sat, 9am-3:30pm Sun & public hols

Constructed around 1315, this Mudéjar-style synagogue is one of three in Spain preserved from that era. The other two are in Toledo. The women's gallery and decorative plasterwork, with Hebrew script, are of particular interest. The synagogue lies in the Judería, the Jewish quarter, which has hardly changed since Moorish times. In a plaza nearby is a bronze statue of Maimónides, a 12th-century Jewish sage who has become a popular local figure.

Did You Know?

The name Córdoba may have derived from *Kartuba*, Phoenician for "prosperous city".

Torre de la Calahorra

⌂ Puente Romano 📞 957 29 39 29 🕐 Oct-Apr: 10am-6pm daily; May-Sep: 10am-2pm & 4:30-8:30pm daily

This 14th-century tower is located at the end of the Puente Romano – an arched bridge with Roman foundations that was rebuilt by the Moors. The tower now houses a museum about the life, culture and philosophy of 10th-century Córdoba, when Abd al Rahman III created an independent caliphate with Córdoba as its capital.

Museo de Bellas Artes

⌂ Plaza del Potro 1 📞 957 01 58 58 🕐 Mid-Jun-mid-Sep: 9am-3pm Tue-Sun; mid-Sep-mid-Jun: 9am-9pm Tue-Sat, 9am-3pm Sun

Located in a former charity hospital, this museum exhibits sculptures by local artist Mateo Inurria and Seville School paintings by Zurbarán.

Palacio de Viana

⌂ Plaza Don Gome 2 🕐 Jul & Aug: 9am-3pm Tue-Sun; Sep-Jun: 10am-7pm Tue-Sat, 10am-3pm Sun 🌐 palacio deviana.com

Tapestries, furniture, porcelain and paintings are displayed in this 17th-century mansion, which was once the home of the affluent Viana family. Purchased by a savings bank in 1981, it has been kept much as the family left it. Outside, you'll find 14 beautiful patios and a delightful garden.

Baños del Alcázar Califal

⌂ Campo Santo de los Mártires 🕐 Hours vary, check website 🌐 banosdel alcazarcalifal.cordoba.es

These Arab baths were once part of the Umayyad palace, which was later replaced by the Alcázar de los Reyes Cristianos. Built under the orders of Al-Hakam II, these 10th-century baths reflect the classical order of Roman baths: cold rooms, warm rooms and hot rooms. There is also a museum, which explores the history of bathing.

EAT

Casa Pepe de la Judería
An enduring favourite since 1928, with a flower-filled patio.

⌂ Calle Romero 1 🌐 restaurantecasapepe delajuderia.com

€€€

Mercado Victoria
This gourmet food court specializes in local dishes and produce.

⌂ Paseo de la Victoria 3 🌐 mercadovictoria.com

€€€

THE MEZQUITA

Calle Torrijos 10 **Mar-Oct: 10am-7pm Mon-Sat, 8:30-11:30am & 3-7pm Sun; Nov-Feb: 10am-6pm Mon-Sat, 8:30-11:30am & 3-6pm Sun** **mezquita-catedraldecordoba.es**

Córdoba's Great Mosque, dating back 12 centuries, embodied the power of Islam on the Iberian Peninsula. As you tread beneath its rows of hallowed arches, you'll be transported back to the affluent age of Moorish rule.

Abd al Rahman I, the founder of the caliphate of Córdoba, built the original mosque on the site of a Visigothic church between AD 785 and 787. The building evolved over the centuries, blending many architectural forms. In the 10th century al Hakam II made some of the most lavish additions, including the elaborate *mihrab* (prayer niche) and the *maqsura* (caliph's enclosure). Later, during the 16th century a cathedral was built in the heart of the reconsecrated mosque, under the orders of Carlos I, to complete the city's "Christianization".

Torre del Alminar, a bell tower 93 m (305 ft) high, is built on the site of the original minaret. Steep steps lead to the top for a fine view of Córdoba.

Orange trees grow in the Patio de los Naranjos – the courtyard where the faithful washed before prayer.

The Puerta del Perdón is a Mudéjar-style entrance gate, built during Christian rule in 1377.

← The Mezquita, seen from across the Río Guadalquivir

The Puerta de San Esteban door is set into a wall that has survived from the Visigothic church.

← Walking among the red-and-white striped Caliphal arches

MOORISH ARCHES

The Visigoths were the first to use horseshoe arches in the construction of churches. The Moors modified these arches and used them as the basis of great architectural endeavours, as seen in the Mezquita. Subsequent arches show more sophisticated ornamentation and the slow demise of the basic horseshoe shape.

Caliphal arch, the Mezquita

Almohad arch, Real Alcázar (p454)

Mudéjar arch, Real Alcázar (p454)

Nasrid arch, the Alhambra (p494)

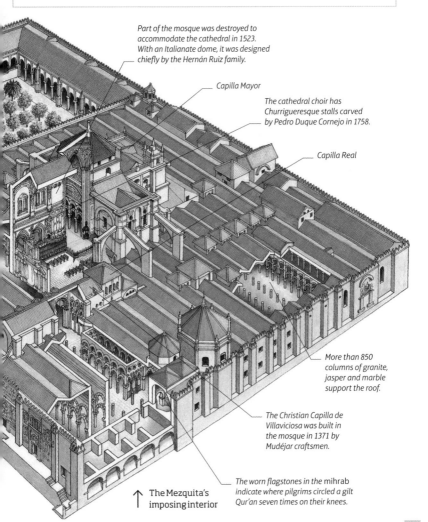

Part of the mosque was destroyed to accommodate the cathedral in 1523. With an Italianate dome, it was designed chiefly by the Hernán Ruiz family.

Capilla Mayor

The cathedral choir has Churrigueresque stalls carved by Pedro Duque Cornejo in 1758.

Capilla Real

More than 850 columns of granite, jasper and marble support the roof.

The Christian Capilla de Villaviciosa was built in the mosque in 1371 by Mudéjar craftsmen.

The worn flagstones in the mihrab indicate where pilgrims circled a gilt Qur'an seven times on their knees.

↑ The Mezquita's imposing interior

A SHORT WALK
CÓRDOBA

Distance 2 km (1 mile) **Nearest train station** Córdoba **Time** 30 minutes

The heart of Córdoba is the old Jewish quarter, situated to the west of the Mezquita's towering walls. A walk around this area gives the sensation that little has changed since the 10th century, when this was one of the greatest cities in the Western world. Wrought ironwork decorates cobbled streets too narrow for cars, where silversmiths create fine jewellery in their workshops. Most of the chief sights are here, while modern city life takes place some blocks north, around the Plaza de Tendillas.

*Built in the Gothic-Mudéjar style, the **Capilla de San Bartolome** is decorated with elaborate tiles.*

*Hebrew script covers the **Sinagoga** (p482). Spain's other major synagogues are in Toledo, Madrid and Barcelona.*

Casa de Sefarad *is a cultural centre with exhibits on Judeo-Spanish history in the heart of the Jewish quarter.*

*Water terraces and fountains add to the tranquil atmosphere of the gardens belonging to the **Alcázar de los Reyes Cristianos** (p482).*

↑ Bright *azulejos* decorating the Capilla de San Bartolome

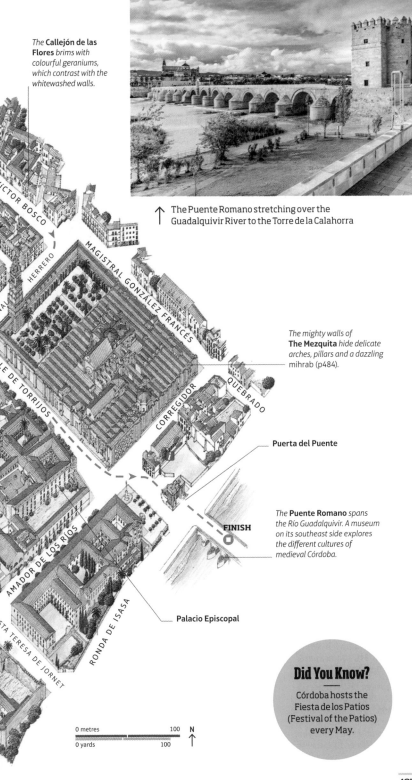

The **Callején de las Flores** *brims with colourful geraniums, which contrast with the whitewashed walls.*

VICTOR BOSCO

HERRERO

MAGISTRAL GONZALEZ FRANCÉS

CALLE DE TORRIJOS

CORREGIDOR

QUEBRADO

AMADOR DE LOS RIOS

RONDA DE ISASA

STA TERESA DE JORNET

↑ The Puente Romano stretching over the Guadalquivir River to the Torre de la Calahorra

The mighty walls of **The Mezquita** *hide delicate arches, pillars and a dazzling mihrab (p484).*

Puerta del Puente

FINISH

The **Puente Romano** *spans the Río Guadalquivir. A museum on its southeast side explores the different cultures of medieval Córdoba.*

Palacio Episcopal

0 metres — 100
0 yards — 100

N ↑

Did You Know?

Córdoba hosts the Fiesta de los Patios (Festival of the Patios) every May.

The imposing façade of the
Hospital de Santiago,
fronted by gardens

ÚBEDA

D5 Jaén Plaza de Andalucía 5; www.
turismodeubeda.com

A UNESCO World Heritage Site, Úbeda is a showcase
of Renaissance magnificence, thanks to the patronage
of some of Spain's most influential men of the 16th
century, including such dignitaries as Juan Vázquez
de Molina. The Old Town is contained within city walls
that were first raised by the Moors in AD 852.

①

Hospital de Santiago

Calle Obispo Cobos
953 75 08 42
8am-1pm & 4-9pm
Mon-Fri, 10am-2pm &
5-9pm Sat Aug: Sat

Created on the orders of
the Bishop of Jaén around
1562, the colossal Hospital
de Santiago was designed
by Andrés de Vandelvira,
who refined the Spanish
Renaissance style into its
more austere characteristics.
Today, the building hosts
cultural exhibitions.

②

Museo Arqueológico

Casa Mudéjar, Calle
Cervantes 6 953 10 86
23 Jul & Aug: 9am-3pm
Tue-Sun (Sep-Jun: to 9pm
Tue-Sat & to 3pm Sun)

This archaeological museum
exhibits artifacts from Neolithic
to Moorish times, including
tombstones from the 1st
century AD. It is located in
the grand Casa Mudéjar, a
15th-century palace.

③

Iglesia de San Pablo

Plaza Primero de Mayo 39
11am-1pm & 6-8pm Tue-
Sat, 11am-1pm Sun

This church has a 13th-century
apse and a 16th-century chapel.
The church is surmounted by a
Plateresque tower that was
completed in 1537.

 GREAT VIEW
Sea of Greenery

Head to the Mirador
del Alcázar for specta-
cular views over the
countryside. A sea of
olive groves is framed
by the Sierras Mágina
to the south and Sierra
de Cazorla to the east.

④
Capilla del Salvador

🏠 Plaza Vázquez de Molina
🕐 11am–2pm & 5–7pm Tue–Sun 🌐 fundacionmedina celi.org

The Capilla del Salvador was designed in the 16th century for Francisco de los Cobos. Although the church was pillaged during the Civil War, it retains a number of treasures, including a golden chalice that was given to Cobos by Carlos I.

Behind the chapel stand Cobos' palace and the Hospital de los Honrados Viejos (Hospital of the Honoured Elders). Both of these buildings can only be visited on a pre-arranged guided tour.

⑤
Santa María de los Reales Alcázares

🏠 Plaza Vázquez de Molina s/n 🕐 10:30am–1:15pm & 5–7:45pm Fri–Sat, 10:45am–1:15pm Sun 🌐 santamaria deubeda.es

Built on the site of an original mosque, this church has a Gothic cloister and a noteworthy Romanesque doorway. Nearby is the Cárcel del Obispo (Bishop's Jail), so-called because nuns who had been punished by the bishop were confined here.

---

⑥
Parador de Úbeda

🏠 Plaza Vázquez de Molina s/n 🌐 parador.es

Built in the 16th century, but much altered in the 17th, this was the residence of Fernando Ortega Salido, dean of Málaga and chaplain of the Capilla del Salvador; the patio is open to visitors.

---

⑦
Palacio de las Cadenas

🏠 Plaza Vázquez de Molina s/n 📞 953 75 04 40 🕐 8am–2:30pm & 4:30–7:30pm Mon–Wed, 8am–2:30pm Thu & Fri

Two stone lions guard Úbeda's town hall, which occupies the Palacio de las Cadenas, a mansion built for Vázquez de Molina by de Vandelvira. It gets its name from the iron chains (cadenas) once attached to the columns supporting the main doorway.

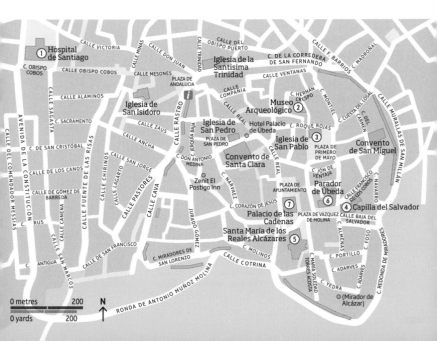

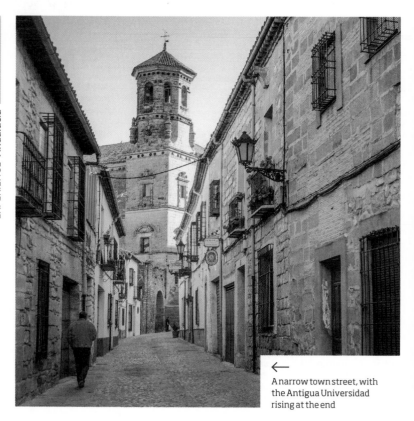

← A narrow town street, with the Antigua Universidad rising at the end

6

BAEZA

 D5 ⬗Jaén ▣▭ ℹ Plaza del Pópulo; 953 77 99 82

Nestled amid the olive groves that characterize much of Jaén province, beautiful Baeza is a small town that's unusually rich in Renaissance architecture. As you wander its winding streets, you'll stumble upon unique examples of this opulent period of building design. With palaces, churches and stately buildings on almost every corner, Baeza is a treat to explore.

Called Beatia by the Romans and later the capital of a Moorish fiefdom, Baeza is portrayed as a "royal nest of hawks" on its coat of arms. It was conquered by Fernando III in 1226 – the first town in Andalucía to be definitively won back from the Moors – and was then settled by Castilian knights. An era of medieval splendour followed, reaching a climax in the 16th century, when Andrés de Vandelvira's splendid buildings were erected. Perhaps the most impressive of these is the town's cathedral, which was rebuilt by de Vandelvira in 1567. Inside, look out for the Capilla Sagrario, within which is a beautiful choir screen by Bartholomé de Jaén. Baeza was designated a UNESCO World Heritage Site in 2003, along with its twin town, the slightly larger Úbeda (p488).

Did You Know?

The province of Jaén is responsible for 20 percent of the world's olive oil production.

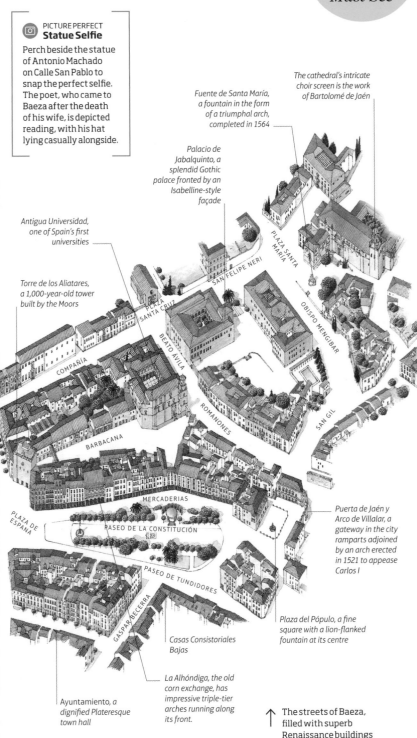

The cathedral's intricate choir screen is the work of Bartolomé de Jaén

Fuente de Santa María, a fountain in the form of a triumphal arch, completed in 1564

Palacio de Jabalquinto, a splendid Gothic palace fronted by an Isabelline-style façade

Antigua Universidad, one of Spain's first universities

Torre de los Aliatares, a 1,000-year-old tower built by the Moors

PLAZA SANTA MARÍA

SAN FELIPE NERI

OBISPO MENGIBAR

PLAZA SANTA CRUZ

BEATO AVILA

COMPAÑÍA

ROMANONES

SAN GIL

BARBACANA

MERCADERIAS

PLAZA DE ESPAÑA

PASEO DE LA CONSTITUCIÓN

PASEO DE TUNDIDORES

GASPAR BECERRA

Puerta de Jaén y Arco de Villalar, a gateway in the city ramparts adjoined by an arch erected in 1521 to appease Carlos I

Plaza del Pópulo, a fine square with a lion-flanked fountain at its centre

Casas Consistoriales Bajas

La Alhóndiga, the old corn exchange, has impressive triple-tier arches running along its front.

Ayuntamiento, a dignified Plateresque town hall

↑ The streets of Baeza, filled with superb Renaissance buildings

↑ The close-packed houses of Granada, with the Alhambra on the hill above them

7

GRANADA

 C6 ⌂ Granada ✈🚃🚌 ℹ Santa Ana 4; www.granadatur.com

The guitarist Andrés Segovia (1893–1987) described Granada as a "place of dreams, where the Lord put the seed of music in my soul". It's not hard to see why as you explore the city's Moorish buildings – reminders of granada's golden period during the rule of the Nasrid dynasty from 1238 to 1492. The most impressive of these monuments are the Alhambra (p494) and Generalife (p496), which sit on the hill above the city.

①

Cathedral

⌂ Calle Gran Vía 5 📞 958 22 29 59 🕐 10am-2pm & 3-7pm Mon-Sat

On the orders of the Catholic Monarchs (p64), work on Granada's cathedral began in 1523, with Enrique de Egas as the architect. The building works continued for over 180 years, with the Renaissance maestro, Diego de Siloé, taking on the job in 1529. De Siloé also designed the façade and the magnificent Capilla Mayor. Under its dome, 16th-century windows depict Juan del Campo's The Passion. The west front was designed by Alonso Cano, who was born in the city and whose tomb lies in the cathedral.

②

Capilla Real

⌂ Calle Oficios 3 🕐 Jun-Sep: 10am-2pm & 3-7pm daily; Oct-May: 10:15am-6:30pm Mon-Sat, 11am-6pm Sun 🚫 1 Jan, Good Fri, 25 Dec 🌐 capillareal granada.com

The Royal Chapel was built for the Catholic Monarchs between 1506 and 1521 by Enrique de Egas, although both monarchs died before it could be completed. A magnificent reja (grille) by Maestro Bartolomé de Jaén encloses the high altar and the Carrara marble figures of Fernando and Isabel, their daughter Juana la Loca (the Mad) and her husband Felipe el Hermoso (the Handsome). Their coffins are in the crypt. Don't miss the sacristy, which is full of a host of artistic treasures, including paintings by Botticelli and Van der Weyden.

③

Monasterio de la Cartuja

⌂ Paseo de la Cartuja 📞 958 16 19 32 🕐 10am-1pm & 4-8pm daily

Founded in 1516 by Christian warrior El Gran Capitán, this monastery has a dazzling cupola by Antonio Palomino, and a Churrigueresque sacristy by Luis de Arévalo and Luis Caballo.

↑ Visitors admiring the sacristy within the Monasterio de la Cartuja

④ Corral del Carbón

🏠 Calle Mariana Pineda 📞 958 57 51 31 🕐 9am–8pm daily

A relic of the Moorish era, this galleried courtyard was a theatre in Christian times. Today it houses a cultural centre.

---

⑤ Casa de los Tiros

🏠 Calle Pavaneras 19 📞 600 14 31 76 🕐 Jun–mid-Sep: 9am–8pm Tue–Sat (to 3pm Sun); mid-Sep–May: 10am–8:30pm Tue–Sat (to 5pm Sun)

Built in Mudéjar style in the 1500s, this palace owes its name to the muskets projecting from its battlements (tiro means "shot"). It originally belonged to the family that was awarded the Generalife (p496) after the fall of Granada. Muhammad XII's sword is carved on the façade.

⑥ Centro Cultural Caja Granada

🏠 Avenida de la Ciencia 2 🕐 Hours vary, check website 🚫 Aug 🌐 caja granadafundacion.es

Set in a stark, white modern building, with a sweeping external staircase, this cultural centre is home to the superb Memoria de Andalucía Museum, which hosts temporary exhibitions, and a theatre and restaurant.

---

⑦ Palacio de la Madraza

🏠 Calle Oficios 14 📞 958 99 63 50 🕐 10am–8pm daily (winter: to 7pm)

Originally an Arab university, this building later became the city hall (the façade dates from the 18th century) and today is a part of Granada University. The Moorish hall has a finely decorated mihrab (prayer niche).

Must See

EAT

Damasqueros
Try the innovative tasting menu at this contemporary restaurant.

🏠 Calle de Damasqueros 3 🌐 damasqueros.com
€€€

Mirador de Morayma
A delightful patio restaurant, offering spectacular views.

🏠 Calle de Pianista Gracia Carrillo 2 🚫 Mon & Tue 🌐 miradordemorayma. com
€€€

La Riviera
Choose from tapas or the à la carte menu.

🏠 Calle Cetti Meriem 7, 9 & 10 📞 958 22 79 69
€€€

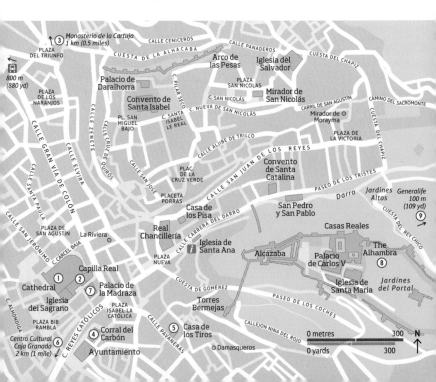

⑧ 🚶 🏛

THE ALHAMBRA

📍 Calle Real de la Alhambra 🚌 C30, C32, C35 🕐 Apr-mid-Oct: 8:30am-8pm daily; mid-Oct-Mar: 8:30am-6pm daily (arrive 1 hour before scheduled visit; allow 3 hours for visit) 🌐 alhambradegranada.org

A visit to the Alhambra – arguably the pinnacle of Europe's Moorish palaces – is a truly special experience. A magical use of space, light, water and decoration characterizes this most sensual piece of architecture.

This palace was built under Ismail I, Yusuf I and Muhammad V caliphs when the Nasrid dynasty ruled Granada. Seeking to belie an image of waning power, they created their idea of paradise on Earth. Modest materials were used (plaster, timber and tiles), but they were superbly worked. The Alhambra complex includes the Palacios Nazaríes, the 13th-century Alcazaba, the 16th-century Palace of Carlos I and the Generalife (p496). Although the Alhambra suffered pillage and decay, including an attempt by Napoleon's troops to blow it up, in recent times it has undergone extensive restoration and its delicate craftsmanship still dazzles the eye.

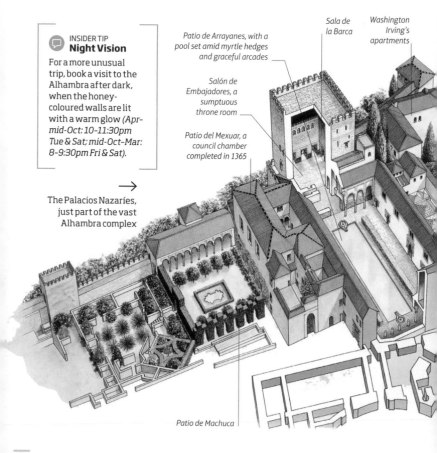

> 💬 INSIDER TIP
> **Night Vision**
>
> For a more unusual trip, book a visit to the Alhambra after dark, when the honey-coloured walls are lit with a warm glow (Apr-mid-Oct: 10-11:30pm Tue & Sat; mid-Oct-Mar: 8-9:30pm Fri & Sat).

→

The Palacios Nazaríes, just part of the vast Alhambra complex

Patio de Arrayanes, with a pool set amid myrtle hedges and graceful arcades

Sala de la Barca

Washington Irving's apartments

Salón de Embajadores, a sumptuous throne room

Patio del Mexuar, a council chamber completed in 1365

Patio de Machuca

The spectacular Alhambra, and *(inset)* a fountain in one of its ornate patios ↑

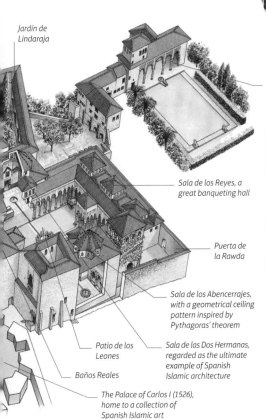

Jardín de Lindaraja

Palacio del Partal, the oldest building in the Alhambra

Sala de los Reyes, a great banqueting hall

Puerta de la Rawda

Sala de los Abencerrajes, with a geometrical ceiling pattern inspired by Pythagoras' theorem

Patio de los Leones

Sala de las Dos Hermanas, regarded as the ultimate example of Spanish Islamic architecture

Baños Reales

The Palace of Carlos I (1526), home to a collection of Spanish Islamic art

↑ Gorgeously intricate Moorish embellishments around a palace window

⑨ ⊘ ⊘

GENERALIFE

📍 Calle Real de la Alhambra 🚌 C30, C32, C35 🕐 Apr–mid-Oct: 8:30am–8pm & 10–11:30pm Tue–Sat, 8:30am–8pm Mon & Sun; mid-Oct–Mar: 8:30am–6pm Sun–Thu, 8:30am–6pm & 8–9:30pm Fri & Sat 🌐 alhambradegranada.org

From the Alhambra's northern side, a footpath leads to the Generalife, the country estate of the Nasrid kings. Here, they could escape from palace intrigues and enjoy tranquillity high above the city.

The name Generalife, or Yannat al Arif, has various interpretations, perhaps the most pleasing being "the garden of lofty paradise". The gardens, begun in the 13th century, originally contained orchards and pastures but have been modified over the years. In contrast to the spectacular architecture and wealth of detail that permeates the Alhambra, the buildings of the Generalife are largely simple, solid structures. Once an idyllic place of respite for kings, today the Generalife provides a magical setting for Granada's annual music and dance festival in late June and July.

> 💬 **INSIDER TIP**
> **Be an Early Bird**
>
> Book the earliest possible morning slot and scoot rapidly through the first couple of rooms – that way you will have the entire palace to yourself and can really appreciate just how tranquil a setting it once was.

Sala Regia

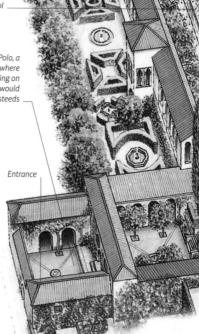

The Patio de la Acequia, an enclosed Persian garden built round a long central pool

The Patio de Polo, a courtyard where visitors arriving on horseback would tether their steeds

Entrance

↑ The Patio de la Acequia, with its central water feature

↑ Visitors wandering the carefully tended gardens of the Generalife

The Patio de los Cipreses, once a secret meeting place for Zoraya, wife of the Sultan Abu-l-Hasan, and her lover

The Escalera del Agua, a staircase with water flowing gently down it

Jardines Altos (Upper Gardens)

Did You Know?

The Generalife sits atop the Cerro del Sol (the Hill of the Sun).

↑ The buildings and extensive gardens of the Generalife

A SHORT WALK

THE ALBAICÍN

Distance 1 km (0.5 miles) **Nearest train station** Estación
Central **Time** 15 minutes

This corner of the city, on the hillside opposite the Alhambra, is
where one feels closest to Granada's Moorish ancestry. Now mostly
pedestrianized, this was the site of the first fortress, built in the
13th century, along with more than 30 mosques. Most of the city's
churches were built over their sites. Along the cobbled alleys stand
cármenes, villas with Moorish decoration and gardens, secluded from
the world by high walls. In the jasmine-scented air of evening, stroll up
to the Mirador de San Nicolás for a magical view over the rooftops of
the Alhambra glowing in the sunset.

Did You Know?

Many street names
start with Cuesta,
meaning "slope".

Casa de los Pisa, *also
known as Museo San Juan de
Dios, displays works of art –
some depicting St John of
God, who died here in 1550.*

START

Built in 1530 by the
Catholic Monarchs, the
Real Chancillería *has a
beautiful Renaissance façade.*

Just north of Plaza Nueva
stands the **Iglesia de Santa
Ana**, *a 16th-century brick
church in Mudéjar style. It has
an elegant Plateresque portal
and, inside, a coffered ceiling.*

FINISH

PLAZA SANTA
ANA

0 metres   50   N
0 yards   50

↑ Walking between the arches in the atmospheric El Bañuelo

Star-shaped openings in the vaults let light into **El Bañuelo**. *These well-preserved Moorish baths were built in the 11th century.*

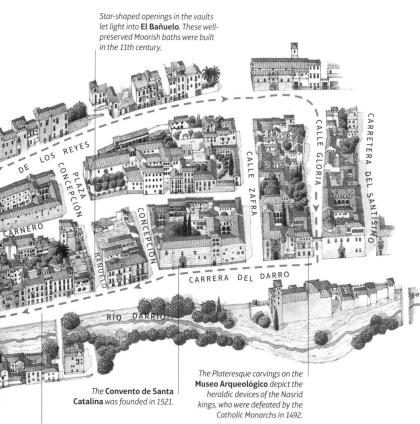

DE LOS REYES

PLAZA CONCEPCIÓN

CARNERO

BAÑUELO

CONCEPCIÓN

CALLE ZAFRA

CALLE GLORIA

CARRETERA DEL SANTÍSIMO

CARRERA DEL DARRO

RÍO DARRO

The **Convento de Santa Catalina** *was founded in 1521.*

The Plateresque carvings on the **Museo Arqueológico** *depict the heraldic devices of the Nasrid kings, who were defeated by the Catholic Monarchs in 1492.*

The **Carrera del Darro** *runs along the Río Darro, past crumbling bridges and the fine façades of ancient buildings, now all restored.*

→ The Carrera del Darro, one of Granada's prettiest streets

EXPERIENCE MORE

EXPERIENCE Andalucía

8

Huelva

△B6 ⋒Huelva 🚌🚍 ⓘCalle Jesús Nazareno 21; 959 65 02 00

Founded as Onuba by the Phoenicians, Huelva had its grandest days as a Roman port. It was almost wiped out in the great Lisbon earthquake of 1755. It is an industrial city today, sprawling around the quayside on the Río Odiel.

Columbus's departure for the Americas *(p65)* from Palos de la Frontera, across the Río Odiel estuary, is celebrated in the excellent **Museo Provincial**, which also charts the history of the Rio Tinto mines. To the east of the centre, the Barrio Reina Victoria is a bizarre example of English mock-Tudor suburban bungalows built by the Rio Tinto Company for its workers in the early 20th century. South of the town, at Punta del Sebo, the Monumento a la Fe Descubridora, a rather bleak statue of a navigator looking towards the Americas, created by Gertrude Vanderbilt Whitney in 1929, dominates the Odiel estuary.

There are three resorts with sandy beaches near Huelva: Punta Umbria, next to the bird-rich wetlands of the Marismas del Odiel; Isla

Cristina, an important fishing port; and Mazagón, with windswept dunes.

Museo Provincial

⋒Alameda Sundheim 13 📞959 65 04 24 🕐9am–8:30pm Tue-Sat, 9am-3:30pm Sun

9

Sierra de Aracena

△B5 ⋒Huelva 🚉El Repilado 🚌Aracena ⓘCalle Pozo de la Nieve s/n, Aracena; 663 93 78 77

This wild mountain range is one of the most remote and least visited corners of Andalucía. Dominated by the ruins of a Moorish fort, the hillside above Aracena is pitted with caverns and in one, the **Gruta de las Maravillas**, is a lake hung with many stalactites.

The village of Jabugo is famed for its ham, *jamón ibérico* or *pata negra*.

Off the A461 are the giant opencast mines at Minas de Riotinto, where iron, copper and silver have been exploited since Phoenician times. The **Museo Minero** traces the history of the Rio Tinto Company.

Gruta de las Maravillas

 ⋒Pozo de la Nieve 📞663 93 78 76 🕐10am–1:30pm & 3-6pm daily

Museo Minero

 ⋒Plaza del Museo 🕐10:30am-3pm & 4-6pm daily 🕐1 & 6 Jan, 25 Dec 🌐parquemineroderiotinto.es

10

Monasterio de la Rábida

△B6 ⋒Huelva 🚌From Huelva 🕐Hours vary, check website 🌐monasterio delarabida.com

The Franciscan Monasterio de la Rábida was founded in the 15th century. In 1491, a dejected Columbus sought refuge here after his plans to sail west to find the East Indies had been rejected by the Catholic Monarchs. Its prior, Juan Pérez, fatefully used his considerable influence as Queen Isabella's confessor to reverse the royal decision.

Inside the monastery there are fine frescoes painted by Daniel Vásquez Díaz in 1930, which glorify the explorer's life and discoveries. Also worth seeing are the Mudéjar cloisters, the gardens and the beamed chapterhouse.

↓ The Monumento a la Fe Descubridora in Huelva

TOP 5 ANDALUCÍAN FIESTAS

Carnival
Residents of Cádiz dress in elaborate costumes for one of Europe's largest and most colourful Carnivals in February or March.

Día de la Cruz
In the first week in May, groups compete to create the most colourful crosses adorned with flowers on Granada and Córdoba's squares and street corners.

Córdoba Patio Fiesta
Flower-decked patios in old Córdoba are opened to the public for displays of flamenco in mid-May.

Columbus Festival
This celebration of Columbus's voyage, held in Huelva in late July or early August, is dedicated to the national music and dance of a different Latin American country every year.

Exaltación al Río Guadalquivir
In late August, horses are raced on the beach at the mouth of the Río Guadalquivir.

 Colourful flags decorating the streets of Moguer's lovely Old Town

⓫ Palos de la Frontera

🅰B6 🚉 Huelva 🚌
🛈 Parque Botánico José Celestino Mutis Paraje de la Rábida; 959 49 46 64

Columbus set sail for the Americas on 3 August 1492 from Palos, the home town of his captains, brothers Martín and Vicente Pinzón.

The 15th-century Iglesia de San Jorge has a fine portal, through which Columbus left after hearing Mass before boarding the *Santa María*.

On the outskirts of town is the **Muelle de las Carabelas**, which contains replicas of the caravels.

Nearby, in the white town of Moguer, treasures include the 16th-century hermitage of Nuestra Señora de Montemayor, and the Neo-Classical town hall. The **Monasterio de Santa Clara** houses the Museo Diocesano de Arte Sacro.

Muelle de las Carabelas
🌣 🚗 Paraje de La Rábida
☎ 959 530 597 🕐 10am–2pm Mon–Fri

Monasterio de Santa Clara
🌣🌣 🚗 Plaza de las Monjas, Moguer ☎ 959 37 01 07 🕐 By guided tour only; Tue–Sun

EAT

Azabache
Expect innovative versions of local dishes at this Huelva spot. The seafood is fresh and there's an extensive wine list.

🅰B6 🚗 Calle Vázquez Lopez 22, Huelva
🌐 restaurante azabache.com

—

El Bodegón
Try the juicy *solomillo a la brasa* (oak-grilled sirloin steak) at this restaurant in Palos de la Frontera.

🅰B6 🚗 Calle Rábida 46, Palos de la Frontera
☎ 959 53 11 05

—

Aires de Doñana (La Choza del Rocío)
This *choza* (thatched hut) in Almonte is known for its *revuelto marismeño* (scrambled eggs with herbs).

🅰B6 🚗 Avenida de la Canaliega 1, Almonte
☎ 959 44 22 89

→

Parading the Virgin, and *(inset)* Iglesia de Nuestra Señora del Rocío

DRINK

Bodegas Barbadillo

Take a tour of this winery to discover how manzanilla sherry has been made here since 1821, before tasting some of this light, dry drink. You can even buy some bottles in the shop.

🅰B6 🏠Calle de Luis de Eguilaz 11, Sanlúcar de Barrameda 🌐barbadillo.com

The Harbour Bar & Restaurant

As the name suggests, this bar has beautiful views of the boats in Marbella's harbour. Come here for a creative cocktail or a glass of refreshing wine on a scorching day.

🅰C6 🏠1st Floor, Club Maritimo, Puerto Deportivo, Marbella 🌐theharbour marbella.com

12

El Rocío

🅰B6 🏠Huelva 🚌 🛈Calle Muñoz y Pavón s/n; 959 026 602

Bordering the Parque Nacional de Doñana *(p476)*, El Rocío is famous for its annual *romería*, when almost a million people converge on the village. Many of the pilgrims travel from distant parts of Spain, some on gaudily decorated oxcarts, to visit the Iglesia de Nuestra Señora del Rocío, where a statue of the Virgin is said to have performed miraculous healings since 1280. Early on the Monday morning of the festival, men from Almonte fight to carry the statue in procession, and the crowd clambers onto the float to touch the image.

13

Sanlúcar de Barrameda

🅰B6 🏠Cádiz 🚌 🛈Calle Calzada Duquesa Isabel s/n; 956 36 61 10

A delightful fishing port standing at the mouth of the Río Guadalquivir, Sanlúcar is overlooked by a Moorish castle. This was the departure point for Columbus's third voyage in 1498 and also for Magellan's 1519 expedition to circumnavigate the globe.

As well as its connection to the conquistadors, Sanlúcar is also known for its light, dry manzanilla sherry made by historic producers, including Bodegas Barbadillo.

The town is a great base for exploring the Parque Nacional de Doñana *(p476)*. Setting sail from the quay, boats take visitors across the river to this wildlife haven.

Chipiona, located a short way along the coast, is a lively little resort town with an excellent beach. The walled town of Lebrija, inland, enjoys views over vineyards. Its Iglesia de Santa María de la Oliva is a reconsecrated 12th-century Almohad mosque.

14 Jerez de la Frontera

AB6 **A**Cádiz **X**🚂🚌 **i**Plaza del Arenal s/n, Edificio Los Arcos; 956 149 863

Jerez is the capital of sherry production and many *bodegas* can be visited. The city is also famous for its **Real Escuela Andaluza de Arte Ecuestre**, an equestrian school with public displays on Thursdays all year (also Tuesdays March to December and some Fridays in summer). On other days you might be able to see the horses being trained. The **Palacio del Tiempo**, nearby, has one of the largest clock collections in Europe. On the Plaza de San Juan, the 18th-century **Palacio de Penmartín** houses the Centro Andaluz de Flamenco, where exhibitions give a good introduction to this music and dance tradition. The partially restored, 11th-century **Alcázar** encompasses a well-preserved mosque, now a church. Just to the north is the cathedral.

Near Jerez, the Monasterio de la Cartuja Santa María de la Defensión is considered one of the most beautiful in Spain.

To the southwest, the port of El Puerto de Santa María has some *bodegas* and a 13th-century castle.

Real Escuela Andaluza de Arte Ecuestre

⊗ **A**Duque de Abrantes **O**Hours vary, check website **W**realescuela.org

Palacio del Tiempo

⊗ **A**Calle Cervantes 3 **C**956 18 21 00 **O**9:30am-2pm Tue-Sun

Palacio de Penmartín

APlaza de San Juan 1 **C**956 90 21 34 **O**11am-1:30pm & 5-8pm Mon-Fri **C**Public hols

Alcázar

⊗⊗ **A**Alameda Vieja **C**650 80 01 00 **O**Jul-Sep: 9:30am-6pm daily; Oct-Jun: 9:30am-3pm daily **C**1 & 6 Jan, 25 Dec

15 Costa de la Luz

AB6 **A**Cádiz **C**Cádiz 🚌Cádiz, Tarifa **i**Paseo de la Alameda s/n, Tarifa; 956 68 09 93

The Costa de la Luz (Coast of Light), which is between Cádiz and Tarifa at Spain's southernmost tip, is an unspoiled, windswept stretch of coast characterized by strong, pure light – the source of its name. From the Sierra del Cabrito, to the west of Algeciras, it is often possible to see the outline of Tangier and the parched Moroccan landscape below the purple-tinged Rif mountains across the narrow Strait of Gibraltar.

Tarifa is named after an 8th-century Moorish commander, Tarif ben Maluk, who landed there with his forces during the Moorish conquest. Later, Tarifa and its 10th-century castle were defended by the legendary hero Guzmán during a siege by the Moors in 1292.

Tarifa has since become the windsurfing capital of Europe. The breezes that blow onto this coast also drive the many wind turbines on the hills.

Off the N340 (E5), at the end of a long, narrow road which strikes out across a wilderness of cacti, sunflowers and lone cork trees, is Zahara de los Atunes, a modest holiday resort with a few

TOP 5 JEREZ SHERRY BODEGAS

Bodegas Álvaro Domecq
Located in the heart of Jerez de la Frontera, this *bodega* is all stone walls and barrels *(www.alvarodomecq.com)*.

Bodegas La Cigarrera
This *bodega* dates back to 1758 *(www.bodegaslacigarrera.com)*.

Bodegas González Byass - Tio Pepe
A complex of patios and gardens in Jerez *(www.tiopepe.com)*.

Bodegas Osborne
The Osborne bull is seen as the unofficial symbol of Spain *(www.osborne.es)*.

Bodegas Sandeman
A well-known brand founded in 1790 *(www.sandeman.eu)*.

hotels. Conil de la Frontera, a little to the west, is busier and more built up.

Close by, off Cabo de Trafalgar, the English admiral Nelson defeated a Spanish and French fleet in the 1805 Battle of Trafalgar, but died during the battle.

↑ Deserted sandy beach, surrounded by dunes, at Bolonia on the Costa de la Luz

GIBRALTAR CONTROVERSY

Britain seized Gibraltar during the War of the Spanish Succession in 1704, and was granted it "in perpetuity" nine years later. As the gateway to the Mediterranean, "the Rock" was essential to Britain in colonial times, and centuries later, in a 1967 referendum, residents voted overwhelmingly to stay under British rule. Tensions over Gibraltar had eased for a while, but confusion caused by Brexit has stirred up renewed conflict.

 16

Gibraltar

🅰C6 🏛British Overseas Territory 🚌 𝑖The Main Guard, 13 John Mackintosh Square; www.visit gibraltar.gi

The high, rocky headland of Gibraltar was signed over to Britain "in perpetuity" in the Treaty of Utrecht, which ended the War of Spanish Succession in 1713. Today, about 4 million people stream across the border annually from La Línea

de la Concepción in Spain. Among the most notable sights of Gibraltar are those testifying to its strategic military importance over the centuries. Halfway up the famous Rock are an 8th-century Moorish castle, whose **keep** was used as a prison until 2010, and 80 km (50 miles) of **siege tunnels** housing storerooms and barracks. **St Michael's Cave**, which served as a hospital during World War II, is now used for classical concerts.

The **Apes' Den**, near Europa Point, which is Gibraltar's southernmost tip, is home to the tailless apes. Legend says that the British will keep the Rock only as long as the apes remain there.

A cable car takes visitors to the Top of the Rock, at 450 m (1,475 ft). **Gibraltar Museum** charts the colony's history.

The Keep, Siege Tunnels, St Michael's Cave, Apes' Den
♿ 🏛Upper Rock Area
📞(+35) 020 04 59 57
🕐9:30am–7:15pm daily

Gibraltar Museum
♿ 🏛18 Bombhouse Lane
🕐10am–6pm Mon–Fri, 10am–2pm Sat ⛔Public hols 🌐gibmuseum.gi

The Rock of Gibraltar, towering over yachts ↓ in the harbour

 17

Algeciras

🅰C6 🏛Cádiz 🚌 𝑖Paseo Río de la Miel s/n; 670 94 87 31

From the industrial city of Algeciras, there are spectacular views of Gibraltar. The city is a major fishing port and Europe's main gateway for ferries to North Africa, especially Tangier and Spain's territories of Ceuta and Melilla.

 18

Marbella

🅰C6 🏛Málaga 🚌 𝑖Glorieta de la Fontanilla, Paseo Marítimo; www. turismo.marbella.es

This resort is frequented by royalty and film stars. There are 24 beaches, including Playa Rio Verde and Playa Nagueles.

Among the delights of the Old Town, with its alleys, squares, shops and restaurants, is the Iglesia de Nuestra Señora de la Encarnación. The **Museo del Grabado Español Contemporáneo** displays some of Pablo Picasso's least-known work.

West along the coast, Puerto Banús is Marbella's ostentatious marina. The expensive shops, restaurants and glittering nightlife reflect the wealth of its clientele.

In complete constrast to Marbella, 31 km (19 miles) southwest, the quiet resort town of Estepona is popular with families with young children. This is most evident early evening, when families gather on the palm-lined promenade. Back behind the coastal road, old squares are shaded by orange trees and retain a charming Spanish atmosphere. At one end of town is a stylish marina with waterside restaurants, beyond which villa complexes stretch out along the coast.

Many golf courses dot the landscape between Marbella and Estepona and are popular all year round.

Museo del Grabado Español Contemporáneo

 Calle Hospital Bazan 9am–2pm Mon & Sat, 9am–7pm Tue–Fri mgec.es

---

19

Arcos de la Frontera

B6 Cádiz Calle Cuesta de Belén 5; 956 70 22 64

Although legend has it that a son of Noah founded Arcos, it was in fact the Iberians. It gained the name Arcobriga in the Roman era and, under the Caliphate of Córdoba, became the Moorish stronghold of Medina Arkosh.

↑ Customers enjoying the view over Arcos de la Frontera from a hotel terrace

It is an archetypal white town, with a labyrinthine old quarter.

On the Plaza de España are the parador and the Iglesia de Santa María de la Asunción, a late Gothic-Mudéjar building noted for its choir stalls and altarpiece. The huge, Gothic Iglesia de San Pedro, perched on the edge of a cliff formed by the Río Guadalete, is a striking building. Nearby is the **Palacio del Mayorazgo**, which has a highly elaborate Renaissance façade. The **ayuntamiento** features a fine Mudéjar ceiling.

In the 15th century the Guzmán family was granted the dukedom of Medina Sidonia, a white town west of Arcos de la Frontera. The area became one of the most important ducal seats in Spain. The Gothic Iglesia de Santa María la Coronada is the town's finest building. It contains a notable collection of Renaissance religious art.

Palacio del Mayorazgo

Calle Nuñez del Prado 956 70 30 13 (Casa de Cultura) 10:30am–1:30pm Mon–Fri, 11am–2pm Sat & Sun

Ayuntamiento

Plaza del Cabildo 947 40 53 32 Mon–Fri, call to check

STAY

Hotel Fuerte

Marbella's very first purpose-built luxury hotel features lush gardens and two outdoor pools, as well as a fitness centre with an indoor pool. It's located close to the beach.

C6 Calle El Fuerte, Marbella fuerte hoteles.com

€€€

Casa Grande

A whitewashed 18th-century mansion on a hill in Arcos de la Frontera, offering great views of the country-side below. Each room is decorated differently, but they are all furnished with gorgeous antiques .

B6 Calle Maldonaldo 10, Arcos de la Frontera lacasagrande.net

€€€

→

People taking in the weathered limestone formations of El Torcal

⑳ El Torcal

C6 🏛Málaga
🚉🚌Antequera
ℹ Antequera; www. torcaldeantequera.com

A massive hump of limestone, which has been weathered into bizarre rock formations and caves, the **Parque Natural del Torcal** is popular with hikers. Marked trails lead from a visitors' centre. The park has fox and weasel populations, colonies of eagles, hawks and vultures, and rare plants and flowers like wild orchids.

Parque Natural del Torcal
☎ 952 24 33 24 ⏱10am–5pm daily (to 7pm Apr–Sep)

㉑ Garganta del Chorro

C6 🏛Málaga 🚉El Chorro
🚌Parque Ardeles ℹ Plaza Fuente de Arriba 15, Álora; 952 06 21 36

Up the fertile Guadalhorce Valley, beyond the village of El Chorro, is a geographical wonder. The Garganta del Chorro is an immense chasm, 180 m (590 ft) deep and in places only 10 m (30 ft) wide, cut by the river through a limestone mountain.

Álora, a classic Andalucían white town with a ruined Moorish castle and an 18th-century church, lies 12 km (7 miles) down the valley.

Along the twisting MA441 from Álora is the village of Carratraca. In the 19th and early 20th centuries, Europe's highest society travelled here for the healing powers of the sulphurous springs. These days, Carratraca has a faded glory – water still gushes out at 700 litres (155 UK and 185 US gal) a minute and the outdoor baths remain open, but they are little used.

> GREAT VIEW
> **Walk This Way**
>
> Take a walk on the Caminito del Rey, a 100-m- (328-ft-) high walkway, clinging to the rock face, which leads to a bridge across the Garganta del Chorro (www.caminitodel rey.info). It's not for sufferers of vertigo!

㉒ Antequera

C6 🏛Málaga 🚉🚌
ℹ Calle Encarnación 4; www.antequera.es

This busy market town was strategically important first as Roman Anticaria and later as a Moorish border fortress defending Granada.

Of its many churches, the Iglesia de Nuestra Señora del Carmen, with its vast Baroque altarpiece, is not to be missed.

The hilltop castle was built in the 13th century on the site of a Roman fort. Walk round the castle walls starting from the 16th-century Arco de los Gigantes. Enjoy the views of Antequera from the Torre del Papabellotas on the best-preserved part of the wall.

In the town below, the 18th-century **Palacio de Nájera** is the setting for the Municipal Museum - the star exhibit is a Roman bronze statue of a boy. The massive dolmens, just

outside the town, are thought to be the burial chambers of tribal leaders and date from around 2500–2000 BC.

Laguna de la Fuente de Piedra, north of Antequera, teems with bird life, including huge flocks of flamingos, which arrive to breed after wintering in West Africa.

Palacio de Nájera
⊛ ⌂ Coso Viejo 📞 952 70 83 00 🕑 Jul-Sep: 9am-2pm Tue-Sun; Oct-Jun: 10am-2pm & 4:30-6:30pm Tue-Sat, 9:30am-2pm Sun

㉓
Málaga
🄰 C6 ⌂ Málaga
🛈 Plaza de la Marina 11;
www.malagaturismo.com

The second-largest city in Andalucía, Málaga, is a thriving port, as it has been since Phoenician times. It also flourished during the 19th century, when sweet Málaga wine was one of Europe's most popular drinks – until phylloxera ravaged its vineyards in 1876.

The cathedral, begun in 1528 by Diego de Siloé, is a bizarre mix of styles. The half-built second tower gave the cathedral its nickname: La Manquita ("the one-armed one").

The **Museo Picasso Málaga** displays works by the local artist, while the Casa Natal de Picasso, where the painter spent his early years, is now the Picasso Foundation. The **Centre Pompidou Málaga** has a good collection of modern and contemporary artworks.

←

The multicoloured, glass-cube building housing the Centre Pompidou Málaga

EAT

El Tintero II
A beachside seafood restaurant in Málaga with no menu – just point at the dishes you fancy when the waiters pass by with their laden trays.

🄰 C6 ⌂ Avenida Salvador Allende 340 (El Palo), Málaga 📞 952 20 68 26

€€€

Mesón Astorga
This classical Malagueeño restaurant serves dishes prepared from fresh market produce. Try the fried aubergine with sugarcane honey.

🄰 C6 ⌂ Calle Gerona 11, Málaga 🅦 meson astorga.com

€€€

Málaga's vast Alcazaba was built between the 8th and 11th centuries. There is a partially excavated Roman amphitheatre by its entrance. Housed in the Palacio de la Aduana, the Museo de Málaga displays archaeological artifacts, including some from the site.

On the hill directly behind the Alcazaba are the ruins of the Castillo de Gibralfaro, a 14th-century Moorish castle.

Museo Picasso Málaga
⊛ ⌂ Calle San Agustín 8 🕑 Hours vary, check website 🗓 1 Jan, 25 Dec 🅦 museo picassomalaga.org

Centre Pompidou Málaga
⌂ Pasaje Doctor Carillo Casaux s/n, Muelle Uno 🕑 9:30am-8pm Wed-Mon 🅦 centrepompidou-malaga.eu

SHOP

Barro de Palma

Stocking Palma del Río's best ceramics, metal-work and screen prints, this is a must-shop. You can also make your own souvenir at one of Barro de Palma's popular ceramic workshops.

B5 ⬒Poligono Industrial Matacaché II 67-68, Palma del Río ⬒barrodepalma.com

---

Alfajar

This light and airy space is the perfect backdrop for Alfajar's characterful ceramics. You can even take a workshop with one of Alfajar's artisans to try your hand at throwing a pot for yourself.

⬒C6 ⬒Calle Císter 1, Málaga ⬒alfajar.es

㉔

Palma del Río

⬒C5 ⬒Córdoba ⬒⬒
ⓘPlaza Mayor de Andalucía s/n; www.palmadelrio.es

The Romans sited a strategic settlement here, on the road between Córdoba and Itálica, almost 2,000 years ago. The remains of the 12th-century city walls are a reminder of the town's frontier days under the Almohads (p449).

The Iglesia de la Asunción, a Baroque church, dates from the 18th century. The Monasterio de San Francisco is now a hotel, and guests can eat dinner in the 15th-century refectory here.

Palma del Río is the home town of El Cordobés, one of Spain's most famous matadors. His biography, *Or I'll Dress You in Mourning,*

↑ Mosaic floor in the Planetarium House at the Roman ruins of Itálica

paints a vivid picture of life in the town and of the hardship which followed the end of the Civil War.

One of the most dramatic silhouettes in Southern Spain is that of the **Castillo de Almodóvar del Río**. The Moorish castle – parts of it dating from the 8th century – stands on a hilltop overlooking the whitewashed town and fields of cotton.

Castillo de Almodóvar del Río

 ⬒11am–2:30pm Mon-Fri, 11am–7pm Sat & Sun ⬒castillodealmodovar.com

---

㉕

Itálica

⬒B6 ⬒Avenida de Extremadura 2, Santiponce, Seville ⬒600 14 17 67 ⬒From Seville ⬒9am–6pm Tue-Sat (Apr–mid-Jun: to 8pm; mid-Jun–mid-Sep: to 3pm), 9am–3pm Sun

Itálica was founded in 206 BC by Scipio Africanus and it grew to become important in the 2nd and 3rd centuries AD. Emperor Hadrian, who was born in the city and reigned from AD 117–138, added marble temples and other grand buildings.

Next to the vast but crumbling amphitheatre is a display of finds from the site.

Traces of Itálica's streets and the mosaic floors of villas can be seen, but little remains of the city's temples or its baths, as most of the stone and marble has been plundered over the centuries.

㉖

Osuna

⬒C6 ⬒Seville ⬒⬒ ⓘCalle Sevilla 37; 954 81 57 32

Osuna was once a key Roman garrison town. It rose again to prominence in the 16th century under the Dukes of Osuna, who wielded immense power. In the 1530s they founded the Colegiata de Santa María, a grand church with a Baroque reredos and paintings by José de Ribera. This was followed in 1548 by the university, a rather severe building with a beautiful patio. Some fine mansions, among them the Palacio del Marqués de la Gomera, also reflect the town's former glory.

To the east lies Estepa, whose modern-day fame rests on its biscuits – *polvorones* and *mantecados*. The Iglesia del Carmen has a black and white, Baroque façade.

→

Alcázar del Rey Pedro, a major landmark at the heart of Carmona

Sierra Morena

🅐C5 🅐Seville & Córdoba
🅡Cazalla, Constantina
🚌Cazalla, Constantina
🛈Plaza Doctor Nosea 1,
Cazalla; www.cazalla.org;
Calle Venero s/n,
Constantina; www.
constantina.org

The Sierra Morena, clad in oak and pine woods, runs across the north of the provinces of Seville and Córdoba. It forms a natural frontier between Andalucía and the plains of neighbouring Extremadura and La Mancha. In 2014, the Sierra was declared a UNESCO Starlight Reserve and the Milky Way spans the night sky.

Fuente Obejuna, north of Córdoba, was immortalized by Lope de Vega (p331) in his play about an uprising in 1476 against a local overlord. The Iglesia de San Juan Bautista in Hinojosa del Duque is a vast church in both Gothic and Renaissance styles. Belalcázar is dominated by the tower of a ruined 15th-century castle.

Storks nest on the church towers of the plateau of Valle de los Pedroches, to the east.

㉘
Carmona

🅐C6 🅐Seville 🚌 🛈Alcázar de la Puerta de Seville; www.turismo.carmona.org

The first major town east of Seville, Carmona's old quarter is built on a hill above the suburbs on the plain. Beyond the Puerta de Sevilla, a gateway in the Moorish city walls, is a dense cluster of mansions, and Mudéjar churches.

The Plaza de San Fernando is characterized by the Renaissance façade of the old **ayuntamiento**. The present town hall, set just off the square, dates from the 18th century; in its courtyard are some Roman mosaics. Close by is the Iglesia de Santa María la Mayor. Built in the 15th century over a mosque, whose patio still survives, this is the finest of Carmona's churches.

Dominating the town are the ruins of the Alcázar del

Did You Know?

Geoffrey Chaucer laments Pedro the Cruel's death in *The Monk's Tale*.

Rey Pedro, once a palace of Pedro I, known as Pedro the Cruel. Parts of it now form a parador.

Just outside Carmona is the **Necrópolis Romana**, the extensive remains of a Roman burial ground. A site museum displays some of the items found in the graves, including statues, glass and jewellery.

Ayuntamiento

🅐Calle Salvador 2 📞954 14 0011 🕙9am-2pm Mon-Fri 🚫Public hols

Necrópolis Romana

🅐Avenida Jorge Bonsor 9 📞600 14 36 32 🕙Apr & May: 9am-8pm Tue-Fri, 10am-8pm Sat, 10am-5pm Sun; Jun-mid-Sep: 9am-3:30pm Tue-Fri, 10am-3:30pm Sat, 10am-5pm Sun; mid-Sep-Mar: 9am-6:30pm Tue-Sat, 10am-5pm Sun 🚫1 Jan, 1 May & 25 Dec

↑ The columns and arches of the House of Y'far at the Medina Azahara

Medina Azahara

🅰C5 🅰Córdoba ⏱Hours vary, check website
🅆medinaazahara.org

Just a few kilometres north of Córdoba lies this once glorious palace. Built in the 10th century for Caliph Abd al Rahman III, it is named after his favourite wife, Azahara. He spared no expense, employing more than 15,000 mules, 4,000 camels and 10,000 workers to bring building materials from as far as North Africa.

The palace is built on three levels and includes a mosque, the caliph's residence and fine gardens. Marble, ebony, jasper and alabaster once adorned the Medina Azahara's many halls, and it is believed that shimmering pools of quicksilver added lustre.

The glory was short-lived. The palace was sacked by Berber invaders in 1010 and over subsequent centuries it was ransacked for its building materials. Now, the ruins give only glimpses of its former beauty – a Moorish main hall, for instance, decorated with marble carvings and a carved wood ceiling. The palace is currently being restored.

Visiting in spring or summer? Book a nighttime visit for a magical experience.

> **Marble, ebony, jasper and alabaster once adorned the Medina Azahara's many halls, and it is believed that shimmering pools of quicksilver added lustre.**

Écija

🅰C5 🅰Seville 🚌 ℹCalle Elvira 1-A, Palacio de Benamejí; www.turismo ecija.com

Écija is nicknamed "the frying pan of Andalucía" owing to its famously torrid climate. In the searing heat, the palm trees on the Plaza de España provide blissful shade and this is the ideal place to sit as well as for evening strolls.

Écija has 11 Baroque church steeples, many adorned with gleaming *azulejos* (p454). The most florid of these is the Iglesia de Santa María, which overlooks the Plaza de España, with the Iglesia de San Juan coming a close second.

Of the many mansions along Calle Emilio Castelar, the Baroque **Palacio de Peñaflor** is well worth a visit. Its pink marble doorway is topped by twisted columns and it has a wrought-iron balcony.

Palacio de Peñaflor
🅰Calle Emilio Castelar 26
📞747 86 72 02 ⏱10am-1:30pm & 4:30-6:30pm Mon, Tue-Fri by appt, 10am-2pm & 5:30-8pm Sat, 11am-2pm Sun

→ The ornate Baroque steeple of the Iglesia de San Juan, Écija

↑ Fuente del Rey, a beautiful sight at the end of Calle del Río in Priego de Córdoba

 31

Priego de Córdoba

C6 **Córdoba** 🚌 **ℹ Plaza de la Constitución 3; www. turismodepriego.com**

Priego de Córdóba's claim to be the capital of Cordoban Baroque is borne out by the dazzling work of carvers, ironworkers and gilders in the many houses, and especially churches, built with wealth generated by a prosperous 18th-century silk industry.

A restored Moorish fortress stands in the whitewashed medieval quarter, the Barrio de la Villa. Close by is the outstanding Iglesia de la Asunción, converted from Gothic to Baroque style by Jerónimo Sánchez de Rueda. Its pièce de résistance is the sacristy, created in 1784 by local artist Francisco Javier Pedrajas. The main altar is Plateresque.

At midnight every Saturday the brotherhood of another Baroque church, the Iglesia de la Aurora, parades the streets loudly singing songs in praise of the Virgin.

Silk merchants built many of the mansions that follow the curve around the Calle del Río. At the street's end is the Baroque Fuente del Rey (King's Fountain). The spouts splash water into three basins adorned with a riot of statuary.

Zuheros, which is perched on a crag in the limestone hills northwest of Priego, is one of Andalucía's prettiest villages.

 32

Montilla

C5 **Córdoba** 🚉🚌 **ℹ Calle Iglesia s/n (in the castle); 957 65 23 54**

Montilla is the centre of an important wine region that produces an excellent smooth white fino. Unlike sherry, it is not fortified. Several *bodegas*, including **Alvear**, the oldest *bodega* in Andalucía, and **Pérez Barquero** will show visitors around by prior arrangement.

The Mudéjar Convento de Santa Clara dates from 1512. The town library is in the Casa del Inca, so named because Garcilaso de la Vega, who wrote about the Incas, lived there in the 1500s.

Overlooking the town is the medieval castle, which houses the tourist office.

Bodega Alvear
Ⓧ 🏠 María Auxiliadora 1 Ⓓ By appt 🔗 alvear.es

Bodega Pérez Barquero
Ⓧ Ⓧ 🏠 Avenida de Andalucía 27 Ⓓ Daily by appt ✖ Aug 🔗 perezbarquero.com

DRINK

Bar Goya
Carmona's oldest bar is set in a 15th-century building but with a thoroughly modern pale blue and crimson paint job.

B6 **Calle Prim 2, Carmona** 🔗 goya tapas.com

Copa Vino
A Swedish-owned bar in Nerja, with a long list of wines available by the glass and colourful oil paintings on display.

C6 **Calle de Almirante Ferrándiz 60, Nerja** 📞 633 95 57 50

Bodegas Lagar Blanco
The owner of this small Montilla *bodega* takes visitors on a tour of the vineyard before pouring out glasses of sherry for tasting.

C5 **Carretera de Cuesta Blanca, km 4, Montilla** 🔗 lagarblanco.es

STAY

Parador de Carmona
This fortress in Carmona is decorated with tapestries and antiques.

B6 Calle Alcazar, Carmona Wparador.es

€€€

Hotel Carabeo
A lovely Nerja hotel, with a leafy pool area, furnished with antiques and artworks.

C6 Calle Hernando de Carabeo 34, Nerja Whotelcarabeo.com

€€€

Hotel Catedral
Almería's 19th-century manor house has large rooms, featuring coffered ceilings.

D6 Plaza de la Catedral 8, Almería Whotelcatedral.net

€€€

33
Lanjarón

D6 Granada
Avenida de Madrid s/n; www.lanjaron.es

Scores of clear, snow-fed springs bubble from the slopes of the Sierra Nevada (p515); their abundance at Lanjarón, on the southern side of this great range of mountains, has given the town a long history as a health spa. From June to October, visitors flock to take the waters for arthritic, dietary and nervous ailments. Bottled water from Lanjarón is sold all over the country throughout the year.

The town's major festival begins on the night of 23 June and ends in an uproarious water battle in the early hours of 24 June, the Día de San Juan. Everyone in the streets gets doused.

The town is on the threshold of Las Alpujarras, a scenic upland area of dramatic landscapes, where steep, terraced hillsides and deep-cut valleys conceal remote, whitewashed villages. Roads to and from Lanjarón wind slowly and dizzily around the slopes.

↑ Visitors admiring the stalactites in a cavern at the Cuevas de Nerja

34
Nerja

C6 Málaga Calle Carmen 1; www.nerja.org

Built on a cliff above sandy coves, the town of Nerja lies at the foot of the Sierra de Almijara. East of the town are the **Cuevas de Nerja**, a series of caverns discovered in 1959. Wall paintings found here are

Europe's Balcony

The Balcón de Europa is a rounded esplanade atop a promontory at the heart of Nerja. Jutting out into the sea, it has views up and down the coast.

believed to be about 20,000 years old. Only a few of the many cathedral-sized chambers are open to the public. One of them has been converted into a vast auditorium.

Cuevas de Nerja

⊘⊛ 🅰 Carretera de las Cuevas de Nerja 🕔 Jul & Aug: 9am–6:30pm daily; Sep–Jun: 9am–4pm daily 🔒 1 Jan, 15 May 🔳 cuevadenerja.es

---

35

Almuñécar

🅰 C6 🅰 Granada 🚌 🅸 Avda Europa; www. almunecarinfo.com

Almuñécar lies on the Costa Tropical, so named because its climate allows the cultivation

of exotic fruit. The Phoenicians founded the first settlement on this fertile land, called Sexi, and the Romans constructed an aqueduct, the remains of which can be seen today. Almuñécar is now a popular holiday resort.

Above the Old Town is the castle, built by the Moors and altered in the 1500s. Below it is the **Museo Arqueológico Cueva de Siete Palacios**, which displays a variety of Phoenician artifacts.

The ancient white town of Salobreña, 31 km (19 miles) southeast of Almuñécar, is set amid fields of sugar cane. Narrow streets lead up a hill to the **Castillo de Salobreña,** which has wonderful views of the Sierra Nevada (*p515*).

Museo Arqueológico Cueva de Siete Palacios

⊛ 🅰 Calle Cueva de Siete Palacios s/n 🄲 607 86 54 66 🕔 10am–1:30pm & 5–7:30pm Tue–Sat, 10am–1pm Sun (Jul–mid-Sep: 6:30–9pm Tue–Sat; Nov–Mar: 4–6:30pm Tue–Sat)

Castillo de Salobreña

⊘⊛ 🅰 Calle Andrés Segovia 🄲 958 61 03 14 🕔 Hours vary, call ahead 🔒 1 Jan, 24, 25 & 31 Dec

---

 36

Montefrío

🅰 C6 🅰 Granada 🚌 🅸 Plaza España 1; www. turismomontefrio.org

The approach to Montefrío from the south offers wonderful views of tiled rooftops and pretty whitewashed houses. This archetypal Andalucían town is topped by the remains of its Moorish fortifications and the 16th-century Gothic Iglesia de la Villa. In the centre of town is the Neo-Classical Iglesia de la Encarnación, designed by Ventura Rodríguez (1717–85). The town is known for its chorizo, as well as its numerous stone crosses, thought to have been constructed in the 16th and 17th centuries.

Santa Fé, 44 km (27 miles) southeast of Montefrío, was built by the Catholic Monarchs at the end of the 15th century. Their army camped here while laying siege to Granada, and this was the site of the formal surrender of the Moors in 1492.

About 40 km (25 miles) south of Montefrío, Loja is known as "the city of water" because of its natural springs.

← Moorish fortifications overlooking whitewashed houses at Montefrío

→

Looking down on the cave dwellings in the troglodyte quarter of Guadix

37

Guadix

 D6 Granada Avenida de la Constitución 15-18; www.guadix.es

The troglodyte quarter, with its 2,000 caves, is Guadix's most remarkable sight. White air vents are one of the only indications of the dwellings below. The **Centro de Interpretación Cuevas de Guadix** and **Cueva Museo de Alfarería la Alcazaba** explore how people live underground.

Centro de Interpretación Cuevas de Guadix

 Plaza de Ermita Nueva s/n 958 66 55 69 10am–2pm & 4–6pm Mon–Fri, 10am–2pm Sat & public hols

---

HIDDEN GEM
Lady of Baza

Impressive evidence of ancient cultures based around the town of Baza, 45 km (28 miles) northeast of Guadix, came to light when a large, seated, female figure was found in a necropolis. She is the Dama de Baza, estimated to be 2,400 years old.

Cueva Museo de Alfarería la Alcazaba

 Calle San Miguel 47 958 66 47 67 10am–2pm & 4:30–8pm daily

38

Laujar de Andarax

D6 Almería Carretera AL-5402 Laujar-Berja, km 1; 950 51 55 35

Situated in the arid foothills of the Sierra Nevada, Laujar looks southwards across the Andarax Valley towards the Sierra de Gádor.

Inside Laujar's 17th-century church, La Encarnación, is a statue of the Virgin by Alonso Cano. Next to the Baroque *ayuntamiento* is a fountain inscribed with some lines written by Francisco Villespesa, a dramatist and poet who was born in Laujar in 1877: "Six fountains has my *pueblo*/He who drinks their waters/will never forget them/so heavenly is their taste." As well as the waters, you can try the area's hearty red wines.

Ohanes, above the Andarax valley further to the east, is an attractive hill town of steep streets and whitewashed houses known for its crops of table grapes.

Did You Know?

Legend has it that Laujar was founded by one of Noah's grandsons.

39

Castillo de La Calahorra

 D6 La Calahorra, Granada 958 67 70 98 Guadix Wed, by appt

Grim, immensely thick walls and stout, cylindrical corner towers protect this castle, which Rodrigo de Mendoza, son of Cardinal Mendoza, had built for his bride between 1509 and 1512. Inside is an ornate, arcaded Renaissance courtyard with pillars and a Carrara marble staircase.

40

Jaén

C5 Jaén Calle Maestra 8; www.turjaen.org

The Moors called Jaén *Geen* – meaning "way station of

caravans" – because of its strategic site on the road between Andalucía and Castile. Their hilltop fortress was rebuilt as the **Castillo de Santa Catalina** after it was captured by King Fernando III in 1246. It is now a parador.

Andrés de Vandelvira, who was responsible for many of Úbeda's fine buildings (p488), designed Jaén's cathedral in the 16th century. Later additions include two 17th-century towers that now flank the west front.

An old mansion, the **Palacio Villardompardo**, houses a museum of arts and crafts, and also gives access to the Baños Árabes, the 11th-century baths of Ali, a Moorish chieftain. These have horseshoe arches, ceilings with star-shaped windows and two ceramic vats in which bathers once immersed themselves. Tucked away in an alley is the Capilla de San Andrés, a Mudéjar chapel founded in the 16th century by Gutiérrez González who, as treasurer to Pope Leo X, was endowed with privileges. A gilded iron screen by Maestro Bartolomé de Jaén is the highlight of the chapel.

The Real Monasterio de Santa Clara was founded in the 13th century and has a lovely cloister dating from the late 16th century. Its church, which has a coffered ceiling, contains a bamboo image of Christ made in Ecuador.

The **Museo Provincial** displays Roman mosaics and sculptures, and Iberian, Greek and Roman ceramics.

Castillo de Santa Catalina
 Camino del Castillo
📞 953 12 07 33 🕐 Jul-Sep: 10am-2pm & 5-9pm Mon-Sat, 10am-3pm Sun; Oct-Jun: 10am-6pm Mon-Sat, 10am-3pm Sun 🚫 1 Jan, 24, 25 & 31 Dec

Palacio Villardompardo
 Plaza Santa Luisa de Marillac 📞 953 24 80 68
🕐 9am-10pm Tue-Sat, 9am-3pm Sun 🚫 Public hols

Museo Provincial
 Paseo de la Estación 29
📞 953 10 13 66 🕐 Jul & Aug: 9am-3pm Tue-Sun; Sep-Jun: 9am-9pm Tue-Sat, 9am-3pm Sun 🚫 1 Jan, 1 May, 25 Dec

---

 41

Sierra Nevada

 D6 🚌 Granada 🚍 From Granada ℹ️ Plaza de Andalucía, Cetursa Sierra Nevada; www.sierra nevada.es

Fourteen peaks more than 3,000 m (9,800 ft) high crown the Sierra Nevada mountain range. The snow lingers on these slopes until July and begins falling again in late autumn, making it a great place to hit the slopes. One of Europe's highest roads, the A395, runs past Solynieve, an expanding ski resort, whose name means "sun and snow", at 2,100 m (6,890 ft), and skirts the two highest peaks, Pico Veleta at 3,398 m (11,149 ft) and Mulhacén at 3,482 m (11,420 ft).

Both the Sierra's proximity to the Mediterranean and its altitude account for the diversity of the indigenous flora and fauna found on its slopes. Look out for golden eagles and rare butterflies.

EAT

Meson Leandro
Set in a lovely city bordering the Parque Natural de Cazorla, this restaurant is renowned for its *carne a la piedra* (stone-baked meat).

 D5 Calle Hoz 3, Cazorla 🌐 meson leandro.com

€€€

Taberna Don Sancho
A lively *taberna* in Jaén serving up imaginative versions of traditional dishes. Ask for the grilled octopus – it's divine.

 C5 Avenida de Andalucía 17, Jaén
📞 953 27 51 21

€€€

Restaurante Valentin
This *marisquería* (restaurant specializing in shellfish) in Almería has been given a nod by the Michelin Guide. Everything is market-fresh.

 D6 Calle Tenor Iribarne 19, Almería
🌐 restaurante valentin.es

€€€

→

Skiers taking to the slopes at a resort in the Sierra Nevada

Walking trail through wonderful scenery in the Parque Natural de Cazorla

Castillo de la Yedra

 🏰 Camino del Castillo, Cazorla ☎ 953 10 14 02 🕐 Jul & Aug: 9am–3pm Tue–Sun; Sep–Jun: 9am–9pm Tue–Sat, 9am–3pm Sun 🕐 1 Jan, 17 Sep, 24, 25 & 31 Dec

---

43

Mojácar

🗺 D6 🏙 Almería 🚌 ℹ Plaza del Frontón 1; www.mojacar.es

From a distance, Mojácar shimmers like the mirage of a Moorish citadel, its white houses cascading over a lofty ridge, 2 km (1 mile) inland from long, sandy beaches.

The village is actually made up of two distinct areas: Mojácar Pueblo (town) and Mojácar Playa (beach). Following the Civil War, Mojácar fell into ruin as most of its inhabitants emigrated, but in the 1960s it was discovered by tourists, giving rise to a new era of prosperity. The old gateway still remains, but otherwise the village has been completely rebuilt, and holiday complexes have grown up along the nearby beaches.

The coast south from Mojácar is among the least built up in Spain, with only small resorts and villages along its length.

42

Parque Natural de Cazorla

🗺 D5 🏙 Jaén 🚌 Cazorla ℹ Plaza de Santa María, Cazorla; www.cazorla.es

This 2,150-sq-km (830-sq-mile) natural park's full name is the Parque Natural de Cazorla, Segura y Las Villas. First-time visitors will be amazed by its abundant wildlife and spectacular scenery of thickly wooded mountains rising to peaks of 2,000 m (6,500 ft).

Access to the park is via whitewashed Cazorla. Among this charming city's many draws is its imposing Moorish **Castillo de la Yedra**, which now houses a folklore museum, and its annual blues festival, which takes place over a few days in July.

From Cazorla, the road winds upwards beneath the ruins of the clifftop castle at La Iruela. After crossing a pass, it then drops down to a crossroads (El Empalme del Valle) in the valley of the Río Guadalquivir. Roads here lead to the river's source and to the quiet modern parador.

If you enjoyed Cazorla's offering, there is also a well-restored Moorish castle at Segura de la Sierra, 30 km (19 miles) from the reserve's northern edge.

CAZORLA WILDLIFE

More than 100 bird species live in this nature reserve, some very rare, such as the golden eagle and the griffon vulture. Cazorla is the only habitat in Spain, apart from the Pyrenees, where the lammergeier lives. Mammals in the park include the otter - active at dawn and dusk - mouflon and wild boar, and a small remaining population of Spanish ibex. The red deer was reintroduced in 1952. Among the flora supported by the limestone geology is the indigenous *Viola cazorlensis*.

44

Cástulo

🅰C5 🅰Carreta Linares-Torreblascopedro (JV-3003), km 3.3 🕐Apr-mid-Jun: 9am-9pm Tue-Sat, 9am-3pm Sun; mid-Jun-mid-Sep: 9am-3pm Tue-Sun; mid-Sep-Mar: 9am-6pm Tue-Sat, 9am-3pm Sun 📅1 & 6 Jan, 24, 25 & 31 Dec 🆆museosdeandalucia.es

The ancient city of Cástulo features relics from as far back as 3000 BC, or the Neolithic period. However, most of its remains – a necropolis, an underground water storage system and residential quarters, including a synagogue – date from the Iberian and Roman civilizations.

After exploring the remains, take in the Monographic Archaeological Museum of Cástulo, which explores the history of the site.

45

Vélez Blanco

🅰D5 🅰Almería 🚌Vélez Rubio 🇮Avenida Marqués de los Vélez; 950 41 95 85

The mighty Castillo de Vélez Blanco was built between 1506 and 1513 by the first Marquis de Los Vélez. The Renaissance interiors are now displayed in the Metropolitan Museum in New York, but there is a reconstruction of one of the patios.

Just outside, the **Cueva de los Letreros** contains paintings from around 4000 BC. One depicts the Indalo, a figure holding a rainbow, which has been adopted as the symbol of Almería.

Cueva de los Letreros

 🅰Camino de la Cueva de los Letreros 📞694 46 71 36 🕐By guided tour only at 4:30pm Wed, Sat & public hols, noon Sun (Jun-Aug at 7pm only); book ahead

46

Andújar

🅰C5 🅰Jaén 🚆🚌 🇮Plaza Santa María Torre del Reloj; 953 50 49 59

Andújar stands on the site of an Iberian town, Iliturgi, which was destroyed in the Punic Wars (*p62*) by Scipio. The Romans built the 15-arch bridge spanning the Río Guadalquivir.

In the central square is the Gothic Iglesia de San Miguel, with paintings by Alonso Cano. The Iglesia de Santa María la Mayor has a Mudéjar tower. Inside it is El Greco's *Christ in the Garden of Olives* (c 1605). In April, people make the 23-km (14-mile) pilgrimage from here to the Santuario de la Virgen de la Cabeza.

Some 29 km (18 miles) northeast of Andújar is the town of Baños de la Encina. On a hill, its fortress stands out thanks to its 15 towers, built in AD 967. Scattered below is a sea of white, red-roofed houses, dominated by a stone church. Further north, the road and railway between Madrid and Andalucía squeeze through a spectacular gorge in the eastern reaches of the Sierra Morena, the Desfiladero de Despeñaperros.

> **From a distance, Mojácar shimmers like the mirage of a Moorish citadel, its white houses cascading over a lofty ridge, 2 km (1 mile) inland from long, sandy beaches.**

↑ Santuario de la Virgen de la Cabeza, near Andújar

Almería

🅐D6 🅐Almería 🅧
🅡🅡 Estación Intermodal
🅘 Parque Nicolás Salmerón;
**www.turismode
almeria.org**

Almería's colossal **Alcazaba**, dating from AD 995, is the largest fortress built by the Moors in Spain. The huge structure bears witness to the city's Golden Age, when it was an important port under the Caliphate of Córdoba, exporting brocade, silk and cotton.

During the *reconquista*, the Alcazaba withstood two major sieges before falling to the armies of the Catholic Monarchs *(p62)* in 1489. The royal coat of arms can be seen on the Torre del Homenaje, built during their reign.

Adjacent to the Alcazaba is the old fishermen's and Romany quarter of La Chanca, where some families live in caves with painted façades.

SHOP

La Jarapa

This is *the* place to buy one of Níjar's ubiquitous rugs. La Jarapa stocks a huge range of designs made in every colour under the sun.

**🅐D6 🅐Avenida
Federico García Lorca
62, Níjar 🅦lajarapa.com**

Mercado Central de Almería

A great place to soak up local life, this lively food market provides the perfect introduction to Almería's gastronomy.

**🅐D6 🅐Calle
Circunvalación Ulpiano
Díaz 14, Almería 🅒950
25 84 53**

Berber pirates from North Africa often raided Almería. Consequently, the cathedral looks almost like a castle, with its four towers, thick walls and small windows. The site was originally a mosque. This was converted into a church, but in 1522 it was destroyed in an earthquake. Work on the present building began in 1524 under the direction of Diego de Siloé, who designed the nave and high altar in Gothic style. The Renaissance façade and the carved walnut choir stalls are by Juan de Orea. Traces of Moorish Almería's most important mosque can be seen elsewhere in the Templo San Juan.

The Plaza Vieja is an attractive 17th-century arcaded square. On one side is the *ayuntamiento*, with a cream and pink façade (1899). In Calle Real, the **Castillo de Tabernas Museo del Aceite de Oliva** illustrates the fine art of making olive oil.

One of Europe's most important examples of a Copper Age settlement is located at **Los Millares**, near Gádor, 17 km (11 miles) north of Almería. As many as 2,000 people may have occupied the site around 2500 BC.

Alcazaba

⊛ 🅐Calle Almanzor
🅞Hours vary, check website
🅡1 Jan, 25 Dec 🅦museos
deandalucia.es

SPAGHETTI WESTERNS

Two towns modelled on America's Wild West lie off the N340 highway west of Tabernas. The *poblados del oeste*, as they are known, were built during the 1960s and early 1970s, when low costs and eternal sunshine made Almería the ideal location for spaghetti westerns. Sergio Leone, director of *The Good, the Bad and the Ugly*, built a ranch here and film sets sprang up in the desert. These areas are still used for TV commercials and series, and by film directors such as Steven Spielberg.

Castillo de Tabernas Museo del Aceite de Oliva

⊛ 🅐Calle Real 15 🅞10am, 11am, noon & 1pm by appt only 🅦castillodetabernas.us

Los Millares

🅐Santa Fé de Mondújar
🅒677 90 34 04 🅞By guided tour only 10am–2pm Wed–Sun 🅡1 & 6 Jan, 1 May, 24, 25 & 31 Dec

48
Tabernas

◩ D6 ◪ Almería
▦ ◪ Carretera N340,
km 464; 950 52 50 30

Tabernas is set in Europe's
only desert. The town's
Moorish fortress dominates
the harsh surrounding
scenery of cactus-dotted,
rugged hills and dried-out
riverbeds, which has provided
the setting for many classic
spaghetti westerns. Two film
sets are now popular theme
parks where you can become
a cowboy for the day: **Oasys –
Parque Temático del Desierto
de Tabernas** and **Fort Bravo
Texas Hollywood**, 1 km
(1 mile) and 4 km (2.5 miles)
from Tabernas respectively.

Sorbas, 25 km (16 miles)
east, sits on the edge of the
chasm of the Río de Aguas. Its
notable buildings are the 16th-
century Iglesia de Santa María
and a 17th-century mansion
said to have been a summer
retreat for the Duke of Alba.

Oasys – Parque Temático del Desierto de Tabernas

⊛ ◪ Carretera N340
◪ Hours vary, check website
◪ oasysparquetematico.com

Fort Bravo Texas Hollywood

⊛ ◪ Carretera N340,
Tabernas ◪ 9am–7:30pm
daily ◪ fortbravo.org

↑ Scenic views of the Mediterranean Sea from
the Parque Natural Cabo de Gata

49
Parque Natural de Cabo de Gata

◩ D6 ◪ Almería ▦ San José
**◪ Centro de Visitantes de
las Amoladeras, Carretera
Alp-202, km 7 (Retamar-
Pujaire); 950 16 04 35**

Towering cliffs formed out
of volcanic rock, rolling sand
dunes, endless salt flats
and secluded coves characterize the 290-sq-km
(110-sq-mile) Parque Natural
de Cabo de Gata.

Within its confines are a
few fishing villages, and the
small resort of San José. A
lighthouse stands at the end
of the *cabo* (cape), which can
be reached by road from the
village of Cabo de Gata. The
park includes a stretch of sea-
bed 2 km (1 mile) wide and

Did You Know?

Cabo de Gata may have
been named after
the precious agate
rock found in
the area.

the marine flora and fauna
protected within it attract
scuba divers and snorkellers.

The dunes and saltpans
between the cape and the
Playa de San Miguel are a
habitat for thorny jujube trees.
Many migrating birds stop
here, and among the 170 or
so bird species recorded are
flamingos, avocets, griffon
vultures and Dupont's larks.

A few kilometres inland off
the A7, set amid citrus trees
on the edge of the Sierra de
Alhamilla, is picturesque Níjar.
This Moorish town gained its
fame from the beautifully
glazed pottery and the hand-
woven *jarapas* – blankets and
rugs – that are made here. The
barren plain between Níjar
and the sea has been brought
under cultivation using vast
plastic greenhouses to
conserve the scarce water.

←
Desert landscape around
Tabernas, reminiscent of
the Wild West

A DRIVING TOUR
AROUND THE PUEBLOS BLANCOS

Length 205 km (127 miles) **Stopping-off points** Ubrique; Zahara de la Sierra; Ronda; Gaucín **Terrain** Well-maintained mountainous roads

Instead of settling on Andalucía's plains, where they would have fallen prey to bandits, some Andalucíans chose to live in fortified hilltop towns and villages. These are known as *pueblos blancos* (white towns) because they are whitewashed in the Moorish tradition. Touring these charming settlements will reveal a host of references to the region's past.

Embalse de Bornos

Prado del Rey

Mojaceite

A384

Arcos de la Frontera

El Bosque

START

A372

Las Abiertas

A373

Logo de los Hurones

After exploring **Arcos de la Frontera's** *beautiful Old Town (p505), embark on your tour of the region's* peublos blancos.

Algar

A2034

↑ The white houses of Arcos de la Frontera, spilling down the hillside

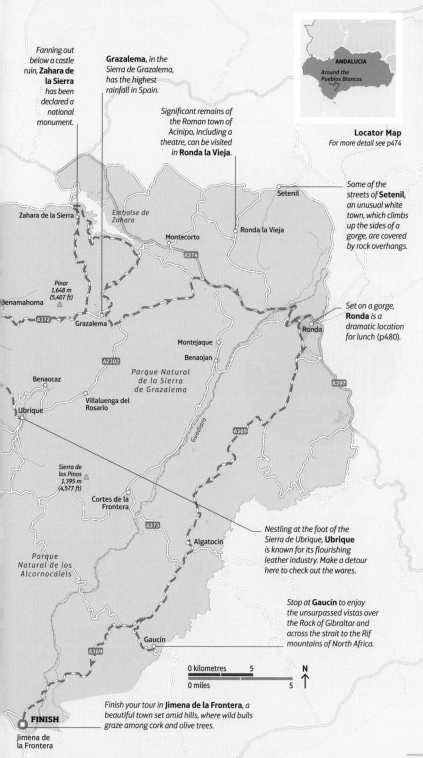

Fanning out below a castle ruin, **Zahara de la Sierra** has been declared a national monument.

Grazalema, in the Sierra de Grazalema, has the highest rainfall in Spain.

Significant remains of the Roman town of Acinipo, including a theatre, can be visited in **Ronda la Vieja**.

ANDALUCIA

Around the Pueblos Blancos

Locator Map
For more detail see p474

Some of the streets of **Setenil**, an unusual white town, which climbs up the sides of a gorge, are covered by rock overhangs.

Setenil

Zahara de la Sierra

Embalse de Zahara

Montecorto

Ronda la Vieja

A374

Pinar
1,648 m
(5,407 ft)

Benamahoma

A372

Grazalema

Set on a gorge, **Ronda** is a dramatic location for lunch (p480).

Ronda

Montejaque

Benaojan

A2302

Parque Natural de la Sierra de Grazalema

Benaocaz

Villaluenga del Rosario

A397

Ubrique

Guadiaro

A369

Sierra de los Pinos
1,395 m
(4,577 ft)

Cortes de la Frontera

A373

Nestling at the foot of the Sierra de Ubrique, **Ubrique** is known for its flourishing leather industry. Make a detour here to check out the wares.

Algatocin

Parque Natural de los Alcornocales

Stop at **Gaucín** to enjoy the unsurpassed vistas over the Rock of Gibraltar and across the strait to the Rif mountains of North Africa.

Gaucín

A369

0 kilometres 5

0 miles 5

N
↑

FINISH

Jimena de la Frontera

Finish your tour in **Jimena de la Frontera**, a beautiful town set amid hills, where wild bulls graze among cork and olive trees.

A DRIVING TOUR
THE COSTA DEL SOL

Length 130 km (80 miles) **Stopping-off points** Estepona; Puerto Banús; Fuengirola; Torremolinos **Terrain** The A7 is a well-maintained, toll-free coastal road

A drive along Spain's sunniest coastline takes in a varied landscape of built-up resorts, where music is piped onto the beaches, and quiet coves, where the scent of barbecuing sardines drifts across the sand. As well as relaxation, the area between Gibraltar and Málaga offers a full range of beach-based activities and watersports, and more than 30 of Europe's finest golf courses lie just inland, so pack your swimming costumes and golf clubs and head for the Costa del Sol.

Marbella's ostentatious marina, **Puerto Banús** *is full of expensive shops. Pause here for a spot of window-shopping to see how the resort's clientele spend their wealth (p504).*

A gleaming yacht moored in the marina at Sotogrande ↑

San Pedro de Alcántara *is a quiet resort with a modern marina and smart holiday developments.*

Estepona's *quiet evenings make it popular with families with young children. It makes a good coffee stop; behind the big hotels are old squares shaded by orange trees (p505).*

Set off after taking in the bright-white boats in the marina at **Sotogrande***, an exclusive resort of luxury villas.*

A397

San Pedro de Alcántara
AP7
A7
Atalaya
Puerto Banús

Ronda del Mar
Estepona
A7

AP7
Sabinillas

Río Guadiaro
Punta de la Chullera
A405
START
Sotogrande
○ Sotogrande Marina
A7

San Roque
A7

○ La Línea de la Concepción
Bahía de Algeciras
GIBRALTAR (UK)
Algeciras
N340
Gibraltar
Punta de Europa

Mediterranean Sea

0 kilometres   10
0 miles   10

N ↑

300

The average days of sunshine a year in the Costa del Sol.

Locator Map
For more detail see p474

ANDALUCIA

The Costa del Sol

Look out for boxes of fresh fish in **Fuengirola**, *which still has an active fishing port, although it is better known today as a package-holiday resort with a chiefly British clientele. It has a spectacular backdrop of steep, ochre mountains.*

El Chapparal

A7

Rincón de la Victoria

El Palo

Málaga

FINISH

A7

AP7

La Capellania

Torremolinos

Benalmádena Costa

A7

Torreblanca

Fuengirola

A355

AP7

Marbella   A7   Cabopino   Cala de Mijas

End your drive at **Rincón de la Victoria**. *This unspoiled beach is famous for its spit-roasted sardines so be sure to try some for dinner.*

A high-rise holiday metropolis, **Torremolinos** *is less brash than it used to be. Huge sums have been spent on new squares, a promenade, green spaces, and improving the beach with millions of tonnes of golden sand. Stop here to relax on the beach.*

Benalmádena Costa *caters almost exclusively for package holidays. Behind the rather rocky beaches and very large marina is a plethora of tourist attractions, such as the Castillo de Colomares and the Buddhist Stupa.*

On a not-too-crowded stretch of coast, **Cabopino** *has a popular nudist beach.*

Mediterranean Sea

↑ Umbrellas and sun loungers on a beach on the Benalmádena Costa

A DRIVING TOUR

LAS ALPUJARRAS

Length 85 km (56 miles) **Stopping-off points** There are bars and restaurants in Órgiva and Trevélez **Terrain** Twisting, narrow mountain roads

The fertile, upland valleys of Las Alpujarras, clothed with chestnut, walnut and poplar trees, lie on the southern slopes of the Sierra Nevada and make for a scenic drive. The architecture of the quaint white villages which cling to the hillsides – compact clusters of irregularly shaped houses with tall chimneys sprouting from flat, grey roofs – is unique in Spain. Be sure to try the local speciality – ham cured in the cold, dry air of Trevélez.

*In the shadow of Mulhacén, mainland Spain's highest mountain, **Trevélez** is famous for its cured ham, so stop here for lunch.*

*Capileira, Bubión and Pampaneira are three villages typical of Las Alpujarras in the pretty **Poqueira Valley**.*

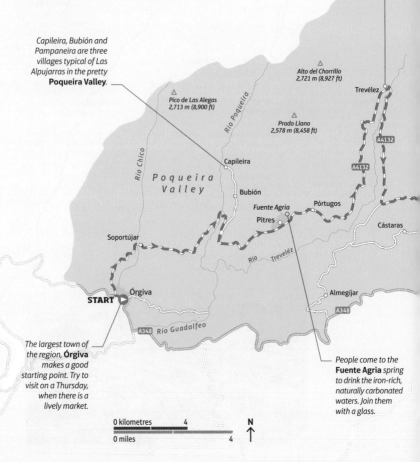

Alto del Chorrillo
2,721 m (8,927 ft)

Trevélez

Pico de Las Alegas
2,713 m (8,900 ft)

Río Poqueira

Prado Llano
2,578 m (8,458 ft)

A4132

A4132

Río Chico

Capileira

Poqueira Valley

Bubión

Fuente Agria

Pórtugos

Pitres

Cástaras

Soportújar

Río Trevélez

Almegíjar

START Órgiva

A348

A348 Río Guadalfeo

*The largest town of the region, **Órgiva** makes a good starting point. Try to visit on a Thursday, when there is a lively market.*

*People come to the **Fuente Agria** spring to drink the iron-rich, naturally carbonated waters. Join them with a glass.*

0 kilometres 4

0 miles 4

N ↑

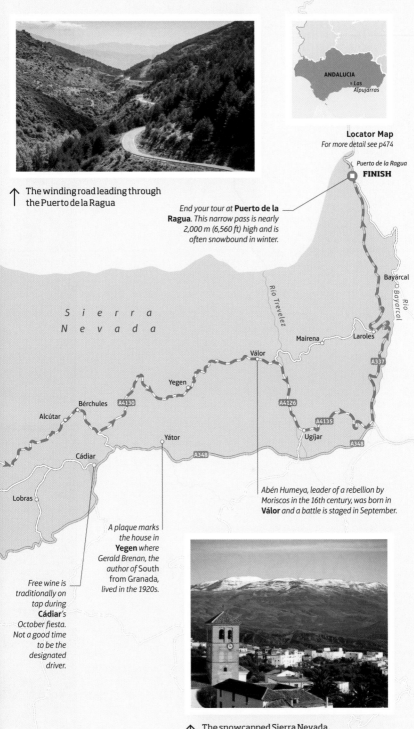

↑ The winding road leading through the Puerto de la Ragua

Locator Map
For more detail see p474

Puerto de la Ragua
FINISH

End your tour at **Puerto de la Ragua**. *This narrow pass is nearly 2,000 m (6,560 ft) high and is often snowbound in winter.*

ANDALUCIA
• Las Alpujarras

Bayárcal

Río Bayárcal

Río Trevelez

*S i e r r a
N e v a d a*

Mairena   Laroles

Válor

A337

Yegen

Bérchules   A4130   A4126

Alcútar

Yátor   A4135

Cádiar   Ugíjar

A348   A348

Lobras

Abén Humeya, *leader of a rebellion by Moriscos in the 16th century, was born in* **Válor** *and a battle is staged in September.*

A plaque marks the house in **Yegen** where Gerald Brenan, the author of South from Granada, lived in the 1920s.

Free wine is traditionally on tap during **Cádiar**'s October fiesta. Not a good time to be the designated driver.

↑ The snowcapped Sierra Nevada, overlooking the village of Válor

525

SPAIN'S ISLANDS

People walking along the Playa de Maspalomas, Gran Canaria

EXPLORE
SPAIN'S ISLANDS

This section divides Spain's Islands into three colour-coded
sightseeing areas, as shown on this map. Find out more
about each area on the following pages.

Portinatx

Sant Vicenç

Sant Antoni

Ibiza

Santa Eulària

Sant Josep

Jesús

Eivissa (Ibiza Town)

Formentera

Fortentera

SPAIN'S ISLANDS

The Balearic
Islands

Western
Canary
Islands

Eastern
Canary
Islands

Atlantic Ocean

La Palma

Santa Cruz
de La Palma

**WESTERN
CANARY ISLANDS**
p554

Santa Cruz
da Tenerife

Tenerife

Agulo

Adeje

Las Palmas de
Gran Canaria

Telde

La Gomera

*La
Frontera*

*Gran
Canaria*

THE BALEARIC ISLANDS
p532

THE BALEARIC
ISLANDS
p532

Mediterranean Sea

Mediterranean Sea

Fornells

Ciutadella   Ferreries   Es Mercadal

Cala Sta Galdana   Alaior

Menorca   Sant Lluís

Binibeca

Pollença   Port de Pollença

Santuario
de Lluc   Alcúdia

Sóller

Fornalutx

Valldemossa   Inca

Artà

Estellencs   Sineu

Andratx   Petra

Palma   Montuïri   *Mallorca*

Manacor

Port
Andratx   S'Arenal

*Badia de
Palma*   Llucmajor   Portocristo

Felanitx   Portocristo

Santanyí   Portopetro

Colònia Sant Jordi

0 kilometres   20

0 miles   20

N

EASTERN CANARY ISLANDS
p564

EASTERN
CANARY ISLANDS
p564

Alegranza

La Graciosa

Lanzarote

Arrecife

Corralejo

Puerto del Rosario   *Atlantic
Ocean*

Antigua

Tarajalejo

Fuerteventura

0 kilometres   50

0 miles   50

N

GETTING TO KNOW
SPAIN'S ISLANDS

Spain's two groups of islands may lie in separate seas – the Balearics in the Mediterranean and the Canaries in the Atlantic – but they have much in common. Blessed with warm climates and clear waters, as well as a whole host of outdoor activities, they are great destinations all year round.

PAGE 532

THE BALEARIC ISLANDS

Chic resorts and glitzy nightclubs may be what comes to mind when you think of the Balearics, but venture inland and you'll soon be rewarded with peaceful villages, awe-inspiring scenery and a wealth of outdoor activities. Mallorca's mountainous interior is snaked by walking and cycling routes, while Menorca is strong on Neolithic remains and beaches, with turquoise-coloured coves around nearly every corner. Despite being renowned for its nightlife, Ibiza, too, has a plethora of secluded spots. Formentera, with its white sands and crystal-clear waters, is perhaps the most alluring island.

Best for
Unspoiled beaches and pumping nightlife

Home to
Mallorca, Ibiza, Menorca, Formentera, Cabrera

Experience
Cycling along the winding road that skirts Mallorca's Cap de Formentor

PAGE 554

WESTERN CANARY ISLANDS

Tenerife is the most visited of the four mountainous islands that make up the western Canaries. Under the shadow cast by Mount Teide, you'll find white-sand beaches, colourful towns and a vibrant underwater world. But the other three islands also have their charms. With rainforests in the north and deserts in the south, La Palma's varied landscape invites exploration. Laid-back La Gomera is also a walker's paradise, while it's the waters off El Hierro that enchant visitors.

Best for
Hiking and climbing

Home to
Tenerife, La Palma, El Hierro, La Gomera

Experience
Stargazing in the clear skies of La Palma

PAGE 564

EASTERN CANARY ISLANDS

The diverse islands of the eastern Canaries make up the province of Las Palma. Gran Canaria has luxurious resorts aplenty, as well as a charming colonial capital – Las Palmas de Gran Canaria. Lanzarote's lunar landscape is the stage for scores of outdoor activities, including cycling, hiking, surfing and diving. And, with long, pristine beaches and strong winds tempering the hot sun, Fuerteventura is an unrivalled destination for windsurfing.

Best for
Watersports

Home to
Lanzarote, Fuerteventura, Gran Canaria

Experience
A buggy ride through Lanzarote's volcanic landscape

THE BALEARIC ISLANDS

The very early history of the Balearic Islands remains shrouded in uncertainty, but the huge stone structures that the Bronze-Age Talayotic people left behind on Mallorca and Menorca offer some insight into the islands' earliest inhabitants.

The Balearics' position in the Mediterranean sea made them a prime target for invasion. The Phoenicians, Carthaginians, Romans and Vandals each stormed the shores to take advantage of the islands' strategic location and used them as a trading port. In the 10th century, the Moors took possession of the islands, but were driven out by Jaime (Jaume) I in the 13th century during the *reconquista*. Catalan settlers soon flocked to the Balearics, bringing their language with them, a dialect of which is still widely spoken. Following the Spanish War of Succession, Menorca was ceded to the British in 1713, who occupied the island for nearly a century, albeit interrupted by a French occupation during the Seven Years' War.

In the mid-20th century, the rest of Europe rushed onto the islands once again, but this time as sun-seeking visitors, largely from the UK and Germany. Today, tourism is the main pillar of the archipelago's economy.

↑ *Barcelona*

Port de Sóller

SÓLLER

ALFÀBIA

VALLDEMOSSA ③

Estellencs

LA GRANJA ⑦

ANDRATX ⑤   **PALMA** ①

Port d'Andratx

Palma Nova   **Palma Mallor**

MA1

MA11

Badia de Palma

Cap Bla

← *Valencia*

Ibiza   Portinatx

Sant Vicenç

SANT ANTONI (SANT ANTONIO) ⑯ ⑰ *ELS AMUNTS*

⑱ **SANTA EULÀRIA DES RIU**

C810

SANT JOSEP (SAN JOSE) ⑭   ⑬   Jesús

Ibiza ⓐ **EIVISSA (IBIZA TOWN)**

C600

⑮ **SES SALINES**

Sant Francesc ㉕ **FORMENTERA**

Es Caló

Cala Saona   *Platja de Migjorn*   *Punta Roja*

Cap de Barbaria

Mediterranean

Sea

| 0 kilometres | 25 |
| 0 miles | 25 |

N ↑

↑ *Barcelona*

Barcelona ↖

Mediterranean Sea

Menorca

Cap de Cavalleria

Fornells

CIUTADELLA FERRERIES

19 **20** **22** ES MERCADAL

ME1

Cala Sta Galdana Alaior

Cap d'Artrutx *Menorca* ✈ **23** MAÓ

CALES COVES **21**

Binibeca Sant Lluís

Mallorca

Cap de Formentor

POLLENÇA Port de Pollença

12

Sa Calobra Alcúdia

6 SANTUARI DE LLUC

Fornalutx Sa Pobla *Badia d'Alcúdia*

MA13

Inca *Cap des Freu*

Sineu Santa Margalida Capdepera Cala Rajada

MA14 Artà Coves d'Artà

Petra *MA15* Son Servera

Manacor

Montuïri *MA15* *Coves dels Hams* Portocristo

S'Arenal **9** PUIG DE RANDA **10** COVES DEL DRAC

Llucmajor *MA14*

Campos **11** FELANITX

8 Castell de Santueri

CAPOCORB VELL Portopetro

Santanyí Cala Figuera

Colònia Sant Jordi

Cap de ses Salines

24 CABRERA

THE BALEARIC ISLANDS

Must See
1 Palma

Experience More
2 Sóller
3 Valldemossa
4 Alfàbia
5 Andratx
6 Santuari de Lluc
7 La Granja
8 Capocorb Vell
9 Puig de Randa
10 Coves del Drac
11 Felanitx
12 Pollença
13 Eivissa (Ibiza Town)
14 Sant Josep (San José)
15 Ses Salines
16 Sant Antoni (San Antonio)
17 Els Amunts
18 Santa Eulària des Riu
19 Ciutadella
20 Ferreries
21 Cales Coves
22 Es Mercadal
23 Maó
24 Cabrera
25 Formentera

↑ Boats lined neatly within Palma's harbour at sunset

1

PALMA

🅰G4 🏝Mallorca ✈9 km (6 miles) E �",🚌⛴ 🅸Plaça Reina 2; www.infomallorca.net

On an island whose name has become synonymous with mass tourism, Palma surprises with its cultural richness. Under the Moors it was a prosperous town of fountains and cool courtyards, and signs of this past wealth are still evident in the sumptuous religious buildings, grand public constructions and fine private mansions that crowd the atmospheric Old Town.

Museu de Mallorca

🅰Carrer de sa Portella 5
🕐10am-6pm Tue-Fri, 11am-2pm Sat & Sun
🆆museudemallorca.caib.es

This museum occupies the Palau Ayamans, a residence built around 1630. The palace was erected on the foundations of a 12th-century Arab house, which is still visible in the underground rooms of the museum. Opened in 1968, the Museu de Mallorca houses a superb collection of works of art associated with Mallorcan history. The collection comprises thousands of exhibits and includes prehistoric artifacts, stone fragments of fallen buildings, priceless Moorish ceramics and jewellery, and medieval and Baroque paintings.

Palau Reial de l'Almudaina

🅰Carrer de Palau Reial
📞971 21 41 34 🕐Apr-Sep: 10am-7pm Tue-Sun; Oct-Mar: 10am-6pm Tue-Sun

Almudaina means "citadel" in Arabic. This royal residence of Jaime (Jaume) II was built after 1309, using the walls of an Arab fortress, and the Gothic palace includes Moorish-style arches and carved wooden ceilings. It is the official residence of the Spanish monarch. Don't miss the graceful Santa Ana chapel.

3

Banys Àrabs

🅰Carrer Can Serra 7
📞637 04 65 34
🕐Apr-Nov: 10am-5pm daily (Dec-Mar: to 6pm)

This 10th-century *hammam* (bathhouse) is one of the few architectural reminders of a Moorish presence on the islands. A horseshoe-arched chamber, it has survived in its original form.

---

④
Castell de Bellver

🏛 Carrer Camilo José Cela 17 ☎ 971 73 50 65 🕐 Apr-Sep: 10am-7pm Tue-Sat, 10am-3pm Sun; Oct-Mar: 10am-6pm Tue-Sat, 10am-3pm Sun

About 3 km (2 miles) from the city centre stands Palma's Gothic castle. Built as a summer residence for Jaime (Jaume) II in the early 14th century, it was then turned into a prison and remained as such until 1915. Today the castle hosts concerts and plays.

---

⑤
Basílica de Sant Francesc

🏛 Plaça Sant Francesc 🕐 10am-2pm Mon-Sat, 9am-12:30pm Sun

Construction of this Gothic church and Franciscan monastery started in 1281 and took 100 years. In the Middle Ages, this was Palma's most fashionable church, and aristocratic families competed to build ever more elaborate side chapels for their dead.

The church's severe façade was embellished around 1680 with a Baroque doorway and stone statues. The dark interior (its Gothic windows have been partially bricked up) contains many fine works of art.

---

⑥
CaixaForum

🏛 Plaça de Weyler 3 🕐 10am-8pm Mon-Sat, 11am-2pm Sun & public hols 🌐 caixaforum.es/palma

The former Grand Hotel was given its present name after the Fundació La Caixa savings bank financed its restoration. Built in 1903, it is the work of Lluís Domènech i Montaner. As a masterpiece of the Modernista style, it has been included on the UNESCO World Heritage list and houses (among other things) a huge collection of Modernista paintings by Hermengildo Anglada-Camarasa.

⑦
Palau Episcopal and Museu Diocesà

🏛 Carrer Mirador 5 🕐 10am-1:30pm Mon-Sat

The Palau Episcopal (Bishop's Palace) dates mostly from the 17th century, though work on it began in 1238. Several rooms house the charming Museu Diocesà, which displays items from various churches in Mallorca.

---

⑧
Fundació Pilar i Joan Miró

🏛 Carrer Joan de Saridakis 29 🕐 Hours vary, check website 🚫 Mon 🌐 miro mallorca.es

When Joan Miró died in 1983, his wife converted his former studio and gardens into an art centre. The building incorporates Miró's original studio, a permanent collection, a shop, a library and an auditorium.

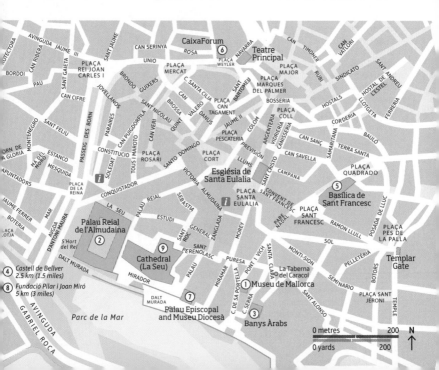

⑨

PALMA CATHEDRAL

🏛 Plaça de la Seu s/n ⏰ Apr-May & Oct: 10am-5:15pm Mon-Fri, 10am-2:15pm Sat; Jun-Sep: 10am-6:15pm Mon-Fri, 10am-2:15pm Sat; Nov-Mar: 10am-3:15pm Mon-Fri, 10am-2:15pm Sat 🚫 Public hols 🌐 catedraldemallorca.org

Combining vast scale with typically Gothic elegance, Palma Cathedral, or La Seu, as Mallorcans call it, is one of the most breathtaking buildings in Spain. One of the best-sited cathedrals anywhere, it is spectacularly poised high on the sea wall, above what was once Palma's harbour.

According to legend, when Jaime (Jaume) I of Aragón was caught in a storm on his way to conquer Mallorca in 1229, he vowed that if God led him to safety he would build a great church in his honour. In the following years the mosque of Medina Mayurqa was torn down and architect Guillem Sagrera (1380–1456) drew up plans for a new cathedral. The last stone was added in 1587, and in subsequent years the cathedral has been rebuilt, notably in the early 20th century when parts of the interior were remodelled by Antoni Gaudí *(p97)*. One particularly notable addition was a bizarre, wrought-iron canopy that Gaudí included above the altar. It incorporates lamps, tapestries and a multi-coloured crucifix. The cathedral's nave is also magnificent; at over 19-m (62-ft) wide it is one of the broadest naves in the world.

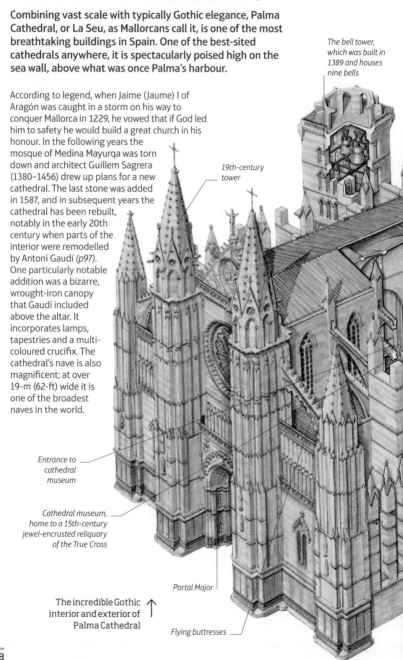

The bell tower, which was built in 1389 and houses nine bells

19th-century tower

Entrance to cathedral museum

Cathedral museum, home to a 15th-century jewel-encrusted reliquary of the True Cross

Portal Major

Flying buttresses

The incredible Gothic interior and exterior of Palma Cathedral ↑

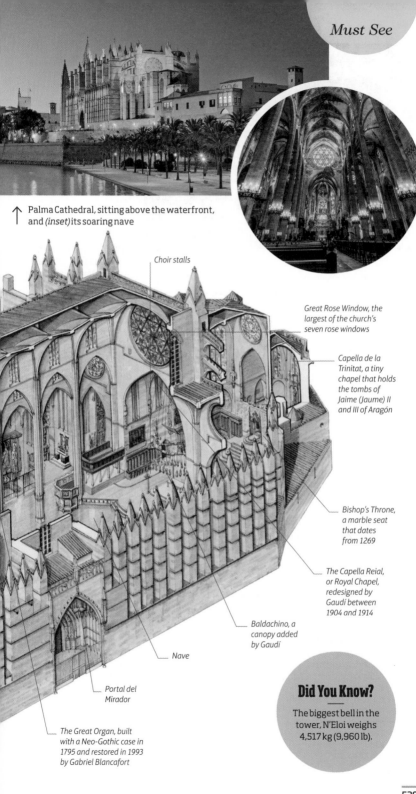

Palma Cathedral, sitting above the waterfront, and *(inset)* its soaring nave

Choir stalls

Great Rose Window, the largest of the church's seven rose windows

Capella de la Trinitat, a tiny chapel that holds the tombs of Jaime (Jaume) II and III of Aragón

Bishop's Throne, a marble seat that dates from 1269

The Capella Reial, or Royal Chapel, redesigned by Gaudí between 1904 and 1914

Baldachino, a canopy added by Gaudí

Nave

Portal del Mirador

The Great Organ, built with a Neo-Gothic case in 1795 and restored in 1993 by Gabriel Blancafort

Did You Know?

The biggest bell in the tower, N'Eloi weighs 4,517 kg (9,960 lb).

A charming narrow-gauge train arriving at Plaça d'Espanya in Sóller

Real Cartuja de Jesús de Nazaret

 Plaça de la Cartuja de Valldemossa ☉ 10:30am-2:30pm Mon-Sat ☒ Nov-Jan ⓦ cartoixadevalldemossa.com

4

Alfàbia

🅰 G4 ⚐ Carretera de Sóller, km 17, Mallorca 🚌 ☉ Mar-Apr: 9:30am-5:30pm Mon-Fri, 9:30am-1pm Sat; Jun-Oct: 9:30am-6:30pm daily ☒ Nov-Feb ⓦ jardines dealfabia.com

Very few *possessiós* in Mallorca are open to the public, which makes Alfàbia worth visiting. The house and garden are an excellent example of a typical Mallorcan aristocratic estate and exude a Moorish atmosphere. Little remains of the 14th-century architecture, but look out for the Mudéjar inscription on the ceiling of the entrance hall and the Hispano-Arabic fountains and pergola.

5

Andratx

🅰 G4 ⚐ Mallorca 🚌 🛈 Avenida de la Cúria 1; 971 62 80 00

This small town lies amid a valley of almond groves in the shadow of Puig de Galatzó, the pyramidical mountain which rises to 1,026 m (3,366 ft). With its ochre and white shuttered houses and the old watchtowers perched high on a hill above the town, Andratx is a very pretty place.

→

Strolling through the manicured gardens of La Granja estate

EXPERIENCE MORE

2

Sóller

🅰 G4 ⚐ Mallorca 🚉🚌 🛈 Plaça d'Espanya 15; 971 63 80 08

Sóller is a little town grown fat on the produce of its olive groves and orchards, which climb up the slopes of the Sierra Tramuntana. In the 19th century Sóller traded its oranges and wine for French goods, and the town retains a faintly Gallic, bourgeois feel.

One of Sóller's best-known features is its delightfully old-fashioned narrow-gauge railway, complete with quaint wooden carriages. The train departs from Palma and ends in Sóller, at the station in the Plaça d'Espanya. From there, an antique tram travels to the fishing village of Port de Sóller, 5 km (3 miles) to the west.

3

Valldemossa

🅰 G4 ⚐ Mallorca 🚌 🛈 Avenida Palma 7; 971 61 20 19

This pleasant mountain town is linked with George Sand, the French novelist who stayed here in the winter of 1838 and 1839 and later wrote unflatteringly of the island in *Un Hiver à Majorque*. Dearer to Mallorcans is the Polish composer Frédéric Chopin (1810–49), who stayed with Sand at the **Real Cartuja de Jesús de Nazaret**. "Chopin's cell", off the monastery's main courtyard, is where a few of his works were written, and still houses the piano on which he composed.

Nearby, a 17th-century pharmacy displays outlandish medicinal preparations such as "powdered nails of the beast". In the cloisters is an art museum with works by Tàpies, Miró and the Mallorcan artist Juli Ramis, as well as Picasso's *The Burial of the Count of Orgaz*, inspired by the El Greco painting of the same name.

 HIDDEN GEM
Seize the Deià

Tucked away on Mallorca's northern coast, in the foothills of the Puig del Teix mountain between Sóller and Valldemossa, lies the sleepy village of Deià. This extremely picturesque village is well worth a visit.

The road southwest leads down to Port d'Andratx, 5 km (3 miles) away. Here, in an almost totally enclosed bay, expensive yachts are moored in rows along the harbour and luxury holiday homes pepper the hillsides. In the past, Port d'Andratx's main role was as the fishing port and harbour for Andratx, but since the early 1960s it has gradually been transformed into an exclusive holiday resort for the rich and famous. When visiting Port d'Andratx, it is a good idea to leave all thoughts of the real Mallorca behind and simply enjoy it for what it is – a chic and affluent resort.

Santuari de Lluc

🗺️ G4 📍 Lluc, Mallorca 🚌 From Palma ⏱️ 10am–2pm Sun–Fri 🌐 lluc.net

High in the mountains of the Sierra Tramuntana, in the remote village of Lluc, is an institution regarded by many as the spiritual heart of Mallorca. The Santuari de Lluc was built mainly in the 17th and 18th centuries on the site of an ancient shrine. The monastery's Baroque church, with its imposing façade, contains the stone image of La Moreneta, the Black Virgin of Lluc, said to

have been found by a young shepherd boy on a nearby hilltop in the 13th century. The sanctuary is home to a children's choir, the Blauets, established in the 16th century. The kids sing the "Salve Regina" at 1:15pm Mon–Fri and 11am Sun (unless they are on tour).

The museum, on the first two floors of the main building, displays paintings and medieval manuscripts. As well as the museum, the monastery now houses a guesthouse.

Along the Camí dels Misteris, the paved walkway up to the hilltop where the sanctuary sits, there are some bronze bas-reliefs by Pere Llimona.

La Granja

🗺️ G4 📍 Carretera de Banyalbufar, km 1.5, Esporles, Mallorca 🚌 ⏱️ Summer: 10am–7pm daily; winter: 10am–6pm daily 🌐 lagranja.net

La Granja is a private estate near the little country town of Esporles. Formerly a Cistercian convent, it is now the property of the Seguí family, who have opened their largely unspoiled 18th-century house to the public as a kind of living museum. Peacocks roam the gardens, salt cod

and hams hang in the kitchen, *The Marriage of Figaro* plays in the ballroom, and the slight air of chaos just adds to the charm of the place.

Capocorb Vell

G4 🏠 Carretera Llucmajor-Cap Blanc (MA-6014), km 23, Mallorca 🚌 El Arenal 🕙10am-5pm Fri-Wed 🌐talaiots capocorbvell.com

Mallorca may not be as rich in megalithic remains as neighbouring Menorca (p551), but this Talayotic village is worth seeing. The settlement, which dates back to around 1000 BC, originally consisted of five *talaiots* (stone tower-like structures with timbered roofs) and another 28 smaller dwellings. Little is known about its inhabitants and the uses for some of the rooms, such as the tiny underground gallery. Too small for living in, this room may have been used to perform magic rituals.

Part of the charm of this place lies in its setting among fields of fruit trees and dry-stone walls. Apart from a snack bar nearby, the site remains undeveloped and quite peaceful.

9

Puig de Randa

G4 🚗 8 km (5 miles) NE of Llucmajor, Mallorca 🚌 To Llucmajor, then taxi 🚉 Calle Terral 23, Llucmajor; 971 66 91 62

In the middle of a fertile plain called the *pla*, Puig de Randa rises 543 m (1,780 ft). It is said that Mallorca's greatest son, the 14th-century theologian and mystic Ramon Llull, came to a hermitage on this mountain to meditate and write his religious treatise, *Ars Magna*. On the way up Puig de Randa there are two small monasteries, the 14th-century Santuari de Sant Honorat and the Santuari de Nostra Senyora de Gràcia, which is built on a ledge under an overhanging cliff.

On the mountaintop is the Santuari de Cura, built to commemorate Llull's time on the *puig*, and largely devoted to his work. A small museum, housed in a 16th-century former school off the central courtyard, which is built in the island's typical beige stone, contains some of Llull's manuscripts.

10

Coves del Drac

G4 🚗 500 m (0.3 miles) S of Porto Cristo, Mallorca 🚌 From Porto Cristo 🕙 By guided tour only, book tickets in advance online 🗓 1 Jan, 25 Dec 🌐 cuevas deldrach.com

Mallorca has numerous caves, from mere holes in the ground to cathedral-like halls. The four vast chambers of the Coves del Drac are reached by a steep flight of steps. At the bottom is the beautifully lit cave, "Diana's Bath". Another chamber holds the underground lake, Martel, 29 m (95 ft) below ground level and 177 m (580 ft) long. Music fills the air of the cave, played from boats on the lake. Equally dramatic are the two remaining caves, charmingly named "The Theatre of the Fairies" and "The Enchanted City".

Alongside, the **Coves d'Hams** are so called because some of their stalactites resemble hooks – *hams* in Mallorcan.

↓ The dramatically lit stalactites in the Coves del Drac

STAY

Hotel Can Mostatxins

This Alcúdian boutique hotel is set in a historic building that dates back to the 15th century. But the spa and champagne bar bring it firmly into the 21st century.

G4 Carrer del Lledoner 15, Alcúdia, Mallorca Whotel canmostatxins.com

€€€

Son Brull

A family-run hotel set in an old farmstead near Pollença, Son Brull will give you a taste of rural life on the island. Each of the rooms is tastefully decorated with subtle Mallorcan touches. The on-site restaurant is excellent.

G4 Carretera Palma-Pollença (PM-220), km 49.8, Pollença, Mallorca Wsonbrull.com

€€€

The caves contain the "Sea of Venice", an underground lake on which musicians sail.

The entrance to the **Coves d'Artà** is near Capdepera. The caves' main attraction is a stalagmite 22 m (72 ft) high.

Coves d'Hams

Carretera Manacor-Porto Cristo, km 11.5
🕐 11am–2:30pm daily
🚫 1 Jan, 25 Dec Wcuevas delshams.com

Coves d'Artà

Carretera Coves s/n, Canyamel 🕐 10am–5pm daily 🚫 1 Jan, 25 Dec Wcuevasdearta.com

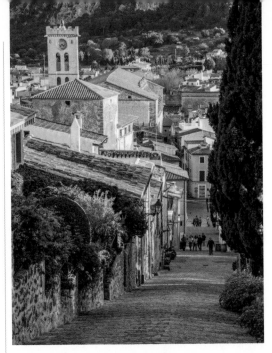

↑ The cobbled steps to El Calvari, lined with stone houses, in Pollença

---

Felanitx

G4 Mallorca 🚌
🚍 Avenida Cala ala Marçal 15, Portocolom; 971 82 60 84

This bustling agricultural town is visited mainly for three reasons: the imposing façade of the 13th-century church, the Esglesia de Sant Miquel; its *sobrassada de porc negre* (a spiced raw sausage made from the meat of the local black pig); and its lively religious fiestas.

Pollença

G4 Mallorca
🚌 🚍 Carrer de Pere J. Cànaves Salas s/n; www.pollensa.com

With its ochre-coloured stone houses and winding lanes, Pollença is picturesquely sited on the edge of fertile farmland. The town has fine churches, including Convent de Santo Domingo, which houses the **Museu de Pollença**. A chapel on the hilltop, El Calvari, is reached either by road or a long climb of 365 steps. On the altar there is a Gothic Christ, carved in wood.

Alcúdia, 10 km (6 miles) to the east, is home to the **Museu Monogràfic de Pollentia** exhibiting statues, jewellery and other remains from the Roman settlement of Pollentia, south of Alcúdia.

Museu de Pollença

Carrer Pere J Salas Cànaves s/n 971 53 11 66
🕐 Summer: 10am–1pm & 5:30–8:30pm Tue–Sat, 10am–1pm Sun; winter: 11am–1pm Tue–Sun

Museu Monogràfic de Pollentia

Carrer de Sant Jaume 30, Alcúdia 971 54 70 04
🕐 Summer: 9:30am–8:30pm Tue–Sat, 9:30am–2:30pm Sun; winter: 10am–3pm Tue–Sat

⑬

Eivissa (Ibiza Town)

🅰F5 🅰Ibiza 🚗🚌⛴
**🅹Plaza de la Catedral;
www.tourism.eivissa.es**

The old quarter of Eivissa (Ibiza Town), known as Dalt Vila, is a miniature citadel guarding the mouth of the almost circular bay. The Portal de ses Taules, a magnificent gateway in the north wall of the 16th-century fortifications, carries the finely carved coat of arms of the kingdom of Aragón, to which the Balearic Islands belonged in the Middle Ages.

Inside the walls stands the stately 16th-century Església de Santo Domingo with its three red-tiled domes. The Baroque interior has a barrel-vaulted ceiling and frescoed walls. Works by Erwin Bechtold, Barry Flanagan and other artists connected with Ibiza are on display in the **Museu d'Art Contemporani**. Art is also on display in the cathedral's Museu Diocesà.

This 13th-century Catalan Gothic building, with 18th-century additions, crowns the whole Dalt Vila.

Under the Carthaginians, the soil of Ibiza was considered holy. The citizens of Carthage deemed it an honour to be buried in the **Necrópolis Púnica del Puig des Molins**. Part of it can be visited by the public.

The crossroads village of Jesús, 3 km (2 miles) north, is worth a visit for its 16th-century church. Originally built as part of a Franciscan monastery, it has an altarpiece from that time created by Rodrigo de Osona the Younger.

Museu d'Art Contemporani

⊗ 🅰Ronda Narcís Puget s/n 🕒Hours vary, check website 🅆eivissa.es/mace

Necrópolis Púnica del Puig des Molins

🅰Via Romana 31 🕒9am-3pm Tue-Thu, 9am-3pm & 5-8pm Fri, 9am-2pm Sat, 10am-2pm Sun 🕒Public hols 🅆maef.es

Did You Know?

Sant Josep's Sublimotion is the world's most expensive restaurant, charging €1,500 per head.

⑭

Sant Josep (San José)

🅰F5 🅰Ibiza 🅹Pere Escanelles (opposite town hall); www.ibiza.travel

The charming village of Sant Josep, the administrative centre of southwest Ibiza, lies in the shadow of Ibiza's highest mountain. At 475 m (1,560 ft), Sa Talaiassa offers a panorama of all Ibiza, including the islet of Es Vedrá, rising from the sea like a rough-cut pyramid.

For the most accessible view of this enormous rock, take the coastal road to the sandy cove of Cala d'Hort, where there are a number of good restaurants and a quiet beach.

↑ Visitors relax in a backstreet café, set up on stone steps in the Dalt Vila, Eivissa

↑ Piles of stacked stones on a rocky beach in Ses Salines, the saline lowlands

Sant Josep is still a traditional village with a good choice of restaurants and bars. The main street has an impressive church where you can sit in the shade of the courtyard trees.

Ses Salines

⚐F5 ⚐Ibiza 🅸Carrer la Revista, Sant Josep de sa Talaia; 971 30 14 60

Situated at the southern end of Ibiza are the saline lowlands called Ses Salines. These natural saltpans provide an extremely important refuge for the local wildlife, and were known as the "Salt Gardens" in Phoenician times.

They are sheltered to the north by the Serra Grossa hills, which rise up to 160 m (520 ft) in some places; to the south they are flanked by the wooded areas of Faló and Corbari. In 1992, the area was given special protection as a nature reserve.

Before tourism, for centuries the revenue from the local salt production provided a large chunk of the island's income. Until quite recently, the place was served by a narrow-gauge railway carrying salt to La Canal – a small port at the southern end of the peninsula. Salt production still continues at Ses Salines, though not on such a grand scale – some 70,000 tonnes of the mineral are exported each year.

Built between the salt lakes is the village of Sant Francesc de S'Estany, where some salt workers still live, which has a small picturesque church. The asphalt road that passes the church leads to a 16th-century watchtower, Torre de sa Salt Rossa, 2 km (1 mile) away. From here there are fine views over nearby Illa Sal Rossa island, the wide beaches of Figueretes (lying to the south of the capital) and Dalt Vila (Old Town) in Eivissa.

Ses Salines' beach, Platja de Ses Salines, is one of the island's most fashionable spots. This long, crescent-shaped sandy beach is bordered by pine woods and has crystal-clear water.

> **Salt production still continues at Ses Salines, though not on such a grand scale - some 70,000 tonnes of the mineral are exported each year.**

EAT

Bebel
An Italian-style Eivissan restaurant, offering both cooked and raw seafood. Tasting menus are available.

⚐F5 ⚐Carrer de Jaume I 4, Eivissa, Ibiza ⓦbebelibiza.com

Tapas Ibiza
Set away from San Antoni de Portmany's busy strip, this lovely restaurant serves tapas, some traditional, some innovative.

⚐F4 ⚐Camino des Reguero 4, San Antoni de Portmany, Ibiza ⓦtapasibiza.com

Montauk Steakhouse
This gorgeous steakhouse is found in Sant Jordi Ses Salines. Here, you can enjoy great food with a nice view of the beach.

⚐F5 ⚐Carretera Platja d'en Bossa 10, Sant Jordi Ses Salines, Ibiza ⓦtheushuaia experience.com

La Paloma
A postcard-pretty garden restaurant, near Eivissa, offering dishes made using organic, local ingredients. The menu features a small range of Italian-inspired dishes.

⚐F5 ⚐Carrer can Pou 4, Sant Llorenç de Balàfia, Ibiza ⓦpaloma ibiza.com

16

Sant Antoni (San Antonio)

🖫F4 🏛Ibiza 🚌🚢
🛈Passeig de Ses Fonts;
www.ibiza.travel

Ibiza's second town, Sant Antoni was known by the Romans as Portus Magnus because of its large natural harbour. Formerly a tiny fishing village, it has turned into a sprawling and exuberant resort. Although it was once over-commercialized, the town has undergone a dramatic face-lift. Nevertheless, the 14th-century parish church of Sant Antoni is practically marooned in a sea of modern high-rise hotels.

To the north of Sant Antoni, on the road to Cala Salada, is

Did You Know?

The Phoenicians dedicated Ibizia to the god of music and dance in 654 BC.

the chapel of Santa Agnès, an unusual early Christian temple (not to be confused with the village of the same name). When this catacomb-like chapel was discovered, in 1907, it contained Moorish weapons and fragments of pottery.

17

Els Amunts

🖫F4 🏛Ibiza 🚌Sant Miquel
🛈Carretera Sant Llorenç
s/n, Sant Joan de Labritja;
971 32 51 41

Els Amunts is the local name for the uplands of northern Ibiza, which stretch from Sant Antoni on the west coast to Sant Vicenç in the northeast. Though hardly a mountain range – Es Fornás is the highest point, at a mere 450 m (1,480 ft) – the area's inaccessibility, due to the lack of infrastructure, has kept Els Amunts virtually unspoiled.

There are very few sights here, apart from the landscape, which consists of pine-clad hills sheltering fertile valleys whose rich red soil is planted with olive, almond and fig trees, and

the occasional vineyard. Tourist enclaves are scarce, except for a handful of small resorts, such as Port de Sant Miquel, Portinatx and Sant Vicenç.

Inland, villages like Sant Joan and Santa Agnès offer an

TOP 5 IBIZA BEACHES

Platja de Ses Salines
A long sandy beach, which is part of a conservation area.

Cala Benirràs
Lively party beach, often with live music

Cala Xarraca
Crystal-clear waters near Portinatx, perfect for snorkelling.

Talamanca
Walking distance from Eivissa, a favourite beach for sunbathing.

Cala Llonga
Large sandy beach near Eivissa, particularly popular with families.

←

Savannah café, overlooking the water on the famous Sunset Strip at Sant Antoni

insight into Ibiza's quiet, rural past. When the almond trees bloom in February, islanders gather in Santa Agnès to admire this spectacle as the whole of the valley is swathed in a covering of silvery-white.

Situated between Santa Agnès and San Antoni, inside the Ses Fontanelles cave are prehistoric paintings, found in 1917 by French archaeologist Henri Breuil. Recent studies date them to the Punic era. The cave is not accessible by the public but there are replicas on site that can be seen from the outside.

The architectural high points of northern Ibiza are several beautiful white churches, like the one in Sant Miquel, which, on Thursdays in summer, hosts a display of Ibizan folk dancing. Outside Sant Llorenç is the tranquil, fortified hamlet of Balàfia, with flat-roofed houses, tiny whitewashed alleys and a watchtower that was used as a fortress during raids by the Turks.

→

The domed roof of Santa Eulària's whitewashed 16th-century church

⑱ Santa Eulària des Riu

🅰F4 🏠Ibiza 🚌🚎 🛈Carrer Mariano Riquer Wallis 4; 971 33 07 28

The characterful town of Santa Eulària des Riu is sited on the island's only river. Its 16th-century church, with its covered courtyard, and the surrounding Old Town were built on the top of a little hill, the Puig de Missa, because this site was more easily defended than the shore below.

Adjacent to the church is the **Museo Etnológico de Ibiza y Formentera**, a folk museum housed in an Ibizan farmhouse. The exhibits include traditional costumes, farming implements, toys and an olive press. A collection of photographs covering 50 years shows how Ibiza has changed.

Two art and craft markets, Punta Arabí (Wed) and Las Dalias (Sat), are held just outside of town and feature hundreds of stalls.

Museo Etnológico de Ibiza y Formentera

♨🕐 🏠Can Ros, Puig de Missa 🅲971 33 28 45 🕐Apr-Sep: 10am-2pm & 5:30-8pm Tue-Sat, 11am-1:30pm Sun; Oct-Mar: 10am-2pm Mon-Sat, 11am-1pm Sun 🗙Mid-Dec-31 Jan

DRINK

Jacaranda Lounge
Chill out on a Balinese bed while sipping a delectable cocktail and listening to live music.

🅰F4 🏠Carretera Cana, Santa Eulària des Ríu, Ibiza 🌐jacaranda-lounge.com

Liquido Cocktail Bar
Overlooking Santa Eulària's marina, this cool bar serves great cocktails accompanied by northern soul and Motown music.

🅰F4 🏠Marina, Santa Eulària des Riu, Ibiza 🅲609 57 22 60

Mirage Restaurant & Cocktail Bar
Pitch up at this lively bar for tasty cocktails or catch a match on the big screen.

🅰F4 🏠Carrer es Joan Rosselló de Son Fortezacripto, Santa Eulària des Riu, Ibiza 🅲692 58 77 03

Ciutadella

 G4 ☐ Menorca 🚌🚌
☐ Plaça des Born 9; www.menorca.es

The key date in the history of Ciutadella is 1558. In that year the Turks, led by Barbarossa, entered and decimated the city, enslaving 3,495 of its citizens and sending them to Constantinople. Of Ciutadella's main public buildings, only the fine Catalan Gothic Església Catedral de Menorca managed to survive this fearsome onslaught in more or less its original condition, only later to be stripped of all its paintings, ornaments and other treasures by Republican extremists during the Civil War.

The nearby Plaça des Born was built as a parade ground for Moorish troops, and from 1558 was gradually rebuilt in Renaissance style. Today it is one of Spain's most impressive squares, containing pleasant cafés and bordered by shady palm trees. At the centre of the Plaça des Born is an obelisk which commemorates the "Any de sa Desgràcia" (Year of Misfortune), when the Turks invaded the city. Around the square are the late 19th-century Teatre Municipal des Born, and a series of aristocratic mansions with Italianesque façades, the grandest of which is the early 19th-century Palau de Torre-Saura. Another one of these impressive palaces, the **Palau Salort**, houses Ciutadella's *ajuntament* (town hall). At set times during the year, you can explore the preserved rooms of this Gothic-style palace, including the kitchen, which has beautiful tiles. From the northern end of the square there is a fine view over the small harbour. If you walk up the Carrer Major des Born past the

HIDDEN GEM
Lithica

Only a few kilometres from Ciutadella, you can visit a restored old quarry, which shows the history of stone-work on the island. Equally impressive here are the beautiful medieval gardens.

cathedral, you come to Ses Voltes, an alley lined on both sides by whitewashed arches. Turn right along the Carrer del Seminari for the Baroque Església dels Socors and the **Museu Diocesà** with its displays of ecclesiastical paraphernalia. The Art Nouveau market, which dates from 1895 and is painted dark green, stands nearby.

The peace of Ciutadella is disturbed every June by the Festa de Sant Joan, a spectacular ritual of horsemanship. During the festival

the local gin *(ginebra)* is drunk copiously and the city comes to a grinding halt.

Museu Diocesà

 ⌂ Carrer del Seminari 7 **☎** 971 48 12 97 **⏰** May–Oct: 10:30am–1:30pm Tue–Sat

Palau Salort

⌂ Plaça des Born 9 **⏰** May–Oct: 10am–4pm daily **⊘** Nov–Apr

---

⑳

Ferreries

△ G4 **⌂** Menorca **🚌** **ℹ** Carrer Mallorca 2; 971 37 45 05

At 142 m (466 ft) above sea level, this picturesque little town is the highest settlement in Menorca. Its name derives from the many blacksmiths *(ferreries)* who once worked around here. At the heart of the town is the Plaça d'Espanya. Here, at a weekly Saturday market, you can buy leather goods as well as produce brought in by local farmers. In Plaça l'Església is the parish church of Sant Bartomeu and the town hall. It is also worth stepping into the Centro de Geología de Menorca, to see a selection of the island's natural wonders.

About 6 km (4 miles) to the north of Ferreries is the Santa Agueda castle. Not much remains of this Moorish stronghold, but the view from the top of the third-highest hill in Menorca justifies the climb up to the fortress.

The bay of Santa Galdana, 10 km (6 miles) to the south of Ferreries, is even prettier. You can take a pleasant walk from the beach inland through the fertile riverbed of Barranc d'Algendar.

> **The peace of Ciutadella is disturbed every June by the Festa de Sant Joan, a spectacular ritual of horsemanship.**

↑ Looking down on the seafront from Ciutadella's Plaça des Born

---

EAT

PiQNiQ

This great little sandwich bar in Ciutadella offers a selection of picnic food. The staff will even pack the food in a cooler bag for you.

△ G4 **⌂** Calle Seminari 10, Ciutadella, Menorca **🌐** piqniq.es

€€€

Cuk-Cuk

Dining at this Ciutadella eatery, self-styled as a "restaurant for foodies", is an unusual experience. Take a look at the menu and pick whatever takes your fancy, then cook the dish yourself with guidance from the chef.

△ G4 **⌂** Calle de Sant Pere Alcantara 13, Ciutadella, Menorca **🌐** cuk-cuk.com

€€€

Can Tanu

Have a craving for seafood? This Fornells restaurant is just the place, serving up grilled fish, paella and rice dishes, as well as the local speciality, *caldreta de llagosta* (lobster stew).

△ G4 **⌂** Carrer Major 16, Fornells, Menorca **🌐** cantanu.com

€€€

Exploring the Cales Coves by boat, and *(inset)* Binibeca

A jumble of white houses and tiny streets, it was designed to look like a *poblat de pescadors* (fishing village).

 21

Cales Coves

🅰️G4 🏝️Menorca 🚌Sant Climent, then 25 mins walk
ℹ️Carrer de Ses Moreres 13, Maó; 971 36 37 90

On either side of a pretty bay can be found Cales Coves – the site of Neolithic dwellings of up to 9 m (30 ft) in length, hollowed out of the rock face. The caves, thought to have been inhabited since pre-historic times, are today occupied by a community of people seeking an alternative lifestyle. Some of the caves have front doors, chimneys and even butane cookers.

About 8 km (5 miles) west, along the coast, lies Binibeca, a tourist village built in a style sympathetic to old Menorca.

22

Es Mercadal

🅰️G4 🏝️Menorca 🚌
ℹ️Carrer Major 16; 971 37 50 02

This small country town – one of the three, with Alaior and Ferreries, that are strung out along the main road from Maó to Ciutadella – is unremarkable in itself, but within reach of it are three places of interest.

El Toro, 3 km (2 miles) to the east, is Menorca's highest hill, at 350 m (1,150 ft). It is also the spiritual heart of the island and at its summit is the Santuari del Toro, built in 1670, which is run by nuns.

About 10 km (6 miles) north of Es Mercadal, the fishing village of Fornells transforms itself every summer into an outpost of St Tropez. In the harbour, smart yachts jostle with fishing boats, and the local jet-set crowd into the Bar Palma. Fornells' main culinary speciality is the *caldereta de llagosta* (lobster stew), but the quality varies and prices can be high.

The road-cum-dirt-track to the Cap de Cavalleria, 13 km (8 miles) north of Es Mercadal, passes through one of the Balearics' finest landscapes. Cavalleria is a rocky promontory, whipped by the tramontana wind from the north. It juts out into a choppy sea which, in winter, looks more like the North Atlantic than the Mediterranean. At the western edge of the peninsula are the remains of Sanisera, a Phoenician village mentioned by Pliny in the 1st century AD. The road leads to a headland, with a lighthouse and cliffs 90 m (295 ft) high, where peregrine falcons, sea eagles and kites ride the wind.

Further west along the coast is a string of fine, unspoiled beaches: La Vall d'Algaiarens, Cala Pregonda and Cala del Pilar are three of the best.

Maó

⚠ G4 **⌂ Menorca** 🚗🚌🚢
🛈 Carrer de Ses Moreres 13; 971 36 37 90

The quietly elegant city of Maó has lent its Spanish name, Mahón, to mayonnaise. It was occupied by the British three times during the 18th century. The legacy of past colonial rule can be seen in sober Georgian town houses, with their dark green shutters and sash windows.

Maó's harbour is one of the finest in the Mediterranean. Taking the street leading from the port to the upper town, you come to the 18th-century Església del Carme, a former Carmelite church whose cool white cloister is now the setting for a fruit and vegetable market. Behind the market is the **Col·lecció Hernández Sanz y Hernández Mora**, which houses Menorcan art and antiques. The nearby Plaça Constitució is overlooked by the church of Santa Maria, which has a huge organ. Next door is the town hall, with its Neo-Classical façade, adorned by the famous clock donated by Sir Richard Kane (1660–1736), the first British governor of Menorca.

Located at the end of the Carrer Isabel II is the Església de Sant Francesc, with an intriguing Romanesque doorway and Baroque façade. This is the venue for the **Museu de Menorca**, which explores the island's Talayotic past. Two minutes' walk south of here will take you to the Plaça de S'Esplanada, behind which is the **Ateneu de Maó**. Inside are collections of local ceramics and maps, and a library. It is advisable to obtain permission before looking around. On the north side of the harbour is a mansion known as Sant Antoni or the Golden Farm. As Maó's finest example of Palladian architecture, it has an arched façade, painted plum red, with white arches, in the traditional Menorcan style. Nelson, the British admiral, is thought to have stayed here. The house has a collection of Nelson memorabilia and a fine library but is closed to the public.

Col·lecció Hernández Sanz y Hernández Mora

♿ ⌂ Carrer Anuncivay 2
📞 971 35 65 23 🕐 May–Oct: 10am–1:30pm & 6–8pm Tue–Sat, 10am–1:30pm Sun; Nov–Apr: 10am–1:30pm & 6–8pm Thu–Sat, 10am–1:30pm Tue, Wed & Sun

Museu de Menorca

⌂ Plà des Monestir 9
🕐 10am–6pm Tue & Thu, 10am–2pm Wed, Fri, Sat & Sun 🌐 museudemenorca.com

Ateneu de Maó

⌂ Carrer Rovellada de Dalt 25
📞 608 02 21 10 🕐 Summer: 9am–2pm Mon–Fri; winter: 4–9:30pm Mon–Fri

ANCIENT MENORCA

Exceptionally rich in prehistoric remains, Menorca has been described as an immense open-air museum. The majority of the sites are the work of the Talayot people who lived between 2000 BC and 1000 BC and are named after the *talaiots* or huge stone towers that characterize the Menorcan landscape. There are hundreds of these Bronze Age villages and structures dotted around the island. Usually open to the public and free of charge, these sites provide an invaluable insight into the ancient inhabitants of the Balearic Islands.

 The harbour on Cabrera island, watched over by the fortress on the hill above

 Cabrera

🅐 G4 🏠 Baleares 🚢 From Colònia Sant Jordi 🚉 Carrer Gabriel Roca s/n, Colònia Sant Jordi; 971 65 60 73

From the beaches of Es Trenc and Sa Ràpita, on the south coast of Mallorca, Cabrera looms on the horizon. The largest island in an archipelago of the same name, it lies 18 km (11 miles) from the most southerly point of Mallorca. Cabrera is home to rare plants, reptiles and sea birds, such as Eleonora's falcon. The waters are important for marine life. All this has resulted in it being declared a national park. Cabrera was once used as a military base and it has a small population. On it stands a 14th-century castle and a simple inn.

㉕ **Formentera**

🅐 F5 🏠 Baleares 🚢 From Ibiza 🚉 Estación Marítima, Puerto de La Savina; www.formentera.es

An hour's boat ride from Ibiza will bring you to this unspoiled island where waters are blue and the way of life is slow.

From the small port of La Savina, there are buses to other parts of the island, or you can hire a car, moped or bicycle from one of the shops.

Sant Francesc Xavier, Formentera's tiny capital, is situated 3 km (2 miles) from La Savina. Most of the island's amenities are in this town. From Sant Francesc, a bumpy minor road leads southwards, ending at Cap de Barbaria, the site of an 18th-century defensive tower and a lighthouse. From the fishing port of Es Caló de Sant Agustí the road winds upwards past the Restaurante Es Mirador, with its panoramic view, to the village of Nostra Senyora del Pilar de la Mola on top of the plateau. About 3 km (2 miles) to the east is a lighthouse, Far de la Mola. Nearby stands a monument to Jules Verne (1828–1905), who used Formentera for the setting of his novel *Hector Servadac*.

One sight worth seeking out is the megalithic sepulchre of Ca Na Costa (2000 BC) near Sant Francesc, the only one of its kind in the Balearics. This circle of upright stone slabs predates the Carthaginians.

The island features some of the Mediterranean's last unspoiled shorelines. Two of the finest beaches are Migjorn and Cala Sahona, southwest of Sant Francesc. Illetes and Llevant are two beaches on either side of a long sandy spit in the far north of the island. To the north is the island of Espalmador, with its natural springs.

STAY

Hotel Entre Pinos
There's a great breakfast, pool and spa at this Formentera option.

🅐 F5 🏠 Avenida Mola, km 12.3, Es Caló, Formentera 🌐 hotelentrepinos.es

€€€

Sa Volta Hotel
This Formentera hotel offers an elegant stay. The rooftop pool has excellent views.

🅐 F5 🏠 Avenida Miramar 94, Es Pujols, Formentera 🌐 savolta.com

€€€

EAT

La Mariterranea Formentera
Although the speciality of this Formentera restaurant is *paellas* and *fideuá* (a noodle dish similar to *paella*), you'll also find a selection of other meat and fish dishes here.

🅿 F5 🏠 Carrer Major 42, Sant Ferràn de ses Roques, Formentera 🌐 mariterranea.com

€€€

Integral
Enjoy inventive veggie and vegan dishes at this welcoming spot. It serves delicious juices and smoothies as well.

🅿 F5 🏠 Carrer de s'Espalmador 39, Es Pujols, Formentera 📞 971 32 91 07

€€€

FORMENTERA'S BEACHES

The beaches of Formentera can easily rival those of Ibiza. The unspoiled natural environment, magnificent sand and clean waters attract an increasing number of visitors. Most have no hotels or clubs nearby and only a few feature bars or restaurants, which for many people only adds to their charm.

OUTDOOR ACTIVITIES

If the thought of just flopping on the sand gives you itchy feet, there are plenty of opportunities to be active on Formentera's beaches. Although the conditions for windsurfing are not as impressive here as they are in the Canary Islands, the gentler winds makes Formentera's beaches a good place for beginners to pick up some basic techniques. Take a lesson with Wet4Fun on Es Pujols beach *(www. wet4fun.com)*. They also offer sailing courses for a range of ages and abilities, kayaking and stand-up paddleboarding (SUP). If you're feeling adventurous, you could even opt for SUP yoga.

Prefer to be underwater? Formentera's clear, clean waters, combined with the diversity of marine life, creates the ideal conditions for diving. Every seaside resort has at least one *centro de buceo* (diving centre), but our favourite is Vellmari Formentera diving in La Savina *(vellmari.com)*.

← Windsurfing on the turquoise waters off Formentera

TOP 5 FORMENTERA BEACHES

Platja de ses Illetes
The most popular beach on the island. The Es Trucadors peninsula stretches to the north.

Platja de Llevant
This beach, occupying the eastern side of the peninsula, is much quieter than Platja de ses Illetes.

Platja de sa Roqueta
Situated next to the only hotel in this area, this beach connects to Platja de Llevant so is perfect for beach walks.

Platja de Tramuntana
A number of small, secluded beaches are tucked among the rocks here.

Es Caló de Sant Agustí
The beaches near this fishing village can be reached via the footbridges that cross the thickets covering the dunes.

↑ A sheltered corner of a secluded beach near the fishing village of Es Caló de Sant Agustí

WESTERN CANARY ISLANDS

At one time the most westerly point of the known world to Europeans, these islands are shrouded in mystery as their early history remains unclear. Discovered and visited sporadically throughout history, concrete records begin with the Spanish conquest in the 15th century, which saw the defeat of the Indigenous Gaunche people who had come to the islands from North Africa in the 10th century BC. Tenerife and La Palma were the last islands in the Canaries to fall to the Spanish. Although little physical evidence of the Guanches remains, their language is immortalized in Tenerife's name itself, which comes from a Guanche word meaning "snowy mountain". Following the Spanish conquest, the colonists planted vines in Tenerife's fertile volcanic soil, and the island was soon awash with vineyards, producing dry wines which became the island's main export.

After the conquest, all seven of the main Canary Islands were considered a single province of Spain, resulting in a tug-of-war for dominance between Gran Canaria and Tenerife, the two largest and most economically important islands. This would continue until 1927, when the current political distinction between east and west was established.

WESTERN
CANARY
ISLANDS

Llano Negro
Los Sauces
Hoya Grande
LP1
Puntagorda
LP1
9 LA PALMA
Santa Cruz de la Palma
Breña Alta
Los Llanos
de Aridane
El Paso
Tazacorte
La Palma
LP2
LP2
Monte de Luna
Las Indias
Los Canarios

Atlantic Ocean

Gomera
Agulo
Villahermoso
GM1
**LA
GOMERA**
Garajonay
1,487 m (4,878 ft) △
11
Vueltas La Calera
GM2
San
Sebastián
Allajero
Playa
Santiago

Hierro
Valverde
Las Puntas
Puerto de la Estaca
Frontera
Sabinosa
10 EL HIERRO
La Restinga

WESTERN CANARY ISLANDS

Must See
1 Parque Nacional del Teide

Experience More
2 La Laguna
3 Puerto de la Cruz
4 Candelaria
5 Los Cristianos
6 Montes de Anaga
7 La Orotava
8 Santa Cruz de Tenerife
9 La Palma
10 El Hierro
11 La Gomera

Visitors filtering into the →
park, at the base of the
imposing Teide mountain

1 🅜 🍽

PARQUE NACIONAL DEL TEIDE

🄰F7 **🄌Tenerife** **🚌348 from Puerto de la Cruz; 342 from Playa de las Américas** **🕒9am–6pm daily** **🎫1 & 6 Jan, 25 Dec** **ℹEl Portillo Visitors' Centre; 922 92 23 71**

Towering over Tenerife and surrounded by a wild volcanic landscape, Pico del Teide is an awesome sight and the Mount Teide National Park is a delight to explore. Follow the marked paths to discover this unique, protected area.

Pico del Teide was once dwarfed by a much larger adjacent cone, until it collapsed over 180,000 years ago, leaving behind its smaller neighbour and La Caldera de Las Cañadas – a wide volcanic crater. A rim of fractured crags forms a pie-crust edge to the 45-km- (28-mile-) long perimeter of this enormous caldera. With this collapse, Pico del Teide, which sits on the northern edge of the Caldera de Las Cañadas, became Spain's highest summit. Teide is still active and nearby Pico Viejo, a volcanic cone also known as Montaña Chahorra, last erupted in the 18th century.

Today volcanic material forms a wilderness of weathered, mineral-tinted rocks, ash beds and lava streams. The flat expanses of the seven *cañadas* (small sandy plateaus) were created by the collapse of ancient craters.

A single road crosses the plateau of Las Cañadas, passing a parador, cable-car station and visitors' centre. Near the Parador de Cañadas del Teide, you'll find Los Roques de García, flamboyantly shaped lava rocks. Other famous rock formations in the park include Los Azulejos, which glitter blue-green because of the copper deposits within them.

WILD FLOWERS

The inhospitable badlands of Las Cañadas are inhabited by some rare and beautiful plants, many of which are unique to the Canary Islands. Most striking is the tall *Echium wildprettii*, a kind of viper's bugloss, whose red flowers reach 3 m (10 ft) in early summer. The best time of year for flower-spotting is May to June. Don't take any plants away with you: all vegetation within the park is strictly protected and must not be uprooted or picked.

←
A cable car traversing the park; the ride takes eight minutes and leaves visitors just short of Teide's summit

 INSIDER TIP
Park Life

Take time to stop by the visitors' centre during your trip. Here, a film and exhibition chart the origins of the park, while displays help identify the wild flowers found across the landscape.

↑ Relaxing in the sunshine at the Parador de Cañadas del Teide, a mountain lodge

EXPERIENCE MORE

La Laguna

🗺 F7 🏝 Tenerife 🚌 ℹ Calle de la Carrera 7; www. webtenerife.com

A bustling university town, La Laguna is the second-largest settlement on Tenerife and a UNESCO World Heritage Site.

Its charming old quarter, which is best explored on foot, has many historic buildings and good museums. Most of the sights lie between the bell-towered Iglesia de Nuestra Señora de la Concepción, which dates from 1502, and the Plaza del Adelantado. The town hall, a convent and the Palacio de Nava stand on this tree-shaded square.

Puerto de la Cruz

🗺 F7 🏝 Tenerife 🚌 ℹ Calle Las Lonjas s/n; www.webtenerife.com

The oldest resort in the Canaries, Puerto de la Cruz first came to prominence in 1706, when a volcanic eruption obliterated Tenerife's main port of Garachico. Puerto de la Cruz took its place, later becoming popular with genteel English convalescents. The town's older buildings give it much of its present character.

The beautiful Complejo Costa Martiánez, an open-air swimming complex designed by the famous Lanzarote architect César Manrique (*p569*), compensates for a lack of good beaches. Lounge or swim in one of its seawater pools, surrounded by palms and fountains.

Outside town, the **Jardín de Orquídeas** is the oldest garden in Tenerife, and has a large orchid collection. For more nature, Icod de los Vinos, a short drive west, has a spectacular ancient dragon tree.

Jardín de Orquídeas

⊗ 🏝 Camino Sitio Litre s/n 🕐 9:30am–5:30pm Wed–Sun 🌐 jardinde orquideas.com

→

Statue of a Guanche chief on the seafront at Candelaria

Candelaria

🗺 F7 🏝 Tenerife 🚌 ℹ Avenida de la Constitución 7; www. webtenerife.com

This coastal town is famous for its shrine to Nuestra Señora de la Candelaria, the Canary Islands' patron saint, whose image is surrounded by flowers and candles in a modern church in the main square. Supposedly washed ashore in pagan times, this gaudy Virgin was venerated before Christianity reached the island. In 1826 a tidal wave returned her to the sea, but a replica draws pilgrims to worship here every August. Outside, stone effigies of Guanche chiefs line the sea wall.

A street in La Laguna's old quarter, a UNESCO World Heritage Site

 5

Los Cristianos

F7 **Tenerife**
Paseo Playa de las Vistas 1; www.webtenerife.com

The old fishing village of Los Cristianos, on Tenerife's south coast, has grown into a town spreading out along the foot of barren hills. Ferries and hydrofoils make regular trips from its little port to La Gomera and El Hierro *(p562)*.

To the north lies the modern expanse of Playa de las Américas, Tenerife's largest development. It offers visitors a cheerful, relaxed, undemanding cocktail of sun and fun.

A brief sojourn inland leads to the much older town of Adeje and to the Barranco del Infierno, a wild gorge with an attractive waterfall (2 hours' round walk from Adeje).

Along the coast to the east, the Costa del Silencio is a pleasant contrast to most of the other large resorts, with its bungalow developments surrounding fishing villages. Los Abrigos has lively fish restaurants lining its harbour.

STAY

Santa Barbara Golf & Ocean Club
This four-star resort near Los Cristianos is excellent value for money.

F7 **Avenida del Atlàntico, Golf del Sur, San Miguel de Abona, Tenerife** santa barbaratenerife.com

€€€

6

Montes de Anaga

F7 **Tenerife** **Santa Cruz de Tenerife, La Laguna**

The rugged mountains north of Santa Cruz are lush, and abound with a range of birds and plants. Walking is popular, and guiding maps are available at the tourist office. A steep road with marker posts climbs up from the village of San Andrés by the artificial beach of Las Teresitas. On clear days there are splendid vistas along the paths.

Winding down through the laurel forests of Monte de las Mercedes and the valley of Tejina, you will first come to the town of Valle de Guerra, where there is an ethnographic museum. Next, you will reach Tacoronte, with its interesting churches and a *bodega*.

7

La Orotava

F7 **Tenerife**
Calle Calvario 4; www.webtenerife.com

Nestled in the fertile hills above the Orotava Valley, La Orotava's historic town clusters around the large Iglesia de Nuestra Señora de la Concepción. This domed Baroque building with twin towers was built in the late 18th century. In the surrounding streets and squares are old churches, convents and grand houses with elaborate wooden balconies. Casa de los Balcones and Casa del Turista, on Calle San Francisco, sell handicrafts and regional food.

 8

Santa Cruz de Tenerife

F7 **Tenerife**
Plaza de España; www.webtenerife.com

Tenerife's capital city, Santa Cruz de Tenerife, hosts one of the world's most popular carnivals, second only to Rio de Janeiro. The city has a deep-water harbour suitable for large ships. Its nicest beach, Las Teresitas, lies 7 km (4 miles) to the north. It was created by importing millions of tonnes of Saharan sand and building a protective reef just offshore..

Santa Cruz boasts many handsome historic buildings. The hub of the city focuses around the Plaza de España, near the harbour. Just off it is the Calle de Castillo, the main shopping street.

Particularly interesting is the **Museo de la Naturaleza y el Hombre**, in the Palacio Insular, where Guanche mummies grin in glass cases. Other attractions include the **Museo de Bellas Artes**, which has old masters. Contemporary sculptures adorn the Parque Municipal García Sanabria, a pleasant park with shady paths.

Museo de la Naturaleza y el Hombre
Calle Fuentes Morales 1 **922 53 58 16** **10am-5pm Mon & Sun, 9am-8pm Tue-Sat**

Museo de Bellas Artes
Calle José Murphy 12 **922 24 43 58** **10am-8pm Tue-Fri, 10am-3pm Sat & Sun**

↑ Carnival parade through the streets of Santa Cruz de Tenerife

Pastel façades and delicate wooden balconies line the streets of Santa Cruz de la Palma on La Palma

9
La Palma

E6 Canary Islands
Santa Cruz de la Palma
Plaza de la Constitución s/n, Santa Cruz de la Palma; www.visitlapalma.es

Reaching an altitude of 2,426 m (7,959 ft), La Palma is the world's steepest island. It lies on the northwestern tip of the archipelago and has a cool, moist climate and lush vegetation. The mountainous interior is covered with forests of pine, laurel and giant fern.

The centre of the island is dominated by the Caldera de Taburiente, a volcano's massive crater, more than 8 km (5 miles) wide. National park status is an indication of its botanical and geological importance. The International Astrophysics Observatory crowns the summit. A couple of roads traverse La Palma's dizzy heights, offering fine views of the craters of La Cumbrecita and Roque de los Muchachos.

Santa Cruz de la Palma, the island's main town and port, is an elegant place of old houses with balconies. In the cobbled street behind the seafront, Calle O'Daly, are the Iglesia El Salvador and the *ayuntamiento*.

The tortuous mountain road southwest of Santa Cruz winds over Las Cumbres mountains to El Paso, known for its silk production and hand-rolled cigars.

In September 2021, a volcanic eruption on La Palma caused significant damage to property and thousands of people were displaced. The last major eruption in the Cumbre Vieja volcano chain was in 1971.

10
El Hierro

E7 Canary Islands
Puerto de la Estaca
Calle Doctor Quintero 4, Valverde; www.elhierro.travel

Due to a lack of sandy beaches, El Hierro has escaped tourist invasions. Instead it has caught the attention of naturalists,

---

> **GREAT VIEW**
> **Interstellar**
>
> A visit to La Palma would not be complete without appreciating the stellar views of one of the world's clearest night skies. Take a trip with La Palma Astronomy Tours *(www.lapalma stars.com)* for insider access to the best spots.

---

with its hilly landscape and unusual fauna and flora. El Hierro is the smallest of the Canaries, and the furthest west.

Valverde, the island's capital, sits at 600 m (2,000 ft) above sea level. Canary pines and peculiarly twisted juniper trees cover El Hierro's mountainous interior, best seen from the many footpaths and scenic viewpoints along the roads. A ridge of woodland, curving east–west across the island, marks the edge of a volcano. The crater forms a fertile depression known as El Golfo.

In the far west is the Ermita de los Reyes, a place of pilgrimage and the starting point of the island's biggest fiesta, held in July every four years.

11
La Gomera

E7 Canary Islands
 Calle Real 32, San Sebastián de la Gomera; www.lagomera.travel

La Gomera is the most accessible of the smaller western

$\rightarrow$

Rock formation rising above the steep gorges that typify the island of La Gomera islands, only 40 minutes by hydrofoil from Los Cristianos on Tenerife (90 minutes by ferry), or by plane from Tenerife or Gran Canaria. Many come to La Gomera for a day only, taking a coach trip. Others hire a car and explore on their own: a scenic but exhausting drive for a single day as the terrain is intensely buckled, and the central plateau is deeply scored by dramatic ravines. Driving across these gorges involves negotiating countless dizzying hairpin bends.

The best way to enjoy the island is to stay a while and explore it at leisure, preferably doing some walking. On a fine day, La Gomera's scenery is glorious. Rock pinnacles jut above steep slopes studded with ferns while terraced hillsides glow with palms and flowering creepers. The best section, the Parque Nacional de Garajonay, is a UNESCO World Heritage Site.

San Sebastián, La Gomera's main town and ferry terminal, is situated on the east coast, a scattering of white buildings around a small beach. Among its sights are some places associated with Columbus (*p65*), who topped up his water supplies here before setting out on his voyages. A well in the customs house bears the grand words "With this water America was baptized". Legend has it that he also prayed in the Iglesia de la Asunción, and stayed at a local house.

Beyond the arid hills to the south lies Playa de Santiago, the island's only real resort, which has a grey pebble beach. Valle Gran Rey, in the far west, is a fertile valley of palms and staircase terraces. Once an enclave for hippies, this area is now a popular retreat for nature lovers and artists. In the north, tiny roads weave a tortuous course around several pretty villages, plunging at intervals to small, stony beaches. Las Rosas is a popular stop-off for coach parties, who can enjoy the visitors' centre and a restaurant with a panoramic view.

The road to the coast from Las Rosas leads through the town of Vallehermoso, dwarfed by the huge Roque de Cano, an impressive mass of solidified lava. Just off the north coast is Los Órganos, a fascinating rock formation of crystallized basalt columns resembling the pipes of an organ.

EASTERN CANARY ISLANDS

The Canary Islands were originally inhabited by the Guanche people, who came over from North Africa around 1000 BC. When Spanish conquerors sailed to the archipelago in the early 15th century, they first reached these eastern isles, with Lanzarote being the first to yield to the invaders in 1402. Fuerteventura fell soon after, followed swiftly by Gran Canaria. Fuerteventura was densely wooded at the time, but European settlers cut down the timber for shipbuilding, and the dry climate and introduction of goats to the island reduced the vegetation to parched scrub.

The geographical position of these islands, coupled with the strong trade winds that blow over them, made them the ideal port of call on Columbus's very first transatlantic journey to the Americas. Casa de Colón on Gran Canaria is said to be where Columbus stayed while one of his ships was being repaired.

Lanzarote began to transform from a land dedicated to agriculture and fishing into a popular tourist destination in the 1960s, a change that was heavily influenced by local artist and architect César Manrique. The island's idiosyncratic white houses and the conspicuous scarcity of high-rise buildings is thanks to him. Along with Fuerteventura and Gran Canaria, Lanzarote is a holiday playground – with winter sun, long beaches and plenty of outdoor activities.

EASTERN CANARY ISLANDS

Experience

1. Playa Blanca
2. Puerto del Carmen
3. Parque Nacional de Timanfaya
4. Costa Teguise
5. Arrecife
6. Teguise
7. Haría
8. Jameos del Agua
9. Caleta de Fuste
10. Puerto del Rosario
11. Betancuria
12. Península de Jandía
13. Corralejo
14. Puerto de Mogán
15. Puerto Rico
16. Maspalomas
17. Agaete
18. Tafira
19. Las Palmas de Gran Canaria

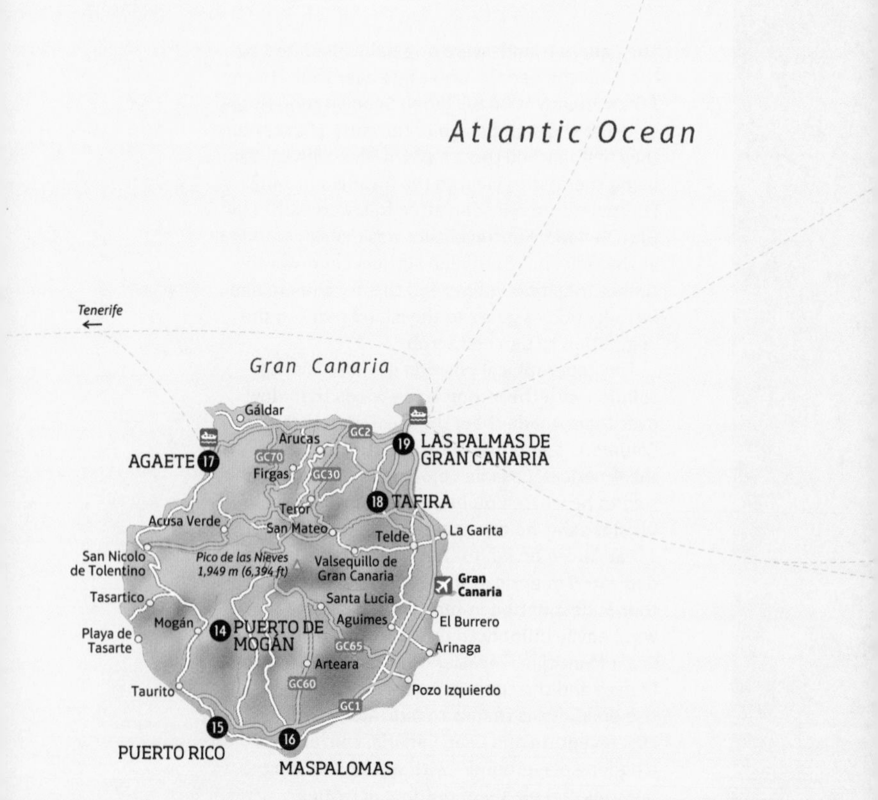

Madeira
Atlantic Ocean
Tenerife
Gran Canaria
Gáldar
Arucas
GC2
19 LAS PALMAS DE GRAN CANARIA
AGAETE 17
GC70
Firgas
GC30
18 TAFIRA
Teror
Acusa Verde
San Mateo
Telde
La Garita
San Nicolo de Tolentino
Pico de las Nieves 1,949 m (6,394 ft)
Valsequillo de Gran Canaria
Gran Canaria
Tasartico
Santa Lucia
Mogán
14 PUERTO DE MOGÁN
Aguimes
El Burrero
Playa de Tasarte
GC65
Arinaga
Arteara
GC60
Taurito
Pozo Izquierdo
GC1
15
PUERTO RICO
16
MASPALOMAS

Alegranza

Montaña Clara

La Graciosa

Órzola

JAMEOS DEL
AGUA ❽

HARÍA ❼

Caleta de
Famara

La Santa

Lanzarote

Tinajo

TEGUISE ❻

Mancha
Blanca

San
Bartolomé

LZ1

COSTA
TEGUISE ❹

PARQUE NACIONDAL
DE TIMANFAYA ❸

Yaiza

ARRECIFE ❺

LZ2

Maciot

PUERTO DEL
CARMEN ❷

PLAYA
BLANCA ❶

Lobos

CORRALEJO ❸

Lajares

El Cotillo

La Oliva

Parque
Holandés

FV1

Tindaya

Puerto Lajas

Puertito de
Los Molinos

FV1

Llanos de
la Concepción

Casillas
del Ángel

FV20

PUERTO DEL ROSARIO ❿

Fuerteventura

✈ Fuerteventura

El Matorral

Antigua

BETANCURIA ⑪

CALETA DE FUSTE ❾

Pajara

Tuineje

Pozo Negro

Tesejérague

Juan Gopar

FV2

La Pared

Gran Tarajal

Costa Calma

Tarajalejo

La Lajita

FV2

Esquinzo

PENÍNSULA
DE JANDÍA ⑫

Morro Jable

*Punta de
Jandía*

Atlantic Ocean

0 kilometres   20

0 miles   20

N
↑

EXPERIENCE

①

Playa Blanca

 G6 Lanzarote 🚌🚢
🚶 Calle Varadero 3; www.
turismolanzarote.com

The fishing village origins of
this resort are readily apparent
around its harbour. Although it
has expanded in recent years,
Playa Blanca remains a family-
oriented place with character.
It has plenty of cafés and
restaurants, shops and bars,
and several large hotels. There
are one or two good stretches
of sand near the town, but the
most enticing lie around
the rocky headlands to the
east, where the clear sea laps
into rocky coves, and clothes
seem superfluous. Playa de
Papagayo is the best known
of these, but a diligent search
will gain you one all to yourself. A four-wheel-drive vehicle
is advisable to negotiate the
unsurfaced roads that lead
to these beaches.

The underwater **Museo
Atlántico** combines art and
conservation. Jason deCaires
Taylor's installations act as an
artificial reef for banks of
sardines and octopuses.

Museo Atlántico

 Puerto Marina Rubicón,
Calle el Berrugo 2 🕒9:30am-
5:30pm Mon-Sat (diving: to
4pm) 🌐underwatermuseum
lanzarote.com

---

②

Puerto del Carmen

G6 Lanzarote 🚌🚢
🚶 Avenida de la Playa; www.
turismolanzarote.com

More than 60 per cent of
Lanzarote's tourists stay in this
resort, which stretches several
kilometres along the seafront.
The coastal road carves its way
through holiday infrastructure,
which is pleasantly designed
and unoppressive, and offers
easy access to a long golden
beach, Playa Blanca. Another
beach nearby is Playa de los
Pocillos. To the north is the
quaint village of Tías and A
Casa José Saramago, the
house-cum-museum where
the Nobel Prize-winning writer
(1922–2010) lived his last
18 years in exile after the
Portuguese government
deemed his work to be
religiously offensive.

③

Parque Nacional de Timanfaya

G6 Yaiza, Lanzarote
🚶 Carretera LZ-67, km 9.6,
Mancha Blanca; 928 11 80
42 🕒9am-5:45pm daily
🚫1 & 6 Jan, 15 Sep, 25 &
31 Dec

From 1730 to 1736, a series of
volcanic eruptions took place
on Lanzarote, burying over

EAT

**La Carmencita
del Puerto**
This Puerto del Carmen
tapas bar is about as
authentically Spanish
as they come.

G6 Avenida de Las
Playas s/n, Puerto del
Carmen, Lanzarote
📞928 51 23 18 🚫Sun

€€€

200 sq km (77 sq miles) of Lanzarote's most fertile land in lava. Miraculously, no one was killed, though many islanders emigrated.

Today, the volcanoes that once devastated Lanzarote provide an enigmatic attraction, aptly known as the Montañas del Fuego (Fire Mountains). They are part of the Parque Nacional de Timanfaya, established in 1974 to protect a fascinating and important geological record. The entrance to the park lies north of the village of Yaiza, where you can enjoy wonderful views across the park. Afterwards, you drive through haunting scenery of dark, barren lava cinders topped by brooding red-black volcano cones. Finally, you will reach Islote de Hilario, whereyou can park at El Diablo panoramic restaurant. From here, buses take visitors for 30-minute tours of the desolate, lunar-like landscapes.

Afterwards, back at Islote de Hilario, guides will provide graphic demonstrations that this volcano is not extinct, but only dormant – brushwood pushed into a crevice bursts instantly into a ball of flame, while water poured into a sunken pipe shoots out in a scorching jet of steam.

 Fishing boats on the water in front of the charming town of Arrecife

❹ Costa Teguise

🅰 G6 🚗 10 km (6 miles) N of Arrecife, Lanzarote
🚌 🛈 Avenida Islas Canarias, Junto Pueblo Marinero; www.turismo lanzarote.com

The contrast between old town Teguise (p570), Lanzarote's former capital, and the exclusive Costa Teguise is striking. Amid the arid, low-lying terrain of this barren ashland, fake greenery and suburban lamps line boulevards filled with timeshare accommodation, leisure clubs and luxury hotels.

❺ Arrecife

🅰 G6 🚗 Lanzarote
✈ 🛈 Avenida la Marina 7; www. turismolanzarote.com

Arrecife, with its modern buildings and lively streets, is the commercial and administrative centre of the island. Despite its modern trappings, the capital retains much of its old charm, with palm-lined promenades, a fine beach and

The waterfront promenade in Playa Blanca, popular for an early evening stroll

two small forts. **Castillo San Gabriel** offers lovely views from a mezzanine, accessed via a stone walkway over the sea. It also houses the Museo de Historia de Arrecife. The 18th-century **Castillo de San José** is now a museum of contemporary art and was renovated by César Manrique. One of his paintings is on display here.

Castillo San Gabriel
🏠 Calle Punta de la Largarta
📞 928 80 28 84 🕐 10am–5pm Mon–Fri, 10am–2pm Sat
🚫 Public hols

Castillo de San José
🏠 Puerto de Naos 📞 901 20 03 00 🕐 10am–6pm daily
🚫 1 Jan, 25 Dec

CÉSAR MANRIQUE

Lanzarote hero César Manrique trained as a painter, and spent time in mainland Spain and New York before coming back to his island home for good in 1968. The artist, sculptor and architect campaigned for traditional and environmentally friendly development on the island, setting strict building height limits and colour requirements. Many tourist sites throughout the Canaries benefited from his talents.

6

Teguise

🅰️G6 🚗Lanzarote
🚌 ℹ️Plaza de la
Constitución; www.
turismolanzarote.com

The island's capital until 1852,
Teguise is a well-kept, old-
fashioned town with wide,
cobbled streets. Visit on a
Sunday, when there is a
handicrafts market and
folk dancing.

Outside Teguise, in the
15th-century castle of Santa
Bárbara, is the **Museo de la
Piratería**, which tells the story
of the pirates who passed
through this area. From here
there are fine views of the
town, as well as a large part
of the island.

If you want to see more of
inland Lanzarote, follow the
central road south of Teguise,
through the strange farmland
of La Geria. Black volcanic ash
covering the landscape has
been scooped into protective,
crescent-shaped pits which
trap moisture to enable vines
and other crops to flourish.
Mozaga, one of the main
villages in the area, is a major
centre of wine production.
Standing on the roadside near
Mozaga is the *Monumento al
Campesino*, César Manrique's
(p569) striking modern sculpture that is dedicated to
Lanzarote's farmers.

Located between Teguise
and Arrecife is the **Fundación
César Manrique**. The former
home and studio of the artist
is a work of art itself. It incorporates five lava caves, some
of his own work and his contemporary art collection.

Museo de la Piratería

⊗ 🚗Montaña de Guanapay
🕐9am–4pm Mon–Sat; 10am–
4pm Sun 🚫1 & 6 Jan, 25 Dec
🌐museodelapirateria.com

Fundación César Manrique

⊗ 🚗Taro de Tahíche
🕐10am–2pm Mon–Fri
🚫1 Jan 🌐fcmanrique.org

↑ Shops and restaurants
set up outside traditional
white houses in Teguise

7

Haría

🅰️G6 🚗Lanzarote
🚌 ℹ️Plaza de la
Constitución 1; www.
turismolanzarote.com

Palm trees and white, cube-
shaped houses distinguish
this picturesque village. It acts
as a gateway to excursions
round the northern tip of the
island. The road to the north
gives memorable views over
exposed cliffs and the 609-m-
(2,000-ft-) high Monte Corona.

From Manrique's **Mirador
del Río** you get excellent
views of La Graciosa, and the
northernmost of the Canary
Islands, Alegranza. To the
south are the Mala prickly
pear plantations, where
cochineal (crimson dye) is
extracted from the insects
which feed on the plants.
Nearby is the **Jardín de
Cactus**, a cactus garden with
around 450 species of cactus,
again designed by Manrique.
The vivid green shade of the
plants stands out against the
blue sky and dark volcano.

> **The island's capital until 1852, Teguise
> is a well-kept, old-fashioned town with
> wide, cobbled streets. Visit on a Sunday,
> when there is a handicrafts market.**

Mirador del Río

⊗ 🅰 Haría 📞 901 20 03 00
🕙 Mid-Jul–mid-Sep: 10am–5pm daily; mid-Sep–mid-Jul: 10am–5:45pm daily

Jardín de Cactus

⊗ 🅰 Guatiza 📞 901 20 03 00
🕙 10am–5pm daily

Jameos del Agua

🅰 G6 🅰 Lanzarote 📞 901 20 03 00 🕙 10am–5pm daily

An eruption of the Monte Corona volcano formed the Jameos del Agua lava caves on Lanzarote's northeast coast. Between 1965 and 1968, these caves were landscaped by César Manrique into an imaginative subterranean complex containing a restaurant, nightclub, a swimming pool edged by palm trees, and gardens of oleander and cacti. Steps lead to a shallow seawater lagoon where a rare species of blind white crab, unique to Lanzarote, glows softly in the dim light. An exhibition on volcanology and Canarian flora and fauna also deserves a look. Folk-dancing evenings are regularly held in this unusual setting.

Another popular attraction is the nearby **Cueva de los Verdes**, a tube of solidified lava stretching 6 km (4 miles) underground. Guided tours of the caves are available, which provide an excellent insight into the peculiarities, secrets and legends that surround these caves.

Cueva de los Verdes

⊗⊗ 🅰 Haría 📞 901 20 03 00 🕙 Mid-Jul–mid-Sep: 10am–4pm daily; mid-Sep–mid-Jul: 10am–5pm daily

DRINK

Ancla2
This chilled-out bar has a huge terrace and direct access to the beach. Try the cava sangría.

🅰 G6 🅰 Avenida de las Playas 38, Puerto del Carmen, Lanzarote 📞 666 86 16 84 🕙 Mon & Tue

---

Lounge Bar
The music and cocktail menu are very good at this cosy spot.

🅰 G6 🅰 Calle Irlanda, Local 6, Playa Blanca, Lanzarote 📞 676 52 15 36

VOLCANIC ISLANDS

The volcanic activity which formed the Canary Islands has created a variety of scenery, from distinctive lava formations to enormous volcanoes crowned by huge, gaping craters. The islands are all at different stages in their evolution. Tenerife, Lanzarote, El Hierro and La Palma are still volcanically active and dramatic displays of flames can be seen in Lanzarote's Montañas del Fuego (p569).

The Canaries are situated above faults in the earth's crust. When magma (molten rock) rises through these cracks, volcanoes are formed. Lanzarote, El Hierro and La Palma are wide, gently sloping shield volcanoes standing on the sea floor. All of them are composed of basalt formed by a hot, dense magma.

In recent years, scientists have worried that La Palma is so volatile that its entire western side may fall into the sea, causing a mega tsunami.

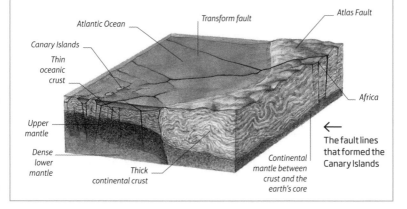

Atlantic Ocean
Transform fault
Atlas Fault
Canary Islands
Thin oceanic crust
Africa
Upper mantle
Dense lower mantle
Thick continental crust
Continental mantle between crust and the earth's core

← The fault lines that formed the Canary Islands

Caleta de Fuste

🗺️ G7 🏝️ Fuerteventura 🚌
ℹ️ Calle Juan Ramón Soto
Morales 10, El Castillo; www.
visitfuerteventura.es

About halfway down the eastern coast lies Caleta de Fuste. The attractive low-rise, self-catering holiday centres surround a horseshoe bay of soft, gently shelving sand.

There are many watersports facilities, as well as the Pueblo Majorero, an attractive "village" of shops and restaurants around a central plaza near the beach. These features make Caleta de Fuste one of Fuerteventura's most relaxed and pleasant resorts.

Puerto del Rosario

🗺️ G6 🏝️ Fuerteventura
✈️🚌🚢 ℹ️ Avenida Reyes de
España; www.turismo-
puertodelrosario.org

Fuerteventura's administrative capital was founded in 1797. Originally known as Puerto de Cabras (Goats' Harbour), after a nearby gorge that was once used for watering goats, it was rechristened to smarten up its image in 1957. The only large port on Fuerteventura, Puerto del Rosario is the base for inter-island ferries and a busy fishing industry.

Betancuria

🗺️ G7 🏝️ Fuerteventura 🚌
ℹ️ Amador Rodríguez s/n;
928 54 96 04

Inland, rugged peaks of extinct volcanoes, separated by wide plains, present a scene of austere grandeur. Scattered, stark villages and obsolete windmills occupy the lowlands, which are occasionally fertile enough to nurture a few crops or palm trees. Beyond, devoid of vegetation, the hills form stark outlines. From a distance they appear brown and grey, but up close the rocks glow with an astonishing range of mauves, pinks and ochres. The richness of colour in this interior wilderness is at its most striking at sunset.

Betancuria is built in a lovely valley here, surrounded by mountains. The village was named after Jean de Béthencourt, Fuerteventura's 15th-century conqueror, who moved his capital inland to thwart pirates. This peaceful oasis is now the island's prettiest village. The Iglesia de Santa María contains gilded altars, decorated beams and sacred relics. Housed in a traditional Canarian house, the **Museo Arqueológico** displays many local archaeological artifacts.

To the south, the village of Pájara boasts a 17th-century church with a curiously decorated doorway. Its design of serpents and strange beasts is believed to be of Aztec influence. Inside, the twin aisles

> 🔍 HIDDEN GEM
> ### Bentan-que
> A few kilometres from Betancuria, at Castillo de Lara, is this delightful picnic spot. There are barbecues you can use (bring your own charcoal) and a kids' play area.

← Playa del Castillo, beside a palm-lined promenade at Caleta de Fuste

both contain statues: one of a radiant Madonna and Child in white and silver, the other a Virgen de los Dolores in black.

La Oliva, to the north, was the site of the Spanish military headquarters until the 19th century. The Casa de los Coroneles (House of the Colonels) is a faded yellow mansion with hundreds of windows and coffered ceilings. The fortified church and the arts centre displaying works of Canary Island artists are also worth a visit.

Museo Arqueológico
⊗ ◪ Calle Roberto Roldán
☎ 928 87 82 41 ⏱ 10am–6pm
Tue–Sat

---

⑫
Península de Jandía

🅐 G7 🅐 Fuerteventura
🚌 Costa Calma, Morro Jable
🚢 Jetfoil from Gran Canaria
🅘 Centro Comercial Cosmo,
Bajo; 928 54 07 76

Excellent beaches of pale sand fringe the Jandía Peninsula in the south of Fuerteventura. A string of *urbanizaciones* (residential developments) now takes up much of the peninsula's sheltered east coast (Sotavento).

Costa Calma, a burgeoning cluster of modern complexes,

offers the most interesting beaches, with long stretches of fine sand interrupted by low cliffs and coves. Morro Jable, a fishing village now swamped by new developments, lies at the southern end of a vast, glittering strand. Beyond Morro Jable, the access road dwindles away into a potholed track leading towards the lonely lighthouse at Punta de Jandía.

Expanses of deserted sand, accessible only by four-wheel-drive vehicle, line the westerly, windward coast (Barlovento) – too exposed for all but the hardiest beach-lovers. A plethora of subtropical marine life in this area makes it popular with scuba divers.

From 1938 to the early 1960s, Jandía belonged to a German entrepreneur and was out of bounds to locals. Even today, rumours of spies and secret Nazi bases circulate.

---

⑬
Corralejo

🅐 G6 🅐 Fuerteventura 🚢
🅘 Avenida Marítima 2;
www.corralejograndes
playas.com

This much-expanded fishing village is now one of the island's two most important resorts. Its main attraction is a belt of sand dunes stretching to the south, resembling the Sahara in places, and protected as a nature reserve – a designation that arrived too late to prevent the construction of two hotels right on the beach.

The rest of the resort, mostly consisting of apartments and hotels, spills out from the town centre. The port area is lively, with busy restaurants and a ferry service to Lanzarote.

Offshore is the tiny Isla de Lobos, named after the once abundant monk seals (*lobos marinos*). Today, scuba divers, snorkellers, sport fishers and surfers claim the clear waters. Glass-bottomed cruise boats take excursionists to the island.

↑ The glorious desert-like sand dunes of Corralejo, stretching south from the town, designated a nature reserve

Did You Know?

Puerto de Mogán's canal system has earned it the nickname "Little Venice".

14

Puerto de Mogán

🅰 F7 🅐 Gran Canaria
ℹ Avenida de Mogán s/n, Puerto Rico; www.gran canaria.com

Situated at the end of the verdant valley of Mogán, this is one of Gran Canaria's most appealing developments – an idyll to many visitors after the lively Playa del Inglés. Based around a small fishing port, it consists of a village-like complex of pretty, white, creeper-covered houses and a similarly designed hotel built around a marina. Boutiques,

bars and restaurants add an ambience without any of the accompanying rowdiness. Development stretches back from the waterfront, but is less instrusive than in other resorts.

The sandy beach, sheltered between the cliffs, is scarcely big enough for all visitors; a car is recommended to reach more facilities at Maspalomas. Ferries provide a leisurely way to get to nearby resorts.

Inland from Puerto Mogán, the road gently climbs through a tropical valley of mangoes, avocados and papaya, to the sleepy white town of Mogán, where terracotta pots litter the roadside. Here, you can sample the rural lifestyle.

15

Puerto Rico

🅰 F7 🅐 Gran Canaria
ℹ Avenida de Mogán, s/n; www.grancanaria.com

The barren steep cliffs that stand west of Maspalomas

now sprout rows of white apartment complexes at every turn. Puerto Rico is an overdeveloped resort popular with families, but has one of the more attractive beaches on the island, a firm crescent of imported sand supplemented by lidos and excellent watersports facilities. It is a great place to learn sailing, diving and windsurfing, or just to soak up the ultraviolet – Puerto Rico enjoys the best sunshine record in the whole of Spain.

16

Maspalomas

🅰 F7 🅐 Gran Canaria 🚌
ℹ Centro Comercial Anexo II 20, Playa del Inglés; www.grancanaria.com

When the motorway from Las Palmas Airport first tips you into this bewildering mega-resort, it seems like a homogeneous blur, but gradually three separate communities

→ Rows of sunbeds and umbrellas lined up on the sand at Maspalomas dunes

emerge. San Agustín, the furthest east, is sedate compared with the others. It has a series of beaches of dark sand, attractively sheltered by low cliffs and landscaped promenades, and a casino.

The next exit off the coastal highway leads to Playa del Inglés, the largest and liveliest resort, a triangle of land jutting into a huge belt of golden sand. Developed from the end of the 1950s, the area is built up with giant blocks of flats linked by a maze of roads. Many hotels lack sea views, though most have spacious grounds with swimming pools. At night the area pulsates with bright disco lights and flashing neon. There are more than 300 restaurants and over 50 nightclubs.

West of Playa del Inglés the beach undulates into the Dunas de Maspalomas.

A pleasant contrast to the hectic surrounding resorts, these dunes form a protected nature reserve. Their western edge (marked by a lighthouse) is occupied by a cluster of luxury hotels. Just behind the dunes lies a golf course encircled by bungalow estates.

Everything is laid on for the package holiday: watersports, excursions, fast food, as well as go-karts and funfairs. One of the most popular attractions is **Sioux City**, a fun-packed Western-themed park, where you can watch stuntmen perform amazing feats.

Sioux City
 🏯 Barranco del Águila, San Bartolomé de Tirajana ⏰10am–3pm Tue–Fri, 10am–4pm Sat & Sun 🆆 siouxcitypark.es

---

TOP 4 CANARY ISLAND FIESTAS

Carnival
Santa Cruz de Tenerife hosts one of Europe's biggest carnivals in February or March. Carnival also takes place on Lanzarote and Gran Canaria.

Corpus Christi
In Tenerife, La Orotava's streets are filled with flowers in striking patterns. The Plaza del Ayuntamiento is covered in copies of works of art that are formed from coloured volcanic sands.

Romería de la Virgen de la Candelaria
Pilgrims visit Candelaria, in Tenerife, in their thousands to venerate the Canary Islands' patroness on 15 August.

Fiesta del Charco
People leap into a large saltwater pond to catch mullet from 7 to 11 September in San Nicolás de Tolentino, Gran Canaria.

↑ Bougainvillea-decked houses in Puerto de Mogán's streets

→ The rocky shore and steep cliffs of the north-east coast near Agaete

 Agaete

🗺 F7 ⚑ Gran Canaria
ℹ Avenida Señora de las
Nieves 1; www.agaete.es

The cloudier northern side of the island is far greener and lusher than the arid south, and banana plantations take up most of the coastal slopes. Agaete, on the northwest coast, a pretty scatter of white houses around a striking rocky bay, is growing into a small resort. Every August, Agaete holds the Fiesta de la Rama, a Guanche rainmaking ritual which dates from long before the arrival of the Spanish. An animated procession of people bearing green branches heads from the hills above the town

down to the coast and into the sea. The revelers beat the water to summon the rain.

The Ermita de las Nieves contains a 16th-century Flemish triptych and model sailing ships. Close by is the **Huerto de las Flores**, a botanical garden.

A brief detour inland up along the Barranco de Agaete takes you through a fertile valley of papaya, mango and citrus trees. North of Agaete are the towns of Guía and Gáldar. Though there is little to see here, both parish churches do contain examples of the religious statuary of the celebrated 18th-century sculptor José Luján Pérez.

Towards the north coast lies the Cenobio de Valerón. This cliff face is pockmarked

with nearly 300 caves beneath a basalt arch. These caverns are believed to have been hideaways for Guanche priest-esses, communal grain stores and refuges from attack.

Huerto de las Flores
🚫 🚫 ⚑ Calle Huertas
📞 928 55 43 82 🕐 10am-
4pm Tue-Sat

 Tafira

🗺 F7 ⚑ Gran Canaria
🚌 ℹ Calle Triana 93,
Las Palmas; www.
grancanaria.com

The hills southwest of Las Palmas have long been desirable residential locations. A colonial air still wafts around Tafira's patrician villas. The **Jardín Canario**, a botanical garden founded in 1952, is the main reason to visit. Plants from all of the Canary Islands can be studied in their own, re-created habitats.

Near La Atalaya lies one of Gran Canaria's most impressive natural sights – the Caldera de la Bandama. This is a volcanic crater 1,000 m (3,300 ft) wide,

---

THE GUANCHES

When Europeans arrived in the Canary Islands in the early 15th century, they found tall, white-skinned people, who lived in caves and later in small settlements on the edges of barren lava fields. Guanche was the name of one group on Tenerife, but it came to be used for all the indigenous people of the islands. The origins of the Guanches are unclear, but it is probable that they arrived on the islands in the 1st or 2nd century BC from Berber North Africa.

STAY

Gold By Marina

This modern adults-only hotel is a short walk from the Playa del Inglés. It has a rooftop terrace with sunbeds, a hot tub and sauna.

F7 Avenida Estados Unidos de America 15, Playa del Inglés, Gran Canaria en.goldbymarina.com

€€€

Casa Mozart

A charming boutique hotel, which balances its buzzy location in the centre of Las Palmas with a calm atmosphere.

F7 Calle Mozart 2, Las Palmas, Gran Canaria casamozart.com

€€€

best seen from the Mirador de Bandama, where you gaze down into the green depression about 200 m (660 ft) deep. Some of the inhabited caves in the Barranco de Guayadeque, a valley of red rocks to the south, were dug in the late 15th century.

Jardín Canario

Carretera de Dragonal, km 7 7:30am-2pm Mon-Fri, 10am-5pm Sat & Sun 1 Jan, Good Fri, 25 Dec jardincanario.org

---

Las Palmas de Gran Canaria

F7 Gran Canaria Calle Triana 93; www.grancanaria.com

The largest city in the Canary Islands, Las Palmas is a bustling seaport and industrial city, with 1,000 ships docking here each month. Although the city has faded somewhat from the days when wealthy convalescents flocked here and glamorous liners called in on transatlantic voyages, it remains a vibrant place to visit.

Las Palmas is built around an isthmus. The modern commercial shipping area, Puerto de la Luz, takes up the eastern side of the isthmus, which leads to the former island of La Isleta, a sailors' and military quarter. On the other side of the isthmus is the crowded Playa de las Canteras, a long stretch of golden beach.

For a scenic tour, begin in the Parque Santa Catalina, near the port. This is a popular, shady square of cafés and newspaper kiosks. In the leafy residential quarter of Ciudad Jardín, you'll find the Parque Doramas, while in the Pueblo Canario visitors can watch folk dancing and browse in craft shops. At the end of town is the Barrio Vegueta, a charming quarter that dates back to the Spanish conquest. At its heart stands the Catedral de Santa Ana, begun in 1500. The adjacent **Museo Diocesano de Arte Sacro** contains works of religious art.

Nearby, the **Casa de Colón** is a 15th-century governor's residence where Columbus stayed. There is a museum here dedicated to his voyages.

For early history, visit the **Museo Canario**, which contains Guanche mummies, skulls, pottery and jewellery.

Museo Diocesano de Arte Sacro

Calle Espíritu Santo 20 928 31 49 89 10am-4:30pm Mon-Fri, 10am-1:30pm Sat

Casa de Colón

Calle Colón 1 928 31 23 73 10am-6pm Mon-Sat, 10am-3pm Sun 1 Jan, 24, 25 & 31 Dec

Museo Canario

Calle Doctor Verneau 2 10am-8pm Mon-Fri, 10am-2pm Sat & Sun 1 Jan, 25 Dec elmuseocanario.com

---

 PICTURE PERFECT
Fruit Pastel

San Juan, a *barrio* of Las Palmas de Gran Canaria, is a pretty collection of multicoloured houses that transforms the hillside into a pastel patchwork, or a game of Tetris brought to life.

←

Casa de Colón, a museum in Las Palmas de Gran Canaria dedicated to Columbus

A DRIVING TOUR
CRUZ DE TEJEDA

Length 45 km (28 miles) **Stopping-off points** Artenara;
Roque Nublo **Terrain** Roads can be narrow with few passing
places; sudden patches of cloud or mist may descend

Gran Canaria's mountainous interior makes for an ideal day
tour, from any part of the island. Choose a fine day or the
views may be obscured. The route from Maspalomas leads
through dry ravines of bare rock and cacti, becoming more
fertile with altitude. Roads near the central highlands
snake steeply through shattered, tawny crags, past
caves and pretty villages to panoramic viewpoints
from which you can see Mount Teide (p558) on
Tenerife. On the north side, the slopes
are much lusher, growing citrus
fruits and eucalyptus trees.

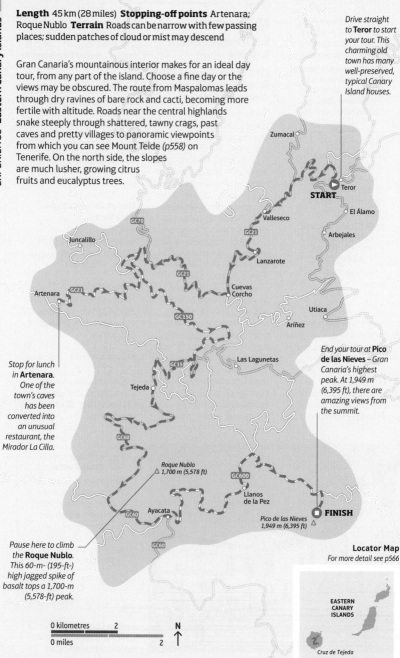

*Drive straight
to **Teror** to start
your tour. This
charming old
town has many
well-preserved,
typical Canary
Island houses.*

*Stop for lunch
in **Artenara**.
One of the
town's caves
has been
converted into
an unusual
restaurant, the
Mirador La Cilla.*

*End your tour at **Pico
de las Nieves** – Gran
Canaria's highest
peak. At 1,949 m
(6,395 ft), there are
amazing views from
the summit.*

*Pause here to climb
the **Roque Nublo**.
This 60-m- (195-ft-)
high jagged spike of
basalt tops a 1,700-m
(5,578-ft) peak.*

Zumacal

Teror
START

El Álamo

Valleseco

Arbejales

Juncalillo

Lanzarote

Artenara

Cuevas
Corcho

Utiaca

Las Lagunetas

Aríñez

Tejeda

Roque Nublo
△ 1,700 m (5,578 ft)

Llanos
de la Pez

Ayacata

FINISH

Pico de las Nieves
1,949 m (6,395 ft)
△

GC70 · GC21 · GC150 · GC15 · GC60 · GC600

Locator Map
For more detail see p566

EASTERN
CANARY
ISLANDS

Cruz de Tejeda

0 kilometres   2
0 miles   2

N
↑

Did You Know?

The mountain's name – Roque Nublo – translates as "Rock in the Clouds".

↑ Looking towards Mount Teide from the summit of Roque Nublo

NEED TO KNOW

Aerial view of the road to Puerto de Confrides, near Guadalest

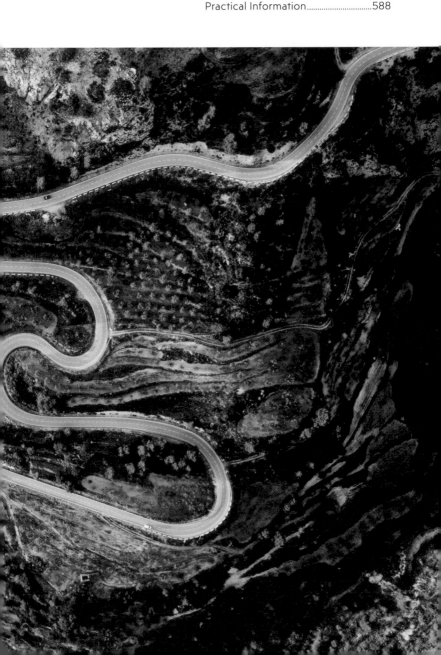

BEFORE
YOU GO

Things change, so plan ahead to make the most of your trip. Be prepared for all eventualities by considering the following points before you travel.

AT A GLANCE

CURRENCY
Euro (EUR)

AVERAGE DAILY SPEND

SAVE	SPEND	SPLURGE
€80	**€150**	**€200+**

BOTTLED WATER	COFFEE	BEER	DINNER FOR TWO
€0.80	**€1**	**€2.50**	**€40**

ESSENTIAL PHRASES

Hello	Hola
Goodbye	Adiós
Please	Por favor
Thank you	Gracias
Do you speak English	¿Habla inglés?
I don't understand	No comprendo

ELECTRICITY SUPPLY

Power sockets are type F, fitting a two-prong, round-pin plug. Standard voltage is 230 volts.

Passports and Visas

For entry requirements, including visas, consult your nearest Spanish embassy or check the **Exteriores** website. EU nationals may visit for an unlimited period, registering with local authorities after three months. Citizens of the UK, US, Canada, Australia and New Zealand can reside without a visa for up to 90 days.
Exteriores
w exteriores.gob.es

Government Advice

Now more than ever, it is important to consult both your and the Spanish government's advice before travelling. The **UK Foreign and Commonwealth Office**, the **US Department of State**, **Australian Department of Foreign Affairs and Trade** and the Spanish Exteriores website offer the latest information on security, health and local regulations.
Australian Department of Foreign Affairs and Trade
w smartraveller.gov.au
UK Foreign and Commonwealth Office
w gov.uk/foreign-travel-advice
US Department of State
w travel.state.gov

Customs Information

You can find information on the laws relating to goods and currency taken in or out of Spain on the **Turespaña** website.
Turespaña
w spain.info

Insurance

We recommend that you take out a comprehensive insurance policy covering theft, loss of belongings, medical care, cancellations and delays, and read the small print carefully.

UK citizens are eligible for free emergency medical care in Spain provided they have a valid European Health Insurance Card (**EHIC**) or UK Global Health Insurance Card (**GHIC**).

EHIC
ⓦ ec.europa.eu
GHIC
ⓦ ghic.org.uk

Vaccinations

For information regarding COVID-19 vaccination requirements, consult government advice *(p582)*.

Booking Accommodation

Spain offers a diverse range of accommodation, including a system of government-run hotels called *paradors*. A useful list of accommodation can be found on the Turespaña website.

Book your accommodation well in advance if you plan to visit in the peak season (July and August). As a winter-sun destination, the Canary Islands are busiest from December to March.

Most hotels quote their prices without including tax (IVA), which is 10 per cent everywhere except on the Canary Islands, where it is 6.5 per cent and called IGIC.

Money

Most urban establishments accept major credit, debit and prepaid currency cards. Contactless payments are common in cities, but it's always a good idea to carry cash for smaller items and to buy train, bus and metro tickets. ATMs are widely available throughout the country, although many charge for cash withdrawals.

Spain does not have a big tipping culture, but it is appreciated and it's common to round-up the bill.

Travellers with Specific Requirements

The Confederación Española de Personas con Discapacidad Física y Orgánica (**COCEMFE**) and **Accessible Spain** provide information and tailored itineraries for those with reduced mobility, sight and hearing.

Spain's public transport system generally caters for all passengers, providing wheelchairs, adapted toilets, ramps and reserved car parking at airports and stations. Metro maps in Braille are available from the Organización Nacional de Ciegos (**ONCE**).

Accessible Spain
ⓦ accessiblespaintravel.com
COCEMFE
ⓦ cocemfe.es
ONCE
ⓦ once.es

Language

Castellano (Castilian) is Spain's primary language, but three others are also widely spoken: *català* (Catalan) in Catalonia, Valencia and the Balearic Islands; *galego* (Galician) in Galicia; and *euskara* (Basque) in the Basque country. As a visitor, it is perfectly acceptable to speak Castilian wherever you are. English is widely spoken in the cities and other tourist spots, but not always in rural areas.

Opening Hours

> **COVID-19** Increased rates of infection may result in temporary opening hours and/or closures. Always check ahead before visiting museums, attractions and hospitality venues.

Lunchtime Many places close for the siesta between 2pm and 5pm.
Monday Many museums, public buildings and monuments are closed all day.
Sunday Churches and cathedrals are closed to the public during Mass.
Public holidays Most museums and many shops either close early or do not open at all.

PUBLIC HOLIDAYS	
1 Jan	New Year's Day
Mar/Apr	Good Friday
1 May	Labour Day
15 Aug	Assumption Day
12 Oct	Spain's National Day
1 Nov	All Saints' Day
6 Dec	Spanish Constitution Day
8 Dec	Feast of the Immaculate Conception
25 Dec	Christmas Day

GETTING
AROUND

Whether you are visiting for a short city break or rural country retreat, discover how best to reach your destination and travel like a pro.

PUBLIC TRANSPORT COSTS

MADRID

€8.40

Day ticket (Zone A)
Metro, bus, trains

BARCELONA

€7.60

Day ticket (Zone 1)
All public transport

SEVILLE

€5.00

Day ticket
Buses and tram

TOP TIP
A day pass for Seville's metro costs €4.50, but buses are the best way to get around.

SPEED LIMIT

MOTORWAYS

120 km/h
(75 mph)

DUAL CARRIAGEWAY

100 km/h
(60 mph)

SECONDARY ROAD

90 km/h
(55 mph)

URBAN AREAS

30 km/h
(20 mph)

Arriving by Air

Madrid, Barcelona and Málaga are the main airports for long-haul flights into Spain. European budget airlines fly to cities across Spain all year round at reasonable prices. They also offer good rates on regular internal flights.

For information on getting to and from Spain's main airports, see the table opposite.

Train Travel

International Train Travel

Spain's international and domestic rail services are operated by state-run Red Nacional de Ferrocarriles Españoles (**Renfe**). Safety and hygiene measures, timetables, ticket information, transport maps, and more can be obtained from the Renfe website. For international train trips, it is advisable to purchase your ticket well in advance. **Eurail** (p589), **Rail Europe** and **Interrail** sell passes (to European non-residents and residents respectively) for international journeys lasting from five days up to three months. Both passes are valid on Renfe trains.

There are several routes to Spain from France. The main western route runs from Paris to the French town of Hendaye, right on the French-Spanish border, from where you can catch one of the regular services to a Spanish town or city. The southern route from Paris runs directly to Barcelona, but you can also choose to travel via Cerbère. At Cerbère, there are connections with services to Valencia, Alicante, Girona and Murcia, as well as the TALGO (Tren Articulado Ligero Goicoechea Oriol), a high-speed luxury train service (operated by Renfe).

There are two main rail routes from Portugal to Spain. The Sud Express departs daily from Lisbon and terminates in Hendaye. Alternatively, Lusitania is a sleeper train from Lisbon, which will take you to Madrid in around nine hours.

Interrail
w interrail.eu
Rail Europe
w raileurope.com
Renfe
w renfe.com

GETTING TO AND FROM THE AIRPORT

Airport	Distance to city	Taxi fare	Public Transport
Barcelona	14 km (9 miles)	€35	Rail (35 mins), bus (25 mins)
Bilbao	12 km (7 miles)	€26	Bus (30 mins)
Madrid	16 km (10 miles)	€30	Bus (20 mins), metro (30–40 mins)
Málaga	8 km (5 miles)	€20	Rail (15 mins), bus (20 mins)
Palma de Mallorca	9 km (5.5 miles)	€25	Bus (15 mins)
Las Palmas de Gran Canaria	18 km (11 miles)	€30	Bus (60 mins)
Santiago de Compostela	10 km (6 miles)	€21	Bus (20–30 mins)
Tenerife Sur – Reina Sofía	64 km (40 miles)	€80	Bus (60 mins)
Valencia	9 km (5.5 miles)	€20	Bus (20 mins)

CAR JOURNEY PLANNER

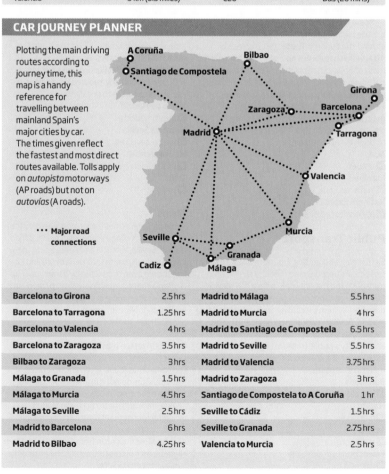

Plotting the main driving routes according to journey time, this map is a handy reference for travelling between mainland Spain's major cities by car. The times given reflect the fastest and most direct routes available. Tolls apply on *autopista* motorways (AP roads) but not on *autovías* (A roads).

••• Major road connections

Barcelona to Girona	2.5 hrs	**Madrid to Málaga**	5.5 hrs
Barcelona to Tarragona	1.25 hrs	**Madrid to Murcia**	4 hrs
Barcelona to Valencia	4 hrs	**Madrid to Santiago de Compostela**	6.5 hrs
Barcelona to Zaragoza	3.5 hrs	**Madrid to Seville**	5.5 hrs
Bilbao to Zaragoza	3 hrs	**Madrid to Valencia**	3.75 hrs
Málaga to Granada	1.5 hrs	**Madrid to Zaragoza**	3 hrs
Málaga to Murcia	4.5 hrs	**Santiago de Compostela to A Coruña**	1 hr
Málaga to Seville	2.5 hrs	**Seville to Cádiz**	1.5 hrs
Madrid to Barcelona	6 hrs	**Seville to Granada**	2.75 hrs
Madrid to Bilbao	4.25 hrs	**Valencia to Murcia**	2.5 hrs

Domestic Train Travel

Renfe is Spain's national rail operator, from whom you can buy tickets online or at stations. They, along with some regional companies, operate a good service throughout the country.

There are several train services. The fastest intercity services are the AVE (operated by Renfe). Tickets can be expensive and should be booked in advance. A cheaper option for travelling between the major cities is the slower TALGO service. Small towns are accessible via *regionales y cercanías* (the regional and local services), which are frequent and inexpensive.

Long-Distance Bus Travel

Often the cheapest way to reach and travel around Spain is by coach. **Eurolines** runs daily services to Barcelona. Check out the website for available offers. In the UK, tickets can be bought from **National Express**, the sister company of Eurolines. The journey from London Victoria Coach Station takes about 24 hours.

Spain has no national coach company, but private regional companies operate routes around the country. The largest of these is **Alsa**, which has routes and services that cover most of Spain. Other companies operate in particular regions – Alsina Graells, for instance, covers most of the south and east of Spain. Tickets and information are available at all main coach stations as well as on company websites, but note that it is not always possible to book tickets in advance.

Alsa
w alsa.es
Eurolines
w eurolines.com
National Express
w nationalexpress.com

Public Transport

Sightseeing and getting around in Spain's towns and cities is best done on foot and by public transport. The majority only offer a bus service, but the larger cities operate multiple public transport systems, including trams. **Barcelona**, **Madrid**, **Seville** and **Valencia** all have efficient metro systems. For up-to-date information about a city's public transport options, as well as ticket advice, check out their individual municipal websites.

Barcelona
w bcn.cat
Madrid
w madrid.es
Seville
w sevilla.org
Valencia
w valencia.es

Metro

The **Metro de Madrid** has 13 lines that serve the whole city and are divided into various zones. You can buy a single ticket for Zona A or a ten-journey ticket, which allows travel on both metro and buses. Tourist tickets providing between one and seven days' unlimited travel can be purchased at train stations or at the airport. The metro runs every day from 6am to 1:30am. Note that there is a €3 supplement for travel to and from the airport.

In Barcelona, a single metro journey will cost you €2.20, or you could get a T10 ticket which, once validated, lets you make 10 combined journeys on the metro, buses, trams and local trains (each combined journey must be taken within 75 minutes). If you plan to use public transport a lot, the more expensive T-2Dias gives you unlimited transport for two days until the end of service. Barcelona's metro, run by **TMB**, is open from 5am to midnight Sundays to Thursdays, until 2am on Fridays and for 24 hours every Saturday.

Metrovalencia is best used to get you to places beyond the city centre, particularly to and from the beach. A metro ticket to any station within the city limits is the same price.

The **Metro de Sevilla** only links the centre with Seville's outlying suburbs, so it is best to use buses to hit the major sights.

Metro de Madrid
w metromadrid.es
Metro de Sevilla
w metro-sevilla.es
Metrovalencia
w metrovalencia.es
TMB
w tmb.cat

Trams

Some of Spain's cities have comprehensive tram networks, including Alicante, Barcelona, Bilbao, Madrid, Seville, Valencia and Zaragoza. In the Canary Islands, Santa Cruz de Tenerife and La Laguna are even connected by a tramway. This is often a cheap and efficient way to travel, and trams are often more accessible than other modes of public transport.

Bus

Buses remain the most common mode of public transport throughout Spain, but they can sometimes follow an erratic timetable. Many services do not run after 10pm, although there are some night buses in the cities.

Bus, tram and metro tickets in Madrid, including tourist tickets, are interchangeable. If you do not have a ticket, you can pay the driver directly. Most buses run from 6am until 11:30pm. Night buses run less frequently. The price is the same as for day tickets.

In Barcelona the T10 and T-2Dias tickets are valid on buses.

Valencia has a good bus network, and buses are the preferred way of travelling for locals. If you are out and about a lot during the day, get a ten-journey *bono* (voucher). You can view a map of the bus routes in the city on the **EMT** website.

Buses are the easiest and cheapest way to get around Seville's main sights. The routes can be found on the **TUSSAM** website.

EMT
w emtvalencia.es
TUSSAM
w tussam.es

Taxis

Taxis are a reasonably priced way to get around if public transport isn't an option. Generally speaking, the journey starts with a flat fee and then increases depending on the distance travelled. Fares tend to be higher at night and also during the weekend and public holidays. Surcharges usually apply for trips to airports, as well as bus and train stations. Barcelona's taxis are yellow-and-black, whereas Madrid's are white with a diagonal red band on the front doors.

Driving

If you drive to Spain in your own car, you must carry the vehicle's registration document, a valid insurance certificate, a passport or a national identity card and your driving licence at all times. You must also display a sticker on the back of the car showing its country of registration and you risk on-the-spot fines if you do not carry a red warning triangle and a reflective jacket with you at all times.

Spain has two types of motorway: *autopistas*, which are toll roads, and *autovías*, which are toll-free. You can establish whether a motorway is toll-free by the letters that prefix the number of the road: A = free motorway; AP = toll motorway.

Carreteras nacionales, Spain's main roads, have black-and-white signs and are designated by the letter N (Nacional) plus a number. Those with Roman numerals start at the Puerta del Sol in Madrid, and those with ordinary numbers have kilometre markers giving the distance from the provincial capital.

Carreteras comarcales, secondary roads, have a number preceded by the letter C. Other minor roads have numbers preceded by letters representing the name of the province, such as the LE1313 in Lleida.

Car Hire

To rent a car, you must be over 21 years of age. The most popular car-hire companies in Spain are **Europcar**, **Avis** and **Hertz**. All have offices at airports and major train stations, as well as in the larger cities. Fly-drive, an option for two or more travellers where car hire is included in the cost of your air fare, can be arranged by travel agents and tour operators. If you wish to hire a car locally for around a week or less, you will be able to arrange it with a local travel agent. A car for hire is called a *coche de alquiler*.

Avis
w avis.com
Europcar
w europcar.com
Hertz
w hertz-europe.com

Rules of the Road

When using a car in Spain, drive on the right and use the left lane only for passing other vehicles.

Most traffic regulations and warnings to motorists are represented on signs by easily recognized symbols. However, a few road rules and signs may be unfamiliar to some drivers.

If you have taken the wrong road, and it has a solid white line, turn round as indicated by a *cambio de sentido* sign. At crossings, give way to all on-coming traffic, unless a sign indicates otherwise.

The blood-alcohol concentration (BAC) limit is 0.5 mg/ml and is very strictly enforced.

Boats and Ferries

Ferries connect the Spanish mainland to the Balearic and Canary Islands, and to North Africa, Italy and the UK. All the important routes are served by car ferries. **Acciona Trasmediterránea** links Barcelona and Valencia to the three main Balearic Islands and also operates a weekly service from Cádiz to the main ports of the Canary Islands. There are also car ferries between various islands and passenger-only services between Gran Canaria, Tenerife and Fuerteventura, and between Tenerife and La Gomera. Book all ferries in advance.

Acciona Trasmediterránea
w trasmediterranea.es

Walking

Arguably, the best way to explore Spain's towns and cities is on foot. By walking, you can take in the architectural details, absorb street life and peek into any church, shop or bar that catches your interest. Many urban areas are pedestrianized, but be aware that pavements can be narrow and uneven in historic centres.

The countryside also rewards walkers with hundreds of short trails and long-distance Gran Recorrido (GR) routes *(p38)*. The most famous GR route is the epic Camino de Santiago, which takes four weeks to complete *(p232)*.

PRACTICAL
INFORMATION

A little know-how goes a long way in Spain. Here you will find all the
essential advice and information you will need during your stay.

EMERGENCY NUMBERS

**GENERAL
EMERGENCY**

112

TIME ZONE

CET/CEST: Central
European Summer
time runs from the last
Sunday in March to the
last Sunday in October.
The Canary Islands
are always one hour
behind mainland Spain.

TAP WATER

Tap water in Spain is
safe to drink unless
stated otherwise.

WEBSITES AND APPS
España
Spain's official tourism website *(www.
spain.info)*.
Eurail
A useful website for planning train
journeys *(www.eurail.com)*.
Moovit
A route-planning app.
WiFi Map
Finds free Wi-Fi hotspots near you
(www.wifimap.io).

Personal Security

Spain is a relatively safe country to visit, but petty
crime does take place. Pickpockets work known
tourist areas, stations and busy streets. Use your
common sense and be alert to your surroundings, and you should enjoy a stress-free trip.

If you do have anything stolen, report the
crime within 24 hours to the nearest police
station and take ID with you. Get a copy of the
crime report *(denuncia)* to make an insurance
claim. Contact your embassy if your passport
is stolen, or in the event of a serious crime.

As a rule, Spaniards are very accepting of
all people, regardless of their race, gender or
sexuality. Homosexuality was legalized in Spain
in 1979 and in 2007, the government recognized
same-sex marriage and adoption rights for
same-sex couples. That being said, the Catholic
church still holds a lot of sway here and some
conservative attitudes prevail, especially outside
of urban areas. If you do feel unsafe, head for
the nearest police station.

Health

Spain has a world-class healthcare system.
Emergency medical care in Spain is free for
all UK and EU citizens. If you have an EHIC or
GHIC *(p582)*, be sure to present this as soon as
possible. You may have to pay after treatment
and reclaim the money later.

For visitors coming from outside the UK
or EU, payment of medical expenses is the
patient's responsibility, so it is important to
arrange comprehensive travel insurance
before travelling.

Seek medicinal supplies and advice for minor
ailments from a pharmacy *(farmacia)*, identifiable
by a green or red cross. Each pharmacy displays
a card in the window showing the address of
the nearest all-night pharmacy.

Smoking, Alcohol and Drugs

Smoking is banned in enclosed public spaces
and is a fineable offence, although you can still
smoke on the terraces of bars and restaurants.

Spain has a relaxed attitude towards alcohol consumption and, in cities, it is common to drink on the street outside the bar of purchase.

Recreational drugs are illegal, and possession of even a very small quantity can lead to an extremely hefty fine. Amounts that suggest an intent to supply drugs to other people can lead to custodial sentences.

ID

By law you must carry identification with you at all times in Spain. A photocopy of your passport should suffice, but you may be asked to report to a police station with the original document.

Local Customs

Regional pride is strong throughout Spain. Be wary of calling Catalans, Galicians and Basque people "Spanish", as this can cause offence.

A famous Spanish tradition is the siesta, which sees many shops closing between 1pm and 5pm.

Bullfighting

Corridas (bullfights) are widely held in Madrid and the south, but the sport is banned in Catalonia and the Balearic Islands and there are few bullrings in the north. Supporters argue that the bulls are bred for the industry and would be killed as calves were it not for bullfighting, while organizations such as the Asociación Defensa Derechos Animal (**ADDA**) hold protests throughout the country. If you do attend a *corrida*, bear in mind that it's better to see a big-name matador because they are more likely to make a clean and quick kill. The audience will make their disapproval evident if they don't.
ADDA
🔲 addaong.org

Visiting Churches and Cathedrals

Most churches and cathedrals will not permit visitors during Sunday Mass. Generally, entrance to churches is free, however a fee may apply to enter special areas, like cloisters. Spain retains a strong Catholic identity. When visiting religious buildings ensure that you are dressed modestly, with knees and shoulders covered.

Mobile Phones and Wi-Fi

Free Wi-Fi is reasonably common in Spain, particularly in libraries, large public spaces, restaurants and bars. Some places, such as airports and hotels, may charge for you to use their Wi-Fi.

Visitors travelling to Spain with EU tariffs are able to use their devices abroad without being affected by roaming charges. Users will be charged the same rates for data, calls and texts as at home.

Some UK networks have reintroduced roaming charges for their customers. Check with your provider before travelling.

Post

Correos is Spain's postal service. Postal rates fall into three price bands: Spain; Europe and North Africa; and the rest of the world. Parcels must be weighed and stamped at Correos offices, which are open 8:30am–9:30pm Monday to Friday; outside the cities they close by 1–2pm on weekdays.

Letters sent from a post office usually arrive more quickly than if posted in a *buzón* (postbox). In cities, *buzóns* are yellow pillar boxes; elsewhere they are small, wall-mounted postboxes.
Correos
🔲 correos.es

Taxes and Refunds

IVA in mainland Spain and the Balearic Islands is normally 21 per cent, but with lower rates for certain goods and services. In the Canary Islands, they have the IGIC tax, which is normally 6.5 per cent, but varies for certain goods and services.

Under certain conditions, non-EU citizens can claim a rebate of these taxes. Present a form and your receipts to a customs officer at your point of departure.

Discount Cards

Some cities offer a visitor's pass or discount card for exhibitions, events and museum entry, and participating restaurants. These are not free, so consider carefully how many of the offers you are likely to take advantage of before purchasing a card.

INDEX

Page numbers in **bold** refer to main entries

A

PHRASE BOOK

IN AN EMERGENCY

Help!	¡Socorro!	soh-**koh**-roh
Stop!	¡Pare!	**pah**-reh
Call a doctor!	¡Llame a un médico!	**yah**-meh ah **oon meh**-dee-koh
Call an ambulance!	¡Llame a una ambulancia!	**yah**-meh ah **oonah** ahm-boo-**lahn**-a-thee-ah
Call the police!	¡Llame a la policía!	**yah**-meh ah lah poh-lee-**thee**-ah
Call the fire brigade!	¡Llame a los bomberos!	**yah**-meh ah lohs bohm-**beh**-rohs
Where is the nearest telephone?	¿Dónde está el teléfono más próximo?	**dohn**-deh ehs-**tah** ehl teh-**leh**-foh-noh mahs **prohx**-ee-moh
Where is the nearest hospital?	¿Dónde está el hospital más próximo?	**dohn**-deh ehs-**tah** ehl ohs-pee-**tahl** mahs **prohx**-ee-moh

COMMUNICATION ESSENTIALS

Yes	Sí	see
No	No	noh
Please	Por favor	pohr fah-**vohr**
Thank you	Gracias	**grah**-thee-ahs
Excuse me	Perdone	pehr-**doh**-neh
Hello	Hola	**oh**-lah
Goodbye	Adiós	ah-dee-**ohs**
Goodnight	Buenas noches	**bweh**-nahs **noh** chehs
Morning	La mañana	lah mah-**nyah**-nah
Afternoon	La tarde	lah **tahr**-deh
Evening	La tarde	lah **tahr**-deh
Yesterday	Ayer	ah-**yehr**
Today	Hoy	oy
Tomorrow	Mañana	mah-**nyah**-nah
Here	Aquí	ah-**kee**
There	Allí	ah-**yee**
What?	¿Qué?	keh
When?	¿Cuándo?	**kwahn**-doh
Why?	¿Por qué?	pohr-**keh**
Where?	¿Dónde?	**dohn**-deh

USEFUL PHRASES

How are you?	¿Cómo está usted?	koh-moh ehs-**tah** oos-**tehd**
Very well, thank you.	Muy bien, gracias.	mwee bee-**ehn grah**-thee-ahs
Pleased to meet you.	Encantado de conocerle.	ehn-kahn-**tah**-doh deh koh-noh-**thehr**-leh
See you soon.	Hasta pronto.	ahs-tah **prohn**-toh
That's fine.	Está bien.	ehs-**tah** bee-**ehn**
Where is/are ...?	¿Dónde está/están ...?	**dohn**-deh ehs-**está/están** ...? **tah**/ehs-**tahn**
How far is it to ...?	Cuántos metros/ kilómetros hay de aquí a ...?	**kwahn**-tohs meh-trohs/kee-**loh**-meh-trohs **eye** deh ah-**kee** ah
Which way to ...?	¿Por dónde se va a ...?	pohr **dohn**-deh seh **bah** ah
Do you speak English?	¿Habla inglés?	ah-**blah** een-**glehs**
I don't understand	No comprendo	noh kohm-**prehn**-doh
Could you speak more slowly, please?	¿Puede hablar más despacio, por favor?	pweh-deh ah-**blahr** mahs dehs-pah-thee-oh pohr fah-**vohr**
I'm sorry.	Lo siento.	loh see-**ehn**-toh

USEFUL WORDS

big	grande	**grahn**-deh
small	pequeño	peh-**keh**-nyoh
hot	caliente	kah-lee-**ehn**-teh
cold	frío	**free**-oh
good	bueno	**bweh**-noh
bad	malo	**mah**-loh
enough	bastante	bahs-**tahn**-the
well	bien	bee-**ehn**
open	abierto	ah-bee-**ehr**-toh
closed	cerrado	thehr-**rah**-doh
left	izquierda	eeth-key-**ehr**-dah
right	derecha	deh-**reh**-chah
straight on	todo recto	toh-doh **rehk**-toh
near	cerca	**thehr**-kah
far	lejos	**leh**-hohs
up	arriba	ah-**ree**-bah
down	abajo	ah-**bah**-hoh

early	temprano	tehm-**prah**-noh
late	tarde	**tahr**-deh
entrance	entrada	ehn-**trah**-dah
exit	salida	sah-**lee**-dah
toilet	lavabos, servicios	lah-**vah**-bohs sehr-**bee**-thee-ohs
more	más	mahs
less	menos	**meh**-nohs

SHOPPING

How much does this cost?	¿Cuánto cuesta esto?	**kwahn**-toh **kwehs**-tah **ehs**-toh
I would like ...	Me gustaría ...	meh goos-ta-**ree**-ah
Do you have ...?	¿Tienen...?	tee-**yeh**-nehn
I'm just looking, thank you.	Sólo estoy mirando, gracias.	soh-loh ehs-**toy** mee-rahn-doh **grah**-thee-ahs
Do you take credit cards?	¿Aceptan tarjetas de crédito?	ah-**thehp**-tahn tahr-**heh**-tahs deh **kreh**-dee-toh
What time do you open?	¿A qué hora abren?	ah **keh** oh-rah **ah**-brehn
What time do you close?	¿A qué hora cierran?	ah keh oh-rah thee-**ehr**-rahn
This one.	Este.	**ehs**-the
That one.	Ese.	**eh**-she
expensive	caro	**kahr**-oh
cheap	barato	bah-**rah**-toh
size, clothes	talla	**tah**-yah
size, shoes	número	no**meh**-roh
white	blanco	**blahn**-koh
black	negro	**neh**-groh
red	rojo	**roh**-hoh
yellow	amarillo	ah-mah-**ree**-yoh
green	verde	**behr**-deh
blue	azul	ah-**thool**
antiques shop	la tienda de antigüedades	lah tee-**ehn**-dah deh ahn-tee-gweh-**dah**-dehs
bakery	la panadería	lah pah-nah-deh-**ree**-ah
bank	el banco	ehl **bahn**-koh
book shop	la librería	lah lee-breh-**ree**-ah
butcher's	la carnicería	lah kahr-nee-theh-**ree**-ah
cake shop	la pastelería	lah pahs-teh-leh-**ree**-ah
chemist's	la farmacia	lah fahr-**mah**-thee-ah
fishmonger's	la pescadería	lah pehs-kah-deh-**ree**-ah
greengrocer's	la frutería	lah froo-teh-**ree**-ah
grocer's	la tienda de comestibles	lah tee-**ehn**-dah deh koh-mehs-**tee**-blehs
hairdresser's	la peluquería	lah peh-loo-keh-**ree**-ah
market	el mercado	ehl mehr-**kah**-doh
newsagent's	el kiosko de prensa	ehl kee-**ohs**-koh deh **prehn**-sah
post office	la oficina de correos	lah oh-fee-**thee**-nah deh kohr-**reh**-ohs
shoe shop	la zapatería	lah thah-pah-teh-**ree**-ah
supermarket	el supermercado	ehl soo-pehr-mehr-**kah**-doh
tobacconist	el estanco	ehl ehs-**tahn**-koh
travel agency	la agencia de viajes	lah ah-**hehn**-thee-ah deh bee-**ah**-hehs

SIGHTSEEING

art gallery	el museo de arte	ehl moo-**seh**-oh deh **ahr**-the
cathedral	la catedral	lah kah-teh-**drahl**
church	la iglesia	lah ee-**gleh**-see-ah
	la basílica	lah bah-**see**-lee-kah
garden	el jardín	ehl hahr-**deen**
library	la biblioteca	lah bee-blee-oh-**teh**-kah
museum	el museo	ehl moo-**seh**-oh
tourist information office	la oficina de turismo	lah oh-fee-**thee**-nah deh too-**rees**-moh
town hall	el ayuntamiento	ehl ah-yoon-tah-mee-**ehn**-toh
closed for holiday	cerrado por vacaciones	thehr-**rah**-doh pohr bah-kah-cee-**oh**-nehs
bus station	la estación de autobuses	lah ehs-tah-see-**ohn** deh owtoh-**boo**-sehs
railway station	la estación de trenes	lah ehs-tah-thee-**ohn** deh **treh**-nehs

STAYING IN A HOTEL

Do you have a vacant room?	¿Tienen una habitación libre?	tee-**eh**-nehn oo-nah ah-bee-tah-thee-**ohn** lee-breh
double room	habitación doble	ah-bee-tah-thee-**ohn** doh-bleh
with double bed	con cama de matrimonio	kohn kah-mah deh mah-tree-**moh**-nee-oh
twin room	habitación con dos camas	ah-bee-tah-thee-**ohn** kohn dohs kah-mahs
single room	habitación individual	ah-bee-tah-thee-**ohn** een-dee-vee-doo-**ahl**
room with a bath	habitación con baño	ah-bee-tah-thee-**ohn** kohn bah-nyoh
shower	ducha	doo-chah
porter	el botones	ehl boh-**toh**-nehs
key	la llave	lah yah-veh
I have a reservation.	Tengo una habitación reservada.	tehn-goh oo-na ah-bee-tah-thee-**ohn** reh-sehr-**bah**-dah

EATING OUT

Have you got a table for ...?	¿Tienen mesa para ...?	tee-**eh**-nehn meh-sah pah-**rah**
I want to reserve a table.	Quiero reservar una mesa.	kee-eh-roh reh-sehr-**bahr** oo-nah **meh**-sah
The bill, please.	La cuenta, por favor.	lah kwehn-tah pohr fah-**vohr**
I am a vegetarian	Soy vegetariano/a	soy beh-heh-tah-ree-**ah**-no/na
waitress/ waiter	camarera/ camarero	kah-mah-**reh**-rah/ kah-mah-**reh**-roh
menu	la carta	lah **kahr**-tah
fixed-price menu	menú del día	meh-**noo** dehl **dee**-ah
wine list	la carta de vinos	lah **kahr**-tah deh **bee**-nohs
glass	un vaso	oon **bah**-soh
bottle	una botella	oo-nah boh-**teh**-yah
knife	un cuchillo	oon koo-**chee**-yoh
fork	un tenedor	oon teh-neh-**dohr**
spoon	una cuchara	oo-nah koo-**chah**-rah
breakfast	el desayuno	ehl deh-sah-**yoo**-noh
lunch	la comida/ el almuerzo	lah koh-**mee**-dah/ ehl ahl-**mwehr**-thoh
dinner	la cena	lah **theh**-nah
main course	el primer plato	ehl pree-**mehr plah**-toh
starters	los entrantes	lohs ehn-tran tehs
dish of the day	el plato del día	ehl **plah**-toh dehl **dee**-ah
coffee	el café	ehl kah-**feh**
rare	poco hecho	**poh**-koh **eh**-choh
medium	medio hecho	**meh**-dee-oh **eh**-choh
well done	muy hecho	mwee **eh**-choh

MENU DECODER

asado	ah-**sah**-doh	roast
el aceite	ah-**theh-eh**-teh	oil
las aceitunas	ah-theh-**toon**-ahs	olives
el agua mineral	ah-gwa mee-neh-**rahl**	mineral water
sin gas/con gas	seen gas/kohn gas	still/sparkling
el ajo	**ah**-hoh	garlic
el arroz	ahr-**rohth**	rice
el azúcar	ah-**thoo**-kahr	sugar
la carne	**kahr**-neh	meat
la cebolla	theh-**boh**-yah	onion
la cerveza	thehr-**beh**-thah	beer
el cerdo	**therh**-doh	pork
el chocolate	choh-koh-**lah**-teh	chocolate
el chorizo	choh-**ree**-thoh	chorizo
el cordero	kohr-**deh**-roh	lamb
el fiambre	fee-**ahm**-breh	cold meat
frito	**free**-toh	fried
la fruta	**froo**-tah	fruit
los frutos secos	**froo**-tohs seh-kohs	nuts
las gambas	**gahm**-bahs	prawns
el helado	eh-**lah**-doh	ice cream
al horno	ahl **ohr**-noh	baked
el huevo	oo-**eh**-voh	egg
el jamón serrano	hah-**mohn** sehr-**rah**-noh	cured ham

el jerez	heh-**rehz**	sherry
la langosta	lahn-**gohs**-tah	lobster
la leche	**leh**-cheh	milk
el limón	lee-**mohn**	lemon
la limonada	lee-moh-**nah**-dah	lemonade
la mantequilla	mahn-teh-**kee**-yah	butter
la manzana	mahn-**thah**-nah	apple
los mariscos	mah-**rees**-kohs	seafood
la menestra	meh-**nehs**-trah	vegetable stew
la naranja	nah-**rahn**-hah	orange
el pan	pahn	bread
el pastel	pahs-**tehl**	cake
las patatas	pah-**tah**-tahs	potatoes
el pescado	pehs-**kah**-doh	fish
la pimienta	pee-mee-**yehn**-tah	pepper
el plátano	**plah**-tah-noh	banana
el pollo	**poh**-yoh	chicken
el postre	**pohs**-treh	dessert
el queso	**keh**-soh	cheese
la sal	sahl	salt
las salchichas	sahl-**chee**-chahs	sausages
la salsa	**sahl**-sah	sauce
seco	**seh**-koh	dry
el solomillo	soh-loh-**mee**-yoh	sirloin
la sopa	**soh**-pah	soup
la tarta	**tahr**-tah	pie/cake
el té	teh	tea
la ternera	tehr-**neh**-rah	beef
las tostadas	tohs-**tah**-dahs	toast
el vinagre	bee-**nah**-greh	vinegar
el vino blanco	**bee**-noh **blahn**-koh	white wine
el vino rosado	**bee**-noh roh-**sah**-doh	rosé wine
el vino tinto	**bee**-noh **teen**-toh	red wine

NUMBERS

0	cero	**theh**-roh
1	uno	**oo**-noh
2	dos	dohs
3	tres	trehs
4	cuatro	**kwa**-troh
5	cinco	**theen**-koh
6	seis	says
7	siete	**see**-eh-the
8	ocho	**oh**-choh
9	nueve	**nweh**-veh
10	diez	dee-**ehth**
11	once	**ohn**-theh
12	doce	**doh**-theh
13	trece	**treh**-theh
14	catorce	kah-**tohr**-theh
15	quince	**keen**-theh
16	dieciséis	dee-eh-thee-**seh-ees**
17	diecisiete	dee-eh-thee-see **eh**-the
18	dieciocho	dee-eh-thee-**oh**-choh
19	diecinueve	dee-eh-thee-**nweh**-veh
20	veinte	**beh**-een-the
21	veintiuno	beh-een-tee-**oo**-noh
22	veintidós	beh-een-tee-**dohs**
30	treinta	**treh**-een-tah
31	treinta y uno	treh-een-tah ee **oo**-noh
40	cuarenta	kwah-**rehn**-tah
50	cincuenta	theen-**kwehn**-tah
60	sesenta	seh-**sehn**-tah
70	setenta	seh-**tehn**-tah
80	ochenta	oh-**chehn**-tah
90	noventa	noh-**vehn**-tah
100	cien	thee-**ehn**
101	ciento uno	thee-**ehn**-toh **oo**-noh
102	ciento dos	thee-**ehn**-toh dohs
200	doscientos	dohs-thee-**ehn**-tohs
500	quinientos	khee-nee-**ehn**-tohs
700	setecientos	seh-teh-thee-**ehn**-tohs
900	novecientos	noh-veh-thee-**ehn**-tohs
1,000	mil	meel
1,001	mil uno	meel **oo**-noh

TIME

one minute	un minuto	oon mee-**noo**-toh
one hour	una hora	**oo**-na oh-rah
half an hour	media hora	**meh**-dee-a oh-rah
Monday	lunes	**loo**-nehs
Tuesday	martes	**mahr**-tehs
Wednesday	miércoles	mee-**ehr**-koh-lehs
Thursday	jueves	hoo-**weh**-vehs
Friday	viernes	bee-**ehr**-nehs
Saturday	sábado	**sah**-bah-doh
Sunday	domingo	doh-**meen**-goh

ACKNOWLEDGMENTS

DK would like to thank the following for their contribution to the previous edition: Sally Davies, Mary-Ann Gallagher, Ben Ffrancon Davies, John Ardagh, David Baird, Vicky Hayward, Adam Hopkins, Lindsay Hunt,Nick Inman, Paul Richardson, Martin Symington, Nigel Tisdall, Roger Williams

The publisher would like to thank the following for their kind permission to reproduce their photographs:

Key: a-above; b-below/bottom; c-centre; f-far; l-left; r-right; t-top

123RF.com: Jose Angel Astor 351, 366-7; Mauro Celio 86cr; Pavel Dudek 42-3t, 50tr; Juan Jimenez Fernandez 30t; Iakov Filimonov 119crb; Francesco Riccardo Iacomino 50-1b; Olena Kachmar 140-1b; Luis Sandoval Mandujano 8clb; Alena Redchenko 16c, 70-1; Elena Solodovnikova 334clb; Zhanna Tretiakova 139br.

4Corners: Francesco Carovillano 378clb; Paolo Giocoso 310bl; Reinhard Schmid 282t, 539tl, 546-7t, 563b, 572-3t; Luigi Vaccarella 382clb.

akg-images: Album / Oronoz / Museo Reina Sofia / *Tête dite «le lapin»* (1930ca) by Julio Gonzalez 325clb.

Alamy Stock Photo: Michael Abid 111; Mauricio Abreu 322cr, 332t; AFLO Co. Ltd. / Nippon News 52tl, D. Nakashima 52-3b; age fotostock / Alfred Abad 168bl, agefotostock / María Galán 362-63b, agefotostock / Felix González 328-29t, / Bruno Almela 26br, / Juanma Aparicio 41cl, 499tr, / Gonzalo Azumendi 26cr, 161tl, 392bl, 394-5b, 550cl, 550-1t, / Tolo Balaguer 283br, 423t, / J. LL. Banús 94bl, / F. J. Fdez. Bordonada 286t, / Rafael Campillo 13br, 276tl, / Angelo Cavalli 135tl, Veryan Dale 54-55b, / Paco Gómez García 318t, / Javier Larrea 184clb, 270clb, 273b, 274crb, 325cra, / Museo Nacional Centro de Arte Reina Sofia / *Guernica* (1937) by Pablo Picasso © Succession Picasso / DACS, London 2019 324t, / David Miranda 254bl, 331tr, 421br, / José Antonio Moreno 505tr, 511t, / Juan José Pascual 422br, / Jesús Nicolás Sánchez 400br, / Richard Semik 285br; AGF Srl / Giuseppe Masci 122cla; Jerónimo Alba 13cr, 392-3t, 409b, 499br; Mark Alexander 492br; Alfie1981 213bl; Alpineguide 487tr; Andreas Altenburger 231tr; Juanma Aparicio 32crb, 455cra; Arco Images GmbH / K. Kreder 560br; Art Collection 3 84cb; Asturimage 38tl; Juan Aunion 142t; Aurelian Images 370bl; Aitor Rodero Aznarez 89cb; Gonzalo Azumendi 56-7t; David Bagnall 488t; Darren Baker 461tr; Cristian Mircea Balate 558-9t; Peter Barritt / Fundacio Pilar Miro / *Personnage Gothique Oiseau eclair sculpture* (1976) by Jown Miro © Successió Miró / ADAGP, Paris and DACS London 2019 37cla; Ben Welsh Premium 39cl; Bildarchiv Monheim GmbH / Gerhard Hagen 343t, 343cra; Stuart Black 512tr; Jordi Boixareu 60clb; Richard Bradley 293bl, 336; Michael Brooks 267cra, 236bc, 468bl; Camila Se 113cra; Cavan / Aurora Photos / David Santiago Garcia 280b, 391b; Michelle Chaplow 525br; Chromorange / Andreas Poertner 503br; Classic Image 63cb, 64br; Sorin Colac 484clb; Colin Palmer Photography 540tl; Richard Cummins 507bl; Ian Dagnall 85tr, 234t, 284tl, 333br, 453tl; Ian G Dagnall 268br; DCarreño 239b, 240b, 241tr, 364-5t, 414crb; Design Pics Inc / Destinations / Ken Welsh 373br; dleiva 327, 439b; Doleesi 46bl; DomonabikeSpain 79cl; Adam Eastland 30bl, 338-9b; Education & Exploration 4 326crb; EFE News Agency 47br, 561br; Elenaphotos 206t; Endless Travel 93bl, 155cr; EnriquePSans 339tl; Eduardo Estellez 63br; Etabeta 301bc; Europe / Peter Forsberg 338br; Greg Balfour Evans 551br; Everett Collection Historical 67cr; Peter van Evert 462b; Factofoto 76b, 126, 350c, 354, 380-1t, 406-7t, 418b; Alexei Fateev 185t, 287tc; 298, 398b; Christophe Faugere 168-9t; Iakov Filimonov 20t; Aaron Fink 85cra; Freeartist 200-1b; Maria Galan 387br, 397crb; David Gato 53br;

geogphotos 480bc; Kevin George 371ca, 418tl; Javier Gil 258-9b; GL Archive 66bc; 131br, 299bc; Paul Christian Gordon 28-9c, 279br; Mikel Bilbao Gorostiaga 49tr; Tim Graham 43cl, 278b; Granger Historical Picture Archive 66tl, 299crb; Matt Griggs 179clb; Gerold Grotelueschen 114br; Susana Guzman 399tr; hemis.fr / Bertrand Gardel 30cr, 210clb, 213tc, 299cr, 330b, / Patrick Frilet 515br, / Ludovic Maisant 12-3b, 124cl, / René Mattes 184b, / Alessio Mamo 300-1b, / Bertrand Rieger 272tl, / Anna Serrano 510tl; Heritage Image Partnership Ltd / Index 62cb, 66crb, 398tr; Peter Horree 332bl, 461bl, / Museum Reina Sofia / Installation shot of *Grün-Blau (793 / 1-4)* (1993) © Gerhard Richter 2019 (12082019) 324-5b, / Museum Reina Sofia / *Untitled (Model for Trench Shaft and Tunnel)* (1978) by Bruce Nauman © Bruce Nauman / Artists Rights Society (ARS), New York and DACS, London 2019 324-5b; Stephen Hughes 545tl; IanDagnall Computing 299bl; imageBROKER / Florian Bachmeier 388-9b, / Barbara Boensch 206cl, 364bl, / Jose Antonio Moreno Castellano 416bl, / Michael Fischer 363t, / Christian Handl 383tr, / olf 374b, / Jochen Tack 59cl, / Moritz Wolf 463tr; incamerastock 319cra; Ingolf Pompe 52 / Museu Picasso Barcelona © Succession Picasso / DACS, London 2019 20crb; Interfoto / © Succession Picasso / DACS, London 2019 91cb; Islandstock 60cl; Ivoha 229tr, 241br; Eric James 301cra; JeffG 307t; JLImages 372t; jmeyersforeman 371tr; Jon Arnold Images Ltd 220c, 222, 264t; Federico Julien 92-3t; John Kellerman 458b, 471t; Andrey Khrobostov 110fcrb; David Kilpatrick 559br; Brian Kinney 78-9t; Jason Knott 416tl; Art Kowalsky / Museo Nacional Centro De Arte Reina Sofia / *Brushstroke* (1996) By Roy Lichtenstein © Estate Of Roy Lichtenstein / DACS, London 2019 104-5; / Museo Nacional Centro De Arte Reina Sofia Designed By Jean Nouvel © Jean Nouvel / ADAGP, Paris and DACS, London 2019 322-3; Lobro 98crb; Look / Ingolf Pompe 201t, / Andreas Strauss 125br; De Luan 299clb; Sabine Lubenow 55cl; Jose Lucas 235bl, 508tr; Cro Magnon 282cla, 397br; Riccardo Mancioli / Museo Guggenheim Bilbao / *The Matter Of Time* (1994–2005) by Richard Serra © ARS, NY and DACS, London 2019 36clb; MARKA / Dario Fusaro 359cra; Stefano Politi Markovina 45br, 88-9t, 89br, 117tr, 276-7b, 539cra, 543tr; Martin Thomas Photography 96-7b; Bob Masters 169b; Mauritius Images GmbH / Walter Bibikow 469tl, / Jose Fuste Raga 203tc; Matt May 49cl; Mehdi33300 352b, 402-3, 412bl; Melba Photo Agency 183tr; Paul Melling 198-9b; Mikel Bilbao Gorostiaga- Travels 275tr; Hercules Milas 75t, 106; Tim Moore 46-7t, 249bl, 275br; Hilary Morgan 61clb, 517b; Motion / Horizon Images 408tl, 458crb; Graham Mulrooney 134clb; Juan Carlos Muñoz 49br; Perry van Munster 42bl; Nature Picture Library / Jose B. Ruiz 250-1b, 477cr; Newscom / BJ Warnick 139tr; Niday Picture Library 64tr; North Wind Picture Archives 65tr; Novarc Images / Nico Stengert 579; B.O'Kane / Museo Nacional Centro de Arte Reina Sofía / *Wheat and Steak* (1981) by Miralda © DACS 2019 322bl; Joris Van Ostaeyen 259tr; Efrain Padro 303; Sean Pavone 316-7b, 482t; Carlos Sanchez Pereyra 101br, 516tl; Will Perrett 471br; peterforsberg 457cla; Photo12 / Archives Snark 66cla; The Picture Art Collection 394cl; MB_Photo 121tr; Pictureproject 118-9t; Prisma Archivo 62t, 62bc, 64tl, 64clb, 110cb, 157cra, 319cr; Prisma by Dukas Presseagentur GmbH / Raga Jose Fuste 171t, 548-9b; Luca Quadrio 138-9t; M Ramírez 251tr, 279t, 415tr, 433cra, 435tr, 562tl; robertharding , / Neale Clark 113tc, / Marco Simoni 552tl, / Michael Snell 210-1t; SCFotos - Stuart Crump Photography 23tr; Science History Images / Photo Researchers 65cra, 65tl; Carmen Sedano 256cb; Alex Segre 317tr, 341br; Keith Skingle 203br; Witold Skrypczak 510br; The Artchives 319bc; Travelscape Images 267t; Jorge Tutor 344bl, 395br, 441tr; UtCon Collection 281br; Humberto Valladares 385br; Lucas Vallecillos 28ca, 43br, 48tl, 57br, 59tl, 100b, 123bl, 164bl, 167bl, 264bc, 342b, 375tl, 490t; Ken Welsh 105tl, 430-1t; Jan Wlodarczyk 85tc, 99clb,104bl; World History Archive 66-7t, 67clb, 157tl, 409tr; World History Archive / AG 110clb; Chun Ju Wu 115b; Yay Media AS / Quintanilla 188bl; zixia 56tc,

artspacetours: 36 – 7t.

AWL Images: Mauricio Abreu 432bl; Jon Arnold 536t; Giordano Bertocchi 237t; Matteo Colombo 271tl, 379br; Michele Falzone 531bl, 564-5; Bertrand Gardel 22-3t; Hemis 317cla, 437tr; Jane Sweeney 504-5b; Travel Pix Collection 117tl.

Bridgeman Images: Private Collection / Photo © AISA / *Design for the Fachada del Nacimiento of the Templo de la Sagrada Familia* by Antonio Gaudi (1852-1926) 110crb; Museu Picasso, Barcelona / *Las Meninas* (1957) by Pablo Picasso © Succession Picasso / DACS, London 2019 91bc.

Used with permission of Casa Batlló (www. casabatllo.es): 12t, 75, 79crb, 98crb, 106-7, 116-7 all.

Cinema Paradiso: 44br.

La Dama - Creative Artisans: 20cr.

Depositphotos Inc: mmedp 520bl; Patryk_Kosmider 208-9t; sujetar 522cl.

Dorling Kindersley: Max Alexander 155br; Joe Cornish 547br.

Dreamstime.com: Claudiu Alexandru 116bl; Alexsalcedo 148c, 150, 221bl, 260-1; Alfonsodetomas 391cra; Steve Allen 157cr; Dolores Giraldez Alonso 47cb; Andreusk 38-9b; Leonid Andronov 22ca, 326br; Valery Bareta 523bl; Sergio Torres Baus 530c, 532; Christian Bertrand 53tr, 60cr, 61cl; Lukas Bischoff 12t; Serjunco Bon 559clb; Bsanchezsobrino 353t, 426-7; Sirio Carnevalino 358clb; Chasdesign1983 215crb; Chiyacat 40tl; Sorin Colac 10-11b, 32t, 492t; Tomasz Czajkowski 497t; Danflcreativo 89bl; Danileon 180-1t; Josema Dieguez 401tl; Ego450 141ca; Elenaphotos 204-5t; Marina Endermar 25tr; Manuel Escudero 191t; Eyeofpaul 30crb; Alejandro Otero Fernández 51cl; Iakov Filimonov 28tl, 63tr, 122t, 164-5t, 202b; Fosterss 60cra; Hans Geel 41br; Yulia Grigoryeva 293t, 312-3; Olivier Guiberteau 484bl; Antonio Guillem 39br; David Herraez 371tc, 414b; Raul Garcia Herrera 12clb, 61tr; Eduardo Huelin 37br; Lukasz Janyst 29tc, 179bl; Jarnogz 24-5c; Kiko Jiménez 447t, 472; Jjfarq 345t; García Juan 65tl, 65br, 84crb; Marcin Jucha 11cr, 417b; Fenlio Kao 329b; Kasto80 302c; Laszlo Konya 233tl; Oleksandr Korzhenko 286-7b; Jan Kranendonk 302bc; Veniamin Kraskov 141cra; Enrique Arnaiz Lafuente 254-5t; Erik Lattwein 320cr; Bogdan Lazar 95t; Leonovo 32cr; Lunamarina 10ca, 38-9t, 29tr, 173br, 519tr, 553clb, 553b; Madrabothair 467tr; Marcorubino 79crb, 114t, 132tl; Carlos Soler Martinez 380bc; minnystock 34bl; Juan Moyano 54-5t, 196t; Roland Nagy 99tr; Nanisimova 133cr; Nataliia Gr 34cr; Olgacov 158t, 166t; Gerardo Onandia 425tl; Sean Pavone 18cb, 309b, 346-7, 376t; Erlantz Perez 182-3b; Perseomedusa 51br, 55crb; Juan Ignacio Polo 24cla; Radub85 11br; Richair 103br Saiko3p 10clb, 26cl, 130-1t, 226t, 256t, 284br; Rui Santos 496bl; Olena Serditova 120-1b; Sigur1 387tc; Vadym Soloviov 24tl; Opreanu Roberto Sorin 13t, 34crb; Rechitan Sorin 63tl; Ivan Soto 63cla; Sssanchez 575tr; Alena Stalmashonak 32bl; Steveheap 525tl; StockPhotoAstur 61crb; Tanaonte 60crb; Barna Tanko 304br; Aleksandar Todorovic 486bl; Tomas1111 99crb; Typhoonski 48-9b, 212t; Stefano Valeri 243crb; Maria Vazquez 186-7b; Venemama 281tl; Alvaro German Vilela 60cla, 270b; Vitalyedush 117cra, 299cra, 306b; Tatyana Vychegzhanina 77t, 136; Cezary Wojtkowski 495cra; Tetiana Zbrodko 155t.

El Celler de Can Roca: Wim Jansen 41tr.

©FC BARCELONA: 139clb.

Getty Images: AFP Contributor 110cr; age fotostock / Eduardo Grund 509b; Anadolu Agency 61cr; AWL Images / Michele Falzone 512-3b; Corbis Documentary / Atlantide Phototravel 379tr, / Frank Lukasseck 570t; De Agostini / DEA / G. Dagli Orti

433tl, 433tr, / C. Sappa 438tl; De Agostini Picture Library 130bl; Pablo Blazquez Dominguez 67tr; Europa Press Entertainment 45cl; Hulton Fine Art Collection / Heritage Images 304t; The Image Bank / Gonzalo Azumendi 560t, / Juan Carlos Munoz 390t; / Silvestre Garcia - IntuitivoFilms 506-7t; Lonely Planet Images / Andrew Bain 386tl, / Dan Herrick 460t; Moment / Luis Dafos 494-5t, / Dominic Dähncke 198tr, / Dhwee 268-9t, / esslingerphoto.com 178-9t, fhm 480-1t, / I just try to tell my emotions and take you around the world 412-3t, / Eve Livesey 420-1t, / QuimGranell 274b, / Daniel Hernanz Ramos 340-1t, / Carmen Martínez Torrón 384-5t, / Zu Sanchez Photography 440b; Moment Open / Dominic Dähncke 360-1b, / Artur Debat 544b, / japatino 238t; Moment Unreleased / Angel Villalba 396t; NurPhoto 56bl, 308tl; Photolibrary / Sylvain Sonnet 300t; Photononstop / Daniele Schneider 188-9t; Andreas Rentz 67bc; Stockbyte / Luis Davilla 360tl; Universal Images Group / Andia 101tl, / Education Images / © PATRIMONIO NACIONAL 439tc, / Prisma by Dukas 518-9b.

Isla Magica: 58-9b.

iStockphoto.com: aluxum 22-3c; Anouchka 86bc; apomares 24-5t; argalis 577bl; Arousa 236b; basiczto 18tl, 288-89; Benedek 68-9; Lux Blue 228bl, 501tr, 514t; CactuSoup 160b; Chalffy 8cla; Cheng NV 11t; Javier Conejero 502cra; Angel Daniel 17t, 144-45; dkgilbey 8cl; E+ / apomares 252-3t; / Eloi_Omella 17bl, 216-7; / ferrantraite 86-7, / Imgorthand 40-1b, 58tl; Ed-Ni-Photo 384bl; Eloi_Omella 141t; Ershov_Maks 119clb; Estellez 423cla; fotoVoyager 292c, 294-5; Gatsi 6-7; holgs 305b; Gerold Grotelueschen 22cla; Ihor_Tailwind 78-9b; jacquesvandinteren 502t; Jareck 19cb, 526-7; Joesboy 559tr; Jorgefontestad 61tl, 190b, 205br; Josanmu 74c, 80-1; Juan-Enrique 541b; Leesle 206-7b; leeznow 411tr; LucVi 149t, 174; LUNAMARINA 149bl, 192-93; ManuelVelasco 249br; MarquesPhotography 221t, 244-5, 248-9t, 249clb; Mediterranean 8-9; merc67 500-1b; Nikada 113tr; Portokalis 119br; RolfSt 574-5b; Ruhey 457t; Juergen Sack 569tr; SeanPavonePhoto 464-5t; Sloot 162-3b; sorincolac 459tr; George-Standen 568-9b; Starcevic 132-3b; stefanopolitimarkovina 20bl, 478-9t; Syldavia 358-9t; Tantarantana 102-3t; titoslack 453tr; TomasSereda 98clb; Trabantos 2-3, 542br; Tramont_ana 44-5t; _ ultraforma_ 531t, 554-5; Vilches 26t; Worledit 38tr; Xantana 22t; xavierarnau 51tr.

Mary Evans Picture Library: 84clb.

© Museo Lázaro Galdiano: 339tr.

© Museo Thyssen-Bornemisza, Madrid: 321tl; Pablo Casares 320-1b.

Museu d'Art Contemporani de Barcelona (MACBA): Miquel Coll Molas 96t.

Museus de Sitges: Photographic Archive of the Consorci del Patrimoni de Sitges Guillem Fernández-Huerta 169cra.

naturepl.com: Jose B. Ruiz 436-7b; Wild Wonders of Europe / Oxford 477clb, 477br.

Museu Picasso: 90-1.

Picfair.com: Hans Geel 172clb; Perry van Munster 446c, 448.

© Gerhard Richter 2019: Installation shot of *Grün-Blau, 1993 (793 / 1-4)* © Gerhard Richter 2019 (12082019) 324-5b.

Robert Harding Picture Library: age fotostock / Jer o Alba 53cl; Charles Bowman 335cl; Kav Dadfar 34t; Maria Galan 242clb; David Santiago Garcia 573br; Christian Kober 576t; Markus Lange 411br; Richard Martin 156t; Arturo Cano Mino 383cra; Roberto Moiola 455t; Juan Carlos Munoz 257b; Ramon

Navarro 476-7t; Nick Servian 230clb; Michael Snell 434-5t; Lucas Vallecillos 163t, 495br; Oliver Wintzen 466-7b.

Shutterstock: Evgeny Kuzhilev 170b; Rubiphoto 318-9b.

Unsplash: Jack Anstey / @jack_anstey 580-1b; beasty / @beastydesign 4; Peter Feghali / @peterf 115tc; Mateusz Plinta / @matplinta 19tl, 443.

Front Flap images
123RF.com: Olena Kachmar t; **Alamy Stock Photo:** age fotostock / Juanma Aparicio bl, / Gonzalo Azumendi cla; Cavan / David Santiago Garcia br; **Dreamstime.com:** Lukasz Janyst cra; Saiko3p c.

Cover
Front and Spine: The scenic Cala Trons at Lloret de Mar, Costa Brava.
AWL Images: Stefano Politi Markovina.
Back: **AWL Images:** Stefano Politi Markovina b; Juan Ignacio Polo tr; **iStockphoto.com:** MarquesPhotography c; TomasSereda cla.

Original cartography Lovell Johns Ltd (Oxford), ERA-Maptec Ltd

For further information see: www.dkimages.com

Illustrators: Stephen Conlin, Gary Cross, Richard Draper, Isidoro González-Adalid Cabezas (Acanto Arquitectura y Urbanismo S.l.), Claire Littlejohn, Maltings Partnership, Chris Orr & Assocs, John Woodcock

This edition updated by
Contributors Lynnette McCurdy Bastida, Adriana Canal, Mary-Ann Gallagher, Candela García
Senior Editor Alison McGill
Senior Designers Tania Da Silva Gomes, Stuti Tiwari
Project Editors Dipika Dasgupta, Rebecca Flynn
Editors Nayan Keshan, Anuroop Sanwalia
Assistant Editor Chhavi Nagpal
Assistant Picture Research Administrator Vagisha Pushp
Jacket Coordinator Bella Talbot
Jacket Designer Ben Hinks
Senior Cartographic Editor Casper Morris
Cartography Manager Suresh Kumar
Cartographic Editor Subhashree Bharati
Senior DTP Designer Tanveer Zaidi
Senior Production Editor Jason Little
Production Controller Kariss Ainsworth
Deputy Managing Editor Beverly Smart
Managing Editors Shikha Kulkarni, Hollie Teague
Managing Art Editor Bess Daly
Senior Managing Art Editor Priyanka Thakur
Art Director Maxine Pedliham
Publishing Director Georgina Dee

First edition 1996
Published in Great Britain by Dorling Kindersley Limited, DK, One Embassy Gardens, 8 Viaduct Gardens, London SW11 7BW

The authorised representative in the EEA is Dorling Kindersley Verlag GmbH. Arnulfstr. 124, 80636 Munich, Germany

Published in the United States by DK Publishing, 1450 Broadway, Suite 801, New York, NY 10018

Copyright © 1996, 2022 Dorling Kindersley Limited
A Penguin Random House Company
21 22 23 24 10 9 8 7 6 5 4 3 2 1

A CIP catalogue record for this book is available from the British Library.

A catalogue record for this book is available from the Library of Congress.

ISSN: 1542 1554
ISBN: 978 0 2415 5936 9

Printed and bound in China.

www.dk.com

A NOTE FROM DK EYEWITNESS

The rapid rate at which the world is changing is constantly keeping the DK Eyewitness team on our toes. While we've worked hard to ensure that this edition of Spain is accurate and up-to-date, we know that opening hours alter, standards shift, prices fluctuate, places close and new ones pop up in their stead. So, if you notice we've got something wrong or left something out, we want to hear about it. Please get in touch at travelguides@dk.com